Lecture Notes in Computer Science   8833

Commenced Publication in 1973
Founding and Former Series Editors:
Gerhard Goos, Juris Hartmanis, and Jan van Leeuwen

T0212950

Lecture Notes in Computer Science 8883

Commenced Publication 1973
Founding and Former Series Editors:
Gerhard Goos, Juris Hartmanis, and Jan van Leeuwen

Editorial Board

David Hutchison
  Lancaster University, UK
Takeo Kanade
  Carnegie Mellon University, Pittsburgh, PA, USA
Josef Kittler
  University of Surrey, Guildford, UK
Jon M. Kleinberg
  Cornell University, Ithaca, NY, USA
Friedemann Mattern
  ETH Zurich, Switzerland
John C. Mitchell
  Stanford University, CA, USA
Moni Naor
  Weizmann Institute of Science, Rehovot, Israel
C. Pandu Rangan
  Indian Institute of Technology, Madras, India
Bernhard Steffen
  TU Dortmund University, Germany
Demetri Terzopoulos
  University of California, Los Angeles, CA, USA
Doug Tygar
  University of California, Berkeley, CA, USA
Gerhard Weikum
  Max Planck Institute for Informatics, Saarbruecken, Germany

Zhenan Sun   Shiguang Shan   Haifeng Sang
Jie Zhou   Yunhong Wang   Weiqi Yuan (Eds.)

Biometric Recognition

9th Chinese Conference, CCBR 2014
Shenyang, China, November 7-9, 2014
Proceedings

 Springer

Volume Editors

Zhenan Sun
Chinese Academy of Sciences, National Laboratory of Pattern Recognition
Institute of Automation, Beijing, China
E-mail: znsun@nlpr.ia.ac.cn

Shiguang Shan
Chinese Academy of Sciences, Institute of Computing Technology, Beijing, China
E-mail: sgshan@ict.ac.cn

Haifeng Sang
Weiqi Yuan
Shenyang University of Technology
School of Information Science and Engineering, Shenyang, China
E-mail: sanghaif@163.com; yuan60@126.com

Jie Zhou
Tsinghua University, Software Engineering Institute, Beijing, China
E-mail: jzhou@tsinghua.edu.cn

Yunhong Wang
Beihang University, School of Computer Science and Engineering, Beijing, China
E-mail: yhwang@buaa.edu.cn

ISSN 0302-9743   e-ISSN 1611-3349
ISBN 978-3-319-12483-4   e-ISBN 978-3-319-12484-1
DOI 10.1007/978-3-319-12484-1
Springer Cham Heidelberg New York Dordrecht London

Library of Congress Control Number: 2014951218

LNCS Sublibrary: SL 6 – Image Processing, Computer Vision, Pattern Recognition, and Graphics

Typesetting: Camera-ready by author, data conversion by Scientific Publishing Services, Chennai, India

Printed on acid-free paper

Springer is part of Springer Science+Business Media (www.springer.com)

Preface

In today's Information Age, identifying a person accurately and protecting information security have become a key social problem to be solved. So far, the most convenient and secure solution is biometric identification technology. In China today, biometric identification offers a great social and economic benefit. For example, a huge population base and increasingly frequent population mobility have made identification a primary factor. Biometric identification has always been used in guaranteeing security , and a large number of workshops on this topic have sprung up in China. Biometric identification has shown an outstanding performance in numerous sectors in the last few years; however, because of various restrictions, biometric identification technologies have advantages but also limitations when put into use.

Many researchers in China concentrating on biometric identification technology, are making great contributions to this area. Therefore, it was necessary to organize an annual conference to bring together leading biometrics researchers and system designers in China to promote the research and development of reliable and practical solutions for biometric authentication. The Chinese Conference on Biometric Recognition (CCBR) has been successfully held in Beijing, Hangzhou, Xi'an, Guangzhou, and Jinan for eight times since 2000. The 9th Chinese Conference on Biometric Recognition (CCBR 2014) was held in Shenyang, during November 7-9, 2014. This volume of conference proceedings contains 63 papers selected from among 90 submissions; all papers were carefully reviewed by three reviewers on average. The papers address: face, fingerprint and palmprint, vein, and iris and ocular biometrics; behavioral biometrics; application and systems of biometrics; multi-biometrics and information fusion; and other biometric recognition and processing issues.

We would like to express our gratitude to all the contributors, reviewers, and Program Committee and Organizing Committee members, who made this conference successful. We also wish to acknowledge the support of the Chinese Association for Artificial Intelligence, Springer, the Chinese Academy of Sciences' Institute of Automation, and Shenyang University of Technology for sponsoring this conference. Special thanks are due to Wei Qiumin, Chang Le, and Yu Xia for their hard work in organizing the conference.

November 2014

Zhenan Sun
Shiguang Shan
Haifeng Sang
Jie Zhou
Yunhong Wang
Weiqi Yuan

Organization

Advisors

Tieniu Tan — Institute of Automation, Chinese Academy of Sciences

Jie Tian — Institute of Automation, Chinese Academy of Sciences

Jingyu Yang — Nanjing University of Science and Technology, China

Xilin Chen — Institute of Computing Technology, Chinese Academy of Sciences

Jianhuang Lai — Sun Yat-sen University, China

General Chairs

Jie Zhou — Tsinghua University, China

Yunhong Wang — Beihang University, China

Wciqi Yuan — Shenyang University of Technology, China

Program Chairs

Zhenan Sun — Institute of Automation, Chinese Academy of Sciences

Shiguang Shan — Institute of Computing Technology, Chinese Academy of Sciences

Haifeng Sang — Shenyang University of Technology, China

Program Committee

Caikou Chen — Yangzhou University, China

Fanglin Chen — National University of Defense Technology, China

Wensheng Chen — Shenzhen University, China

Xi Chen — Kunming University of Science and Technology, China

Zhen Cui — Huaqiao University, China

Weihong Deng — Beijing University of Posts and Telecommunications, China

Xiaoqing Ding — Tsinghua University, China

Fuqing Duan	Beijing Normal University, China
Yuchun Fang	Shanghai University, China
Jufu Feng	Peking University, China
Jianjiang Feng	Tsinghua University, China
Yuqing He	Beijing Institute of Technology, China
Ran He	Institute of Automation, Chinese Academy of Sciences
Qingyang Hong	Xiamen University, China
Dewen Hu	National University of Defense Technology, China
Haifeng Hu	Sun Yat-sen University, China
Mingxing Ja	Northeastern University, China
Wei Jia	Institute of Nuclear Energy Safety Technology, Chinese Academy of Sciences, China
Changlong Jin	Shandong University (Weihai), China
Zhong Jin	Nanjing University of Science and Technology, China
Xiaoyuan Jing	Wuhan University, China
Wenxiong Kang	South China University of Technology, China
Peihua Li	Dalian University of Technology, China
Wei Li	Fudan University, China
Wenhui Li	Jilin University, China
Ziqing Li	Institute of Automation, Chinese Academy of Sciences
Heng Liu	Southwest University of Science and Technology, China
Qingshan Liu	Nanjing University of Information Science and Technology, China
Yuanning Liu	Jilin University, China
Zhi Liu	Shandong University, China
Chaoyang Lu	Xidian University, China
Yuan Mei	Nanjing University of Information Science and Technology, China
Zhichun Mu	University of Science and Technology Beijing, China
Gang Pan	Zhejiang University, China
Hong Pan	Southeast University, China
Dongmei Sun	Beijing Jiaotong University, China
Taizhe Tan	Guangdong University of Technology, China
Ying Tan	Peking University, China
Zengfu Wang	Institue of Intelligent Machines(IIM), CAS, China
Yiding Wang	North China University of Technology, China
Xiangqian Wu	Harbin Institute of Technology, China

Lifang Wu	Beijing University of Technology, China
Xiaohua Xie	Shenzhen Institute of Advanced Technology (SIAT), CAS, China
Yuli Xue	Beihang University, China
Gongping Yang	Shandong University, China
Jucheng Yang	Tianjin University of Science and Technology, China
Wankou Yang	Southeast University, China
Xin Yang	Institute of Automation, Chinese Academy of Sciences
Yingchun Yang	Zhejiang University, China
Yilong Yin	Shandong University, China
Shiqi Yu	Shenzhen University, China
Shu Zhan	Hefei University of Technology, China
Baochang Zhang	Beihang University, China
Lei Zhang	The Hong Kong Polytechnic University, SAR China
Yongliang Zhang	Zhejiang University of Technology, China
Zhaoxiang Zhang	Beihang University, China
Cairong Zhao	Tongji University, China
Qijun Zhao	Sichuan University, China
Hong Zheng	Wuhan University, China
Huicheng Zheng	Sun Yat-sen University, China
Weishi Zheng	Sun Yat-sen University, China
Dexing Zhong	Xi'an Jiaotong University, China
En Zhu	National University of Defense Technology, China

Organizing Committee Chair

Xia Yu	Shenyang University of Technology, China

Organizing Committee

Qiumin Wei	Shenyang University of Technology, China
Hui Song	Shenyang University of Technology, China
Le Chang	Shenyang University of Technology, China
Jing Huang	Shenyang University of Technology, China
Wei Li	Shenyang University of Technology, China
Bo Zhang	Shenyang University of Technology, China
Xiaonan Liu	Shenyang University of Technology, China

Table of Contents

Face

Fingerprint and Palmprint

Vein Biometrics

Iris and Ocular Biometrics

Behavioral Biometrics

Application and System of Biometrics

Multi-biometrics and Information Fusion

Other Biometric recognition and Processing

3D Face Analysis: Advances and Perspectives

Di Huang*, Jia Sun, Xudong Yang, Dawei Weng, and Yunhong Wang

IRIP Lab, School of Comput. Sci. and Eng., Beihang Univ., Beijing, China
dhuang@buaa.edu.cn

Abstract. In the past decade, research on 3D face analysis has been extensively developed, and this study briefly reviews the progress achieved in data acquisition, algorithms, and experimental methodologies, for the issues of face recognition, facial expression recognition, gender and ethnicity classification, age estimation, *etc.*, especially focusing on that after the availability of FRGC v2.0. It further points out several challenges to deal with for more efficient and reliable systems in the real world.

Keywords: 3D face analysis, survey, shape representation, challenges.

1 Introduction

The face has obvious advantages over other biometrics for people identification and verification applications, because it is natural, non-intrusive, contactless and socially well accepted. The past decades have witnessed tremendous efforts first focusing on 2D facial images [1] and more recently on 3D face models or scans [2]. In spite of great progress achieved so far within the field [3] [4] [5] [6] [7], the face presented in the 2D image/video is still not reliable enough as a biometric trait, especially in the presence of illumination and pose variations [8]. With the rapid development in 3D imaging systems, 2.5D or 3D scans have emerged as a major alternative to deal with the unsolved issues in 2D face recognition, *i.e.*, changes in lighting and pose [2] [9]. Meanwhile, 3D data convey exact geometry information of human faces, and they are thus theoretically complementary to 2D images that capture the texture clues.

During the past several years, face analysis in the 3D domain has received increasing attention from both the academia and industrial, along with the release of databases, such as FRGC [10], Bosphorus [11], BU-3DFE [12], and BU-4DFE [13]. The research not only covers 3D shape based face analysis [14] [15] [16] [17], but also includes 3D+2D multi-modal face analysis [18] [19] [20] and 3D aided 2D face analysis (*i.e.* heterogeneous or asymmetric 3D-2D face analysis) [21] [22], involving in various applications, *e.g.* 3D Face Recognition (FR), 3D Facial Expression Recognition (FER), 3D Face based Gender and Ethnicity Classification (GEC), 3D Face based Age Estimation (FAE), *etc.*[1]

In 2006, Bowyer *et al.* presented a comprehensive survey which includes early studies on recognition performed by matching models of the 3D shape of the face,

---

* Corresponding author.

[1] In this study, we mainly focus on solely 3D shape based face analysis. Unless stated, all related applications discussed only make use of 3D geometry clues.

Z. Sun et al. (Eds.): CCBR 2014, LNCS 8833, pp. 1–21, 2014.

either alone or in combination with matching corresponding 2D intensity images [2]. They also pointed out three main research challenges that need to deal with in the future, *i.e.* the need for better sensors, improved recognition algorithms, and more rigorous experimental methodology. This paper is an update and expansion of [2] as well as several contemporaneous work [9] [8], and it extensively reviews recent advances in 3D face analysis (not limited to 3D FR, but embracing other related issues, such as 3D FER, GEC, FAE) from then on, in which the progress on these targeting directions [2] is particularly summarized. Moreover, it also discusses new challenges that we are facing now or probably meet in the future.

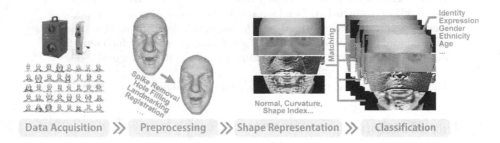

Fig. 1. General framework of 3D face analysis approaches

2   General Framework of 3D Face Analysis

There are a number of 3D face related applications, and although they differ in the specific objective, they generally share the common framework in processing. As depicted in Fig.1, the system of 3D face analysis contains four major steps, *i.e.* data acquisition, preprocessing, shape representation, and classification.

In data acquisition, a 3D imaging system is required to generate 3D facial scans composed of surface shapes and their corresponding textures. Although it is commonly acknowledged that the 3D shape per se is illumination independent, the sensing on it is generally not. Lighting changes can greatly affect the shape that is acquired by a sensor, and artifacts do occur in some areas. As a result, preprocessing is usually launched to produce a "clean" face. Furthermore, landmarking and registration are probably needed for data alignment in the following stages. The core in 3D face analysis lies in the shape representation of 3D facial surfaces, and their geometric characteristics can be described as a variety of features which are application dependent related to different attributes, including identity, gender, ethnicity, age, expression *etc.* Finally, in classification, machine learning techniques are adopted to predict the class label to which the feature of the given 3D face belongs. Additionally, a parallel pipeline is necessary for the 2D intensity in multi-modal 3D+2D face analysis, which can be combined with that of the 3D geometry at data level [24] [25], feature level [26], matching score level [27] [28] [19] [29] [30] [20], decision level [29], or multiple levels [31] [32].

3 Data Acquisition

A 3D imaging device is an instrument that collects 3D coordinates of a given region of a surface [23]. Current 3D scanners roughly fall into two classes, *i.e.* structured light and stereo reconstruction. **Structured light** is an "active" scanning technique, and its basic configuration consists of a camera and a projector under known geometric relationship. The projector emits one or more encoded light patterns onto the scene, and the shape information is extracted by measuring the deformation of light patterns on the surface of the object. Current structured light based scanners can capture static or sequences of 3D face scans along with the 2D intensity images in real-time, or even at a higher speed. While its drawback is that users' faces are restricted into a limited amount of area not only covered by the projected light but also visible to the camera, maybe leading to artifacts [111]. Some representative equipments are the Minolta Vivid 900/910 Series, Inspeck Mega Capturor II 3D, and Kinect Camera *etc.*

Stereo reconstruction based techniques have two branches, namely Multi-view stereo and photometric stereo. The former is a "passive" capturing method, and its setup includes multiple calibrated cameras placed at various viewpoints. Under certain constraints, the point correspondence in different scene images is established and the facial shape is reconstructed. It does not require any flashing lights, as all the cameras can record the same scene simultaneously, with constant lights, allowing more natural behaviour from the subjects being recorded. But accurate reconstruction of smooth surfaces, *e.g.* regions without much natural texture, is very difficult [2]. Additionally, 3D reconstruction should be operated offline due to the huge computational complexity involving this technique. Some commercial examples are the DI3D (Dimensional Imaging) dynamic face capturing system and the 3DMD dynamic 3D stereo system. The latter is an approach to estimate the surface normals of the object through a set of its images captured under different (multi-spectral) illumination conditions. Its advantage is that it can operate at high-speed. However, it is very sensitive to the presence of projected shadows, highlights and non-uniform lighting. Furthermore, instead of point clouds or surface meshes, it only estimates the surface normals of object, and the following integration procedure for surface reconstruction therefore incurs more computation cost and additional errors. A 3D face acquisition system is recently developed using this technique in [112].

More recently, specialized 3D imaging devices for face data acquisition have appeared, *e.g.* Artec Eva, 3DMDface, *etc.* Artec Eva is a handheld scanner with independent light source. It captures up to 16 frames per second, and different frames are automatically aligned to build a 3D model in real-time. 3DMDface is a stereo-based 3D scanner equipped with two projectors and six cameras located in two sides. In each shot, the system merges all the images from different cameras into two texture images of each side and one 3D model.

Using these devices, a number of databases are collected and released to the community for research on different 3D face analysis based topics, which can be summarized in Table 1. Section 6 introduces dataset utilization in various topics.

4   Preprocessing

Existing 3D imaging systems generally capture both the geometry and reflectance properties of an object, and the majority of current 3D face databases displayed in Table 1 provide both the 3D shape and its corresponding (*i.e.* point-to-point registered) 2D texture counterpart of a face. Thereinto, the 3D facial surface is stored in different formats, *e.g.* point-cloud, range image, and triangular mesh. Before feature extraction, the facial surface needs to be preprocessed, including data cleaning, landmarking, cropping, and registration [2].

As explicated in Section 3, artifacts probably appear because of inappropriate illumination conditions and unexpected subject movement, and they tend to occur in face regions such as oily areas that are specular, the eyes, and the ones of facial hair (*e.g.* eyebrows, mustache, or beard) even if the subject remains still under ideal lighting source. The most common types of artifacts can generally be described as "spikes" and "holes", which may incur large errors to the subsequent stages in processing. To clean 3D data, smoothing filters, such as median filter and Gaussian filter, are often adopted to remove spikes, and interpolation techniques are usually exploited to fill holes.

Several distinct anthropometric points shared by human beings are then required for face cropping, pose correction, or feature extraction, and automatically locating these fiducial points is named landmarking in face analysis. Compared with other keypoints, the nose tip is the most widely needed, and relatively easy and efficient to localize, by adopting *e.g.* curvature analysis [128], profile analysis [18], and Spherical Depth Map (SDM) fitting [130], *etc.* Current 3D landmarking techniques can be roughly categorized into two streams, *i.e.* heuristic approaches and learning approaches. The first usually notices a correlation between the local shape and the targeted landmark, which is used to define some rule to select candidate positions on query faces, including curvature extrema based [128] [131] [129], curve extrema based [18] [133], and their combination [134]. Such methods prove effective for rough detection of the most distinctive facial points, but they are generally not competent for highly accurate localization as they follow a set of rules that depend on one another. Furthermore, they are restricted to limited number of specific landmarks. The second derives prior knowledge from a training set, whose samples are with annotations, and it is extensively studied in 2D and becoming popular in 3D especially since the release of big labeled data, such as statistical model based [136] [137], graph matching based [132], and random forest based [135]. These methods are more flexible than heuristic ones, because it is not necessary to provide specific rules for each point. High accuracies are reported on nearly frontal faces and even the ones in large poses [138] [139].

Registration is the process of transforming different 3D facial surfaces (sets of points) into one coordinate system. On the one hand, it can be directly used to compute the similarity of faces for rigid or non-rigid matching in different applications, *e.g.* Iterative Closet Points (ICP) [40], Iterative Closet Normal Points (ICNP) [140], and Thin-Plate-Spline (TPS) [42], *etc.* On the other hand, it can

---

[2] An example preprocessing software: http://pszeptycki.com/tool.html

Table 1. Overview of major databases that are publicly available for 3D face analysis

Database (Year)	Device	#Img.	#Subj.	Data	Variation*
CASIA (2004) [125]	Vivid 910	4624	123	Mesh	E, P
GavabDB (2004) [120]	Vivid 700	549	61	Mesh	E, P
FRGC v1 (2005) [10]	Vivid 910	943	200	Range+2D	-
FRGC v2 (2005) [10]	Vivid 910	4007	466	Range+2D	E, Ti
ND-2006 (2006) [121]	Vivid 910	13450	888	Range+2D	E
BU-3DFE (2006) [12]	3DMD	2500	100	Mesh+2D	E
FRAV3D (2006) [122]	Vivid 700	1696 $^+$	106$^+$	Mesh+2D	P
Bosphorus (2008) [11]	Inspeck 3D Mega II	4666	105	Range+2D	E, O, P
BU-4DFE (2008) [13]	3DMD	60600	101	3D+2D Seq.	E
Texas 3DFRD (2010) [123]	3Q MU-2 system	1149	118	Range	-
3D-TEC (2011) [102]	Vivid 910	428	214	Range+2D	E, Tw
UOY (2011) [124]	N/A	5250	350	Mesh	O, P
SHREC (2011) [144]	Roland Scanner	780	130	Mesh	P
UBM-DB (2011) [126]	Vivid 900	1473	143	Range+2D	E, O
FaceWarehouse (2014)[127]	Kinect	3000	150	Mesh+RGBD	E

* E: Expression, O: Occlusion, P: Pose, Ti: Time, Tw: Twins. $^+$ Figures from [33]

be adopted for pose correction, and with landmarks, facial surfaces, in different poses, can be efficiently aligned for further stages, like shape representation.

5 Shape Representation

Shape representation (*i.e.* geometric feature extraction) is the core issue in 3D face analysis, even though there are many related applications, including Face Recognition (FR), Facial Expression Recognition (FER), Face based Gender and Ethnicity Classification (GEC), Face based Age Estimation (FAE) *etc.* Generally speaking, this step seeks a geometric feature space where the differences of face samples are highlighted and distinguished in specific applications. For instance, in 3D FR, shape features are expected to convey person-distinctiveness while remain stable as facial expression varies [33]. In 3D FER, it is desired to generate geometry features that are able to describe subject-independent properties of facial expressions [34]. In 3D GEC and FAE, gender, ethnicity, and age related clues are extracted to provide enough discrimination [35] [36] [37]. Meanwhile, the shape representation of 3D facial surfaces should also be robust to internal and external occlusions, particularly in 3D FR [38] [39].

Similar to the taxonomy in 2D face analysis [1], 3D face representation methods can also be roughly categorized into two classes, *i.e.* holistic- and feature-based. The **holistic-based** ones employ all data (*i.e.*, entire point-clouds, meshes, or range images) to represent faces, and the similarity between their surfaces can be directly measured using registration approaches, *e.g.* Iterative Closet Points (ICP) [40] [41] [44] and Thin-Plate-Spline (TPS) [42] [43] [45], or subspace based techniques, *e.g.* Principal Component Analysis (PCA) [3] [46] [47], Linear Discriminant Analysis (LDA) [4] [48]. The **feature-based** ones concentrate on local descriptive points [49] [50], curves [51] [52] [53] [54], or regions [55] [56] [57] [58] [59] [60] [61] of faces and compare them in a given feature space for decision.

This taxonomy felicitously summarizes the early studies for this issue; however, recent investigations consistently reveal that feature-based methods perform better than holistic based ones, and the number of feature-based or hybrid (combination of holistic- and feature-based) techniques greatly increases. There thus exist more appropriate categorizations in different applications.

5.1   Progress in 3D FR

Face Recognition (FR) is the most comprehensive and complicated application in automatic face analysis. As in the 2D domain, the representation of 3D facial surfaces tries to deal with a number of intrinsic and external challenges, including expression changes, pose variations (*i.e.*, self-occlusions), ageing, occlusions, cosmetic use, *etc.*, especially in the real world. Among these difficulties, the solutions to facial expression variations have been extensively discussed, because (1) these changes are the most common behaviours in human faces; (2) they elastically deform facial surfaces, not only in non-rigid regions (*e.g.* mouth, cheeks) but in rigid ones (*e.g.* forehead, nose) as well; and (3) 3D methods suffer more from them than 2D ones do. Therefore, we review these studies according to the categorization how they handle the problem of facial expression changes, *i.e.* Deformable Model based, Surface Distance based, and Invariant Region based.

Deformable Model based methods assume that human faces are non-rigid and deformable surfaces that can be elastically transformed into one another or generic models based on certain criteria. The quantifications of deformations or the coefficients in model fitting are adopted as metrics for FR. For example, Lu and Jain propose a robust approach to 3D FR through an expression deformation model by using the TPS function [62] [63], which extends their previous idea of employing ICP and TPS for rigid and non-rigid face matching respectively [64] [45]. Kakadiaris *et al.* [14] introduce an expression robust 3D FR method based on Annotated Face Model (AFM), to which each face is fitted and its geometry image [65] as well as normal map are then generated for feature extraction. In [66], Amberg *et al.* present an expression-invariant 3D FR approach by building and fitting an identity/expression separated 3D Morphable Model (3DMM) [67] to facial surfaces, and expressive faces can be neutralized for similarity measurement computation. Similarly, Mpiperis *et al.* [68] make use of the Bilinear Model [69] to encode identity and expression in independent controlled parameters, and thus perform joint expression-invariant FR and identity-invariant FER. Mian *et al.* [70] suppose that the pure expression deformation can be reconstructed with the minimal error if the probe and gallery faces belong to the same subject, and design a PCA based Expression Deformation Model (EDM) for 3D FR.

Recently, several investigations focus on improving the aforementioned methods in some aspect. Ocegueda *et al.* successively attempt to introduce Markov Random Field (MRF) and LDA to make wavelet coefficients [14] more discriminative and compact [71] [72]. Towards real-world 3D FR, AFM [14] is combined with a statistical model based landmark detector to deal with partial scans, and even for matching profiles of a person [73].

These methods are intuitively attractive, because they usually use parametrical statistical models, and are thus able to find dense (*e.g.* one-to-one) correspondence between face scans for expression morphing, transfer, and neutralization. However, their major drawback lies in the requirement of proper distribution of face samples (neutral and expressive) and a certain number of fiducial landmarks of each face in the training stage (except [14] to deal with nearly frontal faces). Moreover, the iterative fitting (registration) process needs to be well initialized and carefully controlled to balance the performance and computation cost.

Surface Distance based approaches suppose that facial surfaces are two-dimensional, compact, connected, and genus zero manifolds embedded in $\mathbb{R}^3$, and the geodesics, induced by the Riemannian metric as intrinsic geometry quantities, are adopted to construct expression-invariant facial representation. Bronstein *et al.* [74] are the pioneers who put this idea into practice, using an isometric model that facial surfaces with different expressions of the same subject are approximately intrinsically equivalent and such invariant geometry thus contributes to identification. This model is further extended [75], and only metric tensor of the surface is used for geodesic distance computation, instead of Fast Marching on Triangulated Domains (FMTD) in [74], allowing for simple and efficient 3D acquisition techniques like photometric stereo for fast and accurate FR. Another key issue, namely the influence of the embedding space geometry and dimensionality choice, is discussed in [76]. In [77], the isometric-invariant similarity between faces is measured by embedding one facial surface to another, thus ameliorating the ability to handle partially missing data. These methods are greatly challenged by the open mouth that makes the genus zero surface assumption and the isometric-invariant property of geodesic distance invalid. Mpiperis *et al.* [78] solve this problem by mapping the lips to a continuous area on the geodesic plane so that the hole of the mouth vanishes, and introduce a geodesic polar representation. Meanwhile, they point out that the isometry assumption of surface deformation is not valid for large facial expressions.

Different from the above iso-metric surface based approaches, where the entire isometric approximated facial surfaces are utilized for matching, there exist some studies on the isometry of specific facial parts. In Riemannian geometry, if surfaces are differentiable, their tangent spaces are manifolds, and various curves on facial surfaces can be measured for face matching. Daoudi's group follows this idea and propose a set of iso-level curve based methods for facial surface representation, including iso-depth curves [79] and circular curves (iso-geodesic curves) [80] [81]. Iso-depth curves are closed planar curves sampled from pose normalized 2.5D facial depth images, which can be extracted by cutting the depth facial image using a plane parallel to the XY-plane; while circular curves are closed space curves sampled from aligned 3D facial surfaces, which can be generated by incising a facial surface using a sphere centered at the nose tip with a pre-defined radius. Selecting a proper Riemannian metric, the geodesic path between two points can be calculated in the quotient space that is defined based on the pre-shape space constructed by the elements of the velocity functions of curves. Recognition finally performs using the similarity between two surfaces averaging the distances of all pairs of corresponding facial curves. The usage of the iso-level curves has the limitation that each curve goes through different facial regions which makes it difficult to separate local variability. For improvement, they introduce another curve feature, namely radial curves [82] [17], which are open space curves sampled from pose normalized 3D surfaces, produced by slicing a facial surface using a plane passing the nose tip perpendicular to the XY-plane, and it shows the robustness to moderate occlusion and data missing. These approaches provide intrinsic local coordinate systems for facial surfaces and both point- and curve-level correspondence, hence achieving natural elastic metric between deformable and non-rigid facial surfaces. Nevertheless, their performance highly depends on the nose tip, and it is problematic when a large area of the facial surface (especially with the nose tip) is missing. Moreover, the geometric shapes and topological structures of iso-level curves [79] [80] [81] dramatically change when mouth opens, and this impact is weakened in [17] for the quality filter based curve selection and statistical model based curve recovery.

Berretti *et al.* develop an iso-geodesic stripe based approach for 3D FR [83] [84] [85]. Their method first partitions the facial surface into the same number of geodesic stripes and sub-strips of equal width, and the inter- and intra-distances of corresponding strips (or sub-strips) are computed by using 3D Weighted Walkthroughs. They claim that these iso-geodesic strips do not change too much under facial expressions, and slight point-drifting or deformation of strips only yields small variations in 3DWW, thereby making this approach expression insensitive. A facial surface is then described as a graph, in which nodes represent strips (or sub-strips) and edges represent distances between the strips (or sub-strips), and identification is finally achieved by matching graphs. This method shows some tolerance to inaccurate fiducial points and missing data, but like the iso-metric and iso-level curve based ones, mouth opening largely degrades its performance.

Invariant Region based techniques make the hypothesis that when a facial expression occurs, there always exist local areas, either in relatively rigid or elastic facial regions, that keep invariant or vary slightly. Once accurately localized and comprehensively characterized, they can be densely or sparsely matched for 3D FR. In literature, such methods are more extensively studied than the previous two types, which can be further classified into three categories according to the way how the invariant regions are described, namely original data based, sparse representation based, and dense representation based.

In general, original data based ones first separate the rigid and non-rigid regions, and the former are then used for matching to resist expression changes. If multiple regions are adopted, their contributions will be combined. Chang *et al.* [60] [61] propose a method to 3D FR by matching multiple overlapping nose regions that are regarded stable as expression varies. ICP is exploited to compare the gallery face with all regions of a probe respectively, whose Mean Square Errors (MSE) are combined through the product and sum rules. They show that the nose region convey sufficient distinctiveness for identification; however, they also point out that the rigid areas are not so robust since a 10% degradation appears when going from matching neutral expressions to varying expressions. Later, Faltemier et al. [86] present an extended region ensemble method, and the best result is reached when 28 regions distributed over the whole face are selected for ICP matching and Borda Count based fusion. Queirolo et al. [87] introduce a Simulated Annealing-based (SA) surface matching with the Surface Interpenetration Measure (SIM). This approach has a large probability to reach the global optimal solution and works more precisely for the property of SA-based matching process and the superiority of SIM over MSE. Finally, the scores of all the region pairs are fused by the sum rule.

Despite competitive results, registering multiple facial areas causes a disadvantage of high computational cost. Spreeuwers [88] proposes an efficient and accurate multiple region matching based method. To deal with expression changes, 30 overlapping regions are defined in an intrinsic coordinate system, and high resolution range images are generated by resampling. The vectorization form of each region is used as feature, whose dimensionality is further reduced by PCA and LDA, and a likelihood ratio classifier is then adopted for regional feature classification. The majority voting based fusion strategy is utilized for final decision. It achieves better performance than [61] [86] [87], and more importantly, it runs hundreds of times faster. However, similar to other related methods, landmarking largely effects region segmentation. Additionally, there is still no theoretical support on the design (e.g. size, shape, position, etc.) of these regions.

Sparse representation based ones firstly detect repeatable and discriminative keypoints or small regions, and the similarity of two facial surfaces can be then measured by the distance of their keypoint (or region) sets described in certain local shape feature space for FR. Alyuz et al. [15] follow the manner of multiple region matching as in [61] [86] [87]. and comparing region pairs not only in the original coordinate feature space but in the curvature based one. The Average Face Model (AvFM) [89] [29] is extended to independent 15 local regions, which is thus named the Average Region Model (AvRM). The Nearest Neighbor (NN) algorithm is used to compute the similarity in the feature space, and both score-level (sum and product rules) and abstract-level (plurality voting) fusion are considered to combine multiple regions. The authors highlight the advantages in system speed at that period, which is still too slow to meet current requirement. It is worth noting that the performance achieved in the curvature feature space is much better than that in the raw coordinate feature space.

Another stream in sparse representation is inspired by the well-known SIFT-like framework, including the principal steps of keypoint detection, description, and matching. For instance, in 2008, Mian et al. [19] attempt such an approach. It first detects keypoints at locations where shape variations are high, and tensor representation based descriptors (extension of [90] [91]) are then extracted from the keypoints, which are finally associated using Cosine distance, constrained by holistic graph matching. Huang et al. propose to represent original smooth facial range images by a group of intermediate distinctiveness enhanced maps, namely Shape Index (SI) maps [92], Multi-Scale Local Binary Pattern (MS-LBP) maps

[92], and Multi-Scale extended LBP Depth Face (MS-eLBP-DF) [93] [16]. Then, the 2D SIFT operator is applied to these maps for matching. Compared to [19], the discriminative power of keypoints is improved; however, these maps are not totally pose invariant, only robust to moderate pose changes.

Recently, the SIFT-like framework is extended to 3D mesh data, several popular 2D descriptors, *i.e.* SIFT, Daisy, and HOG are generalized to meshSIFT [38] [94], meshDaisy [39], and meshHOG [95] respectively, for 3D FR. These methods are completely rotation invariant and registration free, but their computation cost is generally expensive due to mesh based data processing.

By contrast, dense representation based ones initially extract the local shape feature from each point of the surface, and these features of overlapping or non-overlapping areas that cover the entire face are then encoded in vectors, which are finally correspondingly compared for similarity computation through classifiers in 3D FR. Cook *et al.* [96] perform multi-orientation and multi-scale Log-Gabor filters on facial range images, claiming that Log-Gabor captures more cues of high frequency than Gabor does. The face is divided into a 7×7 grid with 50% overlap in both horizontal and vertical directions. PCA is employed to the filter responses of each region for dimensionality reduction, and the simple sum rule based score level fusion is used to combine the Mahalinobis Cosine distances for prediction. It is then extended by combining the Haar wavelet transformation, Log-Gabor filter, and Discrete Cosine Transform (DCT) for multi-scale face representation [97], that are further projected into PCA and LDA subspace for classification, where the effectiveness of Log-Gabor is highlighted.

Wang *et al.* [98] introduce a Collective Shape Difference Classifier (CSDC) based method. The difference between two facial range images is captured by a Sign Shape Difference Map (SSDM), whose patterns of shape differences are then highlighted in three local feature spaces, *i.e.* Haar-like, Gabor, and Multi-Block LBP (MB-LBP), measuring the change pattern of shape difference, the characteristics of spatial localities and orientations, and the texture characteristics of SSDM respectively. Boosting is finally exploited to select the most discriminative cues to build the final classifier. Besides high performance, this method runs at a high speed. Its main limitation is the possible failure for large data missing.

In [99], Huang *et al.* present a 3D FR method based on Local Shape Patterns (LSP) and Sparse Representation Classifier (SRC). Using Region based ICP (R-ICP), facial surfaces are precisely aligned and their range images are generated. For facial representation, LSP works in the same way as LBP does on the facial range image, but extends it by inducing the orientation factors, thus improving the discriminative power to distinguish similar local shape variations. Meanwhile, it proves that SRC also outperforms other classifiers for histogram based features, which is consistent with the finding in [100] for geometry attribute based features. Li *et al.* [101] introduce the multi-scale and multi-component Local Normal Patterns (LNP) based face representation, which improves the discriminative ability of LBP-like features by embedding normal cues. A weighted SRC is then developed to assign different credits to individual regions, to improve the robustness to expression variations.

5.2 Progress in Other Applications

Besides in 3D FR, great progress on facial representation has also been achieved in other 3D face related applications in recent years, including FER, GEC, FAE, *etc*. Many methods in such topics refer to the successful experience from 3D FR.

Specifically, in 3D FER, the key problem lies in how to highlight shape clues specific to facial expressions while reducing those related to identities. Current techniques in 3D FER form two categories, *i.e.* model-based and feature-based [34]. The idea of the model-based approaches is similar to the deformable model based approaches in 3D FR. A generic 3D face template (usually a neutral face model averaged by a number of training samples) is fitted to an input, and the corresponding coefficients or parameters are then adopted for expression label prediction. Their difference is that FER mainly focuses on how to, from the fitted coefficients or parameters, extract information of shape deformations due to facial expressions rather than identities in FR. Gong *et al.* [105] present a method to define Basic Facial Shape Component (BFSC), which is modeled by a linear combination of neutral faces and thus does not contain any expression cue. The substraction of BFSC from that of an input expressional face scan provides Expressional Shape Component (ESC), to construct the expression feature vector. Zhao *et al.* [113] propose a Statistical Facial feAture Model (SFAM), which consists of multiple features extracted from the regions around 19 key landmarks, to fit the input face, and the parameters are taken as feature vectors.

Feature-based approaches extract expression sensitive geometric features from an input facial scan for label prediction, and many local features originally proposed in 3D FR are directly discussed in 3D FER. For instance, a set of normalized Euclidian distances between some landmarks are adopted as features [117], similar [100]. Berretti *et al.* [118] calculate SIFT-like features in the neighborhood of pre-defined fiducial points on depth facial images. Li *et al.* [114] extract the meshSIFT features [38] from several manual landmarks to characterize local shape variations. In [115], the authors extend their previous LNP based features [116] to 3D FER and apply the Multiple Kernel Learning (MKL) technique to combine the contributions of various components and scales. Please see more technical details in 3D FER from two specific surveys [34] [111].

Compare to the methods in 3D FR and FER, the ones in GEC and FAE are limited. Early tasks try basic features, such as coordinates, normals, curvatures, and wavelets of selected facial patches. While, more recent studies are prone to using features, which have proved competent in 3D FR, to encode the difference of gender, ethnicity, and age. For example, similar to [82], based on the theory of Riemannian geometry, Xia *et al.* [110] analyze the symmetry of 3D face for gender classification, and Deformation Scalar Field (DSF) based on pair-wise shape comparison of corresponding symmetric curves is computed for classification. In [119], Oriented Gradient Maps (OGMs) [20] are investigated in race classification. Xia *et al.* [37] enhance DSF [110] by embedding its spatial and gradient to capture both the face averageness and symmetry for age estimation. Meanwhile, there is still specialized technique. Huang *et al.* [36] propose a Boosted Local Circular Patterns (LCP), an LBP variant, for gender and race classification.

6 Experimental Methodology

In the early days, it is difficult to validate and compare different algorithms due to the lack of appropriate databases and standard experimental protocols. After years of effort, many well-designed datasets are publicly available to address more challenging problems. Meanwhile, standard experimental protocols for different 3D face related topics are established to make fair comparison of methods and access to the state of the art. In the following, we mainly introduce the commonly used experimental settings for datasets for FR, FER, GEC, and FAE in 3D.

In 3D FR, there are two scenarios: verification and identification (see [2] for specific definitions), and verification rate at 0.1% False Accepted Rate (FAR) and rank-one recognition rate are mostly used for comparison in verification and identification respectively. Currently, FRGC v2.0, Bosphorus, BU-3DFE, and 3D-TEC are the most common choices. For identification, their protocols are quite similar. One of the neutral facial scan is selected to compose the gallery set (N subjects) and the remaining ones (M scans) are regarded as probes, thereby generating a $N \times M$ matrix. For example, a 466×3541 matrix in FRGC v2.0 [96] [14] [98] [16], a 105×4561 matrix in Bosphorus [39] [94] [95], a 100×2400 matrix in BU-3DFE [33], a 61×488 matrix in GavabDB [16] [17], and a 214×214 matrix in 3D-TEC [102] [103]. For verification, the entire Bosphorus and Gavab databases are seldom used, since they contain scans with large data missing which dramatically trouble inter-class and intra-class thresholding. In the other three, ROC curves of All *vs.* All similarity matrix (*i.e.* each pair of faces are compared) are usually adopted [98] [102] [33]. Besides, it provides three masks to screen the All *vs.* All matrix (4007×4007) which are of increasing difficulty reflecting the time elapsed between sample acquisition [96] [14] [98] [16].

In 3D FER, the algorithms are generally evaluated by the average recognition rate of all the six expressions of a certain times of repeated experiments. Moreover, the confusion matrix of the six expressions is also concerned to study the precision of each expression and the error between two expressions. The most commonly exploited datasets are BU-3DFE, Bosphorus, and BU-4DFE. The first evaluation on BU-3DFE for 3D FER is given by [104], where 60 unknown subjects with their expressive face scans of level III and IV are selected and in each experiment, the data are randomly divided into 2 subsets: the one of 54 subjects for training and the other of 6 for testing. The experiment is repeated 20 times. However, Gong *et al.* [105] point out that 20 times are not sufficient to produce stable results, and they hence recommend a repetition of more than 100 times. More recently, Zeng et al. [106] claim that randomly selecting 60 subjects at each experiment is more meaningful than using fixed 60 subjects for fair comparison. BU-4DFE is used to validate dynamic 3D FER methods, and the experimental protocol is similar to that of BU-3DFE. Due to the high computational cost on these 3D sequences, existing tasks report their performance based on a round of 10-fold cross validation [108] [109]. Bosphorus is chosen for 3D AU recognition in [107], where a 10-fold person independent cross validation scheme is employed.

Research in other 3D face related applications, *i.e.* GEC and FAE, is not as extensive as that in FR and FER, and FRGC v2.0 is still the most frequently selected for validation. In 3D GEC, gender classification is a typical binary classification problem, but the one for ethnicity classification is generally not the case. However, since the distribution of 3D face samples in current public datasets with ethnicity labels available is unbalanced, it is also often treated as a binary classification problem. For example, a recent study given by Huang et al. [36] select a subset of 3676 scans belonging to 319 white and 99 Asian people from FRGC v2.0 for both gender and ethnicity classification with a 10-fold cross validation scheme, the same as [35]. They also make use of all the scans from BU-3DFE for gender classification and 1875 samples of 51 Whites and 24 East Asians for race classification using the same partitioning in training and testing data. In [110], all face scans from FRGC v2.0 are adopted for gender classification with 10-fold cross validation, and the details of some earlier related tasks (using other databases) are also compared and discussed. In 3D FAE, Xia et al. [37] show the first method which formulates age estimation as a regression problem, and employ FRGC v2.0 for evaluation. Two protocols are adopted: gender-general based using the first scans of all subjects and gender-specific based separating the selected data into male and female groups with a leave-one-person-out scheme.

7 Summary and Discussion

As foreseen by Bowyer et al. [2] in 2006, research involving 3D FR is indeed in a period of rapid expansion in the past several years, reflected by the increasing number of scientific papers as well as the constant launch of advanced 3D scanners. Furthermore, other 3D related topics, c.g. 3D FER, 3D GEC, 3D FAE, etc., are also studied at different levels, which, along with 3D FR, form the domain of 3D face analysis. The progress achieved falls into three aspects in terms of sensors, algorithms, and experimental methodologies, thereby partly showing answers to these challenges discussed in [2].

The key properties of 3D face scanners are the acquisition time, field of view, robustness to ambient illumination, safety of projector, resolution, and accuracy [2]. Compared to the ones at that time, current imaging systems are really much better. The acquisition speed of some devices, such as 3dMDface and Kinect II, is up to tens of millisecond per shot, and even supports to record dynamic 3D sequences. Although still inferior to that of 2D cameras, it is not too far behind. Furthermore, their resolutions can easily achieve the scale at millimeter or even sub-millimeter level which makes each face model contain 200K points or more. Thanks to infrared based projection, the sensitivity to lighting changes weakens and the safety to human eyes is improved.

To assess algorithms, we take FR as an example due to its leading position in 3D face analysis. Facial expression variations are regarded as the major challenge in [2], and as the pervasive technique, registration based methods, e.g. ICP and TPS, are attempted in many ways to solve this problem. The remarkable result through adaptive region selection based matching [60] highlighted in [2] is largely improved by more effective registration alternatives, such as SA [87] and ICNP [140], on the FRGC v2.0 database. Besides, two additional frameworks, namely surface distance based and (sparse or dense) local feature based, are extensively developed, as explicated in Section 5.1. Furthermore, the computational cost of 3D FR approaches is dramatically reduced, and several systems [98] [88] even show their potential in real time processing. Additionally, multi-modal 3D+2D FR techniques [18] [29] [30] are widely investigated as well, far more sophisticated than those preliminary ones mentioned in [2], and emerging FR scenarios appear either to introduce possible extra clues or synergies between the two modalities, including asymmetric (heterogeneous) 3D *vs.* 2D FR [141] [142] [21], 3D assisted 2D FR [143] [22]. On the other hand, increasing attention [39] [94] [95] starts to move towards severe external occlusion and large data missing, aiming to adapt to practical conditions. Similar cases can also be observed in other topics.

Existing databases concern various changes including expression, pose, occlusion, time, *etc.*, and their protocols are either initially setup (*e.g.* FRGC v2.0 and 3D TEC for FR) or gradually updated to the current form (*e.g.* BU-3DFE for FER and FRGC v2.0 for GEC). For each topic defined in this writing, there is some experiment setup to follow (as described in Section 6), to achieve fair comparison with the state of the art. Some datasets can be regard as the enhanced version of another. For example, 3D-TEC extends FRGC v2.0 by providing extremely similar shape clues of identical twins in the presence of smiling, and BU-4DFE upgrades BU-3DFE through dynamic sequences of continuously varying expressions. Therefore, cross-database evaluation [72] can also be explored.

In spite of the fact that the benchmark of 3D face analysis has been tremendously advanced, there is still some distance to see the proliferation of related systems in practical use. Old problems are solved while new ones appear, which requires further effort both in the academia and industrial. For sensors, current devices are able to efficiently provide high quality data, and the bottleneck turns to the price and the size. For algorithms, many teams report almost perfect performance in 3D FR on FRGC v2.0, BU-3DFE, and the frontal subset of Bosphorus, demonstrating that the problem of expression variations is handled at the present stage, unless much larger dataset, at least consisting of thousands of subjects, comes out. The approaches are then expected to show robustness to large pose changes and occlusions, commonly occurring in non-cooperation of users. In 3D FER, a stable result above 90% is still not reached, and the study on 3D FAE is indeed limited. What's more, these issues in 3D face analysis are discussed individually, but these attributes, *i.e.* identify, gender, ethnicity, age, expression, *etc.*, are intuitively related, and the outcomes of different applications should mutually promote, which is another research direction worth investigating. For experimental methodologies, new 3D face databases, of much larger size and even demographic distribution (in particular for ethnicity), captured in a long time span, are needed for more rigorous evaluation schemes.

We are still on the way to address the existing and coming challenges so that these optimistic expressions about the potential of 3D face analysis will have a chance to come true. But compared with [2], we are now closer to the objective.

Acknowledgments. This work was supported in part by the National Basic Research Program of China (No. 2010CB327902), the National Natural Science Foundation of China (NSFC) under Grant 61202237 and Grant 61273263; the Specialized Research Fund for the Doctoral Program of Higher Education (No. 20121102120016); the research program of State Key Laboratory of Software Development Environment (SKLSDE-2013ZX-31); the joint project by the LIA 2MCSI lab between the group of Ecoles Centrales and Beihang University; and the Fundamental Research Funds for the Central Universities.

The authors would like to thank the Committee of CCBR 2014 for inviting this paper. Thanks also go to Dr. Huibin Li, Xi'an Jiaotong Univ., for discussions.

References

1. Zhao, W., Chellappa, R., Phillips, P., Rosenfeld, A.: Face recognition: A literature survey. CSUR 35(4), 399–458 (2003)
2. Bowyer, K., Chang, K., Flynn, P.: A survey of approaches and challenges in 3d and multi-modal 3d + 2d face recognition. CVIU 101(1), 1–15 (2006)
3. Turk, M., Pentland, A.: Eigenfaces for recognition. JOCN 3(1), 71–86 (1991)
4. Belhumeur, P., Hespanha, J., Kriegman, D.: Eigenfaces vs. Fisherfaces: Recognition using Class Specific Linear Projection. TPAMI 19(7), 711–720 (1997)
5. Wiskott, L., Fellous, J.-M., Kuiger, N., Von der Malsburg, C.: Face recognition by elastic bunch graph matching. TPAMI 19(7), 775–779 (1997)
6. Ahonen, T., Hadid, A., Pietikäinen, M.: Face recognition with local binary patterns. In: Pajdla, T., Matas, J(G.) (eds.) ECCV 2004. LNCS, vol. 3021, pp. 469–481. Springer, Heidelberg (2004)
7. Wright, J., Yang, A., Ganesh, A., Sastry, S., Ma, Y.: Robust face recognition via sparse representation. TPAMI 31(2), 210–227 (2009)
8. Abate, A., Nappi, M., Riccio, D., Sabatino, G.: 2D and 3d face recognition: a survey. PRL 28(14), 1885–1906 (2007)
9. Scheenstra, A., Ruifrok, A., Veltkamp, R.C.: A survey of 3D face recognition methods. In: Kanade, T., Jain, A., Ratha, N.K. (eds.) AVBPA 2005. LNCS, vol. 3546, pp. 891–899. Springer, Heidelberg (2005)
10. Phillips, P., Flynn, P., Scruggs, T., Bowyer, K., Chang, J., Hoffman, K., Marques, J., Min, J., Worek, W.: Overview of the face recognition grand challenge. In: CVPR (2005)
11. Savran, A., Alyüz, N., Dibeklioğlu, H., Çeliktutan, O., Gökberk, B., Sankur, B., Akarun, L.: Bosphorus database for 3D face analysis. In: Schouten, B., Juul, N.C., Drygajlo, A., Tistarelli, M. (eds.) BIOID 2008. LNCS, vol. 5372, pp. 47–56. Springer, Heidelberg (2008)
12. Yin, L., Wei, X., Sun, Y., Wang, J., Rosato, M.: A 3d facial expression database for facial behavior research. In: FG (2006)
13. Yin, L., Chen, X., Sun, Y., Worm, T., Reale, M.: A high-resolution 3d dynamic facial expression database. In: FG (2008)
14. Kakadiaris, I., Passalis, G., Toderici, G., Murtuza, M., Lu, Y., Karampatziakis, N., Theoharis, T.: Three dimensional face recognition in the presence of facial expressions: An annotated deformable model approach. TPAMI 29(4), 640–649 (2007)
15. Alyuz, N., Gokberk, B., Akarun, L.: Regional registration for expression resistant 3-d face recognition. TIFS 5(3), 425–440 (2010)

16. Huang, D., Ardabilian, M., Wang, Y., Chen, L.: 3-D face recognition using elbp-based facial description and local feature hybrid matching. TIFS 7(5), 1551–1565 (2012)
17. Drira, H., Ben Amor, B., Srivastava, A., Daoudi, M., Slama, R.: 3D face recognition under expressions, occlusions, and pose variations. TPAMI 35(9), 2270–2283 (2013)
18. Mian, A., Bennamoun, M., Owens, R.: An efficient multimodal 2d-3d hybrid approach to automatic face recognition. TPAMI 29(11), 1927–1943 (2007)
19. Mian, A., Bennamoun, M., Owens, R.: Keypoint detection and local feature matching for textured 3d face recognition. IJCV 79(1), 1–12 (2008)
20. Huang, D., Ben Soltana, W., Ardabilian, M., Wang, Y., Chen, L.: Textured 3d face recognition using biological vision-based facial representation and optimized weighted sum fusion. In: CVPRW (2011)
21. Huang, D., Ardabilian, M., Wang, Y., Chen, L.: Oriented gradient maps based automatic asymmetric 3d-2d face recognition. In: ICB (2012)
22. Chu, B., Romdhani, S., Chen, L.: 3D-aided face recognition robust to expression and pose variations. In: CVPR (2014)
23. Boehler, W., Marbs, A.: 3D scanning instruments. In: International Workshop on Scanning for Cultural Heritage Recording (2002)
24. Papatheodorou, T., Reuckert, D.: Evaluation of automatic 4D face recognition using surface and texture registration. In: FG (2004)
25. Kusuma, G.P., Chua, C.-S.: Image level fusion method for multimodal 2D + 3D face recognition. In: Campilho, A., Kamel, M.S. (eds.) ICIAR 2008. LNCS, vol. 5112, pp. 984–992. Springer, Heidelberg (2008)
26. Arca, S., Lanzarotti, R., Lipori, G.: Face recognition based on 2D and 3D features. In: Apolloni, B., Howlett, R.J., Jain, L. (eds.) KES 2007, Part I. LNCS (LNAI), vol. 4692, pp. 455–462. Springer, Heidelberg (2007)
27. Chang, K., Bowyer, K., Flynn, P.: An evaluation of multimodal 2d + 3d face biometrics. TPAMI 27(4), 619–624 (2005)
28. Husken, M., Brauckmann, M., Gehlen, S., Von der Malsburg, C.: Strategies and benefits of fusion of 2d and 3d face recognition. In: CVPRW (2005)
29. Gokberk, B., Dutagaci, H., Ulas, A., Akarun, L., Sankur, B.: Representation plurality and fusion for 3-D face recognition. TSMCB 38(1), 155–173 (2008)
30. Ben Soltana, W., Huang, D., Ardabilian, M., Chen, L., Ben Amar, C.: Comparison of 2d/3d features and their adaptive score level fusion for 3d face recognition. In: 3DPVT (2010)
31. Li, S.Z., Zhao, C., Ao, M., Lei, Z.: Learning to fuse 3D+2D based face recognition at both feature and decision levels. In: Zhao, W., Gong, S., Tang, X. (eds.) AMFG 2005. LNCS, vol. 3723, pp. 44–54. Springer, Heidelberg (2005)
32. Ben Soltana, W., Ardabilian, M., Chen, L., Ben Amar, C.: Adaptive feature and score level fusion strategy using genetic algorithms. In: ICPR (2010)
33. Smeets, D., Claes, P., Hermans, J., Vandermeulen, D., Suetens, P.: A comparative study of 3-D face recognition under expression variations. TSMCC 42(5), 710–727 (2012)
34. Fang, T., Zhao, X., Ocegueda, O., Shah, S., Kakadiaris, I.: 3D facial expression recognition: A perspective on promises and challenges. In: FG (2011)
35. Toderici, G., OMalley, S., Passalis, G., Theoharis, T., Kakadiaris, I.: Ethnicity- and gender-based subject retrieval using 3-d face-recognition techniques. IJCV 89(2), 382–391 (2010)
36. Huang, D., Ding, H., Wang, C., Wang, Y., Zhang, G., Chen, L.: Local circular patterns for multi-modal facial gender and ethnicity classification. In: IVC (2014)

37. Xia, B., Ben Amor, B., Daoudi, M., Drira, H.: Can 3d shape of the face reveal your age? VISAPP (2014)
38. Maes, C., Fabry, T., Keustermans, J., Smeets, D., Suetens, P., Vandermeulen, D.: Feature detection on 3d face surfaces for pose normalization and recognition. BTAS (2010)
39. Li, H., Huang, D., Lemaire, P., Morvan, J.-M., Chen, L.: Expression robust 3d face recognition via mesh-based histograms of multiple order surface differential quantities. In: ICIP (2011)
40. Besl, P., McKay, N.: A method for registration of 3-d shapes. TPAMI 14(2), 239–256 (1992)
41. Zhang, Z.: Iterative point matching for registration of free-form curves and surfaces. IJCV 13(2), 119–152 (1994)
42. Bookstein, F.L.: Principal warps: thin-plate splines and the decomposition of deformations. TPAMI 11(6), 567–585 (1989)
43. Dryden, I.L., Mardia, K.V.: Statistical Shape Analysis. John Wiley and Sons (1998)
44. Medioni, G., Waupotitsch, R.: Face modeling and recognition in 3-d. In: AMFG (2003)
45. Lu, X., Jain, A.: Deformation analysis for 3d face matching. WACV (2005)
46. Hesher, C., Srivastava, A., Erlebacher, G.: A novel technique for face recognition using range imaging. ISSPA (2003)
47. Heseltine, T., Pears, N., Austin, J.: Three-dimensional face recognition: an eigensurface approach. In: ICIP (2004)
48. Heseltine, T., Pears, N.E., Austin, J.: Three-dimensional face recognition: A fishersurface approach. In: Campilho, A.C., Kamel, M.S. (eds.) ICIAR 2004. LNCS, vol. 3212, pp. 684–691. Springer, Heidelberg (2004)
49. Wu, Z., Wang, Y., Pan, G.: 3D face recognition using local shape map. In: ICIP (2004)
50. Mian, A., Bennamoun, M., Owens, R.: Matching tensors for pose invariant automatic 3d face recognition. In: CVPRW (2005)
51. Cartoux, J., LaPreste, J., Richetin, M.: Face authentication or recognition by profile extraction from range images. In: Workshop on Interpretation of 3d Scenes (1989)
52. Nagamine, T., Uemura, T., Masuda, I.: 3D facial image analysis for human identification. In: ICPR (1992)
53. Wu, Y., Pan, G., Wu, Z.: Face authentication based on multiple profiles extracted from range data. In: AVBPA (2003)
54. Li, C., Barreto, A., Zhai, J., Chin, C.: Exploring face recognition by combining 3d profiles and contours. In: IEEE Southeast Conference (2005)
55. Lee, J.C., Milios, E.: Matching range images of human faces. In: ICCV (1990)
56. Tanaka, H.T., Ikeda, M., Chiaki, H.: Curvature-based face surface recognition using spherical correlation principal directions for curved object recognition. In: FG (1998)
57. Chua, C., Han, F., Ho, Y.K.: 3D human face recognition using point signature. In: FG (2000)
58. Lee, Y., Park, K., Shim, J., Yi, T.: 3D face recognition using statistical multiple features for the local depth information. In: VI (2003)
59. Moreno, A.B., Sanchez, A., Velez, J.F., Diaz, F.J.: Face recognition using 3d surface-extracted descriptors. In: IMVIP (2003)
60. Chang, K.I., Bowyer, K.W., Flynn, P.J.: Adaptive rigid multi-region selection for handling expression variation in 3d face recognition. In: CVPRW (2005)

61. Chang, K.I., Bowyer, K.W., Flynn, P.J.: Multiple nose region matching for 3d face recognition under varying facial expression. TPAMI 28(10), 1695–1700 (2006)
62. Lu, X., Jain, A.: Deformation modeling for robust 3d face matching. In: CVPR (2006)
63. Lu, X., Jain, A.: Deformation modeling for robust 3d face matching. TPAMI 30(8), 1346–1357 (2008)
64. Lu, X., Colbry, D., Jain, A.: Three-dimensional model based face recognition. In: ICPR (2004)
65. Gu, X., Gortler, S.J., Hoppe, H.: Geometry images. In: SIGGRAPH (2002)
66. Amberg, B., Knothe, R., Vetter, T.: Expression invariant 3d face recognition with a morphable model. In: FG (2008)
67. Blanz, V., Vetter, T.: Face recognition based on fitting a 3d morphable model. TPAMI 25(9), 1063–1074 (2003)
68. Mpiperis, I., Malassiotis, S., Strintzis, M.: Bilinear models for 3-d face and facial expression recognition. TIFS 3(3), 498–511 (2008)
69. Tenenbaum, J., Freeman, W.: Separating style and content with bilinear models. Neural Computation 12(6), 1247–1283 (2000)
70. Al-Osaimi, F., Bennamoun, M., Mian, A.: An expression deformation approach to non-rigid 3d face recognition. IJCV 81(3), 302–316 (2009)
71. Ocegueda, O., Shah, S., Kakadiaris, I.: Which parts of the face give out your identity? In: CVPR (2011)
72. Ocegueda, O., Passalis, G., Theoharis, T., Shah, S., Kakadiaris, I.: UR3D-C: linear dimensionality reduction for efficient 3d face recognition. IJCB (2011)
73. Chu, D., Shah, S., Kakadiaris, I.: 3D face recognition for partial data using semi-coupled dictionary learning. In: FG (2013)
74. Bronstein, A., Bronstein, K.R.: Expression-invariant 3d face recognition. In: AVBPA (2003)
75. Bronstein, A.M., Bronstein, M.M., Spira, A., Kimmel, R.: Face recognition from facial surface metric. In: Pajdla, T., Matas, J(G.) (eds.) ECCV 2004. LNCS, vol. 3022, pp. 225–237. Springer, Heidelberg (2004)
76. Bronstein, A., Bronstein, M., Kimmel, R.: Expression-invariant representations of faces. TIP 16(1), 188–197 (2007)
77. Bronstein, A.M., Bronstein, M.M., Kimmel, R.: Robust expression-invariant face recognition from partially missing data. In: Leonardis, A., Bischof, H., Pinz, A. (eds.) ECCV 2006. LNCS, vol. 3953, pp. 396–408. Springer, Heidelberg (2006)
78. Mpiperis, I., Malassiotis, S., Strintzis, M.: 3-D face recognition with the geodesic polar representation. TIFS 2(3), 537–547 (2007)
79. Samir, C., Srivastava, A., Daoudi, M.: Three-dimensional face recognition using shapes of facial curves. TPAMI 28(11), 1858–1863 (2006)
80. Samir, C., Srivastava, A., Daoudi, M., Klassen, E.: An intrinsic framework for analysis of facial surfaces. IJCV 82(1), 80–95 (2009)
81. Ballihi, L., Ben Amor, B., Daoudi, M., Srivastava, A., Aboutajdine, D.: Boosting 3-d geometric features for efficient face recognition and gender classification. TIFS 7(6), 1766–1779 (2012)
82. Drira, H., Ben Amor, B., Daoudi, M., Srivastava, A.: Pose and expression-invariant 3d face recognition using elastic radial curves. In: BMVC (2010)
83. Berretti, S., Del Bimbo, A., Pala, P.: Description and retrieval of 3d face models using iso-geodesic stripes. In: MIR (2006)
84. Berretti, S., Del Bimbo, A., Pala, P.: Analysis and retrieval of 3d facial models using iso-geodesic stripes. In: CBMI (2008)

85. Berretti, S., Del Bimbo, A., Pala, P.: 3D face recognition using isogeodesic stripes. TPAMI 32(12), 2162–2177 (2010)
86. Faltemier, T., Bowyer, K., Flynn, P.: A region ensemble for 3d face recognition. TIFS 3(1), 62–73 (2008)
87. Queirolo, C., Silva, L., Bellon, O., Segundo, M.: 3D face recognition using simulated annealing and the surface interpenetration measure. TPAMI 32(2), 206–219 (2010)
88. Spreeuwers, L.J.: Fast and accurate 3d face recognition using registration to an intrinsic coordinate system and fusion of multiple region classifiers. IJCV 93(3), 389–414 (2011)
89. Gokberk, B., Irfanoglu, M., Akarun, L.: 3D shape-based face representation and feature extraction for face recognition. IVC 24(8), 857–869 (2006)
90. Mian, A., Bennamoun, M., Owens, R.: A novel representation and feature matching algorithm for automatic pairwise registration of range images. IJCV 66(1), 19–40 (2006)
91. Mian, A., Bennamoun, M., Owens, R.: Three-dimensional model-based object recognition and segmentation in cluttered scenes. TPAMI 28(10), 1584–1601 (2006)
92. Huang, D., Zhang, G., Ardabilian, M., Wang, Y., Chen, L.: 3D face recognition using distinctiveness enhanced facial representations and local feature hybrid matching. In: BTAS (2010)
93. Huang, D., Ardabilian, M., Wang, Y., Chen, L.: A novel geometric facial representation based on multi-scale extended local binary patterns. In: FG (2011)
94. Smeets, D., Keustermans, J., Vandermeulen, D., Suetens, P.: meshsift: Local sur face features for 3d face recognition under expression variations and partial data. CVIU 117(2), 158–169 (2013)
95. Berretti, S., Werghi, N., Del Bimbo, A., Pala, P.: Matching 3d face scans using interest points and local histogram descriptors. CG 37(5), 509–525 (2013)
96. Cook, J., Chandran, V., Fookes, C.: 3D face recognition using loggabor templates. In: BMVC (2006)
97. Cook, J., Chandran, V., Fookes, C.: Multiscale representation for 3-d face recognition. TIFS 2(3), 529–536 (2007)
98. Wang, Y., Liu, J., Tang, X.: Robust 3d face recognition by local shape difference boosting. TPAMI 32(10), 1858–1870 (2010)
99. Huang, D., Ouji, K., Ardabilian, M., Wang, Y., Chen, L.: 3D face recognition based on local shape patterns and sparse representation classifier. In: Lee, K.-T., Tsai, W.-H., Liao, H.-Y.M., Chen, T., Hsieh, J.-W., Tseng, C.-C. (eds.) MMM 2011 Part I. LNCS, vol. 6523, pp. 206–216. Springer, Heidelberg (2011)
100. Li, X., Jia, T., Zhang, H.: Expression-insensitive 3d face recognition using sparse representation. In: CVPR (2009)
101. Li, H., Huang, D., Morvan, J.-M., Chen, L., Wang, Y.: Expression-robust 3d face recognition via weighted sparse representation of multi-scale and multi-component local normal patterns. Neurocomputing 133, 179–193 (2014)
102. Vijayan, V., Bowyer, K., Flynn, P., Huang, D., Chen, L., Hansen, M., Shah, S., Ocegueda, O., Kakadiaris, I.: Twins 3d face recognition challenge. IJCB (2011)
103. Li, H., Huang, D., Chen, L., Wang, Y., Morvan, J.-M.: A group of facial normal descriptors for recognizing 3d identical twins. BTAS (2012)
104. Wang, J., Yin, L., Wei, X., Sun, Y.: 3D facial expression recognition based on primitive surface feature distribution. In: CVPR (2006)
105. Gong, B., Wang, Y., Liu, J., Tang, X.: Automatic facial expression recognition on a single 3d face by exploring shape deformation. ACM MM (2009)

106. Zeng, W., Li, H., Chen, L., Morvan, J.-M., Gu, X.: An automatic 3d expression recognition framework based on sparse representation of conformal images. FG (2013)
107. Zhao, X., Dellandrea, E., Chen, L., Samaras, D.: AU recognition on 3d faces based on an extended statistical facial feature model. BTAS (2010)
108. Sun, Y., Yin, L.: Facial expression recognition based on 3D dynamic range model sequences. In: Forsyth, D., Torr, P., Zisserman, A. (eds.) ECCV 2008, Part II. LNCS, vol. 5303, pp. 58–71. Springer, Heidelberg (2008)
109. Drira, H., Ben Amor, B., Daoudi, M., Srivastava, A., Berretti, S.: 3D dynamic expression recognition based on a novel deformation vector field and random forest. In: ICPR (2012)
110. Xia, B., Ben Amor, B., Drira, H., Daoudi, M., Ballihi, L.: Gender and 3d facial symmetry: what's the relationship? In: FG (2013)
111. Sandbach, G., Zafeiriou, S., Pantic, M., Yin, L.: Static and dynamic 3d facial expression recognition: a comprehensive survey. IVC 30(10), 683–697 (2012)
112. Zafeiriou, S., Hansen, M., Atkinson, G., Argyriou, V., Petrou, M., Smith, M., Smith, L.: The photoface database. In: CVPRW (2011)
113. Zhao, X., Huang, D., Dellandrea, E., Chen, L.: Automatic 3d facial expression recognition based on a bayesian belief net and a statistical facial feature model. In: ICPR (2010)
114. Li, H., Morvan, J.-M., Chen, L.: 3D facial expression recognition based on histograms of surface differential quantities. In: Blanc-Talon, J., Kleihorst, R., Philips, W., Popescu, D., Scheunders, P. (eds.) ACIVS 2011. LNCS, vol. 6915, pp. 483–494. Springer, Heidelberg (2011)
115. Li, H., Chen, L., Huang, D., Wang, Y., Morvan, J.-M.: 3D facial expression recognition via multiple kernel learning of multi-scale local normal patterns. In: ICPR (2012)
116. Li, H., Huang, D., Morvan, J.-M., Chen, L.: Learning weighted sparse representation of encoded facial normal information for expression-robust 3d face recognition. IJCB (2011)
117. Tang, H., Huang, T.: 3D facial expression recognition based on automatically selected features. In: CVPRW (2008)
118. Berretti, S., Del Bimbo, A., Pala, P., Ben Amor, B., Daoudi, M.: A set of selected SIFT features for 3d facial expression recognition. In: ICPR (2010)
119. Ding, H., Huang, D., Wang, Y., Chen, L.: Facial ethnicity classification based on boosted local texture and shape descriptions. In: FG (2013)
120. Moreno, A.B., Sánchez, A.: GavabDB: a 3d face database. In: COST275 Workshop on Biometrics on the Internet (2004)
121. Faltemier, T., Bowyer, K., Flynn, P.: Using a multi-instance enrollment representation to improve 3d face recognition. In: BTAS (2007)
122. Conde, C., Serrano, A., Cabello, E.: Multimodal 2d, 2.5d & 3d face verification. In: ICIP (2006)
123. Gupta, S., Castleman, K., Markey, M., Bovik, A.C.: Texas 3d face recognition database. In: SSIAI (2010)
124. Heseltine, T., Pears, N., Austin, J.: Three-dimensional face recognition using combinations of surface feature map subspace components. IVC 26(3), 382–396 (2008)
125. CASIA-3D FaceV1, http://biometrics.idealtest.org/
126. Colombo, A., Cusano, C., Schettini, R.: UMB-DB: A database of partially occluded 3d faces. In: ICCVW (2011)
127. Chen, C., Weng, Y., Zhou, S., Tong, Y., Zhou, K.: FaceWarehouse: a 3d facial expression database for visual computing. TVCG 20(3), 413–425 (2014)

128. Colbry, D., Stockman, G., Jain, A.: Detection of anchor points for 3d face verica-
     tion. In: CVPRW (2005)
129. Szeptycki, P., Ardabilian, M., Chen, L.: A coarse-to-fine curvature analysis-based
     rotation invariant 3d face landmarking. In: BTAS (2009)
130. Liu, P., Wang, Y., Huang, D., Zhang, Z., Chen, L.: Learning the spherical har-
     monic features for 3-d face recognition. TIP 22(3), 914–925 (2013)
131. D'Hose, J., Colineau, J., Bichon, C., Dorizzi, B.: Precise localization of landmarks
     on 3d faces using gabor wavelets. In: BTAS (2007)
132. Romero, M., Pears, N.: Landmark localisation in 3d face data. In: AVSS (2009)
133. Faltemier, T., Bowyer, K., Flynn, P.: Rotated profile signatures for robust 3d
     feature detection. In: FG (2008)
134. Segundo, M., Silva, L., Bellon, O.P., Queirolo, C.: Automatic face segmentation
     and facial landmark detection in range images. TSMCB 40(5), 1319–1330 (2010)
135. Fanelli, G., Dantone, M., Gall, J., Fossati, A., Van Gool, L.: Random forests for
     real time 3D face analysis. IJCV 101(3), 437–458 (2012)
136. Nair, P., Cavallaro, A.: 3-D face detection, landmark localization and registration
     using a point distribution model. TMM 11(4), 611–623 (2009)
137. Zhao, X., Dellandrea, E., Chen, L., Kakadiaris, I.: Accurate landmarking of three-
     dimensional facial data in the presence of facial expression and occlusions using
     a three-dimensional statistical facial feature model. TSMCB 41(5), 1417–1428
     (2011)
138. Perakis, P., Passalis, G., Theoharis, T., Kakadiaris, I.: 3D facial landmark detec-
     tion under large yaw and expression variations. TPAMI 35(7), 1552–1564 (2013)
139. Creusot, C., Pears, N., Austin, J.: A machine-learning approach to keypoint de-
     tection and landmarking on 3d meshes. IJCV 102(1-3), 146–179 (2013)
140. Mohammadzade, H., Hatzinakos, D.: Iterative closest normal point for 3d face
     recognition. TPAMI 35(2), 381–307 (2013)
141. Huang, D., Ardabilian, M., Wang, Y., Chen, L.: Asymmetric 3d/2d face recog-
     nition based on lbp facial representation and canonical correlation analysis. In:
     ICIP (2009)
142. Huang, D., Ardabilian, M., Wang, Y., Chen, L.: Automatic asymmetric 3d-2d
     face recognition. In: ICPR (2010)
143. Toderici, G., Passalis, G., Zafeiriou, S., Tzimiropoulos, G., Petrou, M., Theoharis,
     T., Kakadiaris, I.: Bidirectional relighting for 3d-aided 2d face recognition. In:
     CVPR (2010)
144. Veltkamp, R.C., Van Jole, S., Drira, H., Ben Amor, B., Daoudi, M., Li, H., Chen,
     L., Claes, P., Smeets, D., Hermans, J., Vandermeulen, D., Suetens, P.: SHREC
     2011 track: 3D face models retrieval. EG-3 DOR (2011)

Automatic Two Phase Sparse Representation Method and Face Recognition Experiments

Ke Yan[*], Yong Xu, and Jian Zhang

Shenzhen Graduate School, Harbin Institute of Technology
{yanke401,zpower007}@163.com, yongxu@ymail.com

Abstract. The two phase sparse representation (TPSR) method has achieved promising face recognition performance. However, this method has the following flaw: its recognition accuracy varies with parameter M and at present there is no means to automatically set it. As a consequence, it becomes the bottleneck to apply the TPSR method to real-world problems. In this paper, we propose an improvement to TPSR (ITPSR), which can choose a proper value of parameter M for obtaining the optimal performance. Extensive experiments show that the proposed ITPSR is feasible and can obtain excellent performance.

Keywords: Pattern Recognition, Sparse Representation, Transform Methods.

1 Introduction

Sparse representation methods [1, 2] have attracted tremendous attention and were viewed as a breakthrough of face recognition [3]. Besides face recognition, sparse representation methods were also applied to video analysis [4], image super-resolution [5,6], image recovery [7], image denoising [8], action recognition [9], illumination recovery [10,11] etc. One of the underlying factors to contribute to the good performance of sparse representation methods is that they provide an excellent way to represent face images. Besides sparse representation methods with ℓ_1 norm minimization [12-14], there are many other representation methods such as representation methods with ℓ_2 norm minimization [4-6, 15]. In order to summarize these methods with similar properties, we refer to them as representation-based methods. The methods in [16-21] use the sparse combination of training samples to represent the test samples.

Among previous representation based methods, representation methods with ℓ_2 norm minimization are very easy to implement and are mathematically tractable [22-23]. For example, one of them is the well-known collaborative representation method, which has shown good performance on face recognition [4]. Moreover, by using a very simple strategy, one can exploit representation methods with ℓ_2 norm minimization to obtain sparse representation of the test sample with respect to the

---

[*] Corresponding author.

Z. Sun et al. (Eds.): CCBR 2014, LNCS 8833, pp. 22–30, 2014.

training samples and to obtain very good recognition results. Moreover, the two phase sparse representation (TPSR) method is a sparse representation method with ℓ_2 norm minimization method and obtains remarkable recognition results [9, 11]. However, this method in [24-25] has the following flaw: the recognition accuracy of TPSR severely varies with parameter M , and up to now an automatic choosing strategy of the parameter M is still missing. As a consequence, this parameter is the bottleneck to apply the TPSR method to real-world problems. Actually, almost all representation methods suffer from the problems that the performance of the method varies with the parameter and it is hard to properly set the parameter.

In 2012, the method proposed in [26] proposed a way to set the parameter of TPSR. However, we see that this way does not resolve the problem of TPSR. With this paper, we aim at improving TPSR with the goal of devising an algorithm that can automatically set parameter M for obtaining the optimal performance. With a reasonable criterion, the devised algorithm can properly set parameter M . Extensive experiments show that the proposed improvement to TPSR is feasible and can obtain excellent performance. Moreover, since other representation methods can achieve good performance under the condition that the parameter in it is properly set, the proposed improvement is a good representation method.

2   Description of TPSR

In this section, we will present the details of the proposed TPSR method. We assume that there are L classes and n training samples $x_1...x_n$. If a training sample is from the j th class ($j = 1, 2, ..., L$), we take j as the class label of this training sample.

2.1   The First Phase of the TPSR

The first phase of the TPSR uses all of the training samples to represent each test sample and exploits the representation result to identify the M nearest neighbors of the test sample from the set of the training samples. It first assumes that the following equation is approximately satisfied:

$$y = a_1 x_1 + ... + a_n x_n \tag{1}$$

where y is the test sample and a_i ($i = 1, 2, ..., n$) are the coefficients. We can rewrite Eq(1) into the following equation:

$$y = XA \tag{2}$$

where $A = [a_1...a_n]^T$, $X = [x_1...x_n]$. $x_1...x_n$ and y are all column vectors. If X is a nonsingular square matrix, we can solve A by using $A = X^{-1}y$; otherwise, we can solve it by using $A = (X^T X + \mu I)^{-1} X^T y$, where μ is a small positive constant and I is the identity matrix. Eq(1) shows that every training sample makes its own contribution to representing the test sample. The contribution that the i th training sample makes is $a_i x_i$. The contribution, in representing the test sample, of the i th training sample x_i can be also evaluated by the deviation between $a_i x_i$ and y, i.e. $e_i =\parallel y - a_i x_i \parallel^2$. e_i can be also somewhat viewed as a measurement of the distance between the test sample and the i th training sample. We consider that a small e_i means that the i th training sample has a great contribution in representing the test sample. We exploit e_i to identify the M training samples that have the M   greatest contributions, in representing the test sample and denote them by $x_1, ..., x_M$. We refer to these samples as the M nearest neighbors of the test sample. Let $C = \{c_1, c_2, ..., c_d\}$, a set of some numbers, stand for the set of class labels of the M   nearest neighbors. If a nearest neighbor is from the j th class ($j = 1, 2, ..., L$), we take j as the class label of this nearest neighbor. C must be one subset of set $\{1, 2, ..., L\}$ i.e. $C \subseteq \{1, 2, ..., L\}$. If no neighbor is from the p th class, then the number p must be not an element of C. Consequently, the TPSR will not ultimately classify the test sample into the p th class.

2.2   The Second Phase of the TPSR

The second phase of the TPSR seeks to represent the test sample as a linear combination of the determined M   nearest neighbors and uses the representation result to classify the test sample. This phase assumes that the following equation is approximately satisfied:

$$y = b_1 \tilde{x}_1 + ... + b_M \tilde{x}_M$$

(3)

where $\tilde{x}_i$ ($i = 1, 2, ..., M$) are the identified M nearest neighbors and b_i ($i = 1, 2, ..., M$) are the coefficients. $\tilde{x}_i (i = 1, 2, ..., M)$ are the subset of   set X. We rewrite Eq.(3) into

$$y = \tilde{X}B$$

(4)

where $B = [b_1 ... b_M]^T$, $\tilde{X} = [\tilde{x}_1 ... \tilde{x}_M]$. If $\tilde{X}$ is a nonsingular square matrix, we can solve B by using $B = (\tilde{X})^{-1} y$; otherwise, we can solve it by using $B = (\tilde{X}^T \tilde{X} + \gamma I)^{-1} \tilde{X}^T y$ where γ is a positive constant and I is the identity matrix. After we obtain B, we refer to $\tilde{X}B$ as the representation result of our method. We can convert the representation result into a two-dimensional image with the same size as the original sample image.

Since the neighbors might be from different classes, we calculate the sum of the contribution to represent the test sample of the neighbors from each class and exploit the sum to classify the test sample. For example, if all the neighbors from the r th ($r \in C$) class are $\tilde{x}_s ...$ $\tilde{x}_t$, then the sum of the contribution to represent the test sample of the r th class will be

$$g_r = b_s \tilde{x}_s + ... + b_t \tilde{x}_t \tag{5}$$

We calculate the deviation of g_r from y by using

$$D_r = \| y - g_r \|^2, r \in C \tag{6}$$

We can also convert g_r into a two-dimensional matrix with the same size as the original sample image. When we do so, we also refer to this matrix as a two-dimensional image that stands for the contribution of the r th class. A smaller deviation D_r means a greater contribution to representing the test sample. Thus, we classify y into the class that produces the smallest deviation. In summary, the main steps of the TPSR are as follows:

1. Use the first phase to determine the M nearest neighbors for the test sample.
2. Exploit the M nearest neighbors of the test sample to construct Eq.(3) and solve this equation.
3. Use Eq.(6) to compute deviation D_r which is generated from the r th class $(r \in C)$.
4. Classify the test sample into the class that has minimum deviation. In other words, if $D_q = \min D_r (q, r \in C)$, the test sample will be classified into the $q, r \in C$ th class.

Using the second phase, the TPSR determines the contribution in representing the test sample of different M nearest neighbors and classifies the test sample into the class that makes the largest contribution. The contribution of one nearest neighbor is mainly associated with the corresponding coefficient. If the i th nearest neighbor has a large similarity with the test sample, then the corresponding coefficient probably has a large absolute value. As a result, the i th nearest neighbor probably also makes a large contribution to representing the test sample.

3   The Proposed Method

The main steps of the proposed method are described as follows:

1. To initialize M as M_0.
2. To use the first phase to determine M nearest neighbors for the test sample.
3. To exploit the M nearest neighbors of the test sample to construct Eq.(3) and solve this equation.
4. To use Eq.(6) to compute deviation D_r which is generated from the r th class, $r \in C$.
5. To classify the test sample into the class that has minimum deviation. In other words, if $D_q = \min D_r (q, r \in C)$, the test sample will be classified into the q th class. Let $R_t = sort(D_r)$, i.e. vector R_t is composed of all entries of D_r in ascending order. Let $v_t = \log(R_t(2)/R_t(1))$. $R_t(1)$ and $R_t(2)$ are the first two smallest entries of R_t.

6. After steps 1-5 have been implemented for all test samples, we identify 10 percent of the test samples with the smallest v_t and take the mean of v_t s of these test samples as u_L. If the u_L is less than $0.95 * u_{L-1}$ (u_{L-1} is the mean of v_t s of the test samples obtained in the last loop), then the algorithm is terminated; otherwise, $M = M + M_{step}$ and go to steps 2.

Now we present the reasonability of the proposed method. v_t indicates the confidence of the classification result and larger v_t means greater confidence. Thus, the proposed method takes the M whose changes saint reduction of v_t as the critical point. Because very small v_t usually leads to erroneous classification, we should take the test samples with small v_t into serious account. As a result, it is reasonable to compare the mean of v_t s of 20 percent of the test samples with the smallest v_t. On contrary, if we compare the mean of v_t s of the test samples with great v_t s, the result will be much less significant. As we know, a procedure similar to the one in our method has been successfully used as a reject procedure. Its reasonability is that low v_t means that the possibilities of the test sample truly being from the class with the smallest score and from the class with the second smallest score have no saint difference, so we had better reject to class it. We see that pattern classification methods with the above reject procedure have reputation owing to its promising performance.

Our method also provides better strategy and scheme than previous attempt to add reject function to TPSR. In [15], the authors regarded the ratio of the smallest residual to the deviation between the test sample and the obtained linear combination of the training samples as the criterion to determine M. It seems that this criterion is somewhat feasible but has the following disadvantage: the above ratio almost always varies with the numbers of the classes and training samples as well as the dimensionality of the sample. For example, a large number of classes usually lead to a small ratio. As a consequence, it is indeed hard to properly set M in real-world applications where the numbers of the classes and training samples as well as the dimensionality of the sample are various. On the contrary, for the criterion in our method, the experimental results show that a same threshold applicable for all the experiments on different databases is available.

4   Experimental Results

4.1   Experiments on the ORL Face Database

We firstly use the ORL face database to test our method. This database contains 400 images from 40 person each providing 10 images. For some person, the images were taken at different condition, with varying light, facial expression(smiling or not smiling), facial detail(glass or not glass).We respectively took the 4,5,6,7 face images of each person as training samples, and the other sample as test samples. Table 1 shows the rates of the classification accuracy of different methods. We can see that our proposed method's recognition rates are higher than the other methods. Therefore,

ITPSR can improve LRC, CRC, SRC. The parameters λ of these methods are 0.01. Figure 1 shows the classification accuracies rates of different M nearest neighbors in TPSR. The sub-figures (a-d) respectively correspond to the training numbers of 4,5,6,7. The proposed method's accuracy rate is one of the rates in the TPSR, and then we mark the accuracy rates of ITPSR in the sub-figures (a-d) as black dot. As a result, we can overcome the bottleneck to apply the TPSR method to real-word problems.

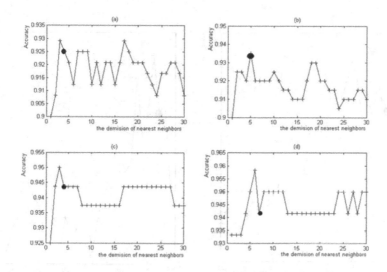

Fig. 1. The classification accuracy rates of different nearest neighbors of TPSR

Table 1. Accuracies (%) of different methods on the ORL database

train_num	4	5	6	7
Proposed method	92.5%	93.5%	94.37%	95%
src	92.08%	92.5%	93.75%	95%
lrc	89.17%	88.5%	91.88%	91.67%
crc	90%	90.5%	92.5%	94.17%

4.2   Experiments on the Feret Face Database

Then we conducted the experiment on the Feret databases[25]. From the Feret database we used a subset of images from 1400 images from 200 person with each subject providing seven images. For some person, the images were taken from different condition, with varying light, facial detail (frontal face and deflection face). We split the database into two halves. One half, which respectively contains 4, 5 face images for each person, was used for training samples, and the other half was used for testing. Table 2 shows the rates of the classification accuracy of proposed method, SRC, LRC and CRC. Because of the number of testing samples is large, the recognition rates of different methods are low. We can see that our method can improve other methods, and the accuracy of ITPSR is the highest in these methods. The parameter λ of SRC is 0.001, and the other methods' λ are 0.01. Figure 2 shows the classification accuracies rate of different M neighbors in TPSR. The sub-figures (a-b) respectively correspond to the training numbers of 4, 5. The proposed method's accuracy rate is one of the rates in the TPSR, and the accuracy rates of ITPSR are marked in the sub-figures (a-b) as black dot. The proposed method can overcome the bottleneck of TPTSR to real-word problems.

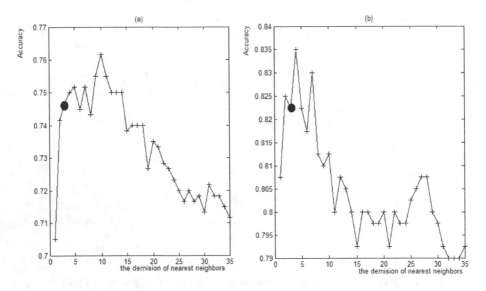

Fig. 2. The classification accuracy rates of different nearest neighbors of TPSR

Table 2. Accuracies (%) of different methods on the Feret database

train_num	4	5
Proposed method	74.67%	82.25%
Src	63.67%	77.75%
lrc	55.33%	68.5%
crc	45.17%	49.5%

5   Conclusions

The proposed ITPSR is able to properly determine a value for the parameter in previous TPSR method. It indeed breaks the bottleneck on real-world applications of previous TPSR method and makes it become a feasible method. The experimental results show that the proposed ITPSR can obtain excellent performance. Moreover, other representation methods almost have parameters that need to be manually set, whereas the proposed ITPSR does not need to do so and can automatically set a good value for the parameter.

References

1. Wright, J., Yang, A.Y., Ganesh, A., Sastry, S.S., Ma, Y.: Robust Face Recognition via Sparse Representation. IEEE Trans. Pattern. Anal. Mach. Intell 31, 210–227 (2009)
2. Wright, J., Ma, Y., Mairal, J., Sapiro, G., Huang, T.S., Yan, S.: Sparse Representation for Computer Vision and Pattern Recognition. IEEE. Proc. 98, 1031–1044 (2010)
3. Kroeker, K.L.: Face Recognition Breakthrough. Commun. ACM. 52, 18–19 (2009)
4. Mairal, J., Sapiro, G., Elad, M.: Learning Multiscale Sparse Representations for Image and Video Restoration. In: Institute for Mathematics and Its Applications (2007)
5. Yang, J., Wright, J., Huang, T.S., Ma, Y.: Image Super-resolution Via Sparse Representation. IEEE. Trans. Image. Process 19, 2861–2873 (2010)
6. Yang, J., Wright, J., Huang, T., Ma, Y.: Image Super-resolution as Sparse Representation of Raw Image Patches. In: IEEE Conference on Computer Vision and Pattern Recognition, pp. 1–8 (2008)
7. Guleryuz, O.G.: Nonlinear Approximation Based Image Recovery Using Adaptive Sparse Reconstructions and Iterated Denoising-part I: theory. IEEE. Trans. Image. Process 15, 539–554 (2006)
8. Dong, W., Li, X., Zhang, D., Shi, G.: Sparsity-based Image Denoising via Dictionary Learning and Structural Clustering. In: IEEE Conference on Computer Vision and Pattern Recognition, pp. 457–464 (2011)
9. Qiu, Q., Jiang, Z., Chellappa, R.: Sparse Dictionary-based Representation and Recognition of Action Attributes. In: IEEE International Conference on Computer Vision, pp. 704–714 (2011)
10. Mei, X., Ling, H., Jacobs, D.W.: Illumination Recovery from Image with Cast Shadows via Sparse Representation. IEEE Trans. Image. Process 20, 2366–2377 (2011)
11. Xu, Y., Zhu, X., Li, Z., Liu, G., Lu, Y., Liu, H.: Using the Original and 'Symmetrical Face' Training Samples to Perform Representation based Two-step Face Recognition. Pattern Recognit. 46, 1151–1158 (2013)
12. Yang, J., Zhang, L., Xu, Y., Yang, J.Y.: Beyond Sparsity: The Role of L1-optimizer in Pattern Classification. Pattern Recognit. 45, 1104–1118 (2012)
13. Mei, X., Ling, H., Jacobs, D.W.: Sparse Representation of Cast Shadows via L1-regularized Least Squares. In: IEEE 12th International Conference on Computer Vision, pp. 583–590 (2009)
14. Donoho, D.L.: For Most Large Underdetermined Systems of Linear Equations the Minimal ℓ1- Norm Solution is also the Sparsest Solution. Communica. Appl. Math. 59, 797–829 (2006)
15. Naseem, I., Togneri, R., Bennamoun, M.: Linear Regression for Face Recognition. Pattern IEEE Trans. Anal. Mach. Intell. 32, 2106–2112 (2010)
16. Wright, J., Ma, Y., Mairal, J., Sapiro, G., Huang, T.S., Yan, S.: Sparse Representation for Computer Vision and Pattern Recognition. Proc. IEEE 98, 1031–1044 (2010)
17. Mairal, J., Bach, F., Ponce, J., Sapiro, G., Zisserman, A.: Supervised Dictionary Learning. In: Neural Information Processing Systems Conference, vol. 21 (2008)
18. Shi, Y., Dai, D., Liu, C., Yan, H.: Sparse Discriminant Analysis for Breast Cancer Biomarker Identification and Classification. Prog. Nat. Sci. 19, 1635–1641 (2009)
19. Dikmen, M., Huang, T.S.: Robust Estimation of Foreground in Surveillance Videos by Sparse Error Estimation. In: 19th International Conference on Pattern Recognition, pp. 1–4 (2008)
20. Elhamifar, E., Vidal, R.: Sparse Subspace Clustering. In: IEEE Conference on Computer Vision and Pattern Recognition, pp. 2790–2797 (2009)

21. Rao, S.R., Tron, R., Vidal, R., Ma, Y.: Motion Segmentation via Robust Subspace Separation in the Presence of Outlying, Incomplete, or Corrupted Trajectories. In: IEEE Conference on Computer Vision and Pattern Recognition, pp. 1–8 (2008)
22. Zhang, L., Yang, M., Feng, X.C.: Sparse representation or collaborative representation: Which helps face recognition? In: IEEE International Conference on Computer Vision, pp. 471–478 (2011)
23. Zhang, Z., Li, Z.M., Xie, B.L., Wang, L., Chen, Y.: Integrating Globality and Locality for Robust Representation Based Classification. Math. Probl. Eng. (2014), doi: http://dx.doi.org/10.1155/2014/415856
24. Xu, Y., Zhang, D., Yang, J., Yang, J.Y.: A Two-phase Test Sample Sparse Representation Method for Use with Face Recognition. IEEE. Trans. Circuit. Syst. Video. Technol. 21, 1255–1262 (2011)
25. Zhang, Z., Wang, L., Zhu, Q., Liu, Z.H., Chen, Y.: Noise modeling and representation based classification methods for face recognition. Neurocomputing (2014), doi: 10.1016/j.neucom.2014.07.058
26. Zhu, Q., Xu, Y., Wang, J., Fan, Z.: Kernel Based Sparse Representation for Face Recognition. In: 21st International Conference on Pattern Recogniton, pp. 1703–1706 (2012)
27. Phillips, P.J., Moon, H., Rizvi, S.A., Rauss, P.J.: The FERET Evaluation Methodology for Face-recognition Algorithms. IEEE Trans. Pattern. Anal. Mach. Intell. 22, 1090–1104 (2000)

Pure Face Extraction from 3D Point Cloud Using Random Forest Skin Classification[*]

Hongbo Huang[1,2], Zhichun Mu[1], Hui Zeng[1], and Mingming Huang[1]

[1] School of Automation and Electrical Engineering, University of Science
and Technology Beijing, Beijing 100083, China
[2] Computing Center, Beijing Information Science and Technology
University, Beijing 100192, China
hauck@sohu.com, mu@ies.ustb.edu.cn,
{hzeng,mmhuang1205}@163.com

Abstract. Using 3D information is expected to handle challenges in 2D face recognition and improve system performance. Extracting pure facial part in face point cloud is usually the first step in a 3D face recognition system, which was mainly operated by manual in most previous studies. In this paper we propose a fully automatic approach for pure face extraction from 3D point cloud. Considering that 3D face point cloud can often be sensed in combination with color information, we use random forest classifiers to classify skin points and non-skin points in 3D point clouds. Usually there will be a few holes in the obtained skin point cloud, which mainly correspond to eyes, mouth, moustache, etc. We propose an approach based on nearest neighbor search method to fulfill the holes. Experiments show that the proposed approach can extract pure faces with different sizes, poses and expressions under various illumination conditions.

Keywords: Face recognition, Random forest, Skin detection, K-nearest neighbor algorithm.

1 Introduction

Face recognition has been highly researched in recent decades. Applying cases can be found in many fields including security monitoring, automated surveillance systems, design of human computer interfaces, multimedia communication, etc.[1] Although great advances have been made technically, face recognition still faces some

---

[*] This paper was supported by (1) National Natural Science Foundation of China under the Grant No. 61170116;61375010; (2) National Natural Science Foundation of China under the Grant No. 61005009; (3) Beijing Municipal Natural Science Foundation under the Grant No. 4102039; (4) Funding Project for Academic Human Resources Development in Institutions of Higher Learning Under the Jurisdiction of Beijing Municipality (PHR201108261). (5) Beijing Higher Education Young Elite Teacher Project under the Grant No. YETP0375. (6) Portions of the research in this paper use the CASIA-3D FaceV1 collected by the Chinese Academy of Sciences' Institute of Automation (CASIA).

Z. Sun et al. (Eds.): CCBR 2014, LNCS 8833, pp. 31–39, 2014.

difficulties. Most of the proposed approaches use 2D images to represent individual faces. Despite these methods perform well in constrained conditions, the recognition rates reduced greatly while there were variations in illumination, pose and facial expressions[2]. In an attempt to address these issues, research has begun to focus on the use of 3D facial data recently. The 3D data collected by a range sensor is less sensitive to the above imaging problems[3]. Accordingly, recognition systems based on 3D face information have the potential for greater recognition accuracy and are capable of overcoming some of the limitations in 2D face recognition systems[4]. Generally, two main representations are commonly used to model faces in 3D applications: range images and point clouds. A range image is often considered as a 2.5D image because it has similar form to intensity 2D image. A range image consists of a two-dimensional representation of a 3D points set (x, y, z), where each pixel in the X–Y plane stores the depth value z, while point clouds representation stores the points set (x, y, z) directly[5]. 3D point clouds are a global description that can represent multi-view of the whole head including face and ear. They are seldom affected by self-occlusions. In this paper, we mainly focus on the preprocessing of 3D face point cloud representation.

In the procedures of face recognition, so as to use 3D point cloud to represent a human face, the first step should be the locating of pure facial part in the point set. It makes sense to remove the points that are corresponding to hair, shoulders, clothes, etc. It would be great help to improve face recognition accuracy. Most literatures in 3D face recognition concentrated on data description, feature extraction or classification. In the research works reported previously, 3D data preprocessing mainly solved by manual operations. Or it was only automatic with frontal faces. Sala Llonch and E. Kokiopoulou proposed an automatic algorithm to extract face, removing irrelevant information from the 3D point clouds[6]. They firstly projected the point cloud to the X-Y plane to formulate a matrix A, and then estimated a vertical projection curve from the point cloud by computing the column sum of the matrix A. Then, they defined two lateral thresholds on the left and right inflexion points of the projection curve, and removed all data points beyond these thresholds. By a predefined Z-value threshold of the histogram, they further removed the points corresponding to the chest. Their method works well for the frontal face data but runs into trouble when the face pose is not frontal. Considering that 3D shape of the face can often be sensed in combination with a 2D color map, that is, the point cloud is often with color information. In this paper, we propose a method that extracts pure 3D face by detecting skin tone in 3D point cloud with a random forest algorithm. The proposed method can deal with any variations of the face pose and is fully automatic. To the best of our knowledge, this kind of methods has however not been investigated in 3D face recognition yet.

The rest of this paper is organized as follows: Section 2 briefly presents the random forest framework. In Section 3, the proposed methodology is described and illustrated. The experiments and results are provided in Section 4. Finally, some concluding remarks are given in Section 5.

2   Random Forest

Random forest is an ensemble leaning method which was firstly introduced by Ho[7] and further developed by Amit, Geman[8] and Breiman[9]. The main idea is a bit like two well-known methods, bagging and boosting, which try to combine weak classifiers to obtain a strong one. In bagging, each tree is independently constructed using a bootstrap sample of the data set. A simple majority vote is taken for prediction. In boosting, successive trees give extra weight to points incorrectly predicted by earlier predictors and a weighted vote is taken for prediction. Random forest first grows a number of tree predictors. Each tree depends on the values of a random vector sampled independently in the training set. Then, each tree votes for a predictor. Finally, the forest chooses the classification with the most votes. In comparison to bagging and boosting, random forest is faster in training and testing and it does not over fit. As has been proved[9], it has a very high generalization accuracy and is more robust with respect to noise. It is successfully used in image classification, image matching, segmentation and recognition[10].

During the procedure of constructing a random forest, a random vector k is selected with replacement from the features, which is independent of the past random vectors 1, ... , k−1 but with the same distribution. Then a tree is grown using the training set and the random vector k, resulting in a classifier h (x, k) where x is an input vector. After a large number of trees are generated, they vote for the most popular class. A single tree classifier may have accuracy only slightly better than a random choice of class. But combining trees using random features can produce improved accuracy[9].

The error of a random forest depends on the strength of the individual trees in the forest and the correlation between them. To improve accuracy, the randomness injected has to minimize correlation while maintaining strength. Randomness can be injected by two means: in subsampling the training data so that each tree is grown using a different subset; and in selecting different features from giving feature space in the node tests. The random forests procedure consists of both of the randomness at each node to grow each tree.

The generalization error is estimated by a method called out-of-bag (OOB) estimate. Consider the method for constructing a classifier from any training set. Given a specific training set T form bootstrap training sets T_i, construct classifiers h (x, T_i) and let these classifiers vote to form the bagged predictor. For each y, x in the training set, aggregate the votes only over those classifiers for which T_i does not containing y, x. This is called out-of-bag classifier. Then the out-of-bag estimate for the generalization error is the error rate of the out-of-bag classifier on the training set. The study of Breiman gives evidence to show that the out-of-bag estimate is unbiased and as accurate as using a test set of the same size as the training set[9].

3   Proposed Methodology

In this paper, our objective is extract pure face part from raw 3D point cloud. To this end, we developed a method by detecting skin tone from colorful 3D point cloud of human faces and removing points that are correspond to hair, shoulders, clothes, etc. We use CASIA 3D face database[12] to evaluate our methodology. CASIA 3D face database consists of 4624 scans of 123 persons using the non-contact 3D digitizer, Minolta Vivid 910. The database also consists of variations of poses, expressions and illuminations. It's difficult to locate face automatically by methods such as eye location, nose location, etc. because in many cases that part of area may be self-occluded. But skin color can be detected robustly by our method in any pose, expression and illumination variations such that we can remove the redundant points from the clouds.

3.1   Color Space Selection

Different color spaces have been proposed for skin detection such as RGB, YUV, HSV, and YCbCr. Generally HSV and YCbCr color spaces are used to retrieve from the intensity variations[13]. Selection of a proper color space can have a profound effect on the skin detection performance. Studies on more than ten common color spaces in [14] indicate that HSV color space provide the best result. So, in our study, we use HSV space to carry out our work. HSV color space represents colors in terms of Hue (or color-depth), Saturation (or color-purity) and intensity of the Value (or color-brightness). In some applications, HSV is also called HSB (Hue, Saturation, and Brightness) or HSI (Hue, Saturation, and Intensity). In this model, hue refers to color type, such as red, blue, or green, etc. It takes values from 0 to 360. Saturation refers to the vibrancy or purity of the color. It takes values from 0 to 100%. The lower the saturation of a color, the more "grayness" the color will appear. Finally, Value component refers to the brightness of the color. It also takes values from 0 to 100% [14].

The transformation from RGB to HSV is non-linear. It can be converted to the following expressions:

$$V = (R+G+B)/3 \tag{1}$$

$$X = -1/sqrt(6)R - 1/sqrt(6)G + 2/sqrt(6)B \tag{2}$$

$$Y = 1/sqrt(6)R - 1/sqrt(6)G \tag{3}$$

$$H = \arctan(Y/X) \tag{4}$$

$$S = (X^2 + Y^2)^{1/2} \tag{5}$$

In practice, we can follow the conversion bellow to execute much more efficiently and fast in a computer:

$$V = \max(R,G,B) \tag{6}$$

$$S = \begin{cases} 0, & if \quad MAX = 0 \\[2ex] 1 - \dfrac{MIN}{MAX}, & Otherwise \end{cases} \tag{7}$$

$$H = \begin{cases} Undefined \quad , \quad if \quad MAX = MIN \\ 60 \times \dfrac{G-B}{MAX - MIN} \quad , \quad if \quad MAX = R \quad and \quad G \geq B \\ 60 \times \dfrac{G-B}{MAX - MIN} + 360 \quad , \quad if \quad MAX = R \quad and \quad G < B \\ 60 \times \dfrac{B-R}{MAX - MIN} + 120 \quad , \quad if \quad MAX = G \\ 60 \times \dfrac{R-G}{MAX - MIN} + 240 \quad , \quad if \quad MAX = B \end{cases}$$

(8)

Where MAX is the maximum of the (R, G, B) values and MIN is equal to the minimum of those values.

3.2   Random Forest Train and Classification

We randomly selected 1256 scans of CASIA 3D face database. From each scan, we manually selected 20 points correspond to skin parts such as face, ear and neck. Then we selected 20 points corresponding to non-skin parts such as hair and clothes. The color information of each point was recorded as (R, G, B). Then the RGB color space was transformed into HSV space. The skin and non-skin points color is demonstrated in Fig.1 and Fig.2, where skin points are marked with 'o' and non-skin points are marked with ' • '. As we can see from Figure 1 and Figure 2, these skin color points gathered, while non-skin color points distributed around them. The skin colors appeared more concentrated and more separable from non-skin colors in HSV color space than in RGB color space. It is not difficult to deduce that we can predict a point to be skin color or non-skin color by decision trees.

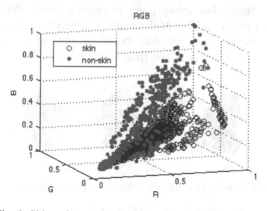

Fig. 1. Skin colors and non-skin colors in RGB color space

Let L be a column vector that contains the known class labels for the selected point colors. Each element of L specifies the group the corresponding point colors belong to, which labels the skin color points as "1" and non-skin color points as "-1". We then use these point colors to train a random forest model. With the trained model, when a color point is given, we can classify it into proper class thus we can tell whether it is a skin point or not.

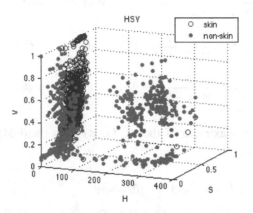

Fig. 2. skin and non-skin colors in HSV color space

3.3   Facial Components Recovery

For a given facial 3D scan, we use random forest method to classify all the points into skin color points and non-skin color points. All the non-skin color points were removed from the original point cloud to keep only skin part. Fig.3 shows one of the results of the processing. Fig.3 (a) is an original point cloud of a scan, and (b) is the points corresponding to skin part. As we can see, some part such as eyebrows, eyes and mouth are removed. But these components are important to a human face so we must try to recover these parts. We propose a method using range search in each point of the original point cloud. For every point in original point cloud, we search its neighbor points in an r radius sphere. If the number of neighbor points is greater than a threshold, we suppose it is a point that should be kept in the final point cloud. Otherwise, it should be removed from the final point cloud.

(a)   (b)   (c)

Fig. 3. Result of 3D face point cloud preprocessing

Fig.3 (c) showed the processed final point cloud of a face. It is clear that the proposed method can recover eyebrows, eyes and mouth, etc. and some noise can be removed too.

4   Experiments

To test the skin color detection method, we conducted a series of experiments on CASIA 3D face database. Firstly, as we stated in section 3.2, we manually selected 1256*20 skin color points and non-skin color points respectively. Then we performed validation on the selected points. In random forests, there was no need for cross-validation or a separate test set to get an unbiased estimate of the test set error. It is estimated internally during the run. Each tree is constructed using a different bootstrap sample from the original data. About one-third of the cases are left out of the bootstrap sample and are not used in the construction of the kth tree. Put each case left out in the construction of the kth tree down the kth tree to get a classification. In this way, a test set classification is obtained for each case in about one-third of the trees. At the end of the run, take j to be the class that gets most of the votes every time case n is OOB. The proportion of times that j is not equal to the true class of n averaged over all cases is due to the OOB error estimate. To test the influence of the number of trees on random forest, we vary the value of tree number from 0 to 500. The OOB error rates obtained are represented by the graph of Fig. 4.

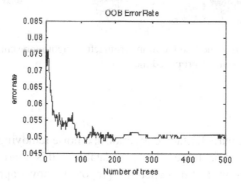

Fig. 4. Influence of the number of trees on random forest

The results show that the random forest model gives good performance and when tree number is about more than100. The performance is relatively stable. Overall, the results are good enough in terms of correct classification.

In the second test phase, 4624 scans in CASIA 3D face database were processed by the proposed method. Almost all skin faces could be extracted from original point clouds. Few scans lost part of points corresponding to eyes, mouths, etc. due to large facial expressions. Few scans made noises due to the fact that the clothes in the scans are similar to skin color. Despite these shortcomings, this method can greatly improve the speed and accuracy of subsequent processing and has a positive role in promoting 3D face feature extraction and recognition. Some results are shown in Fig. 5.

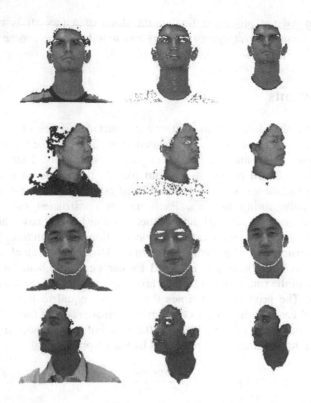

Fig. 5. Examples of proposed method.Columns from left to right represent original point cloud, results of skin filter and results of proposed method.

5   Conclusion

In 3D face recognition, pure 3D face extraction and noise removing are mainly solved by manual operations. For large 3D face database, this kind of work is time-consuming and exhausting. In this paper, we proposed a novel approach for pure 3D face extraction, which can extract faces and ears in any variations of pose and expressions, and it is fully automatic. We trained a random forest model and used this model for skin color classification. To fill holes on the skin filtered point cloud, we performed an approach based on KNN. Experimental results showed that the proposed algorithm could detect faces with different sizes, poses and expressions under different illumination conditions fast and accurately. We believe that this method would be helpful to improve the performances of 3D face recognition.

References

1. Smeets, D., et al.: Objective 3D face recognition: Evolution, approaches and challenges. Forensic. Sci. Int. 201(1-3), 125–132 (2010)
2. Heseltine, T., Pears, N., Austin, J.: Three-dimensional face recognition: An eigensurface approach. In: 2004 International Conference on Image Processing, ICIP 2004, vol. 2. IEEE (2004)
3. Chen, H., Bhanu, B.: 3D free-form object recognition in range images using local surface patches. Pattern Recognition Letters 28(10), 1252–1262 (2007)
4. Bowyer, K.W., Chang, K., Flynn, P.: A survey of approaches and challenges in 3D and multi-modal 3D+2D face recognition. Computer Vision and Image Understanding 101(1), 1–15 (2006)
5. Abate, A.F., et al.: 2D and 3D face recognition: A survey. Pattern Recognition Letters 28(14), 1885–1906 (2007)
6. Sala Llonch, R., et al.: 3D face recognition with sparse spherical representations. Pattern Recognition 43(3), 824–834 (2010)
7. Ho, T.K.: Random decision forests. In: Proceedings of the Third International Conference on Document Analysis and Recognition. IEEE (1995)
8. Amit, Y., Geman, D.: Shape quantization and recognition with randomized trees. Neural Computation 9, 1545–1588 (1997)
9. Breiman, L.: Random Forests. Machine Learning 45(1), 5–32 (2001)
10. Rehanullah Khan, A.H., Stöttinger, J.: Skin detection: A random forest approach. In: 2010 17th IEEE International Conference on Image Processing (ICIP). IEEE (2010)
11. Anna Bosch, A.Z., Muñoz, X.: Image Classification using Random Forests and Ferns. In: IEEE 11th International Conference on Computer Vision, ICCV 2007, pp. 1–8. IEEE (2007)
12. CASIA-3D FaceV1, http://biometrics.idealtest.org/ (accessed June 10, 2014)
13. Chitra, S., Balakrishnan, G.: study for two color spaces HSCbCr and YCbCr in skin color detection. Applied Mathematical Sciences 6(85), 4229–4238 (2012)
14. Chaves-González, J.M., et al.: Detecting skin in face recognition systems: A colour spaces study. Digital Signal Processing 20(3), 806–823 (2010)

A Novel Cross Iterative Selection Method for Face Recognition

Xiuli Dai, Wen-Sheng Chen, Binbin Pan[*], and Bo Chen

College of Mathematics and Computational Science,
Shenzhen Key Laboratory of Media Security,
Shenzhen University, Shenzhen 518160, China
{chenws,pbb,chenbo}@szu.edu.cn

Abstract. To enhance the discriminant power of features in face recognition, this paper builds a novel discriminant criterion by nonlinearly combining global feature and local feature, which also incorporates the geometric distribution weight information of the training data. Two formulae are theoretically derived to determine the optimal parameters that balance the trade-off between global feature and local feature. The obtained parameters automatically fall into interval [0, 1]. Based on the parameter formulae, we design an efficient cross iterative selection (CIS) algorithm to update the optimal parameters and optimal projection matrix. The proposed CIS approach is used for face recognition and compared with some existing methods, such as LDA, UDP and APD methods. Experimental results on the ORL and FERET databases show the superior performance of the proposed algorithm.

Keywords: Face recognition, LDA, LPP, Feature extraction, Parameter determination.

1 Introduction

Facial feature extraction is a crucial problem for Face Recognition (FR). Based on different feature extraction criteria, a large number of FR algorithms have been developed during the past decades. The feature extraction methods are mainly divided into two categories, namely the global feature extraction and the local feature extraction. Linear discriminant analysis (LDA) [1], which depicts the global feature, is a representative method of the first category. LDA pursues a linear mapping which seeks discriminant information maximally by maximizing between-class scatter meanwhile minimizing within-class scatter. So far, many variations of LDA method have been proposed for face recognition [2]-[5]. While for the second category, a typical method is the locality preserving projection(LPP) [6] which displays the local feature embedded in the high dimensional input pattern space. The basic idea of LPP is to find a projection which makes the projected points close when the original data have a small distance. Inspired by LPP method, unsupervised discriminant projection

---

[*] Corresponding author.

Z. Sun et al. (Eds.): CCBR 2014, LNCS 8833, pp. 40–49, 2014.

(UDP) [7], a modification of LPP, is proposed. The aim of UDP is to maximize the global scatter and minimize the local scatter simultaneously. Unlike LPP algorithm, UDP has a direct connection to classification since it utilizes the information of the"non-locality". Hence, UDP outperforms LPP in face recognition tasks. It can be seen that both global feature and the local feature play important roles in facial image classification. However, the methods discussed above either only extract the global feature, or just model the local feature. These single-structural feature based approaches are not able to fully employ the advantages of global feature and local feature simultaneously. To make best use of global feature and local feature, we previously proposed an automatic parameter determination (APD) [8] method by combining LDA and UDP methods. APD performs better than LDA, LPP and UDP in face recognition. But APD still have some drawbacks. On the one hand, the parameters determined by the APD parameter formulae do not always range in [0, 1], it usually causes to interrupt the iteration. On the other hand, APD does not consider the geometric distribution weight information of the training data. Therefore, the performance of APD would be affected.

To address the problems of APD method, this paper presents a new feature fusion method for face recognition. We establish a novel discriminant criterion function which not only fuses the global feature with the local feature, but also incorporates the geometric distribution weight information of the training data. By maximizing the discriminant criterion function, two trade-off parameters are theoretically proven to satisfy the optimal formulae, which are suitable to design a cross iterative selection (CIS) algorithm. It can also be seen that the parameters determined by the optimal formulae automatically range in [0, 1]. This means that the cross iteration can always continue until it encounters the stopping conditions. Our CIS algorithm adopts radial basis function (RBF) with fractional order [9] to model the geometric distribution weight information of the training samples. To evaluate the performance of the proposed CIS algorithm, we select two publicly available face databases, namely ORL and FERET databases, for training and testing. Compared with LDA, UDP and APD algorithms, experimental results demonstrate that the proposed method has the superior performance.

The rest of this paper is organized as follows. Section 2 gives a theoretical analysis on our method and develops a CIS algorithm. Experimental results on two facial databases are reported in section 3. Finally, section 4 draws the conclusions.

2   Proposed CIS Method

2.1   Some Notations

Let c and d be the number of classes and the dimension of sample vector respectively. The total training sample set is $X = [X_1, X_2 ; \cdots, X_c]$, The i th class

$X_i = [x_1^{(i)}, x_2^{(i)}, \cdots, x_{m_i}^{(i)}]$ contains m_i $(1 \leq i \leq c)$ training samples and the total

number of all training is $m = \sum_{i=1}^{c} m_i$, where $x_j^{(i)} \in R^d$ denotes the j as samples in

class i. Assume μ_i is the center of class i. $\mu_i = \dfrac{1}{m_i} \sum_{j=1}^{m_i} x_j^{(i)}$, and the entire mean

$\mu = \dfrac{1}{c} \sum_{i=1}^{c} \mu_i$. The weighted graph matrix $S = (S_{ij}) \in R^{m \times m}$ and matrix

$H = (H_{ij}) \in R^{m \times m}$ which describe the relationship of two points in face space can

be calculated according to the following principles:

$$S_{ij} = \begin{cases} \exp\left(-\dfrac{\|x_i - x_j\|^2}{t} \right), & x_i \in N_{k(x_j)} \text{ or } x_j \in N_{k(x_i)} \\ 0, & \text{otherwise} \end{cases}$$

$$H_{ij} = \begin{cases} 1 - \exp\left(-\dfrac{\|x_i - x_j\|^2}{t} \right), & x_i \notin N_{k(x_j)} \text{ or } x_j \notin N_{k(x_i)} \\ 0, & \text{otherwise} \end{cases}$$

where $N_{k(x)}$ means the k nearest neighbors of data x, $D = diag\{D_{11}, \cdots, D_{mm}\}$ with

$D_{ii} = \sum_j S_{ij}$ and the Laplacian matrix $L = D - S$. Matrices $S_L = XLX^T$ and

$S_D = XDX^T$. Matrix $B = diag\{B_{11}, B_{22}, \cdots, B_{mm}\}$ with $B_{ii} = \sum_j H_{ij}$ and matrix

$N = B - H$, $S_N = XNX^T$. Matrix S_L is called local scatter matrix while S_N in UDP

method is called nonlocal scatter matrix.

The radial basis function $K_\alpha(x)$ with fractional order is given below:

$$K_\alpha(x) = \exp\left(-\|x\|^\alpha \right), \tag{1}$$

above RBF can be viewed as the normalized radial kernel of fractional order. In order to utilize the

geometric distribution weight information, the within-class scatter matrix S_W and

between-class scatter matrix S_B are modified respectively as follows:

$$S_W = \dfrac{1}{m} \sum_{i=1}^{c} \sum_{j=1}^{m_i} \left(x_j^{(i)} - \mu_i \right) \left(x_j^{(i)} - \mu_i \right)^T \cdot K_{\alpha_w} \left(x_j^{(i)} - \mu_i \right), \tag{2}$$

$$S_B = \frac{1}{m} \sum_{i=1}^{c} m_i \left(\mu_i - \mu \right) \left(\mu_i - \mu \right)^T \cdot \left[1 - K_{\alpha_b} \left(\mu_i - \mu \right) \right], \tag{3}$$

where $K_{\alpha_w} \left(x_j^{(i)} - \mu_i \right)$ and $K_{\alpha_b} \left(\mu_i - \mu \right)$ are radial basis functions defined by (1). α_w and α_b are fractional order parameters. It is natural to think that the sample $x_j^{(i)}$, nearby its own class center μ_i, is more important to represent the feature of the class. So, as is shown in (2) and (3), a penalty weight (small weight) will be imposed on the intra-data, if the intra-data is far from its own class center. Similarly, if two different class centers are close to each other, they will be given a small weight as well.

2.2   Proposed Discriminant Criterion

To fuse the global feature with the local geometric feature, we propose a new discriminant criterion function as follows:

$$J_{(a,b,W)} = \frac{tr\left(W^T \left(\left(1-b^2 \right) S_B + \left(2b - b^2 \right) S_N \right) W \right)}{tr\left(W^T \left(\left(a-1 \right)^2 S_W + a^2 S_L \right) W \right)} \tag{4}$$

where S_W, S_B, S_L, S_N are respectively defined in subsection **2.1**, W is the projection matrix, a and b are two parameters which can be adjusted to balance the global feature and local feature. The optimal projection matrix W_{CIS} can be obtained by maximizing the criterion function $J_{(a,b,W)}$. When a, b are given, this problem is equivalent to solve the following generalized eigen-system:

$$\left(\left(1-b^2 \right) S_B + \left(2b - b^2 \right) S_N \right) w = \lambda \left(\left(a-1 \right)^2 S_W + a^2 S_L \right) w,$$

where λ and w are the corresponding eigenvalue and eigenvector, respectively. The projection matrix W_{CIS} is formed with the generalized eigenvectors associated to the top eigenvalues of the above eigen-system. Next, we will show how to determine the optimal parameters a and b. To this end, we have the following theorem.

Theorem 1.   To maximize the discriminant criterion function (4) when W is given, the parameters a
and b must satisfy the following formulae:

$$a = \frac{tr\left(W^T S_W W \right)}{tr\left(W^T \left(S_W + S_L \right) W \right)}, b = \frac{tr\left(W^T S_N W \right)}{tr\left(W^T \left(S_N + S_B \right) W \right)}.$$

$$\tag{5}$$

Proof. The formulae (5) can be derived by direct computation from the equation

$$\nabla_{(a,b)} J_{(a,b,W)} = 0 \, ,$$

where notation $\nabla_{(a,b)}$ means the gradient of $J_{(a,b,W)}$ with respect to (a,b).

It can be seen from (5) that two parameters a and b range in [0, 1]. Based on the equations (5), three cross iterative selection equations are obtained in this paper to automatically determine the optimal parameters and the optimal projection matrix. The simplifier of our algorithm is as follows.

Algorithm **1**

Initialize $a = a_0, b = b_0$

For $K = 0, 1, 2, \ldots$

$$W_k = \arg\max_W J_{(a_k, b_k, W)}$$

$$\tag{6}$$

$$a_{k+1} = \frac{tr\left(W_k^T S_W W_k\right)}{tr\left(W_k^T \left(S_W + S_L\right) W_k\right)}$$

$$\tag{7}$$

$$b_{k+1} = \frac{tr\left(W_k^T S_N W_k\right)}{tr\left(W_k^T \left(S_N + S_B\right) W_k\right)}$$

$$\tag{8}$$

The stopping conditions for the Algorithm **1** are as follows.

1. Set a maximum update number t_0. If the update number k is greater than t_0, then the iteration is stopped.

2. Let r_k, associated to the projection matrix W_k, be the rank one accuracy at the k th iteration. If $|r_{k+1} - r_k| < \varepsilon$ for a given small threshold ε or $r_{k+1} < r_k$, then we interrupt the iteration.

2.3   Detailed Algorithm Design

According to the discussions in previous subsection, our CIS algorithm is designed below.

Step 1:   Calculate matrices S_W, S_B, S_L and S_N defined in subsection **2.1**.

Step 2: Compute covariance matrix $S_T = \dfrac{1}{m}\sum_{i=1}^{c}\sum_{j=1}^{m_i}\left(x_j^{(i)}-\mu\right)\left(x_j^{(i)}-\mu\right)^T$

and perform eigen- value decomposition (EVD) $S_T \overset{EVD}{=} U\Lambda U^T$, where U is an orthogonal matrix,

$$\Lambda = diag\left(\lambda_1,\lambda_2,\cdots,\lambda_\tau,0,\cdots,0\right)\in R^{d\times d} \text{ with } \lambda_1 \geq \lambda_2 \geq \cdots \geq \lambda_\tau > 0.$$

Denote

$$U_T = U\left(:,1:\tau\right)\in R^{d\times\tau} \text{ and then set } W_{PCA} = U_T.$$

Step 3:   Initialization. Let $k = 0, a_k = a_0$, and $b_k = b_0$.

Step 4:   Update matrices $S_1^{(k)}, S_2^{(k)}$ respectively using the following formulae:

$$S_1^{(k)} = \left(1-b_k^2\right)S_B + \left(2b_k - b_k^2\right)S_N \text{ and } S_2^{(k)} = \left(a_k-1\right)^2 S_W + a_k^2 S_L.$$

Step 5: Perform EVD: $W_{PCA}^T S_2^{(k)} W_{PCA} \overset{EVD}{=} U_2\Sigma_2 U_2^T \in R^{\tau\times\tau}$, where U_2 is an orthogonal matrix and Σ_2 is a diagonal matrix.

Step   6:   If $rank\left(\Sigma_2\right) = \tau$,   set

$$S_1^{(k)} \leftarrow W_{PCA}^T S_1^{(k)} W_{PCA}, S_2^{(k)} \leftarrow W_{PCA}^T S_2^{(k)} W_{PCA} \text{ and go to step 7.}$$

Otherwise, update W_{PCA} according to the rule: $W_{PCA}\left(:,1:\tau-1\right), \tau \leftarrow \tau-1$ and go to step 5.

Step 7:   Solve eigen-system $\left(S_2^{(k)}\right)^{-1} S_1^{(k)} w = \lambda w$ and obtain W_k, which is formed with the p

eigenvectors corresponding to the largest p eigenvalues.

Step 8: If the stopping condition is satisfied, we cease the cross iteration and go to Step 9,   Otherwise,

let $k \leftarrow k+1$ and compute a_k, b_k according to (7), (8), then go to Step 4.

Step   9:   Let the optimal projection matrix $W_{CIS} = W_k$.

3   Experimental Results

This section reports the experimental results of our method and some existing FR approaches such as LDA, UDP and APD algorithms. In the following experiments, the values of fractional order parameters are given as $\alpha_w = 0.075$ and $\alpha_b = 0.95$, while the initial values of the trade-off parameters are $a_0 = b_0 = 0.5$. The maximal number of iterations is set to $t_0 = 10$.

3.1   Face Databases

ORL and FERET databases are selected for evaluations. The ORL database contains 400 images of 40 individuals. Each person consists of 10 images with different facial expressions, small variations in scales and orientations. Fig.1. illustrates variations of one individual from the ORL database. For the FERET database, we chose 120 people, 6 images for each individual. The six images were extracted from 40 different sets, namely Fa, Fb, Fc and duplicate. Fa and Fb are sets of images taken with the same camera at the same day but with different facial expressions. Fc is a set of images taken with different cameras at the same day. Duplicate is a set of images taken around 6-12 months after the day taking the Fa and Fb photos. Images from two individuals are shown in Fig. 2.

All facial images from above two databases are aligned by the centers of eyes and mouth with resolution 112x92. After two-level wavelet decomposition using D4 wavelet, they are further compressed down to resolution 30x25 with 256 gray levels per pixel. Finally, each facial image $x \in R^d$ is normalized using the formula $x^* = (x - mean(x)) / std(x)$.

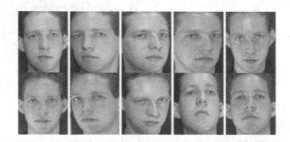

Fig. 1. The images of one person from the ORL database

Fig. 2. The variations of two person from the FERET database

3.2   Comparisons on ORL Database

The training number (TN) n ranges from 2 to 9. The n training images are randomly selected from each individual and the rest $10-n$ images are for testing. The experiments are repeated 10 times and the average accuracies are then calculated. The experimental results are tabulated in Table 1 and plotted in Fig.3. (left). It is observed that the rank one recognition rate of our CIS approach increases from 82.16% with TN=2 to 99.00% with TN=9. The performance for each method is enhanced when the number of training samples increases. The accuracies of LDA, UDP and APD methods increase from 66.34%, 80.25%, 81.28% with TN=2 to 96.50%, 91.00%, 94.25% with TN=9 respectively. Compared with these approaches, it can be seen that our CIS method achieves the best performance on the ORL face database.

Table 1. Recognition rates on ORL database

TN	2	3	4	5	6	7	8	9
LDA	66.34%	75.21%	81.33%	87.80%	91.38%	94.00%	95.13%	96.50%
UDP	80.25%	85.64%	86.75%	86.60%	88.63%	90.42%	91.13%	91.00%
APD	81.28%	87.96%	90.08%	90.85%	93.81%	94.67%	95.13%	94.25%
CIS	82.16%	88.71%	91.96%	93.40%	95.75%	96.58%	97.63%	99.00%

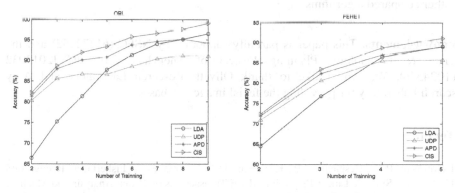

Fig. 3. Rank 1 accuracy versus training number on the ORL face database (right) and FERET face database (left)

3.3   Comparisons on FERET Database

For the FERET database, the number of training images for each person varies from 2 to 5. The experiments also run 10 times and the mean accuracies are then calculated. The experiment results are recorded and tabulated in Table 2 and plotted in Fig.3. (right) respectively. It can be seen that the accuracy of the proposed method increases from 72.31% with TN=2 to 91.08% with TN=5. While the recognition rates of LDA, UDP and APD methods increase from 64.42%, 70.86%, 71.94% with TN=2 to

89.00%, 85.75%, 88.92% with TN=5 respectively. It is obvious that the proposed method outperforms the other methods on FERET database as well.

Table 2. Recognition rates on FERET database

TN	2	3	4	5
LDA	64.42%	76.72%	86.50%	89.00%
UDP	70.86%	80.64%	85.58%	85.75%
APD	71.94%	82.33%	87.00%	88.92%
CIS	72.31%	83.42%	88.71%	91.08%

4   Conclusions

In this paper, a cross iterative selection (CIS) method is proposed to enhance feature discriminant power by nonlinearly combining the global feature and the local feature, and also using the geometric distribution weight information of the training samples. We theoretically obtain two trade-off parameter formulae, which show that the determined optimal parameters always range in [0, 1]. Based on the obtained parameter formulae, our CIS algorithm is developed for face recognition. Two face databases, including ORL and FERET databases are chosen for performance evaluation. Experimental results indicate that our proposed CIS approach surpasses all the other compared algorithms.

Acknowledgments. This paper is partially supported by NSFC (61272252) and the Science & Technology Planning Project of Shenzhen City (JCYJ2013032 6111024546). We would like to thank Olivetti Research Laboratory and Amy Research Laboratory for providing the facial image databases.

References

1. Belhumeur, P.N., Hespanha, J.P., Kriegman, D.J.: Eigenfaces vs. Fisherfaces: Recognition Using Class Specific Linear Projection. IEEE Transactions on Patten Analysis and Machine Intelligence 19(7), 711–720 (1997)
2. Yu, H., Yang, J.: A Direct LDA Algorithm for High-Dimensional Data-with Application to Face Recognition. Pattern Recognition 34(10), 2067–2070 (2001)
3. Chu, D.L., Thye, G.S.: A New and Fast Implementation for Null Space Based Linear Discriminant Analysis. Pattern Recognition 43(4), 1373–1379 (2010)
4. Sharma, A., Paliwal, K.K.: A Two-stage Linear Discriminant Analysis for Face Recognition. Pattern Recognition Letters 33(9), 1157–1162 (2012)
5. Chen, W.S., Zhang, C., Chen, S.: Geometric Distribution Weight Information Modeled Using Radial Basis Function with Fractional Order for Linear Discriminant Analysis Method. Advances in Mathematical Physics 2013, Article ID825861, 9 pages (2013)
6. He, X.F., Niyogi, P.: Locality Preserving Projections. In: Advances in Neural Information Processing Systems, vol. (16), pp. 153–160 (2004)

7. Yang, J., Zhang, D., Yang, J.Y.: Globally Maximizing, Locally Minimizing:Unsupervised Discriminant Projection With Applications to Face and Palm Biometrics. IEEE Trans. Pattern Analysis and Machine Intelligence 29(4), 650–664 (2007)
8. Huang, T.Q., Chen, W.S.: Automatic Parameter Determination Based on Modified Discriminant Criterion for Face Recognition. In: 2011 Seventh International Conference on Computational Intelligence and Security (CIS 2011), pp. 1091–1094 (2011)
9. Li, M., Zhao, W.: Representation of A Stochastic Traffic Bound. IEEE Transactions on Parallel and Distributed Systems 21(9), 1368–1372 (2010)

The Methods of Modeling the Image Sets Based on MEAP and Its Application on Face Recognition

Qian Wang[1], Jian-huang Lai[2], Na Liu[1], and Wei-Shi Zheng[2]

[1] School of Mathematics and Computational Science, Sun Yat-sen University, China
[2] School of Information Science and Technology, Sun Yat-sen University, China
hdwangqian@126.com , stsljh@mail.sysu.edu.cn,
{lindaliumail,sunnyweishi}@gmail.com

Abstract. This paper applies a novel clustering method in the image set-based face recognition, called the Muti-Exemplar Affinity Propagation algorithm (MEAP)[11]. The new method is extended from the affinity propagation (AP). It is a muti-exemplar model which constructs a two-level mapping: φ_1 between the feature points and the exemplars, and φ_2 between the exemplars and the super-exemplars. In this paper, we just use the first-level mapping result, i.e the subclasses to take part in the subsequent face recognition. The experiment results in different databases indicate the excellence of our method and the robustness to face occlusion .

Keywords: Face recognition, the similarity metric matrix, MEAP, super-exemplar, consistent match.

1   Introduction

As the development of the computer technology and the pattern recognition technology for decades, the face recognition system has been applied widely. So far, the face recognition algorithm has been considerably perfect in the controllable environment, however,various face representations such as occlusions and postures in practice give face recognition technology great challenges. In recent years, the image set-based face recognition has brought wide attentions for the widespread applications of video retrieval and surveillance. Compared to the conventional single image-based face recognition, an image set contains more information, so it can achieve better recognition result.

1.1   Review of Related Work

The points of the image set-based face recognition is how to model the image sets and how to measure their similarity. Generally, the approaches to set modeling fall into two ways: parametric and nonparametric representations. The parametric methods mainly express the image sets with distribution function, such as the single Gaussian or Gaussian mixture models, then calculate the similarity between distributions with Kullback-Leibler Divergence. While the nonparametric methods relax the restrictions

Z. Sun et al. (Eds.): CCBR 2014, LNCS 8833, pp. 50–60, 2014.

on data set distributions, and represent the image sets either by a single linear subspace or an intricate manifold in the form of a mixture of linear subspaces. Wang.R and Chen.X proposed a manifold-manifold learning method (MDA) [1,2]. The main idea is that every image set is modeled as a manifold, aiming at maximizing "manifold margin". MDA seeks to learn an embedding space, where manifolds belong to different classes are better separated, and the local data compactness within the same manifold is strengthened. H.Cevilala and B.Triggs state that every image set is charactered by a bounded convex geometric region (the affine or convex hull) spanned by its feature points, then the similarity between two image sets is measured by the geometric distance of their corresponding convex region [3]. Wang.R again proposes a covariance discriminative learning approach and express each image set with its covariance matrix [13]. As the covariance matrix is symmetric positive definite (SPD), the classical learning methods can't be used to take classification in the manifold directly. So the Log-Euclid distance metric is considered and get a kernel function which maps the covariance matrices from the Riemann manifold to the Euclid space, making all the learning methods for the vector space available.

2   Our Method

As a part of the face recognition algorithm, the MEAP plays a key role. In this section, we will systematically introduce the image set-based face recognition algorithm in the sequence of the experimental procedure, and highlight the MEAP in details. For clarity, we divide the procedure into two steps: the expressions of image sets and the metric of their similarity.

2.1   The Expressions of Image Sets

As the original data is video sequences, after transforming into single - frame images, we use the Adaboost operator [5] to detect faces, then align and normalize them.

First of all, we use face sparse descriptor to characterize the image sets. Face sparse descriptors [7] is that the position of the key points and the corresponding feature descriptors are extracted from every face image firstly, then all the positions and the feature descriptors within the same image set constitute two new sets: one consisting of all the positions $X^k = \{x_1^k, x_2^k, ..., x_n^k\}$, the other all the descriptors $Des^k = \{d_1^k, d_2^k, ..., d_n^k\}$. The experiment tells us that if the number of images belonging to one set is too large, the dimension of the achieved descriptor matrix will be very high, thus occupying much time and space. So to ensure the fairness of the experiment, we halve the descriptors so that the number is not more than the given threshold.

As we know, the video sequences from databases are usually taken in uncontrollable situations, so the descriptor sets contain many noise points. We divide the feature points into core points and boundary points by means of the definition of conspicuousness [9] and reject all the boundary points to cluster more accurately.

2.1.1   MEAP [11]

Clustering is an efficient data analysis approach for image set representation and usually processes the data without any prior information about the data, which is called unsupervised learning. In practical applications, we sometimes can get a little prior information, including class labels and the limitation of data partition. How to use the little prior information to do clustering for the enormous data without prior information is what the semi-supervised to do. Also, the supervised learning method is that most of the data have prior information, aimed at the clustering results keep pace with the prior knowledge.

Assumed that $[s_{ij}]_{N \times N}$ is a user-defined similarity matrix, and s_{ij} is the similarity between point i and the potential exemplar. $[l_{ij}]_{N \times N}$ is a linkage matrix, and l_{ij} express the linkage between exemplar j and the super-exemplar k. Then we construct a muti-exemplar model to seek the following two maps: $\psi_1 : \{1,...,N\} \to \{1,...,N\}$ assigning point i to the exemplar $\psi_1(i)$, and $\psi_2 : \{\psi_1(1),...,\psi_1(N)\} \to \{\psi_2(\psi_1(1)),...,\psi_2(\psi_1(N))\}$ assigning exemplar $\psi_1(j)$ to the super-exemplar $\psi_2(\psi_1(j))$. The objective of the model is to maximize $s_1 + s_2$, in which s_1 sums all the similarity between point and its exemplar, and s_2 sums all the linkage between exemplar and its super-exemplar.

The model. Let $C = [c_{ij}]_{N \times N}$ be an assignment matrix, and $c_{ij} \in \{0,1\} (j \neq i)$ is assigned 1 with point j being the exemplar of point i, similarly, $c_{ii} \in \{0,...,N\}$ is not equal to 0 with exemplar c_{ii} being the super-exemplar of exemplar i, i.e.,

$$c_{ij} = \begin{cases} 1, & \text{if point } j \text{ is the exemplar of point } i \\ 0, & \text{else.} \end{cases} \forall i \neq j, \tag{1}$$

$$c_{ii} = \begin{cases} k \in \{1,...,N\}, & \text{if } k \text{ is the super-exemplar of exemplar } i, \\ 0, & \text{if } i \text{ is not an exemplar.} \end{cases} \tag{2}$$

So s_1 and s_2 can be represented as followings:

$$S_1 = \sum_{i=1}^{N} \sum_{j=1}^{N} s_{ij} \cdot [c_{ij} \neq 0] \tag{3}$$

$$S_2 = \sum_{i=1}^{N} l_{ic_{ii}} \cdot [c_{ii} \neq 0] \tag{4}$$

Where $[\cdot]$ is the Iverson notation with $[true] = 1$ and $[false] = 0$.

We define a function matrix $[S_{ij}(c_{ij})]_{N \times N}$, in which the non-diagonal elements are the similarity between data point and the potential exemplar, meanwhile the diagonal elements are the exemplar preference s_{ii} sums the linkage $l_{ic_{ii}}$ between exemplar i and its corresponding super-exemplar, i.e.,

$$S_{ij}(c_{ij}) = \begin{cases} s_{ij}, & \text{if } i \neq j \text{ and } c_{ij} \neq 0, \\ s_{ii} + l_{ic_{ii}}, & \text{if } i = j \text{ and } c_{ii} \neq 0, \\ 0, & \text{else.} \end{cases} \tag{5}$$

According to (3), (4) and (5), we see that $S_1 + S_2 = \sum_{i=1}^{N} \sum_{j=1}^{N} S_{ij}(c_{ij})$.

A probable assignment matrix should satisfy the following three restricts:
① Each data point should be assigned to an exemplar accurately:

$$I_i(c_{i1},...,c_{iN}) = \begin{cases} -\infty, & \text{if } \sum_{j=1}^{N}[c_{ij} \neq 0] \neq 1, \\ 0, & \text{else} \end{cases}$$

② If there exists a point i selecting point j as its exemplar, then point j must be its own exemplar:

$$E_j(c_{1j},...,c_{Nj}) = \begin{cases} -\infty, & \text{if } c_{jj} = 0 \text{ but } \exists i : c_{ij} = 1, \\ 0, & \text{else.} \end{cases}$$

③ If exemplar i selects exemplar k as its super-exemplar, point k must be its own super-exemplar:

$$F_k(c_{11},...,c_{NN}) = \begin{cases} -\infty, & \text{if } c_{kk} \neq k \text{ but } \exists i : c_{ii} = k, \\ 0, & \text{else.} \end{cases}$$

The target of the muti-exemplar is to maximize function $S(C)$:

$$S(C) = S_1 + S_2 + \text{three restrictions}$$

$$= \sum_{i=1}^{N}\sum_{j=1}^{N}S_{ij}(c_{ij}) + \sum_{i=1}^{N}I_i(c_{i1},...,c_{iN}) + \sum_{j=1}^{N}E_j(c_{1j},...,c_{Nj}) + \sum_{k=1}^{N}F_k(c_{11},...,c_{NN}). \quad (6)$$

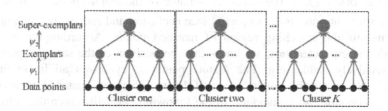

Fig. 1. The model of muti-exemplar. The mapping ψ_1 assigns each data point to the most suitable exemplar, and ψ_2 assigns each exemplar to its most comportable super-exemplar. That is, clusters in the second level are subclasses of the data points.

As shown in the fig.1, the data points, exemplars and super-exemplars form a two-level structure model, and the second level is the refinement of the classification. In experiment, we just use the result of mapping ψ_1, i.e., the subclasses. Compared to the Affinity Propagation, the clustering result of our method makes the classification more detailed.

Similar to AP, the optimization is carried out by a complex max-sum belief propagation process until it is convergent.

Clustering. Let $[S_{ij}]_{m\times n}$ be the stripped feature matrix which is prepared for the clustering, then its similarity matrix can be represented as:

$$Simi = \frac{S^T S}{\sum\limits_{i=1}^{m}\sum\limits_{j=1}^{n} S_{ij}^{2}} \tag{7}$$

The similarity matrix can be applied to similarity measurement of the features between two objects. When the two objects are totally the same, their similarity is 1; conversely, if they have no relations at all, the similarity is 0.

The input of MEAP is the $Simi$ we have calculated above, and the output includes the clustering sets and their corresponding exemplars.So far, the image sets have been represented as the clustering sets.

2.2   The Measurement of Image Sets' Similarity

After clustering for the feature points, the similarity measurement between image sets can be represented as what between clustering sets, i.e., the distance calculation between clustering sets. Before distance computing, we should first match the feature points between two sets. Generally,the matching is completed by computing the distance between the feature points from one set and all the dis-matched feature points from the other set, then selecting the minimum . It is easy to know that the computational cost is $o(n^2)$ (n is the minimum number of the feature points from the two sets). To ensure the robustness to partial face occlusion and reduce the computation, we will narrow the searching region of matched points. According to the facial framework and characteristics, we know that the position of the same property features is relatively stable (e.g. The feature points of eyebrows all lie in the top of the face). So except for isolated cases, if the two points are matched, their corresponding clusters are also coincident. In the following, we will search the coincident clusters [9].

Let $T^{(1)} = \{t_{11}, t_{12}, ..., t_{1m}\}$ and $T^{(2)} = \{t_{21}, t_{22}, ..., t_{2n}\}$ be two cluster sets with $t_{1i} = \{\varsigma_{1i}^{1}, \varsigma_{1i}^{2}, ..., \varsigma_{1i}^{m_i}\}$ and $t_{2j} = \{\varsigma_{2j}^{1}, \varsigma_{2j}^{2}, ..., \varsigma_{2j}^{n_j}\}$ .To find the coincident cluster of t_{1k} in $T^{(2)}$, we compute the distances between t_{1k} and all the clusters in $T^{(2)}$. Note that $v_1^1(k)$ and $v_2^1(k)$ are the cluster indexes having respectively the minimum and sub-minimum distance from t_{1k} to $T^{(2)}$, i.e.,

$$v_1^1(k) = \tau_1 = \arg\min_{\tau} \left\| t_{1k}^{'} - t_{2\tau}^{'} \right\|, \tag{8}$$

$$v_2^1(k) = \tau_2 = \arg\min_{\tau:\tau\neq\tau_1} \left\| t_{1k}^{'} - t_{2\tau}^{'} \right\|, \tag{9}$$

where t'_{1k} and $t'_{2\tau}$ is respectively the exemplar of t_{1k} and $t_{2\tau}$ .Similarly, let $v_1^2(l)$ and $v_2^2(l)$ be what from t_{2l} to $T^{(1)}$.

If cluster t_{1k} and t_{2l} satisfy:

$$(i) \quad v_1^1(v_1^2(l)) = l, \text{ i.e. } v_1^1(k) = l, v_1^2(l) = k, \tag{10}$$

$$(ii) \quad \frac{\left\| t'_{1k} - t'_{2v_1^1(k)} \right\|}{\left\| t'_{1k} - t'_{2v_2^1(k)} \right\|} \leq \eta, \frac{\left\| t'_{2l} - t'_{1v_1^2(l)} \right\|}{\left\| t'_{2l} - t'_{1v_2^2(l)} \right\|} \leq \eta, \text{ we say they are coincident.} \tag{11}$$

Assumed t_{1k} and t_{2l} are coincident, now we calculate the minimum distances from every feature descriptor in t_{1k} to t_{2l} :

$$d(\zeta_{1k}^u, t_{2l}) = \min_{\zeta_{2l}^c \in t_{2l}} \left\| \zeta_{1k}^u - \zeta_{2l}^c \right\|. \tag{12}$$

Note that $d^y(\zeta_{1k}^u, t_{2l})$ is the y th minimum of all the n_1 distances, then the distance from t_{1k} to t_{2l} is represented as the average of the first p minimum distances:

$$d(t_{1k}, t_{2l}) = \frac{1}{p} \sum_{y=1}^{p} d^y(\zeta_{1k}^u, t_{2l}). \tag{13}$$

Above all, the distance from $T^{(1)}$ to $T_{(2)}$ can be calculated as:

$$d(T^{(1)}, T^{(2)}) = \frac{1}{m} \sum_{k=1}^{m} d(t_{1k}, t_{2l}). \tag{14}$$

When in practice, we first compute the number of matched clusters between training image set and testing set, and if it is larger than the given value Ω, the training set is allowed to take part in the distance measurement with the testing set and what has the minimum distance are considered as the same class.

2.3   The Algorithm of Image Set-Based Face Recognition

The whole algorithm applied in experiment is as follows:

Image set-based face recognition algorithm

Input: The stochastically selected face image sets (including gallery sets and testing sets) and their labels.

Output: The recognition rates.

Steps:

1.   With the SURF operator modified from SIFT, we get the image sets' feature descriptor matrices.

2.   while num(descriptors)>threshold

        Num(descriptors)=num(descriptors)/2;
   end

3.   According to the definition of conspicuousness, all the feature points are classified as   the core points and boundary points and the latter are rejected.

4.
$$Simi = \frac{S^T S}{\sum_{i=1}^{m} \sum_{j=1}^{n} s_{ij}^{2}}$$

5.   Clustering with MEAP

6.   Computer the distances between clusters.Get the recognition rate

3   Experiment

3.1   Database

The CMU Mobo database [6] is about the motion of the body and contains 25 individuals walking on a treadmill in the CMU 3D room. The subjects perform four different walk patterns: slow walk, fast walk, inclines walk and walking with a ball. In the experiment, we select one walking pattern from each subject to form the gallery set, and meanwhile select 60 video sequences from the rest .

The Honda/USCD database is constructed for face detection and recognition. It includes two sub-databases and we just use the one containing 20 subjects which has three sub-sets for training, testing and occlusion testing. In the experiment, we select one video sequence from each subject to form the gallery set and select 40 video sequences from the rest. All the selections are random and in each database the final recognition rate is taken from nine times random experiments .

The face images in both databases are as shown in fig.2:

(a) CMU Mobo database

(b) Honda/USCD database   (c) Honda/USCD database with occlusions

Fig. 2. Face samples in each database.

3.2   The Algorithms for Comparison

1. DCC(Discriminative Learning and Recognition of Image Set Classes Using Canonical Correlations) [17];
2. MMD(Manifold-Manifold Distance with Application to Face Recognition based on Image Set) [1];
3. AHISD(Face recognition based on image set) [3];
4. SANP(Sparse Approximated Nearest Points for Image Set Classification) [16].

3.3   The Experiment Results

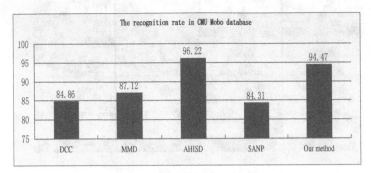

Fig. 3. The recognition rates of each algorithm in CMU Mobo database

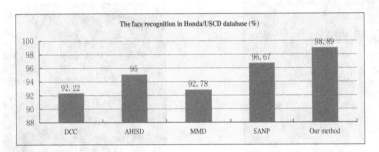

Fig. 4. The recognition rates of each algorithm in Honda/USCD database

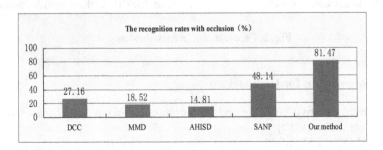

Fig. 5. The recognition rates of each algorithm in Honda/USCD database with occlusions

3.4   The Results Analysis

The above three figures tell us the superiority of our method in each database. Compared to each algorithm, the reasons why our method works excellently are as follows: Firstly, we did not cluster the feature points as soon as the feature descriptors were generated, but rejected the boundary points in advance, thus relieving the disturbance of the false face images. Secondly, the clustering method we use details the classification, thus making the data mining more deeply and improving the recognition rate. Thirdly, in the phase of distance computation between clusters, we matched them in advance so that the false matching was avoided. Moreover, as the compared algorithms use the global feature-based image representation methods but ours is local-based, and in occlusion situations, the global features will be influenced more heavily, this just indicates our method's robustness to occlusion.

In the experiment with CMU Mobo database, the rate of our method is not higher than AHISD. It is because that before clustering, we halved the feature points, thus losing much useful message. Meanwhile, the videos in CMU Mobo includes many incline walking and walking with a ball sequences, the faces in such situations move in a large region, so the recognition errors will exist without enough message. This is also the drawback of our method to be improved.

4 Conclusion

This paper introduces a novel image set representation method: Muti-exemplar Affinity Propagation, and applies it to face recognition. This algorithm is extended from the Affinity Propagation and details the classification of feature points. Experimental results show that our method performs quite well and also proves the robustness to occlusion. In experimental process, the difficulty we meet is that the quantity of extracting feature points is usually so big that time and space costs increase madly, which is our work to be conquered.

References

1. Arandjelović, A., Shakhnarovich, G., Fisher, J., Cipolla, R., Darrell, T.: Face recognition with image sets using manifold density divergence. In: IEEE International Conference on Computer Vision and Pattern Recognition, pp. 581–588 (2005)
2. Wang, R., Chen, X.: Manifold Discriminant Analysis. In: IEEE International Conference on Computer Vision and Pattern Recognition, pp. 429–436 (2009)
3. Cevikalp, H., Triggs, B.: Face recognition based on image sets. In: IEEE International Conference on Computer Vision and Pattern Recognition, pp. 2567–2573 (2010)
4. Ke, Y., Sukthankar, R.: PCA-SIFT: A more distinctive representation for local image descriptors. In: IEEE International Conference on Computer Vision and Pattern Recognition, pp. 506–513 (2004)
5. Viola, P., Jones, M.: Rapid object detection using a boosted cascade of simple features. In: IEEE International Conference on Computer Vision and Pattern Recognition, pp. 511–518 (2001)
6. Gross, R., Shi, J.: The CMU Motion of Body (MoBo) database. Technical Report CMU-RI-TR-01-18, Robotics Institute, Carnegie Mellon University (2001)
7. Liu, N., Lai, J.-H., Zheng, W.-S.: A Facial Sparse Descriptor for Single Image Based Face Recognition, Neurocomputing (93), 77–87 (2012)
8. Liu, N., Lai, J.-H., Zheng, W.-S.: A Sparse Local Feature Descriptor for Robust Face Recognition. In: Chinese Conference on Biometric Recognition
9. Liu, N., Lim, M.-H., Yuen, P.-C., Lai, J.-H.: Image Set-based Face Recogntion: A Local Multi-Keypoint Descriptor-based Approach

10. Liu, N., Lai, J.-H., Qiu, H.-N.: Robust Face Recognition by Sparse Local Feature from a Single Image under Occlusion. In: International Conference on Image and Graphics, ICIG (2011)
11. Wang, C.-D., Lai, J.-H., Suen, C.Y., Zhu, J.-Y.: Multi-Exemplar Affinity Propagation. IEEE Transactions on Pattern Analysis and Machine Intelligence 35(9) (September 2013)
12. Yan, Y., Zhang, Y.-J.: State of the Art on Video Based Face Recognition. Chinese Journal of Computers 32(5) (May 2009)
13. Wang, R., Guo, H., Davis, L.S., Dai, Q.: Covariance Discriminative Learning: A Natural and Efficient Approach to Image Set Classification. IEEE (2012)
14. Yu, X., Jian, Y.: Semi-Supervised Clustering Based on Amnity Propagation Algorithm. Journal of Software 19(11), 2803–2813 (2008)
15. Zhao, X.-J., Wang, L.-H.: Analysis and improvement of semi-supervised clustering algorithm based on affinity propagation. Computer Engineering and Applications 46(36), 168–170 (2010)
16. Hu, Y., Mian, A.S., Owens, R.: Sparse Approximated Nearest Points for Image Set Classification. In: IEEE International Conference on Computer Vision and Pattern Recognition, pp. 121–128 (2011)
17. Kim, T.K., Kittler, J., Cipolla, R.: Discriminative learning and recognition of image set classes using canonical correlations. IEEE Transactions on Pattern Analysis and Machine Intelligence 29(6), 1005–1018 (2007)
18. Križaj, J., Štruc, V., Pavešić, N.: Adaptation of SIFT features for robust face recognition. In: Campilho, A., Kamel, M. (eds.) ICIAR 2010. LNCS, vol. 6111, pp. 394–404. Springer, Heidelberg (2010)
19. Sim, T., Baker, S., Bsat, M.: The CMU Pose, Illumination, and Expression (PIE) Database. In: IEEE International Conference on Automatic Face and Gesture Recognition, pp. 46–51 (2002)
20. Zhu, P., Zhang, L., Zuo, W., Zhang, D.: From Point to Set: Extend the Learning of Distance Metrics
21. Yan, Y., Zhang, Y.-J.: State of the Art on Video Based Face Recognition. Chinese Journal of Computers 32(5) (May 2009)

A Novel Face Recognition Method
Using Vector Projection

Changhui Hu, Xiaobo Lu*, and Yijun Du

School of Automation, Southeast University, Nanjing 210096, China
xblu2013@126.com
Key Laboratory of Measurement and Control of CSE, Ministry of Education,
Southeast University, Nanjing 210096, China
230139132@seu.edu.cn

Abstract. In this paper, we propose a novel face recognition method by using vector projection, which uses vector projection length to evaluate the similarity of two image vectors in face image vector space. The projection length of a test image vector on direction of a training image vector can measure the similarity of the two images. But the decision cannot be made by only a training image which is the most similar to the test one. The mean image vector of each class also contributes to the final classification. Thus, the decision of the proposed vector projection classification (VPC) approach is ruled in favor of the maximum combination projection length. The performance of the proposed VPC approach is evaluated using two standard face databases; a comparative study with the state-of-the-art approaches illustrates the efficacy of the proposed VPC approach.

Keywords: Face Recognition, Image Vector, Combined Projection Length.

1 Introduction

As the great application prospects in commerce, law enforcement, information security, etc. [1-2], face recognition has received significant attention in the past twenty years. Especially in recent years, a tremendous amount of new principles, new methods and new technologies have emerged in an endless stream in face identification literature. Turk and Pentland [3] proposed the eigenfaces method, which was one of the reconstructive approaches in early face recognition. Belhumeur et al. [4] proposed the fisherfaces method, which was a significantly discriminative approach for face identification. It provides better performance than the eigenfaces method yet suffers from the problem limited to simple small size [4-6]. Under the influence of these ideologies in [3,4], Yang et al. [7] proposed the two-dimensional principal component analysis (2DPCA) method, and Xiong et al. [8] proposed the two-dimensional fisher's linear discriminant (2DLDA) method. The two methods directly deal with the 2D images without image to vector transformation, which are not only

---

* Corresponding author.

Z. Sun et al. (Eds.): CCBR 2014, LNCS 8833, pp. 61–69, 2014.
© Springer International Publishing Switzerland 2014

more computationally efficient than the eigenfaces and fisherfaces, but also are avoiding the small simple size problem of the fisherfaces. However, unlike the aforementioned facial feature based methods, the downsampled image based methods have received more attention in recent years. Wright et al. [9] proposed the sparse representation classification (SRC) algorithm, which uses the sparse linear combination of all the training images to represent a test image. Naseem et al. [10] proposed the linear regression classification (LRC) algorithm, which utilizes the linear combination of the training images of the same class to represent a test image.

The main drawback of the facial feature based methods in [3,4,7,8] is carrying out complex training process which consumes a lot of computational time. Although the downsampled image based methods in [9,10] do not need to execute complex training process, the coefficient vector of a linear representation is difficult to compute, especially when the training sample size is very large. To address these problems, we propose a simple but efficient VPC approach for face recognition.

2   Vector Projection Classification Approach

Since face images have similar structure, the face images of the same person have more similarities than those from different persons. It is a proverbial fact that a vector contains two attributes: the length and direction. Intuitively, the more similar the two face images are, the longer the projection length between the two image vectors is in image vector space. Hence, the vector projection length can be used to evaluate the similarity between two image vectors. The principle of the VPC approach is depicted as following.

Fig.1 shows the illustration of the image vector projection. There are two training image vectors, a and b in image vector space, and they are normalized to unit vectors ($|a| = 1$, $|b| = 1$). Suppose that a and b are from different-object classes, y is a test image vector. The angle between y and a is θ_a, and the angle between y and b is θ_b ($\theta_a > \theta_b$).

The length of vector y is defined as below [11]

$$|y| = \sqrt{(y, y)} \tag{1}$$

where (y, y) denotes the inner product of vector y and itself, the projection lengths of the test image vector y on the directions of image vector a and b can be computed respectively as

$$Y_a = |y| \cos(\theta_a) = (y, a) \tag{2}$$

$$Y_b = |y| \cos(\theta_b) = (y, b) \tag{3}$$

It can be seen from Fig.1, the test image vector y is more similar to the image vector b than a, and the projection length Y_b is longer than Y_a. Formula (2) (or (3)) indicates that the projection length Y_a (or Y_b) can measure the similarity of the image vector y and a (or b), and a projection length can be computed by only the inner product of two vectors.

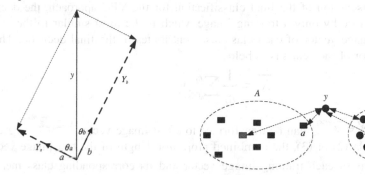

Fig. 1. The image vector projection   **Fig. 2.** The classification using vector projection

Since face images of a single-object class are more similar than those of different-object classes; the projection length of two image vectors from the same object class is longer than that of two image vectors from different object classes. However, under some special conditions, using only the most similar training image can lead to the misclassifying of a test image. Fig.2 shows the classification using image vector projection. Suppose that there are several training images from two classes A (squares) and B (circles), red square and red circle stand for the mean images of the two classes respectively.

The distance (i.e. dotted lines with double arrows in Fig.2) represents the similarity of the two images. The shorter the distance of two images is, the longer the projection length of the two image vectors is. It can be seen that the most similar training image of the test image y is a, which is from class A. However, the test image y really belongs to class B, and y is closer to the mean image of the class B compared with the mean image of the class A. Thus, the most similar training image and its corresponding class mean image are used to decide the final classification together. Based on this principle, the VPC approach for face recognition is presented as below.

Given c classes training samples from n samples, each class contains n_i images with $n=\sum_{i=1}^{c} n_i$. $A_i^j \in \mathbb{R}^{d \times r}$ is the jth image of the ith class in the training set, where $j=1,2,\cdots,n_i$, $i=1,2,\cdots,c$. All the two-dimensional images A_i^j are transformed to one-dimensional image vectors $w_i^j \in \mathbb{R}^{m \times 1}$ via column concatenation, and then all image vectors are normalized using the formula as following

$$v_i^j = \frac{w_i^j}{\left| w_i^j \right|} \quad i=1,2,\cdots,n \tag{4}$$

All the normalized image vectors are used to compose a normalized training set as below

$$V = \left[v_1^1, \cdots, v_i^j, \cdots, v_c^{n_c} \right] \in \mathbb{R}^{m \times n} \tag{5}$$

As previous discussion of the final classification for the VPC approach, the decision cannot be made by only a training image which is the most similar to the test one, the mean image vector of each class also contributes to the final decision. The mean image vector of each class is as below

$$\overline{X_i} = \frac{1}{n_i} \sum_{j=1}^{n_i} v_i^j \tag{6}$$

A test image $Y \in \mathbb{R}^{d \times r}$ can be transformed to a test image vector $y \in \mathbb{R}^{m \times 1}$. According to formula (2) or (3), the combined projection length of the test image vector y on directions of each training image vector and its corresponding class mean image vector is computed as

$$P_i(y) = k \bullet \left(y, v_i^j \right) + (1-k) \bullet \left(y, \overline{X_i} \right) \tag{7}$$

where $0 \le k \le 1$. It is obvious that the parameter k can influence the performance of the proposed VPC approach. In our experiments, $k=0.8$ is adopted, the reason is presented in subsection 3.1.

The final decision rule is made in favor of the maximum combination projection length as

$$\max_i P_i(y), \quad i \in [1, 2, \cdots, c] \tag{8}$$

3   Experiments and Analysis

In this section, experiments are carried out to illustrate the efficacy of the VPC approach using the Yale [12] and ORL [13] databases, which contain pose, illumination, facial expression variations. A comprehensive comparison of the proposed VPC approach with state-of-the-art methods: eigenfaces [3], fisherfaces [4], 2DPCA [7], 2DLDA [8], SRC [9] and LRC [10], is presented by adopting several standard evaluation protocols in the face recognition literature [7,10]. All experiments are executed on the PC with Core(TM)2 Duo 2.99 GHz processor and 1.96GB RAM using Matlab 7.0 software.

3.1   Experiments on the Yale Database

The Yale face database [12] contains 165 images of 15 individuals, with 11 different images for each object class. These images incorporate several variations, including illumination (right-light, center-light and left-light), facial expression (happy, normal, sad, sleepy, surprised and wink), and occlusion (w/glasses and w/no glasses). All images are grayscale and normalized to 231×195 pixels in our experiments. Fig.3 shows the images of one person in the Yale database. The Yale database was used to evaluate the performance of the VPC approach under conditions where both facial expression and illumination are varied.

Fig. 3. The images of one person in the Yale database

Fig.4 shows the recognition rates of the VPC approach with variable values of parameter k in formula (7) on the Yale database, here the first five images of each person is used to train, while the remainder are for testing . It can be seen that, the VPC approach achieves the highest recognition rates when $k=0.8$. Although, the optimal values of k for various face databases may be different. We adopt $k=0.8$ in formula (7) for all the following experiments.

When $k=0$, the VPC approach uses only the projection length between a test image and each class mean image to measure the similarity. When $k=1$, the VPC approach uses only the projection length between a test image and its most similar training image to measure the similarity.

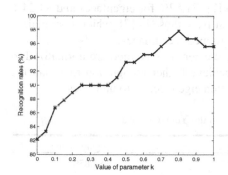
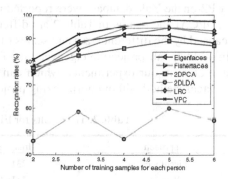

Fig. 4. Recognition rates for variable k **Fig. 4.** Recognition rates for variable samples

Table 1. The results for EP1 on the Yale database

Approach	Image size	Recognition rate
Eigenfaces	231×195	91.11%
Fisherfaces	231×195	94.44%
2DPCA	231×195	88.89%
2DLDA	231×195	60%
SRC	10×8	94.44%
LRC	10×8	94.44%
VPC	231×195	97.78%

Two evaluation protocols as reported in the literature [7,10] are adopted in our experiments. Evolution Protocol 1 (EP1) takes the first five images of each person as the training set, while the rest form the testing set. The VPC approach is comparable to the eigenfaces, fisherfaces, 2DPCA, 2DLDA, SRC and LRC approaches. All images are proportionately downsampled to an order of 10×8 for SRC and LRC algorithms. A detail comparison of the recognition rates for EP1 is summarized in Table 1. The proposed VPC approach copes well with variations of facial expression and illumination, achieving the highest recognition rate of 97.78%. It outperforms the latest LRC and 2DLDA approaches by margins of 3.34% and 37.78% respectively.

Fig.5 shows the recognition rates of the comparable methods on the Yale database under different number of training samples for each person. It can be seen that the VPC approach attains the highest recognition rates under different number of training samples for each person.

For Evolution Protocol 2 (EP2), the "leave-one-out" strategy is adopted. The recognition rates for each algorithm are reported in Table 2. The VPC algorithm achieves a comparable recognition rate of 86.06%, and outperforms the traditional eigenfaces and 2DPCA approaches.

Here, it should be pointed out that all the facial feature based methods such as eigenfaces, fisherfaces, 2DPCA and 2DLDA used all the components (i.e. projection eigenvectors corresponding to all nonzeros eigenvalues) for achieving the maximal recognition rate in our experiments. The recognition rates of eigenfaces and 2DPCA for EP2 on the Yale database were reported in [7] (71.52% for eigenfaces and 84.24% for 2DPCA), the results in Table 2 are different from those in [7], which may mainly be caused by the different sizes and scales of cropped face images.

In addition, all projection eigenvectors of the eigenfaces method are normalized to unit vectors in our experiments, which can achieve higher recognition rate than the eigenfaces method without normalizing projection eigenvectors to unit ones.

Table 2. The results for EP2 on the Yale database

Approach	Image size	Recognition rate
Eigenfaces	231×195	84.85%
2DPCA	231×195	85.45%
LRC	10×8	86.06%
VPC	231×195	86.06%

3.2   Experiments on the ORL Database

The ORL database [13] consists of 40 object classes with 10 images per person. The database contains facial expressions (smiling or nonsmiling, open or closed eyes) and occlusion (glasses or without glasses). It also characterizes a maximum of 20 degree rotation of the face with some scale variations of 10 percent. Fig.6 shows the images of one person in the ORL database. In our experiments, all images are grayscale and normalized to 112×92 pixels. The ORL database is used to evaluate the performance of VPC under conditions where the pose is varied. For the sake of fair comparison to all approaches, all experiments are conducted by downsampling 112×92 images to an order of 10×8.

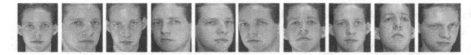

Fig. 6. The images of one person in the ORL database

For EP1, the experiments take the first six images of each person to compose the training set, while the rest four images of each person are designated as testing. The experimental results are shown in Table 3. The VPC approach achieves a comparable recognition rate of 95.63%; even with such posture changes, it outperforms the benchmark fisherfaces. The experimental results on the ORL database indicate that the proposed VPC approach shows excellent performance for moderate pose and scale variations compared to the state-of-the-art approaches.

For EP2, experiments are conducted to verify the VPC approach. The results are summarized in Table 4, including recognition rates and execution time for each approach. The VPC approach achieves a comparable recognition rate of 97.75%.

Here, it should be pointed out that the recognition rates of eigenfaces, fisherfaces, 2DPCA and LRC approaches for EP2 using the ORL database were reported in [7,10], which are 97.50%, 98.50%, 98.30% and 98.75% respectively. As the different sizes and scales of all cropped face images, the recognition rates for the same algorithm differ in [7,10] compared with our results. However, the margins of recognition rates are less than 1% except the margin of 2DPCA is 5.30%, which is explained as that the down-sampled images may decrease the recognition rate of the 2DPCA method.

The execution time for the VPC approach is much less than those of other five approaches on the ORL database, which is about 2 times faster than the best competitor LRC.

Table 3. The results for EP1 on the ORL database

Approach	Image size	Recognition rate
Eigenfaces	10×8	97.50%
Fisherfaces	10×8	94.38%
2DPCA	10×8	96.88%
2DLDA	10×8	97.50%
SRC	10×8	94.38%
LRC	10×8	95.63%
VPC	10×8	95.63%

Table 4. The results for EP2 on the ORL database

Approach	Image size	Execution time	Recognition rate
Eigenfaces	10×8	266.03s	98.50%
Fisherfaces	10×8	5697.80s	98.75%
2DPCA	10×8	346.63s	93%
SRC	10×8	3.77s	96.75%
LRC	10×8	5.11s	98.00%
VPC	10×8	2.50s	97.75%

4   Discussion and Conclusion

In this paper, a novel face recognition method is proposed which addresses the face identification task by using vector projection. The proposed VPC approach is evaluated using two standard databases with a variety of state-of-the-art approaches reported in the face identification literature. Considerable comparative analysis with the benchmark approaches clearly reflects the potency of the proposed VPC approach. To the best of our knowledge, for the simple architecture of the proposed VPC approach, it is the fastest face identification approach in terms of execution time in face identification literature. Also, it breaks through the barrier that face identification approaches are restricted by the dimensionality of face images. Although the proposed VPC approach is efficient for the problem of face identification, the author realized that the robustness issues related to facial expression, illumination and pose variations should be further studied.

Acknowledgments. The authors would like to thank the anonymous reviewers for their constructive comments and suggestions. This work was supported by the National Natural Science Foundation of China (No.61374194), the Program Sponsored for Scientific Innovation Research of College Graduates in Jiangsu Province (No. KYLX_0139) and the Natural Science Foundation of Jiangsu Province (No. BK20140638).

References

1. Zhao, W., Chellappa, R., Phillips, P.J., Rosenfeld, A.: Face recognition: A literature survey. J. ACM Computing Surveys 35(4), 399–458 (2003)
2. Tan, X., Chen, S., Zhou, Z.H., Zhang, F.: Face recognition from a single image per person: a survey. Pattern Recognition 39(9), 1725–1745 (2006)
3. Turk, M., Pentland, A.: Eigenfaces for recognition. Journal of Cognitive Neuroscience 3(1), 71–86 (1991)
4. Belhumeur, P.N., Hespanha, J.P., Kriegman, D.J.: Eigenfaces vs. fisherfaces: Recognition using class specific linear projection. IEEE Transactions on Pattern Analysis and Machine Intelligence 19(7), 711–720 (1997)
5. Swets, D.L., Weng, J.J.: Using discriminant eigenfeatures for image retrieval. IEEE Transactions on Pattern Analysis and Machine Intelligence 18(8), 831–836 (1996)
6. Zheng, W.S., Lai, J.H., Yuen, P.C.: GA-fisher: a new LDA-based face recognition algorithm with selection of principal components. IEEE Transactions on Systems, Man, and Cybernetics, Part B: Cybernetics 35(5), 1065–1078 (2005)
7. Yang, J., Zhang, D., Frangi, A.F., Yang, J.Y.: Two-dimensional PCA: a new approach to appearance-based face representation and recognition. IEEE Transactions on Pattern Analysis and Machine Intelligence 26(1), 131–137 (2004)
8. Xiong, H., Swamy, M.N.S., Ahmad, M.O.: Two-dimensional FLD for face recognition. Pattern Recognition 38(7), 1121–1124 (2005)

9. Wright, J., Yang, A.Y., Ganesh, A., Sastry, S.S., Ma, Y.: Robust face recognition via sparse representation. IEEE Transactions on Pattern Analysis and Machine Intelligence 31(2), 210–227 (2009)
10. Naseem, I., Togneri, R., Bennamoun, M.: Linear regression for face recognition. IEEE Transactions on Pattern Analysis and Machine Intelligence 32(11), 2106–2112 (2010)
11. Tanabe, K.: Projection method for solving a singular system of linear equations and its applications. Numerische Mathematik 17(3), 203–214 (1971)
12. Yale Univ. Face Database (2002),
    http://cvc.yale.edu/projects/yalefaces/yalefaces.html
13. Samaria, F.S., Harter, A.C.: Parameterisation of a stochastic model for human face identification. In: Proceedings of the Second IEEE Workshop on Applications of Computer Vision, December 5-7, pp. 138–142 (1994)

Face Recognition Based on Non-local Similarity Dictionary

Haibin Liao[1], Shejie Lu[1,*], and Qinghu Chen[2]

[1] School of Computer Science and Technology, HuBei University of Science and Technology,
Xianning, 437100, China
`liao_haibing@163.com, aiminglu@163.com`
[2] School of Electronic Information, Wuhan University, Wuhan, 430072, China
`qhchen@whu.edu.cn`

Abstract. With the increasing demand of surveillance camera-based applications, the very low resolution (VLR) problem occurs in many face application systems. Traditional two-step methods solve this problem through employing super-resolution (SR). However, these methods usually have limited performance because the target of SR is not absolutely consistent with that of face recognition. Moreover, time-consuming sophisticated SR algorithms are not suitable for real-time applications. To avoid these limitations, we propose a novel approach for VLR face recognition without any SR preprocessing. Our method based on the linear combination coefficients of non-local image patches is the same regardless of image resolutions inspired by the learning-based face SR method. Experimental results show that the proposed VLR face recognition method is high in recognition accuracy and robust in resolution variations.

Keywords: Super Resolution, Face Recognition, Dictionary Learning, Linear Combination, Non-local Similarity.

1 Introduction

In face recognition system, it is generally assumed that the face region is large enough to contain sufficient information for recognition. With the growing application of surveillance, there is an increasing demand for face recognition especially in Very Low Resolution (VLR) face problem [1]caused by the low resolution of the camera, long distance between people and camera. A potential method to solve the VLR problem is to recover lost high-frequency details in the face images. Therefore, super-resolution (SR) algorithms are employed [2-4] to reconstruct a high-resolution (HR) face image from a VLR observation. Baker and Kanade [5] were the first to propose the term "face hallucination" for face SR. And Liu et al. [6] developed a two-step method integrating a global parametric model and a local non-parametric model to SR. Recently, an effective face hallucination method based on dictionary-learning has been proposed to SR [7,8,9].

---

* Corresponding author.

Z. Sun et al. (Eds.): CCBR 2014, LNCS 8833, pp. 70–77, 2014.

However, the aim of these SR is for visual enhancement. One main concern raised by both Gunturek et al [10] and Nguyen et al [11] is how to apply SR for a specific biometric modality effectively to improve recognition performance, rather than visual clarity. Based on these concerns, feature-domain SR techniques have been proposed for face [10, 11, 12] to improve recognition performance. These features are super-resolved through using a maximum posteriori estimation approach. Specific knowledge of face is incorporated in the form of prior probabilities to constrain the SR process, improving robustness to noise and segmentation errors. What is more, by learning the mapping among faces with different resolutions in a unified feature space, Li et al. [13] found that it was possible to carry out LR face recognition without any SR reconstruction preprocessing.

In order to improve VLR face recognition, we proposed a new method based on resolution scale invariant feature (RSIF). The proposed face recognition method was inspired by learning-based SR method. We carried out LR face recognition without any SR reconstruction preprocessing by learning the correspondences between LR image patches and HR image patches from a training database consisting of LR and HR patch pairs.

2   Multi-scale Linear Combination Consistency

Learning-based image SR methods are mainly on the basis of two laws of image similarity: 1) large available similar information existed in different regions of a certain image; 2) This similarity can preserve in multi-scale resolutions. In fact, image similarity not only exists in local pixels but also in non-local regions. For example, the similar pixels of a certain pixel can be found in the whole image pixel space instead of being restricted to its neighborhood. Generally, an image will contain sufficient repetitive structure as shown in the square and circle windows in Fig.1. Fig.1 shows that there are many pixels with similar local structure in the flat regions as well as the edge regions of the images. From what we discussed above, face image as a specific image, possesses non-local similarity. Then we will prove that the feature of multi-scale linear combination consistency.

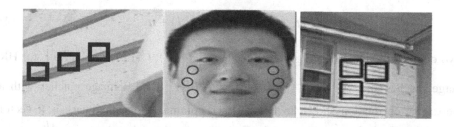

Fig. 1. Image with its non-local similarity paches

Let I^H be an arbitrary HR image, and then the corresponding LR image I^L can be generated by the degradation of I^H :

$$I^L = DHI^H + N \qquad (1)$$

Where, I^H and I^L are column vectors, N is the random Gaussian noise evenly distributed in the image, D and H denotes the down-sampling and blurring filter operator respectively, and the down-sampling factor is s.

Divide these images into patches:

$$P_{i,j}(I^L) = P_{i,j}(DHI^H) + P_{i,j}(N)$$
$$P_{i,j}(I^L) = D_P H_P P_{k,l}(I^H) + P_{i,j}(N) \qquad (2)$$

Where, $P_{i,j}(I^L)$ represents an image patch of $q \times q$ centered on the (i, j) pixel from LR images. Let $I^L(i, j)$ be a column vector of $P_{i,j}(I^L)$ and (i, j) $s.t. (si, sj) = (k, l)$. Because of the uniform distribution of noise in the images, Eq. 2 can be rewritten as:

$$I^L(i, j) = D_P H_P I^H(k, l) + n \qquad (3)$$

In the training phase, we generate a HR and LR patch dictionary pair. Assume that there are M images in HR samples $I_m^H (m = 1, ..., M)$, and the corresponding LR samples can be represented as $I_m^L (m = 1, ..., M)$. Each HR and LR image is divided into image patches with overlap to form HR and LR image patch sets. They are $S^H = \{I_m^H(k, l) \mid m = 1, ..., M; (k, l) \in \Omega^H\}$ and $S^L = \{I_m^L(i, j) \mid m = 1, ..., M; (i, j) \in \Omega^L\}$, Ω^H and Ω^L represent the position ranges of the image patches.

Let $T^H = \|S^H\|$ and $T^L = \|S^L\|$, where $\|\bullet\|$ denotes the set cardinality and evidently $T = T^H = T^L$. Eq. 3 can tell the relationship between the corresponding HR and LR patches:

$$I_m^L(i, j) = D_P H_P I_m^H(k, l) + n \qquad (4)$$

Two coupled dictionaries are generated: $A^H = \left[I^H(1); I^H(2); ...; I^H(T)\right]$ for HR image patches and $A^L = \left[I^L(1); I^L(2); ...; I^L(T)\right]$ for LR image patches with a one-to-one correlation shown in Eq. 4. Each column in the dictionary is a vector formed by pixels in an image patch. For example, the tth column in A^L can be represented as $I^L(t) = A^L e_t$, e_t is a column vector with one for the tth element and zeros for other elements. We have:

$$A^L = D_P H_P A^H + V \qquad (5)$$

Where $V = [n; n; ...]$, and it is the same size as A^L.

Let Y be the testing LR face image, we assume that Y is generated from an unknown HR image X by the degradation processing in Eq. 1. That is:

$$Y = DHX + N \qquad (6)$$

We divide Y into image patches. The image patch $Y(i, j)$ centering on (i, j) can be represented as:

$$Y(i, j) = D_p H_p X(k, l) + n \qquad (7)$$

We define the non-local similar image patch set of $Y(i, j)$ in A^L as: $\Phi_{i,j}^L = \{I_m^L(i', j') \mid m = 1, ..., M; (i', j') \in N_r^L(i, j)\} = A^L F_{i,j}$. Where $N_r^L(i, j)$ is the non-local region in the LR image centered on (i, j) and with a radius of r.

$F_{i,j}$ is a matrix with $\left\| \Phi_{i,j}^L \right\|$ elements of all e_t: $F_{i,j} = \left[...; e_{t(i',j';m)}; ... \right]$, and $t(i', j'; m)$ denotes the serial number of image patch in the mth image centered on (i', j') of A^L.

According to the linear combination theory, $Y(i, j)$ can be represented as the linear combination of its non-local similar image patches.

$$Y(i, j) = \Phi_{i,j}^L W^L = A^L F_{i,j} W^L \qquad (8)$$

Where W^L is the coefficient matrix and its size is determined by $\left\| \Phi_{i,j}^L \right\|$.

Similarly, image patches in HR image X can be represented as the linear combination of its non-local similar patches:

$$X(k, l) = \Phi_{k,l}^H W^H = A^H F_{k,l} W^H \qquad (9)$$

Because of the corresponding relation of HR and LR image patches, we will have $F_{k,l} = F_{i,j}$. By substituting Eq. 9 into Eq. 7, we get:

$$Y(i, j) = D_p H_p A^H F_{i,j} W^H + n \qquad (10)$$

We combine Eq. 10 and Eq. 5 to get:

$$Y(i, j) = (A^L - V) F_{i,j} W^H + n = A^L F_{i,j} W^H - V F_{i,j} W^H + n \qquad (11)$$

Because of $V = [n; n; ...]$, we can further have $V F_{i,j} W^H = n$. Eq. 11 can be simplified as:

$$Y(i, j) = A^L F_{i,j} W^H \qquad (12)$$

Comparing Eq. 8 with Eq. 12, it is evident that $W^H = W^L$. Then, we can conclude that the linear combination of an image patch in terms of its non-local similar patches is consistent in HR and LR spaces. Therefore we have tested the multi-scale linear combination consistency. Notably, when the degradation process of the testing image and the training image are the same, the error between W^L and W^H is theoretically zero regardless of the noise energy.

3   RSIF Face Recognition

In order to improve the recognition performance of VLR face images, this paper proposed a novel face recognition approach based on resolution scale invariant feature (RSIF). Section 2 concluded that the linear combination coefficients of non-local image patches were the same regardless of image resolutions. Therefore these coefficients can be used as facial features for recognition. RSIF consists of three steps: data acquisition, coefficients calculation, recognition.

(a)data acquisition

Public face database CAS-PEAL-R1 [14] is selected for our experiments. We choose representative face images from 500 individuals to form the HR face image space. Firstly, these face images are aligned manually and normalized to the same size. Secondly, the corresponding LR face image space is generated from the degradation of the HR images. Thirdly, these images are divided into patches.

(b) Coefficients calculation

Image patch $Y(i, j)$ can be represented as the linear combination of similar image patches:

$$Y(i, j) = \Phi_{i,j}^L W^L \tag{13}$$

Where $\Phi_{i,j}^L$ is the set of non-local similar image patches in the LR dictionary, we rewrite it as $\Phi_m^L, m = 1, 2, \cdots M$ for the sake of clearness, M is the number of similar patches. W^L is the weight matrix and the weight value w_m^L denotes the contribution of each similar non-local image patch to the corresponding input image patch. Generally, Eq.13 can be rewritten as:

$$Y(i, j) = \sum_{m=1}^{M} w_m^L \Phi_m^L(i, j) + e \tag{14}$$

e is the reconstruction error, and calculating the coefficients W^L means to minimize the reconstruction error e:

$$W^L = \underset{w_m}{\arg\min} \left\| Y(i, j) - \sum_{m=1}^{M} w_m^L \Phi_m^L(i, j) \right\|^2 \tag{15}$$

Eq. 15 is a problem of constrained least square.

(c) Recognition

We represent a face by a set of linear combination coefficients. These coefficients are concatenated to form a vector. Comparing two faces a_1 and a_2 in a vector space, in this paper, we use the nearest neighbor classifier with the distance measure of the cosine of the angle between these two vectors:

$$d = \frac{<a_1, a_2>}{\|a_1\|} \|a_2\| \tag{16}$$

4 Experiments

In this section, we would like to evaluate the performance of the proposed algorithm in terms of recognition accuracy.

Databases and Settings: In this experiment, two public face image databases are used, namely FRGC V2.0 [15] and CAS-PEAL. For the FRGC V2.0 database, we select ten images per person with a near-frontal view and mild expression variations. Those individuals with less than ten applicable images will be discarded. Finally a subset of 311 individuals is selected for our experiments. For the CAS-PEAL database, we select eleven images per person with expression and pose variations. For each person, six images are used as the gallery set while the rest five images are used as the probe set.

First, we evaluate the performance of the proposed RSIF algorithm on images with different resolutions. For the FRGC V2.0 database, images of 7*6, 14*12, and 28*24 are used as the testing LR set and HR images of 56*48 are used as the training set. For the CAS-PEAL database, images of 8*6, 16*12, 32*24, and 64*48 are used as the testing LR set and HR images of 128*96 are used as the training set.

We applied kernel LDA (KLDA) for facial feature extraction and nearest neighbor (NN) for VLR and HR recognition. Our algorithm was directly operated on the VLR images with RSIF feature and NN classifier. The results are shown in Figs. 2, 3 and 4. The proposed method can improve the performances on three different resolutions. For images of 7*6, the recognition rate of RSIF approximates that of the original HR images. For images of 14*12, and 28*24, the performances of RSIF are even better than that of the original HR images. Moreover, the recognition rates of RSIF on three different resolutions are nearly the same. This means that RSIF is robust to resolution variations and can be used to solve VLR face recognition problem.

We further conduct our experiments on the CAS-PEAL face image database. The purpose of this experiment is to compare the proposed RSIF method with other face recognition algorithms, namely Gunturk's method [10], Wilman's method [1]. Face images with different resolutions are used for experiments. The results are shown in Fig. 5. We can conclude that RSIF face recognition method is better than other methods used in this experiment.

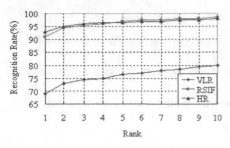

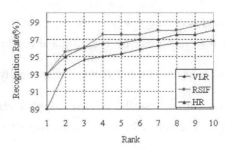

Fig. 2. Recognition results of 7*6 LR images

Fig. 3. Recognition results of 14*12 LR images

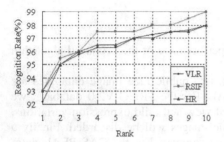

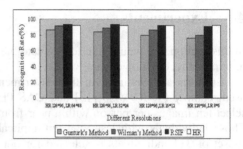

Fig. 4. Recognition results of 28*24 LR images

Fig. 5. Recognition results of face images with different resolutions using different face recognition algorithms

Conclusion

In this paper, non-local similarity and Multi-scale linear combination are defined and proved to be consistent in images with different resolutions. Therefore, it can be applied in SR face recognition. Experimental results show that this new algorithm is better than some existing face recognition methods. The new algorithm is robust to resolution variations.

References

1. Zou, W.W.W., Yuen, P.C.: Very low resolution face recognition problem. IEEE Transactions on Image Processing 21(1), 327–340 (2012)
2. Yang, J., Huang, T.: Image super-resolution: Historical overview and future challenges. In: Milanfar, P. (ed.) Super-Resolution Imaging. ch. 1. CRC Press, Boca Raton (2010)
3. Park, S.C., Park, M.K., Kang, M.G.: Super-resolution image reconstruction: A technical overview. IEEE Signal Process 20(3), 21–36 (2003)
4. van Ouwerkerk, J.: Image super-resolution survey. Image Vis. Computer 24(10), 1039–1052 (2006)

5. Baker, S., Kanade, T.: Hallucinating faces. In: Fourth International Conferences on Automatic Face and Gesture Recognition, pp. 83–89. IEEE Press, Grenoble (2000)
6. Su, C., Zhuang, Y., Huang, L., Wu, F.: Steerable pyramid based face hallucination. Pattern Recognition 38(6), 813–824 (2005)
7. Yang, J.C., Wright, J., Huang, T.S., Ma, Y.: Image super-resolution as sparse representation. IEEE Transactions on Image Processing 19(11), 2861–2873 (2010)
8. Zeyde, R., Elad, M., Protter, M.: On Single Image Scale-Up Using Sparse-Representations. In: Boissonnat, J.-D., Chenin, P., Cohen, A., Gout, C., Lyche, T., Mazure, M.-L., Schumaker, L. (eds.) Curves and Surfaces 2011. LNCS, vol. 6920, pp. 711–730. Springer, Heidelberg (2012)
9. Ma, X., Zhang, J., Qi, C.: Hallucinating face by position-patch. Pattern Recognition 43, 2224–2236 (2010)
10. Gunturk, B.K., Batur, A.Z., Altunbasak, Y., Hayes, M.H., Mersereau, R.M.: Eigenface domain super-resolution for face recognition. IEEE Trans. Image Process. 12(5), 597–606 (2003)
11. Nguyen, K., Sridharan, S., Denman, S., Fookes, C.: Feature-domain super-resolution framework for Gabor-based face and iris recognition. In: 2012 IEEE Conference on Computer Vision and Pattern Recognition, pp. 2642–2649 (2012)
12. Hennings-Yeomans, P., Baker, S., Vijaya Kumar, B.V.K.: Simultaneous super-resolution and feature extraction for recognition of low-resolution faces. In: Proc. IEEE Conference on Computer Vision and Pattern Recognition, pp. 1–8 (June 2008)
13. Li, B., Chang, H., Shan, S., Chen, X.: Low-resolution face recognition via coupled locality preserving mappings. IEEE Signal Process Lett. 17(1), 20–23 (2010)
14. Gao, W., Cao, B., Shan, S.G., Chen, X.L., Zhou, D.L., Zhang, X.H., Zhao, D.B.: The CAS-PEAL large-scale Chinese face database and baseline evaluations. IEEE Transaction on System Man, and Cybernetics (Part A) 38, 149–161 (2008)
15. Phillips, P., Flynn, P., Scruggs, T., Bowyer, K., Chang, J., Hoffman, K., Marques, J., Min, J., Worek, W.: Overview of the face recognition grand challenge. In: Proc. IEEE Int. Conf. Comput. Vis. Pattern Recognit., pp. 947–954 (2005)

Adaptive Weighted Label Propagation for Local Matching Based Face Recognition

Yan Guo[1], Xiaohui Li[2], Yugen Yi[2], Yunyan Wei[2], and Jianzhong Wang[2,*]

[1] Changchun Vocational Institute Of Technology, Changchun, China
[2] College of Computer Science and Information Technology, Key Laboratory of Intelligent Information Processing of Jilin Universities, Northeast Normal University, Changchun, China
wangjz019@nenu.edu.cn

Abstract. In this paper, a new algorithm named Adaptive Weighted Label Propagation (AWLP) which explores the complementary property among sub-patterns from the same face image is proposed for local matching based face recognition. The proposed AWLP first partitions the face images into several smaller sub-images. Then, multiple similarity graphs are constructed for different sub-pattern sets. At last, in order to take correlation among different sub-patterns into account, the graphs obtained by various sub-pattern sets are combined and the procedures of label prediction and graph weight learning are integrated into a unified framework to propagate the class information of the labeled samples to unlabeled ones. Moreover, a simple yet efficient iterative update algorithm is also proposed to solve our AWLP. Extensive experiments on three face benchmark databases show that AWLP has very competitive performance with the state-of-the-art algorithms.

Keywords: face recognition, label propagation, local matching, adaptive weighted label propagation.

1 Introduction

During the past decades, face recognition has become one of the most active and challenging research topics in pattern recognition and computer vision fields [1]. Many researchers have proposed various algorithms to improve the performances of face recognition systems [1]. Based on the availability of label information, face recognition algorithms can be generally classified into two groups, i.e., supervised and unsupervised methods [1]. Though the experimental results showed that the performances of supervised face recognition algorithms outperformed unsupervised ones in most cases, labeling all the training samples often required expensive human labor and much time [2]. To cope with this problem, some semi-supervised learning methods [2] aiming to learn from partially labeled data and abundantly unlabeled data have been proposed.

In this paper, we mainly focus on the label propagation (LP) for the pattern classification tasks such as face recognition because it has been proven to be an effective

---

* Corresponding author.

Z. Sun et al. (Eds.): CCBR 2014, LNCS 8833, pp. 78–85, 2014.
© Springer International Publishing Switzerland 2014

semi-supervised learning approach [3-7]. The key idea behind LP is to first construct a graph in which each node represents a data point and each edge is assigned a weight reflects the similarity between data points. Then, the class labels of the unlabeled samples are predicted by propagating the class information of labeled data to its neighbors in the constructed graph. Hence, constructing the graph structure and esti-mate the similarities between data points play pivotal roles in the label propagation algorithms. Meanwhile, many methods have been proposed for graph construction [3-7]. Although these methods performed well on face recognition tasks, their perfor-mances may be affected by some problematic factors in the real-world face images [8]. The main reason is that they utilized the holistic information of the face images as input for face recognition. Based on the observation that some of the local facial fea-tures do not vary with pose, lighting, facial expression and disguise, some local matching based methods which extract facial features from different levels of locality have been proposed. They have shown more promising results in face recognition tasks [8, 9]. Though the label propagation methods can be straightforward extended for local matching based face recognition by applying them to the sub-pattern sets independently, a main drawback of this kind of extension is that they ignore the latent complementary information of the multiple sub-images from the same face image, which is crucial to improve the recognition performance [9].

Motivated by the recent success of local matching based methods and label propa-gation algorithms, we proposed a new classification algorithm, namely Adaptive Weighted Label Propagation (AWLP) for local matching based face recognition in this paper. In AWLP, the underlying complementary information among different sub-patterns of the same face image is effectively utilized. Specifically, face images are first partitioned into several smaller sub-images to form different sub-patterns. Then, multiple similarity graphs are constructed for various sub-pattern sets. Finally, an adaptive weighted strategy is used to combine the graphs obtained from different sub-pattern sets, the procedures of labels prediction and graph weight learning are integrated into a unified framework. We apply AWLP to face recognition tasks and compare it with several state-of-the-art methods. Extensive experiments on several face benchmark databases (such as Yale, AR and CMU PIE) show that AWLP has very competitive performance with the state-of-the-art algorithms.

The remainder of this paper is organized as follows. In Section 2, we propose our AWLP algorithm. Experimental results on three face databases are illustrated in Sec-tion 3. Finally, Section 4 discusses our conclusion with this work.

2 The Proposed Method

2.1 Adaptive Weighted Label Propagation

2.1.1 Face Image Partition

Like other local matching based face recognition algorithms [8, 9], the first step of our AWLP is to partition the face images into sub-patterns. Let $X=[x_1,...,x_n] \in R^{d \times n}$ denotes n face images belong to c persons, in which the first $l<<n$ samples $X_l=[x_1,...,x_{l+1}] \in R^{d \times l}$ are labeled and the rest n-l samples $X_u=[x_{l+1},...,x_n] \in R^{d \times (n-l)}$ are unlabeled. The size of each face image is $S_1 \times S_2$. After dividing each face image into

M sub-images and then concatenating each sub-image into a column vector, we can get $X^m = [x_1^m, x_2^m, ..., x_N^m](m=1,...,M)$ which denotes the sub-pattern set contains the mth sub-pattern of all input face images.

2.1.2 Graph Construction

For each sub-pattern set, we firstly construct a neighborhood weighted graph on given data by putting an edge between each sample and its k-nearest neighbors. Let $N(x_i^m) = [x_{i,1}^m, x_{i,2}^m ..., x_{i,k}^m]$ be the k-nearest neighbors of x_i^m. the weight matrix can be computed by minimizing the reconstruction error

$$\varepsilon(W^m) = \min \sum_i \| x_i^m - \sum_{j:x_j^m \in N(x_i^m)} W_{ij}^m x_j^m \|^2$$

$$s.t. \quad \sum_{j:x_j^m \in N(x_i^m)} W_{ij}^m = 1, W_{ij}^m \geq 0, W_{ij}^m = 0 \text{ if } x_j^m \notin N(x_i^m)$$

(1)

To ensure symmetry, W^m can be symmetrized as $W_{ij}^m = (W_{ij}^m + W_{ji}^m)/2$ [4].

2.1.3 Label Propagation

For each sub-pattern set, the first aim of AWLP is to ensure that the nearby samples would be assigned similar labels. Therefore, in order to achieve this goal, we minimize the following objective function

$$\min \sum_{i,j=1}^n \| f_i - f_j \|^2 W_{ij}^m = \min 2tr(F^T(D^m - W^m)F) = 2tr(F^T L^m F)$$

(2)

where $F=[f_1, f_2, ..., f_n]^T \in R^{n \times c}$ denotes the predicated label matrix, $f_i \in R^c$ is the predicated label vector of x_i, $D_{ii} = \sum_{j=1}^n W_{ij}$, and $L = D-W$ is the Laplacian matrix.

Then, in order to take the latent complementary information of different sub-patterns from the same face image, the Laplacian matrices obtained by various sub-pattern sets are combined through using an adaptive non-negative weight vector $\lambda=[\lambda_1, \lambda_2,..., \lambda_M]$. Thus, the first objective function of the proposed AWLP is

$$\min \sum_{m=1}^M \lambda_m tr(F^T L^m F) = \min \sum_{m=1}^M tr(F^T \lambda_m L^m F) \quad s.t \ F \geq 0, \sum_{m=1}^m \lambda_m = 1, \lambda_m \geq 0$$

(3)

The second aim of AWLP is to make sure that the predicted labels of data points are consistent with the initial labels. Therefore, similar to traditional label propagation algorithm, the objective function can be defined as

$$\min \sum_{i=1}^n \| f_i - y_i \|^2 U_{ii} = \min tr(F^T UF - 2F^T UY + Y^T UY)$$

(4)

where U is a selecting diagonal matrix whose diagonal element $U_{ii} = \infty$ if x_i is labeled and $U_{ii} = 0$ otherwise.

Now, through combining Equations (3) and (4), the objective function of the proposed AWLP can be formulated as

$$\min \sum_{m=1}^M tr(F^T \lambda_m L^m F) + tr(F^T UF - 2F^T UY + Y^T UY)$$

$$s.t \quad F \geq 0, \sum_{m=1}^M \lambda_m = 1, \lambda_m \geq 0$$

(5)

2.2   Optimization Method

Clearly, the objective function of Equation (5) is a non-convex optimization problem and cannot have a closed form solution. Consequently, we introduce an iterative approach to optimize F and λ alternatively, i.e., fixing the weight λ to update predicted label matrix F; and fixing F to update λ. The two steps are conducted iteratively until convergence or a maximum number of iterations are reached.

We first fix λ and solve F, let $W = \sum_{m=1}^{M} \lambda_m W^m$ and $D = \sum_{m=1}^{M} \lambda_m D^m$, by removing irrelevant items, the optimization problem (5) can be reduced to

$$J(\varphi) = tr(F^T(D-W)F) + tr(F^TUF - 2F^TUY) + tr(\varphi F) \tag{6}$$

where φ_{ij} is the Lagrange multiplier. By taking a derivative of Equation (6) with respect to F and set it to 0, the predicted label matrix of dataset can be obtained as

$$F = F \odot [(WF + UY)/(DF + UF)] \tag{7}$$

Then, we fix F and update λ, by removing irrelevant items, the optimization problem (5) can be reduced to

$$\min tr(F^T \sum_{m=1}^{M} \lambda_m L^m F) \quad s.t \ \sum_{m=1}^{M} \lambda_m = 1, \lambda_m \geq 0 \tag{8}$$

In fact, the solution of λ in Equation (8) is $\lambda_m = 1$ corresponding to the minimum $tr(F^T L^m F)$ over different sub-patterns and other entries in λ equal to 0. It means that only one pattern is selected by this method. In this paper, we adopt a trick utilized in [10] to handle this problem, i.e., we set $\lambda_m \leftarrow \lambda_m^r$ with $r > 1$. Therefore, the Equation (8) can be formulated as

$$\min tr(F^T \sum_{m=1}^{M} \lambda_m^r L^m F) \quad s.t \ \sum_{m=1}^{M} \lambda_m = 1, \lambda_m \geq 0 \tag{9}$$

By using a Lagrange multiplier ζ to take the constraint $\sum_{m=1}^{M} \lambda_m = 1$ into consideration, we get the Lagrange function as follows [10]

$$J(\lambda, \zeta) = tr(F^T \sum_{m=1}^{M} \lambda_m^r L^m F) + \zeta (\sum_{m=1}^{M} \lambda_m - 1) \tag{10}$$

Setting the derivative of $J(\lambda, \zeta)$ with respect to λ_m and ζ to zero, we have

$$\frac{\partial J(\lambda, \zeta)}{\partial \lambda_m} = r\lambda_m^{r-1} tr(F^T L^m F) - \zeta = 0, \frac{\partial J(\lambda, \zeta)}{\partial \zeta} = \sum_{m=1}^{M} \lambda_m - 1 = 0 \tag{11}$$

Therefore, the updating formula for λ_m can be obtained

$$\lambda_m = (1/tr(F^T L^m F))^{1/(r-1)} / \sum_{m=1}^{M} (1/tr(F^T L^m F))^{1/(r-1)} \tag{12}$$

where the parameter r controls λ_m. If $r \to +\infty$, different λ_m will be close to each other, if $r \to 1$, $\lambda_m = 1$ only corresponding to minimum $tr(F^T L^m F)$ over different sub-patterns, and $\lambda_m = 0$ otherwise.

3   Experiments Results and Analysis

In this section, the recognition performances of our AWLP are evaluated and compared with LGC [3], LNP [4], SIS [5], LPSN [6] and GLP [7] on three standard face databases (Yale [11], AR [12] and CMU PIE [13]). To fairly compare the proposed AWLP with other label propagation algorithms, we extend all holistic label propagation methods for local matching based face recognition by performing them on each sub-pattern set independently. Then, a final result is made by majority voting for classification. All experiments are carried out via using MATLAB on a computer with Intel Core i7-2100 CPU at 3.2 GHz and 16 GB physical memory.

3.1   Database Description

The Yale face database [11] was constructed by the Yale Center for Computation Vision and Control. It contains 165 images of 15 individuals (each person has 11 different images). The images demonstrate variations in lighting condition, facial expression   with or without glasses.

The AR face image database [12] consists of more than 4000 frontal images from 126 subjects including 70 men and 56 women. In this study, we choose a subset which contains 50 males and 50 females for our experiment. For each subject, 14 images with only illumination and expression changes are selected.

The CMU PIE face database [13] includes 68 subjects with 41,368 face images as a whole. The face images were captured by 13 synchronized cameras and 21 flashes under varying pose, illumination, and expression. In our experiment, 24 face images of each individual are used.   All images are resized to the resolution of 64×64 pixels.

3.2   Face Recognition Results

In order to take the relations between nearby sub-images into consideration, the overlapping partition way which can connect the adjacent local regions is utilized in our study. However, how to choose the appropriate sub-image size which gives optimal performance is still an open problem. In this work, we will not attempt to deal with this issue. So without losing generality, the sizes of sub-image are set as 16×16, 24×24 and 34×34 for all databases and the overlap between adjacent sub-images is 4 pixels.

As what is suggested in [5, 6], we randomly choose 5, 7 and 10 images from each person as labeled samples for Yale, AR and CMU PIE, respectively. The remaining images are regarded as unlabeled for testing. Meanwhile, the random selection procedure is repeated 10 times in each database. For parameters in our algorithm, we tune their values by a cross-validation way and report the best results in our experiments. The average recognition rates, standard deviations and average running times obtained by different algorithms on three face databases are shown in Tables 1-3. According to these results, it can be found that the proposed AWLP performs consistently better than other algorithms regardless of the sub-image size on all the datasets (especially on Yale and AR databases), which confirms that the complementary information of different sub-patterns' forming a same face are important to improve the recognition performance. The computation costs of SIS, LPSP and GNLP are much higher than LGC, LNP and AWLP. The lower variances of AWLP compared to other methods suggest that the performance of AWLP is more stable.

Then, the performances of the proposed AWLP under different numbers of labeled data samples are evaluated on the three face images databases. The numbers of labeled samples are set as {3, 4, 5, 6} for Yale, {4, 5, 6, 7} for AR, and {8, 10, 12, 14} for CMU PIE, and the rest samples are considered as unlabeled samples for testing. After 10 times random labeled samples selections, the average accuracies of AWLP are shown in Fig. 1. From these results, we can find that with the increase of labeled samples, the recognition results of the proposed AWLP are improved.

Table 1. The average recognition rates (%), standard deviations (%) and average running time (s) of different algorithms on Yale database

Method	16×16	24×24	34×34
LGC	91.78±2.41(0.66)	85.78±2.66(0.28)	81.54±2.68(0.13)
LNP	92.11±2.87(2.28)	87.56±3.07(1.02)	83.00±2.16(0.68)
SIS	92.00±2.19(337)	87.87±2.98(191)	83.11±2.79(108)
LPSN	92.25±2.34(506)	87.44±2.10(237)	82.89±4.20(132)
GNLP	92.44±2.68(10.2)	88.15±2.06(6.83)	83.35±2.72(9.60)
AWLP	95.56±2.15(2.74)	91.67±1.92(1.10)	86.78±1.18(0.71)

Table 2. The average recognition rates (%), standard deviations (%) and average running time (s) of different algorithms on AR database

Method	16×16	24×24	34×34
LGC	95.03±2.48(61.6)	91.89±3.12(24.3)	90.27±2.98(10.6)
LNP	96.13±1.81(74.5)	93.17±2.56(29.5)	92.34±2.78(15.6)
SIS	96.57±2.49(440)	93.02±2.56(324)	92.84±1.84(412)
LPSN	96.03±1.92(4650)	93.72±1.38(1035)	92.44±2.52(768)
GNLP	96.33±2.51(303)	93.53±2.60(131)	92.93±2.33(128)
AWLP	98.76±1.40(179)	96.36±1.62(45.3)	96.27±1.53(25.3)

Table 3. The average recognition rates (%), standard deviations (%) and average running time (s) of different algorithms on CMU PIE database

Method	16×16	24×24	34×34
LGC	90.38±1.66(108)	89.26±1.66(40.1)	88.72±2.04(17.3)
LNP	92.99±1.70(125)	90.15±1.45(46.6)	89.13±1.59(22.5)
SIS	92.43±1.69(953)	90.63±1.83(995)	89.60±2.07(2105)
LPSN	92.70±2.76(2590)	91.04±2.94(1377)	90.53±1.08(2355)
GNLP	93.07±1.77(186)	91.19±1.87(162)	90.48±1.17(152)
AWLP	94.47±1.22(134)	93.07±1.03(54)	91.92±1.05(28.9)

3.3 Performance Analysis on the Parameters

In this subsection, the influences of the parameter values on the proposed algorithm are tested. In the first experiment, We fix the parameter r and set the neighborhood size k from 3 to 15. The average recognition results obtained by our algorithm on the three face databases are shown in Fig. 2. From these results, we can see that a moderate neighborhood size is more preferred for our AWLP.

In the second experiment, we fix the parameter k and tune r from 2 to 10. Figure 3 shows the recognition rates of AWLP under various r values on three face databases. From this figure, it is easy to find that the differences among the recognition results of our method under various r value are small (only about 1%). This means that the proposed AWLP is not very sensitive to the parameter r.

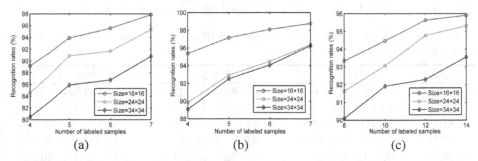

(a)   (b)   (c)

Fig. 1. The average recognition accuracies rate of the proposed AWLP under different number of labeled samples on three face image databases. (a) Yale. (b) AR. (c) CMU PIE.

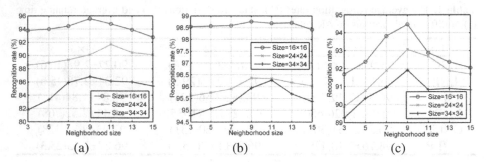

(a)   (b)   (c)

Fig. 2. The average recognition accuracies rate of the proposed AWLP under various sizes of neighborhood on three face image databases. (a) Yale. (b) AR. (c) CMU PIE.

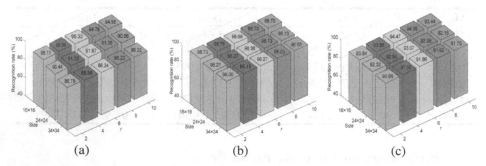

(a)   (b)   (c)

Fig. 3. The average recognition accuracies rate of the proposed AWLP under various parameter r on three faces image databases. (a) Yale. (b) AR. (c) CMU PIE.

4 Conclusions

In this paper, we propose a new semi-supervised learning algorithm called Adaptive Weighted Label Propagation (AWLP) which integrates data labels prediction and weight learning into a unified framework for local matching based face recognition. In our method, the latent complementary information of different sub-patterns is taken into account to improve the performance of label propagation algorithm. Meanwhile, an efficient iterative optimization method for AWLP is also proposed. Extensive experiments are conducted on the three face databases to demonstrate the advantages of our proposed AWLP approach. The experimental results also show that the performance of our proposed AWLP is better than several related works.

Acknowledgment. This work is supported by Fund of Jilin Provincial Science & Technology Department (No. 20130206042GX), Young scientific research fund of Jilin province science and technology development project (No. 20130522115JH, 201201070, 201201063).

References

1. Li, S.Z., Jain, A.K.: Handbook of face recognition. Springer, New York (2011)
2. Belkin, M., Niyogi, P., Sindhwani, V.: Manifold regularization: A geometric framework for learning from labeled and unlabeled examples. The Journal of Machine Learning Research 7, 2399–2434 (2006)
3. Zhou, D., Bousquet, O., Lal, T.N., Weston, J., Schölkopf, B.: Learning with local and global consistency. In: NIPS, pp. 321–328 (2004)
4. Wang, J., Wang, F., Zhang, C., Shen, H.C., Quan, L.: Linear neighborhood propagation and its applications. IEEE Transactions on Pattern Analysis and Machine Intelligence 31(9), 1600–1615 (2009)
5. Cheng, H., Liu, Z., Yang, J.: Sparsity induced similarity measure for label propagation. In: ICCV, pp. 317–324 (2009)
6. Zang, F., Zhang, J.S.: Label propagation through sparse neighborhood and its applications. Neurocomputing 97, 267–277 (2012)
7. Tian, Z., Kuang, R.: Global Linear Neighborhoods for Efficient Label Propagation. In: SDM, pp. 863–872 (2013)
8. Chen, Y., Li, Z.Z., Jin, Z.: Feature extraction based on maximum nearest subspace margin criterion. Neural Processing Letters 37(3), 355–375 (2013)
9. Wang, J.Z., Ma, Z.Q., Zhang, B.X., Qi, M., Kong, J.: A structure-preserved local matching approach for face recognition. Pattern Recognition Letters 32(3), 494–504 (2011)
10. Xia, T., Tao, D., Mei, T., Zhang, Y.: Multiview spectral embedding. IEEE Transactions on Systems, Man, and Cybernetics, Part B: Cybernetics 40(6), 1438–14469 (2010)
11. Yale University Face Database (2002)
12. Martinez, A., Benavente, R.: The AR Face Database, CVC Technical Report 24 (1998)
13. Terence, S., Simon, B., Maan, B.: The CMU pose, illumination, and expression (PIE) database. IEEE Transactions on Pattern Analysis and Machine Intelligence 25(12), 1615–1618 (2003)

An Approach for Pupil Center Location
Using Facial Symmetry

Gang Zhang[1,2], Jiansheng Chen[2], Guangda Su[2], and Ya Su[3]

[1] School of Software, Shenyang University of Technology, Shenyang 110023, China
[2] Department of Electronic Engineering, Tsinghua University, Beijing 100084, China
[3] School of Computer and Communication Engineering,
University of Science and Technology Beijing, Beijing 100083, China
zhang_gang_1973@yahoo.com

Abstract. A novel approach for pupil center location is presented in the paper. It is based on the hypothesis that both of pupil centers are of symmetry about a perpendicular bisector of a face, and uses the center of the face region detected and one of the eye region located to determine another unknown pupil center. To reduce the effect that the center of the face region detected deviates from the perpendicular bisector, the center of the face region is disturbed and two constraints, *i.e.* radial and angular, are used. Thus the pupil center candidates are obtained. Then peak detection, modified least trimmed squares, and PCA-reconstruction-error-minimum are used to select the optimal one. Experimental results show that the approach can be used for pupil center location of faces under pose variations.

Keywords: Face recognition, pupil center location, facial symmetry.

1 Introduction

Eyes are important organs in a face and of significance to face recognition. Pupil centers are notable position in eye regions and can be used for face normalization and alignment constraints which can provide strong support for face recognition, human-computer interaction and gaze estimation. Requirement of automatic face analysis makes importance of pupil centers more prominent. Early algorithms for pupil center location are mainly for a front upright face or approximately. This requires that pose of a face is constrained when it is captured. In recent years, study with tasks as a center begins to steer that with users as a center. But this requires that pose of a face is unconstrained when it is captured. Our work focuses on pupil center location of a face with pose variations.

Usually, pupil center location is built on face detection and eye location, which can reduce pupil center candidates. However, when yaw, especially combination of yaw and pitch, is beyond a threshold, performance of face detection reduces rapidly as well as that of eye location does. A phenomenon is that only a single eye region located roughly in the face region is detected. Our idea is to use the symmetry between pupil centers about a perpendicular bisector of a face to determine unknown pupil

Z. Sun et al. (Eds.): CCBR 2014, LNCS 8833, pp. 86–94, 2014.

center from the known one. Other researchers also attempt to use topology among face organs to constrain each other. All these researchers attempt to determine unknown value from known one.

In recent years, many approaches for pupil center location have been proposed. Valenti *et al.* used isophotes, which were the curves connecting the points of equal intensity, as the features of eye regions [1]. Yuille *et al.* built an eye deformable template using the eye structure which was characterized by edge, peak and valley in the eye region [2]. The approach can be used for faces with pose variation, but is susceptible to illumination variation and self-occlusion. Huang *et al.* designed several deformable templates and selected one by the pose parameters estimated by a 3D face model [3]. Ding *et al.* used eye regions as positive samples and neighboring regions as negative samples to train an eye classifier and located the pupil centers by it [4]. Monzo *et al.* used eye pairs as positive samples to train a SVM eye classifier. Comparatively speaking, the approaches using eye pairs are more stable than those using a single eye region [5]. Bolme *et al.* annotated position of pupil centers for faces in a training set. For each image, filter responses were obtained by convoluting it with correlation filters. A model was built by averaging all of filter responses. For a sample face, the correlation between the model and the Fourier response of the face region was used to locate the pupil centers [6].

Our approach attempts to explore a solution by which unknown values can be estimated via using known ones. It trains classifiers beforehand and uses them to compute the already-known ones. Then facial symmetry is used to determine unknown values. Here it is considered that both pupil centers are of symmetry about the parting line of a face. The center of the known face region is disturbed and two constraints, i.e. radial and angular, are used to constrain pupil center candidates of the unknown eye region. Then peak detection and modified least trimmed squares are used to select possible candidates. Region-merging and PCA-reconstruction-error-minimum are used to obtain the optimal pupil center.

2   Significance Using Symmetry between Pupil Centers

Organs on a face are of good symmetry for a front face or approximately. Although congenital defects of a face and variation of face expression can change it, it usually exists. For a pose face, roll, yaw and pitch are three degrees of freedom which is commonly used. Here roll and pitch variation will not change the symmetry, but yaw will. When a yaw angle is small, the symmetry is kept basically. However, when a yaw angle is beyond a threshold, it is destroyed more and more seriously with the angle increased. Thus the symmetry can be used to constrain pupil center candidates when a yaw angle is less than a special threshold.

From a psychophysiological point of view, a face is of symmetry about its parting line. Thus the parting line needs to be considered beforehand. A reasonable selection is to use the term in medicine, *i.e.* a line passing ophryon, and moreover, plumbing the line which links both pupil centers, as shown in Fig.1. After the parting line is determined, both pupil centers can be determined and verified each other using the symmetry of a face. For example, if the pupil centers Center_L(x_l, y_l) and Center_R(x_r, y_r) are known, and the equation about the parting line, *i.e.* $y = kx + b$, is too, the following relations exist.

$$(y_r - y_l / x_r - x_l) * k = -1 \tag{1}$$

$$|k*x_l - y_l + b| / \text{sqrt}(k \wedge 2 + 1) = |k*x_r - y_r + b| / \text{sqrt}(k \wedge 2 + 1) \tag{2}$$

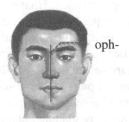

oph-

Fig. 1. Parting line of a face

Thus the unknown pupil center can be determined by equations (1) and (2) after the known pupil center and the parting line are obtained. In previous study, we used region segmentation, convexity analysis, horizontal and vertical projection and feed-filling to estimate possible pupil regions. The center of the pupil region with minimum average gray is used as the known pupil center [7]. Here we propose an approach on computing the parting line. It uses the center of the rectangle surrounding a face obtained by a face classifier. It is supposed that the center is adjacent to the parting line. Thus the line passing it can be treated as the parting line approximately. However, it should be noted that the lines passing a point is not a line, but a family of lines. This means that the unknown pupil center obtained by equation (1) and (2) is not an element, but a set, as shown in fig.2. Suppose that f_c denotes the center of the rectangle surrounding a face, e_c is the known pupil center, the red line is the parting one, then all the points on the circle with f_c as a center and the distance from f_c to e_c as a radius are the unknown pupil center candidates.

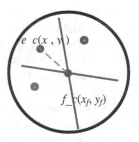

Fig. 2. Unknown pupil center candidates

3   Approach for Pupil Center Location

Here a novel approach for pupil center location is proposed. It uses the symmetry of pupil centers about the parting line of a face. It is useful for pupil center location of a face with pose variations, especially for the case in which a single eye is located in the detected face region.

3.1   Algorithm on Pupil Center Location

Suppose that there only contains a single face in an image, our approach for pupil center location can be denoted as follows. Here input data is an image which contains a face, but output data is the location of both pupil centers.

Algorithm: Pupil center location

---

a)   Using AdaBoost classifiers to detect a face, and then locate eyes in the detected face region.

b)   If the amount of eye regions obtained is larger than 3, detection window overlay and location offset are used. Thus accurate pupil centers can be obtained. If both pupil centers are obtained, then go to step *f*), else continue step *c*).

c)   Using the center in the detected face region and the pupil center which is located accurately to estimate the location of the unknown pupil center by the symmetry of both pupil centers about the parting line of a face. Then pupil center candidates can be obtained.

d)   Peak detection and modified least trimmed squares are used for each pupil center candidate. Thus false candidates can be removed.

e)   Eliminating-maximal-items-away is used to reduce pupil center candidates along with region-merging. PCA-reconstruction-error-minimum is used to obtain the best candidate in the unknown eye region.

f)   For both pupil centers from step *b*), PCA-reconstruction-error-minimum is used. For pupil centers obtained either from step *b*) or step *e*), if minimal reconstruction error is larger than a special threshold, then location failure occurs.

g)   If pupil center location succeeds, then optimize pupil centers.

3.2   Pupil Center Candidates of Unknown Eye Region

Here the approach which determines the pupil center candidates in the unknown eye region will be described. Suppose that the center of the face region is $f\_c(x_f, y_f)$ and the known pupil center is $e\_c(x_e, y_e)$, if $f\_c(x_f, y_f)$ is close to the parting line of a face, the pupil center candidates of the unknown eye region will lie on the circle with

$f\_c(x_f, y_f)$ as a center and the distance from $f\_c(x_f, y_f)$ to $e\_c(x_e, y_e)$ as a radius. Here we attempt to reduce the effect that $f\_c(x_f, y_f)$ deviates from the parting line of a face by disturbing $f\_c(x_f, y_f)$. Our idea is to select a neighborhood with $f\_c(x_f, y_f)$ as a center and ε as a radius. The parameter ε is obtained from experiments. For each point in the neighborhood, a circle can be obtained by using it as a center and the distance from it to $e\_c(x_e, y_e)$ as a radius. Thus some circles are obtained, and all the points on these circles comprise pupil center candidates. In addition, when yaw variation turns out, the distance from the unknown pupil center to $f\_c(x_f, y_f)$ is usually equal to or less than that from $e\_c(x_e, y_e)$ to $f\_c(x_f, y_f)$. Thus we extend each circle to a ring in fig.3(a). When a person faces a video camera, roll variation ranges from 0 degree to 180 degree. Thus each ring can be reduced a semi-ring in fig.3(b) further. However, it needs to be noted that $e\_c(x_e, y_e)$ should lie in the semi-ring.

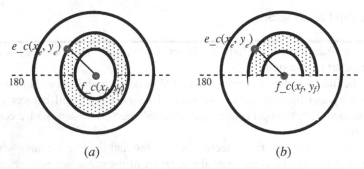

Fig. 3. Pupil center candidates (a) Ring that possible pupil center candidates lies   (b)Semi-ring that possible pupil center candidates lies

3.3 Obtaining Optimal Pupil Center of Unknown Eye Region

Here the approaches that obtain the optimal pupil center from unknown eye region will be described. After peak detection and modified least trimmed squares are carried out for each candidate, the amount of pupil center candidates is reduced. The distribution of the candidates is used to reduce it furtherly. Then PCA-reconstruction-error-minimum is employed to obtain the optimal pupil center.

3.3.1 Selecting Pupil Center Candidates

Here peak detection method [8], which Hallinan *et al.* presented, is used to determine possibility that one element is a pupil center. It is based on the research results of psychophysiology that the region which consists of an iris and a pupil usually has lower gray than other parts of the eye region. Thus a deformable model is built. It consists of two concentric circles and contains four parameters, *i.e.* the center (x_0, y_0), the radius r of the inner circle and the one r' of the outer circle. The model can be evolved by shifting the center and changing the radii. Here it is used only to change the radii. The termination condition of the model evolution is that the average gray of the pixels in the inner circle is lower than that of the pixels in the outer ring. Then the center of the inner circle is regarded as a pupil center candidate.

However, a pupil is not usually round. This means that the inner circle can contain not only the pupil, but also interference pixels. But outer interference, yaw variation, and *etc.* make the problem more serious. Here modified least trimmed squares are used to eliminate interference pixels in the region. Take the inner circle for example. Pixels in it are divided into two kinds, *i.e.* pixels belonging to the pupil and interference pixels. With each pixel in it as a reference, squared difference sum of gray between other pixels and the pixel is computed. From the perspective of clustering, when an interference pixel is used as a reference, squared difference sum of gray is usually greater. Here it can be ensured that the inner circle only contains the pixels belonging to the pupil by removing the interference pixels. The same method can be used to remove the interference pixels in the ring.

After peak detection method together with modified least trimmed squares is used, the pupil center candidates can be reduced further.

3.3.2   Obtaining Optimal Pupil Center Candidate

Here the optimal pupil center candidate will be selected. Observing the reduced location of the pupil center candidates, we can find that these elements are of relatively concentrated distribution. Thus region-merging can be used to reduce pupil-center candidates further. For each element in the pupil center candidates is reduced, the element and the already-known pupil center are used to reduce the effect of roll variation and normalize the face. Then PCA-reconstruction-error-minimum is used to obtain the optimal pupil center candidate. A small neighborhood is selected as a center. The pixels' gray is lower than average one that is kept. Their centroid is used as the pupil center of the unknown eye region.

4   Experiments and Performance Analysis

The verification of the approach is carried out on open head pose database [9]. It includes 2790 images of 15 persons. All images are the color images of size 384*288. There are two groups of images for each person, and 93 images in each group. It contains the face images with yaw and pitch. The range of yaw is $\{\varphi | \varphi \in [-90°, 90°]$ and $\varphi \bmod 15 = 0\}$, and that of pitch is $\{\alpha | \alpha \in [-90°, 90°]$ and α is even multiple of 15 $\}$. It also contains the images where subjects wear glasses.

4.1   Process and Measurement

Here the normalized error [10] is used to measure location performance. Supposed that d_{left} and d_{right} denote the Euclidean distances between left and right pupil centers and their ground truth, respectively, the parameter w denotes the Euclidean distance between the ground truths of the pupil centers, then it can be defined as follows.

$$e = \max(d_{left}, d_{right}) / w \tag{3}$$

Here the parameter e is independent from the size of a face. When e is less than 0.1, the parameter e can be regarded as the distance between the point in the iris and the ground truth of the pupil center. When e is less than or equal to 0.05, the point in the pupil is usually located. The parameter e is the distance between the point in the pupil and the ground truth of the pupil center.

4.2   Test Results for Open Head Pose Database

For open head pose database, after face detection and eye location are carried out, 730 images are obtained. After the above approach is used for pupil center location, 711 images are gained. Some location results are shown in fig.4. The results located successfully are at the first row, and some ones of failure are at the second row.

Fig. 4. Test results for open head pose database

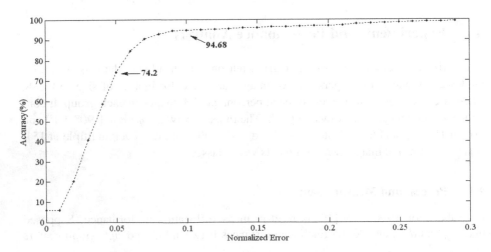

Fig. 5. Statistical error curve for open head pose database

The database has no ground truths of the pupil centers, so we manually annotate the pupil centers and used them as ground truths. It should be noted that a pupil and an iris are difficult to distinguish for some images, which have an effect on accuracy of annotation. The normalized errors are computed, and statistical error curve is shown in fig.5. When e is less than or equal to 0.05, it can be seen that the probability that the pupil centers lie at the range of the pupil is 56.12%. When e is less than or equal to 0.1, the probability that the pupil centers lie at the range of the region, which consists of an iris and a pupil, is 81.29%.

5   Conclusions

In the paper, a novel approach for pupil center location of faces under pose variation is presented. It uses the symmetry of a face about the parting line. The center of the face region is disturbed and two constraints, *i.e.*, radial and angular, are used to constrain pupil center candidates. Peak detection and modified least trimmed squares are used to select possible pupil center candidates. Region-merging and PCA-reconstruction-error-minimum are used to obtain the optimal pupil center. Experiments show that previous approach can be used for pupil center location of faces under pose variation. In the latter work, the following works will be carried out. First, more effective approaches for face detection and eye location will be used. Second, better approach for optimizing a pupil center will be explored.

Acknowledgments. The work was supported by the National Natural Science Foundation of China under Grand No. 61372176, 61305009 and 61101152.

References

1. Valenti, R., Gevers, T.: Accurate Eye Center Location through Invariant Isocentric Patterns. IEEE Trans. Pattern Analysis and Machine Intelligence 34, 1785–1798 (2012)
2. Yuille, A.L., Hallinan, P.W., Cohen, D.S.: Feature Extraction from Faces Using Deformable Templates. International Journal of Computer Vision 8, 99–111 (1992)
3. Huang, W.J., Yin, B.C., Chen, T.B., Kong, D.H.: Eye Feature Extraction Based on 3D Deformable Template. Journal of Computer Research and Development 39, 495–501 (2002)
4. Ding, L.Y., Martinez, A.M.: Features versus Context: An Approach for Precise and Detailed Detection and Delineation of Faces and Facial Features. IEEE Trans. Pattern Analysis and Machine Intelligence 32, 2022–2038 (2010)
5. Monzo, D., Albiol, A., Sastre, J., Albiol, A.: Precise Eye Location Using HOG Descriptors. Machine Vision and Applications 22, 471–480 (2011)
6. Bolme, D.S., Draper, B.A., Beveridge, J.R.: Average of Synthetic Exact Filters. In: IEEE Computer Society Conference on Computer Vision and Pattern Recognition, pp. 2105–2112. IEEE Press, Miami (2009)

7. Zhang, G., Chen, J.S., Su, G.D., Liu, J.: Double-Pupil Location of Face Images. Pattern Recognition 46, 642–648 (2013)
8. Hallinan, P.W.: Recognizing Human Eyes. In: Geometric Methods in Computer Vision, vol. 1570, pp. 212–226 (1991)
9. Gourier, N., Hall, D., Crowley, J.L.: Estimating Face Orientation from Robust Detection of Salient Facial Features. In: International Workshop on Visual Observation of Deictic Gestures, pp. 1–9. Cambridge (2004)
10. Jesorsky, O., Kirchberg, K.J., Frischholz, R.W.: Robust Face Detection Using the Hausdorff Distance. In: Bigun, J., Smeraldi, F. (eds.) AVBPA 2001. LNCS, vol. 2091, pp. 90–95. Springer, Heidelberg (2001)

Disguised Face Recognition Based on Local Feature Fusion and Biomimetic Pattern Recognition

Ying Xu[1], Yikui Zhai[*], Junying Gan, and Junying Zeng

[1] School of Information and Engineering, Wuyi University,
Jiangmen, Guangdong, China
{xuying117,yikuizhai,junyinggan@163.com}, zengjunying@126.com

Abstract. Disguised face recognition (FR) is considered as one of the difficult and important problems in FR field. Rather than disguised modeling, a disguised face recognition algorithm based on local feature fusion and geometry coverage is presented in this paper. Local binary pattern (LBP) and local phase quantization (LPQ) is firstly applied to extract the binary and phase statistics features which are robust to the disguised mode, then hyper sausage neuron based on biomimetic pattern recognition (BPR) theory is adopted to construct high-dimensional geometry coverage of different classes, which makes full use of continuous characteristics of identical class face features while avoids the interruption of the disguised mode. Experiments on AR face database and disguised face database established by police face combination software show that, compared with the state-of-the-art methods, the proposed recognition algorithm can achieve high recognition results under disguised conditions.

Keywords: Disguised face recognition, Local feature fusion, Biomimetic pattern, Geometry coverage.

1 Introduction

Face recognition is one of the most important research topics in pattern recognition and artificial intelligence. Due to the difficulties of overcoming illumination, resolution, expression, pose, age and disguised variations, it has remained a hot research direction [1]. In recent years, many algorithms for robust illumination, pose and expression variations has been proposed [2]. But for the disguised, glasses, and mustache variations, it still remains unsolved [3-4]. For national security recognition circumstances, such as the recognition of criminals or terrorists at large, deliberate face camouflages on mustache, sunglasses, hat, eyebrow, lip, age and et al. are often done to hide their genuine identity. The problem of recognizing these disguised face images are very challenging. Ramanathan et al [3] utilized the feature space of left half face and right half one to seek for relative optimal side for feature projection. But performance for disguised face recognition still needs to be improved. Singh et al [4] proposed a dynamic neural network framework and 2D Log Gabor transform to extract

---

[*] Corresponding author.

Z. Sun et al. (Eds.): CCBR 2014, LNCS 8833, pp. 95–102, 2014.

phase features, and then split these into multi-frames for Hamming matching. We achieved relatively good results. But, these results are not satisfying yet. Different from the methods above, in this paper, we try to solve the disguised face recognition problem from the aspects of more effective features and geometry coverage of the same person in high-dimensional space. In feature extraction process, local binary pattern (LBP) [5] and local phase quantization (LPQ) [6] are adopted to extract effective and stable features for recognizing faces in disguised condition. These features are fused in weighted concatenated way to form a feature vector. While for recognition algorithm, the geometry coverage method is based on biomimetic pattern recognition theory [7], which focuses more on the view of 'reorganization'. 'Classification', is adopted to seek appropriate geometry's coverage in high-dimensional space by the intrinsic continuous characteristic of samples from the same person in term of identifying the disguised faces.

2   Proposed Approach

In the proposed approach, LBP and LPQ histogram features are firstly extracted for effective and stable features respectively. Then they fused in weighted concatenated way for effective and stable features. Geometry coverage model based on BPR is performed for robust disguised face recognition.

2.1   Feature Extraction Based on LBP and LPQ

LBP is widely used in texture analysis and pattern recognition. It has achieved very good performance in the illumination-invariant face recognition task. The LBP operator, as shown in equation (1), extracts information which is invariant to local monotonic grey-scale variations of the image. During the LBP operation, the value of current pixel f_c, is applied as a threshold to each of the neighbours, f_p ($p=0,..., p-1$) to obtain a binary number. A local binary pattern is obtained by first concatenating these binary bits and then converting the sequence into the decimal number. Using circular neighbourhoods and linearly interpolating the pixel values allows the choice of any radius R, and number of pixels in the neighbourhood P, to form an operator

$$LBP_{P.R} = \sum_{P=0}^{P-1} s(g_p - g_c)2^P \tag{1}$$

LPQ descriptor which proposed by Ojansivu [6] has gained reputation in recent years for its outstanding performance in image texture analysis. In LPQ method, fourier phase spectrum is utilized to extract robust features. Firstly, Short time Fourier Transform (STFT) is computed over a $M * M$ local rectangular window N_x at each pixel x of the image $f(x)$ in LPQ, that is

$$F(u,v) = \sum_{y \in N_x} f(x-y)e^{-j2\pi u^T y} = w_u^T f_x \tag{2}$$

w_u is the basis vector of the STFT at frequency u, and f_x is another vector containing all M^2 image pixels from N_x.

Details of LPQ method can be found in Ojansivu [6]. Five LPQ images of a disguised face are calculated under different scales in which LPQ window size takes different value respectively, as shown in Fig.1. To achieve the best performance results, local LPQ window's size is a key parameter in feature extraction.

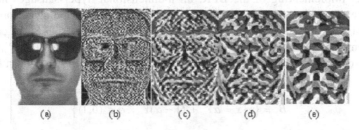

(a)   (b)   (c)   (d)   (e)

Fig. 1. Disguised face image (a) and the corresponding quantized phase features (b-e) obtained by different LPQ local window scale

After extracting the features of LBP and LPQ, we simply fused them in an equal weighted and concatenated way in this paper. We considered that each of the histogram features are important in extracting the feature of disguised face here. For the high dimensionality and information's redundancy brings by feature fusion, simple principal component analysis (PCA) method is adopted to extract the statistically independent information as basis for the geometry coverage method in the following step.

2.2   Geometry Coverage via Biomimetic Pattern Recognition

Biomimetic Pattern Recognition (BPR) [7] was proposed as a new pattern recognition model by academician Wang Shoujue. Different from the "division" concept of traditional pattern recognition, BPR emphasizes the view point of the function and mathematical model of pattern recognition on the concept of "cognition", which is much closer to the function of human being. Moreover, BPR aims at the optimal coverage of the samples of the same type, while traditional pattern recognition aims at the optimal classifications of different types of the samples in the feature space. Particularly, the construction of the subspace of a certain type of samples depends on analyzing the relations between the specific types of samples and utilizing the methods of "coverage of objects with complicated geometrical forms in the high-dimensional space".

An important and essential focus of attention in BPR is the principle of homology-continuity (PHC):

In the feature space R^n, we assume that set A includes all the samples which belong to class A. And if there exist any two samples x and y, there must be a set B for any $\varepsilon > 0$

$$B = \{x_1, x_2, x_3, \cdots, x_n \ | x_1 = x, x_n = y, n \subset N,$$

$$\rho(x_m, x_{m+1}) < \varepsilon, \varepsilon > 0 \ | n-1 \geq m \geq 1, m \subset N\} \qquad (3)$$

where $B \subset A$, $\rho(x_m, x_{m+1})$ is the distance between x_m and x_{m+1}.

According to the principle above, the differences between any two samples from the same class are continuous. In other words, there exists a gradual process for one class including all the possible samples in which one sample may be slightly different from the other.

For easier implementing of the BPR, an n-dimensional hyper-sausages neuron is adopted here. Thus the union of hyper-sausages, which is the topological product of line segments and hyper-surface, can be a suitable basic shape (sets P_i) to cover the region of samples of the same class in the feature space approximately (set P'_a).

Let j neurons cover P_a approximately, and then the covering of i-th neuron P_j is

$$P_i = \left\{ x \mid = \rho(x, y) \leq k, y \in B_i, x \in R^n \right\} \qquad (4)$$

$$B_i = \left\{ x \mid x = \alpha Y' + (1 - \alpha)Y'_{i+1}, \alpha \in (0,1) \right\} \qquad (5)$$

The covering of all j neurons is: $P'_a = \bigcup_{i=0}^{j-1} P_i$.

The function of Hyper-Sausages Neuron (HSN)[6] is

$$f_{HSN}(x) = \mathrm{sgn}\left(2^{\frac{d^2(x, \overline{x_1 x_2})}{r_0^2}} - 0.5\right) \qquad (6)$$

Where

$$d^2(x, \overline{x_1 x_2}) = \begin{cases} \|x - x_1\|^2, & q(x, x_1, x_2) < 0 \\ \|x - x_2\|^2, & q(x, x_1, x_2) > \|x - x_2\| \\ \|x - x_1\|^2 - q^2(x, x_1, x_2), & otherwise \end{cases}$$

$$q(x, x_1, x_2) = \left\langle x - x_1, \frac{x_2 - x_1}{\|x_2 - x_1\|} \right\rangle$$

Where x is feature vector of a testing sample. x_1 and x_2 are feature vectors of two training samples which determine a line segment.

3   Experimental Results

In order to evaluate the effectiveness of proposed recognition approach, two databases are adopted here. The first one is AR face database [8] which is substantially more challenging among the public released databases. AR face database consists of over 4,000 frontal images for 126 individuals. For each individual, 26 images were taken in two separate sessions. These images include more facial variations, such as illumination change, expressions, facial sunglasses occluded disguise and the scarf disguise. A subset of the data set consisting of 50 male subjects and 50 female subjects is chosen for the experiment.

The other database is specially designed by us for performance evaluation by the IQ Biometric Faces Software [9] using the same method as reference [3]. The software is adopted by worldwide police organization including US CIA and FBI, and helps arrest criminals who escaped for over five years successfully. There are lots of disguised modes which have representativeness and authenticity in certain extend. The disguised face database designed (named DS database in the following) consists of 100 individuals. Each individual has 16 face images. One session samples of a person are 1 frontal face image and 15 disguised images. The disguised mode includes variations of sunglasses, mustache, hats, eyebrow, smile and etc. The processed face image is with the resolution of 150*116.

We will demonstrate the robustness of the disguised face recognition algorithm via both of the genuine users and imposters in these two databases. Performance comparison of other state-of-the-art methods is also presented. Here, 70 subjects are randomly selected as genuine users; the left 30 subjects are used as the imposters. Half images of each genuine subjects are randomly selected for training, and the other half are for testing. For reducing the randomness of sample relying, experiments presented here takes the average results from 100 independent experiments. The proposed algorithm is implemented on an Intel Dual Core 2.60 GHz machine and applied with Matlab 2010b image processing toolbox.

3.1   Experimental Results on AR and DS Face Database

Since hyper sausage neural model is adopted to construct high-dimensional space geometry coverage in the proposed algorithm, the hyper sausage neural radius value k is a crucial parameter here. The following experiments will evaluate the performance and relationship of true recognition rate and true rejection rate under varying k value while parameters of LBP and LPQ take the optimal value above respectively. For genuine users, true recognition rate (TRR), false recognition rate (FRR), and false rejection rate (FRR*) are evaluated. While for imposters, true rejection rate (TRR*) and false acceptance rate (FAR*) are evaluated. Results are listed in Table 1 and Table 2. From Table 1, we can see that with the increasing of BPR threshold value k from 510 to 550, the true rejection rate in AR face database declined from 99.43% to 94.15%, while the true recognition rate rose from 97.10% to 98.03%. The geometry coverage of neuron hyperlinks in the feature space is small when BPR threshold k is 510. Thus a good result of true rejection rate has been obtained. But with the increasing of BPR threshold, more and more imposters were covered into the geometry coverage of hyperlinks so that the true rejection rate declined. For DS face database, true recognition rate and true rejection rate hold similar changing principle as these on AR face database under the variation of k value, which is listed in Table 2. For a practical face recognition algorithm, it is both important to achieve outstanding true recognition and rejection performance. Thus we can choose k = 528 and k = 475 as an appropriate BPR threshold value to achieve the balance of true recognition and rejection performance in AR and DS face database respectively, where the proposed algorithm can reach the optimal mean true recognition results of 98.58% and 97.80% respectively.

Table 1. Performance of genuine users and imposters on AR face database via proposed algorithm under varying hyper sausage neuron radius value k, while parameters of LBP and LPQ take the optimal value respectively.

k	Results of Genuine Users			Results of Imposters All Users		
	TRR	FRR	FRR*	TRR*	FAR*	TRR
510	97.10%	0.00%	2.90%	99.43%	0.00%	98.27%
520	97.45%	0.20%	2.35%	99.41%	0.00%	98.43%
525	97.28%	0.10%	2.62%	99.37%	0.63%	98.33%
528	**98.10%**	**0.14%**	**1.77%**	**99.05%**	**0.95%**	**98.58%**
530	97.86%	0.07%	2.07%	98.25%	1.75%	98.06%
540	98.63%	0.16%	1.52%	95.85%	4.15%	97.24%
545	98.27%	0.31%	1.43%	94.44%	5.56%	96.36%
550	98.06%	0.44%	1.49%	94.15%	5.85%	96.11%

Table 2. Performance of genuine users and imposters on DS face database via proposed algorithm under varying hyper sausage neuron radius value k, while parameters of LBP and LPQ take the optimal value respectively.

k	Results of Genuine Users			Results of Imposters All Users		
	TRR	FRR	FRR*	TRR*	FAR*	TRR
460	93.25%	6.75%	0.00%	99.52%	0.48%	96.39%
465	93.69%	6.31%	0.00%	99.93%	0.07%	96.81%
470	94.28%	5.72%	0.00%	99.87%	0.13%	97.08%
475	**95.74%**	**4.26%**	**0.00%**	**99.85%**	**0.15%**	**97.80%**
480	95.28%	4.66%	0.06%	99.31%	0.69%	97.30%
485	94.37%	4.31%	1.32%	98.65%	1.35%	96.51%
490	94.85%	3.50%	1.65%	98.28%	1.72%	96.57%
495	93.28%	5.84%	0.88%	97.99%	2.01%	95.64%

Table 3. Performance comparison of proposed algorithm and other algorithms on AR and DS face database under the same 256-dimensional feature.

Method	AR Database	DS Database
PCA + SVM	90.36%	89.56%
PCA + BPR	91.63%	90.76%
LBP + BPR	97.59%	94.65%
LPQ + BPR	97.94%	95.66%
SRC	94.82%	92.16%
Proposed	98.35%	96.89%

To further demonstrate the performance of the proposed algorithm, Sparse Representation Classifier (SRC) [11], Support Vector Machine (SVM) [12], and PCA based BPR method are adopted here for comparison, where RBF kernel is used in SVM, random sampling dimension reduction method is utilized in SRC, and 96% of the energy of PCA is adopted for PCA plus BPR method respectively. Experiments are all based on the condition of half randomly selected training and testing samples under 256-dimensional feature and the results are taken for the average recognition value of 100 times experiments, as shown in Table 3. It shows that the proposed method outperforms the other three methods in both databases.

4   Conclusions

A novel disguised-face recognition algorithm based on local feature fusion and hyper sausage neural based BPR methods are presented in this paper. The algorithm aims on extracting more robust disguised feature via fusion strategy and building geometry coverage in high-dimensional space to finish the task of recognizing or rejecting disguised faces. Experimental results on both AR face database and disguised face database demonstrate that the proposed disguised face recognition outperforms the other state-of-the-art methods in recognizing disguised faces. However, single scale feature fusion extraction may not be sufficient to utilize all the information of the disguised face images. Therefore, the multi-scale feature fusion can be considered as an improved method in future research to further enhance the recognition's efficiency.

Acknowledgement. This work is supported by the National Natural Science Foundation of China (No. 61072127, 61372193, and 61070167),the NSF of Guangdong Province, PRC (No. S2013010013311, 10152902001000002, S2011010001085, and S2011040004211), the High Level Personal Project of Guangdong Colleges(No. [2010]79) , the Foundation for Distinguished Young Talents in Higher Education of Guangdong, China under Grant No. 2012LYM-0127, and Science Foundation of Young Teachers of Wuyi University(No.2013zk07), and the Opening Project of Zhejiang Key Laboratory for Signal Processing (No. ZJKL-4-SP-OP2014-05).

References

1. Zhao, W., Chellappa, R., Phillips, P.J., Rosenfeld, A.: Face recognition: A literature survey. ACM Computing Survey 35(4), 399–459 (2003)
2. Georghiades, S., Belhumeur, P.N., Kriegman, D.J.: From few to many: illumination cone models for face recognition under differing pose and lighting. IEEE Trans. on Pattern Recognition and Image Analysis 23(6), 643–660 (2001)
3. Ramanathan, N., Chowdhury, A.R., Chellappa, R.: Facial similarity across age, disguise, illumination and pose. In: Proceedings of International Conference on Image Processing, vol. 3, pp. 1999–(2002)
4. Singh, R., Vatsa, M., Noore, A.: Face recognition with disguise and single gallery images. Image Vision Computing 27, 245–257 (2009)
5. Ojala, T., Matti, P., Topi, M.: Multiresolution Gray Scale and Rotation Invariant Texture Classification with Local Binary Patterns. IEEE Trans. on Pattern Analysis And Machine Intelligence 24, 971–987 (2012)

6. Ojansivu, V., Heikkilä, J.: Blur Insensitive Texture Classification Using Local Phase Quantization. In: Elmoataz, A., Lezoray, O., Nouboud, F., Mammass, D. (eds.) ICISP 2008 2008. LNCS, vol. 5099, pp. 236–243. Springer, Heidelberg (2008)

7. Wang, S.J.: Bionic (topological) pattern recognition - õA new model of pattern recognition theory and its applications. Acta Electronica Sinica 30(10), 1417–1420 (2002)

8. Martinez, A., Benavente, R.: The AR Face Database, VC Technical Report 24 (1998)

9. IQ Biometrix Faces Software Ver 4.0, http://www.iqbiometrix.com

10. Wright, J., Yang, A.Y., Ganesh, A., Sastry, S.S., Ma, Y.: Robust Face Recognition via Sparse Representation. IEEE Trans. on PAMI 31(2), 210–227 (2009)

Thermal Infrared Face Recognition
Based on the Modified Blood Perfusion Model
and Improved Weber Local Descriptor

Xiaoyuan Zhang, Jucheng Yang[*], Song Dong, Chao Wang, Yarui Chen, and Chao Wu

College of Computer Science and Information Engineering,
Tianjin University of Science and Technology, Tianjin, China
jcyang@tust.edu.cn

Abstract. In order to extract the robust thermal infrared facial features, a novel method based on the modified blood perfusion model and the improved Weber local descriptor is proposed. Weber local descriptor (WLD) is able to extract a wealth of local texture information, which computes not only the differences between the center pixel and its neighbors but also the gradient orientation information describing the direction of edges in the local area, so it is suitable for texture-based thermal infrared face recognition. In order to make full use of local authentication information, an improved Weber local descriptor is proposed to extract the local features from the blood perfusion image. For improved Weber local descriptor, the Isotropic Sobel operator instead of the traditional method is used to compute the orientation and build more stable feature histograms. Experimental results show that the proposed method could achieve better recognition performance compared to the traditional methods.

Keywords: infrared face recognition, modified blood perfusion model, improved Weber local descriptor.

1 Introduction

The infrared face recognition was first proposed in 1992 by Dr. Prokoski [1]. The use of infrared face images can solve the limitations of visible-spectrum based face recognition, such as invariance to variations in illumination and robustness to variations in pose, which are two major factors affecting the performance of face recognition. Compared with the visible face recognition, the infrared face recognition can get a better recognition rate under illumination variations, face pose variations, facial expression, makeup, photos, fraud and other conditions.

Although thermogram[2] is susceptible to ambient temperature, mood, etc., but each person has unique vascular distribution, which can not be copied, and the features will not be changed with age. Wu et. al. [3] proposed to use the changeless blood perfusion data to replace the facial temperature data that depends on the

---

[*] Corresponding author.

Z. Sun et al. (Eds.): CCBR 2014, LNCS 8833, pp. 103–110, 2014.

ambient temperature, and proposed a face blood perfusion model based on thermodynamics and thermal physiology. Their further research [4] found that some parameters of the model vary or differ from person to person, it is reasonable to ignore these terms to obtain the modified blood perfusion model. Buddharhaju[5] proposed to extract the vascular information from thermal infrared image by using the vascular distribution and cross information for infrared face recognition. Li et. al. [6] proposed a global infrared face recognition method based on PCA, Hua et. al. [7] proposed a global PCA + LDA based thermal infrared face recognition method. In order to extract local features of infrared face image, Li et. al. [8] proposed an infrared face recognition method based on local binary pattern (LBP). The LBP method can extract a wealth of local texture information. However, LBP just computes the differences between the center pixel and its neighbors, while Weber local descriptor (WLD)[9] computes not only the differences between the center pixel and its neighbors but also the gradient orientation information describing the direction of edges, so it is suitable for texture-based thermal infrared face recognition.

In order to make full use of local authentication information, an improved Weber local descriptor is proposed. For the improved Weber local descriptor, the Isotropic Sobel operator instead of the traditional method is used to compute the orientation and build more stable feature histograms.

So, this paper presents a thermal infrared face recognition method based on the modified blood perfusion model and the improved Weber local descriptor. Experimental results show that the proposed method could achieve better recognition performance compared to the traditional methods.

The remaining of this paper is organized as follows: the second section introduces the theory of the modified blood perfusion model and Weber local descriptor; the third section describes the proposed thermal infrared face recognition method based on the modified blood perfusion model and the improved Weber local descriptor; Section four shows the experimental results; the fifth section gives the conclusion.

2   Related Theory

2.1   Modified Blood Perfusion Model

Wu et.al.[4] proposed a modified blood perfusion model to convert thermogram into blood perfusion image. The modified blood perfusion model is as follows:

$$\omega = \frac{\varepsilon \sigma \left(T^{4} - T_{e}^{4}\right)}{\alpha c_{b}\left(T_{a} - T\right)} \tag{1}$$

Where, the meaning of the physical variables are: T_{α} is arterial temperature, T_{s} is ambient temperature, T is skin temperature, $\varepsilon, \sigma, \alpha, c_{b}$ are constant parameters.

Fig. 1. Comparison of thermogram and blood perfusion image

The blood perfusion image indicates not only the features of the thermogram, but also the physiological features of the face between the artery and the skin surface $(T_\alpha - T)$.

2.2 Weber Local Descriptor (WLD)

Weber local descriptor (WLD)[9] has two components: the differential excitation and the orientation, as shown in Fig.2.

The differential excitation is computed as follows: the sum of differences between the center pixel and its surroundings pixels divides the center pixel. The differential excitation is computed:

$$\xi(x_c) - \arctan[\frac{v_s^{00}}{v_s^{01}}] \tag{2}$$

Where v_s^{00} and v_s^{01} is the outputs of filters f_{00} and f_{01} respectively, v_s^{00} is the sum of differences between the center pixel and its surroundings pixels, v_s^{01} is the original picture, x_c is the center pixel. The arctangent function is adopted on the ratio. In order to form a statistical histogram in a simple way, the differential excitation is quantized into M intervals, $\xi_m (m = 0,1,...,M-1)$.

The orientation is the ratio of the change in horizontal directions to that in the vertical direction of an image. The orientation is computed as follows:

$$\theta(x_c) = \arctan(\frac{v_s^{11}}{v_s^{10}}) \tag{3}$$

Where v_s^{11} and v_s^{10} are the outputs of filters f_{11} and f_{10} respectively. The range of orientation $\theta(x_c)$ is $[-\pi/2, \pi/2]$. In order to get more texture information, the range of orientation is expended to $[0, 2\pi]$. The quantization function is as follows:

$$\Phi_t = f_q(\theta') = \frac{2t}{T}\pi, t = \mathrm{mod}\left(\left\lfloor\frac{\theta}{2\pi/T} + \frac{1}{2}\right\rfloor, T\right) \tag{4}$$

We get a 2D histogram $\{WLD(\xi_m, \Phi_t)\}$; $m = 0,1,...,M-1$; $t = 0,1,...,T-1$; M and T represent the number of different excitation intervals and the number of dominant orientations respectively. To obtain a more effective classification, the 2D histogram is converted into the one-dimensional histogram.

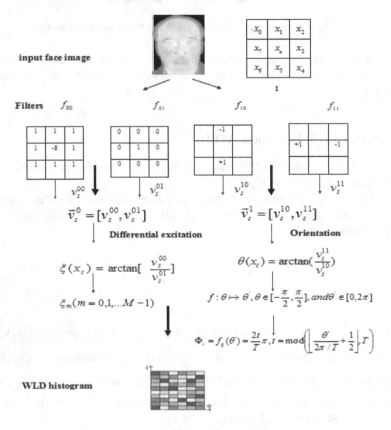

Fig. 2. The Computation diagram of WLD

3   Proposed Method

In this section, we propose a thermal infrared face recognition method based on the modified blood perfusion model and the improved Weber local descriptor, as shown in Fig.3.

The main steps of the proposed method as follows:

Step 1: Converting thermogram into blood perfusion image

We first use the modified blood perfusion model mentioned in section 2.1 to convert the temperature information (thermogram) into the blood perfusion image.

Step 2: Gaussian smoothing
We utilize Gaussian smoothing to make the blood perfusion image smoother:

$$I' = I * G(x, y, \sigma) \tag{5}$$

Where * represents convolution, Gaussian kernel function as follows:

$$G(x, y, \sigma) = \frac{1}{2\pi\sigma^2} \exp\left(-\frac{x^2 + y^2}{2\sigma^2}\right) \tag{6}$$

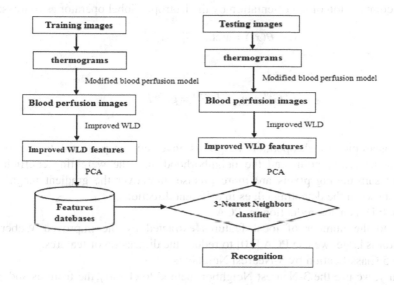

Fig. 3. The diagram of the proposed method

Where σ is the variance of the Gaussian filter, in our experiment, we found that better result were obtained when the value of σ is slightly greater than 1.

Step 3: Local features extraction by the improved Weber local descriptor

We first divide the face image into sub-regions, the purpose is to extract facial local features better, and the face image is divided into $i \times j$ sub-regions. In the computation of the orientation, the original WLD calculated as follows:

$$\theta(x_c) = \arctan(\frac{x_7 - x_3}{x_5 - x_1}) \tag{7}$$

As shown in Fig.4, the input image is I, here we introduce an isotropic Sobel operator to replace the original method to compute the orientation, the templates of Isotropic Sobel operator as follows:

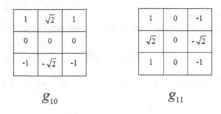

$$g_{10} \qquad\qquad g_{11}$$

Fig. 4. Isotropic Sobel operator

The computation of the orientation by the Isotropic Sobel operator as follows:

$$\theta(x_c) = \arctan(G_s^{11} / G_s^{10}) \tag{8}$$

$$G_s^{10} = g_{10} * I, G_s^{11} = g_{11} * I \tag{9}$$

The isotropic Sobel operator weight is inversely proportional to the distance between the center point and the neighborhood, and the weighting coefficients of different surrounding pixels are more precise, moreover the gradient magnitude is consistent when the detecting edges in different directions.

Step 4: Dimension reduction by PCA

Due to the number of local features extracted by the improved Weber local descriptor is large, we use PCA [10] to reduce the dimension of features.

Step 5:Classification by 3-Nearest Neighbors

Finally, we use the 3-Nearest Neighbor method to classify the features and get the recognition result.

4   Experiments and Results

4.1   Infrared Face Database

All experiments in our paper are carried out on an infrared face database captured by ThermoVision A40 infrared camera[3]. The database contains 1000 images collected under the same conditions, there are 50 individuals, with 20 images per person. Each piece of the original captured image size is 240×320, after face detection and normalization, the image size is 80×60.

4.2   Experiments

The following three experiments are carried out on the infrared face database mentioned in 4.1. In these experiments, for each person, 10 images for training, and the rest 10 images for testing.

Experiment 1: Finding the optimal way to divide the image into blocks

As the dimensions of features depend on the size of blocks, in order to investigate the effect of blocking mode on the recognition performance, we tested the different blocking modes to find the optimal one. Experimental result is shown in Table1.When the blocking mode is 2x3 or 4x2, we obtained the highest recognition rate. And in all the following experiments we use the blocking mode of 2x3.

Table 1. Recognition rate of different blocking modes

Blocking mode	1x1	2x2	2x3	2x4	4x2
Recognition rate	0.974	0.988	0.990	0.988	0.990

Experiment 2: Choosing parameters for improved WLD feature extraction

We quantized differential excitation and orientation into intervals of M and T respectively, here we discuss the effect of the parameters M and T to the recognition performance. As can be seen in Tabel 2, when the parameters M and T changes, although the recognition rate change too, but the change is very small, which shows the method based on the histogram is robust. Here we choose M = 8, T = 8, to obtain a high recognition rate as much as possible while maintaining the feature dimension as low as possible.

Table 2. Recognition rate of different M×T

M×T	6x8	8x8	8x12	6x12
Recognition rate	0.988	0.990	0.990	0.990

Experiment 3: Comparison with the different methods

The comparison of the recognition rates of the proposed method and other methods on the blood perfusion image is shown as Fig.5.We can see that the proposed method and BLOOD+WLD+PCA+LDA get the top two better results. And we found that the performance of BLOOD+WLD+PCA+LDA is nearly the same as the proposed method, while with the increase of training samples, its performance is not better than our proposed method, that is because more and more identification information is lost during the dimension reduction by PCA, the lost information can be valuable for LDA to choose the best projection direction.

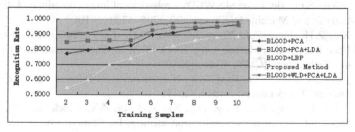

Fig. 5. Comparison experiments of different methods

5   Conclusion

This paper presents a thermal infrared face recognition method based on the modified blood perfusion model and the improved Weber local descriptor, in order to obtain more biometrics information, we firstly convert the infrared face thermogram into the blood perfusion image, and then extract local features by the improved weber local descriptor, which computes the orientation by the Isotropic Sobel operator. Experimental results show that the proposed method gets better recognition results than the traditional methods.

Acknowledgments. This work was supported by the Open Fund of Guangdong Provincial Key Laboratory of Petrochemical Equipment Fault Diagnosis No.GDUPTKLAB201334.

References

1. Hermosilla, G., Javier, R.S., Verschae, R., Correa, M.: A comparative study of thermal face recognition methods in unconstrained environments. J. Pattern Recognition 45, 2445–2459 (2012)
2. Xie, Z.H., W, S.Q., He, C.Q., Fang, Z.J., Yang J.C.: Infrared Face Recognition Based on Blood perfusion Using Bio-heat Transfer Model. In: Chinese Conference on Pattern Recognition 2010, China (2010)
3. Wu, S.Q., Jiang, L.J., Xie, S.L., et al.: Infrared face recognition by using blood perfusion data. In: Audio and Video-based Biometric Person Authentication, New York, pp. 320–328 (2005)
4. Wu, S.Q., Zheng, H.G., Kia, A.C., Sim, H.O.: Infrared Facial Recognition Using Modified Blood Perfusion. In: 9th International Conference on Information and Communications Security, China (2007)
5. Buddharhaju, P.: Physiology-based face Recognition in the thermal infrared spectrum. J. IEEE Transactions on PAML 29(4), 613–626 (2007)
6. L, J., Yu, W.X., Kuang, G.Y., et. al.: The research on face recognition approaches of infrared imagery. J. Journal of National University of Defense Technology 28(2), 73–76 (2006)
7. Hua, S.G., Zhou, Y., Liu, T.: PCA+LDA based thermal infrared imaging face recognition. J. Pattern Recognition and Artificial Intelligence 21(2), 160–164 (2008)
8. Li, S.Z., Chu, R., Liao, S., et al.: Illumination invariant face Recognition using near-infrared images. J. IEEE Transactions on Pattern Analysis and Machine Intelligence 29(4), 627–639 (2007)
9. Chen, J., Shan, S.G., He, C., et al.: WLD: a robust local image descriptor. J. IEEE Trans. Pattern Analysis and Machine Intelligence 32, 1705–1720 (2010)
10. Lu, Y., Xie, Z.H., Fang, Z.J., Yang, J.C., Wu, S.Q., Li, F.: Time-lapse Data Oriented Infrared Face Recognition Method using Block-PCA. In: The International Conference on Multimedia Technology (ICMT), China (2010)
11. Lu, Y., Yang, J.C., Wu, S.Q., Fang, Z.J.: Normalization of Infrared Facial Images under Variant Ambient Temperatures, Austria (2011)
12. Wu, S.Q., Lu, Y., Fang, Z.J., Yang, J.C., Xie, Z.H., Li, Z.X.: Block and the least square method based infrared image normalization method. In: Chinese Conference on Pattern Recognition 2010, China (2010)

Research of Improved Algorimth
Based on LBP for Face Recognition

Mingxing Jia[1], Zhixian Zhang[2], Pengfei Song[3], and Junqiang Du[4]

School of Information Science & Engineering,
Northeastern University, Shenyang 110819, China
jiamingxing@ise.neu.edu.cn

Abstract. Face recognition is one of the research hotspots in the area of computer vision and pattern recognition which has a wide application perspective. In this paper, a research on the classical Local Binary Pattern (LBP) is made and an improved algorithm named double-circle LBP is proposed, which can further enhance the rotation invariant characteristic of LBP. Since LBP descriptor based on the block has good recognition effect, this paper further proposed the strategy of "multiple blocks+middle block" in double-circle LBP descriptor, which can effectively solve the problem that the information around the original block line cannot be extracted completely. Finally, experiments are conducted on Orl, Yale and Extended YaleB face databaseds by comparing the recognition rate by using original LBP and its improved algorithms. The results show that double-circle LBP descriptor and "multiple -block+middle-block LBP descriptor can greatly improve the recognition rate.

Keywords: face recognition, LBP, double-circle LBP, multiple blocks+middle block strategy.

1 Introduction

Face recognition has gone through a very long history, Galton published first two articles about face recognition on a journal named Nature in 1888 and 1910; however, they were not involved in the matter of automatic recognition. Research paper related to automatic face recognition was first seen on an academic report of Panoramic Research Inc made by Chan and Bledsoe in 1965, which has history of nearly five decades. Over the years, face recognition is always in many researchers's good graces, and there emerged a lot of new techniques and methods in this area.

Local Binary Pattern (LBP) is good for extracting local texture feature of a face image. Because it is not sensitive to light and have certain robustness to gesture, it is widely used in dynamic video monitoring [1], image texture analysis [2-4], the massive data retrieval[5], image reconstruction, etc . LBP algorithm was applied in the actual application fields of metal surface detection firstly by Ojala et al. In 2002, Rubio et al applied LBP feature extraction technology to the feature extraction of aerial photograph and Heikkilii et al applied to moving objects detection field [6]. Finally, in 2005, Pietikäinen M [7] firstly employed LBP in face recognition, and this

Z. Sun et al. (Eds.): CCBR 2014, LNCS 8833, pp. 111–119, 2014.

was a milestone in the development of face recognition.With the development of face recognition technology, researchers put forward a lot of LBP variant algorithm [8]. Jin et al. [9] is pointing out that LBP descriptor may lose some local structure information in some cases, so they presented a solution by comparing each pixel including the center pixel with the mean value of all pixels in the image to get the binary-encoding Improved LBP (ILBP). Tan and Triggs [10] found LBP is so sensitive to noise that they raised the mode of local three values (LTP) in order to improve the algorithm. Li et al [11] proposed sub-area neighborhood operation method:to replace the mean operation for a single pixel : multi-scale block local binary pattern .Lior Wolf et al. [12] proposed TP - LBP/FP - LBP, which is also same to LTP by manipulating the blocks around middle pixels; the result showed that it has good effect on face recognition. Zhao and Pietikainen [13] first extended two-dimensional local pattern to the three-dimensional local binary pattern (VLBP). Afterwards, Zhao and Pietikainen [14] promoted VLBP to three-orthogonal pattern (LBP - TOP). Though local binary pattern can express the local texture feature well, it is inevitable to lose some useful local information. Tan and Triggs [15] proposed method local Gabor binary mode (LGBP). Above all, extract Gabor small potter and LBP feature from each pixel; then, reduce dimension of the two feature respectively by PCA; finally connect these two series of face feature [16]. By fusing these two kinds of features, the face image is enriched by different information, and expressed very completely.

However, when images are captured under non-ideal imaging conditions, user doesn't cooperate the recognition system or recognition task is conducted on a large-scale database, these difficulties are still not solved.

2   Local Binary Pattern Algorithm

The basic idea of local binary pattern is through statistical frequency of local structure to express the characteristics of the whole image. The original LBP operator adopts the fixed size of 3×3 rectangular area.

In order to solve two defects of original LBP: fixed scale and limited texture information, Ojala et al. [2] proposed the improved algorithm on the basis of the original LBP operator. The first defect is settled by extending the fixed scale to a larger rectangular or circular area. Namely, the value of radius from center to its neighborhood is not limited to 1 pixel; the number of pixels around the center pixel is not limited to 8 and all the operated pixels don't have to correspond to some fixed pixel in the image. When using a circular neighborhood method, (x, y) is the coordinates of the center pixel g_c, correspondingly, R is the radius value of the neighborhood, P is the number of sampling points.

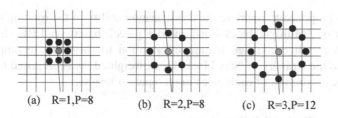

(a)   R=1,P=8   (b)   R=2,P=8   (c)   R=3,P=12

Fig. 1. The LBP operator with different pattern and radius

Encoding formula is given as follows:

$$LBP = \sum_{i=0}^{P-1} s(g_i - g_c) \cdot 2^i \tag{1}$$

We can obtain an image after LBP operation called LBP spectrum, and it usually use histogram to represent to the characteristics of the spectrum. The histogram of the image by the following formula:

$$H = \{ h_j, j = 0, 1, 2, ..., n-1 \} \tag{2}$$

$$h_j = \sum_{x,y} I\{LBP(x,y) = j\}, \, j = 0, 1, 2, ..., n-1 \tag{3}$$

j is a mode value of LBP, and $n = 2^p$ is the maximum value. (x, y) is the coordinates of the center pixel.

I(.) Is the decision function as follows:

$$I(m) = \begin{cases} 1, & when\ m\ is\ ture \\ 0, & when\ m\ is\ false \end{cases} \tag{4}$$

3   Improved Algorithm Based on LBP

The big challenge of face recognition is to find a strong classified facial features representation method to improve the robustness to illumination and posture change. Although the advantage performance of LBP to express the facial feature is obvious, it has some deficiencies. For instant, when there exist great changes in illumination, ambient noise or poseture of a face image. LBP's ability of classification and robustness is restricted. The information extracted by single block of LBP operator is not complete so as to some important Features are not obtained. Aiming at solving the shortcomings mentioned above, the strategy of "double circle" based on LBP algorithm is proposed to improve the classification ability of the rotating LBP feature; the strategy of "Multiple blocks and middle piece" based on LBP algorithm was proposed to enrich the image feature information to solve the incomplete feature problem, and the strategy of "key block+block weighted "was proposed to reasonably arrange the contribution of each piece to recognition results.

3.1   Double-Circle LBP Descriptor

For an image with rotation or small gesture, the performance of traditional LBP is not very good. In order to solve this problem, we proposed double-circle strategy based on LBP algorithm, where the "double circles" means that LBP encoding is round coding and statistical features histogram adopted circular statistical methods. On the one hand, circular encoding solve the problems of the fixed scale in original LBP, on the other hand, the "circular" encoding has a strong robustness to rotate image. The original coding region of LBP is the center pixel and its neighboring 8 pixels. The value of radius from center to its neighborhood is not limited to 1 pixel; the number of pixels around the center pixel is not limited to 8 and all the operated pixels don't have to correspond to some fixed pixel in the image. Circular encoding make the whole relative position of LBP code value and pixel values keep a constant after any angle of rotation and the only change variable is each pixel's position; if using the rectangular encoding instead, with per rotated angle, its encoded value will change dramatically and doesn't have the ability to rotation invariant.

The paper [2] proposed the circular encoding for LBP operator, but histogram statistics still employed rectangular histogram statistics. After a deep understanding of the circular LBP operator encoding principle, this paper puts forward the double-circle strategy: circular encoding and circular histogram statistics. Circular histogram statistics make the relative position of statistics value and pixel values keep a constant after any angle of rotation, and the only change variable is each pixel's position;

This paper puts forward the "circular" histogram statistical approach which has a very good effect for identifying posture change image, using circle encoding and circle statistical histogram method, there is no big difference in statistical histogram when images from one person under different rotation angles. The double-circle LBP proposed in this paper was focused on solving small pose change and other issues in Orl face database. Double- circle LBP algorithm has a good recognition effect on face database in which face images with rotation and small posture.

3.2   Multiple-Blocks +Middle-Block LBP Algorithm

In the process of extracting original feature, the feature vector only reflects the characteristics of the whole image, but cannot describe the details. In addition, facial expressions and illumination change are insensitive to the block image, so we divided the whole face image into some blocks and then take sub image feature vector as recognition features, which will be able to make full use of information about the image. Cascading all sub-features and thus gets the expression of the whole face.

However, while dividing the image into a plurality of sub-images, this will produce a plurality of dividing lines. The features on the edges of the dividing line are not easy to express and only one type of block strategy tends to separate some key part of the image (such as the eyes, mouth, etc.), this will result in the feature of key parts can not be descripted completely and effectively. To solve this problem, this paper proposed Multiple-blocks +middle-block LBP algorithm. The main advantage of this method is the using different ways to segment an image so that the position of dividing lines will be different, which can be effective not only for segmenting the key parts, but also   compensating information of edge feature of the dividing line. Multiple-blocks +middle-block LBP algorithm can extract texture features in more detail.

Relative to LBP operator with only one block and a fixed size template, multiple LBP can obtain a sub-block part of the image block according to demand. For example, for some obvious area with edge information, such as eyes, mouth, nose and other parts in face images, it is needed to divide these key areas into an independent part but without being separated.Fig.2 shows the Schematic diagram of Multiple-block + middle-piece strategy.

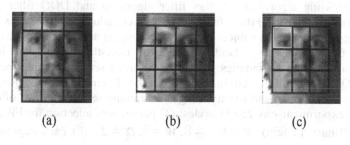

(a)   (b)   (c)

Fig. 2. The Schematic diagram of "Multiple block + middle piece"

Panning the original block image right with a step of half sub-block width, so that we can get 12 blocks (3 x 4) as shown in Figure 2(a). The size of sub-blocks is still 25 × 25 pixels; however, the total block area is reduced. Eye can complete representation by one sub-block after dislocation. In the same way, 4 x 3 blocks can be obtained after downward panning with a step of half sub-block height of the original block image. Particularly, simultaneous operating the two steps above then a 3 × 3 sub-blocks can be obtained as shown in Figure 2(c). It was found that the "middle block strategy by dislocation can Separate eyes, nose and mouth individually; it will be greatly beneficial to the feature matching and recognition. By adding three kinds of chunking strategy proposed in this paper, it effectively compensates missing information caused by dividing line between block and block, enrich the details of the image and significantly improve the recognition rate. The process of Multiple-blocks+Middle-block LBP algorithm is shown in Figure 3.

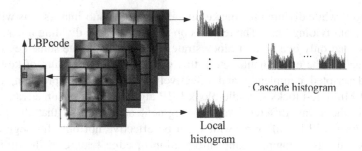

Fig. 3. The implementation process of "Multiple block + middle piece" LBP algorithm

4   The Experiment Results and Analysis of Improved LBP Algorithm

The purpose of this experiment is to verify the superiority of the improved algorithm based on LBP. Experiment supplementary explanation: (1) all images are performed Light preprocessing algorithm: Median filter algorithm and DOG filter algorithm before feature extraction; (2) three face databases were adopted: Orl (each subject has 10 face images), Yale (each subject has 11 face images) and Extended Yale B (each subject has 64 face images). Randomly selected two, three, four, five images as training set, the remaining samples were used as probe set as for experiment on Orl and Yale. Only one difference in experiment on Extended YaleB: Respectively selecting five, ten, fifteen and twenty images as training set; (3) the size of each sub-block in our experiment was 25×25 pixles; (4) parameters selection for FPLBP(Four-Path Local Binary Pattern): $r = 1, s = 8, w = 3, \alpha = 2$; (5) each experiment was randomly repeated 10 times, taking average as the final recognition rate.

The result of Recognition rate on Orl by using different algorithms is shown in Table 1 as follows:

Table 1. Comparison of different algorithms on Orl (%)

Training number of each subject Methods	2	3	4	5
PCA ①	74.50	79.86	86.08	90.70
LDA ②	76.85	82.15	90.74	94.58
LBP ③	88.12	94.21	96.29	97.55
LTP ④	88.87	94.36	96.29	97.65
FPLBP ⑤	86.88	91.07	97.08	96.00
double-circle LBP ⑥	88.69	94.35	96.63	98.70
Multiple block + middle piece LBP ⑦	88.71	94.82	97.33	98.36
Fusion ⑥ + ⑦	91.03	95.56	98.82	99.11

The result of Recognition rate on Yale by using different algorithms is shown in Table 2 as follows:

Table 2. Comparison of different algorithms on Yale (%)

Training number of each subject Methods	2	3	4	5
PCA ①	69.19	76.92	81.52	83.44
LDA ②	71.56	79.00	88.56	89.46
LBP ③	95.48	97.50	98.76	98.78
LTP ④	95.92	97.56	98.74	98.89
FPLBP ⑤	95.78	97.50	98.00	98.44
double-circle LBP ⑥	96.15	97.83	98.95	98.89
Multiple block + middle piece LBP ⑦	97.63	98.92	98.95	98.89
Fusion ⑥ + ⑦	97.93	99.33	99.52	99.78

The result of Recognition rate on Extended YaleB by different algorithms is shown in Table 3 as follows:

Table 3. Comparison of different algorithms on Extended YaleB (%)

Training number of each subject Methods	5	10	15	20
PCA ①	56.47	59.07	63.25	69.58
LDA ②	66.60	72.87	79.17	82.59
LBP ③	91.51	92.43	96.89	98.22
LTP ④	90.57	93.24	95.95	97.25
FPLBP ⑤	91.88	92.56	97.12	97.99
double-circle LBP ⑥	92.01	93.52	97.11	98.26
Multiple block + middle piece LBP ⑦	92.55	94.81	97.61	98.89
Fusion ⑥ + ⑦	92.93	95.13	98.32	99.08

5   Conclusions

LBP algorithm not only has strong capabilities of texture feature extraction and classification, but also its calculation is simple. However, there are still some deficiencies. For example, it is sensitive to illumination and big change in posture. Filtering preprocessing solve the deficiency poor capability of classification when

LBP faces the big change in illumination, noise, and other extreme conditions. This paper proposed "double circle" LBP To increase the robustness to posture, which can further enhance the rotation invariant characteristic of LBP. We put forward multiple-block + middle-block strategy Based on the idea of block LBP, which has been proved has a better recognition effect than LBP. This method effectively compensates for the incomplete information extracted surrounding the dividing line when using original single one block LBP strategy. The experiment results showed that the improved LBP proposed in this paper performed good recognition characteristic and got the highest recognition rate than any other algorithm related LBP.

References

1. Heikkila, M., Pietikainen, M., Heikklia, J.: A texture — based method for modeling the background and detecting moving objects. IEEE Trans. on Pattern Analysis and Machine Intelligence 28(4), 657–662 (2006)
2. Ojala, T., Pietikäinen, M., Maenpaa, T.: Multiresolution gray-scale and rotation invariant texture classification with local binary patterns. IEEE Trans. Pattern Anal. Mach. Intell. 24(7), 971–987 (2002)
3. Nanni, L., Lumini, A., Brahnam, S.: Local binary patterns variants as texture descriptors for medical image analysis. Artificial Intelligence in Medicine 49(2), 117–125 (2012)
4. Pietikäinen, M.: Image analysis with local binary patterns[M]//Image Analysis, pp. 115–118. Springer, Heidelberg (2005)
5. Ahonen, T., Pietikainen, M.: A Framework for analyzing texture descriptors. In: VISAPP 2008: Third International Conference on Computer Vision Theory and Applications, pp. 507–512. Springer, Heidelberg (2008)
6. PietikÄainen, M., Hadid, A., Zhao, G.Y., Ahonen, T.: Computer Vision Using Local Binary Patterns, pp. 193–202. Springer, Heidelberg (2011)
7. Pietikäinen, M.: A texture-based method for modeling the background and detecting moving objects. IEEE Trans. Pattern Anal. Mach. Intell. 28(4), 657–662 (2006)
8. Nanni, L., Lumini, A., Brahnam, S.: Survey on LBP based texture descriptors for image classification. Expert Systems with Applications 39(3), 3634–3641 (2012)
9. Ahonen, T., Pietikäinen, M.: Face description with Local binary patterns: application to face recognition. IEEE Transactions on Pattern Analysis and Machine Intelligence 28(12), 2037–2041 (2006)
10. Zhang, W., Shan, S., Zhang, H., Gao, W., Chen, X.: ulti-resolution histograms of local variation patterns (MHLVP) for robust face recognition. In: Proc. Audio- Video-Based Biometric Person Authent., pp. 937–944 (2005)
11. Zhang, L., Chu, R., Xiang, S., Li, S.Z.: Face detection based onMulti-Block LBP representation. In: Proc. Int. Conf. Biometrics, pp. 11–18 (2007)
12. Wolf, L., Hassner, T., Taigman, Y.: Descriptor Based Methods in the Wild. In: Workshop in ECCV (2008)
13. Zhao, G., Pietikäinen, M.: Dynamic texture recognition using volume local binary patterns dynamical vision. In: Proceedings of European Conference on Computer Vision Workshop on Dynamical Vision, Graz, Austria, pp. 165–177 (2006)
14. Zhao, G., Pietikäinen, M.: Dynamic texture recognition using local binary patterns with an application to facial expressions. IEEE Transactions on Pattern Analysis and Machine Intelligence 29(6), 915–928 (2007)

15. Tan, X., Triggs, B.: Fusing Gabor and LBP Feature Sets for Kernel-Based Face Recognition. In: Zhou, S.K., Zhao, W., Tang, X., Gong, S. (eds.) AMFG 2007. LNCS, vol. 4778, pp. 235–249. Springer, Heidelberg (2007)
16. Zhang, W.C., Shan, S.G., Gao, W., Chen, X.L., Zhang, H.M.: Local gabor binary pattern histogram sequence (LGBPHS):a novel non-statistical model for face representation and recognition. In: Proceedings of the 10th International Conference on Computer Vision, pp. 786–791. IEEE, Beijing (2011)

A Real-Time Face Recognition System Based on IP Camera and SRC Algorithm

JunYing Gan, XiaoJie Liang, YiKui Zhai, Lei Zhou, and Bin Wang

School of Infomation and Engineering, Wuyi University,
Jiangmen, 529020, China
{junyinggan,lxjinwy,yikuizhai,zhouleidz}@163.com,
wb3533366@sina.com

Abstract. We design a real-time face recognition system based on IP camera and SRC algorithm by way of OpenCV and C++ programming development. Meanwhile, we do research on the IP camera and rewrite some function of SDK so that OpenCV can process the video frame. First, AdaBoost algorithm is used to detect face in each frame, and then LBP is used to extract the feature of texture. Finally, we obtain the result by SRC algorithm. Experimental results show that the system can deal with real-time video and have robustness to the illumination.

Keywords: face recognition system, local binary patterns(LBP), sparse representation-based classification(SRC), IP camera.

1   Introduction

Face recognition has been viewed as one of the hot topics in the research fields of biometrics identification technology. As a non-contact certification, it is highly praised by users and researchers. Thus, many algorithms in face recognition were proposed every year. However, the algorithms used in system are stagnant [1-3]. Examples include Principal Component Analysis (PCA), Support Vector Machine(SVM), Fisherface etc. In recent years, John Wright [4] used sparse representation theory, which regarded face recognition as solving linear equations. Based on this, he proposed Sparse Representation Classification(SRC) which had a good performance under occlusion. In this paper, we exploit a face recognition system which uses sparse representation to perform classification.

IP camera, the integration of traditional analog cameras with the network video servers, is an embedded digital surveillance product. Once IP camera is connected to the Internet, you can visit it by every computer in the same Local Area Network(LAN). Because of its high stability and reliability, it appears in many areas of professional surveillance. Currently, the main application for the secondary development of IP camera includes [5-6]: moving target tacking, panoramic images stitching and so on. In this system, we use IP camera and computer vision technology to achieve the intelligence video surveillance.

Z. Sun et al. (Eds.): CCBR 2014, LNCS 8833, pp. 120–127, 2014.
© Springer International Publishing Switzerland 2014

2   Overall Design

The real-time face recognition system based on IP camera and SRC algorithm is composed of image acquisition unit and interface. In image acquisition modules, we use HIKVISON DS-2CD3212D-I5 IP camera. The interface modules consist of real-time preview, registration and face recognition, as shown in Figure 1.

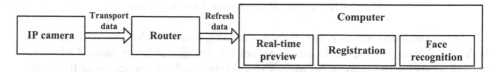

Fig. 1. Schematic diagram of face recognition system

This system is designed by way of C++ and OpenCV. Since HIKVISION's SDK is written in C++ and it does not provide OpenCV interface, we must rewrite some function of SDK so that OpenCV can process video frame. Secondly, the computer and IP cameras are made in the same LAN. Two IP cameras are set up to obtain origin images in which we can use Haar feature and Adaboost cascades classifier to detect face. At the same time, in order to reduce interference such as background and hair, image standardization is used. Furthermore, we save images after extracting the texture feature by LBP algorithm. Finally, we do the same job with all input frame and obtain the result by SRC algorithm, as what is shown in Figure 2.

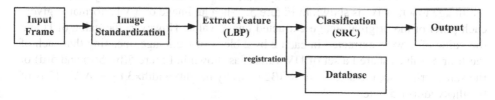

Fig. 2. Algorithm Flowchart

2.1   HIKVISION IP Camera's Data Decoding

If you want to get a frame from USB camera, you just need to type two simple commands under Opencv:

```
CvCapture *pCapture=cvCreateCameraCapture(-1);
IplImage *pFrame=cvQueryFrame(pCapture);
```

Among them, the first statement is to assign video streams to pCapture structure. Another one is to get a frame from pCapture. The command (cvCreateCameraCapture) is a way by which drive is read from local computer. However, HIKVISION IP camera's drive does not exist in the computer. We can only use the SDK for secondary development to get the video streams by rewriting its callback function and decoding function, as shown in Figure 3.

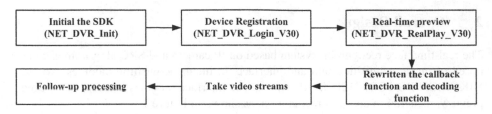

Fig. 3. HIKVISION IP camera development process

The data of video stream is stored in the decoding function. The format of one frame is YV12 that means the Y, U and V values are grouped together instead of interspersed, as shown in Figure 4. So as to YV12 format, all the Y values come first in the memory, followed by all the V values, and finally followed by all the U values.

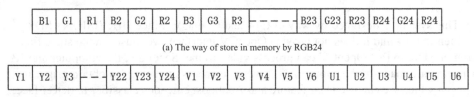

Fig. 4. Example of 4×6 image stored in the memory

In order to adapt to human visual system, we converted the memory which stores the image to a matrix, as shown in Figure 5. When an image of YV12 format is given, each pixel of the original image extracted one Y value. However, the value of U and the value of V were extracted in each 2 by 2 block of the image, meaning that each of the four Y values shared a set of UV values, as shown in Figure 5(b), 5(c) and 5(d) of the same stripe. So, the size of an RGB24 was by height×width×3 byte. A YV12 is of height×width×1.5 byte.

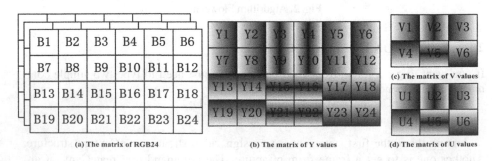

Fig. 5. The matrix of RGB24 and YV12

As we can see, the data of YV12 is only half of RGB24. It can work in previous black-and-white display system, in which Y values are only used. To be able to display color images, we need to convert to RGB24 format and the formula is

$$\begin{cases} R = Y + 1.13983 \times (V - 128) \\ G = Y - 0.39465 \times (U - 128) - 0.58060 \times (V - 128) \\ B = Y + 2.03211 \times (U - 128) \end{cases} \quad (1)$$

According to the method discussed above, we do the same to the HIKVISION IP camera. The results are obtained, as shown in Figure 6. Until now, we can get a frame and convert it to the format that OpenCV can process.

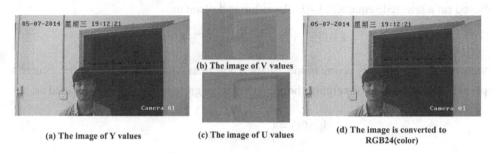

(a) The image of Y values   (c) The image of U values   (d) The image is converted to RGB24(color)

(b) The image of V values

Fig. 6. The image of Y,V,U values and RGB24

2.2   Face Detection and Image Standardization

Face detection modules is to achieve two main functions: determining whether there is a face in each frame; marking the area if it exists. There are many face detection models such as template matching model, skin color model and AdaBoost model[7] at present. AdaBoost is one of the most successful algorithms in face detection. Although the training is slow, it has a high speed and accuracy in detection which can satisfy the real-time requirements. In this paper, we use Haar feature and AdaBoost cascades classifier to detect face. The results are shown in Figure 7(a).

The faces which AdaBoost classifier is used to detect are all located in the center of the image but contain many interference such as background and hair. In order to improve the recognition rate of follow-up, we need to eliminate these disturbances and retain the key information which is useful to face recognition. Face image standardization[8] is used, as shown in Figure 7(b).

(a) The images of face detection   (b) The images of standardization

Fig. 7. Face Detection and Image Standardization

2.3   LBP Algorithm

LBP algorithm[9] aims mainly to compare the size of each pixel value in the image with its neighborhood. It uses binary encoding to describe the texture which has robustness to the illumination. The original LBP operator is defined as a 3 by 3 window, as shown in Figure 8(a). Let the pixel in the center of the window be with a threshold value. If the value around it is bigger than the threshold value, the position of the pixel is marked as 1, otherwise as 0. In the end, binary encoding is implemented based on a selected sequence. LBP algorithm is defined as

$$\text{LBP}(x_c, y_c) = \sum_{r=0}^{8} 2^r \, \text{sign}(P_r - P_c) \tag{2}$$

where (x_c, y_c) and P_c correspond to the coordinates and the value of the center pixel, P_r is the value of neighborhood, sign is a sign function which is defined as

$$\text{sign}(x) = \begin{cases} 1 & \text{if } x > 0 \\ 0 & \text{otherwise} \end{cases} \tag{3}$$

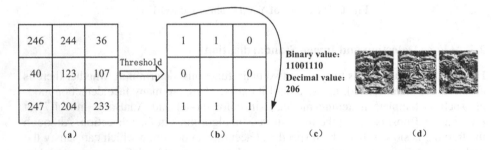

(a)   (b)   (c)   (d)

Fig. 8. LBP operator and feature extraction.((d) comes from Figure 7(b) by LBP to extract texture feature)

2.4   SRC Algorithm

Face image is a matrix in some software. Thus, we convert it to a column vector as $y' \in R^{N \times 1}$. Suppose there are k subjects and each subject has n samples. Now we can make a dictionary $D = [D_{11}, D_{12}, \cdots D_{1n}, D_{21}, D_{22}, \cdots, D_{2n}, \cdots, D_{k1}, D_{k2}, \cdots, D_{kn}]$, where $D_{ij} \in R^{N \times 1} (i = 1, 2, \cdots, k, j = 1, 2, \cdots, n)$. Given a testing sample $y' \in R^{N \times 1}$ belongs to i_{th} subject. Although the testing sample is not absolutely the same as the training sample of i_{th} subject in the dictionary, they have a high correlation than other subjects. Therefore, it can be represented by linear combination of the predefined base approximately.

$$y = Dx \tag{4}$$

where $x = [0,0,\cdots,0,\cdots x_{i1},x_{i2},\cdots,x_{in},\cdots,0,0,\cdots,0]$. The coefficients should be zero except the i_{th} subject. Actually we can only approximate the results that make the coefficients of i_{th} subject as large as possible and others are as small as possible. That is why SRC can be used in face recognition.

The objective function of sparse equation is defined as

$$\hat{x}_1 = \arg\min_x \|x\|_1 \quad \text{subject to } \|y - Dx\|_2 \leq \varepsilon \tag{5}$$

where $\|\bullet\|_1$ denotes the $\ell_1 - $norm and the ε is the error. There are many fast $\ell_1 - $norm algorithms[10] to solve this problem, such as Gradient Projection Sparse Representation(GPSR), Homotopy, Iterative Shrinkage-Thresholding(IST), Truncated Newton Interior-point Method(TNIPM) and Augmented Lagrange Multiplier(ALM). In the paper, we use Homotopy to solve the $\ell_1 - $norm problem. The process of SRC algorithm is as follows.

---

1) Input a matrix of training samples $D = [D_{11}, D_{12}, \cdots, D_{kn}]$ and a testing sample y.

2) Solve the ℓ_1 minimization problem:

   $$\hat{x}_1 = \arg\min_x \|x\|_1 \quad \text{subject to } \|y - Dx\|_2 \leq \varepsilon$$

3) Repeat $i = 1, 2, \cdots, k$

   compute the residuals: $\text{res}(y) = \left\| y - D\delta_i(\hat{x}_1) \right\|$,

   where $\delta_i(\hat{x}_1)$ is a vector whose only nonzero entries are the entries in $\hat{x}_1$ associated with i_{th} subject.

4) Output: $\text{identity}(y) = \arg\min_i \text{res}(y)$.

In addition, as we can not guarantee, everyone has been registered in the database. We can't use the minimal residual to determine someone. Therefore, a threshold value based on the system's environment is set, meaning that when the minimal residual is less than this threshold value, the system outputs the recognition result, otherwise it does not.

3   Experiments

In order to verify the effectiveness of algorithms and the coherence of system, we extract a video sequences in which the resolution of each frame is 640×320. The experimental hardware environment is Intel Core i7 CPU, 3.40GHz, RAM 8GB.

Figure 9(a) is original image and the big blue rectangle is detection region. Figure 9(b) is the results of face detection by using Haar feature and Adaboost cascade classifier, as shown in blue small rectangle. Figure 9(c) is the results of LBP feature extracted from face region. Figure 9(d) is the final result of recognition. For more detail please log: http://v.youku.com/v_show/id_XNzM1MTUzMTAw.

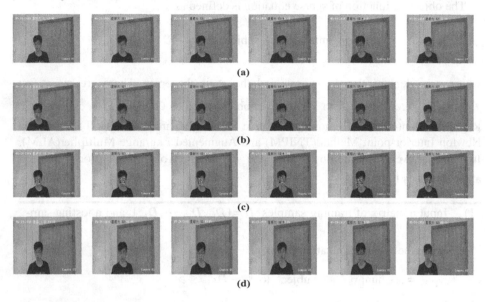

Fig. 9. The results of experimental

4   Summary and Prospect

The system is designed to the Ribbon interface, which overall view is shown in Figure 10(a) and the details in Figure 10(b). As shown in Figure 10(a), the upper two windows are used to show the frame coming from IP camera. The lower two windows are for the identification and only one is open in Figure 10(a).

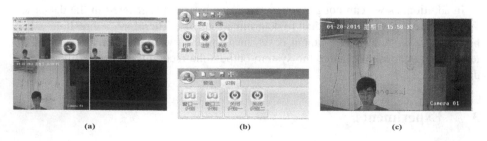

Fig. 10. The interface

Meanwhile, there are 3000 images of 30 subjects in the database, the final result of recognition is shown in Figure 10(c). This system is not only practical and fresh but also it has robustness to the illumination. However, when the two IP cameras are used to identification at the same time, the system will appear delayed phenomenon. So how to make two computers work at the same time and how to share the result of recognition will be the focus of the next phase of work.

Acknowledgements. This work is supported by NNSF (No.61072127, No.61372193), NSF of Guangdong Province, P.R.C. (No.S2013010013311, No.10152902001000002, No.S2011010001085, No.S2011040004211), Science Foundation of Young Teachers of Wuyi University(No.2013zk07), and the Opening Project of Zhejiang Key Laboratory for Signal Processing (No. ZJKL_4_SP-OP2014-05).

References

1. Chen, R.Z., Song, C.Y.: The design of face recognition system based on network. Industrial Instrumentation Automation 6, 43–55 (2013) (in Chinese)
2. Yuan, Z.H.: Face recognition system and key technology research. Master Thesis, Nanjing University of posts and telecommunication (2013) (in Chinese)
3. Jiang, Y.Z., Liu, S.G., Yang, X., Liao, L.B.: Application of fishface algorithm to face recognition system. In: IEEE Conference Anthology, pp. 1–4 (2013)
4. Wright, J., Yang, A.Y., Ganesh, A., Sastry, S.S., Ma, Y.: Robust face recognition via sparse representation. IEEE Transactions on Pattern Analysis and Machine Intelligence 31(2), 210–227 (2009)
5. Chen, L.S.: Design and implement of moving target tracking algorithm based on PTZ cameras. Master Thesis, Sun Yat-sen University (2012) (in Chinese)
6. Zheng, M., Chen, X.L., Guo, L.: Stitching video from webcams. In: Bebis, G., Boyle, R., Parvin, B., Koracin, D., Remagnino, P., Porikli, F., Peters, J., Klosowski, J., Arns, L., Chun, Y.K., Rhyne, T.-M., Monroe, L. (eds.) ISVC 2008, Part II. LNCS, vol. 5359, pp. 420–429. Springer, Heidelberg (2008)
7. Freund, Y., Schapire, R.E.: A desicion-theoretic generalization of on-line learning and an application to boosting. In: Computation Learning Theory, pp. 23–27. Springer, Heidelberg (1995)
8. Gan, J.Y., Huang, Y.M.: A method of face image standardization for face recognition. Journal of Wuyi University (Natural Science Edition) 16(2), 11–15 (2002) (in Chinese)
9. Ojala, T., Pietikainen, M., Maenpaa, T.: Multiresolution gray-scale and rotation invariant texture classification with local binary patterns. IEEE Transactions on Pattern Analysis and Machine Intelligence 24(7), 971–987 (2002)
10. Yang, A.Y., Sastry, S.S., Ganesh, A., Ma, Y.: Fast ℓ1-minimization algorithms and an application in robust face recognition:A review. In: The 17th IEEE International Conference on Image Processing (ICIP), pp. 1849–1852 (2010)

Facial Expression Recognition
Based on Classification Tree

Shuizi Zhou, Gui Feng, and Jingfang Xie

College of Information Science and Engineering of Huaqiao University, Xia Men, China
zsz021227@163.com, fenggui@sohu.com, shitou4320@126.com

Abstract. Most of facial expression recognition systems have a low recognition rate for non specific facial expression. Therefore, a new method of facial expression recognition is proposed based on classification tree. According to the differences in expressions, we classify 7 kinds of expressions from coarse to fine. And at each layer in the classification tree, we set feature vectors into different regions, and extract the most feature vectors for classification by LDA. Experimental results show that the proposed method can achieve a recognition rate of 82.38% on JAFFE database, which verifies the effectiveness of the proposed algorithm.

Keywords: non specific facial expression, classification tree, feature extraction, LDA.

1   Introduction

Most of the general facial expression recognition methods were based on feature clustering, and combined with multiple classifiers. Thus, each classifier could only distinguish one or less than one facial expression.

Ying et al. [1] proposed a method, which uses Adaboost for feature extraction in order to highlight more available LBP features, and using SVM for multiple bi-level classification. The feature extraction algorithm was more effective. Zhang Zheng et al. [2] proposed a method, which combines multi-block local Gabor binary patterns and gray level co-occurrence matrix to describe the local texture. They used C-SVM as the classifier to solve the multi-class problem with the voting strategy and introduced the feature weighting mechanism based on two classifiers. The recognition rate was 76.1% resulted on JAFFE database. Liu Yi et al. [3] proposed a method, which combines facial Gabor feature and Adaboost to improve the performance of the expression classifier. For the multi-classification problem (such as K), K (k-1) /2 1:1 strong classifiers were trained and cascaded for expression classification.

However, there are several points to be improved, such as classifier quantity and recognition speed. In this paper, we present a classification tree method, which has simple, clear structure and requires for less classifiers. According to the sample characteristics, we define multiple sub tasks, and each layer in the classification tree could only complete one task. In such structure, the number of classification samples in each layer could be decreased, which effectively reduces the burden to make upper classifiers. The kind of classification samples could also be reduced, and recognition

Z. Sun et al. (Eds.): CCBR 2014, LNCS 8833, pp. 128–135, 2014.

performance is improved significantly. It is much easier to identify big differences in small samples than to find out slight differences in large samples, which is the essence of this method.

2   Classification Tree

The reasonable definition of sub task in each layer plays an important role in producing the advantages of classification for multi-objective problem. According to reference [4], it is known that recognition rate is high in expressions "happiness" and "surprise" but relatively low in other five expressions. Happiness is easily identified as surprise. Anger and fear are easily identified as disgust. Therefore a classification tree is built to classify expressions from coarse to fine based on the expression characteristics, which is described as below:

1. In the first layer of classification tree, seven expressions are divided into three sub classes, which are {surprise}, {sadness, anger, disgust}, {fear, happiness, neutral}.
2. In the second layer, on the one hand, the class {sadness, anger, disgust} is divided into two sub classes {disgust} and {sadness, anger}. On the other, the class {fear, happiness, neutral} is divided into classes {fear}, {happiness} and {neutral}.
3. In the third layer, class {sadness, anger} is divided into {sadness} and {anger}.

Accordingly, the classification process is shown in Fig. 1.

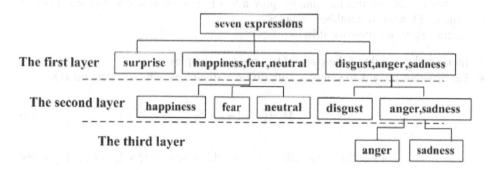

Fig. 1. Classification process

3   Extraction of Classification Feature

3.1   Classified Gabor Features

As we know, facial expression features in different regions of the human face have different contribution for classification, accordingly, for expressions in each layer, feature sets in different regions are extracted to be used for classification, which can reduce classification error. In our method, for each layer of classification tree, different Gabor feature vectors are extracted and increase the weight of regions with the greatest contribution.

3.2   Feature Selection

Gabor feature vectors, mentioned above, have different contributions for different expressions, and the most feature vectors for classification in the layer is obtained by feature selection based on LDA, which is to expand the distance between classes of feature vectors entering this layer, meanwhile to gather the distance within one class.

In this paper, LDA is combined with classification tree to obtain the most feature vector in the condition of each layer of classification tree, which can also avert the overlapping of classes with short distance between each others, such as the confusion of "disgust" and "anger".

The following consideration is that the high feature dimension is larger than the sample. Thus, a fast PCA is adopted to reduce the dimension of the resulted feature, which solves the singular value problem in traditional LDA.

4   K Nearest Neighbor Method

The resulted feature vector will be classified by K nearest neighbor method [4]. That is, firstly find out k nearest neighbor samples in the test samples, then deduce the most frequency expression of the k samples, finally classify test sample into this expression.

However, there are two faults in the traditional method. One is that dominant quantity may dominate the classification result, and it may lead to wrong classification. The other is that the similar samples play a less important role due to the consistent treatment of k nearest neighbor samples.

Accordingly, we improve it in two aspects:

- Increase the weight of the class of less training samples
- Set different weighs to samples with different distances, which is defined as

$$M_i = (k+1-i)/k \tag{1}$$

Where M_i is a weight of the kth nearest neighbor sample $(i = 1,...,k)$. M_1 is the closest sample. With the increasing of i, the distance between nearest neighbor sample and test sample is more and more far.

Finally sum up M_i of the same class, and choose the class with the maximum as the test expression.

5   Experimental Results and Discussion

Fig. 2 shows the experimental process. The proposed method is tested on the JAFFE database. We adopt the Leave-on-out to make sure the test samples do not appear in the training set. Through the scores of cross-validation, the average of the ten is taken for the result.

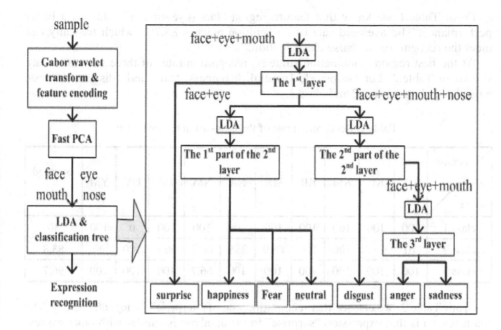

Fig. 2. Expression recognition process based on classification tree

5.1 The First Layer

The purpose of this layer is to divide seven expressions into three classes {surprise}, {neutral, happiness, fear} and {disgust, sadness, anger}. So in this layer, the {surprise} can be recognized.

The feature vector is combined with face, eyes, mouth and constitutes the coarse classified feature vector through LDA. In order to obtain the high recognition rate, the recognition rate of coarse classification must be high as well. Recognition rates in the first layer, adopting feature vectors combined with different facial regions, are listed in Table. 1.

Table 1. Recognition rate in the first layer of feature vector combined with different regions

person feature region	KA	KL	KM	KR	MK	NA	NM	TM	UY	YM	averaged rate
face+eye +mouth	86.36	86.36	100	100	95.23	80.95	71.42	85.71	85.71	95.45	88.72
face	72.72	50	85.71	42.86	90.48	76.19	61.9	66.67	71.43	86.36	70.43
face+eye	86.36	95.45	95.24	85.71	100	85.71	52.38	76.19	76.19	90.91	84.41
face+ mouth	86.36	81.82	95.24	42.86	100	80.95	71.42	71.42	66.67	100	79.67

From Table.1 we know that feature region "face+eye+mouth" achieves a better performance. The averaged rate of recognition reaches 88.7%, which basically can meet the recognition of coarse classification.

At the best region combination strategy, recognition rates of three sub classes are shown in Table.2. Let {surprise}, {neutral, happiness, fear} and {disgust, sadness, anger} for class 1, class 2 and class 3.

Table 2. Recognition rate of three classes in the first layer

person / class	KA	KL	KM	KR	MK	NA	NM	TM	UY	YM	averaged rate
class 1	100	100	100	100	100	0	100	100	0	100	80
class 2	70	66.7	100	100	88.9	88.9	66.7	66.7	100	90	83.8
class 3	100	100	100	100	100	100	66.7	100	100	100	96.7

From Table.2, we can see that recognition rate of "surprise" is not satisfactory. The main reason is that expression "surprise" in the database is similar with other expressions, as shown in Fig. 3.

| nuetral | surprise | happiness | surprise |

Fig. 3. The expression "surprise" in the database

For generalization, in the next two layers, we take average recognition rate of ten persons in the database into consideration rather than specific one face.

5.2   The Second Layer

- The 1st part

The second layer consists of two parts. The 1st part is aimed to divide the first part of class 2 {neutral, happiness, fear} into {neutral}, {happiness} and {fear}. All the three expressions can be recognized at the end of this part.

The feature vector is combined with weighted face, eyes, mouth and constitutes the classified feature vector through LDA. Recognition rates of different regions are shown in Table. 3.

Table 3. Recognition rate of class 2 for fine classification

expression / feature region	fear	happiness	neutral	averaged rate
face+eye+mouth	33.33	80	93.33	68.89
Face	27.5	83.33	96.67	69.17
face+eye	43.33	90	96.67	76.67
face+mouth	28.33	83.33	96.67	69.44

From Table. 3, we know that using feature region "face+eye+mouth" achieves the best performance. Expression "neutral" can basically be recognized, while "fear" cannot, which is primarily because of the low similarity of "fear" of ten persons in the database. Some "fear" expressions change slightly and are almost similar with "neutral", so it is hard to identify.

- The 2nd part

The 2nd part is aimed to divide the second part of class 2{disgust, sadness, anger} into {disgust}, {sadness, anger}. The {disgust} can be recognized at the end of this part.

The feature vector is combined with face, eyes, mouth and constitutes the classified feature vector through LDA. Recognition rates of different regions are shown in Table. 4.

Table 4. Recognition rate of class 3 for fine classification

expression / feature region	disgust	sadness anger	averaged rate
face+eye+mouth	83.51	75	79.26
face	79.93	85	82.46
face+nose	84.95	76.67	80.81
face+eye+nose	83.51	73.33	78.42
face+mouth+nose+eye	90	93.33	92.22

From Table. 4, we know that by adopting feature region "face+mouth+nose+eye", the {disgust} can be better recognized.

5.3 The Third Layer

The purpose of this layer is to divide class 3 {sadness, fear} into {sadness} and {fear}.

The feature vector is combined with face, eye, mouth and constitutes the classified feature vector through LDA. Recognition rates are listed in Table. 5.

Table 5. Recognition rate of the third layer

expression feature region	anger	sadness	averaged rate
face+eye+mouth	93.33	83.33	88.33
face	90	63.33	76.66
face+eye	93.33	66.67	80

From Table. 5, we know that by adopting feature region "face+eye+mouth", {anger} and {sadness} can be well recognized.

5.4   The Final Classification Result

According to the results of classification tree in three layers, we come to the final classification result. As is shown in Table. 6, after ten experiments on different test sets, average recognition rate of seven expressions reaches 82.38%. In terms of several confusing expressions, such as "anger", "disgust" and "sadness", the proposed method can achieve an effective result.

Table 6. Average recognition rate of seven expressions

expression	anger	disgust	fear	happiness	neutral	sadness	surprise	averaged rate
recognition rate	93.33	90	43.33	90	96.67	83.33	80	82.38

6   Conclusions

In this paper, we have presented a new facial expression recognition method based on classification tree. For the multi-classification problem, the expression feature is effectively used in non specific facial expression recognition. At each layer in classification tree, we set different regions for feature vectors, and extract the most feature vectors for classification by LDA. Combination of LDA and classification tree could not only extract the feature most available for classification in each layer, but also do better in identifying several confusing expressions than traditional LDA. In general, the experimental results prove the effectiveness of this method.

References

1. Zilu, Y., Xieyan, F.: Combining lbp and adaboost for facial expression recognition. In: 9th International Conference on Signal Processing, ICSP 2008, pp. 1461–1464. IEEE (2008)
2. Zhang, Z., Zhao, Z., Yuan, T.-T.: Expression recognition based on 2D multi-scale block local Gabor binary patterns. Journal of Computer Applications 004, 964–966 (2010)
3. Liu, Y., Gao, Z., Wang, J.: Facial Expression Recognition Based on Gabor Feature and Adaboost. Modern Scientific Instruments (1), 11–14 (2011)
4. Hu, B.-F., Chen, B.-X., Huang, Y.-C.: Person-independent facial expression recognition based on multi-level classification strategy. Journal of Computer Applications 012, 90–94 (2010)
5. Wang, X.-H., Huang, Y.-Z., Zhang, S.-Q.: Facial Expression Recognition Based on FSVM and KNN. Microelectronics and Computer 30(010), 38–41 (2013)

Multi-Task Learning for Face Ethnicity
and Gender Recognition

Chanjuan Yu, Yuchun Fang[*] and Yang Li

School of Computer Engineering and Science, Shanghai University,200072 Shanghai, China
ycfang@shu.edu.cn

Abstract. Stimulated by multi-task learning method, this paper proposes an algorithm of Feature Selection based on Multi-Task Learning (FS-MTL) for ethnicity and gender recognition with face images. The proposed FS-MTL selects the common features which are shared by multi-tasks are based on the sparse optimization solution of group Least Absolute Shrinkage and Selection Operator (LASSO). Compared with either the classic feature selection algorithm or the single task feature selection, the proposed algorithm can get higher recognition rate through sharing the related information among tasks. At the same time, the stability analysis is introduced to feature selection. With given stability metrics, the results of experiments show that features selected with the proposed algorithm are more stable.

Keywords: Feature selection, Multi-task learning, Stability analysis, Ethnicity recognition, Gender recognition.

1   Introduction

The research on human face ethnicity and gender recognition was firstly studied by psychologists from the perspective of cognitive science [1]. In recent years, the research on computer vision, pattern recognition and artificial intelligence have made extensively studies on this topic. At the same time, the ethnicity and gender classification have extensive application such as identification and retrieval.

In the machine learning, the theory of Single Task Learning (STL) to deal with the single recognition task becomes more and more mature. However, in some cases, the STL cannot solve the multi-task problems. Thus, the multi-task learning (MTL) is proposed. As one of the future developing trend of machine learning, the MTL method makes up the deficiency of STL in many practical applications. With the improvement of the technology and the needs of the application, it is obvious that the trend from STL method to MTL method is inevitable.

MTL can solve the problem of insufficiency of training samples and the problem of training when the testing data sets from different databases. Facing the ethnicity and gender classification, they are two different tasks in face images which share some

---

[*] Corresponding author.

Z. Sun et al. (Eds.): CCBR 2014, LNCS 8833, pp. 136–144, 2014.

common data structure or model. In this paper, we propose a feature selection method (FS-MTL) and apply it to the face ethnicity and gender classification. Compared with the classical feature selection algorithms, the min-Redundancy Max-Relevance (mRMR) [2], and the single task feature selection method, it can not only improve the recognition rate, but also strengthen the robustness.

For feature selection algorithm, previous studies paid more attention to the accuracy and time efficiency, ignoring the stability of the selected subsets of features. In the meanwhile, the classification results will not be credible if the subsets Acknowledgement from high dimensional feature spaces are not stable, such as the microarray analysis in bioinformatics [3]. Therefore, we consider the stability of subsets as one of our research content and make comparison with different feature selection methods. The experimental results show that the proposed FS MTL algorithm has the feature of higher stability.

2   Multi-Task Learning

Multi-task learning is a machine-learning method to solve more than two paralleling problems using a shared representation. The common machine learning algorithms usually learn one task at a time. When facing the complicated learning problems, they can be decomposed into some independent single problems firstly and then learn each sub-problem respectively. Finally, the results are combined into a mathematical model of a complex problem.

As to learn each of the sub-problems, the correlation between different sub-problems is often ignored, where the method based on multi-task learning can concentrate on the correlation between different sub-problems. Therefore, the multi-tasking learning method can improve the prediction's accuracy of complex problems theoretically and overcome the performance bottlenecks of single task learning problems. Also, the multi-task learning method includes the influence of different task learning results. It can not only distinguish the differences of learning tasks, but also share the related features between tasks. So, it uses the correlation between features to improve the learning ability and relieve the over-learning problems with the small high-dimensional samples. Fig.1 shows the framework of STL and MTL method.

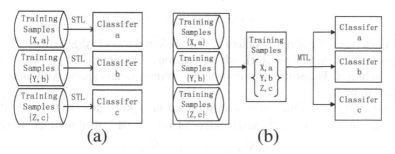

Fig. 1. Framework of (a) STL and (b) MTL

Argyriou et.al [4] believed that, in Reproducing Kernel Hilbert space (RKHS), the normalized problem of nonlinear model could be well solved by using multi-task learning model which obtained excellent performance. In [5], a feature dimension reduction technique was proposed for multi-task problems, which tried to find out the feature space shared among related tasks. The method was divided into two steps: 1) learning the unique features from single task. 2) learning the shared features of multitasks. Also, in [6], it was assumed that there existed a subset of features shared among multitasks. By constructing $l_{2,1}$ convex optimization problem, the MTL problem was proved redefined as a convex optimization problem. Zhang et.al [7] put forward a probability model based on ICA to learn the relevant multitasks, and finally obtained good performance in text classification. Obozinski et.al [8] extended the l_1 - norm normalization of single task to multitask learning, by punishing covariance of different tasks. Their experiment's results proved that the method was better than the feature selection method when based on l_1 -norm. Zhang [9] proposed a robust Multitask Feature Learning algorithm (rMTFL) to obtain the common feature of the related tasks which can recognize abnormal task.

3   Feature Selection with Multi-Task Learning (FS-MTL)

In this paper, we mainly apply the idea of MTL for feature selection, sharing the common features by the correlation between tasks to improve the performance of the feature selection method. Given c relevant learning tasks, the training set denoted as $\{(X_1, y_1), ..., (X_c, y_c)\}$, $X_i \in R^{n_i * d}$ contains training samples of the i -th task. $y_i \in R^{n_i}$ denotes the class label of the i -th task. n_i is the number of training samples of the i -th task. d is the dimension of samples.

Through the mutual learning of c tasks, we hope to get the weight matrix $W = [w_1, ..., w_c] \in R^{d \times c}$. $w_i = \{w_i^1, w_i^2, ..., w_i^d\}$, representing the weight coefficient of the i -th task. For the i -th task, the loss function can be defined as $J_i(w_i, X_i, y_i) = |X_i w_i - y_i|$, to minimize the experience error. So the optimization problem can be described as follows Equation (1).

$$\min_{w_i} J_i(w_i, X_i, y_i) + \lambda \| w_i \|_1 \tag{1}$$

For a single task, the above problem is often referred to as LASSO (Least Absolute Shrinkage and Selection Operator), which is a convex optimization problem with no analytical solution. The solution with iterative optimization is sparse with many of its entries tend to be 0.

The global objective function of solving multi-task problem is consistent with the objective function of solving c tasks independently, as described in Equation (2).

$$\min_{W} \sum_{i=1}^{c} J_i(w_i, X_i, y_i) + \lambda \sum_{i=1}^{c} \| w_i \|_1 \tag{2}$$

$$W = \underset{\text{d Dimension}}{\left.\vphantom{\begin{matrix}w_1^1\\w_1^2\\\vdots\\w_1^d\end{matrix}}\right|}\overbrace{\begin{pmatrix} w_1^1 & w_2^1 & \cdots & w_c^1 \\ w_1^2 & w_2^2 & \cdots & w_c^2 \\ \vdots & \vdots & \ddots & \vdots \\ w_1^d & w_2^d & \cdots & w_c^d \end{pmatrix}}^{\text{C Tasks}}$$

As can be seen, under the constraint of l_1-norm, the tasks are independent to each other. In order to select features in the global feature space, we make some changes to get the equation of the objective function under l_2-norm restriction:

$$\min_{W} \sum_{i=1}^{c} J_i(w_i, X_i, y_i) + \lambda \sum_{k=1}^{d} \| w^k \|_2 \tag{3}$$

$$W = \underset{\text{d Dimension}}{\left.\vphantom{\begin{matrix}w_1^1\\w_1^2\\\vdots\\w_1^d\end{matrix}}\right|}\overbrace{\begin{array}{|cccc|} \hline w_1^1 & w_2^1 & \cdots & w_c^1 \\ w_1^2 & w_2^2 & \cdots & w_c^2 \\ \vdots & \vdots & \ddots & \vdots \\ w_1^d & w_2^d & \cdots & w_c^d \\ \hline \end{array}}^{\text{C Tasks}}$$

Face images contain rich semantic information, which makes it possible for multi-task learning. In our paper, we take different semantics classification as different tasks, and we propose the FS-MTL based on the semantics classification. For a given face image training set, we can obtain data set $\{(X_1, y_1), ..., (X_c, y_c)\}$ which is ranked by c tasks after extracting features. Then through equation (3), we get the optimal solution W. Each column w_i of W is corresponding to the sparse coefficient of a single task. For each column w_i, we need to preset the threshold σ and then we get selected value define as follows.

$$idf_i(j) = \begin{cases} 1 & w_i^j \geq \sigma \\ 0 & w_i^j < \sigma \end{cases} \tag{4}$$

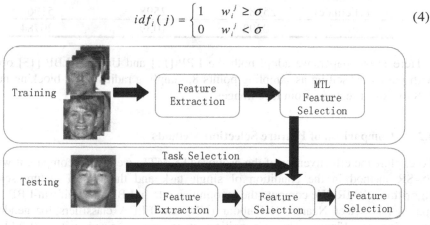

Fig. 2. Framework of FS-MTL

When $idf_i(j) = 1$, it means that the j-th dimension feature of the i-th task is selected, and $idf_i(j) = 0$ means the corresponding feature is not selected. Here, the threshold σ is mainly used to control the sparse degree to feature selection, so the parameter is very important. However, we can select the feature by sorting the sparse coefficients w_i in descending order. The framework of process is shown in Fig. 2. When the number of task $c = 1$, the multi-task learning problem degrades into single task problem. What's more, the feature selection method of single task problem is referred to as the FS-SR.

4   Experimental Analysis

4.1   Data Sets

To verify the effectiveness of the proposed FS-MTL algorithm, we perform experiments on the MORPH-II [10] database, which is one of the biggest face image databases and is abundant with face semantic information such as gender and ethnicity. The race semantics mainly include the black and the white. Other races only account for less than 4%. So we make racial classification only with white and black. Based on the composition of MORPH-II database, the statistics of corresponding semantic images are as listed in Table 1.

Table 1. The distribution of the subset for classification

	B(Black)	W(White)	sum
M(Male)	7794	7794	15588
F(Female)	2598	2598	5196
sum	10392	10392	20784

Here in our paper, we adopt both the LBP [11] and Uniform LBP [13] operator with parameter setting as sampling points 8, sampling radius 2 and blocking number 7*8 to extract features from face images.

4.2   Comparison of Feature Selection Methods

To explore the effectiveness of the proposed FS-MTL, we mainly compare it with the FS-SR method in the condition of single task and the typical feature selection algorithm mRMR. We compute the recognition rate in LBP and Uniform-LBP feature spaces and select Nearest Neighbour (NN) and FLDA classifiers for gender and classification. Finally, the recognition rates are obtained with 10-fold-cross-validation.

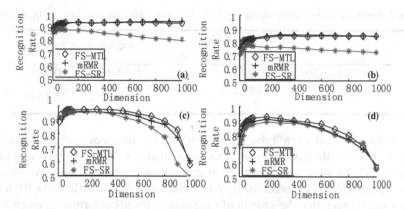

Fig. 3. Recognition rates in LBP feature space with (a) NN classifier for ethnicity classification (b) with NN classifier on gender classification. (c) FLDA classifier for ethnicity classification (d) with FLDA classifier for gender classification.

By Fig.3 and Fig.4, it is obvious that the proposed FS-MTL method is superior to the FS-SR algorithm. It is better than or equivalent to the classic mRMR feature selection method. Recognition rate in low dimension d=100 can reach more than 90%. When in the Uniform-LBP feature space, it is 93.38%.The experimental results prove the fact that FS-MTL shares common feature space between tasks at the same time improvement of the facts.

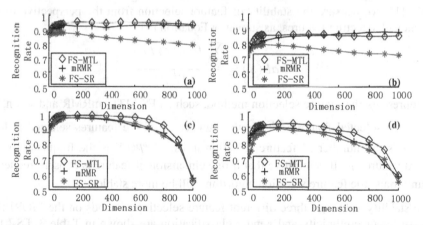

Fig. 4. Recognition rates in ULBP feature space with (a) NN classifier for ethnicity classification (b) NN classifier for gender classification. (c) FLDA classifier for ethnicity classification (d) FLDA classifier for gender classification.

In addition to the recognition rate, we also compare the time efficiency of the three feature selection methods, machine configuration is as follows: Intel (R) Core (TM) i7-2600 @ 3.4 GHZ CPU. Time efficiency of the algorithms is shown in Table 2.

Table 2. Time efficiency comparison of different feature selection methods. (unit: second)

	mRMR		FS-SR	FS-MTL
	d=200	d=600		
Uniform-LBP	65.14	170.98	0.0046	0.3019
LBP	144.23	402.32	10.694	3.1493

As can be observed from Table 2, for mRMR, the time cost increases gradually with the increase of the dimension of the selected features. While the time cost of FS-SR and FS-MTL feature selection method maintain at a relatively low level with the increase of the selected dimensions. By comparing the Uniform-LBP and LBP feature spaces, it can be seen that the growth of time cost of FS-SR algorithm is much higher than that of the FS-MTL algorithm. In conclusion, the efficiency of FS-MTL algorithm is the most optimal, FS-SR algorithm ranks the second, mRMR is the worst.

4.3   Stability of Feature Selection Method

Besides the accuracy and time efficiency, stability is one of the important indicators to measure the quality of feature selection algorithm. The feature selection's result varies with the change of the training set especially with small sample set. According to the characteristics of feature selection in face recognition, we adopt Stab (S) criteria [15] to measure the stability of feature selection from the perspective of the frequency of selecting features, as shown in Equation (5).

$$Stab(S) = \frac{\sum_{r \in F} freq(r) / m}{|F^{'}|} \tag{5}$$

S represents the feature selection method, such as FS-MTL, mRMR and so on, r denotes the selected feature, $|F^{'}|$ is the number of all the features selected at least once. m is the number of feature selection trials. $frep(r)$ is the frequency of the selected feature r. It is intuitive that if one dimension of feature is chosen frequently in many trials, the feature selection algorithm will be more stable.

The stability values of three different feature selection methods on the MORPH-II database for face ethnicity and gender classification are shown in Table 3. FS-MTL feature selection algorithm shows the highest stability.

In conclusion, by comparing the recognition rates, time efficiency and stability of three feature selection methods vary in a great deal. It is obvious that the performance of our FS-MTL algorithm is the optimal.

Table 3. Stability comparison of different feature selection methods

	Dimension d	mRMR	FS-SR	FS-MTL
	200	0.5141	0.3876	0.6969
ULBP	400	0.5435	0.4032	0.6826
	600	0.5639	0.4161	0.6842
	200	0.3623	0.3521	0.5848
LBP	400	0.3806	0.3806	0.5839
	600	0.3919	0.3968	0.5725

5   Conclusion

Inspired by multi-task learning, we propose a feature selection algorithm based on multi-task learning. Since face ethnicity and gender classification can be considered as different tasks, we mainly concentrate on the two tasks to verify the FS-MTL algorithm. The proposed FS-MTL selects the common features shared by multi-tasks based on the sparse optimization solution of group LASSO. Experiments on MORPH-II database show that the recognition rates of FS-MTL method is higher than that of the FS-SR method based on single task learning and the classic mRMR method. From the aspect of time efficiency, FS-MTL is comparable to FS-SR. Both FS-MTL and FS-SR are better than the mRMR method. And the stability analysis of feature selection method shows that the proposed FS-MTL algorithm is superior to the FS-SR algorithm and classic mRMR criterion. Hence, the performance of FS-MTL has been proved. We can conclude that the FS-MTL can be an excellent method applied in feature selection for multi-tasks.

Acknowledgments. The work is funded by the National Natural Science Foundation of China (No.61170155).

References

1. Cottrell, G.W.: Extracting features from faces using compression networks: Face, identity, emotion and gender recognition using holons. In: Connectionist Models: Proceedings of the 1990 Summer School, pp. 328–337 (1990)
2. Peng, H.-C., Long, F., Ding, C.: Feature selection based on mutual information: Criteria of max-dependency, max-relevance, and min-redundancy. IEEE Transactions on Pattern Analysis and Machine Intelligence 27(8), 1226–1238 (2005)
3. Boulesteix, A.L., Slawski, M.: Stability and aggregation of ranked gene lists. Briefings in Bioinformatics 10(5), 556–568 (2009)
4. Evgeniou, T., Pontil, M.: Regularized multi-task learning. In: Proceedings of the Tenth ACM SIGKDD International Conference on Knowledge Discovery and Data Mining, pp. 109–117. ACM (2004)
5. Argyriou, A., Evgeniou, T., Pontil, M.: Multi-task feature learning. In: Advances in Neural Information Processing Systems, vol. 19 (2006)

6. Argyriou, A., Evgeniou, T., Pontil, M.: Convex multi-task feature learning. Machine Learning 73(3), 243–272 (2008)
7. Zhang, J., Ghahramani, Z., Yang, Y.-M.: Learning Multiple Related Tasks using Latent Independent Component Analysis. In: Advances in Neural Information Processing Systems (2005)
8. Obozinski, G., Taskar, B., Jordan, M.: Multi-task feature selection. Statistics Department, UC Berkeley (2006)
9. Gong, P.-H., Ye, J.-P., Zhang, C.-S.: Robust Multi-Task Feature Learning. In: Proceedings of the 18th ACM SIGKDD International Conference on Knowledge Discovery and Data Mining, pp. 895–903. ACM (2012)
10. Ricanek, K., Tesafaye, T.: MORPH: A Longitudinal Image Database of Normal Adult Age-Progression. In: 7th International Conference on Automatic Face and Gesture Recognition, FGR, pp. 341–345. IEEE (2006)
11. Ojala, T., Pietikäinen, M., Mäenpää, T., Harwood, D.A.: Comparative Study of Texture Measures with Classification based on Featured Distributions. Pattern Recognition 29(1), 51–59 (1996)
12. Ahonen, T., Hadid, A., Pietikäinen, M.: Face Description with Local Binary Patterns: Application to Face Recognition. IEEE Transactions on Pattern Analysis and Machine Intelligence 28(12), 2037–2041 (2006)
13. Ojala, T., Pietikäinen, M., Mäenpää, T.: Multiresolution Gray-scale and Rotation Invariant Texture Classification with Local Binary Patterns. IEEE Transactions on Pattern Analysis and Machine Intelligence 24(7), 971–987 (2002)
14. Tan, Y., Fang, Y.-C., et al.: Parameter prediction for RIU-LBP based on PSO-BP algorithm. In: 2011 4th International Congress on Image and Signal Processing (CISP), vol. 3, pp. 1324–1328. IEEE (2011)
15. Davis, C., Gerick, F., et al.: Reliable gene signatures for microarray classification: assessment of stability and performance. Bioinformatics 22(19), 2356–2363 (2006)

A Unified Facial Feature Pointdatabase

Pan Gao, Yuchun Fang[*], Renbi Yu, Wei Jiang

School of Computer Engineering and Science, Shanghai University,
200072 Shanghai, China
ycfang@shu.edu.cn

Abstract. To support the relevant research on face analysis tasks, face image databases with annotated ground-truth are necessary. Although there are many face databases with large amount of images available with increasing research on face analysis, there are few open large face databases with the coordinates of multiple Facial Feature Points (FFPs) provided. In this paper, we build up a large FFP database combining several existing face databases through mapping the known coordinates of the available FFPs to a unified FFP model. The unified model is established based on multiple principles through very thorough analysis of the existing models. The FFPs are mapped to the protocol model with 7 different algorithms. As a result, we obtain a large face database of 70 FFPs labeled with various gender, ethnicity, age and expressions. This new database can be widely used in other relevant researches.

1 Introduction

Relevant researches about facial features detection should be supported by face image databases providing enough samples for training and testing. To establish suitable face image databases that can meet different research requirements, many efforts have been paid by no matter individuals or institutions. These databases are totally different in size (number of subjects and images per subject), types of images (color or gray), collecting conditions(controlled and uncontrolled with lighting and pose variations).There are many popular databases widely used in face recognition, facial expression recognition and other face analysis tasks. The number of images and subjects of these databases are increasing, however, only very little information about the ground truth of Facial Feature Points (FFPs) is proved with these databases.

In most conditions, we need to know the accurate facial features location to perform fine recognition task on facial expression recognition or test the accuracy of an algorithm for automatic facial features alignment. Therefore, some databases provide the relevant files containing the feature point coordinates of face images in their databases. Some of most popular databases equipped with feature points coordinates files are listed in Table 1. Some important shortages of these databases can be summarized through the information shown in Table 1. Firstly, the number of facial feature points in some database is not sufficient. Secondly, the number of images in some databases is not sufficient. Thirdly, most annotation of FFPs is

---

[*] Corresponding author.

Z. Sun et al. (Eds.): CCBR 2014, LNCS 8833, pp. 145–154, 2014.

manually processed, which is of very high cost. To solve the above three problems, it is significant to propose new convenient idea for establishing a large face database annotated with sufficient FFPs. Considering there exist plenty of small face databases with FFPs coordinate information, a combination of multiple face databases may be an effective solution. However, the protocols of ground truth of these databases are different, which makes it impossible to combine them directly.

Table 1. Face databases with groundtruth of multiple FFPs

	Subject	Variation	# of FFPs	Methods
CK+[1]	123	10,734	68	manually
FGnet[2]	82	988	68	AAM
Data Tang[3]	2,000	2,000	95	manually
BioID[4]	23	1521	20	manually
XM2VTSDB[5]	295	2360	68	manually
AR Face [6]	126	>=4000	22	manually
Talking Face[7]	--	5000	68	AAM
IMM [8]	37	37	58	AAM

In order to take advantage of these databases integrated as an entirety, we need to ensure that the facial feature points of images are located according to a uniform model (including the number of point, location and marking order).

In this paper, we establish a model for uniform facial features location by analyzing the characteristics of existing databases. More specifically, we select three databases as our original databases, i.e. the Extended Cohn-Kanade Dataset (CK+), the FGnet Facial Emotions and Expressions Database (FGnet) and Data Tang (DT) Database. Their basic information is illustrated in Table 1. We design a unified model to incorporate facial feature points from multiple databases. The proposed algorithm is designed according to the position relationship between the feature points coordinate provided by the original databases and the target coordinate according to the unified location model. The design of mapping algorithms is based on the principle and technology of computer graphics.

2   Unified FFP Model

To combine facial feature points from multiple databases into a single database, all the face images in the source data sets should be tracked using a uniform model. The model establishment should be on the basis of three basic principles. First, the new model should conserve as much as raw information. Second, it should simplify the re-annotation algorithm as much as possible. Third, it should meet the requirement of related research tasks. Based on these principles, we build the new model with the following four strategies:

— Make the uniform model as close as possible to the original model.
— Keep the common FFPs in source face databases in the new model.
— The number of FFPs in the unified model is no less than the minimum number of FFPs in source databases.
— Keep the FFPs of any face organ be connected in a closed curve.

According to these principles and methods, we establish a 70-point model. This model includes the annotation of five parts in face, i.e. eyebrows, eyes, nose, mouth and face-line. The specific location of these points is shown in Figure 1.

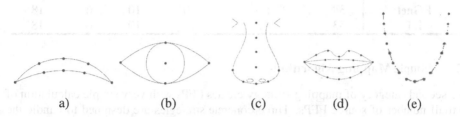

a)   (b)   (c)   (d)   (e)

Fig. 1. Unified FFP Model. (a)8 points for left/right eyebrow (b)5 points for left/right eye (c)9 points for nose (d) 18 points for mouth (e)17 points for face contour.

3   Mapping from Source Database to the Unified Model

Denote the given coordinates of FFPs in the source database as $S = \{o_1 \cdots o_M\}$, o_i $(i = 1,...,M)$ is one FFP. $S_i \subseteq S (i = 1,...,K)$ is a sequence of subsets. The intersection of any two subsets S_i and S_j may not be empty. The set $T = \{t_1, \cdots, t_N\}$ is the N-point FFPs in the unified model. The mapping process can be uniformly defined in Equation (1). For FFPs from different facial areas and databases, it is necessary to design multiple mapping strategies. Taking the three face databases(CK+, FGnet, DT) adopted in this paper as example, we design 7 mapping strategies of 3 categories to map the total 231 FFPs to the unified model. In addition, the size of the subset $|S_i|$ is no more than 4 in most cases.

$$n_i = f(S_j) \tag{1}$$

3.1   Point to Point Mapping Strategy

The first category of mapping algorithm is a direct point to point strategy, meaning to find the corresponding FFPs between the source and the unified model as denoted in Equation (2)

$$t_i = o_j \tag{2}$$

Because the principles of the unified model, keeping the original FFPs as many as possible, over 50 percent of FFPs of the unified model can be decided with point to point mapping from the three adopted source databases. A detailed statistics is listed in Table 2.

Table 2. The point number for direct mapping

	Total	Face Contour	eyebrows	Eyes	Nose	Mouth
Unified model	70	17	16	10	9	18
CK+	58	17	10	4	9	18
FGnet	38	1	10	10	6	18
DT	53	3	16	10	6	18

3.2   Simple Mapping Algorithms

The second category of mapping strategy creates FFPs with very simple calculation of a small number of source FFPs. Three concrete strategies are designed to handle the adopted source databases.

3.2.1   Scale Transform Strategy

This method takes use of the fixed radio of the distances between two points to the candidate point and hence $|S_i| = 2$. To be specific, it uses the ratio r to obtain the target FFP as in Equation (3), in which $d()$ denotes distance. An example is shown in Figure 2(a) with FFPs from the eyebrow in FGnet database, in which the b_t1 is created with b_o1 and b_o2, and b_t2 is created with b_o1 and b_o5. In both cases, $r = 0.25$. Due to fixed composition of FFPs, this strategy is also simple, fast and used most frequently in the whole algorithm except point-to-point mapping.

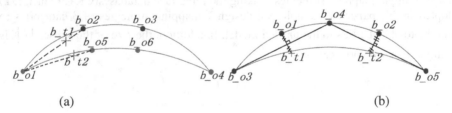

(a)   (b)

Fig. 2. Illustration of eyebrow (a) FFPs in FGnet Database; (b) in CK+ Database (cross denotes the target and dot denotes the source)

$$t = ro_i - (1-r)o_j, \quad r = \frac{d(t,o_i)}{d(o_i,o_j)} \tag{3}$$

3.2.2   Symmetric Mapping Strategy

To make a closed curvature of local organ from an open curve such as eyebrow, we take use of the symmetry in the local region to create target FFPs. An example is shown in Fig. 2(b) of eyebrow in CK+ database, in which b_t1 is symmetric to b_o1 with respect to the line cross b_o3 and b_o4. Similarly, b_t2 is symmetric to b_o2 with respect to the line cross b_o4 and b_o5.

3.2.3   Center of Gravity Strategy

In some cases, the target FFP is the center of gravity of several other source FFPs. For example, to get the center of eye, the center of gravity of several FFPs along the eye contour is a nice solution as illustrated in Fig.3, in which the target e_t is gravity center of e_o1, e_o2, e_o3 and e_o4.

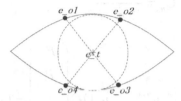

Fig. 3. Eye center of CK+ (cross denotes the target and dot denotes the source)

3.3   Curve Fitting Algorithms

Curve Fitting algorithms use the curvilinear equations to get the coordinates of target points. Normally, more than 4 source FFPs are required for each target FFP.

3.3.1   Polynomial Cubic Interpolation Strategy

The polynomial cubic interpolation strategy is used for the points in the edges of eyes and eyebrows during the mapping process. We use 4 source FFPs to create a curve with the target FFP located in the center of the 4 source FFPs. Between the two compared methods, experiments show that the polynomial cubic strategy is more suitable for FFPs than spline cubic interpolation. To map the FFPS of the adopted three databases, this strategy is used in ten different local regions of face such as the edges of eyes and eyebrows.

3.3.2   Bezier Curve Interpolation Strategy

The Bezier curve interpolation is used to create FFPs along the face contour based on the principle of Bezier curve. Given $n+1$ discrete points $P_i (i = 0,1,\ldots n)$ in a plane, the Bezier curve is defined in Equation (4) or the matrix form in Equation (5), in which C is a symmetric matrix whose value can be calculated directly.

Since the number and the location of FFPs in the three adopted source database are quite different, to unify them into a single model, we take the protocol in the CK+ database as the standard, in which each side of face contour contains 9 FFPs. For the other two source databases, we keep several FFPs along the contour as anchor points, other FFPs are created evenly along the face contour with the Bezier curve interpolation. Taking the contour FFPs in Data Tang as example, for the 7 FFPs along left-/right- half contour, 70 points are actually calculated with the Bezier Curve Interpolation and we select 7 points among them with an even interval 10.

$$P(u) = \sum_{i=0}^{n} B_{i,n}(u) \cdot P_i \qquad (0 \le u \le 1)$$

$$B_{i,n}(u) = C_n^i u^i (1-u)^{(n-i)} \qquad (4)$$

$$C_n^i = \frac{n!}{i!(n-i)!}$$

$$P(u) = \left(u^n, u^{n-1}, \ldots, u, 1 \right) C \begin{pmatrix} P_0 \\ P_1 \\ \vdots \\ P_{n-1} \\ P_n \end{pmatrix} = T(u) \cdot C \cdot P \qquad (5)$$

3.3.3   Piece-Wise Bezier Curve Interpolation Strategy

The piece-wise Bezier Curve Interpolation is an improving version of Bezier Curve Interpolation. Instead of fitting left-/right- face contour with only one Bezier curves, we split the half contour into several sub-curves and fit with separate Bezier curves. The FFPs in each of these sub-curves appear to form a smoother curve, while the intersections of these sub-curves show abrupt variation in different degree. The piece-wise Bezier Curve Interpolation is adopted in cases the half face contour does not appear strictly as a smooth curve, such as the obvious breakpoint in the cheek.

4   Unified FFPs Database

With the strategies in Section 3, we map the FFPs in the three source face database into the unified model and resulted in a very large face database with multiple FFPs labeled. Based on this large FFP database, we train a facial landmark detection model based on the algorithm in [9].The detection results are shown to prove the effectiveness of the database.

4.1   The Unified FFP Database

After mapping the FFPs in three source databases to the defined unified model, a new large face database is created with both the source JPEG image and the text file contains FFP ground truth. The new database is with the following statistics:

— The unified FFP database contains FFPs from a total of 13,722 images (10,734 from the CK+ Database, 988 from the FGnet and 2,000 from the Data Tang).
— The unified FFP database contains FFPs from face images of 2,205 subjects in total. Among them, 2,000 subjects has 1 image/subject, 205 subjects have multiple face images. 123 subjects have face images of different ages. 82

subjects have different facial expressions. The subjects include male and female; different age stages (baby, child, youth, middle-age person, the aged); different ethnicities (White, Yellow, Black, Brown).
— The face images in the database are collected with changing circumstance lighting and pose variations.

4.2   Visual Effect of Multi-strategy Mapping

To show the effect of the FFP mapping results and the changes of FFPs from the source databases to the unified model. We select several face images with old (red circle) and new (cyan cross) FFPs marked as is Fig. 4 to Fig. 6 in the three source database respectively. Compared with the old landmarks, the new landmarks can also well describe the detailed facial feature. Moreover, the new large FFP database make it possible to train better learning model for facial feature detection and other face analysis tasks.

Fig. 4. Examples of old (red circle) and new (cyan cross) FFPs in FGnet database (Images of 1 subject with 4 age variations)

4.3   Visual Effect of Facial Feature Detection with the Unified FFP Database

Based on the new unified FFP database, we train a new facial feature detection model based on the algorithm described in [9] on the LFW face database [10]. Some of the detection results are shown in Fig.7. It can be observed that the model based on the new FFP database can also work on other database.

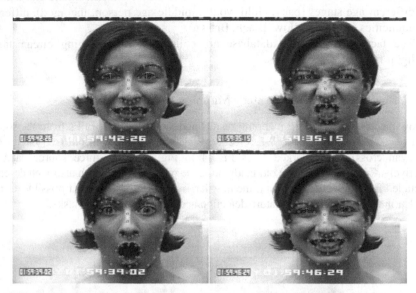

Fig. 5. Examples of old (red circle) and new (cyan cross) FFPs in CK+ database (Images of 1 subject with 4 expressions)

Fig. 6. Examples of old (red circle) and new (cyan cross) FFPs in DT (4 mages of 4 subjects)

Fig. 7. Examples of facial feature detection on LFW database

5   Conclusions

In this paper, we propose a unified facial landmark model based on the observation on several famous face databases with the ground-truth provided. An algorithm contains 7 strategies is applied to map the FFPs in the source databases to the unified model. As a result, a combination database is obtained with uniformly marked FFPs from 13,722 images of 2,205 subjects. The visual effect shows the validation of the proposed multi-strategy FFP mapping algorithm. The facial feature detection model trained with samples from the unified FFP database also shows high quality detection results. The multi-strategy FFP mapping algorithm can also be easily extended to other existing face databases with ground-truth of multiple FFPs. Through such process, the open FFP databases can be unified to a huge or even enormous FFP database alleviating manual label costs and taking great advantage of existing knowledge to well serve the FFP learning tasks in the era of big data.

Acknowledgments. The work is funded by the National Natural Science Foundation of China (No.61170155).

References

1. Lucey, P., Cohn, J.F., Kanade, T., Saragih, J., Ambadar, Z., Matthews, I.: The extended cohn-kanade dataset (CK+): A complete dataset for actionunit and emotion-specified expression. In: 2010 IEEE Computer Society Conference on Computer Vision and Pattern Recognition Workshops (CVPRW), pp. 94–101 (2010)
2. Wallhoff, F.: Technische Univsität München, http://cotesys.mmk.e-technik.tu-muenchen.de/isg/content/feed-database
3. Data Tang, http://www.datatang.com/data/45013
4. Cristinacce, D., Babalola, K.: FGNET Annotation of BioID Dataset, http://personalpages.manchester.ac.uk/staff/timothy.f.cootes/data/bioid_points.html
5. Cootes, T.: XM2VTS 68pt Markup, http://personalpages.manchester.ac.uk/staff/timothy.f.cootes/data/xm2vts/xm2vts_markup.html
6. Ding, L., Martinez, A.M.: Features versus Context: An approach forprecise and detailed detection and delineationof faces and facial features. IEEE Pattern Analysis and Machine Intelligence 32(11), 2022–2038 (2010)
7. Cootes, T.: Talking Face Video (May 2014), http://personalpages.manchester.ac.uk/staff/timothy.f.coo-tes/data/talking_face/talking_face.html
8. Nordstrm, M.M., Larsen, M., Sierakowski, J., Stegmann, M.B.: The IMM Face Database An Annotated Dataset of 240 Face Images (May 13, 2004)
9. Cao, X., Wei, Y., Wen, F., Sun, J.: Face alignment by explicit shape regression. In: 2012 IEEE Conference on Computer Vision and Pattern Recognition (CVPR), pp. 2887–2894. IEEE (2012)
10. Huang, G.B., Ramesh, M., Berg, T.: Labeled faces in the wild: A database forstudying face recognition in unconstrained environments. Technical report, TechnicalReport 07-49, University of Massachusetts, Amherst (2007)

A Novel Iterative Approach to Pupil Localization

Ronghang Zhu, Gaoli Sang, Wei Gao, and Qijun Zhao[*]

National Key Laboratory of Fundamental Science on Synthetic Vision,
School of Computer Science, Sichuan University, Chengdu, China
qjzhao@scu.edu.cn
http://vs.scu.edu.cn/

Abstract. This paper proposes a novel method for localizing the center of pupils. Given a face detected in an image, it first empirically initializes the eye regions in the face, and locates the pupils within the eye regions by using an improved isophote curvature based method. It then updates the eye regions according to the detected pupil centers. In the updated eye regions, the pupil centers are also refined. The above process iterates until the detected pupil centers have sufficiently high consistency with the eye regions. Compared with previous methods, the proposed method can better cope with faces with varying pose angles. Evaluation experiments have been done on the public BioID database and a set of self-collected face images which display various pose angles and illumination conditions. The results demonstrate that the proposed method can more accurately locate pupil centers and is robust to illumination and pose variations.

Keywords: Pupil localization, eye localization, face recognition, gaze estimation.

1 Introduction

Faces play an important role in human communication. Looking at a face, people can perceive plenty of information, such as identity, emotion, and gaze (or attention). Among the various components of faces, eyes are believed to be most expressive. For example, in the Viola and Jones' face detector, it has been found that eyes provide important cues for face detection [1]. In face recognition, interocular distance is often used to normalize face images before feature extraction and matching [2]. In gaze estimation, detecting eyes and localizing the positions of pupils are two important steps [3]. Efficient and effective automated eye/pupil localization algorithms are therefore highly demanded for many face related applications, such as face recognition, gaze estimation, and human-computer interfaces.

A number of automated eye/pupil localization methods have been proposed during the past decades. These methods can be roughly divided into two categories: model-based and feature-based [5][7][8][9][10][11]. Model-based methods assume statistical

---

[*] Corresponding author.

Z. Sun et al. (Eds.): CCBR 2014, LNCS 8833, pp. 155–162, 2014.

models of eye/pupil shapes and appearances. A sufficient number of training samples are required to train the models. Localizing eyes/pupils in face images is completed via fitting the learned models to the images. Feature-based methods, on the contrary, directly localize eyes and pupils based on certain properties of them, e.g., symmetry of eyes, circular contours of pupils, and strong intensity contrast in eye regions. Although model-based methods are generally more stable than feature-based methods, the latter are more easily to apply without requiring training/fitting. More detailed review of existing eye/pupil localization methods can be found in [3][4].

Most pupil localization methods require that faces are firstly detected in the input images. They then empirically determine eye regions within the detected faces, and localize pupils in the eye regions. Obviously, accurate localization of eye regions is crucial for pupil localization. In a recent feature-based method proposed by Valenti and Gevers in [5], the eye regions are estimated according to anthropometic relations, and fixed during the process of localizing pupil centers. As a result, the pupil localization accuracy highly depends on the face detection results and the estimated eye regions. When the face has non-frontal poses, the empirically estimated eye regions might severely deviate from the true regions, which leads to inaccurately localized pupil centers. See Fig 1.

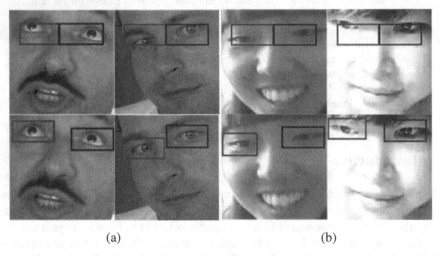

(a)   (b)

Fig. 1. The empirically determined eye regions (first row) and the eye regions estimated with the proposed method (second row) on some example images from the (a) BioID and (b) SCU-EYE databases

In this paper, we aim to improve the pupil localization accuracy particularly for faces with pose variations. To the end, we propose to iteratively update the estimated eye regions according to the estimated pupil centers, and continuously refine the pupil centers until the pupils and the eye regions have sufficiently high consistency. In this way, the pupils can be more accurately located, even when the faces have large pose angles. The contributions of this paper are three folds:

— Proposing a method to iteratively refine the estimated eye regions and the localized pupil centers.
— Improving the state-of-the-art pupil localization method in [5] by using a better weighted voting scheme in determining the center of pupils, and by employing the proposed iterative approach.
— Constructing a set of face images which display various pose angles and whose ground truth eye regions and pupil centers are manually marked. This dataset will be publicly available upon request for research purposes.

The rest of this paper is organized as follows. Section II introduces in detail our proposed method for localizing the center of pupils. Section III reports our experimental results. Finally, Section IV concludes the paper.

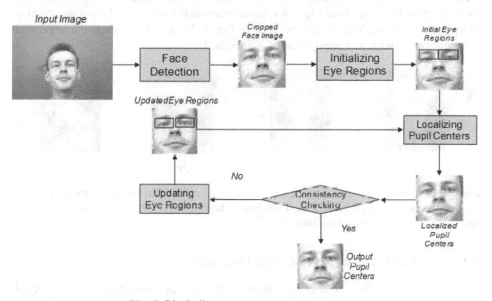

Fig. 2. Block diagram of the proposed method

2   Proposed Method

2.1   Overview

Figure 2 shows the flowchart of the proposed method. As can be seen, it consists of five main steps: face detection, initializing eye regions, localizing pupil centers, consistency checking, and updating eye regions. In this paper, we employ the face detector in [6] to detect the face regions in input images. Once a face region is cropped from the input images, initial eye regions are determined according to anthropometric relations, i.e., the top left corner of the eye region is at 15% height and 10% width of the face region, the right bottom corner of the eye region is at 35% height and 90% width of the face region, and the left and right eyes averagely divide the eye region. Pupil centers are then localized within the eye regions by using an improved isophote curvature based method. The localized pupil centers are then compared with the centers of the eye regions. If the distances between them are smaller than a given threshold (say 4 pixels), the pupils and the eye regions are said to be consistent; otherwise, the eye regions are updated by moving them so that their centers are at the localized pupil centers, and the pupils are re-localized in the updated eye regions. The procedures of localizing pupil centers and updating eye regions are repeated until the pupils are sufficiently consistent with the eye regions.

Compared with previous pupil localization methods, the proposed method has two distinct characteristics. First, the eye regions are iteratively updated. Second, the pupil localization process and the estimation of eye regions are coupled to improve the localization accuracy. Thanks to these characteristics, the proposed method can gradually correct the eye regions when the initially estimated eye regions deviate from the true positions (see Fig.3 for some example). Moreover, the pupils are also more accurately localized as can be seen in Fig. 3. Next, we introduce the improved isophote curvature based pupil localization method.

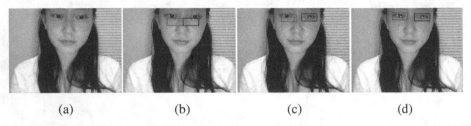

     (a)   (b)   (c)   (d)

Fig. 3. The iterative localization process of the proposed method. (a) An input image, (b) initial eye regions and the pupil centers localized inside the regions, (c) the result after 2 iterations, and (d) the final result after 3 iterations.

2.2   Isophote Curvature Based Pupil Localization

Given an image I, the isophote in it refers to the curves connecting pixels of equal intensity (e.g., the pixels on the contour of a pupil). The isophote curvature at a pixel is defined as

$$k = -\frac{I_y^2 I_{xx} - 2I_x I_{xy} I_y + I_x^2 I_{yy}}{(I_x^2 + I_y^2)^{3/2}} \tag{1}$$

where I_x and I_y are, respectively, the 1st order derivatives along x and y axes, I_{xx}, I_{xy}, and I_{yy} are 2nd order derivatives. The sign of isophote curvature is positive if the outer side of the isophote curve is brighter. For example, the pixels on the contours of pupils and irises have positive isophote curvatures, while the pixels on the contours of eye sockets have negative isophote curvatures.

The isophote curvatures can be used to detect circular patterns in images [5]. Mathematically, the displacement of the center of potential circular pattern at the pixel (x, y) can be computed by

$$\begin{cases} \Delta x = \dfrac{I_x}{\sqrt{I_x^2 + I_y^2}} \cdot \dfrac{1}{k}, \\[4mm] \Delta y = \dfrac{I_y}{\sqrt{I_x^2 + I_y^2}} \cdot \dfrac{1}{k} \end{cases} \tag{2}$$

In other words, there is a circle passing the pixel (x, y), whose center is at the position $(x + \Delta x, y + \Delta y)$. Based on this property of isophote curvatures, we can estimate the center of pupils, which are assumed to be circular patterns in the images of eyes.

Specifically, we use the pixels in an eye region to vote for the pupil center of the eye. Each pixel votes for a center of a potential circular pattern which is computed according to the eq. (2). After all the pixels have cast their votes, the circular center that obtains the highest number of votes is taken as the estimated pupil center in the eye region. As pointed by [5], edge pixels are usually more reliable in determining the pupil centers. Hence, it suggests to weight the votes of pixels with the following edge-ness measurement at their positions,

$$\omega_e = \sqrt{I_{xx}^2 + 2 \cdot I_{xy}^2 + I_{yy}^2}, \tag{3}$$

In our experiments, we have observed that if only using the above-mentioned edge-ness determined weights, the refinement process of pupil centers could become un-stable, i.e., the newly estimated positions of pupil centers might quickly move away from the positions estimated last time. When eyeglass frames appear in the eye regions, this phenomenon can be more frequently observed. Considering that distracts like eyeglass frames are usually near the boundary of eye regions, we propose to include another component into the weight as follows,

$$\omega = \omega_e \times \omega_d, \tag{4}$$

where ω_d is the reciprocal of the distance from the pixel to the currently estimated pupil center. In this way, the pixels that are far from the estimated pupil centers are assigned with small weights, and the stability of the refinement process can be ensured.

3   Experiments

3.1   Databases and Protocols

Two face databases have been used to evaluate the effectiveness of the proposed method: the BioID face image database and a set of face images collected by ourselves (referred to as the SCU-EYE database). The BioID database contains 1,521 grayscale images of 23 subjects. The image size is 384×288 pixels. The self-collected face image database consists of 396 color images of 16 subjects. The size of these

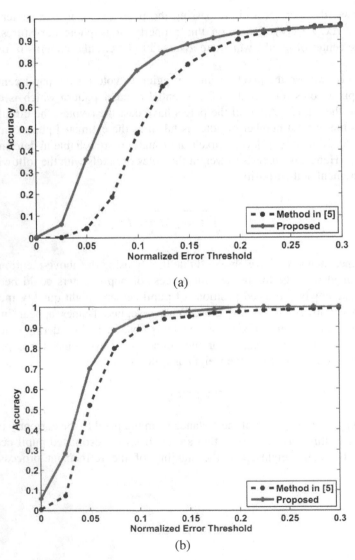

Fig. 4. The pupil localization accuracy on the (a) BioID and (b) SCU-EYE databases

images is 320×240 pixels. They were captured by using web cameras when the subjects were sitting in front of the web cameras and involved in video chats. Note that the subjects were not aware of when the pictures were taken. Consequently, the faces in these images display large variations of scales, pose angles, facial expressions and illumination conditions. The pupil centers in the face images in both databases are manually marked, which are taken as the ground truth.

The faces in these images were automatically detected by using the face detector in [6]. After excluding those images in which the face regions are failed to be correctly detected, we have used 1,198 face images in the BioID database and 396 face images in the SCU-EYE database in our evaluation experiments. We use the normalized error to measure the pupil localization accuracy, which is defined as

$$e = \frac{\max(d_{lfet}, d_{right})}{d_{interocular}},$$

(5)

where $d_{left}(d_{right})$ is the distance between the localized left (right) pupil center and the ground truth left (right) pupil center, and $d_{interocular}$ denotes the distance between the ground truth left and right pupil centers. The pupil localization accuracy at a given normalized error threshold is then computed by dividing the number of face images, for which the pupil localization normalized error is below the threshold, by the total number of testing face images.

(a)   (b)

Fig. 5. Results of the state-of-the-art method [5] (first row) and the proposed method (second row) on some typical images in the (a) BioID and (b) SCU-EYE databases. Green dots represent the ground truth pupil centers, and red dots represent the estimated locations.

3.2   Results

Figure 4 shows the pupil localization accuracy at different normalized error thresholds of the proposed method on the two databases. The results of the state-of-the-art method in [5] are also presented for comparison. It can be clearly seen that the proposed method has higher pupil localization accuracy. The localized pupil centers in some typical face images are given in Fig. 5.

4   Conclusions

In this paper, we have presented a novel iterative method for localizing pupil centers. Instead of using a fixed eye region, the proposed method iteratively updates the eye region according to the estimated pupil center, and further refines the pupil center by considering the updated eye region. This coupled iterative procedure of refining eye regions and pupil centers helps to improve the accuracy of pupil localization, particularly for non-frontal faces with varying pose angles. We have evaluated the proposed method on two databases, and the results prove the effectiveness of the proposed method. In our future work, we are going to incorporate the proposed method with more advanced face detection methods, and to combine it with other model-based methods to further improve the accuracy.

Acknowledgements. This work is supported by grants from the National Natural Science Foundation of China (No. 61202161) and the National Key Scientific Instrument and Equipment Development Projects (No. 2013YQ49087904)..

References

1. Viola, P., Jones, M.: Robust Real-Time Face Detection. Internal Journal of Computer Vision 57(2), 137–154 (2004)
2. Li, S.Z., Jain, A.K.: Handbook of Face Recognition, 2nd edn. Springer, London (2011)
3. Hansen, D.W., Ji, Q.: In the Eye of Beholder: A Survey of Models for Eyes and Gaze. IEEE Transactions on Pattern Analysis and Machine Intelligence 32(3), 478–500 (2010)
4. Song, F., Tan, X., Chen, S., Zhou, Z.: A Literature Survey on Robust and Efficient Eye Localization in Real-Life Scenarios. Pattern Recognition 46(12), 3157–3173 (2013)
5. Valenti, R., Gevers, T.: Accurate Eye Center Location through Invariant Isocentric Patterns. IEEE Transactions on Pattern Analysis and Machine Intelligence 34(9), 1785–1798 (2012)
6. Jesorsky, O., Kirchbergand, K.J., Frischholz, R.: Robust Face Detection using the Hausdorff Distance. In: Third International Conference on Audio- and Video- Based Biometric Person Authentication, Halmstad, Sweden, pp. 90–95 (2001)
7. Ma, Y., Ding, X., Wang, Z., et al.: Robust Precise Eye Location under Probabilistic Framework. In: Proceedings of the Sixth IEEE International Conference on Automatic Face and Gesture Recognition, pp. 339–344 (2004)
8. Kothari, R., Mitchell, J.: L.: Detection of Eye Location in Unconstrained Visual Images. In: International Conference on Image Processing, vol. 3, pp. 519–522 (1996)
9. Asteriadis, S., Nikolaidis, N., Hajdu, A., Pitas, I.: An Eye Detection Algorithm using Pixel to Edge Information. In: Int. Symp. on Control, Commun. and Sign. Proc. (2006)
10. Bai, L., Shen, L., Wang, Y.: A Novel Eye Location Algorithm based on Radial Symmetry Transform. In: ICPR, pp. 511–514 (2006)
11. Jesorsky, O., Kirchberg, K.J., Frischholz, R.W.: Robust Face Detection Using the Hausdorff Distance. In: Bigun, J., Smeraldi, F. (eds.) AVBPA 2001. LNCS, vol. 2091, pp. 90–95. Springer, Heidelberg (2001)

A Pose Robust Face Recognition Approach
by Combining PCA-ASIFT and SSIM

Wei Qi, Yaxi Hou, Lifang Wu[*], and Xiao Xu

School of Electronic Information and Control Engineering,
Beijing University of Technology, Beijing, 100124, China
lfwu@bjut.edu.cn,qiwei7@sina.com,
{xuxiao2013,houyaxi}@emails.bjut.edu.cn

Abstract. Affine Scale Invariant Feature Transform (ASIFT) is robust to scales, rotation, scaling and affine transformation. It could be used for face recognition with pose variation. However, ASIFT requires large data. Could we reduce the data of ASIFT and preserve the face recognition performance? In this paper, we propose an effective face recognition algorithm to combining the structural similarity (SSIM) and PCA-ASIFT (PCA-ASIFT&SSIM).First, we reduce ASIFT dimension using principal component analysis and get PCA-ASIFT. The PCA-ASIFT's discriminative capability drops because of the dimension reduction. It brings about more false SIFT matching. We further introduce the SSIM to reduce the false matching. The experimental results show the efficiency of the proposed approach.

Keywords: Face recognition, dimension reduction, PCA-ASIFT, SSIM.

1 Introduction

Face recognition is one of the active research topics in computer vision and pattern recognition. Recently, face recognition technology has reached a good performance under a controlled imaging condition. But the performance of face recognition with pose variation drops significantly. Scale invariant feature (SIFT) [2] is the local feature with rotating invariance and good robustness. Affine-SIFT (ASIFT) [3] is further proposed to improve the robustness to affine transformation. ASIFT can solve the problem of face recognition under different poses much better.

WU et. Al. [4] proposed a face recognition approach to combining ASIFT and SSIM[4], but they endured heavy storage cost. They obtain roughly 3000 ASIFT points in a face image of 80 × 80. Each ASIFT point has 128dimensiondescriptors. If each dimension is represented by one byte, the data for all ASIFT features from one face image is about 3000 × 128 = 384000bytes. It is much larger than an 80 × 80 face's image data size: 80 × 80 × 3 = 19200 bytes. Therefore, it is necessary to reduce the data. In this paper, dimension reduction is studied.

High-dimensional data is multivariate data obtained by observing. It describes from different angles or method of the same object. Obviously, with the increasing of

---

[*] Corresponding author.

Z. Sun et al. (Eds.): CCBR 2014, LNCS 8833, pp. 163–172, 2014.

data dimension, it provides richer and more detailed information with the emergence of the "curse of dimension" [5].The concept proposed by the Bellman, for the known number of samples, there is a maximum value of the number of feature, when the actual number exceeds the maximum; the performance of the classifier is not improved but degenerated. In order to solve the dimension disaster, dimension reduction is proposed. The basic principle is that the sample points are mapped from the input space to a lower dimensional spacesoastoobtain a compact, low-dimensional representative.

Depending on the mapping method, dimension reduction methods are divided into being linear and being nonlinear. Linear dimension reduction methods include principal component analysis (PCA), projection pursuit (PP), linearly discriminant analysis (LDA), locality preserving projections (LPP),sparsity preservingprojections (SPP) and so on. The principle of linear dimension reduction is to find a linear projection model in high-dimensional dataspace.   It has poor effect on nonlinear high-dimensional data structure. Thus, methods of nonlinear dimension reduction are proposed, like multidimensional scaling (MDS), ISOMAP, KernelBasedPrincipal Component Analysis (KPCA), locally linear embedding (LLE) and so on.

Principal Component analysis (PCA) is to project the high-dimensional data into a low dimension while keeping its spatial features as much as possible. It is a popular dimension reduction method and is usually used in image processing. Therefore, PCA is used in this paper. In our experiments, AISFT feature dimension could be reduced using the PCA, however, it also brings the loss of information and the performance of face recognition with the point that pose variation can't reach the performance of the ASIFT method. Structural similarity (SSIM) is a method used to evaluate the image quality. It is a structural measure based on the similarity between pixels. It can be applied to face recognition and to analyze the similarity of the two facial images. We further introduce SSIM to improve the face recognition performance.

We propose a face recognition approach to combining PCA-ASIFT and SSIM. Firstly, PCA is utilized to reduce the dimension of ASIFT descriptors, and we get PCA-ASIFT. At face recognition stage, the PCA-ASIFT is matched firstly, then for each PCA-ASIFT matching points, its SSIM is used to further filter out the mismatched points, and the face authentication is finished by the average SSIM.

2   The Proposed Approach

We propose a framework of face recognition combining SSIM and PCA-ASIFT. As shown in Fig. 1, we first extract AISFT descriptors from face image, then we utilize principal component analysis (PCA) to reduce AISFT descriptors dimension and obtain a new kind of descriptor with low dimension. We define it PCA-ASIFT descriptors. The method to obtain PCA-ASIFT descriptors is defined as PCA-ASIFT algorithm. For a probe face image, the similarity between it and the PCA-ASIFT of each subject are measured. We do preliminary face features' matching and get pairs of matching points. Then, we utilize structural similarity algorithm to compute the similarity of pairs of local images which is also called face patches. The face patch is window pixels which matching point as the center. The size of window is set to 5×5. After computing the SSIM index, we retain pairs of matching points which are above the threshold. The threshold is set by analyzing the distribution of the SSIM index.

Then we obtain the real matching points. Face recognition is implemented by judge whether the amount of the matching points of the subject is the largest one.

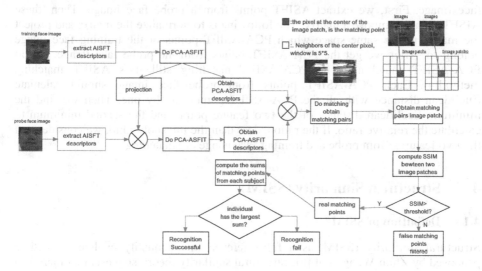

Fig. 1. The flowchart of proposed framework

3   PCA-ASIFT

3.1   Extraction of PCA-ASIFT

PCA-ASIFT uses principal component analysis (PCA) to reduce 128 dimension of ASIFT descriptor. We define an original ASIFT matrix which is composed of all the ASIFT vectors extracted from a face image. We get n ASIFT points from one face image, in which i^{th} ASIFT point is denoted as D_i. Each ASIFT point is 128 dimensional descriptor, so $D_i = \{f_{i1}, f_{i2}, ..., f_{ij}, ..., f_{i128}\}$.And the original matrix can be denoted as $\{D_1, D_2, ..., D_n\}T$,the size of the matrix is n × 128.

Then we do PCA on the original ASIFT matrix. The details are as follows:

1. Normalize the matrix, each column subtracts corresponding average and divide by variance.
2. Get the covariance matrix R.
3. UtilizeJacobialgorithm [8] to calculate the eigenvalues and eigenvectors of matrix R.
4. Put eigenvalues into descending order and get new order of the eigenvalues. Then we use K eigenvalues which is on the order as principal component to form a new matrix. The matrix is defined as projection matrix P.
5. Get the PCA-ASIFT matrix Y, Y is denoted as Y=X×P, the size of the matrix is n×k, k is the dimension of PCA-ASIFT vector after reducing by PCA.

3.2   PCA-ASIFT Matching Based on Euclidean Distance

We measure the distinctiveness of features between training face image and a probe face image. First, we extract ASIFT points from a probe face image. Then, these AISFT points compose a matrix. The following is to normalize the matrix and project the matrix to the same space which PCA-ASIFT points of the training face image belong to. After we get the PCA-ASIFT points from the probe face image, we do PCA-ASIFT matching. The PCA-ASIFT matching still uses ASIFT matching method[4]. Each PCA-ASIFT points from probe face image should calculate Euclidean distance with all the PCA-ASIFT points one by one. Then we find the minimum Euclidean distance of the two feature points and the second minimum to calculate the relative ratio. If the ratio is less than the threshold ratio, we consider that the two features from probe and training face image are matching.

4   Structural Similarity (SSIM)

4.1   Definition of SSIM

Structural similarity (SSIM) is a full-reference image quality evaluation method proposed by Zhou Wang et al [6]. Structural similarity theory suggests that there is a strong correlation between the pixels and the highly structured image. Considering the generation of image, structural information reflects the structure of objects in the scene. It should be independent of the brightness and the contrast. Structural similarity constituted by three factors: brightness, contrast, and structure similarity. Combining the similarity of these three, constitute the reference image x and distorted image y similarity operator, the formula is as follows:

$$SSIM(x,y) = [l(x,y)]^{\alpha} \times [c(x,y)]^{\beta} \times [s(x,y)]^{\gamma} \qquad (1)$$

Where, $l(x, y)$, $c(x, y)$ and $s(x, y)$ are the brightness contrast function, the contrastcontrast function and the structural contrast function respectively.

$$\begin{cases} l(x,y) = \dfrac{2\mu_x\mu_y + C_1}{\mu_x{}^2 + \mu_y{}^2 + C_1} \\[2mm] c(x,y) = \dfrac{2\sigma_x\sigma_y + C_2}{\sigma_x{}^2 + \sigma_y{}^2 + C_2} \\[2mm] s(x,y) = \dfrac{\sigma_{xy} + C_3}{\sigma_x\sigma_y + C_3} \end{cases} \qquad (2)$$

Where μ is the average of image x, y, reflects the brightness information. σ is the variance of image x, y, reflect the contrast information. σ_{xy} is the covariance of image x and y, reflect the structure information.

SSIM index has the following character:

(1) symmetry : $SSIM\ (x, y)\ = SSIM\ (y, x)$

(2) $SSIM \leq 1$

(3) If and only if $x=y$, $SSIM=1$.

4.2   Analysis of SSIM at PCA-ASIFT Points

We utilize structural similarity (SSIM) to filtrate some matching points that are lowly similar after dimension reduction. And we propose SSIM to improve the correct rate for face recognition. Ideally, the value of SSIM between correct matching point and false matching point are obviously different. The ideal state is the distribution of SSIM value is distinct from 0 to 1. In this paper, we set the size of window as 5×5. Fig.2 shows the distribution of SSIM value with the window size of 5×5. And it can distinguish within class pairs from between class pairs.

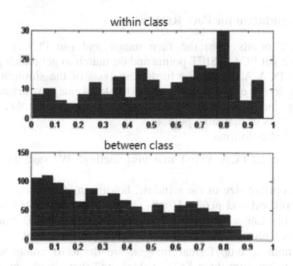

Fig. 2. The distribution of SSIM value with the window size is 5×5 from within and between class pairs

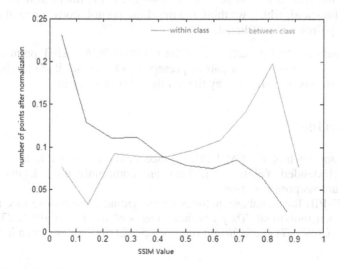

Fig. 3. The distribution of SSIM value within and between class pairs

Why can we use SSIM to improve the performance of face recognition? Fig.3 shows the distributionof SSIM value between within and between class pairs after normalization. We assume the matching pairs from the same subject as within class pairs, other pairs as between class. And we normalize the distribution by the total number so that we could distinguish the matching pairs from the same subject easily. It is obviously observed that the SSIMs of most within class pairs arc bigger than 0.7, while those of between class pairs are smaller than 0.2. It means that they could be discriminated. Therefore, SSIM could be used for further improvement work.

4.3   SSIM Computation for Face Recognition

We extract ASIFT points from the face image and use PCA to do dimension reduction. Then we get PCA-ASIFT points and do match to get match points. SSIM's combination with PCA-ASIFT is for further analysis of the similarity between the matching points pairs. In essence, it is for seeking local image structural similarity of which matching points is the center and we set an appropriate threshold to throw some less-similar pairs of matching points.

SSIM is computed as follows:

1. Matching still use 3.2 PCA-ASIFT matching method. We save the location of the PCA-ASIFT.
2. Select the appropriate size of the window, holding match point as the center and looking for neighborhood pixels. If you choose the pixel neighborhood over the boundaries of the image, edge processing should be done. Definite beyond the boundary points with adjacent positions boundary pixels instead.
3. Because the input is bmp format images, we do RGB components for SSIM respectively, and we sum three SSIM values, and then divide the sum by 3. The result is regarded as the final structural similarity value. The first step to do SSIM is to calculate the average, variance, covariance of the pixels within the window.
4. Compare the final SSIM values with thresholds. If the final SSIM value is greater than the threshold, which we think the matching point is correct one, if it is not, the matching points will be filtered.

We compute SSIM for each pair of the matched PCA-ASIFT points. If SSIM is greater than the threshold, this pair is preserved. Otherwise, it should be discarded. Face recognition is implemented by the number of matched pairs.

5   Experiments

We test our approach on the CMU-PIE [1] face database sand the Extended Yale Face Database B(Extended YaleB) [10]. They are commonly used databases for face recognition across pose variation.

The CMU-PIE face database includes 68 individuals. We choose face images with 5 pose for each individual. They are face images of front view (0° (C27)), up/down rotation 30° (C09/C07) and left/right rotation 25° (C05/C29), as shown in Fig.4.

| C05 | C09 | C27 | C07 | C29 |

Fig. 4. Example face images from CMU-PIE

The Extended Yale Face Database B (Extended YaleB) includes 28 individuals. The data format of this database is the same as the Yale Face Database B [9].Fig.5 shows the face images of the same individual. Face images of front view (0° (P0)) is selected as training face image. The face images of up/down rotation 12°(P1/P5) ,both left and up/down rotation 12°(P2/P4)and left rotation 12°(P3) are selected as probe ones.

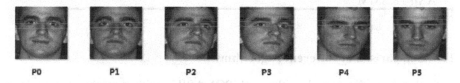

| P0 | P1 | P2 | P3 | P4 | P5 |

Fig. 5. Example face images from Extended YaleB

5.1   Comparison of Different Dimensions

The dimension of ASIFT is reduced to 96, 64and 32 respectively. When PCA algorithm extract main components to generate a new projection space, rateofcontribution S is often considered as standard. Formula 3 shows how to calculate the rateofcontribution S.

$$S = \frac{\sum_{i=1}^{k} \lambda_i}{\sum_{i=1}^{m} \lambda_i} \tag{3}$$

Where, $_i$ is the eigenvalue. When the rate of contribution reaches the standard, we retain features which arecurrently component to compose the low-dimensional projection matrix. The PCA-ASIFT algorithms calculate the rate of contribution for different dimensions is 96 dimensions is roughly 85% -90%, 64dimensions is roughly 65% -70% and 32 dimensions is roughly 40% -45%.

Table 1 shows that we got greater performance after combining with SSIM on both CMU-PIE and extendingYaleB. After we do PCA-ASIFT, we can find that the lower dimension is, the recognition rate gets lower. However, the recognition rate is higher after SSIM combines with PCA-ASIFT and the effect of dimension is not obvious on the two databases. We suggest using PCA-ASIFT which can reduce the dimension of ASIFT descriptor into 64.

Table 1. The Recognition Rates with Different Dimension Before and After do SSIM

Method	PCA-ASIFT Dimension	Average On CMU-PIE database	Average On extended YaleB database
PCA-ASIFT	96	87.9%	92.1%
PCA-ASIFT	64	83.3%	89.3%
PCA-ASIFT	32	70.0%	78.6%
PCA-ASIFT&SSIM	96	89.3%	96.4%
PCA-ASIFT&SSIM	64	90%	97.1%
PCA-ASIFT&SSIM	32	81.3%	92.9%

5.2   Comparison of Different Algorithms

We further compare our algorithms of PCA-ASIFT with dimension of 96(PCA-ASIFT 96), dimension of 64(PCA-ASIFT 64), PCA-ASIFT 96 & SSIM and PCA-ASIFT 64 &SSIM with the original ASIFT on two databases. The compared results are shown in Fig.6 (a). Fig.6 (a) demonstrates that the performance of PCA-ASIFT 96's drops with C29, 64's drops with C29 and C07compare with original ASIFT. However, we can observe that PCA-ASIFT 64& SSIM improves the performance a lot from Fig.6(a). And the original ASFIT gets the best performance. For the other two test face images, the three algorithms get good performance. Fig.6 (b) shows that great performance of PCA-ASIFT&SSIM, both PCA-ASIFT96 &SSIM and PCA-ASIFT64 &SSIMachieve 100% recognition rates with some poses on extended YaleB database. Comparing with the performance of original ASIFT, PCA-ASIFT 96's and 64's drops little with last three poses (P3, P4and P5). After combines with SSIM, we can   obviously   see   that   both   PCA-ASIFT96   &SSIM   and   PCA-ASIFT64&SSIMperformance are improved and are better than original ASIFT algorithm.

Our approach PCA-ASIFT & SSIMachieve great performance and is better than the original ASIFT algorithm and the algorithm of only using PCA-ASIFT to reduce the dimension. We suggest using PCA-ASIFT to reduce the dimension into 64 and then combine with SSIM.

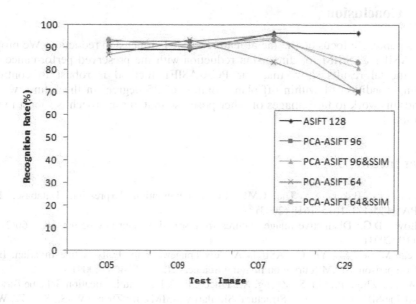

(a)CMU-PIE database

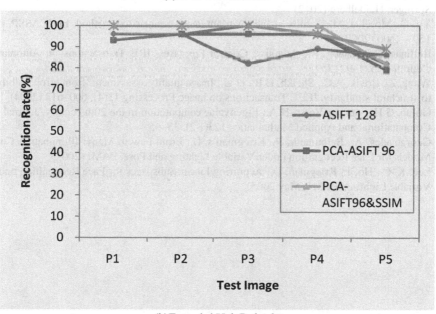

(b)Extended YaleB database

Fig. 6. The performance of different method under controlled imaging condition on two database

6   Conclusion

In this paper, we focus on the facial features ASIFT dimension reduction. We propose PCA-ASIFT & SSIM for dimension reduction with the preserved performance. The experimental results show that our PCA-ASIFT method is robust to controlled imaging condition of within off-plane rotation of 25 degree. In the future, we will extend this work to face images of other poses, so that our approach is robust to pose variation.

References

1. Sim, T., Baker, S.: The CMU Pose, Illumination Expression Database. IEEE PAMI 25(12), 1615–1618 (2003)
2. Lowe, D.G.: Distinctive image features from scale-invariant key points. IJCV 60(2), 91–110 (2004)
3. Jean-Michel, M., Yu, G.: ASIFT: A New Framework for Fully Affine Invariant Image Comparison. SIAM Journal on Imaging Sciences 2(2), 438–468 (2009)
4. Wu, L., Zhou, P., Liu, S., Zhang, X., Trucco, E.: A Face Authentication Scheme Based on Affine-SIFT (ASIFT) and Structural Similarity (SSIM). In: Zheng, W.-S., Sun, Z., Wang, Y., Chen, X., Yuen, P.C., Lai, J. (eds.) CCBR 2012. LNCS, vol. 7701, pp. 25–32. Springer, Heidelberg (2012)
5. Yu, G., Morel, J.-M.: A fully affine invariant image comparison method. In: ICASSP, pp. 1597–1600 (2009)
6. Bellman, R., Kalaba, R.: Adaptive Control Processes. IRE Transactions on Automatic Control 4(2), 1–9 (1959)
7. Wang, Z., Bovik, A.C., Sheikh, H.R., et al.: Image quality assessment: from error visibility to structural similarity. IEEE Transactions on Image Processing 13(4), 600–612 (2004)
8. Golub, G.H., van der Vorst, H.A.: Eigenvalue computation in the 20th century. Journal of Computational and Applied Mathematics 123(1-2), 35–65
9. Georghiades, A., Belhumeur, P., Kriegman's, D.: From Few to Many: Illumination Cone Models for Face Recognition under Variable Lighting and Pose. PAMI (2001)
10. Lee, K.-C., Ho, J., Kriegman, D.: Acquiring Linear Subspaces for Face Recognition under Variable Lighting. PAMI (May 2005)

Live Face Detection by Combining the Fourier Statistics and LBP

Lifang Wu, Xiao Xu, Yu Cao, Yaxi Hou, and Wei Qi

School of Electronic Information and Control Engineering, Beijing
University of Technology, Beijing, 100124, China
lfwu@bjut.edu.cn,
{xuxiao2013,caoyu,houyaxi,qw10020012}@emails.bjut.edu.cn

Abstract. With the development of E-Commerce, biometric based on-line authentication is more competitive and is paid more attentions. It brings about one
of hot issues of liveness detection recently. In this paper, we propose a liveness
detection scheme to combine Fourier statistics and local binary pattern (LBP).
First, The Gamma correction and DoG filtering are utilized to reduce the illumination variation and to preserve the key information of the image. Then the
Fourier statistics and LBP are combined together to form a new feature vector.
Finally, a SVM classifier is trained to discriminate the live and forge face image. The experimental results on the NUAA demonstrate that the proposed
scheme is efficient and robust.

Keywords: Liveness detection, photo spoofing, Fourier statistics.

1   Introduction

With the rapid development of biometrics, fingerprint, face and iris technology were
widely used for on-line authentication. On-line authentication is convenient but it is
easy to be spoofed because the attackers stay far from the public and out of surveillance. Face is one of biometrics which could be easily spoofed. N.M Duc[1] and
others could pass the authentication successfully using only a printed photograph.
Liveness detection could determine if a face image is from the real face lively or from
a photograph, videos of human face [2] or generated 3D faces. It is a resolution to
face spoofing.

Photograph spoofing is usually used by the attackers. They bend and rotate the valid user's photo in front of the image acquisition device, causing an analog legitimate
user to cheat the authentication system. In this paper, we focus on detection of photograph spoofing.

In recent years, more and more algorithms have been proposed for photograph
spoofing detection. These approaches could be generally classified into three classes.

The first one is motion-based approaches. From the view of an observer, the difference between live face and photograph is that the former is a 3-D object, the latter is a
2-D structure, and the motion of both is very different. In [3], the author located a set

Z. Sun et al. (Eds.): CCBR 2014, LNCS 8833, pp. 173–181, 2014.

of automatically facial points firstly, and then exploits geometric invariants for detecting replay attacks. In [4], the author proposed an algorithm based on optical flow to detect the dynamic changes of the human face. Using the information, they implement the liveness detection. It required the user's cooperation. And the estimated depth also has great changes when the impostor bends photograph deliberately. Furthermore, it is easily affected by noise and imaging condition.

The second one is live information-based approaches. The live face characteristics including thermal infrared images, eye blinking and so on are generally used. In [5], the authors explore the appearance features to learn an eye state classifier. In [6], the author detected eyes and computed the moving regions of every eye in the input successive image sequence to implement the liveness detection. Pan[7] trained the live face classifier based on the eye blinking. It required additional equipment.

The third one is texture based approaches. In [8], the authors captured a set of images at different wavelength for feature extraction, and then they extracted gradient-based features to classify genuine and fake face. Andre Anjos[9], and Jukka Maatta[10] analyzed the effectiveness of using LBP to extract features. Jukka Maatta[11] extracted a series of LBPs and trained SVM classifiers to detect the live face. They further proposed an algorithm by fusing LBP, Gabor wavelet and HOG [12]. These algorithms have large feature dimensions and computational complexity. They cost more computation time and store space.

In this paper, we propose a live face detection approach to combining the Fourier statistics and LBP. First, we extract the Fourier statistics and LBP histogram of face images, and then a SVM classifier is trained to distinguish live face and fake face. Experiments on NUAA Photograph Imposter Database showed that the proposed approach was more efficient compared with many previous works. Furthermore, our approach does not require the user's cooperation. It reduces the computational complexity and runs fast.

2   The Proposed Algorithm

For an input image, face detection is first used. And the face image is preprocessed using Gamma correction and DOG respectively. Next LBP histogram and Fourier statistics are extracted respectively, from which the final feature vectors are formed. Finally, a SVM classifier is obtained to discriminate the live or fake face. The frame work is shown in Fig 1.

2.1   Extraction of LBP

Local Binary Patterns (LBP) is a powerful image texture descriptor. It has been widely used in many applications. LBP operator labels each pixel of one image by thresholding a 3×3 neighborhood with the value of central pixel and considering the result as a binary number, of which the corresponding decimal number is used for labeling as shown in Fig 2.

Given a pixel at (x_c, y_c), the resulted LBP can be expressed as follows:

$$LBP(x_c, y_c) = \sum_{i=0}^{7} s(g_i - g_c)2^i \qquad (1)$$

Where i is in the range of [0,7], which represent the 8 neighbors of the central pixel. g_c is the gray level of the central pixel. g_i is the gray-level values of the corresponding neighbouring pixels, and the function $s(x)$ is defined as follows:

$$s(x) = \begin{cases} 1, x > 0 \\ 0, x \le 0 \end{cases} \qquad (2)$$

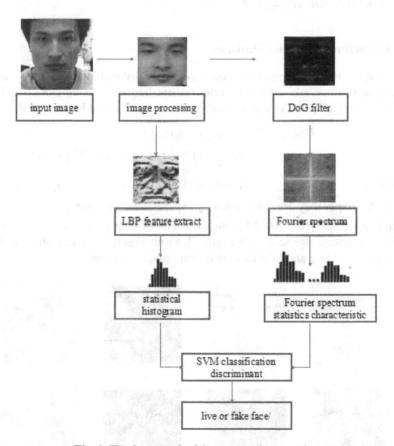

Fig. 1. The framework of the proposed approach

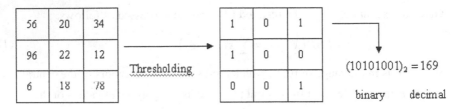

Fig. 2. Illustration of LBP operation

For a face image $f(x, y)$, we could get the LBP histogram. In this paper, we use the uniform LBP. $LBPH_f = \{h_0, h_1, ...h_{58}\}$.

2.2   Extraction of Fourier Statistics

In face images, the high frequency components usually include more noise. In order to reduce such noise, we extract the intermediate frequency using DoG filtering operator as shown in Eq (3), so that as much as information could be preserved.

$$DoG(x, y) = g_1(x, y) - g_2(x, y)$$
$$= G_{\sigma_1}(x, y) * f(x, y) - G_{\sigma_2}(x, y) * f(x, y)$$

(3)

Where, $G_{\sigma_1}(x, y)$ and $G_{\sigma_2}(x, y)$ are Gaussian operator of scale σ_1 and σ_2 respectively. In this paper they are determined by experiments, $\sigma_1 = 0.5, \sigma_2 = 1.0$.

Then Fourier spectrum could be obtained. The Fourier spectra for live face image and fake face image are shown in Figure 3. From Figure3, we can observe that the Fourier spectra of live and fake face images are much different.

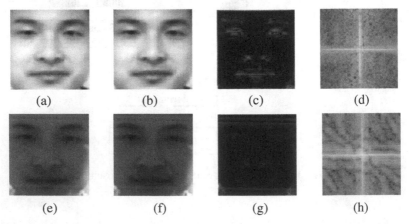

(a)   (b)   (c)   (d)

(e)   (f)   (g)   (h)

Fig. 3. The result of image preprocessing and Fourier Spectra in live face image and fake face image:(a) A live face image; (b) Gama correction result of (a); (c) DOG of (b); (d) Fourier spectra of (c); (e) A fake face image; (f) Gama correction result of (e); (g) DOG of (f); (h) Fourier spectra of (g).

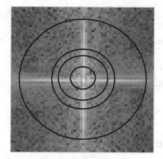

Fig. 4. Illustration of extraction of Fourier statistics

Furthermore, we analyze the variation of frequency components in different face images. We compute the summary of frequency components on a circle as shown in Figure 4, for an image with 64*64 pixels. We could get 32 circles and 32 statistic values in total. The normalized statistic values of live face images and fake face images are shown in Figure 5.

From Figure 5, we can observe that the Fourier statistics of live face image and the fake face image are much different. We further analyze these two kinds of images. A live face is a complex 3-D object, while the photograph can be looked as a planar 2D object. The repeated imaging of printed photo causes a fuzzier feature. These characteristics bring about more low frequency information in the fake face images. A lot of low frequency information is lost; therefore, the Fourier statistics is useful to liveness detection. By now we could get the Fourier statistics $FS_f = \{f_1, f_2 \cdots f_{32}\}$.

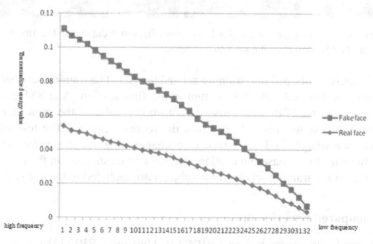

Fig. 5. The normalized Fourier statistics of the live face image and the fake face image

We form the feature vector FV_f of image $f(x,y)$ by connecting the LBP histogram $LBPH_f = \{h_0, h_1, \dots h_{58}\}$ and the Fourier statistics $FS_f = \{f_1, f_2 \dots f_{32}\}$. It is represented as $FV_f = \{h_0, h_1, \dots h_{58}, f_1, f_2, \dots f_{32}\}$.

Based on the feature vector, the liveness detection is implemented by the SVM classifier.

3   Experimental Results

3.1   The Database

We perform our experiments on the NUAA Photograph Imposter Database. This database consists of images of both real client accesses and high quality photographs. The face images of live humans and their photographs were collected in three sessions at intervals of about 2 weeks. During each session, the imaging conditions are different. Some example images are shown in Figure 6.

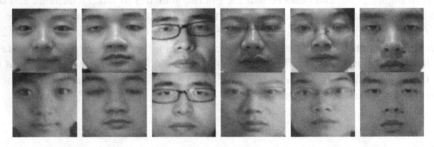

Fig. 6. Example face images in NUAA Photograph Imposter database. The first row: the live face images. The second row: the fake face images.

The database is divided into training set and test set. The training set contains 1743 face images of nine subjects (889 gotten in the first session. And 854 gotten in the second session) and 1748 face images from photographs of the same nine subjects (855 from the first session and 893 from the second session). The test set includes 3362 live face images and 5761 fake face images of 9 subjects gotten in the third session. In order to increase the challenging, only three subjects in the test set are the same as that in the training set. Six new subjects are included in the test set.

3.2   Compared Experiments

We compared our approach with LBPV[14], Uniform LBPV[13] respectively. The compared results are shown in Table 1.

Table 1. The compared detection ratio on NUAA database

Methods	accuracy	live face	fake face	feature dimensions
LBPV[14]	88.03%	91.84%	86.39%	256
Unifom LBPV[13]	86.95%	88.13%	86.25%	59
Our method	96.16%	100%	92.33%	91

From Table 1, we can observe that our approach has much high detection ratio for both live face and fake face. Furthermore, the feature dimension is much smaller than LBPV.

Then, we compare our approach with DoG, HF, LTV fused, LBP, tLBP and mLBP. The results of DoG, HF, LTV fused is gotten from [15]. the LBP, tLBP and mLBP algorithms are implemented by ourselves. The compared results are shown in Fig. 7.

From Fig 7, we can observe that the DoG using middle frequency outperforms HF using the one-third of the highest frequency. It presents that the components in the middle frequency is more discriminative than those in other frequencies. And the proposed approach is better than others because we use both the global and local features and DoG is used for preprocess.

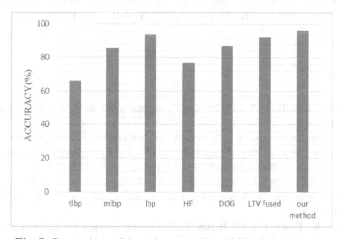

Fig. 7. Comparison of detection rate (%) on NUAA database

3.3 How Does the Occlusion Influence the Results

We further test the way the occlusion influences the detection ratios. The test set is divided into two classes, with glasses and without glasses. We compare our approach with LBP. The results are shown in Table 2.

Table 2. The compared results with/without glasses

Methods	LBP		Ours	
	With glasses	Without glasses	With glasses	Without glasses
Detection Ratio	93.00% (6631/7130)	96.98% (1930/1990)	95.59% (6816/7130)	98.19% (1954/1990)
FRR	7.56% (217/2870)	0% (0/490)	0% (0/2870)	7.37% (314/4260)
FAR	6.62% (282/4260)	4% (60/1500)	0% (0/490)	2.4% (36/1500)

From Table 4. We can observe that both LBP and our approach get higher detection ratio without glasses than with glass. It demonstrates that occlusion influences the performance of both approaches.

4   Conclusion

Spoofing and anti-spoofing has become a hot topic in the biometric recognition. In this paper, we propose a liveness detection approach to combining LBP and Fourier statistics. The experiment obtains results on the NUAA Photograph Imposter. Database confirm the efficiency of the proposed approaches. In this paper, we focus on face images from photographs. Our further work will extend to the video or generated face images.

References

1. Duc, N.M., Minh, B.Q.: Your face is not your password. In: Black Hat Conference, pp. 1–16 (2009)
2. Bharadwaj, S., Dhamecha, T.I., Vatsa, M., et al.: Computationally Efficient Face Spoofing Detection with Motion Magnification. In: 2013 IEEE Conference on Computer Vision and Pattern Recognition Workshops (CVPRW), pp. 105–110. IEEE (2013)
3. De Marsico, M., Nappi, M., Riccio, D., et al.: Moving face spoofing detection via 3D projective invariants. In: 2012 5th IAPR International Conference on Biometrics (ICB), pp. 73–78. IEEE (2012)
4. Kollreider, K., Fronthaler, H., Bigun, J.: Evaluating liveness by face images and the structure tensor. In: Fourth IEEE Workshop on Automatic Identification Advanced Technologies, pp. 75–80 (October 2005)
5. Xu, C., Zheng, Y., Wang, Z.: Eye states Detection by Boosting Local Binary Pattern Histograms. In: ICIP (2008)
6. Jee, H.-K., Jung, S.-U., Yoo, J.-H.: Liveness detection for embedded face recognition system. International Journal of Medicine Science, 235–238 (2006)
7. Pan, G., Sun, L., Wu, Z., Lao, S.: Eyeblink-based Anti-Spoofing in Face Recognition from a Generic Webcamera. In: Proc. 11th IEEE ICCV 2007, pp. 1–8 (2007)

8. Wang, Y., Hao, X., Hou, Y., et al.: A New Multispectral Method for Face Liveness Detection. In: 2013 2nd IAPR Asian Conference on Pattern Recognition (ACPR), pp. 922–926. IEEE (2013)
9. Chingovska, I., Anjos, A., Marcel, S.: On the effectiveness of local binary patterns in face anti-spoofing. In: Bromme, A., Busch, C. (eds.) BIOSIG, pp. 1–7. IEEE (2012)
10. Maatta, J., Hadid, A., Pietikainen, M.: Face Spoofing Detection From Single Images Using Micro-Texture Analysis. In: International Joint Conference on Biometrics (IJCB 2011), Washington DC, USA, pp. 10–17 (2011)
11. Maatta, J., Hadid, A., Pietikainen, M.: Face spoofing detection from single images using texture and local shape analysis. The Institution of Engineering and Technology 2012 (IET Biometrics 2012) 1(1), 3–10 (2012)
12. Tan, X., Triggs, B.: Enhanced local texture feature sets for face recognition under difficult lighting conditions. IEEE Transactions on Image Processing 19(6), 1635–1650 (2010)
13. Kose, N., Dugelay, J.-L.: Classification of Captured and Recaptured Images to Detect Photograph Spoofing. In: ICIEV 2012, pp. 1027–1032 (2012)
14. Yang, J., Lei, Z., Liao, S., Li, S.Z.: Face Liveness Detection with Component Dependent Descriptor. In: ICB 2013, pp. 1–6 (2013)
15. Tan, X., Li, Y., Liu, J., Jiang, L.: Face liveness detection from a single image with sparse low rank bilinear discriminative model. In: Daniilidis, K., Maragos, P., Paragios, N. (eds.) ECCV 2010, Part VI. LNCS, vol. 6316, pp. 504–517. Springer, Heidelberg (2010)

3D Face Recognition by Collaborative Representation Based on Face Feature

Huaijuan Zang, Shu Zhan[*], Mingjun Zhang, Jingjing Zhao, and Zhicheng Liang

School of Computer& Information, Hefei University of Technology, Hefei 230009, China
shu_zhan@hfut.edu.cn

Abstract. To overcome the crucial problem of illumination, facial expression and pose variations in 2D face recognition, a novel algorithm is proposed by fusing global feature based on depth images and local facial feature based on Gabor filters. These two features are fused by residual combined with collaborative representation. Firstly, this approach extracts Gabor and Global feature from 3D depth images, then fuses two features via collaborative representation algorithm. The fused residuals serve as ultimate difference metric. Finally, the minimum fused residual corresponds to correct subject. Extensive experiments on CIS and Texas databases verify that the proposed algorithm is effective and robust.

Keywords: collaborative representation, Gabor feature, global feature, 3D face recognition.

1 Introduction

Face recognition has become an active research topic in the field of biometric recognition. Although 2D face recognition technology is gradually mature, it is susceptible to illumination, pose and facial expression. Therefore, more and more researchers turn to the study of 3D face recognition.

In recent years, sparse representation is a concern in the area of signal processing. Wright et al [1] used sparse representation for face recognition in 2009. They presented sparse representation-based classification (SRC), which showed better robustness. It also achieved good classification results under the occlusion. But some researchers [2-4] have started to question for the role of l_1 norm in image classification. In 2011, Zhang et al [4] presented collaborative representation-based classification (CRC) for face recognition. It solved sparse coefficient by l_2 norm, using similar faces as training dictionary collaboratively, and obtained good recognition effects.

Gabor filter is widely used in the analysis of texture features and image recognition [5] for its good resolution in both time and frequency. In face recognition [6-7] Gabor feature can inhibit illumination, pose and facial expression. The local feature is easy to describe human face, which plays an important role in face recognition.

---

[*] Corresponding author.

Z. Sun et al. (Eds.): CCBR 2014, LNCS 8833, pp. 182–190, 2014.

3D face depth images have good robustness for illumination, expression and pose variations [8]. In this paper, feature selection is fulfilled face recognition combining with collaborative representation. Firstly, this approach extracts global and Gabor feature from 3D face depth images, and then it uses knowledge of collaborative representation to solve sparse coefficient. The minimum fused residual acquired from reconstruction, as the ultimate difference metric, is used to classify.

2   Collaborative Representation Based Classification(CRC)

Zhang et al [4, 9] think that when sparse representation used for face recognition, the key factor is constructing dictionary by multiple samples collaboratively. The dictionary by training samples is often less complete. We can make all training samples together constitute the dictionary. In order to reduce computational complexity, it solves the sparse coefficient by regularized least squares method. But the sparsity is not as strong as l_1 norm. So the classification criterion is improved. It greatly reduces complexity of the algorithm but has no recognition rate impairments. Suppose there are K classes of subjects, and let $X = [X_1, X_2, \cdots X_K]$ as training samples, a test sample for y, then

$$\hat{\rho} = \arg\min_{\rho}\left\{\|y - X\rho\|_2^2 + \lambda\|\rho\|_2^2\right\} \tag{1}$$

λ is regularization parameter, After mathematical derivation, the formula can be transformed into:

$$\hat{\rho} = \left(X^1 X + \lambda \cdot I\right)^1 X^T y \tag{2}$$

Let $P = \left(X^T X + \lambda \cdot I\right)^{-1} X^T$. For a test face image y, it can just simply project y onto P, via $\hat{\rho} = Py$. This makes collaborative representation very fast. Then we reconstruct the test image, calculating the residual with the test image $\left\|y - X_i \hat{\rho}_i\right\|_2$, where X_i and $\hat{\rho}_i$ respectively correspond to the test image matrix and coefficient vector associated with class i. According to the principle of minimum residuals, it puts $\left\|\hat{\rho}_i\right\|_2$ into solving residuals, which provides more discriminant information for classification.

3   Feature Extraction

Gabor feature not only extracts identification components of the low frequency, but also well preserves the integrity information of face. The function of two-dimensional Gabor filters are defined as [6]:

$$\varphi_{u,v}(z)=\frac{\left\|k_{u,v}\right\|^2}{\sigma^2}\exp(-\frac{\left\|k_{u,v}\right\|^2\|z\|^2}{2\sigma^2})[\exp(ik_{u,v}z)-\exp(-\frac{\sigma^2}{2})]$$

(3)

Where $z=(x,y)$ denotes the pixel value of (x,y). u and v denote orientation and scale respectively. Wave vector is defined as $k_{u,v}=k_v e^{i\phi_u}$ with $k_v=k_{max}/f^v$ and $\phi_u=\pi u/8$, $k_{max}=\pi/2$ is the maximum frequency, and f is the spacing factor between kernels in the frequency domain ($f=\sqrt{2}$). σ determines the ratio of the Gaussian window width to wavelength($\sigma=2\pi$).

It can convolute a face image $I(z)$ and the Gabor filter $\varphi_{u,v}(z)$ to get Gabor feature $G_{u,v}(z)$:

$$G_{u,v}(z)=I(z)*\varphi_{u,v}(z)=M_{u,v}(z)\cdot\exp(i\theta_{u,v}(z))$$

(4)

Where, $M_{u,v}(z)$ denotes amplitude and $\theta_{u,v}(z)$ denotes phase information. In this paper, five scales $v=\{0,1,2,3,4\}$ and eight directions $u=\{0,1,2,3,4,5,6,7\}$ are taken to obtain different directions and scales of Gabor feature, denoting $\chi=[a_{0,0}{}^T,a_{0,1}{}^T,...,a_{4,7}{}^T]^T$. The extracted Gabor feature is conducted as input of classifier. From (4) we can see that $G_{u,v}(z)$ is a complex number. In this paper amplitude $M_{u,v}(z)$ is conducted as input because it contains the variation of image local energy which can be used as a measure of local feature.

4   Collaborative Representation Based on Face Feature

3D face depth image not only contains two-dimensional texture but also includes spatial information which is an inherent property of the face. The existence of expression, light, and occlusion will affect the accuracy of feature extraction in global feature. Local feature can divide images into different facial areas and treat them differently. Gabor feature has certain robustness to light, pose and facial expression. Gabor feature also has good spatial locality and orientation selectivity, which can keep local feature of the original data. But Gabor feature is very sensitive to occlusion, so the effect of identification is not very good under the occlusion. Due to the feature that CRC is insensitive to occlusion, an algorithm is presented based on face feature by collaborative representation. It plays advantageous in global and local feature respectively and also makes up its own shortcomings. Whether in the case of pose, facial expression or occlusion, it can greatly improve the recognition performance.

Flow diagram of collaborative representation based on face feature shows in figure 1:

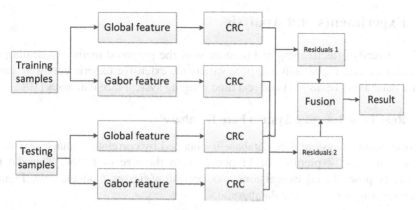

Fig. 1. Flow chart of 3D face recognition by collaborative representation based on face feature

Main steps of the method are as follows:

1) Training set is composed by 3D depth images. Assuming K classes samples, the training samples are $X = [X_1, X_2, \cdots, X_K]$, a test sample is y ;

2) Extract global feature from 3D depth images, then according to (3) and (4), extract Gabor feature which matrices are $G_{global} = [G^{glo}_1, G^{glo}_2, \cdots, G^{glo}_k]$ and $G_{gabor} = [G^{gab}_1, G^{gab}_2, \cdots, G^{gab}_k]$;

3) Project G_{gloK} and G_{gabK} into principal component analysis (PCA) subspace:

$$T^{glo}_r = W^T G^{glo}_r , \quad T^{gab}_r = W^T G^{gab} \tag{5}$$

$$T^{glo}_t = W^T y^{glo} , \quad T^{gab}_t = W^T y^{gab} \tag{6}$$

4) Training samples after reducing dimension constitute the training dictionary:

$$D_{glo} = [T^{glo}_{r1}, T^{glo}_{r2}, \cdots, T^{glo}_{rk}] \text{ and } D_{gab} = [T^{gab}_{r1}, T^{gab}_{r2}, \cdots, T^{gab}_{rk}] ;$$

5) Normalize each column of D_{glo} and D_{gab} , then project a test image to matrix P_1 and matrix P_2 respectively, so we can get the sparse coefficient vector $\alpha_1 = P_1 y$, $\alpha_2 = P_2 y$, where $P_1 = (D_{glo}^T D_{glo} + \lambda \cdot I)^{-1} D_{glo}^T$ and $P_2 = (D_{gab}^T D_{gab} + \lambda \cdot I)^{-1} D_{gab}^T$, I is unit matrix;

6) Calculate the residuals of various classes of samples:

$$e_i^{glo} = \frac{\left\| y - D^{glo}_i \alpha_1 \right\|_2}{\left\| \alpha_1 \right\|_2} \tag{7}$$

$$e_i^{gab} = \frac{\left\| y - D^{gab}_i \alpha_2 \right\|_2}{\left\| \alpha_2 \right\|_2} \tag{8}$$

7) Fused residual is the final measure:

$$e_i = \left| e^{glo}_i \right| + \left| e^{gab}_i \right| \tag{9}$$

8) $identity(y) = \arg\min_i \{ e_i \}$

5   Experiments and Analysis

In order to verify effectiveness and robustness of the proposed method in dealing with illumination, facial expression and pose variations, extensive experiments were carried out on 2 databases: Texas [11] and real time imaging system face databases [10].

5.1   Real Time Imaging System Face Database

Real time imaging system face database is obtained by correlation image sensor. The database contains 77 pictures of 11 people with the size of 64*64. This database incorporates pose, facial expressions and occlusion(glasses / no glasses). Figure 2 shows some subjects from the database.

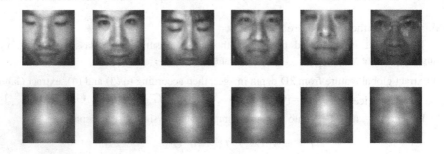

Fig. 2. Some human face intensity images and corresponding depth images in CIS

To some extent, the number of training samples affects recognition rates. 1,2,3,4,5,6 images are randomly selected as training samples of each individual respectively. The last ones are designated as probes. The selected images are 3D depth images. The experimental results are shown in Figure 3 at 4 dimensions.

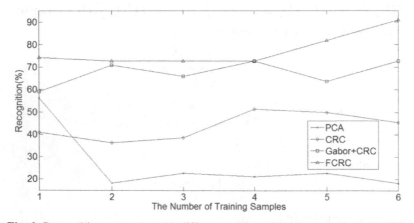

Fig. 3. Recognition rate curve with different number of training samples set in CIS

Since PCA is unable to overcome illumination, facial expression and pose, the recognition result is less effective. While CRC based on global and Gabor feature obtain a better recognition performance. Obviously, the number of training samples affects recognition rates. But it does not change the overall trend. Only the proposed algorithm with the increase numbers of training samples, the recognition rates kept increasing trend. They are significantly higher than several other algorithms. Experimental results show that the proposed method of the FCRC can get the optimal recognition results when choosing a different number of training samples.

In addition, for each subject, 3 depth images were selected as training samples, namely, the resting constitute probe samples. Figure 4 shows the recognition rate curve in different dimensions.

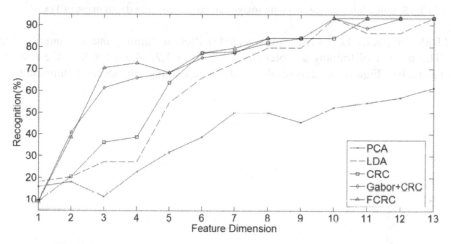

Fig. 4. Recognition rate curve with different feature dimensions in CIS

Linear discriminant analysis (LDA) firstly passes through PCA dimensionality reduction. From Figure 4, it can be observed that in most situations the proposed method outperforms other algorithms. It has reached 93.182% at dimension 10, and since then has maintained this level. While the other algorithms cover up to 93.182% at dimension 12 later, with exception PCA. Experimental results show that collaborative representation based on Gabor and global feature, and fused residuals serving as ultimate difference metric, the proposed method are superior to other algorithms, which proves the robustness of our algorithm.

5.2   Texas 3D Face Recognition Database

Texas 3D Face Recognition Database contains 1149 3D models of 118 adult human subjects. The facial expressions present are smiling or talking faces with open/closed mouths and/or closed eyes. The neutral faces are emotionless. Some human face images are showed in Figure 5.

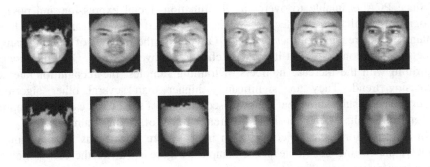

Fig. 5. Some human face intensity images and corresponding depth maps in Texas

1160 pictures of 116 classes are selected. Different training and test samples are set. The number of training samples of each class is 1,2,3,4,5,6,7,8,9, so the rest are used as probes. Figure 6 depicts results for different training samples at 16 dimensions.

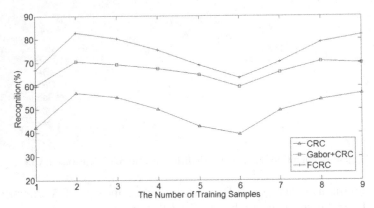

Fig. 6. Recognition rate curve with different size of training samples set in Texas

It can be seen from Figure 6, not training samples are more, and the recognition rates are higher. When the number increases, it will cause the redundancy of information. But no matter how many the training samples are, the proposed algorithm is more effective than other algorithms.

In order to demonstrate robustness of the algorithm in different dimensions, 1 image per person for training, a total of 116, and the other images are used as test samples, a total of 1044. Figure 7 shows the recognition rate curve in different dimensions.

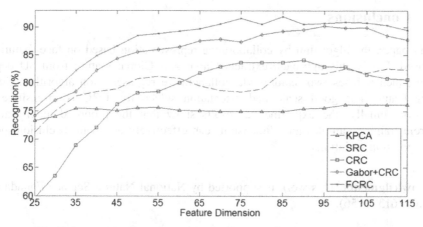

Fig. 7. Recognition rate curve with different feature dimensions in Texas

From Fig 7, with 66D between 112D features, FCRC achieves recognition rates above 90%, while Gabor-CRC reaches 90.134% at 94D features. After this dimension recognition, the rates drop below 90% almost as a whole. On the other hand, the best rates achieved by Kernel PCA (KPCA), SRC, original CRC and Gabor-CRC are 76.149%, 82.57%, 85.153% and 90.23%, FCRC outperforms others achieving a maximum recognition rate of 91.762%. It can be seen that compared with other algorithms, the proposed algorithm has higher recognition rates even when the number of training samples is small.

In order to fully evaluate the performance of the algorithm, the complexities of the various algorithms are analyzed, with Texas database as an example at 30 dimensions. The time consumed in the recognition phase is shown in table 1.

Table 1. Experimental comparison of our proposed method with other methods

Algorithm	TIME(s)
SRC	256
CRC	3
Gabor-CRC	4
FCRC	8

Since most of current face recognition system is offline, so we are comparing the time complexity of algorithms in the recognition phase. Since l_1 norm is more time-consuming to solve sparse coefficient, the time of SRC is the greatest. While CRC-based algorithms use regularized least square to solve the coefficient, time is far less than SRC. So the proposed method is effective.

6   Conclusions

In this paper, the algorithm by collaborative representation based on face feature is proposed. Firstly this approach extracts Gabor and Global feature from 3D depth images, then it fuses two features via collaborative representation algorithm. Since Gabor feature has good scale and orientation selectivity, CRC is insensitive to occlusion. Finally, the experimental results show that the proposed algorithm in different training samples and dimensions can effectively deal with occlusion, pose and expression variations.

Acknowledgments. This work is supported by National Natural Science Foundation of China(61371156).

References

1. Wright, J., Yang, A.Y., Ganesh, A., et al.: Robust face recognition via sparse representation. IEEE Transactions on Pattern Analysis and Machine Intelligence 31(2), 210–227 (2009)
2. Shi, Q., Eriksson, A., Van Den Hengel, A., et al.: Is face recognition really a compressive sensing problem? In: 2011 IEEE Conference on Computer Vision and Pattern Recognition (CVPR), pp. 553–560. IEEE (2011)
3. Rigamonti, R., Brown, M.A., Lepetit, V.: Are sparse representations really relevant for image classification? In: 2011 IEEE Conference on Computer Vision and Pattern Recognition (CVPR), pp. 1545–1552. IEEE (2011)
4. Zhang, L., Yang, M., Feng, X.: Sparse representation or collaborative representation: Which helps face recognition? In: 2011 IEEE International Conference on Computer Vision (ICCV), pp. 471–478. IEEE (2011)
5. Hu, Z.P., Xu, B., Bai, Y.: Sparse representation for image recognition based on Gaborfeature set and discriminative dictionary learning. Journal of Image and Graphics 18(2), 189–194 (2013)
6. Yang, M., Zhang, L.: Gabor feature based sparse representation for face recognition with gabor occlusion dictionary. In: Daniilidis, K., Maragos, P., Paragios, N. (eds.) ECCV 2010, Part VI. LNCS, vol. 6316, pp. 448–461. Springer, Heidelberg (2010)
7. Shu, Z., Qixiang, Z., Jianguo, J., Ando, S.: 3D Face Recognition by Kernel Collaborative Representation Based on Gabor Feature. Acta Photonica Sinica 42(12), 1448–1453 (2013)
8. Drira, H., Ben Amor, B., Srivastava, A., Daoudi, M., Slama, R.: 3D face recognition under expressions, occlusions and pose variations. IEEE Transactions on Pattern Analysis and Machine Intelligence 35(9), 2270–2283 (2013)
9. Chi, Y., Porikli, F.: Classification and Boosting with Multiple Collaborative Representations. IEEE PAMI (2013)
10. Kurihara, T., Ono, N., Ando, S.: Surface orientation imager using three-phase amplitude-modulated illumination and correlation image sensor. In: Electronic Imaging 2003, pp. 95–102. International Society for Optics and Photonics (2003)
11. Gupta, S., Castleman, K.R., Markey, M.K., Bovik, A.C.: Texas 3D face recognition database. In: 2010 IEEE Southwest Symposium on Image Analysis& Interpretation (SSIAI), pp. 97–100. IEEE (2010)

Fake Fingerprint Detection Based on Wavelet Analysis and Local Binary Pattern

Yongliang Zhang[1], Shanshan Fang[1], Yu Xie[2], and Tingting Xu[3]

[1] College of Computer Science & Technology, Zhejiang University of Technology,
Hangzhou, China
[2] Hangzhou Jinglianwen Technology Co., Ltd., Hangzhou, China
[3] School of Computer Science and Technology, Hangzhou Dianzi University, Hangzhou, China
titanzhang@zjut.edu.cn

Abstract. Fake fingerprint detection technology is used for detecting spoof fingerprint attacks in biometric systems. In this paper, an improved software-based fake fingerprint detection approach using wavelet analysis and local binary pattern(LBP) is proposed. Firstly, wavelet analysis is applied to get the denoised image and residual noise image. Then both two images are divided into blocks of the same size to calculate the histogram of LBP as features, which provide more texture information than the features in original wavelet-based method. Finally, support vector machine(SVM) is used for classification. The average rate of accuracy of the proposed approach is 88.53% for all datasets in LivDet2011, and 88.98% in LiveDet2013, while the winner in LivDet2011 is 74.41%, and the winner in LivDet2013 is 86.63%.

Keywords: wavelet analysis, LBP, SVM, fake fingerprint detection.

1 Introduction

Nowadays, fingerprint based biometric systems are widely used. Among all the vulnerabilities of a fingerprint recognition system, the attack directed against the sensor is one of the most important[1]. Fake fingerprints made from inexpensive materials, as well as the improvement of production technology bring risks to the existing fingerprint recognition systems. The ability to identify whether a fingerprint is from a live finger is becoming a challenging research issue.

Several fake fingerprint detection methods are proposed to resist the attack of spoof fingerprint. The first one is called hardware based method, which requires dedicated hardware integrated with the fingerprint system[2]. This method uses the temperature, pulse, blood pressure, odor and other vital signs to detect liveness. But the extra hardware increases the cost and cannot be used in the existing fingerprint authentication systems. In contrast, the software based method can solve these problems and has less intrusive for the user which is an important characteristic for a practical liveness detection solution. Software based approaches can make use of static features being those which require one or more impressions (e.g., the finger is placed and lifted from the sensor one or more times), or dynamic features which are those ex-

Z. Sun et al. (Eds.): CCBR 2014, LNCS 8833, pp. 191–198, 2014.

tracted from multiple image frames (e.g., the finger is placed on the sensor for a short time and a video sequence is captured and analyzed)[3].

In previous research, various types of features have been used as the characteristics to distinguish real fingerprints from spoof ones in feature extraction stage. The main idea of skin distortion-based approach is to recognize the fake fingerprint image by measuring the elasticity difference between the real and the spoof fingerprint[4]. The key to distinguishing is the material elasticity. If the fake material has similar hardness with real skin, it will affect the algorithm performance. The wavelet-based method is to measure the coarseness of the fingerprint surface by calculating the standard deviation of the residual noise of an image[5]. But this method is efficient for sensors with high resolution (1000 dpi, while common commercial sensors only have 500 dpi). A Spatial Surface Coarseness Analysis (SSCA) based method improves the wavelet analysis of the fingertip surface texture by introducing spatial features to the model[6]. It has been proved to achieve great results for Sagem database that's used in the second edition of the Fingerprint Liveness Detection Competition (LivDet2011), comprise only fingerprint images of 500 dpi. But this method only uses coarseness image, and the features are extracted by the standard deviation, which may be incomplete for reflecting local texture information.

This paper proposes an improved algorithm for fake fingerprint detection based on wavelet analysis and LBP. In the following sections, the proposed algorithm will be presented in detail. Section 2 and Section 3 recall the basis of wavelet analysis and LBP, respectively; Section 4 presents the proposed method; Section 5 gives the experimental results and Section 6 presents the conclusion of this paper.

2   Wavelet Analysis

Wavelet analysis is a surface texture analysis of the fingertip for each image region. It can help to minimize the effect of ridge/valley pattern when estimating the surface coarseness because it allows investigation of the input signal at different scales[5]. Suppose the surface coarseness of fingerprint image is a kind of Gaussian white noise. The residual noise $\gamma(x, y)$ can be expressed as:

$$\gamma(x, y) = f(x, y) - f'(x, y) \ . \tag{1}$$

Where $f(x, y)$ represents the original image, and $f'(x, y)$ is the denoised image. Each fingerprint image is denoised by the following steps:

Step1: Two levels of stationary wavelet decomposition are performed to the fingerprint image to achieve one approximation and six details $g_k(x, y), k = 1, 2, ..., 6$.

Step2: Wavelet shrinkage is performed by applying soft-thresholding to each of the six details:

$$g'_k(x, y) = \text{sgn}(g_k(x, y))\sqrt{(g_k(x, y)^2 - \delta^2)_+} \ . \tag{2}$$

$$\delta = \sqrt{2\log(N)}\sigma \ . \tag{3}$$

Where sgn(a) is the signal of a, $(a)_+$ is the maximum value between a and zero. N is the length of each detail; σ is the standard deviation of the three details obtained in the first level of decomposition.

Step3: $f'(x, y)$ is obtained by wavelet reconstruction from the approximation and the denoised details.

As shown in Fig.1 are the original fingerprint image, denoised image and the corresponding residual noise image.

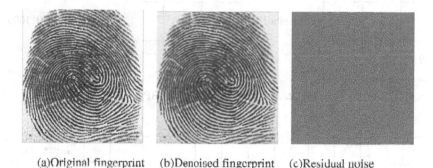

(a)Original fingerprint   (b)Denoised fingerprint   (c)Residual noise

Fig. 1. An example of image denoising.

3   Local Binary Pattern

The Local Binary Pattern (LBP) operator is an effective image texture operator firstly proposed by Ojala et al[7]. It is an efficient rotation-invariant texture classification technique. It uses the center pixel as threshold, compares the neighborhood pixels with the threshold and results in a list of binary values. If the neighborhood pixel is smaller than the threshold, the value in the corresponding position of the list of binary values is set to 0, or to 1 in other cases. The LBP value is calculated by element-wise multiplication of the list of binary values with weights and summing up the results.

The original LBP uses 3*3 operator, as shown in Fig.2, but it may not capture the key texture characteristics. Ojala et al. extended the operator to use circular neighborhoods and linearly interpolated the pixel values in the image, which allows any radius and number of pixels in the neighborhood[9]. $LBP_{P,R}$ represents a circularly symmetric neighbor set of P members on a circle of radius R, as shown in Fig.3. $LBP_{P,R}$ operator is by definition invariant against any monotonic transformation of the gray scale ,i.e., as long as the order of the gray values in the image stays the same, the output of the $LBP_{P,R}$ operator remains constant. The $LBP_{P,R}$ value of the center pixel g_c can be calculated by:

$$LBP_{P,R} = \sum_{p=0}^{P-1} s(g_p - g_c) \times 2^p \ . \tag{4}$$

Where

$$s(t) = \begin{cases} 1, t \ge 0 \\ 0, t < 0 \end{cases} . \tag{5}$$

$g_p (p = 0, \ldots, P-1)$ is the circularly symmetric neighborhood.

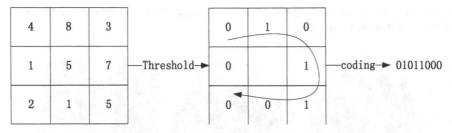

Fig. 2. An example of original LBP operator

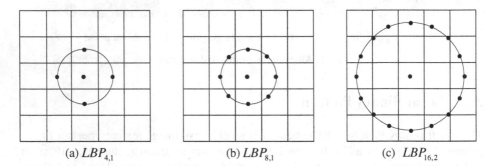

(a) $LBP_{4,1}$ (b) $LBP_{8,1}$ (c) $LBP_{16,2}$

Fig. 3. Examples of circular neighborhoods

4   The Proposed Method

Given an input fingerprint image, the vitality information is represented by a set of features that are extracted to train a pattern classifier. Such classifier is able to compute the probability of the vitality of fingerprint and determine whether the image is from a fake finger or not. In this paper, for a fingerprint image to be judged, wavelet analysis is applied to get denoised image and residual noise image after image segmentation, and then LBP features are extracted from these images. Support Vector Machine (SVM) is used to get classification criterion and obtain the final result.

4.1   Image Segmentation

For a training set or a testing set, calculate the amount of images that the background area is more than half of the image, if the result is greater than 50%, a cutting function is applied:

$$f = CUT(F, \mathrm{h}, \mathrm{w}) \ . \tag{6}$$

Where F is the input image, h, w is the height and width of the processed image. The values of h, w are obtained by cross validation. Image segmentation is used to remove the background that does not provide useful information for fake fingerprint detection.

4.2   Feature Extraction

After image segmentation, wavelet analysis is used to get the denoised image and residual noise image. Firstly, the original image is decomposed into two levels using discrete wavelet transform to get one approximation and six details. Each one of the details is denoised using the hyperbolic shrinkage method. Then the denoised image is obtained by wavelet reconstruction from the approximation and the details previously denoised. The difference value of the original image and the denoised image is the residual noise image.

For the reason that the features extracted from the whole image are mainly global information rather than local information. In order to get more local information, the denoised image and the residual noise image are divided into $P_x \times P_y$ portions. The most suitable values for P_x and P_y are determined using cross validation. Each portion of the denoised image and the residual noise image is used to calculate the histogram of LBP code to get features. The histogram of LBP can get more information than standard deviation used in [5] in local regions. The values of P and R are obtained by cross validation. And uniform pattern and rotational invariance are applied to reduce the dimension of features. The definitions of uniform pattern and rotational invariance are as follows:

Uniform pattern: If the number of spatial transitions in the list of binary values $U(\mathrm{LBP}_{P,R})$ is not bigger than 2, the LBP corresponds uniform pattern. Uniform pattern can be verified by :

$$U(\mathrm{LBP}_{P,R}) = |\, s(g_{P-1} - g_c) - s(g_0 - g_c)\,| + \sum_{i=1}^{P-1} |\, s(g_i - g_c) - s(g_{i-1} - g_c)\,| \tag{7}$$

Rotational invariance: When the image is rotated, the gray values g_p will correspondingly move along the perimeter of the circle around g_0. In order to remove the effect of rotation, rotate the image to get a series of LBP value, choose the minimum value as the LBP value of the center pixel:

$$LBP_{P,R}^{ri} = \min\{ \mathrm{ROR}(\mathrm{LBP}_{P,R}, i) \,|\, i = 0, 1, \ldots, P-1\} \ . \tag{8}$$

Where $ROR(e, i)$ performs a circular bit-wise right shift on the P-bit number e i times.

Finally, all the features are normalized by:

$$X_i' = \frac{X_i}{\sum X_j} \tag{9}$$

X_i is the original component of the feature vector, while $X_i^{'}$ is the normalized component of the feature vector. The features are obtained from all the portions make up the feature vector of the fingerprint image.

4.3   Classification

After features are extracted, SVM is used to distinguish fake fingerprints from real ones. In the training stage, SVM based on polynomial kernel is used to obtain classification criteria. The kernel function is determined by cross validation. And in the testing stage, SVM is applied to make the decision.

5   Experiments

In this paper, we evaluated the proposed method on the databases of LivDet2011 and LivDet2013. LivDet2011 consists of images from four different devices: Biometrika, Digital Persona, Italdata and Sagem[10]. There are 4000 images for each of these datasets, 2000 live images and 2000 spoof images (400 of each of 5 spoof materials). LivDet2013 consists of images from four different devices: Biometrika, Crossmatch, Italdata and Swipe[11]. There are 4000 or more images for each of these devices as detailed in Table 1.

Table 1. Training and testing set in LivDet2013(samples/numbers of fingers)

Dataset	Live training samples	Live testing samples	Fake training samples	Fake testing samples
Biometrika	1000/200	1000/100	1000/50	1000/50
Italdata	1000/200	1000/100	1000/50	1000/50
Crossmatch	1250/500	1250/440	1000/125	1000/100
Swipe	1250/500	1250/500	1000/125	1000/100

FerrLive, *FerrFake* and *ACE* are used for evaluating the liveness detection method. *FerrLive* is the rate that the algorithm produced a false rejection of a live subject, while *FerrFake* is the rate that the algorithm produced a false acceptance of a spoof image. *ACE* is defined as $ACE = (FerrLive + FerrFake)/2$, it means the average classification error rate. And the average rate of accuracy is $1 - ACE$.

As shown in Table2-4 are the *FerrLive*, *FerrFake* and average rate of accuracy of the proposed method compared with winner in LivDet2011 and SSCA method proposed in [6], While the *FerrLive*, *FerrFake* and the average rate of accuracy compared with winner in LivDet2013 are shown in Table5-7. The experimental data shows that the proposed method gets better results than the SSCA based method for Sagem database in LivDet2011. The average rate of accuracy of the proposed approach is 88.53% for all datasets in LivDet2011, and 88.98% in LiveDet2013, which are superior to winners in LivDet2011 and LivDet2013.

Table 2. Comparison of *FerrLive* on LivDet2011

Databases(columns) Algorithm(rows)	Biometrika	Digital Persona	ItalData	Sagem	Average
Winner2011	38.00%	6.20%	15.10%	13.80%	26.60%
SSCA in [6]	—	—	—	14.40%	—
The proposed method	12.40%	3.30%	17.00%	6.10%	9.70 %

Table 3. Comparison of *FerrFake* on LivDet2011

Databases(columns) Algorithm(rows)	Biometrika	Digital Persona	ItalData	Sagem	Average
Winner2011	42.00%	11.60%	40.10%	13.10%	24.50%
SSCA in [6]	—	—	—	11.30%	—
The proposed method	8.00%	16.60%	15.30%	13.10%	13.25 %

Table 4. Comparison of average rate of accuracy on LivDet2011

Databases(columns) Algorithm(rows)	Biometrika	Digital Persona	ItalData	Sagem	Average
Winner2011	60.00%	91.10%	60.00%	86.55%	74.41%
SSCA in [6]	—	—	—	87.20%	—
The proposed method	89.80%	90.05%	83.85%	90.40%	88.53%

Table 5. Comparison of *FerrLive* on LivDet2013

Databases(columns) Algorithm(rows)	Biometrika	Crossmatch	ItalData	Swipe	Average
Winner2013	3.00%	31.28%	2.10%	11.45%	11.96%
The proposed method	2.2%	41.12%	0.10%	3.99%	11.85 %

Table 6. Comparison of *FerrFake* on LivDet2013

Databases(columns) Algorithm(rows)	Biometrika	Crossmatch	ItalData	Swipe	Average
Winner2013	6.40%	31.10%	4.90%	16.10%	14.62%
The proposed method	2.6%	16.9%	9.8%	9.1%	9.6%

Table 7. Comparison of average rate of accuracy on LivDet2013

Databases(columns) Algorithm(rows)	Biometrika	Crossmatch	ItalData	Swipe	Average
Winner2013	95.30%	68.80%	96.50%	85.93%	86.63%
The proposed method	97.60%	69.64%	95.05%	93.64%	88.98%

6   Conclusion

In this paper, an improved algorithm based on wavelet analysis and local binary pattern is proposed. We extend the method in [5], apply wavelet analysis to obtain the residual noise image, as well as the denoised image. Then the images are divided into blocks of size $P_x \times P_y$ to calculate the LBP histogram, instead of standard deviation, to get more local texture information. P_x and P_y are determined by cross validation. SVM is used to make the final decision. And the proposed method is suitable for common commercial sensors with 500dpi resolution. The approach has been tested on the datasets used in LivDet2011 and LivDet2013. The experimental results show that the proposed approach is more efficient than the best algorithm submitted to LivDet2011 and LivDet2013, and the SSCA method proposed in [6]. The average rate of accuracy on LivDet2011 is 88.53%, and the average rate of accuracy on LivDet2013 is 88.98%

Acknowledgments. Supported by the Science Technology Department of Zhejiang Province (2012C24009) and Morpho (Safran).

References

1. Espinoza, M., Champod, C.: Risk evaluation for spoofing against a sensor supplied with liveness detection. Forensic Science International 204, 162–168 (2011)
2. Tan, B., Schuckers, S.: Spoofing protection for fingerprint scanner by fusing ridge signal and valley noise. Pattern Recognition 43, 2845–2857 (2010)
3. Galbally, J., Alonso-Fernandez, F., Fierrez, J., Ortega-Garcia, J.: A high performance fingerprint liveness detection method based on quality related features. Future Generation Computer Systems 28, 311–321 (2012)
4. Antonelli, A., Cappelli, R., Maio, D., Maltoni, D.: Fake finger detection by skin distortion analysis. IEEE Transactions on Information Forensics and Security 1, 360–373 (2006)
5. Moon, Y.S., Chen, J.S., Chan, K.C., So, K., Woo, K.S.: Wavelet based fingerprint liveness detection. Electronic Letters 41, 1112–1113 (2005)
6. Pereira, L.F.A., Pinheiro, H.N.B., Cavalcanti, G.D.C., Ren, T.I.: Spatial surface coarseness analysis: technique for fingerprint spoof detection. Electronics Letters 49, 260–261 (2013)
7. Ojala, T., Pietikäinen, M., Harwood, D.: A comparative study of texture measures with classification based on featured distributions. Pattern Recognition 29, 51–59 (1996)
8. Ahonen, T., Hadid, A., Pietikäinen, M.: Face Recognition with Local Binary Patterns. In: Pajdla, T., Matas, J(G.) (eds.) ECCV 2004. LNCS, vol. 3021, pp. 469–481. Springer, Heidelberg (2004)
9. Ojala, T., Pietikainen, M., Maenpaa, T.: Multiresolution gray-scale and rotation invariant texture classification with local binary patterns. IEEE Transactions on Pattern Analysis and Machine Intelligence 24(7), 971–987 (2002)
10. Yambay, D., Ghiani, L., Denti, P., Marcialis, G., Roli, F., Schuckers, S.: LivDet 2011 - Fingerprint Liveness Detection Competition 2011. In: IAPR/IEEE Int. Conf. on Biometrics, pp. 208–215 (2012)
11. Ghiani, L., Yambay, D., Mura, V., Tocco, S.: LivDet 2013 Fingerprint Liveness Detection Competition 2013. In: International Conference on Biometrics (ICB). Biometrics Compendium, pp. 1–6 (2013)

Fingerprint Quality of Rural Population and Impact of Multiple Scanners on Recognition

Kamlesh Tiwari* and Phalguni Gupta

Department of Computer Science and Engineering,
Indian Institute of Technology Kanpur,
Kanpur U.P., 208016, India
{ktiwari,pg}@cse.iitk.ac.in

Abstract. Fingerprint is a popular biometric trait for designing an automatic human recognition system. These systems are commonly benchmarked over fingerprints of the urban population whereas their practical deployment involves majority of rural population. Living standards of the rural population is not as high as urban ones. They are mostly involved in hard work and less careful about their skin conditions. Therefore, it is desirable to explore the average quality of fingerprint and the performance of automatic fingerprint recognition system for rural population. This paper analyses the (1) age-group and gender wise quality of fingerprint and (2) recognition performance under cross scanner settings. To justify the analysis, 41400 fingerprints are collected from 1150 participants living in rural areas and actively involved in physically hard work. Participants are from age group of 18 to 70 years. Samples have been collected in two phases with a gap of two months with the help of three different fingerprint scanners. Every participant has provided multiple fingerprint samples in each phase on all three scanners.

Keywords: Biometrics, Fingerprint, Quality, Minutiae, CRR, EER.

1 Introduction

Fingerprint is one of the most accepted biometric trait because of its properties like uniqueness, permanence and universality. It is an impression produced on a surface getting in touch with the upper part of a human finger skin. Black lines of this impression are called ridges while white region between two ridges is called valley. A point where a ridge terminated or meets with another ridge is called minutiae. A single fingerprint contains several minutiae points which are used as a feature of the fingerprint. Fingerprint matchers such as MCC [3] uses minutiae features to determine the similarity between two fingerprints. Biometric systems are designed to identify humans based on their physiological or behavioral characteristics such as fingerprint [9,15,13], palmprint [2,11,10] *etc.* Like any other trait, the performance of a fingerprint based human recognition system is also affected by the quality of the acquired fingerprint image samples. Quality of a fingerprint image [4,6,5,14] is usually defined as a measure of the clarity of the ridges and valley structures, as well as the extractability of features.

---

* Corresponding author.

Z. Sun et al. (Eds.): CCBR 2014, LNCS 8833, pp. 199–207, 2014.
© Springer International Publishing Switzerland 2014

Table 1. Device Specifications of Fingerprint Scanners

Specification	Device $\mathcal{D}_1$	Device $\mathcal{D}_2$	Device $\mathcal{D}_3$
Image Resolution (DPI)	500	500	500
Image Size (pixel)	352×544	260×300	320×480
Effective Sensing Area (mm)	17.5×27.5	12.7×14.9	16.26×24.38
Light Source	Blue LED	Red LED	Infrared LED

Generally, the quality depends on many factors like (1) finger conditions such as dry, wet, creased/wrinkled, abraded, finger slide or rotation, (2) type of biometric scanner used [16], (3) data collection environment, (4) quality of biometric trait available with the user, (5) behavior of the user with the sensor, (6) aging [7], *etc*. A good quality fingerprint image consists of clear dark ridge lines separated by white valley along its orientation. Bad quality fingerprint image is generally affected by noise, blur, deformation, contrast deficiency *etc.* which result in spurious and missed features. Such samples are less usable to security systems [17,12]. In [8], a study is presented to determine the effect of fingerprint image quality on the performance of AFRS with a database of 189 subjects which was collected in one session. There is a need of comprehensive study on general population.

This paper explores three important parameters *viz*. (1) quality of fingerprint pertaining to general peoples living in rural area (2) performance of an automatic fingerprint recognition system (AFRS) for this population and (3) performance of AFRS when images are acquired by different scanners. It uses multiple fingerprint scanners of different manufacturers having good market presence. Quality parameters considered for the test are NIST quality score, number of acquired minutiae points and their quality. The paper is organized as follows. Section 2 discusses various quality measures, explains the experimental setup and presents the detailed report on the experiment of the fingerprint quality of general population. Section 3 discusses the performance of an automatic fingerprint recognition system on the database under cross sensor setting. Conclusion is presented in the last section.

2   Fingerprint Quality Observations

Three fingerprint scanners having good market presence have been used in the study. Their specifications are given in Table 1. Let these devices be $\mathcal{D}_1$, $\mathcal{D}_2$, $\mathcal{D}_3$. Fingerprint scanner $\mathcal{D}_1$ uses an advanced CMOS sensor technology and precise optical system. It claims to meet the rigorous requirements on fingerprint image quality. It can reject spoof fingers made from silicone rubber, play-doh, *etc*. Fingerprint sensor $\mathcal{D}_2$ is equipped with liveness detection technology adaptable against spoof threats. It uses multiple types of light to capture an image of external and internal fingerprint. The type of sensor $\mathcal{D}_3$ is a high-quality, rugged optical fingerprint sensor with ultra-precise resolution. It has a very hard fingerprint contact area that is resistant to scratches, impact, corrosion and electrostatic discharge (ESD).

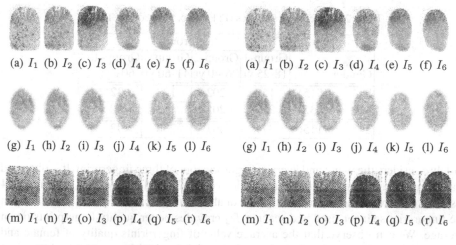

(a) I_1 (b) I_2 (c) I_3 (d) I_4 (e) I_5 (f) I_6 (a) I_1 (b) I_2 (c) I_3 (d) I_4 (e) I_5 (f) I_6

(g) I_1 (h) I_2 (i) I_3 (j) I_4 (k) I_5 (l) I_6 (g) I_1 (h) I_2 (i) I_3 (j) I_4 (k) I_5 (l) I_6

(m) I_1 (n) I_2 (o) I_3 (p) I_4 (q) I_5 (r) I_6 (m) I_1 (n) I_2 (o) I_3 (p) I_4 (q) I_5 (r) I_6

Fingerprint Images of Phase-1   Fingerprint Images of Phase-2

Fig. 1. Fingerprint images of a person acquired on scanner device D_1, D_2 and D_3. First three images in a row are from thumb and next three from pointer finger.

Scanners D_1, D_2, D_3 are used to acquire fingerprints from 1150 subjects living in rural area. These subjects are actively involved in hard work. Fingerprint impressions of thumb and point finger of right hand are acquired. Participants are divided into four groups based on their age to study the effect of age propagation. Table 2 shows participant statistics of different age groups. It can be seen that the gender ratio is nearly same across the groups. Data is collected in two phases with a gap of two months. Three impressions are taken at each phase from each finger. Every participant has provided his fingerprint in both phases on all three devices. Fig. 1 show sample fingerprints of a particular participant in both the phases. There are 1150 participants who have provided the fingerprints and hence, total number of fingerprints is 41, 400.

2.1 Fingerprint Quality

Quality of a fingerprint is evaluated by using *nfiq* routine of NBIS software provided by National Institute of Standards and Technology (NIST) [1]. This routine produces quality values lying between 1 and 5 where 1 corresponds to the highest and 5 is the worst quality. Fig. 2 shows the distribution of fingerprint quality across three scanners. It can be seen that device D_2 has produced maximum number of fingerprint images belonging to quality 1. Out of 13, 800 images, 4268 images are classified as of quality 1. But this is not the case with device D_3. Only 23 of its images are categorized of quality 1.

Table 3 presents the average of the highest, the lowest and the average quality values of fingerprints at different age groups classified by different fingerprint devices. The row *Hi* signifies the scenario when only the best fingerprint out of the three provided by the user per finger per device per phase of all users is considered for analysis. Similarly *Lo*

Table 2. Participants statistics (F: Female, M: Male, T: Total)

Gender		Age group			
		Group-1 18-25 yr	Group-2 26-40 yr	Group-3 41-60 yr	Group-4 60+ yr
F	(515)	159	202	122	32
M	(635)	212	205	158	60
T	(1150)	371	407	280	92

and Av considers the worst and average fingerprint out of three fingerprint. It is observed that average quality of all participants on device D_1, D_2 and D_3 are 2.20, 1.32 and 3.14 respectively. This basically means that the quality of fingerprint acquired depends upon the fingerprint scanner used and scanner D_2 provides better quality fingerprints on an average. We can observe that the average value of fingerprints quality of female and male participants acquired with the help of D_2 is 1.28 and 1.36 respectively. Also on an average, fingerprint impression of female population is slightly better than that of male population. It can also be observed that the similar trend is found to be present in all age-groups except 60+.

Fingerprint quality of male or female participants acquired by D_2 is high but decreases with age. Observation for age-group 60+ shows that the average of best quality of fingerprint for male and female is 1.21 and 1.34 which means that quality of fingerprints of male population is slightly better than that of female participants. This may be due to the fact that after the age of 60, males are not much involved in physical labor whereas female continues with their daily house hold work.

2.2 Number of Minutiae

Number of minutiae extracted by NIST routine is also considered for analysis. Minutiae points for each fingerprint are calculated using minutiae detection software *mindtct* of NBIS. Table 4 presents average of the highest, the lowest and the average number of minutiae points present in the fingerprint images of different age-groups found by different fingerprint devices. It can be observed that the average number of minutiae points extracted from fingerprint images of all users by D_3 is minimum. Surprisingly, in most of the cases, the average number of minutiae points of fingerprints of female users acquired by D_2 is more than that of male users. It is also observed that the average number of minutiae points extracted by *mindtct* of female/male users in all age groups increases with age. This is due to false minutiae which appear by virtue of poor quality.

2.3 Quality of Minutiae

Table 5 presents average of the highest, the lowest and the average quality of minutiae points for different age groups against different fingerprint devices. This parameter is also calculated by using NIST routine. Quality of minutiae takes value from 0 to 100 where higher value corresponds to better quality. It can be observed that average quality of minutiae of all participants depends upon the kind of fingerprint scanner used.

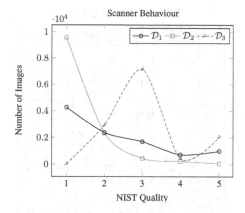

Fig. 2. Scanner Behavior According to NIST Quality Scores

Table 3. NIST Quality (F: Female, M: Male, T: Total)

Age		Device $\mathcal{D}_1$			Device $\mathcal{D}_2$			Device $\mathcal{D}_3$		
		F	M	T	F	M	T	F	M	T
18-25	Hi	2.32	2.08	2.18	1.38	1.55	1.48	3.48	3.32	3.39
	Av	1.69	1.54	1.61	1.16	1.26	1.22	2.94	2.80	2.86
	Lo	1.23	1.17	1.20	1.02	1.05	1.03	2.50	2.36	2.42
26-40	Hi	2.98	2.73	2.85	1.50	1.66	1.58	3.69	3.56	3.62
	Av	2.23	2.05	2.14	1.22	1.33	1.28	3.17	3.04	3.11
	Lo	1.63	1.53	1.58	1.04	1.09	1.06	2.71	2.60	2.65
41-60	Hi	3.59	3.17	3.35	1.83	1.85	1.84	4.09	3.79	3.92
	Av	2.91	2.46	2.65	1.40	1.43	1.41	3.51	3.24	3.36
	Lo	2.29	1.89	2.06	1.11	1.13	1.12	2.98	2.75	2.85
60+	Hi	4.23	3.96	4.05	2.22	2.31	2.27	4.43	4.24	4.31
	Av	3.67	3.30	3.43	1.72	1.63	1.66	3.85	3.66	3.73
	Lo	3.13	2.73	2.87	1.34	1.21	1.26	3.17	3.08	3.11
T	Hi	3.00	2.74	2.85	1.59	1.73	1.67	3.77	3.60	3.67
	Av	2.31	2.10	2.20	1.28	1.36	1.32	3.22	3.07	3.14
	Lo	1.76	1.61	1.68	1.07	1.10	1.08	2.74	2.60	2.66

Quality of minutiae points of scanner $\mathcal{D}_2$ is found to be better. On an average, quality of minutiae obtained through fingerprint impressions of male population by $\mathcal{D}_2$ is slightly better than that of the female population. Similar trend is found to be present in all age-groups except 26-40.

Average quality of minutiae points for female or male participants within different age-groups acquired through $\mathcal{D}_2$ decreases with age. For age-group 18-60, quality average of minutiae points of fingerprint of female users is better than that of the male users on device $\mathcal{D}_1$. Quality of $\mathcal{D}_2$ is not only consistent but also better than others. However, quality in all cases is found to be decreasing as the age increases.

3 Performance of an AFRS

An AFRS can work in two modes. First is the verification, when it decides whether the two given fingerprints belongs to same subject or not while second is the identification, where it searches the stored database to find another fingerprint which matches the most with the the given fingerprint. Nearly $\sim$428,490,000 number of comparisons are done to study the performance of an AFRS by using *bozorth3* matcher of NIST. Standard parameters to measure verification or identification performance are equal error rate (EER) and correct recognition rate (CRR) respectively. At a given threshold, the probability of accepting the impostor is known as false acceptance rate (FAR) and probability of rejecting the genuine user known as false rejection rate (FRR). Equal error rate (EER) is the value of FAR for which FAR and FRR are equal. EER is a good indicator of system performance. It represents the point where false acceptance rate and false reject rate are same. Lower the value of EER better is the system.

Table 6 presents EER of the AFRS when fingerprints of the first phase are matched with those of second phase acquired with the help of different fingerprint scanning devices. EER values when two images which are acquired through the device $\mathcal{D}_2$ are matched is found to be minimum. It also justifies the different quality values obtained

Table 4. Minutia Count

Age		Device $\mathcal{D}_1$			Device $\mathcal{D}_2$			Device $\mathcal{D}_3$		
		F	M	T	F	M	T	F	M	T
18-25	Hi	86.9	84.6	85.6	75.3	71.5	73.0	49.9	45.4	47.3
	Av	70.9	70.6	70.7	64.1	61.3	62.5	40.9	37.0	38.7
	Lo	5.9	5.9	5.9	6.0	6.0	6.0	5.7	5.7	5.7
26-40	Hi	83.9	85.9	84.9	76.7	74.8	75.7	46.3	42.5	44.3
	Av	68.5	71.5	70.0	65.1	63.7	64.4	36.8	34.3	35.5
	Lo	5.8	5.9	5.9	6.0	6.0	6.0	5.6	5.6	5.6
41-60	Hi	89.9	85.5	87.4	83.9	77.4	80.2	46.5	41.6	43.7
	Av	71.9	70.8	71.3	71.0	65.1	67.6	36.3	32.5	34.1
	Lo	5.7	5.8	5.7	6.0	6.0	6.0	5.4	5.5	5.5
60+	Hi	93.8	102.4	99.3	99.6	90.4	93.6	44.9	46.0	45.6
	Av	73.6	83.4	80.0	82.5	74.9	77.5	33.8	34.5	34.3
	Lo	5.2	5.7	5.5	6.0	6.0	6.0	4.9	5.2	5.1
T	Hi	86.8	86.9	86.9	79.4	75.8	77.4	47.4	43.6	45.2
	Av	70.4	72.1	71.4	67.3	64.3	65.6	37.7	34.8	36.1
	Lo	5.7	5.9	5.8	6.0	6.0	6.0	5.5	5.6	5.6

Table 5. Minutia Quality

Age		Device $\mathcal{D}_1$			Device $\mathcal{D}_2$			Device $\mathcal{D}_3$		
		F	M	T	F	M	T	F	M	T
18-25	Hi	57.7	60.3	59.1	57.0	57.3	57.2	32.6	35.3	34.1
	Av	47.8	48.4	48.1	52.2	53.0	52.7	27.7	29.6	28.8
	Lo	5.7	5.4	5.6	6.0	6.0	6.0	5.7	5.7	5.7
26-40	Hi	51.4	55.2	53.4	56.2	56.0	56.1	31.0	32.6	31.9
	Av	41.0	44.3	42.7	51.3	51.2	51.3	25.9	27.0	26.5
	Lo	5.4	5.6	5.5	6.0	6.0	6.0	5.6	5.6	5.6
41-60	Hi	45.6	49.6	47.9	53.6	54.6	54.1	28.6	30.8	29.8
	Av	35.5	38.5	37.2	48.5	49.8	49.2	23.3	25.3	24.4
	Lo	5.4	5.4	5.4	6.0	6.0	6.0	5.5	5.6	5.5
60+	Hi	37.9	41.6	40.3	50.6	50.5	50.5	24.3	27.0	26.1
	Av	28.8	32.0	30.9	44.5	45.2	44.9	18.9	21.3	20.5
	Lo	4.9	5.2	5.1	6.0	6.0	6.0	5.1	5.4	5.3
T	Hi	51.1	54.2	52.9	55.5	55.6	55.6	30.5	32.5	31.6
	Av	41.0	43.0	42.1	50.5	50.9	50.7	25.4	26.9	26.2
	Lo	5.5	5.5	5.5	6.0	6.0	6.0	5.6	5.6	5.6

for $\mathcal{D}_2$. While matching the fingerprints of two specific devices, it is found that the value of EER increases for higher age-group, $i.e.$ the performance of the AFRS decreases as the age of the users increases. In cross sensor setting when the fingerprints acquired through two different devices are matched, we have two observations. First, if the EER value of intra-device fingerprints matching of the two devices is comparable then the EER value of their inter-device AFRS increases. For example, consider an AFRS which matches a fingerprint acquired through $\mathcal{D}_1$ with another fingerprint of $\mathcal{D}_1$, it has EER of 9.0%. Again, EER for matching an image acquired through $\mathcal{D}_2$ with another image of $\mathcal{D}_2$ is 7.9%. Thus both EERs are comparable. Now if the fingerprints acquired on $\mathcal{D}_1$ are matched with those of $\mathcal{D}_2$, EER is 9.9% and when fingerprints acquired on $\mathcal{D}_2$ are matched with those of $\mathcal{D}_1$, EER is found to be 10.0%. In both of these cross sensor settings, performance of the AFRS decreases. Second, if EER of intra-device fingerprint matching of the two devices involved is not comparable, EER of inter device AFRS is decreases for the poorer device which signifies betterment of the system. For example, consider matchings of a fingerprint acquired on $\mathcal{D}_1$ with another on $\mathcal{D}_1$, it has EER as 9.02%, similarly when fingerprint acquired on $\mathcal{D}_3$ are matched with that of $\mathcal{D}_3$ it has EER as 22.73% both of them are not comparable as they have large difference. Now if fingerprint acquired on $\mathcal{D}_1$ are matched with that of $\mathcal{D}_3$ the value EER is 20.75% and when fingerprint acquired on $\mathcal{D}_1$ are matched with that of $\mathcal{D}_3$ the value EER is found to be 20.80%. In this cross sensor setting the performance of the AFRS increases for $\mathcal{D}_3$.

Table 7 presents CRR of AFRS when fingerprints of first phase are matched with those of second phase with the help of different fingerprint scanning devices. Higher the value of CRR better is the system. It can be observed that CRR of $\mathcal{D}_1$ and $\mathcal{D}_2$ is higher than that of $\mathcal{D}_3$. Also, the identification accuracy of $\mathcal{D}_2$ is slightly better than that of $\mathcal{D}_1$ at most of the places. CRR decreases for the higher age-group for any cross device setting. In cross sensor setting when the fingerprints acquired from two different devices are matched, we have two kind of observations. First, if the CRR value of intra device fingerprints matching of the two devices involved is comparable then the CRR value of their inter device AFRS decreases. For example consider an AFRS which matches a

Table 6. Equal Error Rate (%)

Age		Device D_1			Device D_2			Device D_3		
		F	M	T	F	M	T	F	M	T
18-25	D_1	4.5	4.4	4.6	4.9	5.6	5.2	16.5	14.8	15.4
	D_2	5.8	5.3	5.5	4.1	4.0	4.0	14.4	14.2	14.2
	D_3	15.0	14.5	15.7	14.1	13.9	13.9	18.6	18.6	17.5
25-40	D_1	7.7	8.2	7.3	8.4	9.8	8.4	20.5	17.2	18.6
	D_2	8.5	8.8	9.1	7.1	6.5	6.7	18.1	19.1	17.5
	D_3	20.8	20.0	20.3	18.8	21.9	19.1	20.8	19.9	20.9
41-60	D_1	15.5	8.2	11.9	16.6	12.3	13.9	27.1	23.1	24.6
	D_2	15.6	11.4	13.0	9.8	9.9	10.2	22.7	24.8	25.1
	D_3	24.4	22.7	21.9	21.1	21.2	21.9	24.9	24.3	25.7
60+	D_1	19.7	18.3	19.1	22.2	19.9	19.0	34.7	33.1	33.9
	D_2	19.8	20.4	20.7	12.0	14.5	14.2	35.9	31.5	32.8
	D_3	33.6	33.6	31.6	30.3	32.2	32.0	36.9	35.8	37.1
T	D_1	10.2	8.3	9.0	9.2	9.9	10.0	21.4	19.2	20.1
	D_2	10.5	9.6	9.9	7.0	8.1	7.9	18.6	20.7	20.8
	D_3	19.6	20.0	20.7	18.8	21.2	18.8	21.8	22.0	22.7

Table 7. Correct Recognition Rate (%)

Age		Device D_1			Device D_2			Device D_3		
		F	M	T	F	M	T	F	M	T
18-25	D_1	95.8	95.9	95.3	94.4	91.4	92.1	72.4	77.7	72.8
	D_2	92.9	93.6	93.0	94.8	94.0	93.8	78.2	78.6	76.8
	D_3	78.3	81.3	78.2	80.5	77.3	77.5	68.2	74.7	69.9
25-40	D_1	91.6	92.0	90.9	87.2	83.8	84.4	67.7	70.3	67.4
	D_2	90.7	88.7	88.3	89.5	89.0	88.9	72.7	66.5	68.0
	D_3	71.8	71.0	69.4	69.0	67.6	66.5	62.9	65.8	62.3
41-60	D_1	78.2	89.3	83.1	72.5	81.7	76.1	52.2	61.5	55.2
	D_2	77.5	84.9	80.6	82.3	86.6	83.0	58.7	62.0	58.9
	D_3	63.1	66.0	63.2	63.6	64.8	62.6	51.9	59.6	54.1
60+	D_1	72.3	73.8	69.3	63.9	67.5	64.1	37.8	52.4	45.0
	D_2	65.0	66.5	64.2	78.6	72.7	72.4	48.5	47.6	45.8
	D_3	47.1	44.3	43.5	51.7	50.5	48.8	39.3	40.7	38.5
T	D_1	87.0	89.2	87.4	82.3	82.2	81.2	59.8	65.1	61.1
	D_2	85.5	85.0	84.1	87.4	86.3	86.0	66.3	64.4	63.5
	D_3	66.9	68.1	66.0	67.2	65.4	64.6	56.3	61.7	57.4

fingerprint acquired on D_1 with another of D_1 it has CRR as 87.42%, similarly when fingerprint acquired on D_2 are matched with that of D_2 it has CRR as 86.00% both of them are comparable as they do not have much difference. Now if the fingerprint acquired on D_1 are matched with that of D_2 the value of CRR is found to be 84.11% and when fingerprint acquired on D_2 are matched with that of D_1 the value of EER is found to be 81.17%. In both of these cross sensor setting the identification performance of the AFRS decreases. Second, if the performance of intra device fingerprints of the two devices involved is not comparable. We have observed that the CRR value of inter device AFRS is boosted for the poorer device. For example, consider matchings of a fingerprint acquired on D_1 with another on D_1, it has CRR as 87.42%, and when fingerprint acquired on D_3 are matched with that of D_3 it has CRR as 57.39% both of them are not comparable as they have large difference. Now if fingerprint acquired on D_1 are matched with that of D_3 the value CRR is 61.12% and when fingerprint acquired on D_1 are matched with that of D_3 the value CRR is found to be 66.09%. In this cross sensor setting the performance of the AFRS increases as compared to D_3.

4   Conclusion

In this paper, we have used three fingerprint scanners to realize fingerprint image quality in the non-controlled field environment of the common people from villages. Fingerprint images have been collected from 1150 people of age 18-70 years in 2 phases. We have got images of thumb and point fingers of right hand using three scanning device. There is a time gap of 60 days between two phases so that difference between two fingerprint of each user can be studied. In each phase, we acquired multiple images using each device.

Fingerprint image quality is measured by considering *mindtct* quality score, number of minutiae points in the image and quality of minutiae points present in the image. It has been observed that on an average quality of fingerprint impression of female population is slightly better than the male population. A trend towards lower quality of fingerprint in higher age group has been observed. Quality of fingerprint of age-group 18-25 is found to better than older age-groups for any device. It may be a reason of introduction of spurious minutiae as supported by the observation of higher number of minutiae points reported by feature extractor in higher age groups. We have observed that on same set of users one device is producing highest quality images mostly where as fingerprint images of another device is classified mostly of average quality. This clearly indicates that the fingerprint scanning technique has a significant impact on the acquired fingerprint quality. Quality of fingerprint depends upon the kind of fingerprint scanner used. Maximum number of fingerprint images with quality 1 are produced by device $\mathcal{D}_2$ whereas for device $\mathcal{D}_3$, it has been observed that most of the images are of quality 3.

Performance of an AFRS is studied by carrying out ~428M comparisons. In our experiments we have observed that a small increase in the quality of the fingerprint by using different sensor does not favorably improve the performance of AFRS, instead it may decreases the system performance. Improvement in fingerprint quality using cross sensor setting only helps if the improvement is large. If the EER of intra-device fingerprints matching of the two distinct devices is comparable then the EER of their inter-device increases. Similar is the case with CRR.

References

1. NIST biometric image software, http://www.nist.gov/itl/iad/ig/nbis.cfm
2. Badrinath, G.S., Tiwari, K., Gupta, P.: An efficient palmprint based recognition system using 1D-DCT features. In: Huang, D.-S., Jiang, C., Bevilacqua, V., Figueroa, J.C. (eds.) ICIC 2012. LNCS, vol. 7389, pp. 594–601. Springer, Heidelberg (2012)
3. Cappelli, R., Ferrara, M., Maltoni, D.: Minutia cylinder-code: A new representation and matching technique for fingerprint recognition. IEEE Transactions on Pattern Analysis and Machine Intelligence 32(12), 2128–2141 (2010)
4. Chen, Y., Dass, S.C., Jain, A.K.: Fingerprint quality indices for predicting authentication performance. In: Kanade, T., Jain, A., Ratha, N.K. (eds.) AVBPA 2005. LNCS, vol. 3546, pp. 160–170. Springer, Heidelberg (2005)
5. Feng, J., Zhou, J., Jain, A.: Orientation field estimation for latent fingerprint enhancement. IEEE Transactions on Pattern Analysis and Machine Intelligence 35(4), 925–940 (2013)
6. Hong, L., Wan, Y., Jain, A.: Fingerprint image enhancement: algorithm and performance evaluation. IEEE Transactions on Pattern Analysis and Machine Intlgent. 20(8), 777–789 (1998)
7. Lanitis, A.: A survey of the effects of aging on biometric identity verification. Intrenational Journal of Biometrics 2(1), 34–52 (2010)
8. Modi, S.K., Elliott, S.J.: Impact of image quality on performance: Comparison of young and elderly fingerprints. In: Sirlantzis, K. (ed.) International Conference on Recent Advances in Soft Computing, pp. 449–454. IEEE (2006)
9. Singh, N., Tiwari, K., Nigam, A., Gupta, P.: Fusion of 4-slap fingerprint images with their qualities for human recognition. In: World Congress on Information and Communication Technologies, pp. 925–930. IEEE (2012)
10. Tiwari, K., Arya, D.K., Badrinath, G.S., Gupta, P.: Designing palmprint based recognition system using local structure tensor and force field transformation for human identification. Neurocomputing 116, 222–230 (2013)

11. Tiwari, K., Arya, D.K., Gupta, P.: Palmprint based recognition system using local structure tensor and force field transformation. In: Huang, D.-S., Gan, Y., Gupta, P., Gromiha, M.M. (eds.) ICIC 2011. LNCS, vol. 6839, pp. 602–607. Springer, Heidelberg (2012)
12. Tiwari, K., Gupta, P.: Biometrics based observer free transferable e-cash. In: ACM Workshop on Information Hiding and Multimedia Security, pp. 63–70. ACM (2014)
13. Tiwari, K., Gupta, P.: An efficient technique for automatic segmentation of fingerprint ROI from digital slap image. Neurocomputing (in press, 2014)
14. Tiwari, K., Gupta, P.: No-reference fingerprint image quality assessment. In: Huang, D.-S., Jo, K.-H., Wang, L. (eds.) ICIC 2014. LNCS, vol. 8589, pp. 846–854. Springer, Heidelberg (2014)
15. Tiwari, K., Mandal, J., Gupta, P.: Segmentation of slap fingerprint images. In: Huang, D.-S., Gupta, P., Wang, L., Gromiha, M. (eds.) ICIC 2013. CCIS, vol. 375, pp. 182–187. Springer, Heidelberg (2013)
16. Tiwari, K., Mandi, S., Gupta, P.: A heuristic technique for performance improvement of fingerprint based integrated biometric system. In: Huang, D.-S., Bevilacqua, V., Figueroa, J.C., Premaratne, P. (eds.) ICIC 2013. LNCS, vol. 7995, pp. 584–592. Springer, Heidelberg (2013)
17. Tiwari, K., Siddiqui, E.A., Gupta, P.: An efficient image database encryption algorithm. In: Huang, D.-S., Gupta, P., Zhang, X., Premaratne, P. (eds.) ICIC 2012. CCIS, vol. 304, pp. 400–407. Springer, Heidelberg (2012)

Fingerprint Match Based on Key Minutiae
and Optimal Statistical Registration

Yongliang Zhang[1], Shanshan Fang[1], Bing Zhou[1], Congmin Huang[2], and Yuanhong Li[1]

[1] College of Computer Science and Technology,
Zhejiang University of Technology, Hangzhou, China
[2] Hangzhou Jinglianwen Technology Co., Ltd, Hangzhou, China
titanzhang@zjut.edu.cn

Abstract. Fingerprint recognition technology as a promising high-tech has been widely applied in many fields. Fingerprint matching is one of the most important aspects. The biggest challenge is how to improve the recognition performance, when fingerprint images are with low quality and nonlinear deformation. An improved fingerprint match algorithm is proposed in this paper, which is based on key minutiae and optimal statistical registration. First, this algorithm not only combines the global matching with local matching, but also uses the optimal statistical idea to evaluate the best parameters of rotation and translation between two images. Second, this paper uses local greedy method to get the corresponding key minutia pairs. Experimental results show that the proposed algorithm can rival those advanced algorithms in the world.

Keywords: Fingerprint match, Key minutiae, Optimal statistical registration, Minutiae-based matching.

1   Introduction

Matching fingerprint images is a very difficult problem, mainly due to the large variability in different impressions of the same finger[1]. The main cause of falsely non-matched is a very small overlap, high elastic distortion and very different skin condition. Meanwhile, falsely matched is caused by quite similarities in terms of local minutia structures, local ridge orientation, etc. Fingerprint matching can be classified into three major classes: correlation-based matching[2][3], minutiae-based matching[4][5] and non-minutiae feature-based matching[6][7]. Minutiae-based matching, which can be viewed as a point pattern matching problem, is certainly the most well-known and most widely used method for fingerprint matching. The local minutiae structure has invariance in translation and rotation and therefore is suitable for matching without a priori global alignment. In our earlier studies, the minutiae matching based on the octantal nearest-neighborhood structures (ONNS) was developed, which weighed up the low computational complexity and high distortion tolerance[8]. Over the last few years, this algorithm has been applied to practical automated fingerprint verification system[9]. In order to further reduce the false match rate (FMR), an improved algorithm is proposed in this paper, which is based on key minutiae and optimal statistical registration.

Z. Sun et al. (Eds.): CCBR 2014, LNCS 8833, pp. 208–215, 2014.

In the following sections, we will describe in detail our improved fingerprint match algorithm. Section 2 addresses the main steps of our improved algorithm. Experimental results are described in Section 3. Section 4 is the conclusion.

2   Fingerprint Match

As shown in Fig.1, the proposed algorithm mainly includes the following steps: ONNS construction, local matching, optimal statistical registration, global matching, and similarity calculation.

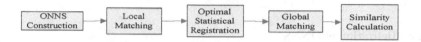

Fig. 1. The flow chart of the proposed algorithm

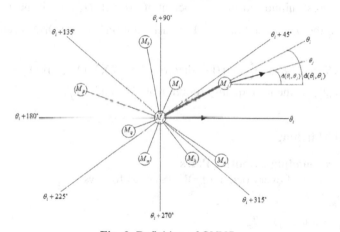

Fig. 2. Definition of ONNS

2.1   ONNS Construction

2.1.1   Rotation and Translation Invariants

Let $\Gamma^S = \{M_i = (X_i, Y_i, \theta_i, Q_i)\}_{i=1}^{N_S}$ be the minuti,set of,e sample image F_S, where , θ_i and Q are the location, the direction and quality of M_i, respectively. Likewise, let $\Gamma^T = \{M'_p = (X'_p, Y'_p, \theta'_p, Q'_p)\}_{p=1}^{N_T}$ be the minutiae,t of t,template image F_T, where , θ'_p and Q'_p are the location, the direction and quality of M'_p, respectively. The rotation and translation invariants are defined as follows:

1) Distance between two different minutiae and M_j:

$$D_{ij} = \sqrt{(X_i - X_j)^2 + (Y_i - Y_j)^2} \ . \tag{1}$$

2) The angle difference $d(\theta_i, \theta_j)$ of two different minutiae:

$$d(\theta_i, \theta_j) = \begin{cases} \theta_i - \theta_j, & if \theta_i - \theta_j \geq 0 \\ 360 + (\theta_i - \theta_j), & else \end{cases} . \tag{2}$$

3) The angle difference $d(\theta_i, \theta_l)$ of the given minutiae and the line between two minutiae, where θ_l is the angle of the directed blue line $\overrightarrow{M_i M_j}$, as shown in Fig.2.

2.1.2   Definition of ONNS

As shown in Fig.2, M_i as the center and θ_i as the x-axis, the image is divided into octants by counterclockwise, and every octant has 45 degrees; then the nearest minutia in each octant is selected, if the minutia exists. That's to say, $O_{ik} = j$ means that M_j is the nearest minutia in the kth octant of M_i; if $O_{ik} = 0$, it means there isn't any minutia in the kth octant of M_i. For each minutia M_i, its ONNS can be defined as follows:

$$ONNS_i = \{ONNS_{ik}\}_{k=1}^8 = \{(D_{ij}, d(\theta_i, \theta_j), d(\theta_i, \theta_l), \Upsilon(Q_i, Q_j)), O_{ik} = j\}_{k=1}^8 \ . \tag{3}$$

where $\Upsilon(Q_i, Q_j)$ is the joint quality function of M_i and M_j.

2.2   Local Matching

2.2.1   Corresponding Minutiae Pairs

The matching rules of every octant of ONNS are as follows:

1) $|D_{ij} - D'_{pq}| < T_D$,

2) $|d(\theta_i, \theta_j) - d(\theta'_p, \theta'_q)| < T_\theta$,

3) $|d(\theta_i, \theta_l) - d(\theta'_p, \theta'_l)| < T_\theta$,

where T_D and T_θ are two thresholds, θ'_l is the angle of the directed line $\overrightarrow{M'_p M'_q}$, D'_{pq} is the distance between the minutia M'_p and M'_q of F_T, M_j and M'_q both are the kth nearest minutiae of M_i and M'_p respectively. The similarity of two $ONNS_{ik}$ and $ONNS_{pk}$ is calculated:

$$S_{ip}^k = (1 - \frac{|D_{ij} - D'_{pq}|}{T_D}) \times (1 - \frac{d(d(\theta_i, \theta_j), d(\theta'_p, \theta'_q))}{T_\theta}) \times (1 - \frac{d(d(\theta_i, \theta_l), d(\theta'_p, \theta'_l))}{T_\theta}) \tag{4}$$

The similarity S_{ip} between the $ONNS_i$ of M_i and the $ONNS'_p$ of M'_p is calculated:

$$S_{ip} = \frac{\Upsilon(Q_i, Q_p')}{\lambda_{ip}} \times \sum_{k=1}^{8} S_{ip}^k \tag{5}$$

where λ_{ip} is the number of matched octants, that's to say, $O_{ik} > 0$ and $O_{pk} > 0$. If $S_{ip} > T_S$, M_i and M_p' are the corresponding minutiae pair, where T_S is a given threshold. Let $\Psi = \{ <i, p >| S_{ip} > T_S \}$ be the corresponding minutiae pairs, and $L = |\Psi|$ is the number of the corresponding minutiae pairs.

2.2.2   Local Greedy Criterion

For the given minutia M_i of F_S, more than one minutia of F_T may be its corresponding minutiae. In fact, M_i only has at the most one corresponding minutia. Here, the local greedy criterion is applied to remove these one-to-many corresponding minutiae pairs:

1) Order corresponding minutia pairs with the descending of similarity:

$$\Psi' - \{ S_{i_1 p_1}', S_{i_2 p_2}', \cdots, S_{i_L p_L}' \}, \tag{6}$$

where $S_{i_u p_u} \geq S_{i_{u+1} p_{u+1}}$ and $<i_u, p_u> \in \Psi$ and $<i_{u+1}, p_{u+1}> \in \Psi$.

2) $H^S = \{i_1\}$, $H^T = \{p_1\}$, $H^M = \{\langle i_1, p_1 \rangle\}$

3) For each corresponding minutia pair $<i_u, p_u> \in \Psi'$ in ascending order of u, if $i_u \notin H^S$ and $p_u \notin H^T$, then H^S, H^T and H^M are updated as follows:

$$H^S = H^S \cup \{i_u\}, \quad H^T = H^T \cup \{p_u\}, \quad H^M = H^M \cup \{\langle i_u, p_u \rangle\}.$$

Obviously, $H^M \subseteq \Psi$ and one-to-many or many-to-one corresponding minutia pair no longer exists in H^M.

2.3   Optimal Statistical Registration

2.3.1   Definition of Key Minutiae

M_i is considered as a key minutia, if the following conditions are satisfied:

1) $Q_i > T_Q$, i.e. the key minutia can't be a poor quality minutia;

2) $i \in H^S$, i.e. the key minutia has the corresponding minutia;

3) $S_{ip} > T_{max}$, $\langle i, p \rangle \in H^M$, i.e. the similarity between the key minutia and its corresponding minutia should be bigger than the given threshold;

By definition, H^M, H^S and H^T are updated:

$$H^M = \{\langle i, p \rangle | \langle i, p \rangle \in H^M \wedge Q_i > T_Q \wedge Q_p' > T_Q \wedge S_{ip} > T_{max}\} . \tag{7}$$

$$H^S = \{i | \langle i, p \rangle \in H^M\} . \tag{8}$$

$$H^T = \left\{ p \mid \langle i, p \rangle \in H^M \right\} . \tag{9}$$

Where Λ is the logical AND operator.

2.3.2   Statistical Registration

The translation parameter $(\Delta x, \Delta y)$ and the rotation parameter $\Delta \theta$ between F_S and F_T can be estimated as follows:

1) Let (x_i, y_i) be the location of the key minutia M_i of F_S, (x_p', y_q') is the corresponding key minutia M_p' of F_T, and $L = |H^M|$ is the number of the corresponding key minutia pairs. The mass center (x_0, y_0) of F_S and (x_0', y_0') of F_T can be estimated:

$$\begin{bmatrix} x_0 \\ y_0 \end{bmatrix} = \frac{1}{L} \begin{bmatrix} \sum\limits_{i \in H^S} x_i \\ \sum\limits_{i \in H^S} y_i \end{bmatrix}, \quad \begin{bmatrix} x_0' \\ y_0' \end{bmatrix} = \frac{1}{L} \begin{bmatrix} \sum\limits_{p \in H^T} x_p' \\ \sum\limits_{p \in H^T} y_p' \end{bmatrix} . \tag{10}$$

2) $(\Delta x, \Delta y)$ is evaluated:

$$\begin{bmatrix} \Delta x \\ \Delta y \end{bmatrix} = \begin{bmatrix} x_0' - x_0 \\ y_0' - y_0 \end{bmatrix} . \tag{11}$$

3) $\Delta \theta$ is estimated:

$$\Delta \theta = \arg\max_{\vartheta} \sum_{d(\vartheta, d(\theta_i, \theta_p')) \leq \zeta, <i, p> \in H^M} (\zeta + 1 - d(\vartheta, d(\theta_i, \theta_p'))) S_{ip} . \tag{12}$$

where ζ is a given threshold.

2.4   Global Matching

According to the above evaluated optimal parameters in the statistical sense, each key minutia $M_i = (X_i, Y_i, \theta_i, Q_i)$ of F_S is translated and rotated to get the registered minutia $M_i^R = (X_i^R, Y_i^R, \theta_i^R, Q_i^R)$:

$$\begin{bmatrix} x_i^R \\ y_i^R \end{bmatrix} = \begin{bmatrix} \cos(\Delta\theta) & \sin(\Delta\theta) \\ -\sin(\Delta\theta) & \cos(\Delta\theta) \end{bmatrix} \begin{bmatrix} x_i - x_0 \\ y_i - y_0 \end{bmatrix} + \begin{bmatrix} x_i + \Delta x \\ y_i + \Delta y \end{bmatrix} . \tag{13}$$

$$\theta_i^R = \theta_i + \Delta\theta, \quad Q_i^R = Q_i . \tag{14}$$

If $|x_i^R - x_p'| > T_D$ or $|y_i^R - y_p'| > T_D$ or $d(\theta_i^R, \theta_p') > T_\theta$, then $<i, p>$ can't be considered as the corresponding key minutiae pair and H^M is updated:

$$H^M = \left\{ <i, p> \mid |x_i^R - x_p'| \leq T_D, |y_i^R - y_p'| \leq T_D, d(\theta_i^R, \theta_p') \leq T_\theta, <i, p> \in H^M \right\} . \tag{15}$$

2.5   Similarity Calculation

The final similarity Sim between F_S and F_T can be calculated:

$$Sim = \sum_{<i,p> \in H^M} S_{ip}, \qquad (16)$$

If $Sim \leq T_{sim}$, then $Sim = 0$, where T_{sim} is a given threshold.

3   Experimental Results

FVC (Fingerprint Verification Competition) is a common benchmark, allowing companies and academic institutions to unambiguously compare performance and track improvements in their fingerprint recognition algorithms[1]. Three databases were created using different state-of-the-art sensors and a fourth database was artificially generated. Our proposed algorithm was tested on this common benchmark, and the test results are as follows, where EER (Equal Error Rate) is an important indicator to denote the error at the threshold for which both FMR and false non-match rate (FNMR) are identical; The rank of our proposed algorithm is between that of Algo-1 and Algo-2, where EER-1 and EER-2 are the EER of Algo-1 and Algo-2, and Rank-1 and Rank-2 are the rank of Algo-1 and Algo-2, respectively. For example, Algo-1 is SAG2 and Algo-2 is CETP for FVC2000 DB1-A; Algo-1 is PA08 and Algo-2 is PA45 for FVC2002 DB1-A. As shown in Table.1, the value of each parameter used in this paper is set according to the experience. As shown in Table.2 to Table.6, the performance of our proposed algorithm can rival those advanced algorithms in the world.

Table 1. The value of those parameters in this paper

The parameter	T_D	T_θ	T_S	T_Q	T_{max}	ζ	T_{sim}
The value	16	12	0.5	0.5	0.8	3	5

Table 2. The tested results on FVC2000

	EER	Algo-1	Rank-1	EER-1	Algo-2	Rank-2	EER-2
DB1_A	0.0146	Sag2	2	0.0117	Cetp	3	0.0506
DB2_A	0.0100	Sag2	2	0.0082	Cspn	3	0.0275
DB3_A	0.0513	Sag2	2	0.0401	Cspn	3	0.0536
DB4_A	0.0362	Sag2	2	0.0311	Cspn	3	0.0504
Average	0.0280	Sag2	2	0.0228	Cspn	3	0.0519

Table 3. The tested results on FVC2002

	EER	Algo-1	Rank-1	EER-1	Algo-2	Rank-2	EER-2
DB1_A	0.0117	PA08	8	0.0098	PA45	9	0.0117
DB2_A	0.0068	PA08	4	0.0052	PB05	5	0.0069
DB3_A	0.0359	PA45	10	0.0348	PA13	11	0.0399
DB4_A	0.0225	PA26	11	0.0199	PA45	12	0.0303
Average	0.0192	PB35	9	0.0142	PA13	10	0.0218

Table 4. The tested results on FVC2004

	EER	Algo-1	Rank-1	EER-1	Algo-2	Rank-2	EER-2
DB1_A	0.0552	P071	8	0.0437	P026	9	0.0554
DB2_A	0.0443	P016	11	0.0439	P048	12	0.0467
DB3_A	0.0401	P067	14	0.0386	P049	15	0.0403
DB4_A	0.0347	P026	19	0.0338	P120	20	0.0353
Average	0.0436	P103	13	0.0433	P048	14	0.0441

Table 5. The tested results on FVC2006

	EER	Algo-1	Rank-1	EER-1	Algo-2	Rank-2	EER-2
DB1_A	0.1397	P124	25	0.13817	P095	26	0.14929
DB2_A	0.0038	P090	14	0.00374	P024	15	0.00474
DB3_A	0.0452	P124	18	0.03991	P060	19	0.04778
DB4_A	0.0257	P053	19	0.02393	P022	20	0.02868
Average	0.0536	P060	19	0.04839	P124	20	0.05514

Table 6. The tested results on FVC ongoing

	EER	Algo-1/rank	EER-1	Algo-2/rank	EER-2
STD	0.0085	Qianbang Yang/15	0.00841	MuhammadAli Jinnah, University/16	0.0086
HARD	0.0284	APRO TECHNOLOGY CO., LTD./12	0.02552	Robert Vaz an/13	0.0368

4   Conclusion

An improved fingerprint match algorithm is proposed in this paper, which is based on key minutiae and optimal statistical registration. A consolidation stage (global matching) is applied to verify the ONNS-based local minutiae matching hold at global level. Through thus improvement, false match rate (FMR) can be further reduced caused by fewer error corresponding minutiae pairs and higher distinctiveness. Experimental results show that the proposed algorithm can rival those advanced algorithms in the world.

Acknowledgments. This work is supported by the Science Technology Department of Zhejiang Province (2012C24009).

References

1. Maltoni, D., Maio, D., Jain, A.K., Prabhakar, S.: Handbook of Fingerprint Recognition, 2nd edn. Springer (2009)
2. Bazen, A.M., Verwasijen, G.T.B., Gerez, S.H., et al.: A Correlation-based Fingerprint Verification System. In: Proc. Workshops on Circuits, Systems, Signal Processing (ProRISC 2000), pp. 205–213 (2000)

3. Lindoso, A., Entrena, L., Liu-Jimenez, J., San Millan, E.: Correlation-Based Fingerprint Matching with Orientation Field Alignment. In: Lee, S.-W., Li, S.Z. (eds.) ICB 2007. LNCS, vol. 4642, pp. 713–721. Springer, Heidelberg (2007)
4. Deng, H., Huo, Q.: Minutiae Matching Based Fingerprint Verification Using Delaunay Triangulation and Aligned-Edge-Guided Triangle Matching. In: Kanade, T., Jain, A., Ratha, N.K. (eds.) AVBPA 2005. LNCS, vol. 3546, pp. 270–278. Springer, Heidelberg (2005)
5. Chen, J.S., Moon, Y.S.: A Statistical Evaluation Model for Minutiae-Based Automatic Fingerprint Verification Systems. In: Zhang, D., Jain, A.K. (eds.) ICB 2005. LNCS, vol. 3832, pp. 236–243. Springer, Heidelberg (2005)
6. Ross, A., Jain, A.K., Reisman, J.: A hybrid fingerprint matcher. Pattern Recognition 36(7), 1661–1673 (2003)
7. Jain, A.K., Prabhakar, S., Hong, L., Pankanti, S.: Filterbank-based fingerprint matching. IEEE Transactions on Image Processing 9, 846–859 (2000)
8. Zhang, Y.: Algorithm Study on Swipe Fingerprint Mosaicking and Fingerprint Matching. Shanghai Jiaotong University (2006)
9. Hangzhou Jinglianwen Technology Co., Ltd., http://www.jinglianwen.com

One-Class SVM with Negative Examples for Fingerprint Liveness Detection

Xiaofei Jia, Yali Zang, Ning Zhang, Xin Yang, and Jie Tian[*]

Institute of Automation, Chinese Academy of Sciences, Beijing 100190, China
{jiaxiaofei,zangyali,zhangning}@fingerpass.net.cn,
xin.yang@ia.ac.cn,tian@ieee.org

Abstract. The study of the artificial fingerprint detection has lasted for a decade. With full prior knowledge of the spoof attack, researchers extract discriminative features and apply some two-class classifiers to detect the spoof. However, we don't know the materials of fake fingerprints used by the attackers in the real world. It means that the traditional evaluation is not scientific. In this paper, we proposed to measure the security of fake fingerprint detection systems by the inter-operability performance across various materials. Fake fingerprints made of various materials have diverse feature distributions. The traditional binary SVM over-fits the training negative data. We proposed a novel model named one-class SVM with negative examples (OCSNE) to solve the problem. In order to simulate the real environment, we modified the structure of the Liveness Detection Competition 2011 (LivDet2011) database accordingly. The experimental results on the LivDet2011 modified database showed OCSNE outperforms the traditional SVM.

Keywords: Fake fingerprint detection, Inter-operability performance, One-class svm.

1   Introduction

The study of the artificial fingerprint detection has lasted for a decade. Academics have extracted a great many of discriminative features only from fingerprint images to detect the fingerprint liveness [1] [2] [3]. Among these algorithms, the first type of multi-scale local binary pattern (MSLBP1) is one of algorithms which have impressive performance and low calculation complex. In this way, we extracted MSLBP1 in our countermeasures.

There is a place where most people typically slip up in research. The materials of spoof fingerprints are the same for training and testing in the current fake fingerprint detection research. With full prior knowledge of fake fingerprints, people extract discriminative features and optimize two-class classifiers to detect artificial fingerprints. In fact, the materials and techniques of the spoof fingerprints used by the attackers are unpredictable. Thus the traditional measurement is not scientific. We suppose the

---

[*] Corresponding author.

Z. Sun et al. (Eds.): CCBR 2014, LNCS 8833, pp. 216–224, 2014.
© Springer International Publishing Switzerland 2014

inter-operability performance across different materials of artificial fingerprints is more persuasive and scientific to measure the security of fake fingerprint detection system. It means that spoof fingerprints are made of different materials in the training and testing parts. We are trying to distinguish the artificial fingerprints made of any materials, even the unknown materials, from the live.

To the best of our knowledge, spoofing fingerprints made of various materials may have different feature distributions. As the distributions feature of spoof fingerprints in training and testing may be different, negative data in our training can be considered to be incompletely sampled. The traditional binary SVM requires adequate samples in the training parts so as to satisfy the same distribution with the testing data. Otherwise, it over-fits the training data, enduring poor performance. The over-fitting is caused by the following reasons. The "missing" negative data may lie in the learned margin. If so, the positive instances should be closer to the "ideal" boundary. What's worse, the negative instances in training may give bad cues about the orientation of the hyperplane.

In order to reduce the over-fitting, we introduced one-class SVM theory to detect spoof fingerprints. Scholkopf et al. [4] suggested the SVM methodology to train the classifier using only positive data. It is called "one-class" SVM. Scholkopf's model treats the origin as the negative data unseen and separates the origin from the positive with the maximum margin. D.M.J. Tax et al. [5] [6] developed another type of one-class SVM called support vector domain description (SVDD). It uses balls with "soft margin" to describe the data in feature space. It has been proved that SVDD and one-class SVM are equal in certain situations [4] [6] . In [6] , D.M.J. Tax added some negative examples to tighten the boundary of SVDD. Since one-class SVM provides a way to describe the positive data and decreases the phenomenon of over-fitting, we extended Scholkopf's one-class SVM with negative examples (OCSNE) to improve the inter-operability performance. The negative data in training is just applied to make the description of positive data tighter. The origin is used to adjust the orientation of the hyperplane. In this way, OCSNE reduces over-fitting on fake fingerprints. In addition, there is a serious drawback in Scholkopf's model and D.M.J. Tax's theory which restricts their wide application. However, our model solves it by adding a constraint.

In order to simulate the real environment and test the performance of various countermeasures, we modified the structure of the Liveness Detection Competition 2011 (LivDet2011) database [7] accordingly. We chose the fake fingerprints made of a specific type of material to train and used the fake fingerprints made of other types of materials to attack. The experimental results showed OCSNE outperforms traditional binary SVM and two types of one-class SVM.

In a word, our contribution consists of the following points. I) We propose an innovative evaluation on the security of artificial fingerprint detection system which is inter-operability performance across different materials. II) As far as we know, it is the first time to introduce one-class theory to detect fake fingerprints. III) OCSNE model based on one-class theory is proposed to improve the inter-operability performance. OCSNE model reduces over-fitting on negative data in training and makes the boundary more accurate than traditional binary SVM.

The rest of the paper is organized as follows. Section 2 explains inter-operability performance across different materials. Section 3 describes one-class SVM with negative examples. The experimental results are shown in section 4. Section 5 concludes this paper.

2   Inter-operability Across Different Materials

The printing area is by 122 mm × 193 mm. The text should be justified to occupy the full line width so that the right margin is not ragged, with words hyphenated as appropriate. Please fill pages so that the length of the text is no less than 180 mm, if possible.

As discussed before, we extracted MSLBP1 in our countermeasure. MSLBP1 distributions of fake fingerprints made of diverse materials in some LivDet2011 training datasets are shown in Figure 1. From Figure 1, we can see both the type of sensor and the materials to produce the artificial fingerprints influencing the distributions deeply. There is a big gap for most of spoof fingerprint feature distributions. In a word, we can't ignore the influence of various materials to make the fake fingerprints.

In the real world, the exact nature of spoof attacks is never known in advance, thus the traditional evaluation which applies spoof fingerprints made of the same materials to train and to test, is not scientific enough to evaluate the security of fake fingerprint detection. We proposed inter-operability across different materials to evaluate the performance of resisting the fake fingerprint attack. The inter-operability across materials means we use a specific material of fake fingerprints during training, and other materials of fake fingerprints during evaluation. Compared with current measurement, it can test whether the artificial fingerprint detection methods over-fit the fake fingerprints used in training. At the same time, it is easy to make some spoof fingerprints, although these fake fingerprints may be generated by different materials from the testing ones used by the attackers. We try to enhance the security of our system by rationally using these negative examples in training. Thus, our simulation environment is in line with reality. Inter-operability across different materials is a scientific and reasonable evaluation to measure security of fake fingerprints detection system.

The principle of the traditional two-class classifier in machine learning is to estimate the probability distribution of the data or to compute a discriminative function to distinguish the data. The main drawback of this approach is that it requires enough samples in the training part satisfied the same probability distribution with the testing data. If not, it over-fits the data seen in training and thus lacks of generalization [7]. As for the fingerprint liveness detection, if we obtain robust features from enough of the live fingerprints, we can describe the feature distribution of the live fingerprints. But our fingerprint liveness detection system faces the challenge of fake fingerprints producing by some unknown materials. We cannot guarantee all the fake fingerprints in training and testing made of various materials satisfy the same probability in distribution. In this way, the spoof fingerprints in training can be considered to be incompletely sampled. Thus when considering of the inter-operability across various materials, we do not think the traditional two-class classifier as the optimal choice.

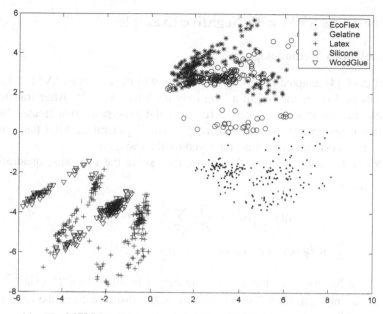

(a)   The MSLBP1 distribution in LivDet 2011 Italdata train spoof dataset

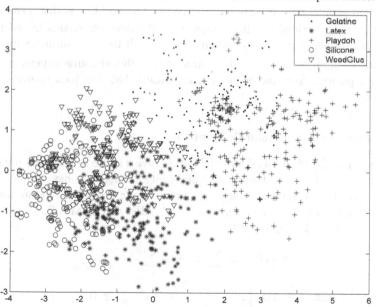

(b)   The MSLBP1 distribution in LivDet 2011 Italdata train spoof dataset

Fig. 1. The feature distribution of artificial fingerprints made of various materials

3   One-Class SVM with Negative Example

3.1   Scholkopf's Methodology

Scholkopf et al. [4] adapted the SVM methodology to the one-class SVM. It just uses positive data and treats the origin as the only negative example. After transforming the data into feature space via a kernel function, the hyperplane that creates the maximum distance between the origin and the positive is generated. After that, the standard two-class decision function is employed for the test data.

To separate the data set from the origin, they solve the following quadratic program:

$$\min \frac{1}{2} \|\omega\|^2 + \frac{1}{v^* l} \sum_{i \in l^+} \xi_i - \rho$$
$$\text{subject to } \omega^T \cdot \phi(x_i) \geq \rho - \xi_i, \xi_i \geq 0$$

(1)

Here, v is a hyper-parameter. l is the number of positive data. The slack variable ξ_i is penalized in each objective function. ρ is the distance from the origin to the hyperplane.

There is a serious flaw in Scholkopf's theory. The problem is that ω maybe is a zero vector in the optimal solution, even when the data are separable and the lack variables are infinitely penalized. When ω, ρ and all the lack variables are zero in the optimal solution, it meets all the constraints. If this situation occurs, we cannot separate the positive from the negative successfully. The drawback restricts its wide applications.

3.2   Support Vector Domain Description

D.M.J. Tax et al. [5] [6] defined a model which gave a circle to describes the positive data, which could be proved equal to Scholkopf's model in some certain situation. When the RBF kernel function is applied or all data are normalized to unit norm vectors, the linear kernel function is selected [5] [6]. After that, D.M.J. Tax applied negative data to tight the description [6].

$$\min R^2 + c_+ \sum_{i \in l^+} \xi_i + c_- \sum_{j \in l^-} \xi_j$$
$$\text{subject to } \|x_i - c\|^2 \leq R^2 + \xi_i, \xi_i \geq 0$$
$$\|x_j - c\|^2 \geq R^2 - \xi_j, \xi_j \geq 0$$

(2)

Here, x_i and x_j belong to the positive data and negative data separately. When we apply the RBF function or all data are normalized to unit norm vectors, the linear function is selected, and the results of k(x,x) for each x are constant. If so, c maybe zero in the optimal solution and result in the data being indistinguishable.

3.3 Outlier Methodology

We solve the defect by adding the positive t in the constraint and proposed the one-class SVM with negative example (OCSNE) model. The optimization equations are changed into the following way:

$$\min \frac{1}{2}\|\omega\|^2 + c_+ \sum_{i \in I^+} \xi_i + c_- \sum_{j \in I^-} \xi_j - c\rho \tag{3}$$

$$\text{subject to } \omega^T \cdot \phi(x_i) \geq \rho - \xi_i, \xi_i \geq 0$$

$$\omega^T \cdot \phi(x_j) \leq \rho - t + \xi_j, \xi_j \geq 0, t > 0$$

c_+, c_- and t are all hyper-parameters which are larger than zero. The decision boundary is close to the positive data in training, while the function distances from negative examples in training to the decision boundary are larger than t. In the OCSNE model, if the data are separable and ω is a zero vector, it breaks the constraint in the programming (3).

By adding t, our model actually has some similarity with binary SVM. But our model derives from the one-class SVM. It has two big differences with traditional SVM. At first, our boundary is closer to the positive data. In this way, if unseen nega-tive data in training lie in the margin, the accuracy rate is not much affected. Compared with the traditional binary classifiers, the spoof fingerprints are just used to tighten the boundary without excessive over-fitting. Secondly, we also penalize the function distance from the origin to the boundary. The origin is treated as the unseen negative data to correct the orientation. Parameter c_+, c_- and c give the tradeoff among the errors of data and the distance from the hyperplane to the origin. In our experiment, c_+, c_- and t are set to be 1.

4   Experiment

The database we used is the database of the Liveness Detection Competition 2011 [7]. 4000 images are acquired by each of the following sensor: (i) Biometrika FX2000, (ii) Digital persona 4000B, (iii) ItalData ET10 and (iv) Sagem MSO300. Half of them are live fingerprint images and the others are spoofs. The training part is 50% of the whole data. The spoof fingerprints are made of ecoflex (platinum-catalyzed silicone), gelatine, latex, silicone and wood glue for Biometrika, ItaData, gelatine, latex, Play-Doh, silicone, wood glue for Digital Persona and Sagem. There are 400 spoof finger-print images made for each of the five materials in each dataset. As the inter-operability performance is more persuasive and scientific to reflect the capabili-ty of protecting the systems against the attackers, we reconstructed the LivDet2011 database accordingly. For each sub-dataset, we chose the fake fingerprints made of a specific type of material to train and used the fake fingerprints made of other types of materials to attack. As the number of spoof fingerprints in training is too small, we doubled it by adding the fake fingerprints made of the same materials in the LivDet 2011 testing parts to our training parts. Thus there were 400 spoof fingerprint images in training. We had five tests in each sub-datasets. Eac test took artificial fingerprints made of different types of materials to train. The spoof fingerprints generated by the other types of materials were applied to attack. So there were 1000 live fingerprints and 400 spoof fingerprints made of a specific type of materials to train and 1000 live fingerprints and 800 spoof fingerprints made of other types of materials to test. The average performance of five tests was taken as the evaluation in each sub-datasets.

In our experiment, we extracted MSLBP1 as features in our countermeasures. The scale of MSLBP1 was set to 5, which is the same with [2]. Four classifiers were compared in our experiments, including Scholkopf' one-class SVM [4], SVDD with negative examples [6], traditional binary SVM, OSNCE.

The performance of the proposed method is estimated by Average Classification Error (ACE) [7] and the Area under receiver operating characteristic (ROC) (AUC). ACE is defined as ACE=(FLR+FFR)/2, where the FLR (False Living Rate) represents the percentage of fake fingerprints misclassified as real, and the FFR (False Fake Rate) represents the percentage of live fingerprints misclassified as fake. To draw an ROC curve, only the true positive rate (TPR) and false positive rate (FPR) are needed. The TPR defines the number of correct positive results occuring among all positive samples available during testing. FPR, on the other hand, defines how many incorrect positive results occur among all negative samples available during testing. AUC is the area under the ROC.

The results of each countermeasure are shown in table 1 and table 2. Figure 2 are the ROC curves for each dataset. From the above tables and figures, we observed that:

Table 1. The ACE of MSLBP1 in (%)

	Scholkopf's SVM	SVDD	binary SVM	OSNCE
Biometrika	46.3	50.1	16.9	9.8
Digital	51.9	35.8	46.1	36.6
Italdata	47.9	51.6	27.1	23.5
Sagem	52.4	25.4	33.7	24.4
mean	49.6	40.7	30.9	23.6

Table 2. The AUC of MSLBP1 in (%)

	Scholkopf's SVM	SVDD	binary SVM	OSNCE
Biometrika	59.2	54.2	95.9	96.8
Digital	41.9	69.1	64.2	66.4
Italdata	58.0	47.1	84.2	84.8
Sagem	36.9	83.9	82.4	83.9
mean	49.0	63.6	81.7	83.0

I)   Scholkopf's SVM is the only model which does not use any fake fingerprint information. Compared with other models, it gets much worse performance. It reflects the importance of fake fingerprints existing in training. Although we don't know the materials and techniques used by attackers, we should make some spoof fingerprints and use them rationally to enhance the performance of fake fingerprint detection system.

II) OSNCE provides the best results on three sub-datasets out of four, and very close to the best on the other one sub-dataset. Therefore it is also the best on the average. Compared with traditional binary SVM, the negative data in OSNCE model are just applied to make the boundary more accurate. In this way, they reduce the reliance on negative data. Beside these, the origin is applied to correct the orientation of hyperplane to some extent.

III) Although compared with traditional SVM, OSNCE has a significant performance improvement, their results are not ideal enough. We should introduce more robust classifiers to detect fake fingerprints in the next research.

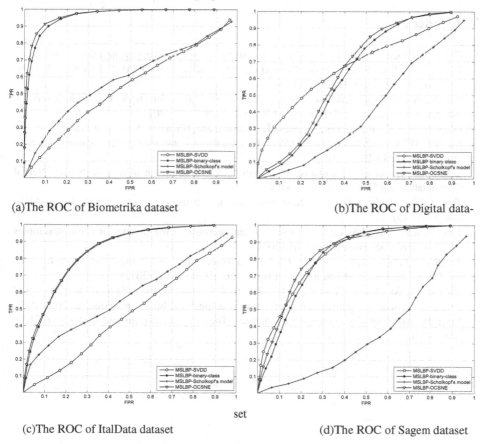

(a)The ROC of Biometrika dataset   (b)The ROC of Digital data-

                                                      set
(c)The ROC of ItalData dataset   (d)The ROC of Sagem dataset

Fig. 2. The ROC of each dataset

5   Conclusion

In this paper, we raised a serious issue. The traditional security evaluation measurement of fake fingerprints detection is not scientific, as we don't know in advance the materials and techniques used by attackers. We proposed a novel and more reasonable measurement which is the inter-operability performance across different materials to make fake fingerprints. The traditional SVM over-fits the negative data in training, enduring poor inter-operability performance. We introduced a novel method named the one-class SVM with negative examples (OCSNE). It makes a description of positive data and negative data are just applied to make the boundary tighter. In this way, we reduce the reliance on the negative data. In addition, OCSNE also treats the origin as the negative data unseen to correct the orientation of the boundary. Experimental results on LivDet2011 modified database showed that they outperform binary SVM and two types of one-class SVM.

References

1. Ghiani, L., Denti, P., Marcialis, G.L.: Experimental results on fingerprint liveness detection. In: Perales, F.J., Fisher, R.B., Moeslund, T.B. (eds.) AMDO 2012. LNCS, vol. 7378, pp. 210–218. Springer, Heidelberg (2012)
2. Jia, X., et al.: Multi-scale local binary pattern with filters for spoof fingerprint detection. Information Sciences: an International Journal 268, 91–102 (2014)
3. Ghiani, L., et al.: Fingerprint Liveness Detection using Binarized Statistical Image Features. In: 2013 IEEE Sixth International Conference on Biometrics: Theory, Applications and Systems (BTAS). IEEE (2013)
4. Schölkopf, B., et al.: Estimating the support of a high-dimensional distribution. Neural Computation 13(7), 1443–1471 (2001)
5. Tax, D.M.J., Duin, R.P.W.: Data domain description using support vectors. In: ESANN, vol. 99 (1999)
6. Tax, D.M.J.: One-class classification; Concept-learning in the absence of counterexamples ASCI dissertation series number 65 (2001)
7. Yambay, D., et al.: LivDet 2011—Fingerprint liveness detection competition 2011. In: 2012 5th IAPR International Conference on Biometrics (ICB). IEEE (2012)
8. Alegre, F., Amehraye, A., Evans, N.: A one-class classification approach to generalised speaker verification spoofing countermeasures using local binary patterns. In: 2013 IEEE Sixth International Conference on Biometrics: Theory, Applications and Systems (BTAS). IEEE (2013)

A New Approach to Palmprint Mainline Restoration Based on Gaussian Distribution

Bing Kang, Fu Liu, and Lei Gao

College of communications Engineering, Jilin University, Changchun 130022, China
liufu@jlu.edu.cn

Abstract. In order to solve the problem of discontinuous palmprint mainline, this paper presents a novel algorithm which can make the discontinuous mainline continuous. The algorithm consists of four steps: energy expansion based on the Gaussian function, calculation of texture probability distribution, acquisition of texture pixel values based on the exponential function and determination of the iteration. Compared with traditional methods, the distinct advantage of the algorithm is the palmprint mainline restoration with directional properties. Therefore, wrong palmprint mainline restoration could be reduced effectively. The results illustrate that the proposed algorithm is feasible and valid.

Keywords: Palmprint, Mainline restoration, Automatic iterative process.

1   Introduction

There are usually three palmprint mainlines in human palm, namely heartline, headline and lifeline. During recent years, Wang YK found the relationship between the abnormal changes of mainlines and the tumor combined with clinical observation. Characteristics of palmprint mainlines may provide a new reference for the early diagnosis of tumors [1].Hence, the way to extract the characteristics of mainlines accurately is very important. But for now, palmprint image acquisition instrument is not yet mature. The palmprint images often contain some noise, making some areas of the palm of the mainline lines not obvious. Therefore, the extraction in such palmprint images is often intermittent and incomplete.

There are many existing palmprint mainlines extraction methods [2-8]. Although these algorithms have achieved some results of mainlines extraction, for some uneven illumination and relatively shallow mainline, mainlines extraction is still intermittent. The traditional way to solve such problems is the morphological expansion and thinning and the expansion basing on the template [9], which can cause the wrong mainline connection or the disability to connect over a long distance. The repair algorithm in [10] can get the repaired mainlines. But, it is complex and the points of interest will affect the accuracy of the robust regression due to the process noise. The mainline restoration algorithm mentioned in [11], uses the known intermittent main line and searches from the center point bi-directionally on the gray image. It can repair the main line, but it still has two limitations: ①the shallow mainlines still can't be repaired;②there will be some glitch after mainline is repaired.

Z. Sun et al. (Eds.): CCBR 2014, LNCS 8833, pp. 225–233, 2014.

In order to solve previous problems, this paper presents a new Gaussian model, which is able to repair intermittent palm mainline. And the experiments verified the proposed method can repair the intermittent palm mainline effectively.

2   ROI of Palmprint Preprocessing

For the three palmprint mainline lines extraction, the first step is to select region of interest (ROI). The current paper selects the method in [12]. ROI region is shown in Figure 1(b).

There are many methods for palmprint mainline extraction now. This paper uses grey value feature extraction algorithm in [13] for the crude extraction of palmprint mainline. The mainline rough extraction is shown in Fig.1(c). The palmprint mainline after processing basing on literature [13] is shown in Figure 1(d).

The mainline in Fig.1(d) was not continuous. There are lots of burrs on it. According to method in [14], the burrs were removed as shown in Fig.2(a).

3   The Principle of the Algorithm

3.1   Image Connected Domain Separation

Assuming that S is an image of palmprint mainline, as shown in Figure 3(a).

Since energy of each image is a single connected domain, it is necessary to separate the connected domain of S, as shown from Fig.3 (b)-3(l). $S_i (i = 1, 2, \ldots N)$ are the separation of the sub images. N is the number of connected domain.

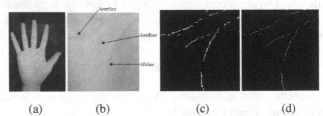

(a)   (b)   (c)   (d)

(a) original image   (b) ROI   (c) The mainline crude extract   (d) morphological processing

Fig. 1. Selection and process of ROI

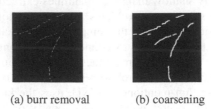

(a) burr removal   (b) coarsening

Fig. 2. Pretreatment of ROI

3.2   Connected Regional Energy Expansion

Assuming S_i' are points in gray image, $X_i(y,x) \in S_i'$. A straight line is made across the point $X_i(y,x)$ with the angle of α. In order to make the energy in all direction expansion, we choose $\alpha \in \{n * \pi / 12 \mid n = 0.....11\}$.

$C_{i_\alpha}(y,x)$ is the set of points on the line with angle α. $C_{i_\alpha}'(y,x)$ is the set of the points on the line that the gray value is 0 (the set of all the black points on the line).So $C_{i_\alpha}'(y,x)$ belongs to $C_{i\alpha}(y,x)$, but not to S_i'.

$P_{i_\alpha}'(y,x)$ is the set of points on the line that the gray value is 256(that is the set of all the white points on the line). It belongs to the intersection of $C_{i\alpha}(y,x)$ and S_i'.

$X_{i_\alpha}'(y,x)(n)$ belongs to $C_{i_\alpha}'(y,x)$. $X_{i_\alpha}'(y,x)(n) \in C_{i_\alpha}'(y,x)$. n represents the order of points, which belongs to $C_{i_\alpha}'(y,x)$. $n = 1$ and $n = 2$ represent the closest and second closest distance between the points on plane S_i and $X_i(y,x)$.

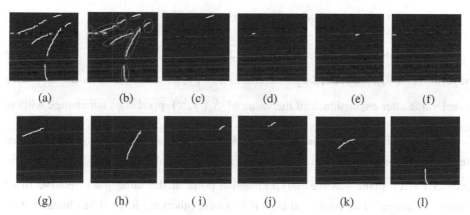

(a) separate images (b) Schematic diagram of separation (c) sub image S1 (d) sub image S2 (e) sub image S3 (f) sub image S4 (g) sub image S5 (h) sub image S6 (i) sub image S7 (j) sub image S8 (k) sub image S9 (l) sub image S10

Fig. 3. Connected domain separate

$n = -1$ and $n = -2$ represents the points on the negative plane with the closest and second closest distance to $X_i(y,x)$. In Fig.4, the line passes the point $X_3(217,218)$ with the angle of $\pi/4$ in the sub image S_3'. $C_{i_\alpha}'(y,x)$ is the set of gray pixel points, $P_{i_\alpha}'(y,x)$ is the set of yellow and green pixel points.

In this paper, three steps are designed for each element expansion processing in $P_{i_\alpha}'(y,x)$:

(1) Select the Gauss function $f(x)$ as the energy expansion standard.

$$f(x) = \frac{1}{\sqrt{2\pi}\sigma} e^{-\frac{(x-\mu)^2}{2\sigma^2}}$$

$$(1)$$

After repeated experiments, the optimal parameters are $\mu=0$, $\sigma=2$.

(2) Then use formula (4) to conduct expansion process for S_i.

$$X_{i_\alpha}'(y,x)(n) = \begin{cases} f(\ln/N|+0.5) & -2N \leq n \leq 2N \\ 0 & else \end{cases}$$

$$(2)$$

Where N is the number of elements in $P_{i_\alpha}'(y,x)$.

(3) Make $X_{i_\alpha}'(y,x)(n)$ linear mapping to [0, 255].

$$X_{i_\alpha}'(y,x)(n) = X_{i_\alpha}'(y,x)(n) \times 255 / f(0)$$

$$(3)$$

However, for each point expanded in 12 directions, $S_i(y,x)$ may correspond to several $X_{i_\alpha}'(y,x)(n)$. The largest value in $X_{i_\alpha}'(y,x)(n)$ is taken as the $S_i(y,x)$ pixel value after expansion, and the value of $S_i(y,x)$ pixel does not change without expansion.

In order to avoid the connected region's influencing and the subsequent generated texture probability distribution, each sub image S_i should be judged by whether for any $S_i(y,x)$ pixel was the only expansion point at the same place relative to all other sub images. The value will be 0 if it is true, otherwise it won't be changed. This decision's principle is from formula (4):

$$S_i(y,x) = \begin{cases} 0 & S_j(y,x)=0 \ (j=1,\ldots,N, j \neq i) \\ S_i(y,x) & else \end{cases}$$

$$(4)$$

3.3   The Probability Distribution of the Texture and Regression of Pixels

In order to obtain the mainline probability distribution of the image, the probability distribution S_i' of black points in each sub image need to be calculated.

Then the joint probability distribution of the black point S'' would be calculated. N was the number of sub images in Formula (8).

$$S_i'(y,x) = 1 - S_i(y,x)/255 \tag{5}$$

$$S''(y,x) = \prod_{i=1}^{N} S_i'(y,x) \tag{6}$$

Finally, the probability distribution of white points in the image is calculated according to equation (7).

$$P(y,x) = 1 - S''(y,x) \tag{7}$$

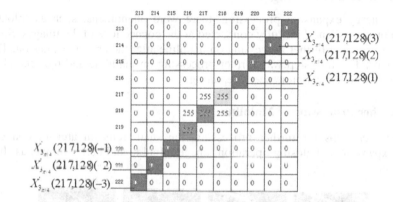

Fig. 4. Set diagram

The probability of inter-connected domain connection area is large and probability distribution is relatively dense. In order to increase the difference between the pixels, the exponential function chooses to make it between 0 and 255, so P' pixel becomes gray scale images for level 256 according to the exponential function.

$$P'(y,x) = 255^{P(y,x)} \tag{8}$$

After binarization on P', the higher value pixel points is mainline. The lower value pixel points are black background. After many times experiments, intermittent mainline was connected best in formula (9) when $T = 220$.

$$Q(i,j) = \begin{cases} P'(y,x) & 220 \le P'(y,x) \\ 0 & else \end{cases} \tag{9}$$

Fig. 5. Result of Experiment

After processing Figure 3 (e) with the mentioned algorithm, the experiment results were shown in Figure 5. Since the algorithm was similar to the process of the energy expansion, it was also called energy expansion algorithm.

4   Further Processing

After the energy expansion processing, there were phenomena, such as 'bloated', 'slim', 'more burrs' and 'not fully connected at the connections of the images. So it is necessary to conduct further processing on mainline after the energy expansion. There are two steps. The first step was further processing on mainline and the second step was to judge whether mainline needs repairing.

4.1   Further Processing of Mainline

There are four steps for further processing, the small removal area of connected regions, expansion and closing operation, image thinning and burr removal, as shown in Figure 6.

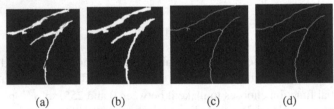

(a)   (b)   (c)   (d)

(a) A small area removal (b) Expansion and closing operation (c) Thinning (d) Burr removal

Fig. 6. The main line further processing

4.2   Repairing Mainline

Count the number of connected region. If it is equal to the number of connected region in actual image, it ends and keeps iteration. Otherwise, Steps are as follows:

1. Energy expansion algorithm;
2. Further processing on mainline;
3. Judging whether the number of connected region was N. If it is, end the iteration and go to step (1) if not;

Generally $N = 2$ is enough for the most situation.

5   The Experiment Results

In order to prove the performance of method in this paper, the same hand image was done for the experiment. The compared results are shown in Fig.7. Fig.7(a) is repaired palmprint mainline. Fig.7(b) and (c) are both morphological thinning algorithm results. Fig.7(b) is the result of minimum expansion for the most far intermittent thread connection. Figure 7 (c) is the largest expansion without the missing repair. Method in [9] could not solve the problem of the far intermittent thread connection, which is solved by this paper, as shown in Fig.7(f).

Under the condition of natural light, 50 pieces of palmprint images were acquired. The experiment results were shown in Table 1.

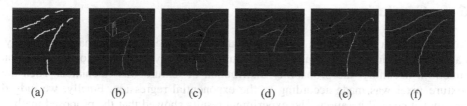

| (a) | (b) | (c) | (d) | (e) | (f) |

(a) the mainline repair   (b) Morphological algorithm 1   (c) Morphological algorithm 2 (d) The literature [9] algorithm   (e) The literature [11] algorithm   (f) The proposed algorithm

Fig. 7. Comparison of various algorithm

Table 1. Experimental results

Total	No need to repair	One times expansion can repair	Two times expansion can repair	Beyond repair
50	4	28	10	8

After the experimental analysis, the mainline repair usually requires energy expansion algorithm only once or twice. For the large intermittent distance of palmprint mainline, energy expansion algorithm could not achieve the repair effect for several times iteration because the intermittent distance exceed the maximum range which each energy expansion algorithm could reach. The one-time energy expansion algorithm could repair the mainline. The result was shown in figure 8. Two times energy expansion algorithm could repair the mainline. The result was shown in figure 9.

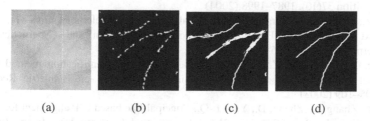

| (a) | (b) | (c) | (d) |

(a)RIO (b) The mainline coarse extraction (c) One times repair (d) Image post processing

Fig. 8. The mainline repaired once

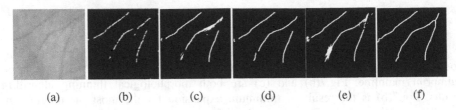

(a)   (b)   (c)   (d)   (e)   (f)

(a)RIO (b) The mainline coarse extract (c) One times repair (d) The mainline post processing(e) Two times repair   (f) The mainline post processing

Fig. 9. The mainline repaired twice

6   Conclusion

In this paper, a new method was proposed to repair the palmprint mainline. Firstly, each of the connected domains was expand by energy according to the Gaussion function. Secondly, the probability distribution of texture was calculated. Then the texture pixel was made according to the exponential regression. Finally, we judged whether it needed iteration. The experiment results showed that the proposed method could repair the intermittent palmprint mainline effectively.

References

1. Wang, Y.K.: Dermatoglyphics and Clinic, pp. 3–4. World Publishing Co. Ltd., Beijing (1999)
2. Yuan, W.-Q., Lin, S., Tong, H.-B.: A Detection Method of Palmprint Principal Lines Based on Local Minimum Gray Value and Line Following. In: The International Conference on Hand-Based Biometrics, pp. 1–5 (2011)
3. Zhang, D.-P., Shu, W.: Two novel characteristics in plamprint verification. Pattern Recognition 32(4), 691–702 (1999)
4. Zheng, P., Sang, N.: Using Phase and Directional Line Features for Efficient Palmprint Authentication. In: The 2nd International Congress on Image and Signal Processing, pp. 1–5 (2009)
5. Han, C.-C., Cheng, H.-L., Lin, C.-L., Fan, K.-C.: Personal authentication using palm-print features. Pattern Recognition 36(2), 371–381 (2003)
6. Wu, X.-Q., Zhang, D., Wang, K.-Q.: Palmprint classification using principal lines. Pattern Recognition 37(10), 1987–1998 (2004)
7. Lei, Z., Zhang, D.: Characterization of palmprints by wavelet signatures via directional context modeling. IEEE Transactions on Systems Man and Cybernetics Part B (Cybernetics) 34(3), 1335–1347 (2004)
8. Wang, T., Li, W.-X., Zhao, W.-N.: A new palmprint identification method based on wavelet transformation. In: The 4th Chinese Conference on Biometric Recognition, pp. 105–109 (2003)
9. Li, W., Zhang, L., Zhang, D., Yan, J.-Q.: Principal line based ICP alignment for palmprint verification. In: The 2009 16th IEEE International Conference on Image Processing, pp. 1961–1964 (2009)

10. Huang, S., Xu, C.-Q., Jing, H.: Principle Line Extraction and Restoration Based on Wavelet Theory. Journal of Image and Graphics 11(8), 1139–1148 (2008)
11. Yuan, W.-Q., Dong, Q., Sang, H.-F.: Hand shape contour tracking method based on directional gradient extremum. Optics and Precision Engineering 18(7), 1675–1683 (2010)
12. Li, W.-X., You, J., Zhang, D.: Texture-based palmprint retrieval using a layered search scheme for personal identification. IEEE Transactions on Multimedia 7(5), 891–898 (2005)
13. Li, W.-X., Xia, S.-X., Zhang, D.-P.: A New Palmprint Identification Method Using Bi-Directional Matching Based on Major Line Features. Journal of Computer Research and Development 41(6), 996–1002 (2004)
14. Ning, Y.-H., Lei, X.-Q., Wang, G.-X.: Improved template-based method of burr removal. Journal of Computer Applications 31(1), 58–64 (2011)

A Survey of Finger Vein Recognition

Lu Yang, Gongping Yang, Yilong Yin*, and Lizhen Zhou

School of Computer Science and Technology, Shandong University,
Jinan, 250101, P.R. China
yangluhi@163.com, gpyang@sdu.edu.cn,
ylyin@sdu.edu.cn, hizlz@126.com

Abstract. As a new biometric technique, finger vein recognition has attracted lots of attentions and efforts from researchers, and achieved some progress in recent years. A survey of progress in finger vein recognition is given in this paper. It mainly focuses on three aspects, i.e., the general introduction of finger vein recognition, a review of the existing research work on image acquisition and feature extraction methods. We finally present the key problems and future directions in order to enlighten finger vein recognition research domain.

Keywords: Biometrics, finger vein recognition, survey, future directions.

1 Introduction

Finger vein recognition is a personal physiological characteristics-based biometric technique, and it uses vein patterns in human finger to perform identity authentication. Near-infrared light (wavelengths between 700 and 1,000 nanometers) is usually used to capture finger vein image [1, 2]. The principle is that, near-infrared light can be absorbed intensively by the hemoglobin in the blood of vein, but transmits other tissues of finger easily, therefore vein pattern in finger will be captured as shadows.

As a biometric characteristic, finger vein has several desirable properties, such as universality, distinctiveness, permanence and acceptability. In addition to, compared with other biometric characteristics (for example, face, gait, fingerprint and so on), it has other distinct advantages in the following two points [1]: (1) Living body identification. It means that only vein in living finger can be captured, and further used to perform identification. (2) Internal characteristic. It is hard to copy or forge finger vein, and very little external factor can damage finger vein, which guarantee the high security of finger vein recognition. These two advantages make finger vein an irreplaceable biometric characteristic, and attract more and more attentions from research teams. A typical finger vein identification system mainly includes image acquisition, preprocessing, feature extraction and matching, as shown in Fig.1.

Kono et al [3], Japanese medical researchers, proposed finger vein based identity identification, and gave an effective feature extraction method. Yanagawa et al [4]

---

* Corresponding author.

Z. Sun et al. (Eds.): CCBR 2014, LNCS 8833, pp. 234–243, 2014.

proved the diversity of human finger vein patterns and the usefulness of finger veins for identity identification on 2, 024 fingers of 506 persons. They show that, two finger vein patterns are identical if and only if they are from the same finger in the same hand of the same person. These two literatures are the foundation of finger vein recognition, which open the era of finger vein recognition. In the early days of finger vein recognition, there are two significant literatures, which are all from Miura et al. The first one [1] is about a feature extracted method, named repeated line tracking. Line tracking starts at various positions, and moves along the direction of vein pattern pixel by pixel. In the second literature, in order to overcome the influence of vein patterns' various widths and brightness, maximum curvature [5] was developed to extract the centerlines of vein.

Fig. 1. Typical finger vein identification system

By the development of the past decade, finger vein recognition ushers in the evolution period now. The most representative literature is Ref. 6, in which authors used Gabor to extract finger vein patterns, and fuse finger vein and finger texture. Beside, Yang et al [7] proposed to use the width of phalangeal joint as a soft biometric trait to enhance the recognition accuracy for finger vein. Although, there are some valuable works in finger vein recognition, lots of key problems are unsolved, for example, the acquisition of high quality image, the high recognition rate, the large scale applications.

In this paper, first we comprehensively review main techniques of finger vein recognition, which include image acquisition devices, existing public databases and some typical feature extraction and matching methods. And then, the unsolved key problems and potential development directions in finger vein recognition are analyzed. Last, we conclude this paper.

2   Image Acquisition and Public Databases

In this section, we mainly describe image acquisition and public finger vein databases. In detail, two ways of image acquisition, one typical device and its acquired images are given firstly. Next, the existing public databases are shown, the comparison between different databases, about the number of images, the size of image and so on, are presented.

There are two ways of finger vein image acquisition, i.e., light reflection method and light transmission method [2], as shown in Fig.2. The main difference between two methods is the position of near-infrared light. In detail, in light reflection method, near-infrared light is placed in finger palmar side, and finger vein pattern is captured by the reflected light from finger palmar surface. Conversely, near-infrared light is placed in finger dorsal side in light transmission method, and the light will penetrate finger. Compared with light reflection method, light transmission method can capture high-contrast image, so most of image acquisition devices employ light transmission method [1, 5, 6, 8, 9, 10].

A typical device of light transmission method [8] is introduced. The schematic cross-section of device, practical imaging device and the captured images are shown in Fig.3. The near-infrared light is on the top plate, and finger will be placed in the groove of the device below the top plate.

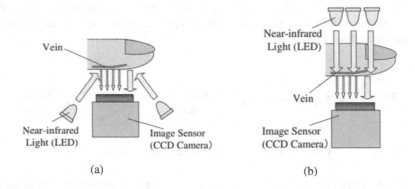

Fig. 2. Two ways of finger vein image acquisition [2]:
(a). Light reflection; (b). Light transmission.

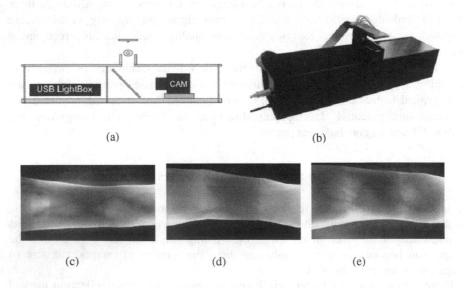

Fig. 3. A typical image acquisition device and the captured images [8]: (a). The schematic cross-section of device; (b). The practical imaging device; (c, d, e). The captured images by (b).

There are multiple public finger vein databases, and five typical databases are introduced in the Table 1. The first one was built by Shandong University, named SDUMLA-FV database, and it was a part of a homologous multimodal database [11]. Another finger vein database was published by Ajay and Zhou [6], and it also was a part of a homologous multimodal database. We call it HKPU-FV database in the following. The third database was from University of Twente, abbreviated UTFV database. Recently, two finger vein databases were published, which were from Tsinghua University [12] and Chonbuk Nation University [13] respectively. The previous database is a part of a homologous multimodal database, and we call it THU-FV database in this paper. The other one is named MMCBNU_6000 database. In Table 1, light transmission-based image acquisition advice was used on all three databases. And for three databases, the number of subject/finger is limited. Besides, images from different databases have different sizes, different contrast, different backgrounds, and different quality.

Table 1. The comparison between typical public finger vein databases.

Database	Acquisition way	Subject number	Finger number per subject	Image number per finger	Image size (pixels)	Typical image
SDUMLA-FV[11]	light transmission	106	6	6	320×240	
HKPU-FV[6]	light transmission	156	2	12/6*	513×256	
UTFV[8]	light transmission	60	6	4	672×380	
THU-FV[12]	light transmission	610	1	2	200×100	
MMCBNU_6000[13]	light transmission	100	6	10	640×480	

* Only 105 subjects turned up for the imaging during the second session, so each of fingers from these subjects has 6 images, but other fingers each has 12 images.

3   Feature Extraction and Matching

Feature extraction is one key process in finger vein recognition. In this section, some feature extraction methods and corresponding matching methods are listed. These feature extraction methods can be classified into three groups, i.e., vein pattern-based methods, dimensionality reduction-based methods and local binary-based methods. Methods in each group and their corresponding matching methods are introduced in the following.

3.1   Vein Pattern-based Methods

There are six typical vein pattern-based feature extraction methods, including repeated line tracking [1], maximum curvature [5], Gabor [6], mean curvature [14], region growth [15], and modified repeated line tracking [16].This group of method is the mainstream in finger vein extraction. In these methods, the vein patterns are segmented firstly, and then the geometric shape or topological structure of vein pattern is used for matching.

Repeated line tracking, maximum curvature, region growth and modified repeated line tracking all use the cross-section of image to extract vein pattern. This is due to the fact that the cross-section of vein pattern looks like a valley, and these methods make use of this point to demerge vein pattern from images, but the special methods of recognizing vein pixel are different. However, mean curvature views the intensity surface of finger vein image as a geometric object, and pixels with negative mean curvature will be seen as vein pattern. Different from the above methods, which extract vein pattern in spatial domain, Gabor transforms image into frequency domain to extract vein pattern.

The vein patterns, extracted by this kind of methods, are binary, so the matched pixel ratio is general used in matching. The matched pixel ratio means the ratio of the number of the matching vein pixels to the total number of the vein pixels in the two vein patterns. As image acquisition is non-contact, finger displacement, i.e., finger rotation and translation, make genuine matching score small. Therefore, in matching, the best match among the pixel-by-pixel translations and rotation with certain degree of testing image are adopted.

3.2   Dimensionality Reduction-based Methods

Subspace learning methods usually transform image into low-dimensional space to classify. In transformation, they keep discriminating information and remove noises. In finger vein recognition, PCA [17], LDA [18], $(2D)^2$PCA [19], and manifold learning [20]have been used. These methods need the training process to learn a transformation matrix. When there are new enrolled users, the transformation matrix need to learn again. So this kind of methods may be not very practical. Classifiers are used in matching for these methods. For example, neural network technique is used in Ref. 17 and 18, and Ref. 19 used k nearest neighbor.

3.3   Local Binary-based Methods

Methods in last group are based on local area, and the extracted features are in binary formation. The local binary pattern (LBP) [9, 23], the local line binary pattern (LLBP) [21], the personalized best bit maps (PBBM) [10], personalized weight maps (PWM) [29] and the local directional code (LDC) [22] are all in this group. In LBP and

LLBP, the local binary code is obtained by compare the gray level of the current pixel and its neighbors. PPBM and PWM further explore the stability of the binary codes, and use the stable binary codes in matching. Different from the four methods, LDC codes the local gradient orientation information. For most of these methods, hamming distance (HD) was used to measure the similarity between the enrolled and input binary vein features.

3.4　Performance and Discussions

In this section, we make a summary and comparison for all methods about the size of used databases, the equal error rate (EER) or recognition rate (RR), and processing time, shown in Table 2.From the table, we can see that some methods, for example, maximum curvature [5] and PBBM [10], report promising performance. At the same, there are two problems: (1)The size of databases are general limited, so it cannot be predict how the performance will be on a large scale database; (2)The processing time is long, although they can be used in real time applications. Beside, as vein patterns

Table 2. Summary and comparison of finger vein recognition methods

Group	Method	Database	EER/RR	Time
vein pattern-based methods	repeated line tracking [1]	678 fingers × 2 images	EER= 0.145%	450ms
	maximum curvature[5]	678 fingers × 2 images	EER= 0.0009%	N/A
	Gabor [6]	312 fingers × 6 or 12 images*	EER=0.65%	N/A
	mean curvature [14]	320 fingers ×5 images	EER=0.25%	118ms
	region growth [15]	125 fingers × 9 images	EER= 0.0369%	210 ms
	modified repeated line tracking [16]	200 images	N/A	N/A
dimensionality reduction-based methods	PCA [17]	10 fingers × 10 images	RR=99%	45 s
	LDA [18]	10 fingers × 10 images	RR=98%	0.0156 s
	(2D)^{2}PCA [19]	80 fingers × 18 images	RR=99.17%	N/A
	manifold learning [20]	328 fingers × 70 images	RR=97.8% EER=0.8%	N/A
local binary-based methods	(LBP) [9]	240 fingers × 10 images	EER=0.21%	44.7 ms
	(LLBP) [21]	204 fingers × 10 images	EER= 3.845%	67.1ms
	(PBBM) [10]	106 fingers × 14 images	EER=0.38%	439.9 ms
	(PWM)[31]	136 fingers ×20 images	EER=0.41%	455.7 ms
	(LDC) [22]	136 fingers × 30 images	EER=1.02%	28 ms

* The first 210 fingers each has 6 images, but the remainder 102fingers each has 12 images.

are the main discriminating information used in finger vein recognition, so in our opinion vein pattern-based methods are the mainstream. Other methods in the second and third groups employ whole image to perform recognition, but it is questionable whether there are the discriminating information in background area of image, i.e., non-finger vein area. In addition, in large scale applications, dimensionality reduction-based methods may be not a good choice, as transformation matrix learning will be a big problem with lots of users.

4   Key Problems and Future Directions

Although some advancements have been made, there are still some problems in finger vein recognition. The first problem is the distinctiveness of finger vein pattern. Yanagawa et al [4] proved the diversity of human finger vein patterns on 2, 024 fingers of 506 persons, but medical evidence is not enough. So, in large scale applications, we cannot confidently predict how the recognition rate will be and if the classification result is reliable. And it also concerns if finger vein can be used in judiciary like fingerprint and face. Besides, the medical evidence about the stability of finger vein is not enough, either. In practical applications, the corresponding problem is the effectiveness of the enrolled finger vein template. In other word, it means if it is necessary to replace the enrolled template every 5 or 10 years. And if the surrounding environment and diseases can affect the finger vein pattern is uncertain.

The second problem is about image acquisition. The price of finger vein acquisition device is still high now, which is one factor that limits the application of finger vein recognition. In public databases, there are some common issues about image quality, for example, low contrast, image blurring, excessive brightness, excessive dark and stains. So, there is a space for the performance improvement of image acquisition device. Dai et al [29] used nonuniform intensity infrared light to capture finger vein image, and the quality of captured image has been improved at certain extent. In total, the device with low price and high performance will vastly promote the development of finger vein recognition.

The third problem is finger displacement during image acquisition. Finger displacement can be divided into 2 dimensional posture changes, i.e. shift along x-axis, y-axis and z-axis, and 3 dimensional posture changes, i.e., rotation around x-axis, y-axis, z-axis [24, 25].Compared with 2 dimensional posture changes, it is harder to handle 3 dimensional posture changes. Transformation models, which were based on binary finger vein pattern [24] and minutia points [25], were used to finger alignment. And some works align displaced fingers in preprocessing [26, 27, 28], but these methods mainly focus on overcoming 2 dimensional posture changes. It may be easier to handle this problem from device, for example, adding a groove to fix finger.

The last one is lack of large scale practical application. Hitachi LTD. has researched finger vein recognition since 1997, and applied finger vein recognition into many domains, for example, ATM automatic teller machine and car lock. The inland industrial communities, which research product of finger vein recognition, start late, and the scale of application is relatively small.

There are many remains to be done on finger vein recognition to further improve its performance, and promote its practical application. Two main remaining problems are discussed here. The first is about large scale applications. A large scale public finger vein database is needed to build, which can be used to evaluate the existing and new methods in laboratory environment. And finger vein image classification and indexing are also very meaningful for large scale applications. The second is liveness detection. Finger vein lies in the inside of finger, but liveness detection is still an urgent work for the application of finger vein recognition. Nguyen et al [30] used fourier and wavelet transforms to detect fake finger vein image. Although it performs preliminary study, there are some shortcomings.

5   Conclusions

In this paper, we review the recent development of finger vein recognition, and give some representative works in this field. In particular, we focus on the technique employed in image acquisition and feature extraction. Besides, we present some key problems of finger vein recognition, and analysis its potential development directions.

Acknowledgments. This work is supported by National Natural Science Foundation of China under Grant No. 61173069, 61472226 and Shandong Natural Science Funds for Distinguished Young Scholar under Grant No. JQ201316.

References

1. Miura, N., Nagasaka, A.: Feature extraction of finger-vein pattern based on repeated line tracking and its application to personal identification. Machine Vision and Applications 15(4), 194–203 (2004)
2. Hashimoto, J.: Finger vein authentication technology and its future. In: Proceedings of the VLSI Symposium on Circuits, Honolulu, HI, pp. 5–8 (2006)
3. Kono, M., Ueki, H., Umemura, S.: A new method for the identification of individuals by using of vein pattern matching of a finger. In: Proceedings of the 5th Symposium on Pattern Measurement, Yamaguchi, Japan, pp. 9–12 (2000)
4. Yanagawa, T., Aoki, S., Ohyama, T.: Human finger vein images are diverse and its patterns are useful for personal identification. MHF Preprint Series, Kyushu University, pp. 1–7 (2007)
5. Miura, N., Nagasaka, A., Miyatake, T.: Extraction of finger-vein patterns using maximum curvature points in image profiles. IEICE Transactions on Information and Systems E90-D(8), 1185–1194 (2007)
6. Kumar, A., Zhou, Y.B.: Human identification using finger images. IEEE Transactions on Image Process 21(4), 2228–2244 (2012)
7. Yang, L., Yang, G.P., Yin, Y.L., Xi, X.M.: Exploring soft biometric trait with finger vein recognition. Neurocomputing 135, 218–228 (2014)
8. Ton, B.T., Raymond, N.V.: A high quality finger vascular pattern dataset collected using a custom designed capturing device. In: Proceedings of International Conference on Biometrics, Madrid, Spain, pp. 1–5 (2013)

9. Lee, E.C., Jung, H., Kim, D.: New finger biometric method using near infrared imaging. Sensors 11(3), 2319–2333 (2011)
10. Yang, G.P., Xi, X.M., Yin, Y.L.: Finger vein recognition based on a personalized best bit map. Sensors 12(2), 1738–1757 (2012)
11. Yin, Y.L., Liu, L.L., Sun, X.W.: SDUMLA-HMT: a multimodal biometric database. In: Sun, Z., Lai, J., Chen, X., Tan, T. (eds.) CCBR 2011. LNCS, vol. 7098, pp. 260–268. Springer, Heidelberg (2011)
12. Yang, W.M., Huang, X.L., Zhou, F., Liao, Q.M.: Comparative competitive coding for personal identification by using finger vein and finger dorsal texture fusion. Information Sciences 268(6), 20–32 (2013)
13. Lu, Y., Xie, S.J., Yoon, S., Wang, Z., Park, D.S.: An Available Database for the Research of Finger Vein Recognition. In: Proceedings of International Congress on Image and Signal Processing, Hangzhou, China, pp. 386–392 (2013)
14. Song, W., Kim, T., Kim, H.C., Choi, J.H., Kong, H.J., Lee, S.R.: A finger-vein verification system using mean curvature. Pattern Recognition Letter 32(11), 1541–1547 (2011)
15. Qin, H.F., Yu, C.B., Qin, L.: Region growth–based feature extraction method for finger-vein recognition. Optical Engineering 50(5), 057208–057208 (2011)
16. Liu, T., Xie, J.B., Yan, W., Li, P.Q., Lu, H.Z.: An algorithm for finger-vein segmentation based on modified repeated line tracking. The Imaging Science Journal 61(6), 491–502 (2013)
17. Wu, J.D., Liu, C.T.: Finger-vein pattern identification using principal component analysis and the neural network technique. Expert Systems with Applications 38(5), 5423–5427 (2011)
18. Wu, J.D., Liu, C.T.: Finger-vein pattern identification using SVM and neural network technique. Expert Systems with Applications 38(11), 14284–14289 (2011)
19. Yang, G.P., Xi, X.M., Yin, Y.L.: Finger vein recognition based on $(2D)^2$PCA and metric learning. Journal of BioMedicine and Biotechnology 2012, 1–9 (2012)
20. Liu, Z., Yin, Y.L., Wang, H., Song, S., Li, Q.: Finger vein recognition with manifold learning. Journal of Network and Computer Applications 33(3), 275–282 (2010)
21. Rosdi, B.A., Shing, C.W., Suandi, S.A.: Finger vein recognition using local line binary pattern. Sensors 11(12), 11357–11371 (2011)
22. Meng, X.J., Yang, G.P., Yin, Y.L., Xiao, R.Y.: Finger vein recognition based on local directional code. Sensors 12(11), 14937–14952 (2012)
23. Lee, H.C., Kang, B.J., Lee, E.C., Park, K.R.: Finger vein recognition using weighted local binary pattern code based on a support vector machine. Journal of Zhejiang University Science C 11(7), 514–524 (2010)
24. Huang, B.N., Liu, S.L., Li, W.X.: A finger posture change correction method for finger-vein recognition. In: Proceedings of Symposium on Computational Intelligence for Security and Defence Applications, Ottawa, Canada, pp. 1–7 (2012)
25. Lee, E.C., Lee, H.C., Park, K.R.: Finger vein recognition using minutia-based alignment and local binary pattern-based feature extraction. International Journal of Imaging Systems and Technology 19(3), 179–186 (2009)
26. Yang, J.F., Shi, Y.H.: Finger-vein ROI localization and vein ridge enhancement. Pattern Recognition Letters 33(12), 1569–1579 (2012)
27. Yang, L., Yang, G.P., Yin, Y.L., Xiao, R.Y.: Sliding window-based region of interest extraction for finger vein images. Sensors 13(3), 3799–3815 (2013)
28. Lu, Y., Xie, S.J., Yoon, S., Yang, J.C., Park, D.S.: Robust finger vein ROI localization based on flexible segmentation. Sensors 13(11), 14339–14366 (2013)

29. Dai, Y.G., Huang, B.N., Li, W.X., Xu, Z.Q.: A method for capturing the finger-vein image using nonuniform intensity infrared light. In: Proceedings of Congress on Image and Signal Processing, Sanya, China, pp. 501–505 (2008)
30. Nguyen, D.T., Park, Y.H., Shin, K.Y., Kwon, S.Y., Lee, H.C., Park, K.R.: Fake finger-vein image detection based on fourier and wavelet transforms. Digital Signal Processing 23(5), 1401–1413 (2013)
31. Yang, G.P., Xiao, R.Y., Yin, Y.L., Yang, L.: Finger Vein Recognition Based on Personalized Weight Maps. Sensors 13(9), 12093–12112 (2013)

Performance Evaluation of Finger Vein Verification Algorithms in PFVR2014

Ran Xian and Wenxin Li

AILAB, Peking University
No.5 Yiheyuan Road, 100871 Beijing, China
{xianran,lwx}@pku.edu.cn

Abstract. This paper concerns about the performance evaluation of finger vein verification algorithms. A finger vein verification competition was held by the author of this paper in the 9th Chinese Conference on Biometrics Recognition. The competition itself is called PKU Finger Vein Recognition. This competition aims at studying the state-of-the-art performance of finger vein verification algorithms, mainly in China. This competition used a general recognition algorithm evaluation platform called RATE developed by the author. RATE provides systematic solutions for database management, benchmark generation, and equipped with a distributed computation system for algorithm evaluation. This paper will discuss RATE platform, the data sets and test protocols of the competition, and the analysis of the competition results.

Keywords: Finger vein verification, biometrics verification, algorithm evaluation, RATE, CCBR.

1   Introduction

Finger vein verification is a new biometrics technology. Over the decades, this technology has made significant achievements. In 2000, Finger vein images are captured using near infrared ray by medical scientist Kono and Ueki [1]. Within the next 10 years, Japanese researchers have invented and proposed many devices and algorithms [2]. In 2010, B.N Huang etc. proposed an algorithm based on wide line detector. It gives impressive performance with EER of 0.87% in a ten thousand level database [3]. Finger vein verification is thought to be a very promising biometrics technology. It uses information hidden under human body, and therefore is stable to outside environment and very difficult to be counterfeited.

Performance evaluation, benchmarks and public database are very important to the development of biometrics verification technologies. For finger print verification, Fingerprint Verification Competition [4] is a competition that has shared its database and evaluation metrics. FVC has then become an ongoing automated evaluation system [5] where researchers can submit algorithms and get performance evaluation without other helps. There are also various face recognition competitions [6] and high quality public database [7] available.

Z. Sun et al. (Eds.): CCBR 2014, LNCS 8833, pp. 244–251, 2014.

By far there are no evaluation systems, publicly recognized benchmarks or database available for the field of finger vein verification. In this condition, we developed an automated performance evaluation system called RATE (Recognition Algorithm Test Engine) for finger vein verification. RATE has 3 parts.

1. Database. The database contains finger vein image samples. These samples are captured by real applications. Peking University has deployed finger vein verification devices for over 5 years. The whole database contains 80,000 fingers, with average 40 samples per finger, and all the samples are well annotated.
2. View and benchmark management tools. A view is a collection of samples with special features, e.g. we may select all females' fingers in the database and form a view for female finger study. Benchmark is based on views - it describes the task for the verification algorithm. More specifically, benchmarks describe matches between samples in a view. The results of running a benchmark can be used to calculate FMR, FNMR, and other metrics.
3. Distributed computation system. Image processing is a time-consuming job compared to text and numerical processing. This system is responsible for running algorithms. It is easy be deployed with a client software, which can be run on general PCs in a plug-and-play fashion.

This competition, which is the first competition of finger vein verification in China, is held on RATE. It is organized by AILAB, Peking University, and lasts from May 1st 2014 to July 1st 2014. Most of the participants are from Peking University.

The task for participants can be simplified as given two images of finger vein, participants will write algorithms to output similarity measurement between these two images. From the similarity measurements, several metrics are evaluated, including False Non-Match Rate FNMR, False Match Rate FMR and Equal Error Rate EER. The final results are represented by EER. Rank is also determined by EER.

A summary of the competition is listed in Table 1. Notice that there are 15 participants but only 4 final submissions. This may be caused by two reasons: one is that some of the algorithms are the products of group work, each group member may have registered and submitted different algorithms; the other is that some algorithms perform not so well so the authors decided not to send them as final submissons. Many algorithms are submitted owing to RATE's quick feedback, which enables the participants to develop and improve algorithms rapidly.

The rest of this paper is organized as follows: Section 2 describes the data sets and benchmarks used in the competition. Section 3 describes the testing protocol and evaluation metrics. Section 4 presents the results and has a discussion. Section 5 draws the conclusions and discusses future works.

Table 1. Summary of the PFVR2014 competition

First place	YANNAN Tech.
Second place	Carlisle
Third place	Jinxing Yu
Participants	15
Algorithm submitted	462
Final submission	4
Best EER	1.684%

2   Data Sets and Benchmarks

The images in the RATE database are captured by devices manufactured by YANNAN Tech. The images are captured in an outdoor environment without guidance. Images are in 8 bit gray scale BMP format. Resolution is 512 × 384. Fig. 1 shows examples of 3 different finger vein images.

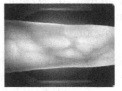

Fig. 1. Example images of finger veins

The data sets used in the competition are generated from RATE database. There are 3 data sets concerned with the competition. The first two data sets are used for developing and testing algorithms. The third data set is used for final evaluation. The detail of each data set is listed in Table 2[1].

Table 2. data sets used in the competition

Name	Size	Comments
PFVR2014-Train-50	50×5	Small data set for quick test and algorithm validation
PFVR2014-Train-100	100×5	Medium data set
PFVR2014-Test-1000	1000×5	Big data set for final evaluation

The PFVR2014-Train-X data set was released immediately after the start of the competition. Participants can submit algorithms and get feedback at any time. These two data sets are for the purpose of developing, validating and tuning algorithms. PFVR2014-Test-1000 was released in the middle of the competition at July 15th. Each participant can only submit one algorithm on this

---

[1] 50×5 means 50 classes, 5 samples per class.

data set, and performance on this data set would be the final performance for the participant.

Benchmarks are generated from each data set. For each data set, all images are going to be matched with other images of the same finger. This kind of match is called genuine attempt. For each data set, the first image of each finger is going to match with every first image of other fingers. This kind of match is called imposter attempt. In general, imposter attempts are a lot more than genuine attempts, so we randomly choose from imposter attempts to make these two matches have the same number of matches.

3   Testing Protocol and Evaluation Metrics

3.1   Testing Protocol

In order to make a submission, participants were asked to register at http://rate.pku.edu.cn. A submission consists of two Win32 executables, Enroll.exe and Match.exe. Enroll.exe is for enrolling a finger vein image and producing a template file. Match.exe is for comparing two template files and producing a similarity score.

The two executables should read input from the command line then print results to standard output or a designated file, finally exit with the right exit value. The executables obey the protocol listed in Table 3.

Table 3. Protocol for the executables

Executable	Enroll.exe	Match.exe
Description	Extract template	Match two templates
Input from command line	Path of the input image and path of the output template file	Paths of two templates for matching
Standard output	None	Similarity degree indicated by a float number between [0-1.0], with 0 meaning not similar at all, and 1 meaning exactly the same
Exit value	0: success, else: failed	0: success, else: failed

3.2   Evaluation Metrics

The final result only depends on the performance of the first submission on data set PFVR2014-Train-1000. Rank is determined by EER. Metrics evaluated in this competition are:

- False Non-Match Rate FNMR.
- False Match Rate FMR.
- Failure to Enroll Number. Number of failures during enrollments.
- Failure to Match Number. Number of failures during matches.
- FMR-FNMR curve.
- ROC curve.
- Equal Error Rate EER.
- Score histogram of genuine and imposter attempts.
- FMR100, FMR1000, ZeroFMR.
- Average enroll time, average match time.

4   Competition Results

Results for the 4 final submissions on PFVR-Train-1000 are showed in table 4.

Table 4. Competition results of the 4 final submissions on PFVR-Train-1000

Submission	YANNAN	Carlisle	Jinxing Yu	Yongxuan Liu
EER(%)	1.684	5.556	7.444	7.741
FMR100(%)	3.307	64.037	83.963	77.74
FMR1000(%)	40.63	75.63	98.259	94.296
ZeroFMR(%)	6.593	35.259	23.22	29.222
#FTE	0	0	0	0
#FTM	0	0	0	0
Avg. Enroll Time(ms)	50.7	62.3	81.2	299.9
Avg. Match Time(ms)	19.4	48.2	568.2	359.6

We could see that the YANNAN algorithm beats all other algorithms obviously from all aspects. This algorithm is one of the core algorithms at YANNAN Tech. We could also see the FTE and FTM are all zeros, which indicates that all algorithms have no fatal bugs.

Although only 4 algorithms were finally submitted, the best algorithm still achieves an outstanding performance. What is worth noting is that except for the best algorithm submitted by a company, all other algorithms are submitted by undergraduate students from Peking University, which is an extraordinary work for these students within 2 months. This indicates in some way that high performance finger vein verification algorithms can be developed in a short time, and there is a good potential to achieve even higher performance if more effort is put.

Score histograms are showed in Fig. 2. FMR-FNMR graphs and ROC curves are drawn in Fig. 3 and Fig. 4.

It's important to see that RATE is also able to assist researchers to develop algorithms more efficiently. Take the second place participant as an example. Fig. 5 shows the evolution of algorithm on PFVR-Train-50 and PFVR-Train-100. For PFVR-Train-50, EER begins at 20%, within 30 evolutions, the EER is

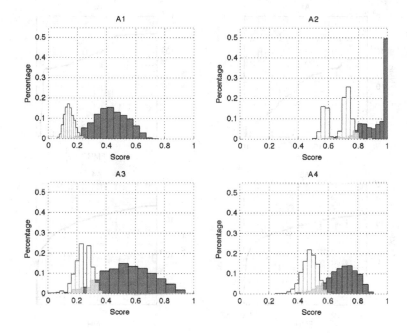

Fig. 2. Score histograms

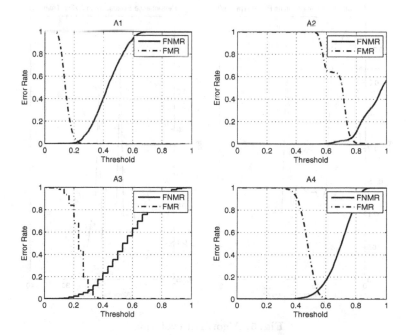

Fig. 3. FMR-FNMR graph

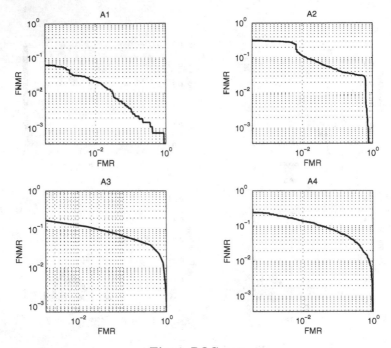

Fig. 4. ROC curve

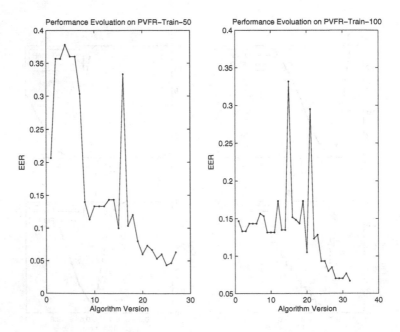

Fig. 5. Algorithm evolution

then below 5%. For PFVR-Train-100, similar results can also be obtained. This proves that RATE is a powerful and promising evaluation platform. By quick feedback on submitted algorithms, researchers are able to concentrate more on core algorithm developing, and try different ideas without worrying about time-consuming experiments.

5   Conclusions

Performance evaluation is important for biometrics verification. Platforms, database and benchmarks used in this competition could be further used for research, and RATE is able to be a general framework for finger vein verification algorithm development and performance evaluation. In this competition, although potential participants are not fully covered, the best algorithm still achieves outstanding performance (EER of 1.684%), proving finger vein verification to be a promising future biometrics technology. Meanwhile, implementation detail of algorithms is not gathered, and runtime memory efficiency is not evaluated. Deeper analysis could also be carried out such as exploiting the potential to combine several algorithms together for higher performance. Future works will focus on providing more comprehensive evaluation and deeper analysis, releasing a high quality large-scale database, and modifying RATE for evaluation of general biometrics recognition algorithms.

References

1. Kono, M., Ueki, H., Umemura, S.: A new method for the identification of individuals by using vein pattern matching of a finger. In: Proceedings of the 5th Symposium on pattern Measurement, Yamaguchi, Japan, pp. 9–12
2. Website of Hitachi, Ltd., http://www.hitachi.co.jp/products/it/veinid/global/products/index.html
3. Huang, B., Dai, Y., Li, R., Tang, D., Li, W.: Finger-Vein Authentication Based on Wide Line Detector and Pattern Normalization. In: 2010 20th International Conference on Pattern Recognition (ICPR), August 23-26, pp. 1269–1272 (2010)
4. Cappelli, R., Maio, D., Maltoni, D., Wayman, J.L., Jain, A.: Performance evaluation of fingerprint verification systems. IEEE Pattern Analysis and Machine Intelligence
5. FVC Ongoing, https://biolab.csr.unibo.it/fvcongoing/UI/Form/Home.aspx
6. Competition on face recognition in mobile environment using the MOBIO database, https://www.beat-eu.org/evaluations/icb-2013-face-recognition-mobio
7. The Facial Recognition Technology (FERET) Database, http://www.itl.nist.gov/iad/humanid/feret/feret_master.html

Capacity Analysis of Hand-Dorsa Vein Features Based on Image Coding

Yiding Wang and Xi Cao

College of Information Engineering
North China University of Technology, Beijing-100144, China
Chinawangyd@ncut.edu.cn, caoxi19890820@163.com

Abstract. This paper presents a method to calculate capacity of hand vein features by coding divided sub-images. An image coding model is proposed in this paper, including gray level inertia moment extraction and feature coding. The proposed method is tested on a database of 1000 images from 100 individuals built up by a custom-made acquisition device. The experiment results indicate that the capacity of hand vein features supports over 100 thousand individuals.

Keywords: Feature capacity, Gray Level Co-occurrence Matrix, Inertia moment, Image encoding.

1 Introduction

With an increasing demand of biometric systems for automatic and secure personal identification, an increasing number of biometric modalities are available. The adoption of a particular biometric system will need to consider the biometric identification capacity, defined as the maximum number of individuals that can be reliably identified, especially for large-scale personal identification. There are various factors affecting the achievable biometric identification capacity, such as individuality linked to modality, image quality linked to acquisition system, and feature discriminatory power linked to processing methodology. Based on the overlapping probability among uniformly distributed minutiae points, individuality has been investigated for fingerprint [1]. By modeling the chain of biometric identification processing as information transmission through a noisy channel [2], the capacity constrained by image quality and feature representation has been formulated for iris and face based on global image features in the low dimensional projected space [3], as well as for palmprint and hand shape based on local image features in the frequency domain and shape geometry [4]. Although these information theoretic approaches provide a good capacity bound, the computation complexity is high due to the requirement of evaluating probability distributions of biometric features in high dimensions. In this paper, an alternative framework is presented based on adaptation of transform coding which is normally used for image compression. Through the coding of image texture features, the statistical variability of the resulting binary codes is considered as a measure of biometric identification capacity. Also presented are the results obtained from the application of

Z. Sun et al. (Eds.): CCBR 2014, LNCS 8833, pp. 252–259, 2014.

the proposed method to near-infrared hand vein images with no prior work on estimation of its identification capacity.

The layout of this paper is as follows. Section 2 introduces an image coding model. The estimation of feature capacity is given in Section 3. Section 4 demonstrates the experiment results. Conclusions are given in the last section.

2   Image Coding Model

To estimate the capacity of hand vein's images, an image coding model including inertia moment and feature coding is used in this paper. The proposed method aims to calculate the top limit of feature capacity of DHV images. The key steps of image coding are shown in Fig. 1, and each step is described in detail in the following text.

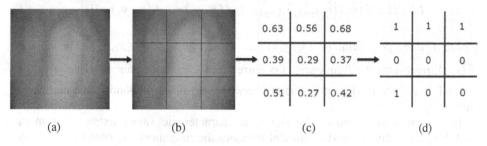

| (a) | (b) | (c) | (d) |

Fig. 1. Key steps of image coding

Step1. A database of hand-dorsa vein images is established using custom-made device. A CCD camera and near infrared (NIR) light source are employed for image acquisition (as shown in Fig. 2(a)). While Fig. 2(b) displays some image samples taken from the vein image acquisition device. The database contains 1000 grey images of 381×381 from 100 individuals in which 50 are female and 50 are male [5]. To test the image coding model, the DHV image database is selected as test image sets. A vein image sample is shown in Fig. 1(a), which has been geometrically corrected. The regions of interest in sample image are also extracted.

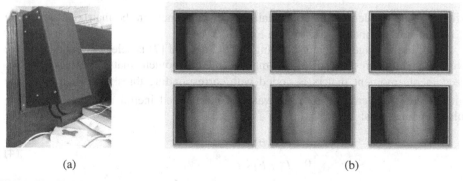

| (a) | (b) |

Fig. 2. The DHV capture system. (a) Vein Iimage Acquisition Device (b) The Hand-dorsa Vein Images in the Database

Step2: Due to the ununiformity of grey distribution, the image sample is divided into several non-overlapping sub-regions to highlight the textural information, as shown in Fig. 1(b). However, if the number of partition is too big, the gray distribution within sub-region will be uniformed. The size of sub-region will be too small to recognize, which makes image partition less meaningful. Therefore, the calculation of optimal number of sub-region is necessary. Besides, a robust textural feature is also needed.

Step3: In the search of textural feature, grey level co-occurrence matrix is selected to transform image sets into arrays based on textural features. Grey Level Co-occurrence Matrix is one of the earliest methods for texture feature extraction proposed by Haralick [6] in 1973. Given an image $f(x,y)$, and (x_1,y_1) and (x_2,y_2) are two pixels in the image. The generalized co-occurrence matrix $P(i,j)$ is given:

$$P(i,j\mid d,\theta) = \#\left\{\left[(x_1,y_1),(x_2,y_2)\right]\mid f(x_1,y_1)=i, f(x_2,y_2)=j\right\}\tag{1}$$

where i is the gray value of (x_1,y_1), and j is gray value of (x_2,y_2). The value of $P(i,j)$ represents the frequency of occurrence of gray value pair (i,j) in $f(x,y)$, d and θ are the deviation and angle between two pixels, # denotes the number of frequency.

Inertia moment is one of the statistical characteristic values extracted from the GLCMs. The value of inertia moment indicates the roughness and complexity of texture feature. Let d be 1 and θ be $0°$, inertia moment of each sub-region is given as:

$$I = \sum_{i=1}^{L}\sum_{j=1}^{L}(i-j)^2 P(i,j)\tag{2}$$

where L denotes image grey level. In order to simplify the calculation, the inertia moment of each sub-region $I(a,b)$ is divided by the mean value of all inertia moments of the matrix to achieve normalized inertia moments:

$$\hat{I}(a,b) = \frac{I(a,b)}{\bar{I}}\tag{3}$$

where a and b denote the coordinate of inertia moment in the matrix. An example of inertia moment matrix is shown in Fig. 1(c).

Step4: In the stage of feature coding, OTSU method [7] is selected to calculate the average coding threshold of all normalized inertia moment matrices. Every normalized inertia moment matrix is coded with corresponding thresholds. Let ϕ_i be the binary code transferred from each value of normalized inertia moment, the coding rule is organized as:

$$\phi_i = \begin{cases} 1 & \hat{I}(a,b) \geq t \\ 0 & \hat{I}(a,b) < t \end{cases}\tag{4}$$

For example, if the threshold is 0.5, the result of image coding is shown in Fig. 1(d).

3   Estimation of Feature Capacity

3.1   Calculation of Optimal Number of Sub-region

Combined with conclusions mentioned in step2, the most important part of image coding is to find the number of optimal sub-region. To estimate the number of optimal sub-region, every image in test image sets is divided into multiple regions ranging from 1×1 to $n \times n$. The calculation of optimal partitions should satisfy that the inter-class variances of inertia moment matrices and inter-class code distance are simultaneously maximized. Therefore, two steps are respectively carried out to estimate the optimal number of partition; the flow chart is shown in Fig. 2:

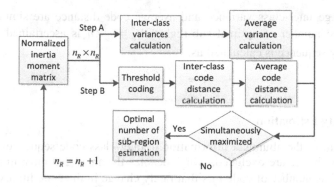

Fig. 3. Estimation of optimal number of sub-region

For step A, the average inter-class variance of all 1000 normalized inertia moment matrices with same partition is calculated. The variance calculation of single $n_R \times n_R$ normalized matrix is given:

$$V = \sum_{a=1}^{n_R} \sum_{b=1}^{n_R} \left[\hat{I}(a,b) - t \right]^2 \quad (1 < n_R \le n) \tag{5}$$

where t is the coding threshold achieved by OTSU method, which correspond to the number of sub-region. After cycling the partitions from 1×1 to $n \times n$, n average variances are acquired.

In step B, all 1000 inertia moment matrices with same partitions are coded by corresponding thresholds. In the knowledge of hamming distance, the average inter-class code distance indicates the dispersion degree of inter-class codes, which is achieved by calculating the average hamming distance of 1000 code sequences. An example of hamming distance calculation is shown in Fig. 3. By comparing different code bits of two code sequences, the hamming distance is 5 between individual A and B.

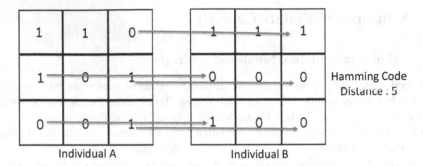

Fig. 4. Example of hamming distance

If the average inter-class variance and average code distance are simultaneously maximized, the number of optimal sub-region $N_o = n_o \times n_o$ is ascertained. The total possible binary sequence is calculated as:

$$N = 2^{N_o} \tag{6}$$

3.2   Capacity Estimation

In order to remove the abundant information in inter-class code sequences, the code bits that rarely change are excluded, which denotes the areas that most images share with. Take N' as number of code bits that rarely change in the code library, the total number of valid code sequences is estimated as:

$$N'_o = 2^{N_o - N'} \tag{7}$$

Finally, the feature capacity C is estimated as:

$$C = \frac{N'_0}{l} \tag{8}$$

The value of C represents the number of individuals that can be supported when the total valid code length is N'_o and valid code length of single individual is l.

4   Experiment Procedure and Results

Firstly, 100 individuals' data from DHV image database were selected as test image sets, each individual has 10 vein images. Secondly, by using the image coding model, each vein image is divided into multiple regions range from 1×1 to 50×50. Thirdly, the normalized inertia moment is used to present the textural complexity of each sub-region. Then, OTSU method is utilized to calculate the average threshold of every normalized inertia moment matrix. The result of step A in calculating the number of optimal sub-region is shown in Fig. 5(a). It is seen that the average inter-class variance reaches its peak when each image is divided into 20×20 rectangular partitions.

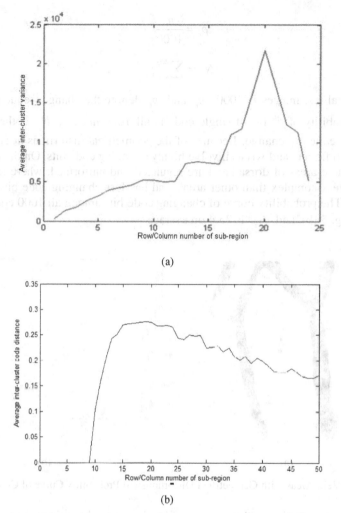

Fig. 5. Optimal Number of Sub-region Calculation: (a)Variance Curve (b) Normalization of code distance

The result of step B is shown in Fig. 5(b). To simplify the statistics, the average inter-class code distance is divided by corresponding partition to achieve normalized code distance. It's observed that the normalized code distance is maximized when partition ranges from 15×15 and 25×25. Combined with the results of step A and step B, 20×20 is selected as optimal number of sub-region. The corresponding coding threshold is 0.41, which is acquired by OTSU method. The normalized code distance is 0.2675 when partition is 20×20. Therefore, the average code distance of single individual indicates as $l = 0.2675 \times 400 = 107$.

To exclude the common code bits that rarely change among the code library, all the 400 code bits in each code sequence are traversed. The calculation of weighted changing bits is respectively given by:

$$p_i = \frac{n_i}{1000} \qquad (9)$$

$$N_c = \sum_i^{400} p_i \qquad (10)$$

while the total test images is 1000, n_i and p_i denote the change frequency and the change probability of ith bit of single code in all 1000 images, N_c is the total code points that frequently change. Because of the geometrical distortions at cross points, veins close to fingers and wrists involve highly changing code bits. On the other hand, veins in middle areas of dorsa-hand are regulated and uniformed, where textural distribution is less complex than other areas, and has less changing code bits, as shown in Fig 5(a). The probability curve of changing code bits among all 1000 coded images is seen in Fig. 5 (b), and N_c is 25.4 on average.

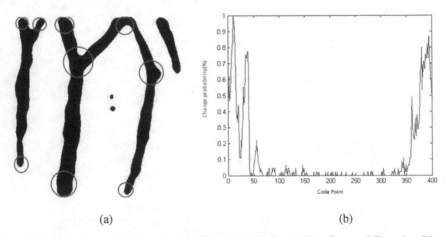

(a)   (b)

Fig. 6. (a): Vein Areas with Geometrical Distortions;(b):Probability Curve of Changing Bits

According to equation 8, the capacity of hand vein can be estimated as:

$$\frac{2^{25.4}}{107} = 413788 \qquad (11)$$

Equation 11 indicates the capacity scale of hand-dorsa vein is about 100 thousand magnitude.

In addition, the method has been applied to fingerprints. Based on the fingerprint images of 80 individuals from CASIA database with each image of size 328×356 pixels partitioned to 25×25 a block, following the same application procedure gives the estimated capacity of 11,146,983 individuals, which is in good agreement with the results reported in [8].

5   Conclusion

This paper proposed a measure of capacity calculation based on hand-dorsa vein images and obtained satisfactory results. The experiment results indicated that the hand vein image has capacity of at least 413788. The result is conservative due to the tested database contains only images of 100 subjects. The algorithm performance can be further improved by using larger-sample database.

References

1. Sharath, P., Salil, P., Anil, K.J.: On the Individuality of Fingerprints. IEEE Trans. Pattern Analysis and Machine Intelligence. 24(8), 1010–1025 (2002)
2. Frans, W., Ton, K.: On the Capacity of a Biometrical Identification System. In: Proceeding of Information Theory, p. 82. IEEE Xplore, Japan (2003)
3. Schimid, N.A.: On Empirical Recognition Capacity of Biometric Systems Under Global PCA and ICA Encoding. IEEE Transactions on Information Forensics and Security 3, 512–528 (2008)
4. Jay, B., Ajay, K.: On estimating performance indices for biometric identification. Pattern Recognition 42, 1803–1815 (2009)
5. Wang, Y.D., Fan, Y., Li, K.F.: Hand Vein Recognition based on multi-scale LBP and wavelet. In: International Conference on Wavelet Analysis and Pattern Recognition, pp. 214–218 (2011)
6. Haralick, R., Shanmugam, K., Dinstein, I.: Texture Features for Image Classification. IEEE Trans. on Systems, Man and Cybernetics 3(6), 610–621 (1973)
7. Otsu, N.: A threshold selection method for gray-level histograms. IEEE Trans. Systems 9(1), 62–66 (1979)
8. Biometrics Ideal Test: CASIA Fingerprint Image Database Version 5.0, http://biometrics.idealtest.org/ (accessed 2014)

Finger-Vein Recognition by Using Spatial Feature Interdependence Matrix Weighted by Probability and Direction

Wenming Yang, Yichao Li, Chuan Qin[*], and Qingmin Liao

Shenzhen Key Lab. of Information Sci&Tech/Shenzhen Engineering Lab. of IS&DRM
Department of EE/Graduate School at Shenzhen, Tsinghua University, China

Abstract. The spatial feature interdependence matrix (SFIM) has been proposed for face representation, which encodes feature interdependences between local patches. However, not all patches are equally important for classification purposes. For finger-vein identification, patches that contain vein lines contribute more to classification. Inspired by this, we propose a weighted SFIM based on probability and direction (PDSFIM). Both the probability and direction of vein lines in a patch are integrated into the SFIM. The experimental results demonstrate the superiority of the proposed method after comparison with various state-of-the-art methods.

Keywords: finger vein, feature interdependence, weighted patch, probability of vein, direction of vein.

1 Introduction

Finger-veins have been increasingly utilized for personal identification due to their enhanced security and immunity to fraud. Finger-vein images are captured under infrared light, which usually has low contrast and contains irregular shading produced by the varying thicknesses of the finger bones and muscles. Thus, classical finger-vein recognition algorithms always segment the finger-veins first. Since the regions that contain veins are relatively dark, in [1], finger-vein points are extracted by repeatedly tracking local dark lines. This method does not extract thin vein lines well because the points on thin vein lines are statistically insignificant. This problem has been solved by [2], which extracted the maximum curvature points of cross-sectional profiles. Besides the information of the line position, the orientation of lines is also important for identification. [3] have developed a competitive coding scheme to extract line orientation information by using Gabor filters. Texture information has also been researched by [4]. By integrating the information from line position and orientation, the method in [5] has a promising performance on our database. However, the discriminative information of ambiguous regions is discarded due to thresholding and the prediction of line direction is unstable because it only uses four pixels in the computing of the depth of current pixel values on a cross-sectional brightness profile.

---

[*] Corresponding author.

Z. Sun et al. (Eds.): CCBR 2014, LNCS 8833, pp. 260–265, 2014.

More recently, the spatial feature interdependence matrix (SFIM)[6] has been proposed for face recognition. The SFIM utilizes the underlying feature interdependences between local region pairs for face representation. Motivated by the observation that the features of patches that contain finger-vein lines are more discriminative, in this research work, SFIM is weighted by the probability that a local patch contains a finger-vein line and the direction of the line.

2   PDSFIM

2.1   SFIM

The SFIM firstly divides images into spatially non-overlapped rectangular patches of the same size. Histograms of LBP (HLBP) of each local patch are used to represent the patch. Then the feature interdependences between each patch pairs are defined as the chi-square distance of their HLBP:

$$a_{ij} = \sum_{n=1}^{K} \frac{(H_i(n) - \overline{H}(n))^2}{\overline{H}(n)}, \tag{1}$$

Where

$$\overline{H}(n) = \frac{H_i(n) + H_j(n)}{2}, \tag{2}$$

and K is the dimension of HLBP (set to 256 in our experiment), H_i is the HLBP of patch i. $a_{i,j}$ encodes the strength that patches tend to depend on each other. The feature interdependences vector formed by all patch pairs is then feed into nearest neighbor classifier for recognition purposes. All patch pairs are treated equally in SFIM, which is unreasonable and inefficient for highly structured images. To address this problem, we propose two ways to weight patch pairs based on the structure of finger vein images.

2.2   Weight Based on Probability

In finger-vein images, the textures of patches that contain finger-vein lines are more important for recognition purposes. To identify regions that contain finger-vein lines, we checked whether the region has a dominant orientation by applying Gabor filters of J orientations to the image. By using the maximum and minimum responses of the J orientations, the probability that a pixel belongs to a finger-vein line is defined as:

$$w_p(x, y) = \frac{abs(\max(R) - \min(R))}{\max(abs(\max(R)), abs(\min(R)))}, \tag{3}$$

where $R = \{R_k \mid k \in (0,...,J-1)\}$ and R_k is the Gabor filtering response at orientation k at pixel (x,y):

$$R_k = I(x,y) * G_R(x,y,\theta_k), \tag{4}$$

where I(x,y) is the original vein images, G_R is the real part of Gabor filters as defined in [3], $\theta_k = \{k\pi / J \mid k \in (0,...,J-1)\}$ is the orientation of the filters.

$w_p(x,y)$ indicates the probability that pixel (x,y) has a dominant orientation, which also shows the probability that it belongs to a finger-vein line. The probability for a patch is computed as the mean probability of all pixels in the patch:

$$p_i = \frac{1}{|S_i|} \sum_{(x,y) \in S_i} w_p(x,y), \tag{5}$$

where S_i is the set of points in patch i, and $|S_i|$ is the number of pixels in patch i. The weight K_{ij}^p is defined as the mean probability of the two patches:

$$K_{ij}^p = \frac{p_i + p_j}{2}. \tag{6}$$

2.3   Weight Based on Direction

In addition to utilizing the probability that the current patch has a dominant orientation, we were able to find which of the neighbour patches also contain a finger-vein line, by using the finger-vein line direction. The direction of the finger-vein line could be predicted by the dominant orientation of the current patch. To do this, we utilize a Winner-take-all rule[3]:

$$d(x,y) = \arg \min_k R_k(x,y), \tag{7}$$

where R_k is defined in Eq. (4).

The highest peak in the orientation histogram of a local patch was then selected as the direction of this patch. If the direction of the line that connected patch j and center patch i was the same as the center patch's orientation d_i, then patch j is very likely to contain a finger-vein line too. So we define

$$K_{ij}^d = \begin{cases} 1, & if\ D(x_j - x_i, y_j - y_i) = d_i \\ 0, & others \end{cases} \tag{8}$$

where D is the direction matrix. Fig.1 shows the direction matrix when J is set to 4, which also shows an example of K_{ij}^d when the direction of the center patch is 2. Because the length of a finger-vein line segment is within some range, patch j that was not in a window W of the center patch was not considered, which also makes the dimension of the feature vector low.

If the d_i of two images were different, we set all K_{ij}^d to 1. This may happen when two images belong to the same class, but the direction of patch i is ambiguous in either one of them. In such ambiguous regions, their feature interdependences with all of their neighbour patches contain more discriminative information than the direction.

Finally, we fuse the two kinds of weights by using their product:

$$K_{ij} = K_{ij}^p \times K_{ij}^d. \tag{9}$$

3 3	2	1 1	0 0	1	0 0
3 3	2	1 1	0 0	1	0 0
0 0	center	0 0	0 0	center	0 0
1 1	2	3 3	0 0	1	0 0
1 1	2	3 3	0 0	1	0 0

Fig. 1. Left: direction matrix D, Right: K_{ij}^d when d_i=2

2.4   PDSFIM

Once we have weights of every patch pairs, we can use them in the calculation of distance between two images:

$$d(a^1, a^2) = \sum_{i=1}^{N} \sum_{j=1}^{N} K_{ij} \frac{2(a_{ij}^1 - a_{ij}^2)^2}{a_{ij}^1 + a_{ij}^2}, \tag{10}$$

where N is the number of local patches, a^1, a^2 are the feature interdependence vectors of two images, which have a size of N^2. $a_{ij}^k (k = 1, 2)$ is the feature interdependence between the i_{th} patch and the j_{th} patch as defined in Eq. (1).

In the original SFIM, the feature interdependences of all patch pairs were calculated by setting all K_{ij} to 1, which is time-consuming and produces feature vectors with very high dimensions. For a 200*100 image divided into patches of size 10*10, the dimension of the feature vector is 200*200 = 40000. In PDSFIM, only the feature interdependences between the center patch and its 25 neighbors are used, so the dimension is dramatically reduced to 25*200 = 5000. PDSFIM also integrates finger-vein probability and orientation information into SFIM by weighting these feature interdependences. Patches that contain finger-vein lines are given a larger weight because they provide more discriminative power. In addition, patch pairs along the same finger-vein line are also given a larger weight because their feature interdependences are more stable.

3   Experimental Results

Experiments were conducted on a database established by using a device that we had developed earlier[7]. Our early smaller database was extended to include 150 people, who each provided images of their left index and middle fingers, and right index and middle fingers. We collected samples in two separate sessions. In total, the database contains 1232 images from 616 different fingers. The images have a size of 200*100 pixels. Fig.2 shows ROI of some captured vein images.

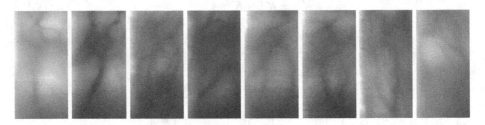

Fig. 2. Vein image samples

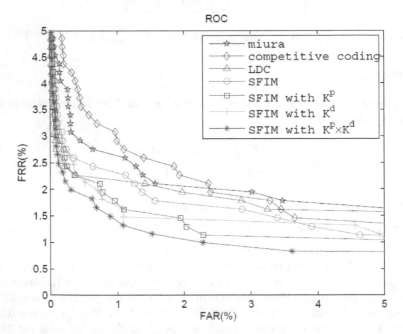

Fig. 3. ROC curves of different methods

In our experiment, each image was matched against all images in the database, producing 1232 genuine macthings and 1,516,592 imposter matchings. The window W is set empirically 5*5, J is set to 6 as in [3]. When computing direction weight, we quantize the direction to 4 to simplify the definition of direction matrix. We compared our method with Miura[2], competitive coding[3], and location and direction coding (LDC)[5]. We also compared the performance of each individual weight. The receiver operating characteristic (ROC) curves are plotted in Fig.3, which demonstrates the superiority of our method.

4   Conclusion

By considering that the regions which contain finger-vein lines are more discriminative, we propose a PDSFIM for finger-vein recognition. We identify the patches by considering the probability that they have a dominant orientation and find other patches that contain finger-vein lines by using the dominant orientation. The experimental results show that our method is promising.

Acknowledgments. The authors would like to thank the support of the Shenzhen Basic Research Project (NO.JC201006030866A).

References

1. Miura, N., Nagasaka, A., Miyatake, T.: Feature extraction of finger-vein patterns based on repeated line tracking and its application to personal identification. Machine Vision and Applications 15(4), 194–203 (2004)
2. Miura, N., Nagasaka, A., Miyatake, T.: Extraction of finger-vein patterns using maximum curvature points in image profiles. IEICE Transactions on Information and Systems 90(8), 1185–1194 (2007)
3. Kong, A.W.K., Zhang, D.: Competitive coding scheme for palmprint verification. In: Proceedings of the 17th International Conference on Pattern Recognition, ICPR 2004, vol. 1, pp. 520–523 (2004)
4. Yang, J., Shi, Y., Yang, J.: Personal identification based on finger-vein features. Computers in Human Behavior 27(5), 1565–1570 (2011)
5. Yang, W., Rao, Q., Liao, Q.: Personal identification for single sample using finger vein location and direction coding. In: 2011 International Conference on Hand-Based Biometrics (ICHB), pp. 1–6. IEEE (2011)
6. Yao, A., Yu, S.: Robust Face Representation Using Hybrid Spatial Feature Interdependence Matrix. IEEE Transactions on Image Processing 22(8), 3247–3259 (2013)
7. http://www.sz.tsinghua.edu.cn/labs/vipl/thu-fvfdt.html

A Database with ROI Extraction for Studying Fusion of Finger Vein and Finger Dorsal Texture

Wenming Yang, Chuan Qin*, and Qingmin Liao

Shenzhen Key Lab. of Information Sci&Tech/Shenzhen Engineering Lab. of IS&DRM
Department of Electronic Engineering/Graduate School at Shenzhen,
Tsinghua University, China

Abstract. In this paper, a database of finger vein(FV) and finger dorsal texture(FDT) region of interest(ROI) images named by THU-FVFDT2 is described in detail. The database is provided as an aid in studying fusion strategy of finger vein and finger dorsal texture images. Furthermore, on account of ROI extraction and manually coarse alignment during construction of the database, it facilitates using the database for research. Moreover, some algorithms of finger vein and finger dorsal texture authentication are tested in our database to ensure the reliability of the database and make research performed with the database as consistent and comparable as possible.

Keywords: fusion of finger vein and finger dorsal texture, multiple modalities, performance.

1 Introduction

Nowadays, research of fusing multiple modalities is more and more popular, such as fusion of hand shape and texture[1], fusion of fingerprint and palmvein[2], fusion of face and fingerprint[3],fusion of finger vein and fingerprint[4] and fusion of finger vein and finger dorsal texture[5,6]. Among them, features based on finger have lower device requirements, smaller device volume and more alternatives. With unique stability and anti-counterfeiting capability, fusion using finger vein is more and more general. In comparison with finger print, finger dorsal texture is a better choice to fuse with finger vein due to their inherent, unique position relationship. Thus, the fusion of finger vein and finger dorsal texture is promising research.

However, no large database of finger vein and finger dorsal texture images is published. In our previous work, a small database[10] of 220 different subjects without image registration is established. In this work, a larger and better(extracted ROI) database of 610 different subjects is built. The database can be viewed and downloaded at the following web address:

\\http://www.sz.tsinghua.edu.cn/labs/vipl/thu-fvfdt.html.

Figure 1 shows some examples of the database images.

---

* Corresponding author.

Z. Sun et al. (Eds.): CCBR 2014, LNCS 8833, pp. 266–270, 2014.

The report is organized as follows. In Section 2, some properties of the database are presented. In section 3, we describe image acquisition, how to obtain the ROI and performance of some algorithms obtained in our database. In Section 4, we conclude this paper.

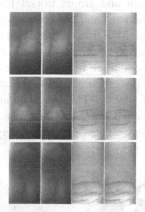

Fig. 1. Matched pairs of finger vein and finger dorsal texture

2   Properties of Database

The main motivation of our new database, which we call Tsinghua University Finger Vein and Finger Dorsal Texture Database2 (THU-FVFDT2), is to provide a large set of realistic finger vein and finger dorsal texture images for more in-depth research. Since captured with interval ranging from about dozens of seconds to one week, the images in the database show a range of variation, including obscure, lighting, slight deformation and translation that corresponds with reality. In addition, measuring algorithm is convenient due to ROI extraction during construction of the database. Some statistics and characters of the database are presented in detail as follows:

1. The database contains 2440(610*4) images. For each subject, there are four images, in which one finger vein and one finger dorsal texture image are for training and the other two are for testing.
2. The images are all ROI of finger vein and finger dorsal texture with manual coarse alignment, the first 220 ROI of which are extracted from THU-FVFDT1 [10]. See Section 3 for details.
3. The finger vein and finger dorsal texture pair of each sample is aligned to ensure their inherent, unique position relationship. See Section 3 for details.
4. The training and testing sample pair of each subject is manually aligned to simplify matching step. A small range of translation in matching step can overcome the translation variation.
5. Some algorithms of finger vein and finger dorsal texture authentication are tested in our database to ensure the reliability of the database. See Section 3 for details.

3   Generation of Database

3.1   Image Acquisition

Figure 2 shows our finger vein and finger dorsal texture imaging device which consists of two low-cost gray cameras and two columns of near infrared LEDs (wavelength 890 nm). The camera(JSP MODEL:DF-2112) on the top plays a role in obtaining finger dorsal texture images and the one on the bottom captures the finger vein images with a near infrared light filter in which the cutoff wavelength is 850 nm. They capture the two types of images simultaneously under control of one computer for higher immunity to spoof-attacks. The two columns of infrared LEDs are set above the finger on both sides. The infrared light penetrates the finger and passes through the filter for finger vein images generation. Figure 3 shows the process of image generation.

Fig. 2. Proposed finger vein and finger dorsal texture imaging device

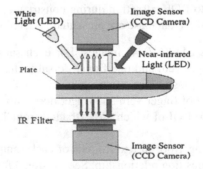

Fig. 3. The process of image generation

3.2   ROI Extraction[5]

An example of raw image is shown in figure 4. At first, the finger vein and finger dorsal texture pair registration should be accomplished. It can be reasonably assumed that the two cameras are approximately parallel. Hence, one homography matrix can describe the projection from the plane of the bottom camera to the top camera. Those salient points that visible in both images can be utilized to calculate the homography matrix as control points. We manually selected four such points. Then Finger is segmented by gradient and the ROI of finger is cropped and stretched to a rectangle. See Figure 4 for details. Finally, the manually coarse alignment is done in each ROI pair.

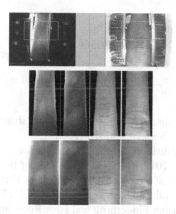

Fig. 4. Four control points and process of ROI generation

3.3   Intended Usage

Given a testing sample, fusion of finger vein and finger dorsal texture category should be decided. Generally, there are three categories of fusion schemes[7], namely pixel, feature and score level fusions. Then the given sample should match with all the train samples in order to find the most similar sample. In this paper, the performance of unimodal and multimodal algorithms in our database is proposed in Table 1.

Accuracy of either single modality is not high because the images should be aligned more precisely. However, the fusion algorithm can obtain more than 0.99 accuracy which certifies the database is reliable and fusion strategy can overcome the drawback of either modality.

Table 1. Performance

	Yang W[8] for FV	Kong A W K[9] for FV	Kong A W K[9] for FDT	Yang W[5] for fusion
Accuracy(%)	98.5	98.36	96.07	99.34
EER	0.0113	0.0161	0.0187	0.0075

4   Conclusion

The main contribution of this paper can be summarized as follows. Firstly, a large database of finger vein and finger dorsal texture images is provided for future research. Secondly, images in the database are all ROIs extracted from the raw images. Finally, Some algorithms of finger vein and finger dorsal texture authentication are tested in our database to ensure the reliability of the database and make research performed with the database as consistent and comparable as possible.

We hope this will accelerate the research in fusion of finger vein and finger dorsal texture.

Acknowledgments. The authors would like to thank the support of the Shenzhen Basic Research Project (NO.JC201006030866A).

References

1. Kumar, A., Zhang, D.: Personal recognition using hand shape and texture. IEEE Transactions on Image Processing 15(8), 2454–2461 (2006)
2. Yamada, S., Endoh, T.: Evaluation of independence between palm vein and fingerprint for multimodal biometrics. In: 2012 BIOSIG-Proceedings of the International Conference of the Biometrics Special Interest Group (BIOSIG), pp. 1–4. IEEE (2012)
3. Joshi, H.D.: BIOMET: A Multimodal Biometric Authentication System for Person Identification and Verification using Fingerprint and Face Recognition. International Journal of Computer Applications 51 (2012)
4. Yang, J., Zhang, X.: Feature-level fusion of fingerprint and finger-vein for personal identification. Pattern Recognition Letters 33(5), 623–628 (2012)
5. Yang, W., Huang, X., Liao, Q.: Fusion of finger vein and finger dorsal texture for personal identification based on Comparative Competitive Coding. In: 2012 19th IEEE International Conference on Image Processing (ICIP), pp. 1141–1144. IEEE (2012)
6. Wenming, Y., Guoli, M.A., Fei, Z., et al.: Feature-Level Fusion of Finger Veins and Finger Dorsal Texture for Personal Authentication Based on Orientation Selection. IEICE Transactions on Information and Systems 97(5), 1371–1373 (2014)
7. Faundez-Zanuy, M.: Data fusion in biometrics. IEEE Aerospace and Electronic Systems Magazine 20(1), 34–38 (2005)
8. Yang, W., Rao, Q., Liao, Q.: Personal identification for single sample using finger vein location and direction coding. In: 2011 International Conference on Hand-Based Biometrics (ICHB), pp. 1–6. IEEE (2011)
9. Kong, A.W.K., Zhang, D.: Competitive coding scheme for palmprint verification. In: Proceedings of the 17th International Conference on Pattern Recognition, ICPR 2004, vol. 1, pp. 520–523 (2004)
10. Tsinghua University Finger Vein and Finger Dorsal Texture Database1THU-FVFDT1, http://www.sz.tsinghua.edu.cn/labs/vipl/thu-fvfdt.html

Local Vein Texton Learning for Finger Vein Recognition

Lu Yang, Gongping Yang, Yilong Yin*, and Lumei Dong

School of Computer Science and Technology, Shandong University,
Jinan, 250101, P.R. China
yangluhi@163.com, {gpyang,ylyin}@sdu.edu.cn,
dongcomeon@gmail.com

Abstract. In finger vein recognition, the input image is generally labeled in accordance with the nearest enrolled neighbor. However, it is so rigid that it is inadequate for some cases. This paper explores a modified sparse representation method for finger vein recognition. In the method, each block in a finger vein image will be sparsely represented by dictionary textons, not simply labeled by the nearest enrolled block, and the representation coefficients of all blocks are arranged to be a two-dimensional histogram to model the image. As textons is learned from local vein pattern, not global vein pattern. Therefore, for encode global geometric information of finger vein pattern, the representation coefficient histogram is projected to different lines, and then connected in parallel to generate more powerful image features. Extensive experiments on the HKPU finger vein database show the effectiveness of the modified sparse representation method in finger vein recognition.

Keywords: Finger vein recognition, texton learning, linear projection.

1 Introduction

Finger vein, a new physiological biometric trait, has been explored for personal identity by research groups in recent years. As near-infrared light can be absorbed by the hemoglobin in finger vein, but can transmit other finger tissues, it is used to capture finger vein pattern, which will be shown as shadow patterns in image [1]. Like other biometric traits, finger vein has several desirable properties, for example, universality, distinctiveness, permanence and acceptability. In addition to, it has other distinct advantages in living body identification, noninvasive and noncontact image capture and spoofing resistance.

In the post, several algorithms for finger vein feature extraction have been proposed, which can be categorized into three groups: (1) Vein pattern based algorithms, for example, repeated line tracking [2], maximum curvature point [3], mean curvature [4] and Gabor filter [5]. These algorithms first segment vein network, and then use the topological structure of vein network as vein feature. However, the segmental results are often unsatisfying in low quality images. (2) Local binary pattern based algorithms,

---

* Corresponding author.

Z. Sun et al. (Eds.): CCBR 2014, LNCS 8833, pp. 271–280, 2014.

for example, local binary pattern (LBP) [6], local line binary pattern (LLBP) [7] and personalized best bit map (PBBM) [8]. These methods are less practical in finger vein recognition, because they do not distinguish vein area and background area of image in feature extraction. (3) Minutia based algorithm [9]. As the number of minutiae in finger vein is limited, the recognition result of this kind algorithm is defective.

Although some advancements have been made, a phenomenon may be a hindrance to the development of finger vein recognition, that the input finger vein image is generally labeled in accordance with the nearest enrolled neighbor. This kind of nearest neighbor based classification is so rigid that it is inadequate for some cases. For example, if the distances between the input image and two or more enrolled images are very approximate, it is obviously inappropriate to label the input image based on the nearest enrolled image. Hence, rigid nearest neighbor based classification may be not optimal.

Recently, the theory of sparse representation (SR) has been successfully used in pattern recognition. Wright et al. [10] introduced a sparse representation framework for robust face recognition, in which the original face samples are used as dictionary to sparsely represent input face image. Yang et al. [11] use the metafaces, learned from original face images, to represent input face image under the framework of sparse representation. Xie et al. [12] uses textons learned from image patches to model texture images in texture classification. Xin et al. [13] introduced sparse representation for finger vein recognition, in which the dimensionality of finger vein image is firstly reduced by sparsity preserving projection (SPP), and then SR is used for finger vein representation in low dimensional space. The method in [13] is based on the sparse property of finger vein image, but only if the number of training images is large enough, images can show sparse property.

In finger vein image, some local vein patterns look similar at a certain extent, and these patterns appear in images at high frequencies, which perhaps can be used as textons. So, like patch-based sparse texton learning [12], in this paper, we try to use the combination of blocks in enrolled images to model the input image. But different from texture image, finger vein patterns have obvious geometric structure. To further encode geometric information of finger vein pattern, we incorporate the idea of linear projection [14] into SR, and generate a series of line features.

In detail, in the new SR method, textons in dictionary are learned from blocks in training images in training process. For an input finger vein image, we first model it by representing each block in it over all learned textons. Thus, for the input image, a two-dimensional SR coefficients histogram is achieved. And then, in order to encode geometric information of finger vein pattern, the two-dimensional histogram is projected to different lines to generate more powerful line features. Last, the line feature will be used in matching. The proposed method will meet two goals in finger vein recognition: 1) the local finger vein pattern can be adequately represented by the dictionary of textons, and 2) the global spatial information of finger vein pattern can be encoded effectively by linear projection.

The rest of the paper is organized as follows. Section 2 reviews the concepts of SR. Section 3 describes the proposed SR method in detail. The experimental results and analysis are shown in section 4, and section 5 concludes this paper.

2   Sparse Representation Based Classification

SR based classification takes root in visual perception mechanism, i.e., that visual neurons generate sparse representation for visual perception. SR can be used as a feature descriptor, and its aim is to seek sparse representation for testing signal over training signals.

Assume there are k classes, and each class i has n_i training samples, denoted by $A_i=[s_{i,1}, s_{i,2}, ..., s_{i,ni}]$, where $s_{i,j}, j=1,2,...,n_i$, is an m-dimensional vector stretched from the jth sample of the ith class. Denote by $A=[A_1, A_2, ..., A_k] \in R^{m \times n}$ the set of training samples from all classes, where $n=n_1+n_2+...+n_k$, is the number of training sample. For a new sample y from the ith class, if it can be approximately coded as a linear combination of all training samples: i.e., $y=A\alpha$, where $\alpha = [\alpha_1, ..., \alpha_i, ..., \alpha_k] = [\alpha_{1,1}, \alpha_{1,2}, ..., \alpha_{1,n_1}, ..., \alpha_{k,n_k}]$, meanwhile most coefficients in α are nearly zero and only coefficients in α_i have significant values, we say y has a sparse representation over training set A. The sparse representation based algorithm [10] is summarized as follows.

1. Normalize the columns of A to have unit $l2$-norm.

2. Solve the l1-minimization problem to get representation coefficients of y:

$$\hat{\alpha}_1 = \arg \min_{\alpha,A} \| A\alpha - y \|_2 + \lambda \| \alpha \|_1.$$

3. Compute the residuals
$$r_i(y) = \| y - A\delta_i(\hat{\alpha}_i) \|_2, i = 1,2,...,k.$$

where $\delta_i : R^n \rightarrow R^n$ is the characteristic function that selects the coefficients associated with the ith class.

4. Output $identity(y) = \arg \min_i r_i(y)$.

3   Modified Sparse Representation

We present the modified SR method in this section. It mainly includes three steps: local texton learning, feature descriptor and matching. The textons in dictionary is the fundamental of the proposed method, which is learned from local finger vein pattern. In feature descriptor, SR coefficients of all blocks in an image constitute a two-dimensional representation coefficient histogram, and the histogram is projected onto different lines to generate a series of line features, which is seen as image feature. In matching, in order to overcome the translation and/or rotation in finger vein images, multiple model histograms are built for each class.

3.1   Local Vein Texton Learning

Local vein texton learning is illustrated in Fig. 1, and we will present the learning process at great length in the following.

Before texton learning, all training images are partition into blocks, and some typical blocks are selected and initialized as dictionary texton. In detail, the image, randomly selected from database, is partitioned into nonoverlapping blocks with size of $p \times p$ pixels, and the block is stretched to a w-dimensional vector ($w = p \times p$). Hence, using all selected training images, we can construct a training block dataset $B = [B_1, B_2, ..., B_s]$, where B_i, $i = 1, 2, ..., s$, is all blocks in ith image. For an image, $B_i = [b_{11}, b_{12}, ..., b_{CR}]$, where b_{cr}, $c = 1, 2, ..., C$ and $r = 1, 2, ..., R$, is one block in a training image.

Assume there are 100 images selected from database, and each image is partitioned into 100 blocks, it is totally 10, 000 blocks. If all blocks are used to learning texton, two limitations will be caused: 1) as the number of blocks is so large that learning process is very time-consuming, and 2) as the vein pattern in blocks are redundancy, the learned textons are not representative, which may not represent images well. So, K-means algorithm is used to determine l typical blocks. The mean vectors of all clusters are initialized as dictionary, denoted by $D = [d_1, d_2, ..., d_l] \in R^{w \times l}$.

After dictionary initialization, sparse representation is used to optimize dictionary D and SR coefficients denoted by $\Lambda = [\beta_1, \beta_2, ..., \beta_l]$, and the optimization objective can be written as

$$\arg\min_{D, \Lambda} \| B - D\Lambda \|_F^2 + \lambda \| \Lambda \|_1, \tag{1}$$

This joint optimization problem is solved according to the method proposed in [11, 15]. The optimized dictionary D is based on the image block, not the whole image, and its texton is local vein pattern, not whole vein pattern in finger. Therefore, we call this learning process local texton learning.

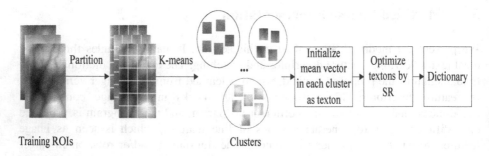

Fig. 1. Dictionary learning. K-means is used to gain typical image blocks and initialize as texton; and SR is used to optimize textons to get the dictionary

3.2   Feature Extraction

Dictionary learning has been introduced in the above section, and in this section we will describe how to use learned dictionary to represent finger vein image. In feature descriptor of finger vein image, we not only seek the effective representation of image block in locality, but also encode the spatial relationship of blocks from global perspective.

For a given finger vein image, we first partition it into nonoverlapping blocks with size of $p{\times}p$ pixels like training blocks, and then the learned dictionary is used to sparsely represent each block. The following problem is solved to get the SR coefficients:

$$\arg\min_{\beta_{ij}} \parallel b_{ij} - D\beta_{ij} \parallel_2^2 + \lambda \parallel \beta_{ij} \parallel_1 \qquad (2)$$

We use the method proposed [15] to solve this problem. Thus, for block b_{ij} at ith row and jth column of an image, we can obtain a coefficient vector β_{ij} saved in sub-histogram h_{ij}. And we arrange the sub-histogram h_{ij} according to the position of the block b_{ij} in image. So, for an image, a two-dimensional SR coefficient histogram can be achieved, shown in Fig. 2.

Although the locality of finger vein image is sought by sparsely representing each block over the learned dictionary, the global geometric information of finger vein pattern, i.e., the spatial relationship of blocks, has not been encoded. Hence, the idea of liner projection is used to encode geometric information of finger vein pattern from global perspective. For the achieved two-dimensional SR coefficient histogram, we project it onto lines with arbitrary angle to get a family of one-dimensional histogram, called line features, which is can depict the geometric information of global finger vein pattern. In finger, vein pattern is always parallel to finger, or grows at 45^0 or 135^0 angle with finger. Hence, projections with 0^0, 45^0, 90^0 and 135^0, are taken to maximize the geometric information of finger vein pattern, receiving four one-dimensional histograms H^0, H^{45}, H^{90} and H^{135}, shown in Fig. 2. Projection is a process of sum calculation for above achieved two-dimensional SR coefficient histogram along certain direction. We take H^{90} as an example to explain the projection process. For each column of above achieved two-dimensional histogram, we calculate the sum of the column as one element in H^{90}. All line features will be connected in parallel to be two-dimensional histogram H as the feature of an image.

3.3   Matching

As the feature of finger vein image is in two-dimensional histogram, Chi-square distance is used to measure the similarity between the input and enrolled images, as following:

$$d_{chi-square}(H_i, H_y) = \sum \frac{(H_i - H_y)^2}{H_i + H_y}, \qquad (3)$$

where H_i, $i=1,2,...,k$, denotes the model histogram of the enrolled image. Similarly, H_y is the SR coefficient histogram of the input image.

The random of finger placement in image acquisition causes translation or/and rotation in finger vein image. In order to overcome this shortcoming, for each enrolled class we use multiple model histograms calculated from multiple images of this class, and the minimum value of matching scores between multiple model histograms and the input histogram is used.

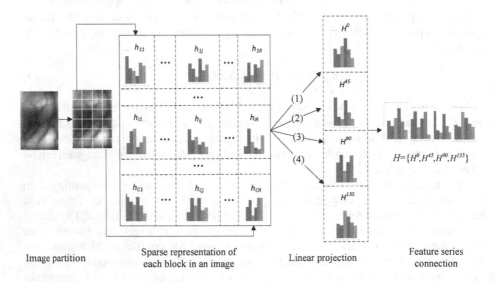

Image partition   Sparse representation of   Linear projection   Feature series
                          each block in an image   connection

Fig. 2. Feature descriptor. For one image, two-dimensional SR coefficient histogram is first achieved, and then the histogram is projected to four directions, last, features in four direction are connected.

3.4   Discussions

In this section, we discuss the relationship between our proposed sparse representation method and one related work: the existing sparse representation based finger vein recognition [13].

The differences between the existing method and our method mainly focus on three aspects. First, in existing sparse representation based finger vein recognition, the dictionary is learned from whole images, while textons in our dictionary are learned from image blocks. In addition, each image has its class label, but for one image block, it does not have class label, which creates the second difference. In existing method, each class has one sub-dictionary, and the global dictionary consists of all sub-dictionaries. In other word, the existing method learn class-specific dictionary. However, the dictionary in our method has no class label, which is a common dictionary. Last, the third aspect is related to the way of identify. In detail, residual of sparse representation is used to identify the input finger vein image in existing method, but we make use of SR coefficient histogram to perform finger vein recognition.

4   Experimental Results

In this section, we evaluate the effectiveness of our proposed SR method in finger vein recognition.

4.1   Experimental Settings

We perform experiments on one public finger vein database from the Hong Kong Polytechnic University [5]. The HKPU database contains 3, 132 finger vein images of 156 subjects captured in two separate sessions. In each session, each subject provided six finger vein images from the left index finger to the left middle finger, respectively. As only 105 subjects turned up for image acquisition in second session, we use 2, 520 images (i.e., 105 subjects×2 fingers×6 images×2 sessions) in our experiment. The training set used to learn dictionary includes one random selected image with 210 classes (In this paper, each finger is seen as one class.). For each class, 8 model histograms are built from 8 images, and remaining 4 images are used to test. The region of interest (ROI) of each image is segmented and normalized into 96×64 pixels using method proposed in [16]. Some typical finger vein images and the corresponding ROIs are shown in Fig. 3.

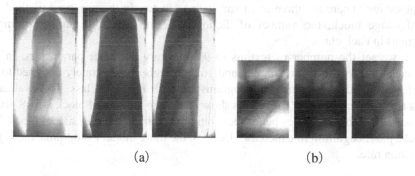

(a)   (b)

Fig. 3. (a) Some typical finger vein images. (b) The corresponding ROIs

4.2   Comparison with Other Methods

In this subsection, we compare the proposed method with four existing methods. In the four methods, one is the existing sparse representation based finger vein recognition [13], and each of three others are selected from each of three feature extraction algorithm groups depicted in Introduction. We fix the parameters as presented in above subsection. Besides, there are some parameters in SR, and we adjust them to get the best performance: λ =0.1, the size of image block is set as 8×8 pixels, and 90 textons are learned. We compare the recognition rates of all methods. The results are shown in Table 1. We can see from the results that the proposed method achieves a better recognition rate than other methods. The reason is that the proposed method seeks a sparse representation for modeling input image over the learned dictionary, and uses representation coefficients to perform classification, which is more flexible than nearest neighbor based classification. In addition, the proposed method encodes both the local vein pattern and the global spatial information, which cannot be done by other methods.

Table 1. Performance comparison of different methods

Methods	Recognition rate (%)
Mean Curvature [4]	0.9298
LBP [6]	0.9393
Minutia [9]	0.7887
Existing SR method [13]	0.9418
Proposed method	0.9524

4.3   Investigation of Parameter Values

We study the performance of the proposed method with different parameter values in this subsection. There are three main varying parameters in the proposed method: the size of image block, the number of dictionary textons and the number of model histograms in each class.

First, we set the number of textons to 90, but vary the other parameters. In this experiment, 8×8 pixels, 12×12 pixels and 16×16 pixels are separately assigned to the size of block, and 4, 6, 8 model histograms are built for each class. The evaluation results are given in Table 2. The results show that when the size of block is 8×8 pixels, the proposed method achieves better recognition rate, and the larger size of block does not make the recognition rate increase. Besides, the more model histograms, the higher recognition rate.

Table 2. The recognition rate (%) of different blocks and models

	8×8 pixels	12×12 pixels	16×16 pixels
4 models	0.8655	0.8452	0.8440
6 models	0.9286	0.9190	0.9131
8 models	0.9524	0.9488	0.9345

Then, we study the influence of the number of dictionary textons on the performance of the proposed method. Here we fix the size of block as 8×8 pixels, but vary the number of dictionary textons and the number of model histograms. The number of dictionary textons varies from 70 to 150, and the number of models in each class varies from 4 to 8. Fig. 4 illustrates the recognition rate of different textons and models. We can clearly see from this figure that when the number of textons is 90, the proposed method achieves best accuracies. After that, with the increase of number of textons, the recognition rate keeps unchanged on the whole. And, the more model histograms, the higher recognition rate, which is same with above experiment.

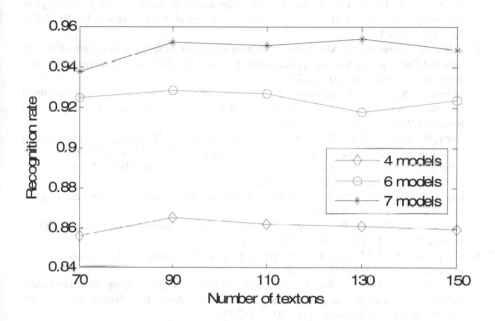

Fig. 4. The recognition rate (%) of different textons and models

5   Conclusions

In this paper, we proposed a modified sparse representation method for finger vein recognition. In the proposed method, textons in dictionary are learned from image blocks, and the image is modeled as distributions over the learned textons. The locality of finger vein pattern is sought by sparsely representing each image block over the learned textons, and the global geometric information of finger vein pattern is also encoded by the liner projections of four directions. Besides, to overcome the translation and/or rotation of finger vein image, we built multiple enrolled models for each class. The proposed method achieves better recognition rate than other methods. However, textons in dictionary are learned from finger vein image, and there are all kinds of noises in image, which are harmful for recognition performance. So, applying the proposed method on feature of finger vein image may be an interesting future issue.

Acknowledgments. This work is supported by National Natural Science Foundation of China under Grant No. 61173069, 61472226 and Shandong Natural Science Funds for Distinguished Young Scholar under Grant No. JQ201316. The authors would particularly like to thank the anonymous reviewers for their helpful suggestions.

References

1. Hashimoto, J.: Finger Vein Authentication Technology and Its Future. In: Proceedings of the Symposium on VLSI Circuits Digest of Technical Papers, Honolulu, HI, USA, pp. 15–17 (2006)
2. Miura, N., Nagasaka, A., Miyatake, T.: Feature extraction of finger vein patterns based on repeated line tracking and its application to personal identification. Machine Vision and Applications 15(4), 194–203 (2004)
3. Miura, N., Nagasaka, A., Miyatake, T.: Extraction of finger-vein patterns using maximum curvature points in image profiles. IEICE Transactions on Information and Systems E90-D(8), 1185–1194 (2007)
4. Song, W., Kim, T., Kim, H.C., Choi, J.H., Kong, H.J., Lee, S.R.: A finger-vein verification system using mean curvature. Pattern Recognition Letter 32(11), 1541–1547 (2011)
5. Kumar, A., Zhou, Y.B.: Human identification using finger images. IEEE Transactions on Image Processing 21(4), 2228–2244 (2012)
6. Lee, E.C., Jung, H., Kim, D.: New finger biometric method using near infrared imaging. Sensors 11(3), 2319–2333 (2011)
7. Rosdi, B.A., Shing, C.W., Suandi, S.A.: Finger vein recognition using local line binary pattern. Sensors 11(12), 11357–11371 (2011)
8. Yang, G.P., Xi, X.M., Yin, Y.L.: Finger vein recognition based on a personalized best bit map. Sensors 12, 1738–1757 (2012)
9. Yu, C.B., Qin, H.F., Zhang, L., Cui, Y.Z.: Finger-vein image recognition combining modified hausdorff distance with minutiae feature matching. Interdisciplinary Sciences: Computational Life Sciences 1(4), 280–289 (2009)
10. Wright, J., Yang, A.Y., Ganesh, A., Sastry, S.S., Ma, Y.: Robust face recognition via sparse representation. IEEE Transactions on Pattern Analysis and Machine Intelligence 31(2), 210–227 (2009)
11. Yang, M., Zhang, L., Yang, J., Zhang, D.: Metaface learning for sparse representation based face recognition. In: 17th IEEE International Conference on Image Processing (ICIP), pp. 1601–1604 (2010)
12. Xie, J., Zhang, L., You, J., Zhang, D.: Texture classification via patch-based sparse texton learning. In: 17th IEEE International Conference on Image Processing (ICIP), pp. 2737–2740 (2010)
13. Xin, Y., Liu, Z., Zhang, H.X., Zhang, H.: Finger vein verification system based on sparse representation. Applied Optics 51(25), 6252–6258 (2012)
14. Cao, Y., Wang, C.H., Li, Z.W., Zhang, L.Q., Zhang, L.: Spatial-bag-of-features. In: IEEE Conference on Computer Vision and Pattern Recognition (CVPR), pp. 3352–3359 (2010)
15. Kim, S.J., Koh, K., Lustig, M., Boyd, S., Gorinevsky, D.: A method for large-scale l1-regularized least squares. IEEE Journal on Selected Topics in Signal Processing 1(4), 606–617 (2007)
16. Yang, L., Yang, G.P., Yin, Y.L., Xiao, R.Y.: Sliding window-based region of interest extraction for finger vein images. Sensors 13(3), 3799–3815 (2013)

Palm Vein Identification Based on Multi-direction Gray Surface Matching

Wei Wu[1], Wen Jin[1], and Jin-Yu Guo[2]

[1] Information Engineering Department Shenyang University Shenyang, China
{wuwei429,jinwencomeon}@163.com
[2] Information Engineering Department,
Shenyang University of Chemical Technology, Shenyang, China
shandong401@sina.com

Abstract. In order to improve the recognition accuracy with high speed, a palm vein identification method based on multi-direction gray surface matching is proposed. The algorithm extracts region of interesting (ROI) of palm vein image firstly. Then, it computes the multi-direction gray scale's difference in the matching of surface of two ROI. The variances of the multi-direction grayscale difference surface are calculated and the minimum of variance is considered as the distance between two feature surfaces. At last, the algorithm decides whether these two images come from the same hand or not according to the distance. In the self-build palm vein database, the recognition rate of this method reaches 98.48% and the speed is 21.8ms. Comparing with other typical palm vein recognition methods, the proposed approach improves CCR and decreases FAR.

Keywords: biometrics, palm vein identification, multi-direction, gray surface matching.

1   Introduction

Private information is traditionally protected by using passwords or Personal Identification Numbers (PINs), which are easy to implement but is vulnerable to the risk of exposure or being forgotten. Biometrics, which uses human physiological or behavioral features for personal identification, has attracted more and more attention and is becoming one of the most popular and promising alternatives to the traditional password or PIN based authentication techniques. Currently, many R&D resources have been devoted to a burgeoning topic in biometrics: palm vein recognition[1-5]. Palm vein is a kind of network of blood vessels underneath a person's palm skin. It is a permanent and unique physiological feature of human [6-7]. Compares with palm-dorsa vein (hand vein) or finger vein, palm vein is richer and denser for recognition and impossible to forgery. Compares with the palm print, palm vein is not influenced by palm skin off. Compares with face, palm vein can distinguish twins easily. Compares with iris, palm vein is more user-friendly.

Z. Sun et al. (Eds.): CCBR 2014, LNCS 8833, pp. 281–287, 2014.
© Springer International Publishing Switzerland 2014

Nowadays, most of the palm vein's identification methods are utilizing the strategy that extracts the feature information from the palm vein image firstly and then encode feature data for matching. But there are some problems with these methods. Firstly, some captured NIR palm vein images are not clear because of some physiological reason [8]. As the result, the feature extraction method can't extract feature information exactly. Secondly, some complex feature extraction methods decrease the efficiency of the recognition.

This paper proposes a novel palm vein recognition method which discards the operating of feature extraction. Palm vein image is a grayscale surface in three-dimensional gray spaces. If two palm vein images come from the same hand, their grayscale surfaces are similar. If they come from different hands, their grayscale surfaces are different. The paper computes the multi-direction grayscale's different surface of two images to be matched. The variances of the multi-direction grayscale difference surface are calculated and the minimum of variance is considered as the distance between two feature surfaces. At last, the algorithm decides whether these two images come from the same hand or not according to the distance.

The remainder of the paper is organized as follows. Image collection and preprocessing are presented in Section 2 and Section 3. Section 4 presents a detailed description of our method based on Multi-direction Gray Surface Matching. The Experiments and Results are given in Section 5. Finally, Section 6 concludes the paper.

2   Image Collections

The image is captured in the illumination of 850nm LED set. A long wave-pass filter of 750nm is added in front of the camera to avoid the influence of visible light. During image acquisition, we request the user to fix his/her hand above the sensor with the palm facing the sensor. The user has to slightly stretch his/her fingers apart. The distance between hand and camera is 10cm or so. The image resolution is 768×554 pixels.

3   Image Preprocessing

In order to reduce the influence of image deformation and increase the recognition accuracy, the region of interest (ROI) in the palm vein image is extracted. After low pass filter and image binarization, we find the outline of the palm. Then, we seek for the maximal inscribed circle nearest to the wrist side (WSMIC, Wrist Side Maximal Inscribed Circle) in the palm image outline. The radius of WSMIC is R. As shown in Fig.1, point A is the tangent point of WSMIC with thumb side outline. Point O is the center of WSMIC. Connect point A and point O, we obtain line AO. Take point O as middle point of DE, and then draw a square BCDE with side of $(2*\sqrt{5}*R/5)$ pass point B and C in WSMIC. Side of BE parallels with line AO. Then, we extract the square BCDE and normalized it to the size of 128×128. The square is the ROI. The ROI is on the thenar of palm[9].

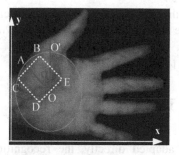

Fig. 1. Schematic diagram of ROI

4   Multi-direction Gray Surface Matching

This paper establishes a three-dimension space, which takes the horizontal direction of image as x axis, the vertical direction of image as y axis and gray value of pixel as z axis. That is the distribution surface of palm vein image in three-dimension space. The three-dimensional gray surface of palm vein image can be used to express the texture feature of palm vein. The fluctuation of palm vein's image on the three-dimensional gray surface has an obvious corresponding relationship with the texture distribution of palm vein, as shown in Fig. 2.

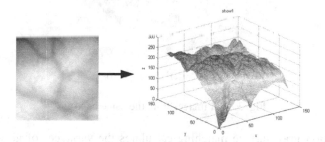

Fig. 2. Gray surface of palm vein ROI image

If two palm vein images come from the same hand, their gray surfaces must coincide or parallel. Their difference can be measured by calculating the variance between gray surfaces. Firstly, it computes the gray difference of two pixels from two different images (eg. R and S) and gets the gray difference surface (eg. D), as shown in Equation (1).

$$D_{ij} = R_{ij} - S_{ij} \qquad (1)$$

Dij represents the gray difference of point (i,j) on gray difference surface D. Rij, Sij represent the gray value of surface R and S on the point(i,j) ,i,j=0,1,2,...,W. W represents the wide of ROI.

Secondly, it calculates the variance of the gray difference surface and considers this variance as the distance between two images. , as shown in Equation (2).

$$\begin{cases} Var = \dfrac{1}{W^2}\displaystyle\sum_{i=1}^{W}\sum_{j=1}^{W}\left(\left|D_{ij}\right|-\overline{X}\right)^2 \\ \overline{X} = \dfrac{1}{W^2}\displaystyle\sum_{i=1}^{W}\sum_{j=1}^{W}\left|D_{ij}\right| \end{cases} \tag{2}$$

But if the variance is adapted directly, the recognition accuracy is not good enough. The reason is that some slight translation between images from same hand is ignored. To solve this question, the paper proposed multi-direction gray surface matching.

Through the comparison experiment, there are slight differences between ROI images from the same hand. They offset mostly between 1-4 pixels, as shown in Fig. 3, but the direction is so different.

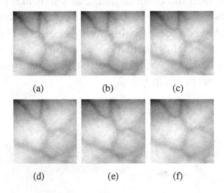

(a)   (b)   (c)

(d)   (e)   (f)

Fig. 3. ROI images from the same hand

Multi-direction gray surface matching calculates the variances of gray difference surface with offsetting 1-4 pixels in the directions of up, down, left and right. Then the algorithm selects the minimum of variance as the result to decide whether the two images come from the same hand.

5   Experiments and Results

5.1   Image Database

In order to test the performance of the proposed method, a palm vein database is built. The database contains 600 palm vein images which belong to 100 individuals with 6 different images each left hand. Image acquisition requirement includes the wrist exposed region with more than 1.5cm. Only rigid deformation is allowed in the collection process. Four images in our database are shown in Fig.4.

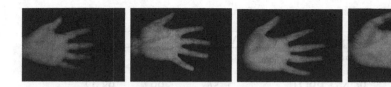

Fig. 4. Images from self-built image database

5.2   Matching Result

The experiments are performed under the Matlab 2011b programming environment with Windows 7 system and Intel(R) Xeon(R) CPU X5687 CPU of 3.6GHz and 32GB. A total of 44850 (50×49×6×6/2+50×6×5/2) comparisons are performed, in which 750 (50×6×5/2) comparisons are intra-class matching. Intra-class matching is the matching of different images coming from the same hand. Inter-class matching refers to matching the images coming from different hands. According to the Euclidean distance distributions of inter-class matching and intra-class matching, the threshold value T will be gained for palm vein matching. If the distance is less than T, the two images belonging to the same hand else belong to different hands. False rejection rate (FRR), false acceptation rate (FAR) and correct recognition rate (CRR) are used for recognition the measurement of performance [10].

$$FRR = \frac{NFR}{NAA} \times 100\% \tag{3}$$

$$FAR - \frac{NFA}{NIA} \times 100\% \tag{4}$$

$$CRR = \frac{the\ time\ of\ right\ result}{the\ total\ time\ of\ experiment} \times 100\% \tag{5}$$

NAA and NIA are the trying times for genuine and imposter separately; NFR and NFA are the times for false rejection and false acceptation separately.

We compare the traditional palm vein recognition method of SIFT[1],Gabor[2], PCA+LPP[3]   and Block gray surface[4]. Table 1 shows the recognition accuracy for different algorithms.

Table 2 shows the recognition times for different algorithms.

From Table 1, we can see that this method is superior to the traditional method in FAR, and CRR. From Table 2, we can see that the proposed method decreases compute complexity by discarding the feature extraction stage. The matching time is not the fastest but is fast enough.

Table 1. Performance comparison of proposed algorithm with other algorithms

Algorithm	FAR(%)	FRR(%)	CRR(%)
SIFT[1]	22.53	11.45	88.46
Gabor[2]	3.52	15.73	96.37
PCA+LPP[3]	1. 56	5.99	98.42
Block Grayscale surface[4]	1.9672	5.8138	97.94
Proposed	1.4880	5.8632	98.48

Table 2. Performance comparison of proposed algorithm with other algorithms

Algorithm	Feature extraction time (ms)	Matching time (ms)	Total time (ms)
SIFT[1]	101.9	0.6569	102.56
Gabor[2]	290.3	900	1192.2
PCA+LPP[3]	4.4	0.0337	4.43
Block Grayscale surface[4]	0.0158	0.1476	0.163
Proposed	**0**	**21.8**	**21.8**

6   Conclusion

This recognition method orientates ROI based on the thenar. We extract feature of palm vein based on multi-direction gray surface matching. The recognition performance reaches: CRR: 98.48%, FAR: 1.4880%, FRR: 5.8632%. Comparing with traditional palm vein's recognition method, this method increases the performance of recognition by decreasing the complexity of compute.

Acknowledgements. This work is supported by Education department of Liaoning province (L2013444),(L2012139).

References

1. Pan, M., Kang, W.: Palm vein recognition based on three local invariant feature extraction algorithms. In: Sun, Z., Lai, J., Chen, X., Tan, T. (eds.) CCBR 2011. LNCS, vol. 7098, pp. 116–124. Springer, Heidelberg (2011)
2. Lee, J.C.: A novel biometric system based on palm vein image. Pattern Recognition Letters 33(12), 1520–1528 (2012)
3. Wang, J., Yau, W., Suwandy, A., et al.: Fusion of palmprint and palm vein images for person recognition based on "Laplacianpalm" feature. Pattern Recognition 41(5), 1514–1527 (2008)
4. Wu, W., Yuan, W., Lin, S., Song, H., Shang, H.: Fast Palm Vein Identification Algorithm Based on Grayscale Surface Matching. Acta Optica Sinica 33(10), 1015004 (2013)

5. Watanabe, M., Endoh, T., Shiohara, M., et al.: Palm vein authentication technology and its applications. In: Proceedings of the Biometric Consortium Conference, pp. 19–21. IEEE Press, Arlington (2005)
6. Wang, L., Leedham, G.: Near-and far-infrared imaging for vein pattern biometrics. In: Proceedings of the Video and Signal Based Surveillance, pp. 52–57. IEEE Press, Sydney (2006)
7. Watanabe, M.: Palm Vein Authentication in Advances in Biometrics, pp. 75–88. Springer, Heidelberg (2008)
8. Lee, E.C., Park, K.R.: Image restoration of skin scattering and optical blurring for finger vein recognition. Opt. Lasers Eng. 49, 816–828 (2011)
9. Wu, W., Yuan, W.Q., Lin, S., et al.: Study of ROI selection and location for palm vein recognition. Journal of Optoelectronics·Laser 24(1), 152–160 (2013)
10. Wu, X., Zhang, D., Wang, K.: Palmprint Recognition, pp. 9–10. Science Press, Beijing (2006)

A Brief Survey on Recent Progress in Iris Recognition

Haiqing Li, Zhenan Sun, Man Zhang, Libin Wang, Lihu Xiao, and Tieniu Tan

Center for Research on Intelligent Perception and Computing (CRIPAC),
National Laboratory of Pattern Recognition (NLPR),
Institute of Automation, Chinese Academy of Sciences (CASIA),
No. 95, Zhongguancun East Road, Beijing 100190, China
{hqli,znsun,zhangman,lbwang,lhxiao,tnt}@nlpr.ia.ac.cn

Abstract. Great progress of iris recognition has been achieved in recent years driven by its wide applications in the world. This survey summaries the progress in iris image acquisition, segmentation, texture analysis, classification and cross-sensor recognition from 2008 to 2014. The core ideas of various methods and their intrinsic relationships are investigated to obtain an overview and insights in the development of iris recognition. The future research work to improve the usability, reliability and scalability of iris recognition systems is also suggested.

Keywords: Iris recognition, iris image acquisition, iris image segmentation, iris texture analysis, iris classification, cross-sensor.

1 Introduction

Iris is one of the most reliable biometric traits due to its uniqueness and stability. The uniqueness of iris texture comes from the random and complex structures such as furrows, ridges, crypts, rings, corona, freckles etc. which are formed during gestation. The epigenetic iris texture remains stable after 1.5 years old or so. Iris recognition has been widely applied in large-scale identity management systems, such as the border control systems in United Arab Emirates and the UID project of the Unique Identification Authority of India (UIDAI). The research of iris recognition has achieved great progress driven by its real world applications. And some new problems of iris recognition are arisen from practical requirements such as cross-sensor iris recognition and iris indexing for efficient large-scale identification.

Bowyer et al. [1,2] have given a review of iris recognition in 2010. This paper is intended to mainly investigate the progress of iris recognition from 2008 to 2014. The purpose of this survey is not to list all research papers in details, but try to summarize the core ideas of various methods and their intrinsic relationships. This paper focuses on the main modules in iris recognition, such as iris image acquisition, iris segmentation, iris texture analysis and some new topics such as iris image classification and cross-sensor iris recognition. The following sections will introduce the research ideas of these problems one by one.

Z. Sun et al. (Eds.): CCBR 2014, LNCS 8833, pp. 288–300, 2014.

2 Iris Image Acquisition

Accurate iris recognition depends on high resolution iris images. However, it is difficult to capture iris images because human iris is a small imaging target with only 11 mm in diameter [3]. And near infrared (NIR, 700-900 nm) illumination is needed to illustrate clear texture details of Asian subjects.

An iris imaging system's capture volume and standoff distance are closely related to its ease of use. The early iris imaging devices such as Panasonic's BM-ET300 and IrisGuard's IG-H100 have limited capture volume in close-up range so that they require significant user cooperation. In order to enlarge the capture volume, auto-focus lens and pan-tilt-zoom (PTZ) units are employed, such as Panasonic's BM-ET500, OKI's IRISPASS-M and the prototype systems proposed in [4,5,6,7,8,9]. These systems usually contain a wide field of view (FOV) camera for scene imaging and a narrow FOV camera which is mounted on a PTZ unit for iris imaging. Typically, the 2D position of a detected face in the wide FOV camera is combined with the face's depth information to adjust the narrow FOV camera towards iris. Yoon et al. [4] adopt light stripe projection and face detection to obtain the 3D location of a user. An optical rangefinder is integrated in Eagle-Eyes [6] for depth estimation. Wheeler et al. [5] use a stereo pair of fixed wide FOV surveillance cameras to locate the 3D position of a face. Boehnen et al. [9] employ a stereo camera and reconstruct the stereo information on the field-programmable gate array (FPGA). Dong et al. [7] use linear regression to coarsely estimate the geometric relationship between the wide FOV camera and the narrow FOV camera, which avoids 3D estimation and speeds up the PTZ adjustment.

Even though auto-focus lens and PTZ units extend the capture volume significantly, the mechanical adjustment of narrow FOV cameras is still too slow to track the human movement. Matey et al. [10] develop an iris on the move system which can identify subjects while they walk through a portal at a normal pace. Two narrow FOV and fixed focal length cameras are vertically stacked to provide a larger capture volume. Unlike the aforementioned systems, some iris imaging systems based on computational photography consider iris imaging and image processing simultaneously. The depth of field of an iris imaging system can be extended by wavefront coded lens [11] and light field cameras [12]. McCloskey et al. [13] utilize flutter shutter technique to avoid motion blur.

In addition to a large capture volume, a long standoff distance is also a desirable feature for an iris imaging system. Fancourt et al. [14] present the first study of iris recognition at a distance. They capture iris images with a telescope and infrared camera at up to 10 m standoff distance. Their experiments report no performance degradation with distance. But this system requires the subject's head to be positioned in a chin rest. The iris on the move system [10] can capture iris images at 3 m standoff distance with the benefits of high resolution cameras and high power NIR strobed illumination. Eagle-Eyes [6] demonstrates iris recognition at 3-6 m standoff distance using a well-designed laser illuminator. The systems presented by Dong et al. [7] and Boehnen et al. [9] are capable of acquiring iris images of sufficient quality for iris recognition at a distance 3 m and 7 m respectively.

Iris image acquisition is still a bottleneck for iris recognition. Great efforts are needed to develop innovative iris imaging systems that can safely and quickly acquire high quality iris images in a large capture volume and at a long distance.

3   Iris Segmentation

Human iris is small in size and always in motion, so it is difficult to capture an image only containing the iris region. Iris cameras usually capture a large area around the human eyes, which means that an iris image may contain not only the iris texture regions but also some neighborhood background regions such as pupil, sclera, eyelids, eyebrow, nose, forehead and eyeglasses. To define valid iris image regions for feature extraction and classification, it is necessary to segment the iris texture regions from others in iris images and represent the boundaries of these ROIs (region of interest) with proper models.

The early work on iris segmentation mainly focuses on locating circular or elliptical iris boundaries. The approaches proposed by Daugman and Wildes motivated most segmentation methods in the past two decades. Daugman's integro-differential operators [3,15] exhaustively search over the parameter space of curves for the maximum in the blurred partial derivative. Camus and Wildes [16] define a component-goodness-of-fit metric, which plays a similar role as integro-differential operators, to find the parameters that maximize gradient strengths and uniformities measured across rays radiating from a candidate central point. The estimated center location is updated in a gradient descend way to reduce the search space. Tan et al. [17] further extend the idea of gradient descent and design an integro-differential constellation which significantly accelerates the original exhaustive search nearly without reduction of accuracy.

Different from integro-differential operators, Wildes [18] creates a binary edge-map via edge detectors at first and then localizes iris boundaries by Hough transforms. Much attention has been paid on edge detection because Hough transforms can be misled by noisy edge points caused by non-iris boundaries. Liu et al. [19] use intensity thresholds to select candidate edge points. Proença and Alexandre [20] detect edges not in original but in clustered images to create more accurate edge maps. Tang and Weng [21] train a SVM classifier for limbic boundary detection using gradient and shape features. Li et al. [22] employ Adaboost to learn class-specific boundary detectors for left/right pupillary boundary and left/right limbic boundary detection. In order to speed up traditional Hough transforms, Uhl and Wild [23] use weighted adaptive Hough transforms to find the center of concentric circles considering both gradient magnitude and orientation. On the other hand, other techniques rather than Hough transforms are adopted to determine the parameters of iris boundaries after well-designed edge detection. Ryan et al. [24] detect edge points on rays and then estimate the parameters in a RANSAC-like manner. He et al. [25] find edge points in polar coordinates and fit the points by a pulling and pushing model. Edges are detected in polar or ellipsopolar coordinates by Gabor filters in the fine localization stage of [23]. Li et al. [26] take advantage of shape information and learned iris boundary detectors to extract genuine pupillary contour segments.

Because the iris texture regions are often partly occluded by eyelids and eyelashes, it is necessary to detect upper and lower eyelid boundaries and eyelashes after iris boundary localization. Even though integro-differential operators and Hough transforms can be straightforwardly generalized for eyelid boundary localization by adopting suitable curves, such as spline [15] and parabolic curves [18], accurate and robust eyelid localization remains unsolved due to eyelids and other occlusions. He et al. [25] use horizontal rank filtering and histogram filtering successively for noise removal. Liu et al. [27] combine an integro-differential parabolic arc operator and a RANSAC-like algorithm for eyelid detection. Li et al. [22] detect eyelid edge points using learned boundary detectors. Eyelashes are hard to be modeled by any parametric shapes because of their random appearance. Daugman [28] excludes eyelashes by statistical inference according to the difference between the intensity histograms of the upper and lower parts of an iris. He et al. [25] detect eyelashes and shadows via a learned prediction model which indicates the amount of occlusions according to the intensity histogram dissimilarity of two iris regions. Zuo and Schmid [29] estimate eyelashes by smearing the horizontal edge. In addition to eyelids and eyelashes detection on original iris images, these occlusions can be detected in normalized images. Huang et al. [30] fuse the edge information obtained through phase congruency and region information to localize the occlusions. Li and Savvides [31] use Gaussian mixture models to model the probabilistic distributions of the Gabor features extracted from both valid and invalid iris regions.

Iris boundaries can be approximated by circles or ellipses in many cases, but sometimes they present irregular shapes and need to be fitted by flexible curves. A popular way to solve this problem is to evolve active contours towards iris boundaries. There are mainly two kinds of representations of active contours, i.e. snakes and level sets. Daugman [28] describes iris boundaries in terms of snakes based on Fourier series expansions of the contour data, while some researchers use level sets to represent iris boundaries [32,33,34]. The major concern in applying active contours to iris segmentation is to design suitable energy functions for curve evolution. Different energy functions are proposed in [32,33]. Nevertheless, active contours tend to be trapped by highly textured regions. Hence Zhang et al. [34] create semantic iris contour maps to remove most iris textures before adopting active contours.

Apart from localizing iris boundaries to isolate valid iris regions, some work directly classifies each pixel in iris images into iris or non-iris regions. Pundlik et al. [35] model an iris image as a Markov random field and use a graph cut based energy minimization algorithm to separate eyelash pupil, iris and background regions. Proença [36] classifies pixels into sclera, iris and background by neural networks using location and color information in the neighborhood of pixels. Tan and Kumar [37] extract Zernike moments around pixels and then use SVM classifiers to identify the iris and non-iris regions. After pixel classification, these methods will fit iris boundaries using parametric curves for segmentation refinement or iris normalization.

4   Iris Texture Analysis

The uniqueness of iris pattern comes from the discriminative information of iris texture. Iris texture analysis plays a core role in the whole recognition system, and remains unsolved for iris images captured in less constrained environments.

Daugman [3] proposes the first effective algorithm for iris recognition, in which Gabor filters are applied to extract the phase information, and then the phase value is quantized into binary codes. At the matching stage, the dissimilarity of two iris codes is measured by Hamming distance. Wildes et al. [38] use Laplacian pyramids to describe iris texture, and employ correlation filters to match two iris feature patterns. Considering iris texture as one dimensional signals, zero-crossing points [39,40] or local sharp variations [41] are detected over the signals. Then, the Euclidean distance of feature points position or the Hamming distance of encoded features are used for matching.

Great progress has been made on iris texture analysis in the past decades. Ma et al. [42] represent iris features using a bank of spatial filters. Noh et al. [43] adopt Haar wavelet decomposition to obtain iris features. In [44], discrete cosine transform (DCT) is employed to extract features from iris texture. These methods obtain similar performance compared to Gabor filters. Sun and Tan [45] propose a general framework for iris texture analysis based on ordinal measures (OMs) which encode the ordinal intensity relationship between several image patches using binary codes. Their experiments show that OMs achieve state-of-the-art performance both in accuracy and efficiency.

In order to deal with the low-quality iris images captured in uncontrolled conditions, more robust iris texture representation methods are introduced. OMs encoded covariance matrices [46] are proposed to capture the correlation of spatial coordinates, intensities, 1st and 2nd-order partial derivatives. Rahulkar and Holambe [47] present a shift, scale and rotation-invariant technique for iris feature-representation and fuse post-classification to improve the accuracy and efficiency of the iris-recognition system. Dynamic features in [48] can capture the properties of iris images under NIR and visible-light illuminations. Advanced image-based correlation [49,50,51] is also a popular approach which can take advantage of the global features. The band-pass geometric features and low-pass ordinal features are fused in [52] to handle the pupillary deformation problem. Zhang et al. [53,54] introduce Daisy features and key-point selection for matching the deformed iris texture.

The recognition performance is closely related to the parameters of filters. Traditionally, the parameters are determined manually, which is often time-consuming and sub-optimal. It is desirable to design an algorithm that can find the optimized parameters driven by training data. He et al. [55] propose an Adaboost based algorithm, namely SOBoost, to select the most effective OMs features. Wang et al. [56,57] formulate the feature selection problem in a linear programming model, which can select a compact and discriminative feature subset by using sparsity regularization.

Sparse representation based iris recognition is first proposed by Pillai et al. [58]. Later, Kumar and Chan [59] model iris representation problem as quaternionic sparse coding problem. However, spare representation has a basic assumption that a test image can be linearly represented by the training samples from the same class. Then, one possible limitation is the acquisition and storage of adequate training samples for each class.

The original Hamming distance of binary iris code treats every bit equally [3]. However, some bits are more stable and some bits tend to be more easily effected by deformation or occlusions. Various strategies are proposed to adaptively set each bit a weight according to different considerations. Daugman [15] proposes a mask to ignore bits occluded by eyelids and eyelashes, where occluded bits are masked by zeroes and the visible bits are reserved by ones. Chen et al. [60] consider that local iris image regions with better quality have better classification capability and vice versa. They incorporated the local quality measures (or local energy) as weights to compute the matching score. Hollingsworth et al. [61] mask the real (imaginary) bits from complex numbers too close to the imaginary (real) axis as fragile bits. Dong et al. [62] present a personalized iris matching strategy by using a class-specific weight map learned from the training images of the same iris class. The importance of each bit in an iris feature is determined by its performance in the training dataset. In [63], Liu et al. focus on recognition of motion blurred iris images and propose a blur mask to adaptively weight each bit in an iris code based on its blur situation. Depending on whether there are available training samples, two mask generation methods are proposed. Extensive experiments are conducted to find the iris regions which are robust to motion blur. Afterwards, penalty coefficients are adaptively assigned based on the robustness.

5   Iris Image Classification

In contrast to iris recognition, iris image classification does not concern the identity label of an iris image. It aims to classify an iris image to an application specific category (genuine vs. fake, Asian vs. non-Asian, etc.). Recently, Sun et al. [64] discuss iris image classification systematically and propose a general framework for iris image classification based on hierarchical visual codebook which encodes the texture primitives. A comprehensive literature review of iris image classification for three kinds of typical applications, i.e. iris liveness detection, race classification and coarse iris classification, has been presented in [64]. The core content of the review is abstracted as follows.

1) Iris liveness detection. In highly secure applications of iris recognition, iris liveness detection is extremely important to prevent attacks of forged iris. Daugman [3] and Wildes [18] suggest pupillary athetosis as the evidence of liveness. The properties of iris imaging have been exploited for liveness detection, such as Purkinje images [65] and the relationship of reflectance ratio between iris and sclera [65]. Most of liveness detection approaches are based on iris texture analysis. He et al. [66] propose to detect printed iris images via frequency analysis. Many well-designed texture features, including gray level co-occurrence matrix [67], statistical distribution of iris texture primitive [68], local binary patterns (LBP) [69] and weighted-LBP [70], are used to describe the discriminative appearance between the genuine and fake iris images. Recently, Galbally et al. [71] detect liveness using quality related measures.

2) Race classification. Race information of a subject is useful for many applications, such as advertising and human computer interface. Although iris texture is significantly different for subjects at micro scale, it presents some similarities at macro scale for the same race. Qiu et al. [72] propose the first texture analysis based racial iris image classification method. A bank of multichannel 2-D Gabor filters is used to extract the global texture information and Adaboost is used to train the classifier. In their later work [73], Iris-Textons are trained to represent the visual primitives of iris texture to classify Asian and no-Asian iris images. Zhang et al. [74] take advantages of supervised codebook and locality-constrained linear coding for race classification. Lyle et al. [75] encode the periocular regions by LBP for gender and race classification.

3) Coarse iris classification. Coarse iris classification divides a large enrolled iris image database into a number of sub-datasets to speed up personal identification. Yu et al. [76] calculate the fractal dimension value in iris blocks for coarse iris classification. Fu et al. [77] use artificial color filter to detect the color information of iris images, and employ margin setting to classify iris images into proper categories. In [78], iris images are grouped into five categories based on statistical description of learned Iris-Textons. Mehrotra et al. [79] use energy based histogram of multi-resolution DCT to group iris images. Sunder et al. [80] extract scale-invariant feature transform (SIFT) features to represent iris macrofeatures (structures such as moles, freckles, nevi, and melanoma) for iris retrieval and matching.

6   Cross-Sensor Iris Recognition

Various iris imaging devices have been developed with the large scale deployments of iris recognition. Different illuminators, lens and sensors of different imaging devices result in cross-sensor variations in iris images. These variations tend to increase the intra-class distance between samples that are captured by different devices. Therefore, the interoperability of different iris imaging devices becomes increasingly important. Bowyer et al. [81] investigate cross-sensor comparisons of two LG iris recognition systems. The experiments demonstrate that performance degradation of cross-sensor iris recognition is mainly caused by the shift of intra-class distribution. Connaughton et al. [82,83] conduct more experiments for interoperability of iris sensors on three commercially available sensors and three matching algorithms. They conclude that the relationship between sensors, algorithms and acquisition environment should be considered to develop a robust iris recognition system.

In order to alleviate performance degradation in cross-sensor iris recognition, several algorithms have been proposed. Arora et al. [84] first predict the source camera and then enhance images accordingly to minimize the appearance difference between images acquired by different cameras. Xiao et al. [85,86] propose feature selection solutions to represent the intrinsic features of iris images from different sensors. A coupled feature selection method is proposed in [86] to select coupled features simultaneously. They utilize $l_{2,1}$ regularization to model the problem and solve the formulation by an efficient algorithm based on a half-quadratic optimization. In [85], the coupled feature weighting factors is learned by a margin based feature selection method. The problem is formulated and solved by linear programming. Pillai et al. [87] propose a kernel learning method for sensor adaption. The learnt transformations on binary iris code can reduce the intra-class distance and increase inter-class distance of cross-sensor comparisons. On the other hand, Xiao et al. [88] fuse the iris and periocular biometrics to improve the performance of cross-sensor identification, where multi-directions ordinal measures are used for feature extraction.

7 Future Research Directions

Several promising research directions can be observed as follows.

1) Iris image acquisition. Currently, commercial iris recognition systems still require high user cooperation to capture iris images of sufficient quality. Although some prototype systems can work at a distance or on the move, their capture volume and imaging speed are unsatisfactory for practical applications, e.g. surveillance. Therefore, iris image acquisition is still a bottleneck for the wide deployment of iris recognition. One solution is to develop better NIR cameras and optical design, or to improve the accuracy and speed of the control units for PZT cameras. Another solution is to consider iris imaging and image processing simultaneously as in computational photography.

2) Iris recognition algorithms. It is inevitable to capture many iris images of low quality in less constrained environments, which brings many difficulties to recognition algorithms. Large occlusions, off-axis gaze and blur will mislead iris segmentation and increase the intra-class variations. Traditional knowledge based iris recognition algorithms are hard to model these large variations and will suffer from large performance degradation. Machine learning methods, such as Adaboost, SVM and neural networks, are powerful tools to automatically learn the optimal parameters for representation and classification. They have successfully improved the robustness and accuracy of iris recognition and will continue demonstrating their capacity at all levels.

3) Large-scale iris recognition Large-scale applications of iris recognition introduce many new challenges. Although the comparisons of binary iris codes are very fast, it is time-consuming for exhaustive search in national-scale databases, e.g. the UID project in India. Iris indexing or coarse classification can select a subset from the large database for comparison and will speed up the search. Another challenge is the interoperability of different iris imaging devices.

On one hand, we should develop more robust recognition algorithms that are insensitive to sensor variations. On the other hand, international standards are needed to reduce the differences among images captured by different sensors. These emerging problems have not been systematically investigated and remain far from solved.

4) Privacy and security The privacy and security issues become increasingly important nowadays, especially in wireless and mobile networks where personal data often faces malware attacks. Therefore, biometric templates should be protected by well-designed encryption algorithms which have negligible influence on the performance of recognition. Irreversibility and unlinkability are two major requirements of biometric template protection. However, the techniques to enhance the irreversibility and unlinkability may reduce the performance of iris recognition.

5) Multi-biometrics The major limitation of iris recognition is its usability. As it is convenient to capture iris and face images simultaneously, it is expected to develop a more accurate, secure and easy-to-use recognition system by combining iris and face biometrics. In addition, iris can be fused with other biometric traits, such as fingerprint and palmprint. However, it remains unsolved to efficiently and effectively unite the complementary advantages of different biometric modalities

8   Conclusions

In this paper, a brief review of some subareas of iris recognition, namely iris image acquisition, segmentation, texture analysis, classification and cross-sensor recognition, has been presented. Several trends of next-generation iris recognition have been concluded. Some important subareas, such as iris image quality assessment and multi-biometrics involving iris, are omitted in this survey due to limited space and will be included in our later survey.

Acknowledgements. This work is supported by the National Natural Science Foundation of China (Grant No. 61273272) and the Instrument Developing Project of the Chinese Academy of Sciences (Grant No. YZ201266).

References

1. Bowyer, K.W., Hollingsworth, K., Flynn, P.J.: Image understanding for iris biometrics: A survey. CVIU 110(2), 281–307 (2008)
2. Bowyer, K.W., Hollingsworth, K., Flynn, P.J.: A survey of iris biometrics research: 2008-2010. In: Handbook of Iris Recognition. Advances in Computer Vision and Pattern Recognition. Springer (2013)
3. Daugman, J.: High confidence visual recognition of persons by a test of statistical independence. IEEE TPAMI 15(11), 1148–1161 (1993)
4. Yoon, S., Jung, H.G., Suhr, J.K., Kim, J.: Non-intrusive iris image capturing system using light stripe projection and pan-tilt-zoom camera. In: CVPR (2007)

5. Wheeler, F.W., Perera, A., Abramovich, G., Yu, B., Tu, P.H.: Stand-off iris recognition system. In: Biometrics: Theory, Applications and Systems (2008)
6. Bashir, F., Casaverde, P., Usher, D., Friedman, M.: Eagle-eyes: A system for iris recognition at a distance. In: IEEE Conference on Technologies for Homeland Security (2008)
7. Dong, W., Sun, Z., Tan, T., Qiu, X.: Self-adaptive iris image acquisition system. In: Proc. of SPIE (2008)
8. Dong, W., Sun, Z., Tan, T.: A design of iris recognition system at a distance. In: Chinese Conference on Pattern Recognition (2009)
9. Boehnen, C., Barstow, D., Patlolla, D., Mann, C.: A multi-sample standoff multimodal biometric system. In: Biometrics: Theory, Applications and Systems (2012)
10. Matey, J., Naroditsky, O., Hanna, K., Kolczynski, R., LoIacono, D., Mangru, S., Tinker, M., Zappia, T., Zhao, W.Y.: Iris on the move: Acquisition of images for iris recognition in less constrained environments. Proc. of the IEEE 94(11), 1936–1947 (2006)
11. Narayanswamy, R., Silveira, P.E.X., Setty, H., Pauca, V.P., van der Gracht, J.: Extended depth-of-field iris recognition system for a workstation environment. In: Proc. of SPIE (2005)
12. Zhang, C., Hou, G., Sun, Z., Tan, T., Zhou, Z.: Light field photography for iris image acquisition. In: Chinese Conference on Biometric Recognition (2013)
13. McCloskey, S., Au, W., Jelinek, J.: Iris capture from moving subjects using a fluttering shutter. In: Biometrics: Theory, Applications and Systems (2010)
14. Fancourt, C., Bogoni, L., Hanna, K.J., Guo, Y., Wildes, R.P., Takahashi, N., Jain, U.: Iris recognition at a distance. In: Kanade, T., Jain, A., Ratha, N.K. (eds.) AVBPA 2005. LNCS, vol. 3546, pp. 1–13. Springer, Heidelberg (2005)
15. Daugman, J.: How iris recognition works. IEEE TCSVT 14(1), 21–30 (2004)
16. Camus, T., Wildes, R.: Reliable and fast eye finding in close-up images In: International Conference on Pattern Recognition (2002)
17. Tan, T., He, Z., Sun, Z.: Efficient and robust segmentation of noisy iris images for non-cooperative iris recognition. IVC 28(2), 223–230 (2010)
18. Wildes, R.: Iris recognition: an emerging biometric technology. Proc. of the IEEE 85(9), 1348–1363 (1997)
19. Liu, X., Bowyer, K., Flynn, P.: Experiments with an improved iris segmentation algorithm. In: IEEE Workshop on Automatic Identification Advanced Technologies (2005)
20. Proença, H., Alexandre, L.: Iris segmentation methodology for non-cooperative recognition. IEE Proc. of Vision, Image and Signal Processing 153(2), 199–205 (2006)
21. Tang, R., Weng, S.: Improving iris segmentation performance via borders recognition. In: International Conference on Intelligent Computation Technology and Automation (2011)
22. Li, H., Sun, Z., Tan, T.: Robust iris segmentation based on learned boundary detectors. In: International Conference on Biometrics (2012)
23. Uhl, A., Wild, P.: Weighted adaptive hough and ellipsopolar transforms for real-time iris segmentation. In: International Conference on Biometrics (2012)
24. Ryan, W., Woodard, D., Duchowski, A., Birchfield, S.: Adapting starburst for elliptical iris segmentation. In: Biometrics: Theory, Applications and Systems (2008)
25. He, Z., Tan, T., Sun, Z., Qiu, X.: Toward accurate and fast iris segmentation for iris biometrics. IEEE TPAMI 31(9), 1670–1684 (2009)
26. Li, H., Sun, Z., Tan, T.: Accurate iris localization using contour segments. In: International Conference on Pattern Recognition (2012)

27. Liu, X., Li, P., Song, Q.: Eyelid localization in iris images captured in less constrained environment. In: Tistarelli, M., Nixon, M.S. (eds.) ICB 2009. LNCS, vol. 5558, pp. 1140–1149. Springer, Heidelberg (2009)

28. Daugman, J.: New methods in iris recognition. IEEE TSMC, Part B 37(5), 1167–1175 (2007)

29. Zuo, J., Schmid, N.: On a methodology for robust segmentation of nonideal iris images. IEEE TSMC, Part B 40(3), 703–718 (2010)

30. Huang, J., Wang, Y., Tan, T., Cui, J.: A new iris segmentation method for recognition. In: International Conference on Pattern Recognition, vol. 3 (2004)

31. Li, Y.H., Savvides, M.: An automatic iris occlusion estimation method based on high-dimensional density estimation. IEEE TPAMI 35(4), 784–796 (2013)

32. Vatsa, M., Singh, R., Noore, A.: Improving iris recognition performance using segmentation, quality enhancement, match score fusion, and indexing. IEEE TSMC, Part B 38(4), 1021–1035 (2008)

33. Shah, S., Ross, A.: Iris segmentation using geodesic active contours. IEEE TIFS 4(4), 824–836 (2009)

34. Zhang, X., Sun, Z., Tan, T.: Texture removal for adaptive level set based iris segmentation. In: IEEE International Conference on Image Processing (2010)

35. Pundlik, S., Woodard, D., Birchfield, S.: Non-ideal iris segmentation using graph cuts. In: CVPR Workshop (2008)

36. Proença, H.: Iris recognition: On the segmentation of degraded images acquired in the visible wavelength. IEEE TPAMI 32(8), 1502–1516 (2010)

37. Tan, C.W., Kumar, A.: Unified framework for automated iris segmentation using distantly acquired face images. IEEE TIP 21(9), 4068–4079 (2012)

38. Wildes, R., Asmuth, J., Green, G., Hsu, S., Kolczynski, R., Matey, J., McBride, S.: A machine-vision system for iris recognition. In: Machine Vision and Applications (1996)

39. Boles, W., Boashash, B.: A human identification technique using images of the iris and wavelet transform. IEEE TSP 46(4), 1185–1188 (1998)

40. Sanchez-Avila, C., Sanchez-Reillo, R.: Two different approaches for iris recognition using gabor filters and multiscale zero-crossing representation. PR 38(2), 231–240 (2005)

41. Ma, L., Tan, T., Wang, Y., Zhang, D.: Efficient iris recognition by characterizing key local variations. IEEE TIP 13(6), 739–750 (2004)

42. Ma, L., Tan, T., Wang, Y., Zhang, D.: Personal identification based on iris texture analysis. IEEE TPAMI 25(12), 1519–1533 (2003)

43. Noh, S.I., Bae, K., Park, Y., Kim, J.: A novel method to extract features for iris recognition system. In: Kittler, J., Nixon, M.S. (eds.) AVBPA 2003. LNCS, vol. 2688, pp. 862–868. Springer, Heidelberg (2003)

44. Monro, D.M., Rakshit, S., Zhang, D.: Dct-based iris recognition. IEEE TPAMI 29(4), 586–595 (2007)

45. Sun, Z., Tan, T.: Ordinal measures for iris recognition. IEEE TPAMI 31(12), 2211–2226 (2009)

46. Li, P., Wu, G.: Iris recognition using ordinal encoding of log-euclidean covariance matrices. In: International Conference on Pattern Recognition (2012)

47. Rahulkar, A., Holambe, R.: Half-iris feature extraction and recognition using a new class of biorthogonal triplet half-band filter bank and flexible k-out-of-n:a postclassifier. IEEE TIFS 7(1), 230–240 (2012)

48. da Costa, R., Gonzaga, A.: Dynamic features for iris recognition. IEEE TSMC, Part B 42(4), 1072–1082 (2012)

49. Thornton, J., Savvides, M., Vijayakumar, B.V.K.: Robust iris recognition using advanced correlation techniques. In: Kamel, M.S., Campilho, A.C. (eds.) ICIAR 2005. LNCS, vol. 3656, pp. 1098–1105. Springer, Heidelberg (2005)

50. Li, Y.H., Savvides, M., Thornton, J., Kumar, B.V.K.V.: Iris recognition using correlation filters. In: Encyclopedia of Biometrics (2009)

51. Zhang, M., Sun, Z., Tan, T.: Perturbation-enhanced feature correlation filter for robust iris recognition. IET Biometrics 1(1), 37–45 (2012)

52. Zhang, M., Sun, Z., Tan, T.: Deformed iris recognition using bandpass geometric features and lowpass ordinal features. In: International Conference on Biometrics (2013)

53. Zhang, M., Sun, Z., Tan, T.: Deformable daisy matcher for robust iris recognition. In: IEEE International Conference on Image Processing (2011)

54. Alonso-Fernandez, F., Tome-Gonzalez, P., Ruiz-Albacete, V., Ortega-Garcia, J.: Iris recognition based on sift features. In: International Conference on Biometrics, Identity and Security (2009)

55. He, Z., Sun, Z., Tan, T., Qiu, X., Zhong, C., Dong, W.: Boosting ordinal features for accurate and fast iris recognition. In: CVPR (2008)

56. Wang, L., Sun, Z., Tan, T.: Robust regularized feature selection for iris recognition via linear programming. In: International Conference on Pattern Recognition (2012)

57. Sun, Z., Wang, L., Tan, T.: Ordinal feature selection for iris and palmprint recognition. IEEE TIP 23(9), 3922–3934 (2014)

58. Pillai, J., Patel, V., Chellappa, R., Ratha, N.: Secure and robust iris recognition using random projections and sparse representations. IEEE TPAMI 33(9), 1877–1893 (2011)

59. Kumar, A., Chan, T.S.: Iris recognition using quaternionic sparse orientation code (qsoc). In: CVPR Workshop (2012)

60. Chen, Y., Dass, S.C., Jain, A.K.: Localized iris image quality using 2-D wavelets. In: Zhang, D., Jain, A.K. (eds.) ICB 2005. LNCS, vol. 3832, pp. 373–381. Springer, Heidelberg (2005)

61. Hollingsworth, K., Bowyer, K., Flynn, P.: The best bits in an iris code. IEEE TPAMI 31(6), 964–973 (2009)

62. Dong, W., Sun, Z., Tan, T.: Iris matching based on personalized weight map. IEEE TPAMI 33(9), 1744–1757 (2011)

63. Liu, J., Sun, Z., Tan, T.: Recognition of motion blurred iris images. In: Biometrics: Theory, Applications and Systems (2013)

64. Sun, Z., Zhang, H., Tan, T., Wang, J.: Iris image classification based on hierarchical visual codebook. IEEE TPAMI 36(6), 1120–1133 (2014)

65. Lee, E.C., Park, K.R., Kim, J.H.: Fake iris detection by using purkinje image. In: Zhang, D., Jain, A.K. (eds.) ICB 2005. LNCS, vol. 3832, pp. 397–403. Springer, Heidelberg (2005)

66. He, X., Lu, Y., Shi, P.: A fake iris detection method based on fft and quality assessment. In: Chinese Conference on Pattern Recognition (2008)

67. He, X., An, S., Shi, P.: Statistical texture analysis-based approach for fake iris detection using support vector machines. In: Lee, S.-W., Li, S.Z. (eds.) ICB 2007. LNCS, vol. 4642, pp. 540–546. Springer, Heidelberg (2007)

68. Wei, Z., Qiu, X., Sun, Z., Tan, T.: Counterfeit iris detection based on texture analysis. In: International Conference on Pattern Recognition (2008)

69. He, Z., Sun, Z., Tan, T., Wei, Z.: Efficient iris spoof detection via boosted local binary patterns. In: Tistarelli, M., Nixon, M.S. (eds.) ICB 2009. LNCS, vol. 5558, pp. 1080–1090. Springer, Heidelberg (2009)

70. Zhang, H., Sun, Z., Tan, T.: Contact lens detection based on weighted lbp. In: International Conference on Pattern Recognition (2010)
71. Galbally, J., Ortiz-Lopez, J., Fierrez, J., Ortega-Garcia, J.: Iris liveness detection based on quality related features. In: International Conference on Biometrics (2012)
72. Qiu, X., Sun, Z., Tan, T.: Global texture analysis of iris images for ethnic classification. In: Zhang, D., Jain, A.K. (eds.) ICB 2005. LNCS, vol. 3832, pp. 411–418. Springer, Heidelberg (2005)
73. Qiu, X., Sun, Z., Tan, T.: Learning appearance primitives of iris images for ethnic classification. In: IEEE International Conference on Image Processing (2007)
74. Zhang, H., Sun, Z., Tan, T., Wang, J.: Ethnic classification based on iris images. In: Sun, Z., Lai, J., Chen, X., Tan, T. (eds.) CCBR 2011. LNCS, vol. 7098, pp. 82–90. Springer, Heidelberg (2011)
75. Lyle, J., Miller, P., Pundlik, S., Woodard, D.: Soft biometric classification using periocular region features. In: Biometrics: Theory, Applications and Systems (2010)
76. Yu, L., Zhang, D., Wang, K., Yang, W.: Coarse iris classification using box-counting to estimate fractal dimensions. PR 38(11), 1791–1798 (2005)
77. Fu, J., Caulfield, H.J., Yoo, S.M., Atluri, V.: Use of artificial color filtering to improve iris recognition and searching. PRL 26(14), 2244–2251 (2005)
78. Qiu, X., Sun, Z., Tan, T.: Coarse iris classification by learned visual dictionary. In: Lee, S.-W., Li, S.Z. (eds.) ICB 2007. LNCS, vol. 4642, pp. 770–779. Springer, Heidelberg (2007)
79. Mehrotra, H., Srinivas, B.G., Majhi, B., Gupta, P.: Indexing iris biometric database using energy histogram of DCT subbands. In: Ranka, S., Aluru, S., Buyya, R., Chung, Y.-C., Dua, S., Grama, A., Gupta, S.K.S., Kumar, R., Phoha, V.V. (eds.) IC3 2009. CCIS, vol. 40, pp. 194–204. Springer, Heidelberg (2009)
80. Sunder, M., Ross, A.: Iris image retrieval based on macro-features. In: International Conference on Pattern Recognition (2010)
81. Bowyer, K., Baker, S., Hentz, A., Hollingsworth, K., Peters, T., Flynn, P.: Factors that degrade the match distribution in iris biometrics. Identity in the Information Society 2(3), 327–343 (2009)
82. Connaughton, R., Sgroi, A., Bowyer, K., Flynn, P.: A cross-sensor evaluation of three commercial iris cameras for iris biometrics. In: CVPR Workshop (2011)
83. Connaughton, R., Sgroi, A., Bowyer, K., Flynn, P.: A multialgorithm analysis of three iris biometric sensors. IEEE TIFS 7(3), 919–931 (2012)
84. Arora, S.S., Vatsa, M., Singh, R., Jain, A.: On iris camera interoperability. In: Biometrics: Theory, Applications and Systems (2012)
85. Xiao, L., Sun, Z., He, R., Tan, T.: Margin based feature selection for cross-sensor iris recognition via linear programming. In: IAPR Asian Conference on Pattern Recognition (2013)
86. Xiao, L., Sun, Z., He, R., Tan, T.: Coupled feature selection for cross-sensor iris recognition. In: Biometrics: Theory, Applications and Systems (2013)
87. Pillai, J., Puertas, M., Chellappa, R.: Cross-sensor iris recognition through kernel learning. IEEE TPAMI 36(1), 73–85 (2014)
88. Xiao, L., Sun, Z., Tan, T.: Fusion of iris and periocular biometrics for cross-sensor identification. In: Zheng, W.-S., Sun, Z., Wang, Y., Chen, X., Yuen, P.C., Lai, J. (eds.) CCBR 2012. LNCS, vol. 7701, pp. 202–209. Springer, Heidelberg (2012)

An Effective Iris Recognition Method Based on Scale Invariant Feature Transformation

Guang Huo[1,2], Yuanning Liu[1], Xiaodong Zhu[1], Hongye Wang[1,3], Lijiao Yu[1], Fei He[1], Si Gao[1], and Hongxing Dong[1]

[1] College of Computer Science and Technology, Jilin University, Changchun 130012, China
[2] Informatization Office, Northeast Dianli University, Jilin 132012, China
[3] The department of information engineering, Shijiazhuang Vocational College for Scientific and Technical Engineering, Shijiazhuang 050800, China
{huoguang12,lyn,zhuxd,wanghy11,ljyu13,
hefei10,gaosi13,donghx13}@jlu.edu.cn

Abstract. The parameter selection of SIFT operator is the premise and difficulty of feature extraction with SIFT. Based on a analysis of the change regulation between each parameter of SIFT operator and the valid key points in detail, a variety of parameter selection ways to fit to extract iris texture features are put forward in this paper. A new set of feature matching method is designed and realized according to the features. According to the experimental results from three public iris databases, including CASIA V1.0, CASIA-V3-Interval and MMU, compared with classical SIFT method of Lowe, the method we proposed has been proven to increase by 2% to 5% in recognition accuracy. It shows that the method we proposed has strong robustness and high recognition ability.

Keywords: Iris recognition, feature extraction, SIFT, feature matching.

1 Introduction

Iris recognition has attracted many attentions of the scholars as a representative of the biometric technologies. There are many fairly representative algorithms in classical algorithms. For instance, Daugman made use of 2D-Gabor filters to extract texture phase feature of the iris and used Hamming distance for matching[1][2]. Boles and Boashash detected zero crossings of one-dimensional wavelet transform over concentric circles on the iris. Both the position and magnitude information of zero-crossing representations were used for matching[3]. These algorithms mostly base on local features of the iris. These algorithms' downside is that algorithm's performance would drop significantly with too much interference. Given this, a kind of global iris recognition algorithm is designed to reduce the effects of local interferences on the whole recognition algorithm's performance.

SIFT operator was proposed for the first time by David G. Lowe[4] in 1999.It extracts the key point feature of being invariant to the scale and rotation of image. It has strong adaptability to illumination variation and anamorphoses. At the same time, this feature has high distinguishability in favor of the subsequent matching. Therefore,

Z. Sun et al. (Eds.): CCBR 2014, LNCS 8833, pp. 301–310, 2014.

SIFT operator is applied successfully in many fields, such as target recognition[5], panorama splicing[6] and structure from motion etc. However, in terms of the literatures we can refer to, it's scant to apply SIFT to research on iris recognition at present.

This article introduces the SIFT[4] into the iris recognition system. We put forward the corresponding improvement scheme on the basis of detailed analysis of the classical SIFT. With the experimental results, the recognition accuracy of our proposed algorithm is improved markedly than before.

2   SIFT Method for Iris Feature Points Matching

2.1   The Iris Image Segmentation

The function of iris image segmentation is separating iris texture region from the image in order to reduce the effects of interferences which is caused by eyelids and eyebrows etc on feature extraction. Considering the complexity of the iris localization and irregularity of iris band, this paper adopts C-V level-set, namely the localization method combined Chan with Vese (C-V in short) and minimizes the energy function in curve evolution of C-V level set.

The image $I(x, y)$ is defined on the domain Ω and closed boundary C, image $I(x, y)$ is divided into two parts: C_0 and C_b, which represents two regions respectively: target and background. The average gray in above two regions is represented respectively by C_0 and C_b. The computational formula of energy function is as follows:

$$E(C, C_o, C_b) = \mu L(C) + v S_o(C) + \lambda_o \iint_{C_o} |I - C_o|^2 dxdy + \lambda_b \iint_{C_b} |I - C_b|^2 dxdy \quad (1)$$

Among them, l_b is the length of the closed boundary C, and $S_o(C)$ is the area of C_0, namely, the interior area of C. $\mu, v \geq 0$, $\lambda_o, \lambda_b > 0$ indicate weight of each energy term. When the contour C locates in the boundary of two regions, $E(c)$ would get a minimum value.

Fig.1 shows the original images and localized images by level-set, namely, (a), (b) and (c) are the original images. (d), (e) and (f) are the localized images. Obviously, level-set can segment the iris band area successfully. In the meantime, the external edge of band gotten by level-set would change with the shape of the band and both inside and outside edges need not to be round. So, the level-set can effectively avoid the problems of non-circular pupil and eyelid shade in traditional ways.

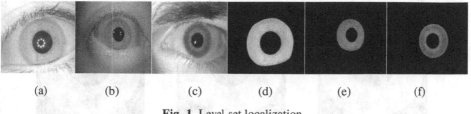

| (a) | (b) | (c) | (d) | (e) | (f) |

Fig. 1. Level-set localization

2.2   Parameter Selection of SIFT Operator

2.2.1   The Scale of the Gaussian Function

Each of iris images in the algorithm of Lowe and Liu needs a Gaussian pyramid of 6 groups and 6 layers, namely $O = 6$. It needs different operation and feature extraction. The algorithm involves 36 images, in which calculation[7] is very large. After experiments, we noticed that the calculation of SIFT can be greatly lessened by reducing the groups of Gaussian pyramid and the extraction of pseudo key points outside the band on the premise of not affecting the extraction of key points in iris band. Finally this paper selects $O = 4$ as the groups of Gaussian pyramid, as shown in Fig.2

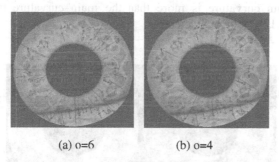

(a) o=6   (b) o=4

Fig. 2. Key point extraction in different groups

2.2.2   Contrast Threshold

In SIFT, the varied numbers of feature points can be extracted on each layer of the image pyramid. As inappropriate number of feature points may result in degradation of recognition performance of algorithm in subsequent matching[8] so the number of feature points depend on actual requirements. Therefore, we regulate the number of feature points with contrast threshold in practice. The feature points that are lower than the threshold value will be deleted.

Due to the fact that iris image contrast is generally lower, if the threshold is set to 0.04 as D. Lowe, the number of key points extracted is limited to match algorithm. Therefore, in the threshold contrast experiment when the contrast threshold is set to 0.01, the number of feature points is within 100-200, and the accuracy of subsequent matching algorithm is the highest. When the value of threshold is less than 0.008 or higher than 0.02, the recognition rate of algorithm will decline substantially. As shown in Fig.3.

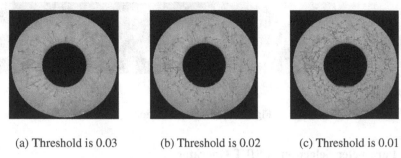

(a) Threshold is 0.03   (b) Threshold is 0.02   (c) Threshold is 0.01

Fig. 3. Key point's extraction in different contrast threshold

2.2.3   Curvature Threshold

Since the DOG operator would cause the strong response of the edges, it produces a large number of pseudo key points on the eyelid's edges[9][10][11], as shown in Fig.4.Considering that the main curvature of DOG response peak is usually large in horizontal direction of edge and small in the vertical direction of edge. So we can control the number of noise points of edge produced by the difference operation through regulating the size of the main curvature threshold. Namely, the feature points whose main curvature is more than the main curvature threshold will be marked as pseudo keys and be deleted.

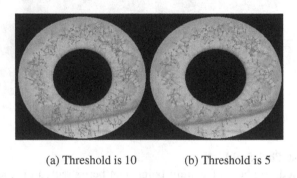

(a) Threshold is 10   (b) Threshold is 5

Fig. 4. The key point's extraction under different main curvature threshold

Experimental results show that the curvature threshold can effectively reduce the number of pseudo key points in eyelid when the curvature threshold is set to 5. The following is shown in Fig.4, figure (a) and (b). The curvature threshold is respective 5 and 10. We can see the second image's pseudo point decrease significantly in eyelid edge.

3 Feature Matching of SIFT Method

The process of SIFT feature matching is divided into the following three steps. The first step is the calculation of the distance of all feature points between two iris images. The second step is the matching judgment of feature points with distance threshold method. The third step is iris feature matching with percentage threshold.

3.1 Distance Calculation of Feature Points

In the process of SIFT feature points matching, we need to calculate the vector distance of every two feature points. Considering the point that the large number of feature points and computational complexity are caused by the description of each feature point by 128-dimensional vector, this paper uses the city-block distance instead of Euclidean distance of Lowe in feature matching. The experimental result on iris databases shows that the feature points obtained by two calculation methods of the distance are basically the same. Only the time spent on calculation is reduced significantly. The specific calculation formula is as follows:

$$L_O = \sqrt{\sum_{i=1}^{n} (x_i - y_i)^2} \qquad (2)$$

L_O represents Euclidean distance, and n represents the dimension of the feature vector.

$$L_J = \sum_{i=1}^{n} |x_i - y_i| \qquad (3)$$

L_J represents city-block distance, according to its definition[12], we can know that L_j has a less time square root calculation than L_o because of the great number of SIFT features. Such change proves to be meaningful.

3.2 Matching Judgment of Feature Points

We calculate the nearest neighbor block distance vals(1) and the sub-nearest neighbor block distance vals(2) of one-dimensional vector L, the smallest two values of L. We judge whether vals(1)< NNRatio*vals(2). If satisfied, two feature points match or otherwise. NNRatio is distance ratio threshold for measuring whether the two feature points match.

Mismatching ratio would reduce with the decrease of NNRatio. But at the same time, more correct matching ratio is given up. On the contrary, when the NNRatio increases, the mismatching ratio increases, affecting the accuracy of iris recognition[13].

In the classical SIFT algorithm, Lowe set the value to 0.8 according to experiments, which may not apply to all objects for feature recognition. For given iris images, a large number of experiments must be carried out to obtain the most suitable distance ratio threshold for iris images. Finally, after cyclic selection of distance ratio threshold on the interval [0.65, 0.95] in TEST template library, the best one we get is 0.85.

3.3   Iris Image Matching of SIFT Method

Since the contrast threshold differs between different iris images, the direct result is that the feature points vary greatly with the same parameters, as shown in Fig.5(a) and (b) --iris image from CASIA-V1.0, and (c) and (d) -- iris image from MMU. The numbers of feature points in four images under the same parameters are respectively 77, 181, 574, and 912, which shows a big gap in the number of feature points in different or even same libraries. Hence, in the classical SIFT, through comparing the matching numbers of feature points in two images [14][15], it is not applicable to iris images. We put forward ratio threshold, as follows, in which η represents the ratio threshold. n_1 and n_2 represent the number of feature points in two images, m represents the number of feature points matching in two images. If η is larger than a fixed threshold η_0, matching is successful, on the contrary, the outcome is otherwise.

$$\eta = m / \min(n_1, n_2) \qquad (4)$$

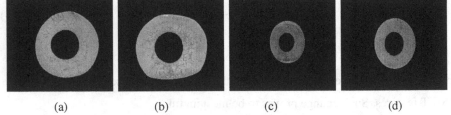

(a)   (b)   (c)   (d)

Fig. 5. Feature extraction of different images

Based on the TEST template library, the cyclic selection is used for the determination of the threshold value η_0, as shown in Fig.6. FAR and FRR touch in the spot where η equals 0.211. Apparently both the separability and the recognition rates are at a high level. Therefore, this paper finally sets the value of η_0 to 0.211. The final match result is shown in Fig.7.

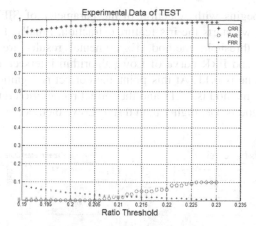

Fig. 6. The experimental data of TEST iris database ratio threshold

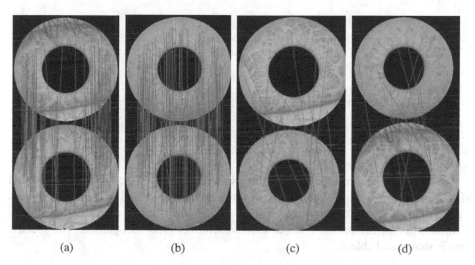

(a)   (b)   (c)   (d)

Fig. 7. The comparison of intra-class and inter-class

4   The Experimental Results

In this paper, experiments are carried out in the following three databases:CASIA-V1.0(108×7 images), CASIA-V3-Interval(126×10 images), and MMU V1.0(90×5 images). To be more specific, we chose the first-generation CASIA-V1.0 of Chinese Academy of Sciences whose separability D was the largest by Lowe algorithm. Moreover, 12×7 images are drawn at random as a template image library (TEST) for threshold optimization experiment.

Our experiment begins with selection of the parameter of SIFT operator in iris databases.Upon this, we starts the iris feature extraction. Finally, feature matching is performed by ratio threshold method. Experimental results are shown in Fig.8. Namely, FAR curve and FRR curve of Lowe algorithm intersect at the place where the rate threshold value is 0.11. At this point, the correct recognition rate is 92.91%. EER of our proposed method is 0.211 and the correct recognition rate is 97.85%. EER of our proposed method is 5%, higher than that of Lowe method.

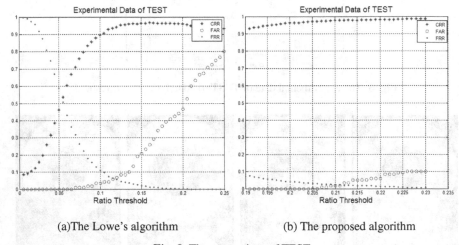

(a)The Lowe's algorithm   (b) The proposed algorithm

Fig. 8. The comparison of TEST

The experimental results in iris database CASIA-V1.0, CASIA-V3-Interval and MMU are shown in Fig.9 The results of Lowe method are listed on the left, and ours on the right. It is obvious that the EER of our method is lower than that from Lowe method .This further proves that our method achieves great recognition. The specific data is shown in Table 1.

Table 1. Experimental data of comparison of different iris database

Iris database	EER	
	Lowe's method	The proposed method
CASIA-V1.0	7%	5%
CASIA-V3-Interval	13%	9%
MMU	15%	14%

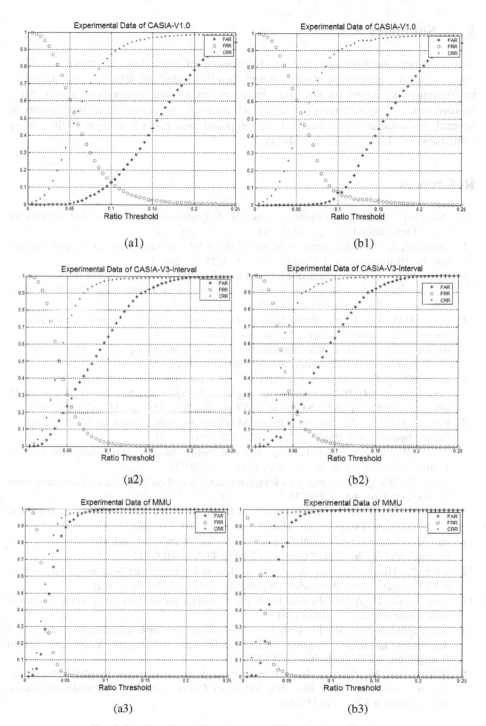

Fig. 9. Results of experimentation in different iris databases

5   Summary

In this paper, we first analyzed the importance of some key parameters of SIFT operator in iris recognition algorithm and then illustrated the selection of parameters in experiments. Based on specific characteristics of iris recognition, a new SIFT feature matching was proposed. Finally, according to the comparative experiments in several iris databases, the method we proposed was proven in term of its strong robustness and high recognition ability.

References

1. Daugman, J.: How iris recognition works. IEEE Transactions on Circuits and Systems for Video Technology 14(1), 21–30 (2004)
2. Daugman, J.: Statistical richness of visual phase information:update on recognizing persons by iris patterns. Int. J. Comput. Vis. 45(1), 25–38 (2001)
3. Boles, W.W.: A wavelet transform based technique for the recognition of the human iris. In: International Symposium on Signal Processing and its Applications, Gold Cost, Australia, August 25-30, pp. 601–604 (1996)
4. Lowe, D.G.: Distinctive image features from scale invariant key points. International Journal of Computer Vision 60(2), 91–110 (2004)
5. Brown, M., Lowe, D.G.: Recognising Panoramas. In: Proceedings of the 9th International Conference on Computer Vision (ICCV 2003), Nice (October 2003)
6. Schaffalitzky, F., Zisserman, A.: Multi-view Matching for Unordered Image Sets, or How Do I Organize My Holiday Snaps? In: Heyden, A., Sparr, G., Nielsen, M., Johansen, P. (eds.) ECCV 2002, Part I. LNCS, vol. 2350, pp. 414–431. Springer, Heidelberg (2002)
7. Bai, Y., Hou, X.: An Improved Image Matching Algorithm Based on SIFT. Journal of Beijing Institute of Technology 33(6), 622–627 (2013)
8. Gao, J., Wu, Y., Wu, K., et al.: Image matching method based on corner detection. Chinese Journal of Scientific Instrument 34(8), 1717–1725 (2013)
9. Wang, G., Wang, Y.: Research on Image Retrieval Based on SIFT. Radio Communication Technology 39(4), 64–66 (2013)
10. Zhao, Y., Zhang, K.: Research on a SAR Image Matching Method Based on Improved SIFT Algorithm. Computer and Modernization (6), 108–115 (2013)
11. Xu, X., Zhang, H.: Iris identification method based on local and global features. The Research and Application of Computer 29(11), 4378–4380 (2012)
12. Yang, X., Huang, Y., Han, X., et al.: A Method for Improving Matching Efficiency of SIFT Features. China Mechanical Engineering 23(11), 1297–1301 (2012)
13. Zeng, L., Gu, D.: A SIFT Feature Descriptor Based on Sector Area Partitioning. Journal of Automation 38(9), 1513–1519 (2012)
14. Ke, Y., Sukthankar, R.: PCA-SIFT: A more distinctive representation for local image descriptors. In: IEEE Computer Society Conference on Computer Vision and Pattern Recognition, vol. 2, pp. II-506–II-513 (2004)
15. Wan, J., Sun, M., Zeng, Z.: Improvement on adaptive distance ratio threshold of scale invariant feature transform algorithm. Journal of China University of Petroleum: Natural Science Edition 37(4), 71–75 (2013)

A Fast Robustness Palmprint Recognition Algorithm[*]

Danfeng Hong[1], Xin Wu[2,**], Zhenkuan Pan[1], Jian Su[3],
Weibo Wei[1], and Yaoyao Niu[1]

[1] College of Information Engineering, Qingdao University, Qingdao
[2] School of Information and Electronics, Beijing Institute of Technology, Beijing
[3] School of Communication and Information Engineering,
University of Electronic Science and Technology of China, Chengdu, China
040251522wuxin@163.com

Abstract. We propose a novel fast robustness palmprint recognition algorithm based on the Curvelet transform and local histogram of oriented gradient (CLHOG) for the poor curve and direction description in the traditional wavelet transform. Curvelet transform is firstly used to obtain four images with the different scales. Then, an algorithm based Local Histogram of Oriented Gradient (LHOG) is designed to extract the robust features from those different scale images. Finally, a Chi-square distance is introduced to measure the similarity in the palmprint features. The experimental results obtained through using the proposed method on both PolyU and CASIA palmprint databases are robust and superior in comparison to some high-performance algorithms.

Keywords: Palmprint recognition, Curvelet, Local Histogram of Oriented Gradient, chi-square distance.

1 Introduction

Palmprint recognition, as a branch of biometric research, gradually becomes a hotspot in recent years [1-3]. Most palmprint recognition methods are discussed in frequency domain, such as wavelet transform. What's more, it has obtained the better identification. HAFIZ et al [4] proposed wavelet-based dominant feature extraction algorithm for palmprint recognition. However, wavelet can only describe characteristics in the local region or singular points, and fail to represent multi-directional edge, texture and other geometric properties of two-dimension images. Therefore, it cannot be an optimal selection for palmprint [4-5]. Zhou et al [5] proposed face recognition algorithm based on adaptive local Gabor algorithm of energy. But a larger feature dimension can limit the real-time requirement. So they reduced the dimension using principal component analysis (PCA) to deal with this problem, while the recognition accuracy still needed further improvement.

[*] This work was supported in part by the Natural Science Foundation of China under Grant No. 61170106 and A Project of Shandong Province Higher Educational Science and Technology Program No.J14LN39.
[**] Corresponding author.

Z. Sun et al. (Eds.): CCBR 2014, LNCS 8833, pp. 311–318, 2014.

Later on, Wang et al [6] designed a novel palmprint identification based on Curve-let transform decision fusion. Curvelet transform has a good description for curve. Also, each layer image from the Curvelet transform can show the direction informa-tion clearly. But, it seldom considers the main orientation, namely, the orientation trend for palmprint image. In order to solve the problem, we propose a fast robustness palmprint recognition algorithm based on Curvelet local histogram of oriented gra-dient (CLHOG), which can not only obtain a desirable recognition result, but also meet real-time requirement. After simple preprocessing, we need to decompose palmprint into four layers by Curvelet transform and extract the direction histogram for the local palmprint image by local histogram of oriented gradient (LHOG). Final-ly, we use Chi-square distance to measure the similarity. The proposed algorithm is tested on PolyU and CASIA palmprint databases and the experimental results show that the recognition accuracy is optimal by comparing with some previous palmprint recognition methods, so as to meet real-time applications.

2   Fast Robustness Palmprint Recognition Algorithm

2.1   Fast Discrete Curvelet Transforms

E. J. Candes and D. L. Donoho [7] developed a multi-scale and multi-direction trans-form called curvelet transform in 2003. The image can be represented and approached with a series of curves via Curvelet transform. There are some original parameters of Curvelet transform listed in [7], which are proved to be optimal. Therefore, we use them in this paper.

More specifically, a pair of windows W(r) and V (t) is used in the first stage, which is called the "radial window" and "angular window," respectively. They can be shown as follows.

$$\sum_{j=-\infty}^{\infty} W^2\left(2^j r\right)=1, r\in(3/4,3/2); \qquad \sum_{l=-\infty}^{\infty} V^2\left(t-l\right)=1, r\in(-1/2,1/2); \qquad (1)$$

Then, for each $j \geq j_0$, the frequency window U_j is defined in the Fourier domain by

$$U_j\left(r,\theta\right)=2^{-3j/4}W\left(2^{-j}r\right)V\left(\frac{2^{\lfloor j/2 \rfloor}\theta}{2\pi}\right) \qquad (2)$$

where $\lfloor j/2 \rfloor$ is the integer part of $j/2$, U_j is a polar "wedge" defined by the W and V, which is applied with scale-dependent window widths for each direction.

These digital transformations are linear and are considered as input Cartesian arrays of the form $f\left[t_1,t_2\right](0\leq t_1,t_2 < n)$, and a collection of coefficients $c^D\left(j,l,k\right)$ as output can be obtained by the digital simulation in the following.

$$c^D\left(j,l,k\right)=\sum_{0\leq t_1,t_2 < n} f\left[t_1,t_2\right]\overline{\varphi_{j,l,k}^D\left[t_1,t_2\right]} \qquad (3)$$

where each $\varphi_{j,l,k}^D$ is a digital curvelet waveform and D stands for "digital".

2.2   Fast Robustness Palmprint Recognition Algorithm

2.2.1   Local Histogram of Oriented Gradient

In order to have a better description on the orientation the palmprint, we use the local histogram of oriented gradient (LHOG) [9] to extract the feature of orientation from each layer image obtained by using Curvelet transform.

We first obtain an orientation map of palmprint image by utilizing the gradient operator, which can be computed by

$$f_x = I * W \qquad f_y = I * W^T \tag{4}$$

$$Mag(i,j) = \sqrt{f_x^2(i,j) + f_y^2(i,j)} \qquad Ang(i,j) = \tan^{-1}\left(\frac{f_y(i,j)}{f_x(i,j)}\right) \tag{5}$$

Where I stands for original image with the size of $M \times M$, '*' is the operator of convolution, W=[-1,0,1] is a mask of convolution, $Mag(i,j)$ and $Ang(i,j)$ are gradient magnitude and angle of $I(i,j)$, $-\pi/2 < Ang(i,j) < \pi/2$. Here, Ang is considered as the orientation map of I.

Then, LHOG is formed by utilizing Ang, each pixel added to the histogram is weighted by using $Mag(i,j)$, and N stands for the orientation number utilized to cover the 360 degree range of orientation. Hence, the LHOG is obtained as follows

$$F_k = F_k + Mag(i,j) \quad if \quad (k-1) \times (2\pi/N) < Ang(i,j) < k \times (2\pi/N) \tag{6}$$

where $k = 1, 2, \ldots\ldots N$, F_k represents the value corresponding to each orientation number of LHOG. Therefore, the feature of LHOG is shown as

$$LHOG = (F_1, F_2, \cdots\cdots F_N) \tag{7}$$

In order to improve the robustness for illumination and noise, LHOG is usually normalized as $LHOG = LHOG / \sum_{k=1}^{N} F_k$. Fig.1 shows the example of LHOG.

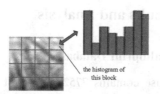

the histogram of
this block

Fig. 1. The histogram of one block of LHOG

According to the principle of Curvelet transform, a palmprint ROI image with a size of 128*128 can be divided into four layers containing the texture and structure information, namely, coarse layer, detail1 layer, detail2 layer and fine layer. The structure information is distributed on the coarse layer. Detail1 and detail2 layers have part structure information, while the fine layer is usually removed because it has a lot of noises.

Next, we divide each layer image into non-overlapped blocks of equal size to reduce the interference of translation and improve the distinguish ability of extracted features. And then LHOG is extracted from each block. So we can obtain $(128 \times 128)/(s \times s)$ blocks from each image. The final LHOG can be defined as follows.

$$LHOG = \left(LHOG_{block1}, LHOG_{block2}, \cdots\cdots LHOG_{(128 \times 128)/(s \times s)} \right) \tag{8}$$

The flow chart of the proposed algorithm is as shown in the Fig.2.

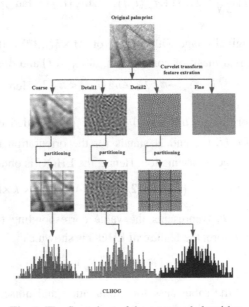

Fig. 2. The flow chart of the proposed algorithm

3   Experimental Results and Analysis

3.1   PolyU and CASIA Palmprint Database

The PolyU palmprint database contains 7752 palmprint images, which is captured from 386 different palms, and CASIA palmprint database contains 5,502 palmprint images captured from 312 subjects. For each subject, CASIA database collects palmprint images from both left and right palms. In our paper, we randomly select 900 samples (150 people, everyone has 6 samples, where one image is considered as the train image, the others are test images) from each database to test the performance of the proposed method.

The ROI (Region of Interest) image is cropped from the original palmprint image by using the method of [10]. Some examples are showed in Fig 3 and each of them contains 128×128 pixels with 256 gray levels per pixel.

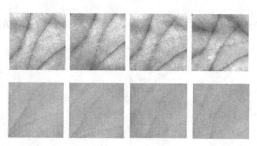

Fig. 3. Some examples of palmprint ROI images in the PolyU (top line) and CASIA (bottom line)

3.2   Identification

In this section, we carry out a series of experiments in order to show the performance of the proposed method on two palmprint databases, PolyU and CASIA palmprint databases. The genuine recognition rate (GRR) is used as an evaluation index. Each of the test images is matched with all of training images in the database. If the test palmprint image and the training image are from the same palm, the matching is considered as a correct matching, vice versa. Particularly, in order to prove the superiority of the proposed approach comparing with the traditional high performance methods, there are four experiments are performed in the following stage.

Experiment 1: We make a comparison with the pattern of different fusion in order to obtain the optimal one. The result of Table.1 shows that the GRR of the former three layers images of the two databases is the best. So we just use the former three layers images to complete the next experiments.

Table 1. The recognition result under the pattern of different fusion for the different layers

Different layer selection	GRR%(PolyU)	GRR%(CASIA)
Coarse	87.00%	83.56%
Coarse+Detail1	98.67%	93.67%
Coarse+Detail1+Detail2	99.22%	97.33%
Coarse+Detail1+Detail2+Fine	80.53%	76.11%

Experiment 2: The aim of this experiment is to choose the optimal orientation. The block size ($s*s$) and the divided orientation number (N) have an enormous impact on the proposed method. Here, the blocks with different sizes ($4*4, 8*8, 16*16$, $32*32$) and different orientation numbers (N=4,6,8,9,10,12) are used to perform some experiments in order to obtain the optimal parameters for the two palmprint databases. When experiments are performed, we respectively fix the block size and

orientation number to compare the GRR. As is shown in Fig.4, when the block size is 16*16 and the orientation number is 12, the GRR of two palmprint databases achieves the highest value.

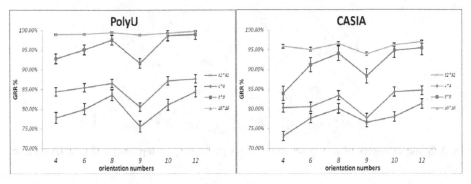

Fig. 4. the GRR of different size and orientation numbers on two palmprint databases

Experiment 3: This experiment is to compare our algorithm with some existing researches which have a good description of direction, scale and texture, such as Gabor transform [11], Curvelet, LBP [12] and LGBP [13]. Fig.5 depicts the chart of comparative result. The GRR of proposed algorithm is higher than the existing research. Distinguished information of scale is obtained by Curvelet, and the main direction characteristics are obtained via LHOG. Through verification test in two palmprint databases, the proposed algorithm has not only lower dimension, but also robustness to the rotation, translation, and illumination of palmprint.

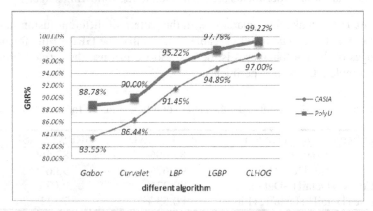

Fig. 5. The chart of comparative result

Experiment 4: On the basic of Experiment 3, this experiment compares the real-time of the algorithm mentioned above. The experiments for the proposed approach are conducted on a personal computer with the Pentium CPU 2.70 GHz and 4G RAM configured with Microsoft Windows 7 and Matlab2009a with image processing toolbox. The execution time for feature extraction, matching and total are listed in

Table 2. We can see that the total time of our algorithm on PolyU and CASIA database are 63.1369ms and 65.1112ms respectively, which is fast enough to meet the real-time requirement.

Table 2. The execution times for feature extraction, matching and total of different algorithm

Algorithm	Feature extraction/ms	Matching/ms	Total/ms
Gabor	84.3121	2.1008	86.4129
LBP	51.1285	28.5037	79.6322
LGBP	214.3269	15.3778	229.7047
CLHOG(CASIA)	43.5787	21.5325	65.1112
CLHOG(PolyU)	42.1843	20.9526	63.1369

4   Conclusions

In this paper, we proposed a CLHOG algorithm for palmprint recognition. LHOG could extract the direction features from palmprint, which were robustness for the rotation, translation, and illumination. The different scale features obtained by Curvelet could improve the recognition accuracy to larger extent. The experimental results on both PolyU and CASIA palmprint databases demonstrated the effectiveness and superiority of the proposed algorithm. By comparing with the previous high-performance palmprint recognition methods, the proposed algorithm had desirable recognition accuracy and a faster recognition rate. In the future, we will continue to improve the proposed approach, making it possible to use in some larger databases and other biometric applications.

References

1. Lin, S., Yuan, W.Q., Wu, W., et al.: Blurred Palmprint Recognition Based on DCT and Block Energy of Principal Line. Journal of Optoelectronics·Laser 23, 2200–2206 (2012)
2. Sun, Z., Wang, L., Tan, T.: Ordinal Feature Selection for Iris and Palmprint Recognition. IEEE Transactions on Image Processing 23, 3922–3934 (2014)
3. Hong, D.F., Wei, W.B., Wu, X., et al.: A Novel Palmprint Recognition Algorithm Based on Region Texture Description. In: International Symposium on Signal Processing, Biomedical Engineering, and Informatics (SPBEI 2013), pp. 636–645. IEEE Press, New York (2013)
4. Hafiz, I., Shaikh, A.F.: A Wavelet-based Dominant Feature Extraction Algorithm for Palmprint Recognition. Digital Signal Processing 23, 244–258 (2013)
5. Zhou, L.J., Ma, Y.Y., Sun, J.: Face Recognition with Adaptive Local-Gabor Gestures Based on Energy. Journal of Computer Applications 33, 700–703 (2013)
6. Wang, X.C., Yue, K.H., Liu, Y.M.: Palmprint Recognition Based on Curvelet Transform Decision Fusion. Procedia Engineering 23, 303–309 (2011)
7. Candes, E.J., Donoho, D.L.: Curvelets – a Surprisingly Effective Nonadaptive Representation for Objects With Edges. In: Rabut, C., Cohen, A., Schumaker, L.L. (eds.) Curves and Surfaces, pp. 105–120. Vanderbilt University Press, Nashville (2000)

8. Hong, D.F., Pan, Z.K., Wu, X.: Improved Differential Box Counting With Multi-scale and Multi-direction: A new palmprint recognition method. Optik-International Journal of Light Electron Optics 125, 4154–4160 (2014)
9. Hong, D.F., Su, J., Hong, Q.G., et al.: Blurred Palmprint Recognition Based on Stable-Feature Extraction Using a Vese–Osher Decomposition Model. PLoS One 9, e101866 (2014)
10. Zhang, D., Kong, W.K., You, J., et al.: Online Palmprint Identification. IEEE Transactions on Pattern Analysis and Machine Intelligence 25, 1041–1050 (2003)
11. Guo, J.Y., Liu, Y.Q., Yuan, W.Q.: Palmprint Recognition Using Local Information from a Single Image Per Person. Journal of Computational Information Systems 8, 3199–3206 (2012)
12. Guo, Z.H., Zhang, L., Zhang, D.P., et al.: Hierarchical Multiscale LBP for Face And Palmprint Recognition. In: IEEE International Conference on Image Processing, ICIP, pp. 4521–4524. IEEE Press, New York (2010)
13. Lian, Q.S., Liu, C.L.: Hierarchical Palmprint Identification Based on Gabor Filter and LBP. Computer Engineering and Applications 43, 212–215 (2007)

Eyelash Removal Using Light Field Camera
for Iris Recognition

Shu Zhang, Guangqi Hou, and Zhenan Sun

Center for Research on Intelligent Perception and Computing,
National Laboratory of Pattern Recognition, Institute of Automation,
Chinese Academy of Sciences, Beijing 100190, China
{shu.zhang,gqhou,znsun}@nlpr.ia.ac.cn

Abstract. Eyelash occlusions pose great difficulty on the segmentation and feature encoding process of iris recognition thus will greatly affect the recognition rate. Traditional eyelash removal methods dedicate to exclude the eyelash regions from the 2D iris image, which waste lots of precious iris texture information. In this paper we aim to reconstruct the occluded iris patterns for more robust iris recognition. To this end, a novel imaging system, the microlens-based light field camera, is employed to capture the iris image. Beyond its ability to refocus and extend the depth of field, in this work, we explore its another feature, i.e. to see through the occlusions. And we propose to reconstruct occluded iris patterns using statistics of macro pixels. To validate the proposed method, we capture a unique light field iris database and implement iris recognition experiments with our proposed methods. Both recognition and visual results validate the effectiveness of our proposed methods.

Keywords: iris recognition, eyelash removal, light field, occlusion.

1 Introduction

Iris recognition [1] is one of the most popular biometrics due to the stableness and uniqueness of iris patterns. However, there still exist several issues that severely affect the recognition procedure. The occlusions of eyelashes is one of them, it will pose great difficulty to the process of segmentation and feature encoding and finally degrade the overall recognition rate. Traditional researches on eyelash removal methods [3] [4] [5] try to remove the eyelash region from the acquired image with rule based methods. Although they can facilitate improvement in the recognition rate, they sacrifice too much precious iris information (iris patterns occluded by eyelashes), so they are less reliable in practical use. However, in this paper we aim to find solutions that can reconstruct occluded iris information rather than exclude them from the recognition process. The thriving of the computational photography offers us a chance to effectively achieve that goal. Nowadays, there exist more options of devices for iris image acquisition, especially some device with the ability to capture the light field [15]. One of the device that come to our attention is the microlens-based light field camera.

Z. Sun et al. (Eds.): CCBR 2014, LNCS 8833, pp. 319–327, 2014.

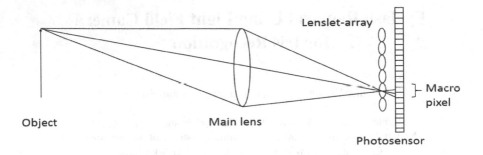

Fig. 1. Microlens-based light field camera model

The microlens-based light field camera (LFC) which was introduced in 2006by Ng [7] with a microlens assembled between the main lens and photo sensor of a conventional camera can capture 4D light field. The captured image (Fig.2 (a))consists of microlen images or may be called macro pixels (marked in a black rectangle) which correspond to pixels underneath each microlens that represent the directional information of the ray in space. The raw light field can alsobe represented using a 4D representation [7] as illustrated in Fig.2 (b). Each image in 4D light field represents an image taken from a certain viewpoint and it is called the sub-aperture image. According to Ng [7], the LFC have two features compared to conventional cameras: (1) extended depth of field (DoF)with decoupled trade-offs between DoF and aperture size; (2) generating photos focused at a range of depth after the photo was taken (also known as refocus).Researches on biometrics with LFC [6] [13] [14] verify that the camera's feature on extended DoF and flexible refocusing may actually benefit the biometrics application. However, the LFC have much more potential to be explored on biometric research.

The superiority of the LFC relies on its ability to capture the 4D light field or the additional directional information. Using similar imaging system, researchers in the synthetic aperture [2] and integral imaging [9] [10] [11] [12] community try to use this kind of additional information to see through occlusions and reconstruct occluded information. Inspired by their work, in this paper, we dedicate to explore the LFC's ability on eyelash removal to benefit the iris recognition task. Unlike previous work [9] [11] [12] which implement the reconstruction mainly based on stereo matching of sub-aperture images, we propose a novel method based on the observation of the refocusing process and the prior knowledge of eyelash occlusions. Specifically, we explored other statistics of macros pixels rather than the mean, which is utilized by the refocus process, to reconstruct iris information occluded by eyelashes. To evaluate the proposed method, we capture a near infrared (NIR) light field iris database using a microlens-based LFC, and implement iris recognition test with the proposed method on this database. Compared to previous works, this paper has three major contributions: (1) we propose to address the eyelash occlusion problem with a novel camera model, i.e. the LFC, breaking through the limitations of conventional camera; (2) we explore to process the captured light field image in a novel way compared to previous work [6] [13] [14] to reconstruct the occluded iris information; (3) we capture a unique light field iris database to evaluate our proposed methods. To the best of our knowledge, this is the first work that try to address eyelash occlusions in iris recognition with a LFC. Our work proves that LFC is a promising trend for the acquisition of iris images in iris recognition and there's more to expect about its potential.

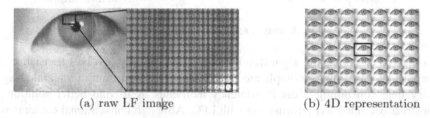

(a) raw LF image   (b) 4D representation

Fig. 2. Two types of representation for LF images

2   Related Works

In the research of eyelash removal, most algorithms follow the procedure of firstly detecting the eyelash regions and then excluding them from iris recognition. Many rule-based methods have been proposed to detect the eyelash regions. Kong and Zhang [4] categorized eyelashes into two groups, and they adopted 1-D Gabor filter and the variance of intensity in a small window to detect separable and multiple eyelashes respectively with database dependent thresholds. Kangand Park [3] introduced the measurement of focus score to decide an adaptive threshold. He et al. [5] proposed a statistically learned prediction model to get the adaptive thresholds. Those methods all aimed at detecting the eyelash regions and excluded them from the recognition procedure, which is a great waste of information. However, we try to find ways to reconstruct occluded iris patterns using novel acquisition devices.

Recently, LFC is gaining traction in biometrics. Zhang [6] explored its ability on iris recognition, comparable recognition rate can be obtained to a conventional camera. In [13] [14], LFC were also adopted for the iris and face recognition, recognition results validated its outstanding ability on extended DoF and refocusing. Novel imaging systems like synthetic aperture [2], integral imaging [9] can also capture light field in one snapshot. As those imaging systems can also capture images from different points of view, they all carry features of the multi-view vision system, like capable of seeing the occluded information. Methods to see through occlusion are well explored in those research areas. In [2], Vaish et al. used a focal-sweep process and some modified cost functions to estimate the depth of the occluded objects. For the reconstruction of occluded information, median color are used. In the integral imaging community, researchers [10] [11][12] tried to remove occlusions and reconstruct occluded information by explicitly detect occlusion regions with stereo matching algorithm in sub-aperture images, and mask them off in the following computational process, so that the resultantimages are occlusions free.

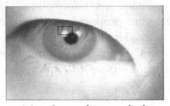

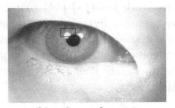

(a) refocused on eyelash   (b) refocused on iris

Fig. 3. Images refocused on different depth

Compared to refocusing algorithm [7] in LFC which only involves translation and superposition, resorting to complicated stereo matching algorithm in integral imaging is very time consuming. This inefficiency motivates us to find better solutions to reconstruct occluded iris information with LFC. Although conventional cameras with a very large aperture are also capable of seeing through occlusions [8], they suffer from very small DoF and thus can't acquire clear iris images without strong restrictions. Another drawback of using conventional cameras lies in the fact that they can't capture enough information to facilitate the accurate reconstruction.

The rest of the paper is organized as follows: Section 3 gives the detailed description of the proposed method; Section 4 states the experiment setup and presents the experiment results; Section 5 concludes this paper with possible future research direction.

3   The Proposed Method for Eyelash Removal

We've given some important information about LFC in previous sections, a detailed overview of the light field camera can be found in [14] [17]. Generally, we decode a raw light field image (which consists of macro pixels) shown inFig.2 (a) to 4D light field representation (which consists of sub-aperture images)[15] [16], as illustrated in Fig.2 (b) for further implementation. Note that, these two kinds of image representations are significant to the understanding of our proposed methods and they can be easily converted to each other once we have properly calibrated the LFC camera [16]. To solve the eyelash occlusion problem, instead of operating on the 4D representation with a complicated stereo matching scheme, we seek methods to operate on the raw light field image, where we use novel statistics of the macro pixels to reconstruct the occluded regions.

3.1   A Different View of Refocus

Based on the 4D representation and ray tracing diagram inside the camera, Ng[17] developed a digital refocusing algorithm after the picture is taken. This algorithm can be formulated as follows:

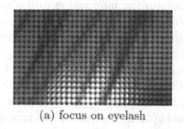

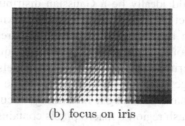

(a) focus on eyelash   (b) focus on iris

Fig. 4. Comparison of raw light filed (LF) image focused on different depth. The cropped raw LF is taken from the rectangle in Fig. 3 of two raw LF image respectively.

$$E_{(\alpha F)}(x',y') =$$

$$\frac{1}{\alpha^2 F^2} \iint L_{F^{(u,v)}} (u(1-\frac{1}{\alpha})+\frac{x'}{\alpha}, v(1-\frac{1}{\alpha})+\frac{y'}{\alpha})dudv \tag{1}$$

Where $E_{(\alpha F)}(x',y')$ is the refocused image; $L_{F^{(u,v)}}$ is a sub-aperture image at the coordinates of (u,v), and u indicates the row index, v indicates the column index; α denotes the ratio of the refocus depth to the current depth. The refocusing implementation is basically a shifting and adding process of the sub-aperture images(as previously mentioned, each sub-aperture image represents a picture taken under a specific viewpoint), and the amount of shifting determines the refocusing depth. This simple implementation benefits from the compact structure of the camera, which keep it from complicated stereo matching manipulation. If we see this process in the view of raw light field images, the refocusing process is simply taking the mean value of macro pixels after converting the shift edsub-aperture images to a raw light field image. In the refocused image, the mean value is adopted to represent pixels on each spot. This view inspires us to find alternative estimation other than the mean value to better reconstruct occluded regions.

If the object is in-focus, then pixels in each macro pixel represent the same object (as in Fig.4 (a), the black line indicate in-focused eyelash), so the information is redundant; otherwise, the pixel in each macro pixel represent different objects (as in Fig.4 (b), iris is in focus, eyelash pixels spread in many different macro pixels), thus taking the mean value will blur this area. Fig.3 illustrates the refocused images, which are obtained simply by taking the average of each macro pixel in Fig.4. Those two raw light field images can be obtained by translating the sub-aperture images and converting them back to a raw light field image. As we can easily convert between those two representations, we don't need to specify where the camera focus on when the picture is taken.

As we have mentioned above, macro pixels which corresponds to in-focus region have redundant information of the same object (the pixel values in one macro pixel should ideally be a Gaussian distribution if it captures the information of the same object), so the mean a good approximation of this region's information. Benefiting from this redundancy, we may represent the refocused images with other statistics without degrading the image quality. Specifically, we can suppress the superimposition of the eyelash pixels in each macro pixel from the raw light field image focused on iris to increase the fidelity of the occluded region. Supposing now we have a raw light field image focused on iris, like the one in Fig.4 (b). Then, the eyelash region's macro pixels contains both iris and eyelash information. So now, one question comes up, can we find a better statistics to represent iris information when it is occluded by eyelashes? Based on prior knowledge that the gray level of eyelash is darker than iris region, the max value of the macro pixels seems to be a good estimate. Although taking the max value is able to exclude eyelash pixels completely, it is less robust too utliers compared to the mean value, this indicates that the max value might not perform well for iris recognition purpose. To increase the robustness and exclude eyelash at the same time, we consider the mean of pixels bigger than the median value of the macro pixels. As the median value is a better estimate of the central tendency than the mean value when occlusions are less than 50%,it might suffice our demands. This statistics is denoted as MBM in this paper.

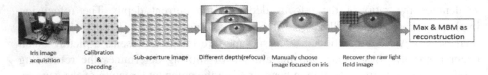

Fig. 5. Proposed eyelash removal method

3.2   Block Diagram of Eyelash Removal

Using some novel statistics, our proposed method is summarized in a block diagram in Fig.5. Firstly, we capture a NIR iris database with a specially designed microlens-based LFC. Note that we don't need to capture images strictly focused on iris, post refocus can help us do that. Then with preprocess like calibration and decoding [16], sub-aperture images are obtained to facilitate the refocus process to calculate images focused on different depth. From those refocused images we manually choose images focused on iris (auto-refocus methods can also be derived to determine the translation step before the refocus process, but we will defer this to future work, since discussion of this very complicated issue is out of the scope of this paper) and convert them back to raw light field images. Then we can use the proposed statistics of the macro pixels mentioned before (MAX and MBM) to reconstruct the occluded information. And finally the reconstructed images are eyelash free and can be used for iris recognition.

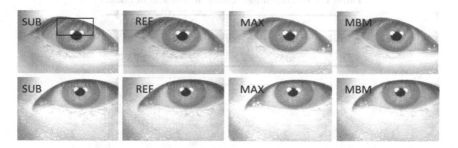

Fig. 6. Visual results of four sets of images. Each row of image come from the same eye, it is obvious our proposed method can remove the eyelashes with reconstructed iris information.

4   Experiments and Results

To verify the effectiveness of our proposed method, we capture a new NIR light-field iris database and experiment our method on this database. Using a specially designed microlens-based LFC, we capture NIR iris images of 21 subjects, 42eyes with over half the images suffering from severe eyelash occlusions. As for the preprocess, calibration methods in [16] are implemented to identify the center of each microlen image and get the decoded 4D representation. Proposed method are implemented to get two sets of pictures, the max images (denoted as MAX)and images consisting of mean of pixels bigger than median (denoted as MBM).For comparison purpose, we also get refocus image focused on iris (denoted as REF), which is adopted in [6] [14] and the middle sub-aperture images (denoted as SUB), which can be seen as a picture taken by a hypothetical conventional camera.

We compare the visual effects of the four sets of images in Fig.6. Our proposed reconstructions have a significant increase in the fidelity of the occluded regions compared to sub-aperture and refocused image. The MAX image looks best as it is able to exclude most part of the eyelash pixels while the MBM image may still be affected when eyelash occlusion is more than 50%. We evaluate our method on iris recognition task with comparison to other two sets of images. To emphasize the effectiveness of reconstruction of the occluded regions, we use only the upper half of iris images (as illustrated in the first image of Fig.6 with a black rectangle) for the test, as eyelashes only affect the upper half of iris regions most of the time. We implement the iris localization and segmentation process following the work of Li et al. [18]. Ordinal features introduced by Sun et al. [19] are adopted for the feature encoding procedure and the hamming distance of two iris codes are calculated to measure the similarity. Table.1 illustrates the recognition results on these four sets of images. Our proposed two sets of images outperform the sub-aperture and refocus images in both Equal Error Rate (EER) and discriminative index, which are two major evaluation criterions for the iris recognition task. Fig.7 shows the ROC curve of the recognition test. Both visual and recognition results verify the proposed method's superiority over previous refocused image [6] [14] and conventional camera image in iris recognition task with sever eyelash occlusions.

Table 1. Iris recognition results on four sets of images

	SUB	REF	MAX	MBM
EER	9.02%	6.79%	6.1%	**5.76%**
DI	2.3035	2.6761	2.7543	**2.7557**

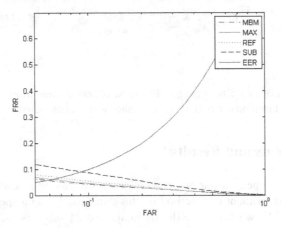

Fig. 7. Roc curve of the iris recognition test

5   Conclusion

To address the eyelash occlusion problem in iris recognition, we adopt a new yet powerful iris sensor for acquisition of iris image and propose a novel method to reconstruct iris information occluded by eyelashes. To the best of our knowledge, this the first time that the LFC is used for eyelash removal in iris recognition research. Compared to conventional eyelash removal methods, our proposed method can exploit more texture information of iris regions for accurate iris recognition; compared to previous works on biometrics with the LFC, we explore its ability to reconstruct occluded information and get better visual and recognition results. Our future works might include exploring glare reduction and auto-refocus using the light field camera for automatic and accurate iris recognition.

Acknowledgement. This work is funded by the National Natural Science Foundation of China (GrantNo. 61273272, 61302184) and the Instrument Developing Project of the ChineseAcademy of Sciences (Grant No. YZ201266).

References

1. Daugman, J.G.: Biometric personal identification system based on iris analysis. U.S.Patent (March 1, 1994)
2. Vaish, V., Levoy, M., Szeliski, R., et al.: Reconstructing occluded surfaces using synthetic apertures: Stereo, focus and robust measures. In: IEEE Conference on Computer Vision and Pattern Recognition, pp. 2331–2338 (2006)

3. Kang, B.J., Park, K.R.: A robust eyelash detection based on iris focus assessment. Pattern Recognition Letters 28(13), 1630–1639 (2007)
4. Kong, W.K., Zhang, D.: Accurate iris segmentation based on novel reflection and eyelash detection model. In: IEEE International Symposium on Intelligent Multimedia, Video and Speech Processing, pp. 263–266 (2001)
5. He, Z., Tan, T., Sun, Z., et al.: Toward accurate and fast iris segmentation for iris biometrics. IEEE Transactions on Pattern Analysis and Machine Intelligence 31(9), 1670–1684 (2009)
6. Zhang, C., Hou, G., Sun, Z., Tan, T., Zhou, Z.: Light Field Photography for Iris Image Acquisition. In: Sun, Z., Shan, S., Yang, G., Zhou, J., Wang, Y., Yin, Y. (eds.) CCBR 2013. LNCS, vol. 8232, pp. 345–352. Springer, Heidelberg (2013)
7. Ng, R., Levoy, M., Brdif, M., et al.: Light field photography with a hand-held plenoptic camera. Computer Science Technical Report CSTR 2(11) (2005)
8. Favaro, P., Soatto, S.: Seeing beyond occlusions (and other marvels of a finite lensaperture). In: IEEE Conference on Computer Vision and Pattern Recognition, pp. 579–586 (2003)
9. Hong, S.H., Jang, J.S., Javidi, B.: Three-dimensional volumetric object reconstruction using computational integral imaging. Optics Express 12(3), 483–491 (2004)
10. Xiao, X., Daneshpanah, M., Javidi, B.: Occlusion Removal Using Depth Mapping in Three-Dimensional Integral Imaging. Journal of Display Technology 8(8), 483–490 (2012)
11. Shin, D.H., Lee, B.G., Lee, J.J.: Occlusion removal method of partially occluded 3Dobject using sub-image block matching in computational integral imaging. Optic Express 16(21), 16294–16304 (2008)
12. Jung, J.H., Hong, K., Park, G., et al.: Reconstruction of three-dimensional occludedobject using optical flow and triangular mesh reconstruction in integral imaging. Optics Express 18(25), 26373–26387 (2010)
13. Raja, K.B., Raghavendra, R., Cheikh, F.A., et al.: Robust iris recognition usinglight-field camera. In: Colour and Visual Computing Symposium (CVCS), pp. 1–6 (2013)
14. Raghavendra, R., Yang, B., Raja, K.B., et al.: A new perspective Face recognition with light-field camera. In: IEEE International Conference on Biometrics (ICB), pp. 1–8 (2013)
15. Levoy, M., Hanrahan, P.: Light field rendering. In: ACM Proceedings of the 23rd Annual Conference on Computer Graphics and Interactive Techniques, pp. 31–42 (1996)
16. Dansereau, D.G., Pizarro, O., Williams, S.B.: Decoding, calibration and rectification for lenselet-based plenoptic cameras. In: IEEE Conference on Computer Vision and Pattern Recognition, pp. 1027–1034 (2013)
17. Ng, R.: Digital light field photography. Stanford university PhD thesis (2006)
18. Li, H., Sun, Z., Tan, T.: Robust iris segmentation based on learned boundary detectors. In: 5th IAPR International Conference on Biometrics (ICB), pp. 317–322. IEEE Press (2012)
19. Sun, Z., Tan, T.: Ordinal measures for iris recognition. IEEE Transactions on Pattern Analysis and Machine Intelligence 31(12), 2211–2226 (2009)

Extraction and Analysis of Texture Information of the Iris Intestinal Loop

Weiqi Yuan and Jing Huang

School of Information Science and Engineering,
Shenyang University of Technology,Shenyang 110870, China
hj4393@gmail.com

Abstract. The iris health evaluation emphasizes the detecting and analyzing of local variations in the characteristics of irises. Therefore, to accurately extract intestinal loop region of iris and objectively represent the texture feature is a prerequisite for gastrointestinal health evaluation based on iris. Based on the Canny operator approach, this paper presents adaptive Canny operator's partition for the extracting of intestinal loop region. This paper presents the measurement method of gray level co-occurrence matrix for representing texture information of irregular intestinal loops and the calculating the 6 texture measure. As the input is to establish the support vector machine model, we solve the classification of different kinds of people. Experiments were performed in collected samples. The detection method can effectively extract different types of the iris intestinal loop region. At the same time, the classification model shows that the proposed texture feature works as a measurement of effective health evaluation basis.

Keywords: the iris intestinal loop region, partition adaptive Canny operator, GLCM, SVM, health evaluation.

1   Introduction

Biometric methods identify people or analyze the status of human health based on physical or behavioral characteristics [1]. Most biometric methods measure human body's surface characteristics, such as finger prints, palm prints, face, irises, tongue, breath, etc. The iris is rich in blood vessels. Nerve fibers comprise 70% of the iris. The fact that an iris contains a large amount of characteristic information in terms of complex and precise structural and textural details makes iris recognition and iris diagnosis (iridology) two important directions in biometrics study.

Textural changes in intestinal loop of irises are caused by gastrointestinal diseases [2-3]. The region from pupil to the collarette is called intestinal loop. The collarette is an annular texture on irises [4]. Fig.1 gives iris collarette.

This paper focuses on the studying of textural representations and the analysis in the intestinal loop area. Extracted collarette is the precondition for the representation and the analysis of texture. The texture of the iris is very complicated. Gray-level of collarette is changing slowly within the scope of a certain pixel. There are some

Z. Sun et al. (Eds.): CCBR 2014, LNCS 8833, pp. 328–338, 2014.

differences between the internal and external texture. But this edge can be observed. In recent years, collarette extraction methods are often extracted. Xin Guodong proposed a gray gradient on normalized iris images by searching for the maximum gray gradient [5]. Yu Li proposed an improve snake model [6].The conventional methods of edge detection have good effect on clear collarette image. The iris image of most people is fuzzy collarette. Aimed at this problem, in this paper, a method of studying collarette extraction by using canny adaptive and partition threshold is introduced. The description method of image texture's features can be summarized as: statistical method, structure method, model method and spectrum method. Gray-level co-occurrence matrix (GLCM) can be used to describe the gray distribution. In this paper, a gray level co-occurrence matrix model is presented for the texture analysis and discrimination of an image. And 6 texture parameters are calculated by using this model for each image. We use the 6 features of each individual to train a SVM classifier so that they are applied to the subsequent evaluation based on iris feature of human body health.

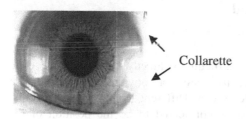

Collarette

Fig. 1. Iris Collarette

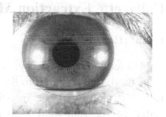

Fig. 2. Result of iris Localization

2   Image Preprocessing

2.1   Location

The iris's position and size are very important in human eye's image during the extracting of collarette. In this paper, we propose an accurate and fast iris location method based on the features of human eyes. Firstly, according to the gray features of pupil, we find a point inside the pupil using a gray value summing operator. Next, starting from this point, we find three points on the iris inner boundary using a boundary detection template designed by us. Then, we calculate the circle parameters of iris inner boundary according to the principle that three points, which are not on the same line, can define a circle. Finally, we find other three points on the iris outer boundary utilizing the similar method and obtain the circle parameters [7-8]. (See Fig 2)

2.2   Image Normalization

The human eye images are of different sizes of iris because the effects of light and other factors may cause changes in the iris area. Iris image must be normalized for extracting collarette. Two borders of the iris ring are mapped to texture map [9]. This map was normalized Iris images. So diagram is shown in Figure 3.

The iris area from the inner radius to outer radius is divided into 150, and then by using the methods above the iris image is normalized; the normalized image's size is by 360*150. Figure 4 is a normalized result.

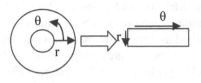

Fig. 3. Illustration of the elastic model   **Fig. 4.** Normalized iris image

3   Collarette Extraction Method

3.1   Collarette

Most people's collarette is fuzzy, so it is difficult to directly carry with the edge detection method. Observed from the image, there are more obvious differences inside and outside the texture of the intestinal loop area. Different location is actually the outside edge of the intestinal loop area. It is considered to be the position of the collarette. So the range of texture can be used to determine the location of the collarette. This work proposes a method for Canny so that it can be used as an edge detector.

3.2   Canny

The Canny edge detector is based on the hysteresis concept; it primarily consists of determining a high threshold that allows a group of pixels to be classified as edge points without using information about their connectivity [9]. A low threshold then determines which pixels will not be edge points and permits only those points that increase the connectivity of the previously determined edge points to be aggregated as edge points. The hysteresis process uses spatial information and thus is a better method than thresholding for edge detection. The method is as follows:

(1) Calculate the gradient image expectation. N is the original image pixels, l is the gray level , t_j is the gray level-gradient. n_j is the gradient image pixels. Probability is $p_j = {n_j}\big/{N}$ 。 An expectation is obtained.

$$E = \sum_{j=1}^{l} t_j \cdot p_j \tag{1}$$

(2) Take 2 levels (p, q) in the gray gradient series ($1 < p < q < l$),Their gray level-gradient is t_m、 t_k. They put the gray-level gradient into three regions. They represent the original image of the edge points, the possible edge points and the edge points.

(3) Expectations of the gray-level gradient are calculated respectively $E_1(1, p)$, $E_2(p,q)$、 $E_3(q,l)$.

$$E_1(1,p) = \frac{\sum_{i=1}^{p} t_i \cdot p_i}{\sum_{i=1}^{p} p_i} \qquad E_2(p,q) = \frac{\sum_{i=p+1}^{q} t_i \cdot p_i}{\sum_{i=p+1}^{q} p_i} \qquad E_3(q,l) = \frac{\sum_{i=q+1}^{l} t_i \cdot p_i}{\sum_{i=q+1}^{l} p_i} \tag{2}$$

(4) Calculating variance between two classes $\sigma^2(p,q)$。 Their maximum corresponds to gray level-gradient t_p, t_q.

$$\sigma^2(p,q) = \left(E(1,p) - E\right)^2 \cdot \sum_{i=1}^{p} p_i + \left(E_2(p,q) - E\right)^2 \cdot \sum_{i=p+1}^{q} p_i + \left(E_3(q,l) - E\right)^2 \cdot \sum_{i=q+1}^{l} p_i \tag{3}$$

(5) Demarcation point p and q are regarded as the high and low threshold.

3.3   Collarette Extraction

We have the following procedure to implement the proposed above algorithm. The adaptive canny edge detector extracts the texture of the intestinal loop area. It is given in Fig5

(1) On the extraction results, 7 * 1 template is established. The template is sided along a column direction, and statistics the summation of pixels in the template.

(2) if the summation is zero, this sub-block is marked. The center of the template sub-block is the edge point.

(3) For all the columns to repeat step (2) until all boundary point are found in the whole image.

(4) all boundary point are lined. It is the collarette of this image.

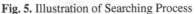

Fig. 5. Illustration of Searching Process   **Fig. 6.** Results of the collarette extraction

In addition, according to a lot of the samples we found that gray scale was smaller on the upper part of image than the lower part of image. The main reason is that the eyelid shade makes uneven illumination, which sits in relative dark. If used the same threshold to the canny operation. The texture detection's effect is not ideal. So it can cause a deviation in the collarette extraction.

Aimed at this problem, this paper proposed partition method based on the canny for extracting the collarette. The method as follows:

（1）Using the proposed adaptive canny operator threshold algorithm to calculate threshold on the whole image of the iris;

（2）Normalized iris image region can be divided into two areas;

（3）Extracting texture on the upper and the lower part of image by canny. According to a large number of experiments, select threshold of the upper part is 0.95 times of the original threshold and select threshold is 1.15 times.

（4）At last, collarette is extracted. It is given in Fig6.

4 Intestinal Loop Information Representation Based on GLCM

4.1 Texture Information Representation

A pair of pixel gray appeared on certain statistical regularity from a direction of image. From a certain extent, it can reflect the texture features of the image. This statistical regularity can be described by a matrix (the gray level co-occurrence matrix) [10]. Gray level co-occurrence matrix (W) reflects the comprehensive information about the direction and the distance of image gray variation. By the gray level co-occurrence matrix, images can be analyzed according to local mode and arrangement rules. But generally, it does not directly use the co-occurrence matrix but get the statistics on the basis of the matrix.

In the image, we take a point (x, y) and another point (x+a, y+b). There is a pair of points. Its gray is (i, j), which is the gray of point(x, y) is i, point(x+a, y+b)is j. A and B are constant. Point(x, y) is moved in the whole image. So, it can be get all kinds of (i, j). In the whole image, Statistical frequency of occurrence for each is P(i, j ,d,θ). So W= [P(i,j,d,θ)]g*g is a gray level co-occurrence matrix. g is the image gray level. The commonly used texture analysis and co-occurrence matrix feature parameters are as follows:

(1) The mean

$$m = \sum_{i=0}^{g-1}\sum_{j=0}^{g-1} ip(i,j,d,\theta)$$

(4)

Mean to represent the average brightness of image. In general, the average brightness of the larger texture rough.

(2) Standard deviation

$$\sigma = \sum_{i=0}^{g-1}\sum_{j=0}^{g-1}(i-m)^2 p(i,j,d,\theta)$$

(5)

Standard deviation is used to represent the image average contrast. In general, texture rough average contrasts larger.

(3) Smoothness

$$R = 1 - \frac{1}{1+\sigma^2}$$

(6)

Smoothness is used to express the relative smoothness measure luminance image in the area.

(4) Three moments

$$\mu_3 = \sum_{i=0}^{g-1}\sum_{j=0}^{g-1}(i-m)^3 p(i,j,d,\theta)$$

(7)

Three moments are used to represent the image gray level's distribution of offset. In general, the three moments of rough texture is big.

(5) Consistency

$$U = \sum_{i=0}^{g-1}\sum_{j=0}^{g-1} p^2(i,j,d,\theta)$$

(8)

Measure the consistency of image texture, when all the gray values are equal, the maximum consistency.

(6) Entropy

$$e = \sum_{i=0}^{g-1}\sum_{j=0}^{g-1} p(i,j,d,\theta)\log_2 p(i,j,d,\theta)$$

(9)

Entropy is used to represent random texture measurement. In general, texture's rough entropy is bigger.

4.2   The Classification Model

The supporting vector-machine method [11] is to establish a learning theory of VC dimension theory and structural risk minimization principle on the basis of statistics. According to the limited sample information, the model complexity (i.e. the learning accuracy of specific training sample) and learning capability (i.c., crror free samples to identify any capacity of) is to find the best compromise in order to obtain the best generalization ability. In this paper, the 6 features above obtained as input. The establishment of a model based on support vector machine.

5   Experiments Results and Discussion

5.1   Iris Database Used for Our Research

Our iris image capture device uses a HM9918 handheld iris instrument. This equipment can collect 24-bit color image. Image's size is by 800*600. Our clinical iris database contains normal and abnormal irises. The iris images were taken from student volunteers at the Shenyang University of Technology. A normal iris refers to the iris image of a healthy individual. To ensure that the irises came from healthy individuals, we made our selection by asking several questions about the current health status and family genetic history of the volunteers.

An abnormal iris (pathological iris) refers to the iris of a patient with a clear medical diagnosis. The information was mainly taken from the Central Hospital Affiliated to Shenyang Medical College. Diagnostic conclusion is obtained while providing health information from a collector or a doctor.

Currently, the iris image's database has irises from 200 healthy individuals and 800 patients diagnosed with gastrointestinal diseases. The image is divided into three categories, as shown in the following table1.

Table 1. Image sample classification

	healthy individuals	Sub healthy individuals	patients
sample	200	619	181

5.2   Collarette Boundary Localization

5.2.1   Localization
Most of people the intestinal loop are with clear texture. But the contour of collarette cannot be seen clearly. The experiment was carried out on Canny operator based on texture. The experimental procedure is as follows. Fig.7(a) shows a normalized image of a normal iris. Then iris texture is extracted by the partition image adaptive Canny

operator. Fig.7 (b) shows the final result of the proposed approach and the 3.3 section's searching algorithm to texture outer boundary points and the connections to obtain the collarette. Its effect is shown in Fig.7(c) shows. Figs.7(d) and (e) are not partitioning the result of traditional model. Such can be seen by the use of comparing method. No partitioned makes curling half iris appear under the extraction errors. Some places increased significantly. The extraction method of partitioning is better in the intestinal region of the collarette iris.

(a) Normalized iris image

(b) Extracting texture by partition   (c) Extracting collarette by
     adaptive Canny operator   partition adaptive Canny operator

(d) Extracting texture by   (e) Extracting collarette by
     the traditional Canny operator   the traditional Canny operator

Fig. 7. Performance of partition adaptive Canny operator for extracting collarette

5.2.2   Different Types of Collarette Detection

Table 1 mentioned three kinds of iris images collarette extraction experiment. The results are as shown in Figure8.

(a) Results for healthy individuals

(in this paper)

(b) Results for healthy individuals

(gradient method)

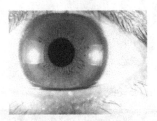

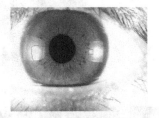

(c) Results for sub-healthy individuals
(in this paper)

(b) Results for sub-healthy individuals
(gradient method)

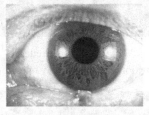

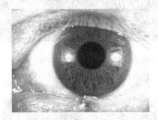

(e) Results for patients
(in this paper)

(b) Results for patients
(gradient method)

Fig. 8. Results of collarette extraction

Among them, Fig8(a), 8(c), 8(e) are extraction results in this paper; Fig8(b), 8(d), 8(f) extraction results in the method for maximum gray level gradient. The results can be seen that the gray gradient method for blur boundary extraction is not ideal, which is unable to obtain the real collarette position.

5.3   The Experimental Results Based on GLCM of Intestinal Loop Information Representation

In accordance with the above calculation method, the results were calculated by different categories of iris image in terms of the gray level and the co-occurrence matrix intestinal loops. We obtain the corresponding eigenvalue, as shown in table 2.

Table 2. Different populations of intestinal loop region texture

	Mean	Standard deviation	Smoothness	Three moments	Consistency	Entropy
Healthy Individuals	9.523101	48.34978	0.034703	8.48273	0.928098	0.229986
Sub-healthy Individuals	15.49412	60.91742	0.053988	12.7842	0.885861	0.330459
Patients	15.86275	61.59037	0.055122	13.0252	0.883326	0.336144

Table 2 shows different populations of intestinal loop region texture. For example, intestinal loop texture with gastrointestinal diseases roughly. The entropy is bigger than that in healthy people. While the figure is less clear among the sub-healthy people between these two classes of entropy. This area's pixel values of the randomness are bigger than other two areas. In this case, the mean and the standard deviation are higher. In addition, this kind of crowd of iris intestinal loop region is smooth and consistent in term of minimum. So, the smoothness and consistency of the maximum value of the minimum is spotted. The population of intestinal loop region's gray level offset in distribution. So is the distribution in the three order moments of maximum.

5.4   Classification Model Results Based on Intestinal Loop Texture Information

The experimental sample is of 300 randomly selected images as training samples in order to establish the model of support vector machine. The other 700 images remained as samples for testing. The results are shown in table 3.

Table 3. Classification performance on typical person

	Healthy Individuals	Sub-healthy Individuals	Patients
Recognition Rate	85.8%	87.6%	89.9%

The SVM method may be the best in recognition. But taking into account more features in the experiment requires the combination of prior knowledge and more direction. Its recognition's performance is lacking in quantity.

6   Conclusion

A critical analysis of iris intestinal loop information is the intestinal loop region localization. That is to say, it detected collarette on the intestinal loop's upper boundary. Detection method of partitioning adaptive based on Canny operator is proposed in this paper, which can effectively extract the iris intestinal loop regions of different types of people. Using gray level co-occurrence matrix is to achieve irregular bowel loop region in term of texture measure. This measure results as input.

The support to vector machine model is established based on the information of the iris intestinal loops so as to achieve a classification of different kinds of people. The model provides basis for computer health evaluation system based on iris.

Acknowledgments. This work was supported by the National Natural Science Foundation of China (No. 61271365).

References

1. Simon, A., Worthen, D.M., Mitas, J.A.: An Evaluation of Iridology. JAMA 242(13), 56–58 (1979)
2. Daugman, J.G.: High confidence visual recognition of persons by a test of statistical independence. IEEE Trans. on Pattern Analysis and Machine Intelligence 15(11), 1148–1161 (1993)
3. Daugman, J.G.: How iris recognition works. IEEE Transactions on CSVT 14(1), 21–30 (2004)
4. Li, F.: System of the ophthalmology. People's Medical Publishing, Beijing (1996)
5. Xin, G.-D., Wang, W.: Study on collarette extraction. Computer Engineering and Design 29(9), 2290–2292 (2008)
6. Yu, L., Wang, K., Zhang, D.: Extracting the autonomic nerve wreath of iris based on an improved snake approach. Neurocomputing (70), 743–748 (2007)
7. Yuan, W.-Q., Xu, L., Lin, Z.-H.: Iris Localization Algorithm Based on Gray Distribution Features of Eye Images. Journal of Optoelectronics. Laser. 17(2), 226–230 (2006)
8. Yuan, W.-Q., Xu, L., Lin, Z.-H.: An accurate and fast iris location method based on the features of human eyes. In: Wang, L., Jin, Y. (eds.) FSKD 2005. LNCS (LNAI), vol. 3614, pp. 306–315. Springer, Heidelberg (2005)
9. Medina-Carnicer, R., Munoz-Salinas, R., Yeguas-Bolivar, E., Diaz-Mas, L.: A novel method to look for the hysteresis thresholds for the Canny edge detector. Pattern Recognition 44, 1201–1211 (2011)
10. Wang, H.: Research on the Pattern Recognition Methods of Wood Surface Texture Based on GLCM. Northeast Forestry University (2007)
11. Cheng, J., Wang, K.: Active learning for image retrieval with Co-SVM. Pattern Recognition (1) (2006)

Pupil Contour Extraction Method of Anti-light Spot Interference for Iris Image Captured in Visible Light

Xia Yu, Jian Song, and Weiqi Yuan

School of Information Science and Technology, Shenyang University of Technology,
No.111, Shenliao West Road, Economic & Technological Development Zone,
Shenyang, 110870, P.R. China
yuxia@sut.edu.cn

Abstract. Point light sources always reflect on color iris image captured by portable color iris image capturing device, which will affect the pupil contour extraction. A pupil's contour extraction method of anti-light spot interference is given in this paper to solve the problem. Firstly, the expanded pupil region is unfolded into a rectangle image. Secondly, all the light spot regions in the rectangle image are positioned by projecting method of axial directions after binarization and median filtering. Thirdly, these regions are filled by image inpainting technique based on fast marching method. Then, pupil contour extraction can be launched. Next, those regions which are close to contour line are repaired so that the entire exact pupil contour is finally extracted out. In addition, the experiment about this method is conducted with 200 color iris images. The results show that this method has considerable validity and adaptability.

Keywords: image processing, iris recognition, pupil contour extraction, light spot interference.

1   Introduction

With rich and stable texture features, iris recognition technology is widely applied in biometric recognition field [1~4]. Besides iris texture features, the morphological feature of pupil can also be applied in paramedical field, such as health status detection [5]. But an exact and complete extraction of pupil contour is needed as the precondition of extracting these features.

At present, there are many methods to position pupil, such as the circular detection algorithm proposed by Daugman [1,2]; Edge detection algorithm combining the Hough transform is proposed by Wildes [4]; Research on iris boundary position in different lights was proposed by Tian Qichuan et al [6]; A method combining a gray projecting and circle equation is proposed by Wu Jianhua et al [7]; An improved iris positioning algorithm based on specific sense region sampling was proposed by Liu Yang et al [8]. An iris location algorithm based on gray distribution features of eye images was proposed by Yuan Weiqi et al [9,10]; Kyong et al   proposed an algorithm for iris positioning based on straight line

Z. Sun et al. (Eds.): CCBR 2014, LNCS 8833, pp. 339–346, 2014.

[11]; Li Xia et al proposed an iris location algorithm based on straight line [12]. However, all these methods above used ideal circles to position inner and outer boundary of iris in order to acquire iris region instead of intentionally acquiring the exact pupil contour. According to the fact that the pupil is not an ideal circle, a new iris edge extraction method proposed by Yuan Weiqi et al [13] can effectively solve the problem of acquiring exact pupil contour.

Unfortunately, the applied object of this method is the iris image captured in infrared light as shown in Fig. 1(a). This picture lacks color features that can be used to aid health status detection. In addition, this method uses the light spots in the pupil(as shown in Fig.1(a)) to position pupil, while most visible light iris images(as shown in Fig. 1(b)) have no such light spots. Therefore, a new method to extract pupil contour in visible iris image is needed.

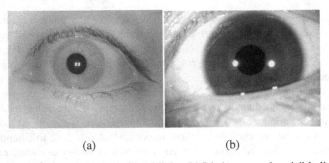

(a)   (b)

Fig. 1. (a) Iris image under infrared light. (b) Iris image under visible light.

Meanwhile, due to the nature of the device itself, the positions of light spots can hardly be determined when an image is captured, as shown in Fig. 2.

These light spot region can be divided into three types, according to the relative positional relationship between the light spot and pupil. The first type is away from the pupil (named Type 1). The second type is close to the pupil edge (named Type 2). And the last one is light spot covering on the pupil edge (named Type 3). Three types of light spot are showed in Fig. 2 (a), (b), (c) respectively.   Fig. 2(b) and Fig. 2(c) are bound to make a mistake in extracting the pupil contour without any processing. Therefore, this article aims to give a pupil contour extraction method of anti-light spot interference for iris image captured in visible light.

2   Methodology

According to the shape and positional characteristics of light spots, the proposed method consists of following four steps to extract the pupil contour.

   (1) Acquire and unfold pupil region.
   (2) Position light spot regions.
   (3) Fill light spot regions and extract pupil contour.
   (4) Search for those light spot regions close to contour line
   (5) Repair the contour extracted in (3).

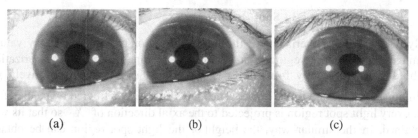

(a)   (b)   (c)

Fig. 2. The relative positional relationship between light spots and pupil. (a) Type 1. (b) Type 2. (c) Type 3.

2.1   Acquiring and Unfolding Pupil Region

Firstly, the pupil is positioned on iris image by algorithm proposed in [6, 9, 10]. Since the pupil region is only a small part of the whole iris image, in order to accelerate the pupil contour extraction speed, small-scale expanded is made before it is unfolded into a rectangle image. The schematic diagram of transformation is shown in Fig. 3. Δr is the expanded length and its value is 50 in this paper.

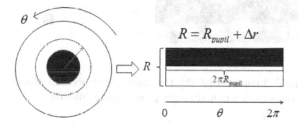

Fig. 3. The schematic diagram of extended pupil area transformation

It should be noted that the method is used for a grayscale image, and the grayscale image generates from the red component of the color image. It can be seen in Fig. 4 that the red component grayscale image make a minimal light spot interference on the halation compared with green and blue components.

(a)   (b)

(c)   (d)

Fig. 4. Different grayscale images from original iris image
(a) Gray. (b) Green   component.   (c) Blue component.   (d) Red component.

2.2   Positioning the Light Spot Regions

Firstly, using the characteristic that the light spot region presents high gray value in the image, all light spot regions can be isolated by binarization. The binarizational threshold is expressed by formula 1. $value_{max}$ and $value_{min}$ are respectively gray maximum and minimum in the image. The high gray noise is filtered by median filter. Next, every light spot region is projected to the axial direction of X so that its width is obtained. In the similar way, the height of the light spot region can be obtained from the projection in the axial direction of Y. According to the width and the height, the accurate position of every light spot region can be confirmed in the image. Fig. 5(b) shows the result of the position of every light spot region in Fig. 5(a).

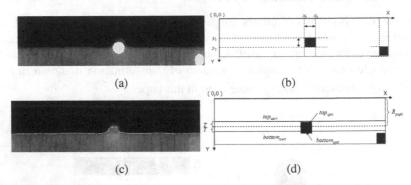

Fig. 5. (a)The unfolded pupil image. (b) The result of the position of every light spot region. (c) The result of contour extraction. (d) a design of judging criterion.

2.3   Fill the Light Spot Regions and Extract Pupil Contour

All the light spot regions are filled by an image inpainting technique based on the fast marching method [14]. And then the pupil contour is extracted by the method in [13]. This would effectively eliminate the light spot impact in Type 1 mentioned above. The results are shown in Fig. 5(c).

2.4   Searching for the Light Spot Regions Impact Directly Contour

The light spot region that impacts contour directly refers to Type 2 and Type 3 above. For searching them out, a search criterion should be designed. The design is shown in Fig. 5(d). The baseline height is R_{pupil}. T is the vertical offset expressed by Equation 1. S is the standard deviation of all the contour points that do not belong to the light spot region. top_{alert} and $bottom_{alert}$ expressed by formula 2. Judgment of the light spot regions belonging to Type 2 and Type 3 is expressed by formula 3.

$$\frac{2}{3}\left(value_{max} - value_{min}\right) \tag{1}$$

$$T = 15 \times \left(1 + \frac{S}{R_{pupil}} \right) \tag{2}$$

$$Top_{alert} = R_{pupil} - T \tag{3}$$

$$bottom_{alert} = R_{pupil} + T$$

$$Spot_{Type1\&2} = \{ region_{spot} | top_{spot} \leq bottom_{alert} \cap bottom_{spot} \geq top_{alert} \} \tag{4}$$

2.5   Repairing the Contour

The process steps of repairing the light spot regions in Type 2 and Type 3 are described as follows.

(1)   The slopes k_0 and k_2 of $Q_0 P_0$ and $Q_2 P_2$ are respectively calculated.

(2)   If $|k_0 - k_2| \leq T_k$, it means that $Q_0 P_0$ and $Q_2 P_2$ will be parallel with each other. Connecting point P_0 and point P_2 by straight line to complete the repair.

(3)   If $|k_0 - k_2| > T_k$, to obtain intersection point P_1 of extension cord $Q_0 P_0$ and extension cord $Q_2 P_2$ and then complete the repair by a quadratic Bezier curve is defined by P_0, P_1, P_2.

The diagram of repairing contour is shown in Fig. 6(a) N_{left} and N_{right} are respectively the number of contour points on left side and right of the light spot region. The value of the number is 10 in this paper. Fig. 6(b) shows the result of repairing contour.

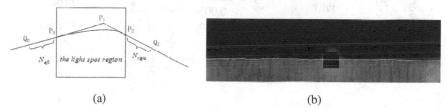

(a)   (b)

Fig. 6. (a) The diagram of repairing contour. (b) The result of repairing contour.

3   Experiment

The study uses a kind of portable color iris image capture device shown in Fig. 8. The image is 24-bit true color image and the resolution is 800 multiplied by 600. The images come from college students and patients in the hospital for gastroscopy and one image per person and per eye captures. Fig. 7 shows the landscape of capturing image process by the portable color iris image capture device. This paper randomly selected 200 images from the iris pictures captured for algorithm experiments. The experiment environment is shown as follows.

(1) Computer system: windows 7(32).
(2) CPU: Intel(R) Core(TM)2 Duo T6570 @ 2.10GHz
(3) RAM: 2.00GB

Fig. 7. The landscape of capturing image process by the portable color iris image capture device

Firstly, according to the number of the light spot existing in the unfolded pupil image, 200 pictures are classified into three classes as shown in Fig. 8(a). The result shows that most of pictures are impacted by light spots. Then, do respectively three times in repeating the experiments in these three classes by three processes. The chart of success rate for contour extraction is shown in Fig. 8(b). The result shows the method in this paper keeps a higher success rate for pictures in any class.

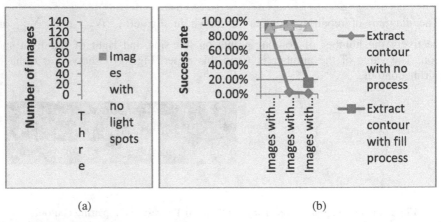

(a)   (b)

Fig. 8. (a) The chart of pictures numbers of three classes. (b) The chart of success rates for contour extraction by three processes

A method for pupil contour extraction is proposed in [15]. So a comparative test between the method in this paper and the method mentioned by [15] is done with these 200 pictures. The result in Table 1 shows that two methods have similar success rate. But the method in this paper has less average time consumption per image.

Table 1. Comparison of two method

methods	accuracy	operation time
The method in [15]	93%	680.5ms
The proposed method	93.5%	224.3ms

Fig. 9(a) shows the comparative image between some partial views without proposed method and corresponding ones with proposed method. Fig. 9(b) exemplifies some results of marked contour by recovery process.

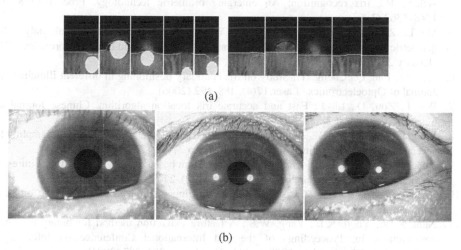

(a)

(b)

Fig. 9. (a)A comparative image between some partial views without proposed method and corresponding ones with proposed method. (b) Some results of marked contour by recovery process.

According to the analysis, the Processing failure comes from quality problems of images captured. In addition, when iris images of some with vitreous opacity is captured, light reflection makes the pupil high bright so that the contour extraction algorithm in this paper can not find the exact boundary.

4   Conclusion

According to different positional characteristics of light spots on iris images, this paper proposes a pupil contour extraction method of anti-light spot interference for iris image captured in visible light. The expanded pupil region of the iris image is unfolded into a rectangle region and all the light spots regions are positioned, according to relative distance between light spot regions and unfolded pupil edge in the region filling and contour repairing process. The experiment about proposed method is conducted with 200 images and the result shows that the success rate is 93.5%. This demonstrates that proposed method in this paper has considerable validity and adaptability and this method is helpful for color image contour extraction in future.

References

1. Daugman, J.G.: Wavelet demodulation codes, statistical independence, and pattern recognition. In: Proc. 2nd Institute of Mathematics and its Applications, IMA-IP, pp. 244–260 (2000)
2. Daugman, J.G.: The importance of being random: statistical principles of iris recognition. Pattern Recognition 36(2), 279–291 (2003)
3. Daugman, J.G.: Demodulation by complex-valued wavelets for stochastic pattern recognition. International Journal of Wavelets, Multiresolution and Information Processing 1(1), 1–17 (2003)
4. Wildes, R.: Iris recognition: An emerging biometric technology. Proc. IEEE 85(9), 1348–1363 (1997)
5. Ma, L., Zhang, D., Li, N., Cai, Y., Zuo, W., Wang, K.: Iris-based medical analysis by geometric deformation features. IEEE Journal of Biomedical and Health Informatics 17(1) (January 2013)
6. Tian, Q., Pan, Q., Cheng, Y.: Study on iris boundary positioning in different illumination. Journal of Optoelectronics · Laser 17(4), 488–492 (2006)
7. Wu, J., Zou, D., Li, J.: Fast and accurate iris location algorithm. Chinese Journal of Scientific Instrument 28(8), 1469–1473 (2007)
8. Yang, L., Xia, L., Na, W., et al.: An improved iris location algorithm based on sampling to special regions of interesting. Acta Photonia Sinica 37(6), 1277–1280 (2008)
9. Yuan, W., Xu, L., Lin, Z.: Iris positioning algorithm based on gray distribution features of eye images. Journal of Optoelectronics · Laser 17(2), 226–230 (2006)
10. Yuan, W., Xu, L., Lin, Z.: An iris block-encoding method based on statistic of local information. Acta Optica Sinica 27(11), 2047–2053 (2007)
11. Nam, K.W., Yoon, K.L., Yang, W.S.: A feature extraction method for binary iris code construction. In: Proceedings of the 2nd International Conference on Information Technology for Application (ICITA 2004), Harbin, pp. 284–287 (2004)
12. Li, X., Yu, L., Wang, N.: A fast iris location algorithm based on line detection. Journal of Computer-Aided Design & Computer Graphics 18(8), 1155–1159 (2006)
13. Yuan, W., Bai, X.: A new iris edge extraction method. Acta Photonia Sinica 8(29), 2158–2163 (2009)
14. Telea, A.: An image inpainting technique based on the fast marching method. Journal of Graphics Tools 9(1), 25–36 (2004)
15. Liu, W., Fan, Y., Lei, T.: Eye corneal reflection removal based on boundary initial position detection. Computer Engineering and Applications 49(17), 1–5 (2013)

Couple Metric Learning Based on Separable Criteria with Its Application in Cross-View Gait Recognition

Kejun Wang, Xianglei Xing, Tao Yan, and Zhuowen Lv

College of Automation, Harbin Engineering University, Harbin 150001, China
{wangkejun,xingxl}@hrbeu.edu.cn

Abstract. Gait is an important biometric feature to identify a person at a distance. However, the performance of the traditional gait recognition methods may degenerate when the viewing angle is changed. This is because the viewing angle of the probe data may not be the same as the viewing angle under which the gait signature database is generated. In this paper, we introduce the separable criteria into the couple metric learning (CML) method, and apply this novel method to normalize gait features from various viewing angles into a couple feature spaces. Then, the gait similarity measurement is conducted in this common feature space. We incorporate the label information into the separable criteria to improve the performance of the traditional CML method. Experiments are performed on the benchmark gait database. The results demonstrate the efficiency of our method.

Keywords: cross-view gait recognition, couple metric learning, separable criteria.

1   Introduction

Over the past decade, the human gait recognition has attracted much attention in the communities of biometric recognition and computer vision since gait is an important biometric feature to identify a person at a distance. Unlike other biometric features, the gait of a person can be captured from a distant camera without drawing the attention of the observed subject. Therefore, gait recognition can be widely applied to visual surveillance in security-sensitive environments such as airports, platforms, and banks. However, the performance of gait recognition system can be affected by many covariate factors, such as light illumination, duration, clothing, load carrying, varying of view angles and so on. Among the above factors, the change of viewing angle is one of the main difficulties since the 2-D gait will appear in significantly different ways under various views. The performance of most existing gait recognition algorithms may drop significantly when viewing angle changes.

To solve the problem which is caused by view change, a variety of methods have been proposed. They can be classified into three main categories. Approaches in the first category are to extract the gait feature which is invariant to viewing angles change. Kale *et al.* [1] proposed a method to generate a side-view of gait from any arbitrary view. Their methods contain two techniques, which are based on the

Z. Sun et al. (Eds.): CCBR 2014, LNCS 8833, pp. 347–356, 2014.

perspective projection model and the optical flow structure. Jean *et al.* [2] developed a method to compute view-normalized trajectories of body parts which were obtained from monocular video sequences. This method efficiently works only within a limited range of views. Han *et al.* [3] extracted view-invariant features from gait energy image (GEI). Only parts of overlapped gait sequences between views were selected for constructing a representation of cross-view gait matching. The methods in the first category can only be applied to a few limited viewing angles and their feature extraction processes can disrupt due to occlusion.

Approaches in the second category are adopted to construct 3-D gait information through multiple calibrated cameras. Shakhnarovich *et al.* [4] proposed an image-based visual hull (IBVH) to render visual views for gait recognition. They computed IBVH from a set of monocular views captured by multiple calibrated cameras. Canonical visual camera positions were estimated. Then rendered images obtained from these viewpoints were used for the normalization of the view. Bodor *et al.* [5] used image-based rendering on a 3-D visual hull model to automatically reconstruct gait features under any required viewing angle. Zhang *et al.* [6] proposed a view-independent gait recognition method on a 3-D linear model and the Bayesian rule. The approaches in the second category require costly complicated setup of calibrated multi-camera system and heavy computational resources for expensive computation which are not suitable for real-time application.

Methods of the third category aim at learning projecting or mapping relationship of gait features under different viewing angles. These methods learn the trained relationship, which may normalize gait features from various viewing angles into shared feature spaces before the gait similarity can be carried out. Compared with other categories, this category has two key advantages: (1) It only requires uncalibrated single-camera system. Rather, it does not need frame synchronization; (2) It is fast in the testing phase and it is suitable for real time applications. Makihara *et al.* [7] introduced a view transformation model (VTM) which can transform frequency domain gait features from different views into the same view. VTM was established through a matrix factorization processed by the applying singular value decomposition. The gait matrix in the training dataset can be decomposed into the subject-independent matrix and the viewing independent matrix. The subject-independent matrix was used to construct VTMs. Instead of adopting the Fourier feature, Kusakunniran *et al.* [8] created VTM based on GEI which was optimized by linear discriminant analysis. The above methods assume that the gait feature matrix in the training dataset can be decomposed into two independent matrices without overlapping elements. However, this assumption has not been clearly verified mathematically. Therefore, it could not guarantee to obtain an optimized VTM. Bashir *et al.* [9] applied canonical correlation analysis (CCA) to model the correlation of gait sequences from different viewing angles. They first projected gait features from two different views onto two learned feature spaces that were optimally correlated based on CCA. Then, the correlation strength was employed to measure gait similarity. Compared with VTM, CCA can cope with feature mismatch across views and is more robust against feature noise. However, CCA is an unsupervised dimensionality reduction. Therefore, it does not take the label information into account.

In this paper, we introduce the separable criteria into the couple metric learning (CML) [10] method and apply this novel method to normalize the gait features from various viewing angles into a couple feature spaces. The label information is employed to improve the performance of the traditional CCA and CML methods. The rest of this paper is organized as follows. In Section 2, we briefly review the traditional CML method. We introduce our novel method to incorporate the separable criteria into CML in Section 3. Gait feature extraction is explained in Section 4. Experimental results are reported in Section 5 and the conclusion is drawn in Section 6.

2   Couple Metric Learning

Given two sets $X \subset \mathbf{R}^{D_x}$ and $Y \subset \mathbf{R}^{D_y}$. Obviously, some common distances (e.g., Euclidean distance) cannot be computed directly since the dimensionalities of the two sets may not be equal. The basic idea of couple metric learning (CML) is to learn the couple map functions f_x and f_y, which in fact map X and Y to a common subspace $\mathbf{R}^{D_c}$, and then introduce the definition of the traditional distance measure in this couple subspace:

$$d^c(x,y) = \sqrt{(f_x(x) - f_y(y))^T A(f_x(x) - f_y(y))}, \qquad (1)$$

Where x, y denotes the point from the data set X and Y, respectively; A denotes a real symmetrical matrix corresponding to different distance function. (e.g., when A is the identity matrix, d^c becomes a function of the Euclidean distance.) Let $A = W_a W_a^T$, we can reformulate (1) as:

$$\begin{aligned} d^c(x,y) &= \sqrt{(f_x(x) - f_y(y))^T W_a W_a^T (f_x(x) - f_y(y))} \\ &= \sqrt{(W_a^T f_x(x) - W_a^T f_y(y))^T (W_a^T f_x(x) - W_a^T f_y(y))} \end{aligned} \qquad (2)$$

The key principle of CML aims at keeping the point pairs, which are within the set of similar relation in the original space as close as possible in the couple subspace. This principle could be formulated by the following objective function:

$$\min J = \min \sum_{(i,j) \in C} \left\| W_a^T f_x(x_i) - W_a^T f_y(y_j) \right\|^2 \qquad (3)$$

where C denotes the similar relation matrix of sets X and Y. For each point $x_i \in X$ and each point $y_j \in Y$. Suppose the class labels are c_{x_i} and c_{y_j}, respectively. Then, the similar relation matrix can be defined as: $C_{ij} = \begin{cases} 1, c_{x_i} = c_{y_j} \\ 0, c_{x_i} \neq c_{y_j} \end{cases}$.

Li et al. [10] considers two linear functions to specify the mapping functions as $f_x(x) = W_x^T x$ and $f_y(y) = W_y^T y$, respectively. In this context, (3) can be reformulated as:

$$\min J = \min \sum_{(i,j) \in C} \left\| W_a^T W_x^T x - W_a^T W_y^T y \right\|^2 \tag{4}$$

Let $P_x = W_x W_a$, $P_y = W_y W_a$, we have

$$\min J = \min \sum_{(i,j) \in C} \left\| P_x^T x_i - P_y^T y_j \right\|^2 \tag{5}$$

Thus, the CML based on linear mapping is simply a matter of two linear transformations: P_x and P_y.

3   Improved Couple Metric Learning Based on Separable Criteria

The CML ensures the pairs of points. They have similar relation in the original two sets as close as possible in the couple subspace. However, the CML cannot ensure that the projected points in the couple subspace could be well separated according to the class labels.

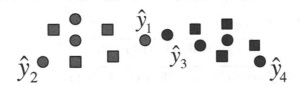

Fig. 1. □denotes set X, ○denotes set Y; red color represents class one, blue color represents class two

As we can observe from Figure 1, although the projected points $\hat{y}_1$, $\hat{y}_2$, $\hat{y}_3$, and $\hat{y}_4$ are close to the corresponding projected points from set X, which have similar relation in the original two sets, the distance between the projected points $\hat{y}_1$ and $\hat{y}_3$ (coming from different classes) is too small to be well separated. In other words, the CML cannot ensure that the projected points belong to the same class which is as close as possible. While the projected points belonging to different classes should be far from each other.

In order to solve this problem, we propose to incorporate the separable criteria into the traditional CML. We first define the within-class relation matrix from each original set as: $C_{x,ij} = \begin{cases} 1, c_{x_i} = c_{x_j} \\ 0, c_{x_i} \neq c_{x_j} \end{cases}$ and $C_{y,ij} = \begin{cases} 1, c_{y_i} = c_{y_j} \\ 0, c_{y_i} \neq c_{y_j} \end{cases}$. Obviously, C_x and C_y

are all real symmetrical matrix. Let the projected point in the couple subspace be $z \in Z$, where $Z \subset R^{Dc}$. Then, we can define the within-class relation matrix and the between-class relation matrix in the couple subspace as $C_{z,ij} = \begin{cases} 1, c_{z_i} = c_{z_j} \\ 0, c_{z_i} \neq c_{z_j} \end{cases}$, and

$C_{z,ij}^- = \begin{cases} 0, c_{z_i} = c_{z_j} \\ 1, c_{z_i} \neq c_{z_j} \end{cases}$, respectively. We introduce the total mean squared distance in the couple subspace as:

$$J_d = \frac{1}{2(N_x + N_y)^2} \sum_{i=1}^{N_x+N_y} \sum_{j=1}^{N_x+N_y} \|z_i - z_j\|^2 = \frac{1}{2(N_x + N_y)^2} \sum_{(i,j) \in C_z} \|z_i - z_j\|^2 + \frac{1}{2(N_x + N_y)^2} \sum_{(i,j) \in C_z^-} \|z_i - z_j\|^2 \tag{6}$$

where N_x and N_y denote the number of the set X and Y, respectively. The first term of the right hand side of (6) represents the mean squared distance within the same class. The second term is the mean squared distance representing the mean squared distance between different classes. We can define the within-class mean squared distance as:

$$J^+ = \frac{1}{N} \sum_{(i,j) \in C_z} \|z_i - z_j\|^2 = \frac{2}{N} \sum_{(i,j) \in C} \|P_x^T x_i - P_y^T y_j\|^2 +$$
$$\frac{1}{N} \sum_{(i,j) \in C_x} \|P_x^T x_i - P_x^T x_j\|^2 + \frac{1}{N} \sum_{(i,j) \in C_y} \|P_y^T y_i - P_y^T y_j\|^2 \tag{7}$$

where $N = 2(N_x + N_y)^2$. Employing some deductions of linear algebra, we can reformulate the objective function (7) into a new form as (8):

$$J^+(P_x, P_y) = Tr \left[\frac{2}{N} (P_x^T XG_x X^T P_x + P_y^T YG_y Y^T P_y - P_x^T XCY^T P_y - P_y^T YC^T X^T P_x) + \right.$$
$$\left. \frac{1}{N} (P_x^T XG_{xx} X^T P_x - P_x^T XC_x X^T P_x) + \frac{1}{N} (P_y^T YG_{yy} Y^T P_y - P_y^T YC_y Y^T P_y) \right] \tag{8}$$

Where Tr denotes the trace operator of a matrix, G_x and G_y are both diagonal matrices and the elements of their diagonals are the summation of the corresponding rows and columns of the similar relation matrix C, which reflects the similar relation between the sets X and Y. G_{xx} and G_{yy} are both diagonal matrices. The elements of their diagonals are the summation of the corresponding rows of C_x and C_y, respectively. Furthermore, we can rewrite the objective function (8) as:

$$J^+(P_x,P_y)=Tr\left(\begin{bmatrix}P_x\\P_y\end{bmatrix}^T\begin{bmatrix}X&\\&Y\end{bmatrix}\begin{bmatrix}\frac{2}{N}G_x+\frac{1}{N}(G_{xx}-C_x)&-\frac{2}{N}C\\-\frac{2}{N}C^T&\frac{2}{N}G_y+\frac{1}{N}(G_{yy}-C_y)\end{bmatrix}\begin{bmatrix}X&\\&Y\end{bmatrix}^T\begin{bmatrix}P_x\\P_y\end{bmatrix}\right) \quad (9)$$

Let $P=\begin{bmatrix}P_x\\P_y\end{bmatrix}$, $Z=\begin{bmatrix}X&\\&Y\end{bmatrix}$, and $\Omega^+=\begin{bmatrix}\frac{2}{N}G_x+\frac{1}{N}(G_{xx}-C_x)&-\frac{2}{N}C\\-\frac{2}{N}C^T&\frac{2}{N}G_y+\frac{1}{N}(G_{yy}-C_y)\end{bmatrix}$, we

obtain a concise form as:

$$J^+(P_x,P_y)=Tr\left(P^TZ\Omega^+Z^TP\right)$$

Similar deduction with (7) to (9), we can define the between-class mean squared distance J^-. Our final objective function can be defined as:

$$\min J = \min(\frac{J^+}{J^-}) = \min Tr(\frac{P^TZ\Omega^+Z^TP}{P^TZ\Omega^-Z^TP}) \quad (10)$$

It is easy to prove that (缺内容) and $F=Z\Omega^-Z^T$ are both symmetrical matrix. The solution to the above optimization problem with respect to P can be computed by D_c, the smallest eigenvectors of the generalized eigenvalue problem $EP=\lambda FP$. According to the definition of $P=\begin{bmatrix}P_x&P_y\end{bmatrix}^T$, we can obtain the projecting matrices P_x and P_y corresponding to the data sets X and Y, respectively.

4   Gait Feature Extraction

In this paper, we choose to use the well known gait energy image (GEI) [11] as a gait feature. Since GEI holds several key information of human gait including the motion frequency, the temporal and spatial changes of human body and global body shape statistic. GEI well reflects the gait rhythm and has been reported as a good feature which is robust to both the silhouette errors and image noises. We first use the method in [12] to extract and segment the human silhouette from image sequences. Then, we normalize the silhouettes to be the same size. The gait period of each gait sequence is determined by the method in [13]. In a window of complete walking cycle(s), GEI is obtained as follows:

$$G(x,y)=\frac{1}{M}\sum_{i=1}^{M}B_i(x,y)$$

Where $B_i(x,y), i=1,2,...,M$ represent a set of gait images, $B_i(x,y)$ is a pixel at position (x,y) of gait image B_i and M is the total number of gait images from complete gait period(s). Figure 2 shows the GEIs of a subject walking under different viewing angles. As we can see , GEIs of the same subject appear in significantly different ways under different viewing angles. So, it is difficult and inefficient to directly measure similarity of GEIs across viewing angles.

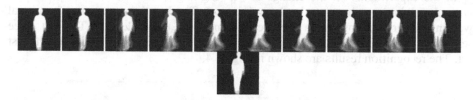

Fig. 2. GEIs of a subject walking under different viewing angles (0°,18°,36°,54°,72°,90°,108°,126°,144°,162°,180°).

In this paper, we propose to use the CML which is based on separable criteria to project GEIs under two different viewing angles to a common feature space before gait similarity is measured. The training process of our method is shown in Figure 3.

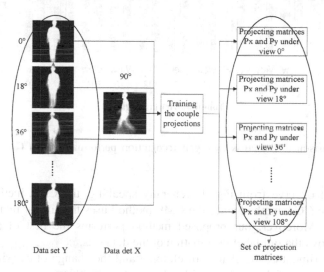

Fig. 3. The training process of our method

5   Experiments

The publically available CASIA gait database B [14] is used in our experiments. The CASIA gait database B is a large multi-view gait dataset that contains 124 subjects from 11 views, namely 0°,18°,36°,54°,72°,90°,108°,126°,144°,162°,and 180°. For each viewing angle of each particular subject, ten gait sequences are captured for each person including six sequences in normal walking, two sequences in walking when carrying a bag and two sequences in walking when wearing a coat. We first use the PCA algorithm to reduce the dimensions of the GEIs features. The reduced dimensionality is equal to 300, and 99% of the total energy is preserved. We employ the nearest neighbor classifier to recognize different subjects. We compare our proposed method with the Canonical Correlation Analysis (CCA) [9] and the couple metric learning (CML) [10] algorithms.

In the experiments on the change of viewing-angle, the first three sequences in normal walking are chosen to be the training set. The last three sequences in normal walking under viewing angle 90° are chosen to be the gallery set.The last three sequences in normal walking under the other viewing angles are chosen to be the test set. The recognition results are shown in Figure 4.

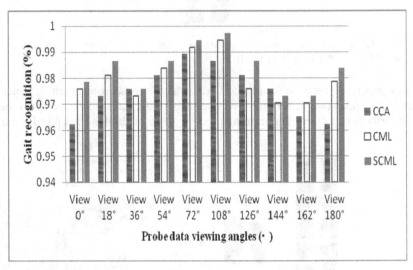

Fig. 4. Comparison of the cross-view gait recognition performances of CCA, CML and our SCML

As we can observe from Fig. 4, generally speaking, the CML method performs better than the CCA method since the CML method uses the similar relation between the two sets. Moreover, our proposed method performs the best of all since our method employs the full label information of the data sets.

In the experiment of the change of clothing and the change of carrying condition, the first sequences of the walking with a bag and the walking with a coat are chosen to be both the training set and the gallery set. The last sequences of the walking with a bag and walking with a coat are chosen to be the test set. The viewing angles for all the sets are chosen to be 90°. The conditions for the training set and the gallery set are chosen to be 'bag + bag', 'coat + coat', 'bag + coat', and the conditions for the test set are bag, coat, 'bag + coat', respectively. The recognition results are shown in Table1.

As we can observe from Table 1, our proposed method performs the best of all. The CML algorithm does not perform well in this experiment, since these is only a single sample of each subject in the training set. Our method improves the performance of the CML by incorporating the label information into the objective function. It also performs the best of all the methods in this experiment.

Table 1.   The gait recognition rate (%) of several algorithms

Method	Training and gallery conditions		
	bag + bag	coat + coat	bag + coat
	Test conditions		
	bag	coat	Bag
PCA	84.68	89.52	——
CCA	84.68	93.55	89.11
CML	83.06	94.35	88.71
SCML	87.10	94.35	90.73

6   Conclusion

In this paper, we propose to incorporate the separable criteria into the traditional couple metric learning method and apply this novel method to the cross-view gait recognition problem. Our method employs the label information to improve the performance of the traditional CCA and CML methods. Experiments on the CASIA-B database demonstrate the proposed method can achieve satisfactory results in covariate conditions across views.

References

1. Kale, A., Chowdhury, A.K.R., Chellappa, R.: Towards a view invariant gait recognition algorithm. In: IEEE Conference on Advanced Video and Signal Based Surveillance, pp. 143–150 (2003)
2. Jean, F., Bergevin, R., Albu, A.B.: Computing and evaluating view-normalized body part trajectories. Image and Vision Computing 27, 1272–1284 (2009)
3. Han, J., Bhanu, B., Roy-Chowdhury, A.: A study on view-insensitive gait recognition. In: IEEE International Conference on Image Processing, ICIP 2005, III-297–III-300 (2005)
4. Shakhnarovich, G., Lee, L., Darrell, T.: Integrated face and gait recognition from multiple views. In: IEEE Computer Society Conference on Computer Vision and Pattern Recognition, vol. 1, pp. I-439–I-446 (2001)
5. Bodor, R., Drenner, A., Fehr, D., Masoud, O., Papanikolopoulos, N.: View-independent human motion classification using image-based reconstruction. Image and Vision Computing 27, 1194–1206 (2009)
6. Zhang, Z., Troje, N.F.: View-independent person identification from human gait. Neurocomputing 69, 250–256 (2005)
7. Makihara, Y., Sagawa, R., Mukaigawa, Y., Echigo, T., Yagi, Y.: Gait recognition using a view transformation model in the frequency domain. In: Leonardis, A., Bischof, H., Pinz, A. (eds.) ECCV 2006. LNCS, vol. 3953, pp. 151–163. Springer, Heidelberg (2006)
8. Kusakunniran, W., Wu, Q., Li, H., Zhang, J.: Multiple views gait recognition using view transformation model based on optimized gait energy image. In: IEEE 12th International Conference on Computer Vision Workshops (ICCV Workshops), pp. 1058–1064 (2009)
9. Bashir, K., Xiang, T., Gong, S.: Cross View Gait Recognition Using Correlation Strength. In: BMVC, pp. 1–11 (2010)

10. Li, B., Chang, H., Shan, S.: Low-resolution face recognition via coupled locality preserving mappings. IEEE Signal Processing Letters 17(1), 20–23 (2010)
11. Han, J., Bhanu, B.: Individual recognition using gait energy image. IEEE Trans. on Pattern Analysis and Machine Intelligence 28(2), 316–322 (2006)
12. Kim, K., Chalidabhongse, T.H., Harwood, D., Davis, L.: Background modeling and subtraction by codebook construction. In: International Conference on Image Processing, pp. 3061–3064 (2004)
13. Wang, L., Tan, T., Ning, H., Hu, W.: Silhouette analysis-based gait recognition for human identification. IEEE Transactions on Pattern Analysis and Machine Intelligence 25, 1505–1518 (2003)
14. Yu, S., Tan, D., Tan, T.: A framework for evaluating the effect of view angle, clothing and carrying condition on gait recognition. In: IEEE 18th International Conference on Pattern Recognition, vol. 4, pp. 441–444 (2006)

Enhancing Human Pose Estimation with Temporal Clues

Jianliang Hao, Zhaoxiang Zhang, and Yunhong Wang

State Key Laboratory of Virtual Reality Technology and Systems,
School of Computer Science and Engineering, Beihang University, Beijing 100191, China
zxzhang@buaa.edu.cn

Abstract. We address the challenging problem of human pose estimation, which can be adopted as a preprocessing step providing accurate and refined humanpose information for gait recognition and other applications. In this paper, we propose a method and augmented Pose-NMS to process the human pose estimation in the consecutive frames based on a reasonable assumption. The poses between the adjacent frames have small changes. Firstly we merge the multiple estimated pose candidates in a single frame to get the representative pose candidates. Then we propagate the final candidate backward and forward to increase the number of the confident candidates based on the Bayesian theory. We apply our method to the Buffy Video dataset and obtain the competitive result to the state-of-art.

Keywords: Human pose estimation, Augmented Pose-NMS, Temporal clues.

1 Introduction

With the development of the intelligent system, human pose estimation has an important role in the computer vision fields. The pose estimations from the static images and the motion videos have lots of various computer vision applications such as the motion capture[1], action recognition[2] and human computer interaction[3]. The more accurate pose configuration can help to analyze the gait information from the body structure. However, the traditional methods suffer from the problem of the lower accuracy and the great challenges including the diversity and uncertainty of the body position, the occlusion, the clutter backgrounds etc. In terms of pose estimation from the still images and pose tracking from the videos, the former lacks of the temporal information and the latter may be better if the poses' configurations in every frame have been known. If we incorporate the information from multiple frames and propagate them to the adjacent frames, we may not only use the advantage of the space relation among the pose candidates in the still images but also combine the temporal relation between adjacent frames to mitigate the effects of the challenges. So we can improve the pose estimation performance by incorporating the raw results from the still images and the poses sequence from the continuous frames.

Z. Sun et al. (Eds.): CCBR 2014, LNCS 8833, pp. 357–365, 2014.

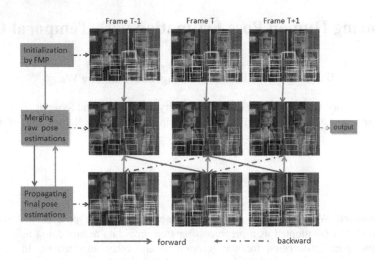

Fig. 1. The flowchart of our method

Our paper mainly focuses on the post-processing pose estimation process. Our contribution is to make full use of the space and temporal information of the pose candidates to improve the human pose performance. Our method, augmented Pose-NMS, based on[4], can take advantage of interframe information and get the more accurate results on the extremely difficult pose parts (elbow and wrist) than [4].Compared with [5].We use the simple and efficient way to propagate the pose configuration between the adjacent information instead of using theoptical flow. We make an assumption that the human poses in the adjacent frames don't change violently, which can be also seen in Figure[2]. We will add the final pose estimations from frame T-1 and T+1 into the candidates in frame T directly when we process the pose estimation of the T frame.We only need the approximately accurate locations when we merge the candidates in a single frame. It is unnecessary to get the more confident candidates by optical flow or other methods with the efficiency considered. The reason why we don't add pose estimations of more previous frames is that correlation of them has weakened(see Figure[2].Several raw pose estimations of every frame will be disturbed if more candidates of previous frame are added. Processing the merging and propagating iteratively can also overcome the disadvantage of the only final candidate added. Although we test the upper body's estimation, the method can be also applied to the whole body estimation.

Figure[1] is the framework of our paper. Firstly, we initialize the raw pose estimation by Flexible Mixtures of Parts model.Then,we merge the raw pose estimates across space and time on every frame to produce the final pose estimations. After that, we propagate the final pose estimation forward and backward and process the merging and propagating iteratively until it reaches the maximum iterations. In the paper, we also introduce the related work and the detail of our proposed method in Section2 and Section3 separately. The experimental results are shown and discussed in Section4. Finally, we draw the conclusion in Section5.

2   Related Work

Human Pose Estimation from Still Images. Human pose estimation based on 2D still images has been an active research field that lots of international and domestic academics are interested in. The traditional model is pictorial structures (PS) models because of its simplicity in the process of inference and learning[13]. The improvements based on the PS model mainly focus on the improved structure of the model based on symmetry and similarity using the cascade model and adding the latent node. Another important model is the Flexible Mixtures of Parts (FMP) model, which produces the state-of-the-art result for human pose estimation [12]. We will use the FMP model to provide an initialization on every video frame due to its computational efficiency and the ability to detect people at different scales.

Human Pose Tracking from Videos. The theme means the combination of the posed estimation with tracking under a sequence of monocular video images. In early work, Ramanan et al[6] assumed that people tended to take on certain canonical poses. Based on the accurate detection, they could build a discriminative appearance model and apply it to each frame. Similarly, Buehler et al[7] exploited temporal tracking with identifying key frames where configurations could be correctly inferred. Ferrari[8] performed simultaneous pose estimation by an integrated spatiotemporal model covering multiple frames based on the static image likelihoods. Compared with [8], Sapp et al[9] andFragkiadaki et al[10] exploited optical flow to locate foreground contours, the segmenting body parts and the propagated information over time.

Human Pose Improvement from Video. Surprisingly, little work has been done about the interesting problem which is how to incorporate pose information across the time. S. Zuffi et al [5] used the Bayesian theory to combine the optical flow [11], hand detector, contour descriptor and the color descriptor. Although the author showed state-of-the-art performance on dataset of TV video sequences, the method was time-consuming. X.P.Burgos-Artizzu et al [4] took into account relation of the pose candidates and then used the Pose-NMS method, whose thought is similar to the weighted k-means and achieve good results. We will improve the method [4] based on the Bayesian theory to propagate the useful pose configuration over time.

3   Model and Method

3.1   Flexible Mixtures of Parts model

Flexible Mixtures of Parts (FMP) model, which is first proposed by Yi Yang et al in [12], shows state-of-the-art performance with the optimistic time cost. We will briefly introduce FMP method and you we see [12]in detail. For the classic Pictorial Structure (PS) Model [13], the candidates' pose scores are defined with the pose configurationL of the image I as follows:

$$S(I, L) = \sum_{i \in V} \alpha_i * \phi(I, l_i) + \sum_{i,j \in E} \beta_{ij} * \psi(l_i, l_j) \qquad (1)$$

Here, $\phi(I, l_i)$ means the local image features at location of part l_i and $\psi(l_i, l_j)$ means the spatial features between part l_i and l_j. The coefficients, α_i and β_{ij} stand for the unary template for part i and pairwise springs between part l_i and l_j respectively.

As the variety of posture and spatial relations considered, Yi Yang et al proposed the FMP model to augment standard spring models, which could capture contextual co-occurrence relations between parts. The updated pose scores are similar with Eqn1 except a new term added to express the typesof pose part (closed eyes or open eyes, smiling or frown). So Eqn1 would change to the following format.

$$S(I, L, M) = \sum_{i \in V} \alpha_i^{m_i} * \phi(I, l_i) + \sum_{i,j \in E} \beta_{ij}^{m_i m_j} * \psi(l_i, l_j) + \sum_{i,j \in E} b_{ij}^{m_i m_j} \qquad (2)$$

In Eqn2, M means the mixture of part i, so $\alpha_i^{m_i}$ and $\beta_{ij}^{m_i m_j}$ mean the unary template for part i with mixture m_i and pairwise springs between part l_i with mixture m_i and part l_j with mixture m_j. The third sum can be interpreted as the Co-occurrence "Bias". $b_{ij}^{m_i m_j}$ stands for the pairwise co-occurrence between part l_i withmixture m_i and partl_j withmixturem_j.In the next steps,α, β, b are learned by implementing their own proposed coordinate-descent solver or other solver (such as SVMStruct[14]) then we can proceed pose estimations based on the Eqn2 and choose the most highest score candidate as the prediction.

3.2   Augmented Pose-NMS

Given a video containing T frames, we can get the pose candidates by FMP,$X^t = \{x_1^t, ..., x_{n^t}^t \mid x_i^t \in R^D, 1 \leq t \leq T\}$ and their associated confidence scores $S^t = \{s_1^t, ..., s_{n^t}^t \mid s_i^t \in R, 1 \leq t \leq T\}$, where n^t is the number of the candidates in frame t and each candidate is parameterizedusing D dimensions. Pose-NMS [4] aims to compute trajectories$Y^t = \{y_1^t, ..., y_K^t \mid y_k^t \in R^D\}$, which are close to the raw pose estimates in each frame. Here K is the number of the human appeared in the video.

For the single-frame, the initialized pose estimates of the K persons can be got by the FMP model and a robust clustering of the raw pose estimates is proceeded to result in more accurate performance than any of the individual ones while simultaneously solving the correspondence problem. The squared Euclidean distance $d(x, y) = ||x - y||_2^2$ are used to measure the distance between two parts. If given X^t and S^t, the loss of the prediction $Y^t = \{y_k^t \mid 1 \leq k \leq K\}$ can be defined as following:

$$L_{space}(Y^t) = \frac{1}{s^t} \sum_{i=1}^{n^t} \min_k d_{bd}(x_i^t, y_k^t) s_i^t \text{, where } s^t = \sum_{i=1}^{n^t} s_i^t \qquad (3)$$

Eqn3 can get appropriate centroids that represent the boundedpose estimation and the satisfying prediction y^k. All the raw pose estimations are correspondingly around the actual location of the different pose. So the threshold is added to limit the maximum distance and avoid the influence of the fairly far apart candidates. The representation of distance then become the $d_{bd}(x, y) = \min(z, \|x - y\|_2^2)$ and the loss of prediction are modified into Eqn4.

$$L_{space}(Y^t) = \frac{1}{s^t} \sum_{i=1}^{n^t} \min_k d_{bd}(x_i^t, y_k^t) s_i^t \qquad (4)$$

Compared with Eqn3, Eqn4 only replacesthe d with d_{bd}. So we can discard the estimation x_i^t which is far from the any prediction y^t to ensure y^t can account for a large number of nearby detections but not any distant ones. In addition, the constant z is set to the average object width in pixels.

Now we give an intuitive explaination to the Eqn3. If we regard the prediction y^t as the cluster and L_{space} as the loss function, then Eqn 3 can be comprehended as the process of weighted k-means. So Eqn3can also reduce the loss step by step and make the raw pose estimations smooth. The new representation of the distanced_{bd}makes the loss reduce to z if x_i^t is far from y^t Therest case is the same with Eqn3. In consequence, Eqn4 can also lead to the descent of the loss and improve the performance.

$$L(Y) = \sum_{t=1}^{T} L_{space}(Y^t) + \lambda \frac{1}{K} \sum_{i=1}^{K} (d(y_k^{t-1}, y_k^t) + d(y_k^t, y_k^{t+1})) \qquad (5)$$

X.P.Burgos-Artizzu et al also improves the method combing the multi-frame information(see Eqn5).But the mean performance maintains similar pose quality on the single-frame.It appears thatthe extra loss added from the multi-frame may have less effect on L_{space}. The pose informations across time play a weak role in the merging the pose candidates. Next, we will introduce how to make full use of the temporal information.

$$s_{n^t+1}^t \propto p(X_{n^t+1}^t) \propto p(X_{n^t+1}^t \mid Y^{t-1}) * p(Y^{t-1}) \qquad (6)$$

For our method, we only need the approximately correct and weight pose oneswhen we merge the pose estimation candidates.In addition, with the time efficiency considered, we will add the previous and next final pose estimations directly instead of the prediction by the tracking method. From Figure2 we can know that the pose keypoints of adjacent frames have changed slightly. If we can get the relatively accurate pose at frame T-1 and then we can add the extra influential candidates and get the score by the Eqn6. $p(X_{n^t+1}^t \mid Y^{t-1})$is the prior knowledge which has been shown in Figure2 and $p(Y^{t-1})$ will be set to 1. So far, every step leads to decrease the loss and we can improve the pose performance by the several times iteration.

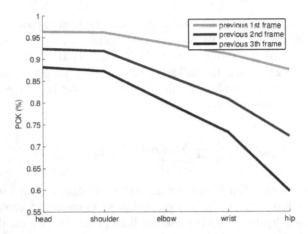

Fig. 2. The relationship of the adjacent frame. 'Previous 1st frame' means the Percentage of Correct Keypoints (PCK) get by using the ground truth of frame T-1 as the prediction of the T frame. The results can be regarded as the prior knowledge by training and will be used when propagating the pose configuration forward and backward. The other lines get the similar meanings.

4   Experimental Results and Analysis

Buffy Stickmen dataset [8][15] is the most widely used dataset for human pose estimation. However the original dataset doesn't contain any temporal information. Luckily, X.P.Burgos-Artizzu et al extends the dataset and creates the Buffy Video dataset [4] by collecting 50 short clips using the same episodes as the original set. The beginning and ending points of the 5 body parts (head, shoulder, elbow, wrist and hip) are benchmarked as before. We will test our augmented Pose-NMS method on the Buffy Video dataset. In order to evaluate our method, we will follow the evaluation criteria called Percentage of Correct Keypoints (PCK) proposed in [12] :   a keypoint is accepted as a correct estimation only if itfalls within $0.2 * \max(h, w)$ pixels of the ground-truth keypoint, where h and w are the height and width of the bounding box.

4.1   Testing on Buffy Video Dataset

To illustrate the performance of our augmented Pose-NMS, We test our method on the Buffy Video dataset. In our experiment, we keep all original pose candidates and use T = 50 just the same as[4]. T is the amount of prior temporal information.As mentioned before, we only add the final pose estimation in frame T-1 to the T frame. Each frame will be optimized in turn, starting from the first frame and proceeding forward for all the frames then backwards. Therefore the temporal smoothness λ will

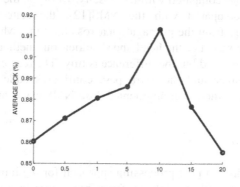

(a) Average accuracy with different λ

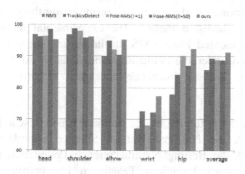

(b)Accuracy of human parts (λ = 10)

Fig. 3. The Accuracy Comparison.Figure3(a) shows the average accuracy with different temporal smoothness λ.Figure3(b) shows the comparison of correct estimation rates between different methods when λ equals 10

be different because of the importance of the temporal information. We increase temporal smoothing λand get the result shown in Figure3(a), from which we canget the satisfied and competitive performance especially on wrist and hip when λ = 10. λ > 1 tells us that temporal term is moreeffectivethan the spatial term. The interpretation can fit our augmented Pose-NMS method, which emphasizes the importance of the temporal information.We will set λ = 10 in the next reported experiment.

4.2   Comparison with Other Methods

We compare our results with raw pose estimation and Pose-NMS, which are obtained by [12], [4] respectively. From Figure3(b), we can see that data driven approaches can help integrate the candidates and improve the performance. The average accuracy outperforms the other method and improves 5.5% than the raw average pose estimation. As we know, arms and hands are relatively small and difficult to localize.

We improve at least 5% compared with the Pose-NMS [4] on the elbow, wrist and hip and at least 10% compared with the NMS[12], the state-of-art method. The improvement is mainly from the propagation across the time, which can help process the occlusion in some way. For the head and shoulder, our method gets the poor result compared with other method,but the difference is tiny. The reason is that both of them have higher performance and the extra pose configures added from the adjacent frames may react. As a whole, our augmented Pose-NMS can achieve better results.

5   Conclusions

In this paper, we address a post-processing approach for the human pose estimation. We make use of the closeness of the different pose parts in a single frame and the relationship of pose estimation from the adjacent frames. We merge the pose estimates in a single frame by clustering and propagating the pose estimates forward and backward by the Bayesian theory. The experimental results demonstrate the advantages of our augmented Pose-NMS. In the future, we will try to improve the human pose estimation under the occlusion conditions by some time sequence. We will also consider the heuristic inference strategy to improve the accuracy of the human parsing method.

Acknowledge. This work is funded by the National Basic Research Program of China (No. 2010CB327902), the National Natural Science Foundation of China (No. 61375036, 61005016), the Beijing Natural Science Foundation (No. 4132064), the Program for New Century Excellent Talents in University, the Beijing Higher Education Young Elite Teacher Project, and the Fundamental Research Funds for the Central Universities. Zhaoxiang Zhang is the corresponding author of this paper.

References

1. Moeslund, T.B., Granum, E.: A survey of computer vision-based human motioncapture. CVIU (2001)
2. Poppe, R.: A survey on vision-based human action recognition. Image and Vision Computing (2010)
3. Pavlovic, V.I., Sharma, R., Huang, T.S.: Visual interpretation of hand gestures forhuman-computer interaction: A review. PAMI (1997)
4. Burgos-Artizzu, X.P., Hall, D., Perona, P., Dollár, P.: Merging pose estimates acrossspace and time. In: BMVC (2013)
5. Zuffi, S., Romero, J., Schmid, C., Black, M.J.: Estimating human pose with flowingpuppets. In: ICCV (2013)
6. Ramanan, D., Forsyth, D.A., Zisserman, A.: Strike a pose: Tracking people by finding stylized poses. In: CVPR (2005)
7. Buehler, P., Everingham, M., Huttenlocher, D.P., Zisserman, A.: Upper bodydetection and tracking in extended signing sequences. IJCV (2011)
8. Ferrari, V., Marin-Jimenez, M., Zisserman, A.: Progressive search space reductionfor human pose estimation. In: CVPR (2008)

9. Sapp, B., Weiss, D., Taskar, B.: Parsing human motion with stretchable models. In: CVPR (2011)
10. KaterinaFragkiadaki, Han Hu, J.S.: Pose from flow and flow from pose. In: CVPR (2013)
11. Xu, L., Jia, J., Matsushita, Y.: Motion detail preserving optical flow estimation. PAMI (2012)
12. Yang, Y., Ramanan, D.: Articulated pose estimation with flexible mixtures-ofparts. In: CVPR (2011)
13. Felzenszwalb, P.F., Huttenlocher, D.P.: Pictorial structures for object recognition. IJCV (2005)
14. Finley, T., Joachims, T.: Training structural svms when exact inference is intractable. In: ICML (2008)
15. Eichner, M., Marin-Jimenez, M., Zisserman, A., Ferrari, V.: 2d articulated humanpose estimation and retrieval in (almost) unconstrained still images. IJCV (2012)

A Simple Way to Extract I-vector
from Normalized Statastics

Zhenchun Lei, Jian Luo, and Yingen Yang

School of Computer and Information Engineering,
Jiangxi Normal University, Nanchang, China
{zhenchun.lei,luo.jian}@hotmail.com, ygyang@jxnu.edu.cn

Abstract. In the i-vector model, the utterance statistics are extracted from features using universal background model. The utterance is mapped to a vector in the total variability space, which is called i-vector. The total variability space provides a basis to obtain a low dimensional fixed-length representation of a speech utterance. But, the processing is complicated for the interweaving of the statistics and machine learning method. So, we considered separating them and proposed a simple way to extract i-vector by classical principal component analysis, factor analysis and independent component analysis from normalized statistics. The results on NIST 2008 telephone data show that the performance is very close to the traditional method and they can be improved obviously after score fusion.

Keywords: speaker verification, principal component analysis, factor analysis, independent component analysis.

1 Introduction

I-vector has become the state of the art technique for text-independent speaker recognition [1] in recent years. Dehak [2] proposed a single space that modeled the speaker and channel's variabilities and named it the total variability space, which was a low-dimension space of the Gaussian Mixture Model (GMM) [3] supervector[4] space. The vectors in the low-dimensional space are called i-vectors, which are smaller in size and can get recognition performance similar to that obtained by Joint Factor Analysis (JFA) [5].

In conventional methods, the total variability matrix is processed by following a similar process to that of learning the eigenvoice [6] matrix of JFA, in which a variant of the Probabilistic Principal Component Analysis (PPCA) [7] approach is introduced for estimating the parameters. The process is very complicated. Some researchers proposed methods to simplify it [8, 9]. We consider that the statistic and the machine learning method are interwoven, so we try to separate them so as to simplify the extractor. On the other side, any other machine learning method can also be applied easily.

Z. Sun et al. (Eds.): CCBR 2014, LNCS 8833, pp. 366–374, 2014.
© Springer International Publishing Switzerland 2014

This paper is organized as follows: We review the i-vector model in section 2. We present our method for extracting i-vector in section 3. Section 4 provides the results of our experiments. Finally, section 5 is devoted to the main conclusions and our future work.

2 I-vector Model

The supervector is consisted of the mean vectors in GMM. In I-vector model, the supervector can be modeled as follows:

$$M = M_0 + T \cdot w \tag{1}$$

where M_0 is a speaker- and channel-independent supervector, usually the universal backgroundmodel(UBM)supervector is a good choice. T is a low rank matrix, which represents a basis of the reducedtotal variability space and w is a normaldistributed vector which are referredto as i-vector. The M is assumed to be normally distributed with mean vector M_0 and covariancematrix$T \cdot T^T$.

A variant of the PPCA approach is used in training the total variability matrix T. The featurevector associated with a given recording is the MAP estimation of w, and the matrix T isestimated using the EM algorithm described in Kenny's paper [6].The likelihood function as the estimation criterion is:

$$\prod_s \max P(O(s)|M_0 + T \cdot w(s), \Sigma) \tag{2}$$

where s ranges over the recordings in the training set, $O(s)$ is the recording data and$\Sigma$is the covariance matrix of GMM.

2.1 I-vector Extractor

The i-vector can be extracted from the Baum-Welch statistics on UBM for a given utterance. The total factor w can be definedby its posterior distribution, which is aGaussian distribution and the mean ofthis distribution corresponds exactly to our i-vector. Suppose we have a sequence of L frames $\{y_1, y_2, ..., y_L\}$ and an UBM composed of C mixture components definedin some feature space of dimension D. The Baum-Welch statistics needed to estimate the i-vector for a given speech utterance u are obtained by

$$N_c = \sum_{t=1}^{L} P(c|y_t, \Sigma_c) \tag{3}$$

$$F_c = \sum_{t=1}^{L} P(c|y_t, \Sigma_c)y_t \tag{4}$$

Where $c = 1, ..., C$ is the Gaussian index and $P(c|y_t, \Sigma_c)$ corresponds to the posterior probability of mixture componentc generating the vector y_t .In order to estimate the i-vector, we also need to compute the centralized first-order Baum-Welch statistics based on the UBM mean mixture components

$$\tilde{F}_c = \sum_{t=1}^{I,} P(c|y_t, \Sigma_c)(y_t - m_c) \tag{5}$$

where m_c is the mean of UBM mixture component c. The i-vector for a given utterance can be obtained through using the following equation:

$$w(u) = (I + T^t\Sigma^{-1}N(u)T)^{-1} \cdot T^t\Sigma^{-1}\tilde{F}(u) \tag{6}$$

We define $N(u)$ as a diagonal matrix of dimension CD × CD whose diagonal blocks are $N_cI(c = 1, ..., C)$. $\tilde{F}(u)$is asupervector of dimension CD × 1 obtained by concatenatingall first-order Baum-welch statistics $\tilde{F}_c$ for a given utteranceu. Σ is a diagonal covariance matrix of dimension CD × CDestimated during factor analysis training and it modelsthe residual variability not captured by the total variabilitymatrix T.

The total variability matrix T estimated by follows:

$$\sum_u N(u) \cdot T \cdot E[w(u)w(u)^t] = \sum_u F(u) \cdot w(u) \tag{7}$$

where $E[w(u)w(u)^t]$is the expectation of $w(u)w(u)^t$

$$E[w(u)w(u)^t] = w(u)w(u)^t + (I + T^t\Sigma^{-1}N(u)T)^{-1} \tag{8}$$

The model is estimated using the EM algorithm, and we don't update Σ in the UBM for simplification. The optimization proceeds by iterating the following two steps: For each training recording u, we use the estimate of T and equation (6) to find the i-vector w(u); The M-step: Estimate a new total variability space T given the old space and the new i-vectors over all recordings in the training set using equation (7). For a new recording, the i-vector can be extracted only using equation (6).

2.2   Classifier

2.2.1   PLDA Classifier

Probabilistic Linear Discriminant Analysis(PLDA)[10, 11, 12]is used in face recognition firstly, and has been introduced for speaker recognition. PLDA model the i-vectors, and assumes that the j-th utterance of the i-th speaker can be decomposed as

$$w_{ij} = \mu + Vy_i + z_{ij} \tag{9}$$

where μ is the mean of all i-vectors, V is the speaker variability space, y_i is the speaker factor and has a standard normal distribution, z_{ij} modelsthe residual variability and be normally distributed with covariance matrixZ.

$$y_i \sim N(0, I) \tag{10}$$
$$z_{ij} \sim N(0, Z)$$

For two new i-vectors w_1 and w_2 in a trial, we have two hypotheses: θ_{tar} that both w_1 and w_2 share the same speaker identity, or θ_{non} that w_1 and w_2 were generated using different identity. The score between w_1 and w_2 can be computed as

$$score = \log \frac{p(w_1, w_2 | \theta_{tar})}{p(w_1, w_2 | \theta_{non})} \tag{11}$$

where $\Sigma_{tot} = V \cdot V^T + \Sigma$, $\Sigma_{ac} = V \cdot V^T$, we can get

$$score = w_1^T Q w_1 + w_2^T Q w_2 + 2 w_1^T P w_2 + const \tag{12}$$

where

$$Q = \Sigma_{tot}^{-1} - (\Sigma_{tot} - \Sigma_{ac} \Sigma_{tot}^{-1} \Sigma_{ac})^{-1} \tag{13}$$
$$P = \Sigma_{tot}^{-1} \Sigma_{ac} (\Sigma_{tot} - \Sigma_{ac} \Sigma_{tot}^{-1} \Sigma_{ac})^{-1}$$

2.2.2 Length Normalization

PLDA assumes that the i-vectors have a Gaussian distribution. But some empirical evidence of non-Gaussian behavior has been provided in literature. So the length normalization [13] is proposed, and the transformation is following:

$$\widetilde{w} = \frac{w}{\|w\|} = \frac{w}{\sqrt{w^T w}} \tag{14}$$

2.2.3 Cosine Similarity Scoring

The simple cosine similarity metric [10, 11] has been applied successfully in the total variability space to compare two supervectors for making a speaker detection decision. Given two i-vectors via the projection of two supervectors in the total variability space and the WCCN compensation for inter-session variabilities, a target w_{target} from a known speaker and a test w_{test} from an unknown speaker, the cosine similarity score is given as:

$$score(w_{target}, w_{test}) = \frac{(w_{target})^T \cdot w_{test}}{\|w_{target}\| \cdot \|w_{test}\|} \begin{array}{c} \geq \\ < \end{array} \theta \tag{15}$$

where θ is the decision threshold.

3   Simple Way to Extract I-vector

i-vector models the speaker and channel-variabilities together, which is a low-dimension space of the GMM super vector space. I-vector extractor transforms the high-dimension statistics into low-dimension vector. The processing is complicated. We try to simplify the processing and use the dimensionality reduction technique as an extractor. Another benefit is that the time consumption can be reduced for extracting an i-vector from statistics.

3.1   Statistic Normalization

In the classical i-vector model, two statistics N and $\tilde{F}$ are computed and be inputted to the extractor. We can get new statistics after normalizing the statistics $\tilde{F}$ using N and the UBM parameters. For the c-th Gaussian component in UBM

$$\widetilde{N}_c = \frac{N_c}{\sum_i N_i}$$

$$S_c = \left(\frac{\tilde{F}_c}{N_c}\right) \cdot \left(\frac{\sqrt{\widetilde{N}_c}}{\sqrt{\Sigma_c}}\right)$$

(16)

where $\widetilde{N}_c$ isnormalized N_c, and$\Sigma_c$isthe covariance of the Gaussian component. Like the supervector, the whole S can be got by concatenating all S_c. After converting every utterance to a fix-size vector, we can use some classical deimensionality reduction techniques to extract the i-vector in a low-dimension space, such as PCA, FA and ICA.

3.2   Principal Component Analysis

Principal component analysis (PCA) [14] is a widely used dimensionality reduction technique in data analysis. PCA captures the largest information in the first few principal components, guaranteeing minimal information loss and minimal reconstruction error in a least squares sense. PCA attempts to find a linear mapping M which maximizes the cost function$trace(M^T cov(X)M)$, where $cov(X)$ is the sample covariance matrix of data X. It can be shown that this linear mapping is formed by the d principal eigenvectors of the sample covariance matrix of the zero-mean data.

The i-vector model can be viewed as a dimensionality reduction technique, whose inputs are the statistics and output of the i-vector. The dimension of statistic is larger than i-vector's. So we can reduce the dimension of statistic using classical PCA. We use the normalized statistic to improve the performance.

3.3   Factor Analysis

Factor Analysis (FA) [15] is also a dimensionality reduction technique, which originates in psychometrics. FA describes variability among observed and the correlated variables in terms of a potentially lower number of unobserved variables called factors. The observed variables are modeled as linear combinations of the potential factors, plus "error" terms. The information gained about the interdependencies between observed variables can be used later to reduce the set of variables in a dataset. Computationally, this technique is equivalent to low rank approximation of the matrix of observed variables.

Given a dataset $X = \{x_1, x_2, \ldots, x_n\}$, we can model it using latent variables:

$$x_i = W \cdot y_i + \mu + \epsilon \tag{17}$$

The vector y_i is called latent because it is unobserved. ϵ is considered a noise term distributed according to a Gaussian with mean 0 and covariance Ψ (i.e. $\epsilon \sim N(0, \Psi)$), μ is some arbitrary offset vector. Such a model is called generative as it describes how x_i is generated from y_i.

Like PCA, we also use FA to extract i-vector from the normalized statistics.

3.4   Independent Component Analysis

The third dimension reduction technique is Independent Component Analysis (ICA) [16], which separates a multivariate signal into additive subcomponents that are maximally independent. ICA can also be used as yet another nonlinear decomposition. It has been used in face recognition. Here, we employ the point of view of optimal information transfer in neural networks with sigmoidal transfer functions.

4   Experiments

4.1   Experimental Setup

The features were derived from the waveforms using 13 mel-frequency cepstral coefficients on a 20 millisecond frame every 10 milliseconds. Delta and delta-delta coefficients were computed via making up a thirty nine dimensional feature vector. And the band limiting was performed by retaining only the filter bank outputs form the frequency range 300-3400 Hz. Mean removal, pre-emphasis and a hamming window were applied. The energy-based end pointing eliminated non-speech frames.

Our experiments were performed on the 2008 NIST SRE dataset. NIST SRE2004 1side training corpus was used to train two gender-dependent UBMs with 512 Gaussian components. The rank of the total variability matrix T was chosen to be 400. NIST SRE2004, SRE 2005, and SRE 2006 telephone datasets were used for estimating the total variability space. For measuring the performance, we used equal error rate (EER) and the minimum decision cost function (DCF).

4.2   Results on Phonecall Condition

The first experiment was run on the 1conv-1conv 2008 SRE core phonecall condition, and the classifier is PLDA classifier. Table 1 show the results. We can see that the performance of our new simple extractors is comparable with the classical method. After fusion, the performance can be improved obviously. The FA method is the best among three dimensionality reduction techniques. But it is maximal in time consuming. The PCA has minimum time consuming, which take only some minutes to construct the principal components while estimating the classical total variability matrix needs a lot of hours. Our methods need less training time than the classical extractor. This may be another benefit.

Table 1. Performance comparison of the i-vector extractors. The results are on the 1conv-1conv 2008 SRE core telephone condition using PLDA classifier

i-vector extractor	gender	EER()	DCF
classical	male	4.7	0.024
new statistic + PCA	male	5.2	0.024
new statistic + FA	male	5.0	0.025
new statistic + ICA	male	5.0	0.023
fusion (classical + new FA)	male	4.5	0.021
classical	female	6.4	0.032
new statistic + PCA	female	6.5	0.032
new statistic + FA	female	6.6	0.033
new statistic + ICA	female	6.7	0.033
fusion (classical + new FA)	female	6.2	0.031

4.3   Results for Cosine Similarity Scoring

Table 2 shows the performance of cosine similarity scoring. LDA and WCCN are applied to i-vectors. zt-norm is applied to get the final scores. The performance is worse than that of PLDA. But the performances are more similar for all extractors.

Table 2. Performance comparison of the i-vector extractors. The results are on the 1conv-1conv 2008 SRE core telephone condition using cosine similarity scoring.

i-vector extractor	gender	EER(%)	DCF
classical	male	5.4	0.026
new statistic + PCA	male	5.4	0.026
new statistic + FA	male	5.2	0.026
new statistic + ICA	male	5.4	0.026
fusion (classical + new FA)	male	5.0	0.025
classical	female	7.0	0.036
new statistic + PCA	female	7.3	0.036
new statistic + FA	female	7.1	0.035
new statistic + ICA	female	7.5	0.037
fusion (classical + new FA)	female	6.7	0.035

5   Conclusions

In the classical i-vector model, the extractor is complicated and the processing is time consuming. We propose a new method to simplify the extractor, which separates the statistic and the machine-learning method. We use three classical machine-learning methods (PCA, FA, and ICA). The result shows that the performance of our method is comparable to the classical i-vector extractor. In our method, any other machine learning method can be integrated easily. So we will consider another machine learning method to improve the performance in future. The new normalized statistic form will also be researched.

Acknowledge. This work is supported by National Natural Science Foundation of P.R.China (61365004), Educational Commission of Jiangxi Province of P.R.China (GJJ12198).

References

1. Kinnunena, T., Li, H.: An overview of text-independent speaker recognition: From features to supervectors. Speech Communication 52(1), 12–40 (2010)
2. Dehak, N., Kenny, P., Dehak, R., Dumouchel, P., Ouellet, P.: Front-End Factor Analysis for Speaker Verification. IEEE Transactions on Audio, Speech and Language Processing 19(4), 788–798 (2011)
3. Reynolds, D.A., Quatieri, T., Dunn, R.: Speaker verification using adapted Gaussian mixture models. Digital Signal Processing 10(3) (2000)
4. Campbell, W.M., Sturim, D.E., Reynolds, D.A., Solomonoff, A.: SVM based speaker verification using a GMM supervector kernel and NAP variability compensation. In: Proc. ICASSP, vol. 1, pp. 97–100 (2006)
5. Kenny, P., Boulianne, G., Ouellet, P., Dumouchel, P.: Joint factor analysis versus eigenchannels in speaker recognition. IEEE Transactions on Audio, Speech and Language Processing 15(4), 1435–1447 (2007)
6. Kenny, P., Gilles, B., Pierre, D.: Eigenvoice Modeling With Sparse Training Data. IEEE Trans. Speech and Audio Proc. 13(3), 345–354 (2005)
7. Tipping, M., Bishop, C.: Mixtures of probabilistic principal component analyzers. Neural Computation 11, 435–474 (1999)
8. Glembekl, O., et al.: Simplification And Optimization of I-Vector Extraction. In: Proceedings of the IEEE International Conference on Acoustics, Speech, and Signal Processing, Prague, Czech Republic, May 22-27, pp. 4516–4519 (2011)
9. Li, M., et al.: Speaker Verification Using Simplified and Supervised I-Vector Modeling. In: Proceedings of the IEEE International Conference on Acoustics, Speech, and Signal Processing (2013)
10. Prince, S.J.D., Elder, J.H.: Probabilistic Linear Discriminant Analysis for Inferences About Identity. In: IEEE 11th International Conference on Computer Vision (2007)
11. Jiang, Y., Lee, K.A., Tang, Z., Ma, B., Larcher, A., Li, H.: PLDA Modeling in I-vector and Supervector Space for Speaker Verification. In: Annual Conference of the International Speech Communication Association, Interspeech (2012)
12. Machlica, L., Zajıc, Z.: An efficient implementation of Probabilistic Linear Discriminant Analysis. In: IEEE International Conference on Acoustics, Speech, and Signal Processing (2013)
13. Garcia-Romero, D., Espy-Wilson, C.Y.: Analysis of i-vector length normalization in speaker recognition systems. In: Annual Conference of the International Speech Communication Association (Interspeech), pp. 249–252 (2011)

14. Martinez, A.M., Kak, A.C.: PCA versus LDA. IEEE Transactions on Pattern Analysis and Machine Intelligence 23(2), 228–233 (2004)
15. Johnson, R.A., Wichern, D.W.: Applied Multivariate Statistical Analysis, 6th edn. Pearson Education (2007)
16. Hyvärinen, A., Oja, E.: Independent Component Analysis: Algorithms and Applications. Neural Networks 13(4-5), 411–430 (2000)

A Novel and Efficient Voice Activity Detector Using Shape Features of Speech Wave

Qiming Zhao, Yingchun Yang[*], and Hong Li

Zhejiang University,
College of Computer Science and Technology, Hangzhou, China
{zqm1111,yyc,lihong}@zju.edu.cn

Abstract. A voice activity detector (VAD) is the prerequisite for speaker recognition in real life. Currently, we deal with the VAD problem at the frame level through short time window function. However, when tackling with the VAD problem manually, we can easily pick out the speech segments containing several words. Inspired by this, we firstly use IIR filter to get the envelope of the waveform and divide the envelope into separate sound segments. And then we extract shape features from the obtained segments and use K-means to cluster the data featured by the amplitude of the wave crest to discard the silent part. Finally, we utilize other shape features to discard the noise part. The performance of our proposed VAD method has apparently surpassed the energy-based VAD and VQVAD with a relative 20% decrease in error rate, While the computation time of the proposed VAD method is only 30% less than that of VQVAD. We also get an encouraging result utilizing our VAD method for speaker recognition with about 3% average decrease in EER.

Keywords: Speaker recognition, Shape feature, GMM-UBM, VAD, Speech wave.

1   Introduction

Voice activity detection (VAD) is essential in speech processing system, which is to locate the speech segments in an utterance. Currently the VAD methods can be grouped into two types. One type is energy-based VAD, which is intuitively simple. Zero-crossing rate and short-time energy are computed with the assumption that speech frames have relatively higher energy than nonspeech frames. Assigned a threshold relative to maximum or average energy of the utterance, speech frames can be distinguished from the nonspeech frames. But this type of VAD has a well-known shortcoming of sensitivity to additive noise. So before using the energy-based VAD, some speech enhanced processing is necessary, e.g spectral subtraction and Wiener filter. The other type is model-based VAD, using statistical model to do the speech nonspeech classification. Speech model and noise model should be separately trained beforehand and classification is done by comparing the score of frame given speech

---

[*] Corresponding author.

Z. Sun et al. (Eds.): CCBR 2014, LNCS 8833, pp. 375–384, 2014.

model and noise model. The main bottleneck is that there are too many kinds of noise and other unknown factors that affect the speech and noise modeling results. In these methods, some frequency statistics features are extracted through Fourier transform. The utilized models include SVM, HMM, GMM, etc. [5].

All these methods deal with the VAD problem at the level of frame [1], which is computed by the window function. With the frame, many kinds of acoustic features can be extracted for speech / non-speech frame discrimination. But how do we human do the VAD job manually? We never do it at the level of frame.

We just treat some adjacent frames as a unit which we call the speech segment. The speech segment may contain several words which are very close (liaison phenomenon), or just one, such as "hello", "bye". The speech segment can be represented by the envelope of voice part which reflects the way people speak. For example, higher the volume of speaking is, the higher the peak of the envelop is. There may be several waves in a speech segment which we call `slice'. One of the reasons that we do the VAD job in the level of segments is that the interval between words is important which can reflect a person's speech custom in some way.

Here is an example of the speech segment. The speech content is "But your home all about it you know", and there are two liaisons in it ("home all" and "about it"). So we have five speech segments in this speech, which are "But", "your", "home all", "about it", and "you know".

When we see the waveform of a speech recording, in our intuition we recognize the segment with high amplitude of the wave crest as speech segment in the case of quiet condition, and it is in truth. We don't need any exercise before, and we can be a good voice activity detector easily.

But if you just look at local part of a whole speech waveform, we can't distinguish whether it is a speech segment or not. The waveform of a speech segment and a noise segment is similar. In fact, they both contain a certain amount of sample points which constitute a waveform. We are confused by the details.

As the way human do the VAD problem, on the basis of shape and trend of the envelope, the algorithm can locate the segments and find the differences between speech segments and noise segments. So the proposed VAD method is designed to use the shape feature to represent speech segment, and use statistic method to find the difference between the form characteristic of speech segments and noise segments.

When we get the envelope of the speech, if the peak of one segment is high, this segment has big chance to be a speech segment, or a noise segment, which both have high energy. Anyway, we detect the segments with high energy at first. Then we find the differences between noise segments and speech segments, for example, the length of the sound of a ring is short and the height-width ratio of it is also different from that of a speech segment. We can use these useful information to detect the noise segments. Besides, if the area of the sound segment is big or the average amplitude of the sound segment is high, this waveform is possible to be a speech segment. The length of speech interval is also useful. Although these shape features are similar, the differences with each other can help to discard the noise segments.

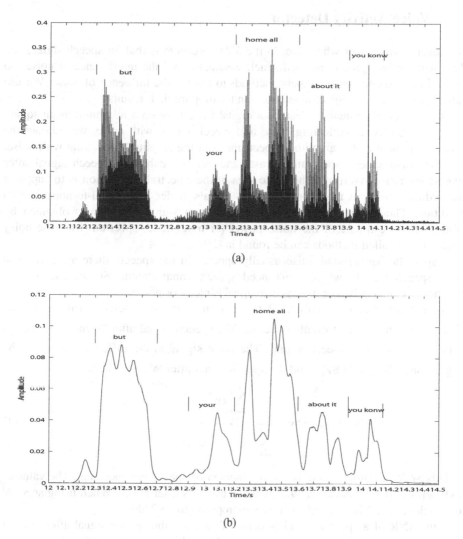

Fig. 1. (a) original speech wave (b)envelop of speech wave

Because an absolute quiet environment is always seldom, the amplitude of the `silent' part is not zero. Therefore, we may get a lot of tiny speech interval. We can combine the adjacent speech segments together, on the base that a complete segment has similar amplitudes in the beginning and end of the segment. Suppose the speaking rate of human is 200 words per minute which is very quick, the time of speaking one word is 0.3s. We can discard the segments with too short length.

2   Voice Activity Detectors

The ideal environment where we do the VAD problem is that all speech signals are clear without background noise. In fact, we can't avoid the interference of noise. So we will need speech enhancement methods to reduce the influence of noise. We use both Wiener filter and Spectral subtraction to compare their results.

The Wiener filter method designs a digital filter base on a minimum mean-square error criterion. After collecting noise and speech signal with noise, we subtract the noise component of the amplitude spectrum from the amplitude spectrum with noise, add the noise speech spectrum phrase, and get the enhanced speech signal after inverse Fourier converting. The basic idea of the Spectral subtraction is to suppress the additive noise in the corrupt speech signals under low signal-to-noise (SNR) condition. The estimate of the original and clean signal spectrum is obtained by subtracting an estimate of the noise power (or magnitude) spectrum from the noisy signal. The detailed methods can be found in [2][3].

Despite the background noise usually appears in the speech, there are still some clean speech signals which don't need speech enhancement. So we use a SNR threshold to judge whether this speech signal is clean or not.

We get the speech signal's SNR through an estimation method. Taking Wiener Filter for example. The formula is below. The speech signal after Wiener filter (sy_i) is taken as the clean speech signal. The noise signal is the difference between the original speech signal (sx_i) and the speech signal after Wiener filter.

$$SNR = 10 \times \log_{10} \frac{\sum_{i=1}^{m} sx_i^2}{\sum_{i=1}^{m} (sx_i - sy_i)^2} \tag{1}$$

This SNR threshold is relative to the method of speech enhancement. The value of SNR threshold T is chosen as 9.2dB when using Wiener Filter. When using spectral subtraction, the SNR threshold is more appropriate to be 22db.

If the SNR of a speech signal is below T, we use the speech signal after Wiener filter to replace the original speech signal. After this step, we get the clean speech signal without background noise. The shape features are extracted from envelop of the clean speech signals. The first feature is the biggest amplitude of peak among the sound segments (E_{peak}). The second one is the area of the sound segment (Area). The length of a sound segment (Len) and the ratio between the length and height ($\frac{R_{Len}}{E_{peak}}$) of a sound segment are the third and the fourth feature, respectively. And the mean amplitude of all sample points in a sound segment is the last feature (MeanE).Then we can use K-means to classify the five shape feature and pick out the speech segments. If the voting number of the five K-means result is bigger than the voting threshold, this segment is a speech segment.

Here is the pseudocode of the proposed VAD method.

Input: Speech signal $\mathbf{sx}_i$ Outputs: VAD lables

1. // Speech enhancement of the speech signal

    $\mathbf{sy}_i \leftarrow$ speech enhancement

2. // Compute SNR of the speech signal

    SNR=Eq(1)

    If SNR<T //T is the SNR threshold

    $\mathbf{sx}_i \leftarrow \mathbf{sy}_i$

3. //Calculate the envelope of the speech signal

    $S_{env} \leftarrow$ IIR filter $(\mathbf{sx}_i)$

4. //Get slice of the envelop, the part between two minimum amplitudes is a slice

    $P_{min} \leftarrow$ FindMinimum (S_{env}) //positions of all minimum amplitudes

    $Seg_{slice} \leftarrow [P_{min}[j], P_{min}[j+1]]$

5. //Combining adjacent slices, get segments

    $E_{peak} \leftarrow S_{env}[P_{peak}]$ //Amplitude at the peak of a slice, P_{peak} is position of the peak of a slice

    $E_{start} \leftarrow S_{env}[P_{start}]$ //Amplitude at the the start position of a slice, P_{start} is start position of a slice

    While $(abs(E_i - E_{start}) > E_{peak}*0.1)$//amplitudes of start and end of a segment isn't symmetry

    $E_i \leftarrow S_{env}[P_{end_i}]$ //Amplitude at the end position of adjacent slice, P_{end_i} is the position of the end of the ith adjacent slice

    i++ //next adjacent slice

    $P_{end} \leftarrow P_{end_i}$ //the position of the end of this segment

    $Seg \leftarrow (P_{start}, P_{end})$

6. //Extract shape features from segments

    $X \leftarrow$ ExtractShapeFeature(E_{peak}, Area, Len, $R_{Len/Height}$, MeanE)

    $E_{peak} \leftarrow$ MaxPeak(Seg) //biggest peak of the slices in a segment

    $Area \leftarrow \int_{P_{start}}^{P_{end}} S_{env} dt$ //using difference to compute the area of a segment

    $Len \leftarrow P_{end} - P_{start}$ //length of a segment

    $R_{Len/Height} \leftarrow \dfrac{Len}{E_{peak}}$ //ratio of length versus height of a segment

MeanE $\leftarrow \dfrac{1}{n} \sum\nolimits_{P_{start}}^{P_{end}} S_{env}$ //mean of all amplitudes in a segment, n is the number

of sample points in the segment

7.   //For all segments, pick out the speech segments

X_i ←Sort the ith shape feature from large to small, i=1,2,3,4,5

lable $_i$ ←K-means(X_i ,5)//classify X_i into 5 parts

lable $_i$ =0 if the centroid of the cluster which this segment belongs to is smallest

lable $_i$ =1 if the centroid of the cluster which this segment belongs to isn't smallest

Voting ←Sum(*lable_i*)

if *Voting*[*j*] > VotingThre shold , *Seg_j* is speech segment

8.   //Combine the adjacent speech segments with interval less than 0.1s

Seg ←Combine (*Seg*)

3   Experiment Setup

We conduct two experiments. First, we get the optimized parameters for the proposed VAD algorithm. Then, we use the endpoint information from the optimized VAD in a speaker verification system.

3.1   VAD Development Set

We use the data of the NIST 2004, 2006 speaker recognition evaluation (SRE), with supplementary automatic speech recognition (ASR) transcripts provided by NIST, as our datasets. We only conduct VAD experiments in three parts of these data. They are the telephone and microphone recordings of the male part of the NIST data. The three parts are telephone recordings of the train part in the NIST 2004 speaker recognition evaluation (04-train-tel), telephone recordings of the train part in the NIST 2006 speaker recognition evaluation (06-train-tel) and telephone recordings of the test part in the NIST 2006 speaker recognition evaluation (06-test-tel). To ensure that the reproduction of your illustrations is of a reasonable quality, we advise against the use of shading. The contrast should be as pronounced as possible.

The VAD experiments are conducted in three methods, the proposed VAD, VQVAD [4] and Energy VAD. The Energy VAD is from open source platform ALIZE [10]. The feature in VQVAD and Energy VAD is 16 MFCCs and 1 energy followed by delta (34 dimensions) extracted with 20ms frame length at a 10ms frame rate.

The methods to evaluate the performance of VAD method is in [4]. The accuracy of a VAD is evaluated by comparing the predicted VAD labels with a clean reference segmentation obtained from the ASR transcripts provided by NIST. Let

$y_t(n) \in \{0,1\}$ and $Y_t(n) \in \{0,1\}$, respectively, denote the predicted and ground truth VAD label of frame t in file n, and let $T(n)$ denote the total number of frames in utterance n. $S_1(n)$ denote the total number of points of the predicted endpoint in utterance n. $S_2(n)$ denote the total number of points of the ground truth VAD endpoint in utterance n. Our primary metric for VAD tuning is average total error rate (ε),

$$\varepsilon = \frac{1}{N_{utt}} \sum_{n=1}^{N_{utt}} \frac{1}{T(n)} \sum_{t=1}^{T(n)} I\{y_t(n) \neq Y_t(n)\} \tag{2}$$

where $I\{\bullet\}$ is an indicator function and N_{utt} is the number of utterances.

3.2   Speaker Recognition Experiments

We use the base GMM-UBM model to perform the speaker recognition experiment. If the EER of these experiment using different kinds of endpoint provided by VQVAD, Energy VAD and proposed VAD is different, the endpoint information which results in lower EER is better.

To test the robustness of the proposed VAD method, we conduct Speaker recognition experiments in three different datasets. The first dataset is the data used in the VAD performance test before. The second dataset is telephone data of the train part in the NIST 2008 speaker recognition evaluation (08-train-tel), telephone data of the train part in the NIST 2010 speaker recognition evaluation (10-train-tel) and telephone data of the test part in the NIST 2010 speaker recognition evaluation (10-test-tel). The third dataset is microphone data of the test part in the NIST 2008 speaker recognition evaluation (08-test-mic), microphone data of the train part in the NIST 2010 speaker recognition evaluation (10-train-mic) and microphone data of the test part in the NIST 2010 speaker recognition evaluation (10-test-mic). The feature is as same as that in VAD experiment using VQVAD and Energy VAD. We use gender-dependent UBM containing 512 Gaussians by Expectation Maximize (EM) algorithm.

The experiment is conducted in personal computer, in which the CPU is Core i3-2130 (3.3GHz), and the RAM is 8GB DDR3.

Table 1. Experiment dataset: Column 1 is the name of the experiment, Column 2 is the data trained for universal background models (UBMs), Column 3 represents the data trained for the speaker UBM model, column 4 gives the data for testing.

Experiment	UBM	Train	Test
04-06-tel	04-train-tel	06-train-tel	06-test-tel
08-10-tel	08-train-tel	10-train-tel	10-test-tel
08-10-mic	08-test-tel	10-train-mic	10-test-mic

4   Result

We get good results in the following two kinds of experiments.

4.1   VAD Experiment

In table 2, with the increasing of the number of the voting, the amount of segments which are seen as noise segments is bigger. If the speech is long enough, even we can set a bigger voting number, we can get enough speech segments to train and test. But if the speech is relatively short, a small voting number is more appropriate.

And in table 3, we can see clearly that the proposed VAD method gets an encouraging result.

Although the time cost of Energy VAD is the least, its performance is the worst. The processing time of the proposed VAD method with Wiener Filter is 16% less than Energy VAD, and its' error rate outperforms the latter by a relative 25% decrease. And the processing time of the proposed VAD method with Spectral Subtraction is 45% less than Energy VAD, while its error rate outperforms the latter by a relative 31% decrease.

Table 2. Proposed VAD (voting number ranging from 1 to 4) with Wiener Filter (WF) and Spectral Subtraction (SS), average error rate (%) in three datasets.

voting	04-train-tel		06-train-tel		06-test-tel	
	WF	SS	WF	SS	WF	SS
1	11	11	10	10	11	10
2	11	11	10	10	11	10
3	11	11	10	10	11	10
4	13	13	12	12	13	12

Table 3. Proposed VAD (voting number:4) with Wiener Filter(WF) and Spectral Subtraction(SS) , VQVAD and Energy VAD , time cost (s) and average errors (%) in three datasets.

Type	Prop.(WF)		Prop.(SS)		VQVAD		Energy VAD	
	Time	Error	Time	Error	Time	Error	Time	Error
04-train-tel	3.52	13	2.38	**11**	4.32	16	**0.86**	20
06-train-tel	3.70	12	2.37	**10**	4.36	16	**0.82**	19
06-test-tel	3.64	13	2.39	**10**	4.38	17	**1.04**	19

4.2   Speaker Recognition Experiment

The speaker recognition results (male trials only), in terms of equal error rate (EER, %) using the proposed VAD are shown in Table 4.

The results of the proposed VAD using Wiener Filter (WF) and Spectral Subtraction (SS) have similar trend. We get better performance with the increasing of voting number threshold.

We choose the result of number of voting, 4, as our final result. Now we seemly get two different conclusions in table 2 and 4. But with the increasing of voting number, more and more segments are seen as noise segments which may be speech segments in fact. To guarantee the purity of the speech segments, we choose the result of voting number as 4 as the best result. For the rest of the experiments, we use wiener filter to enhance energy only.

The reason why the result of 04-06-tel is best is because the speech data in 2004 and 2006 is very clean, with little noise.

The comparison of speaker recognition results (male trials only), in terms of equal error rate (EER, %) using the proposed VAD's, VQVAD's and Energy VAD's endpoint is shown in Tables 5.

Except that the result of 08-10-mic is not good enough as that of VQVAD with little gap, the other two results of EER are both less than these of VQVAD and Energy VAD. Especially as we get about 4.5% decrease in the EER of 04-16-tel experiment.

Table 4. Speaker recognition EER: proposed VAD (voting number ranging from 1 to 4) with Wiener Filter (WF) and Spectral Subtraction (SS), average errors (%) in three datasets.

voting	04-06-tel		08-10-mic		08-10-tel	
	WF	SS	WF	SS	WF	SS
1	10.78	**10.46**	**16.87**	17.48	**15.10**	15.44
2	10.78	**10.40**	**16.72**	17.64	15.77	**15.10**
3	1065	**10.33**	**17.18**	18.10	**15.10**	16.11
4	**9.66**	10.46	**16.41**	16.10	**14.09**	14.43

Table 5. Speaker recognition result (EER, %) on three datasets with three VAD algorithms: proposed VAD with Wiener Filter (Prop.(WF)),VQVAD and Energy VAD

Experiment	Prop.(WF)	VQVAD Energy	VAD
04-06-tel	**9.66**	14.18	18.26
08-10-tel	**16.41**	17.24	20.40
08-10-mic	14.09	**13.76**	17.79

5   Conclusions

The proposed VAD method utilizes the shape features of the speech envelop to detect the endpoint information and somehow discard the noise part. The performance of the method in VAD, and the speaker recognition experiment with endpoint information are both encouraging. Although we get better score in the VAD experiments, we have further work to do when applying the endpoint information to the speaker recognition baseline experiment. The way we get the envelope of the speech record is not the best, we are testing a new method to get the envelope which can better represent the trend of the speech.

Acknowledgment. This work was supported by the National Basic Research Program of China (2013CB329504)

References

1. Haigh, J.A., Mason, J.S.: Robust voice activity detection using cepstral features. In: IEEE Region 10 Conference on Computer, Communication, Control and Power Engineering, pp. 321–324. IEEE Press, New York (1993)
2. Boll, S.: Suppression of acoustic noise in speech using spectral subtraction. IEEE Transactions on Acoustics, Speech and Signal Processing 27, 113–120 (1979)
3. Vaseghi, S.V.: Spectral Subtraction. In: Advanced Signal Processing and Digital Noise Reduction, pp. 242–260. Springer, Heidelberg (1996)
4. Kinnunen, T., Rajan, P.: A practical, self-adaptive voice activity detector for speaker verification with noise telephone and microphone data. In: IEEE International Conference on Acoustics, Speech, and Signal Processing (ICASSP), pp. 7229–7233. IEEE Press, New York (2013)
5. Sohn, J., Kim, N.S., Sung, W.: A statistical model-based voice activity detection. IEEE on Signal Processing Letters 6, 1–3 (1999)
6. Sun, H.W., Ma, B., Li, H.Z.: Frame selection of interview channel for NIST speaker recognition evaluation. In: 7th International Symposium on Chinese Spoken Language Processing (ISCSLP), pp. 305–308. IEEE Press, New York (2010)
7. Burget, L., Matejka, P., Schwarz, P.: etal: Analysis of feature extraction and channel compensation in a GMM speaker recognition system. IEEE Transactions on Audio, Speech, and Language Processing 15, 1979–1986 (2007)
8. Martin, R.: Noise power spectral density estimation based on optimal smoothing and minimum statistics. IEEE Transactions on Speech and Audio Processing 9, 504–512 (2001)
9. VOICEBOX: Speech Processing Toolbox for MATLAB,
http://www.ee.ic.ac.uk/hp/staff/dmb/
voicebox/voicebox.htmlAppendix
10. ALIZE: Open Source platform for biometrics authentification,
http://mistral.univ-avignon.fr/index_en.html

A Robust Speaker-Adaptive and Text-Prompted Speaker Verification System

Qingyang Hong[*], Sheng Wang, and Zhijian Liu

Department of Cognitive Science and Fujian Key Lab of Brain-Like Intelligent System
Xiamen University, Xiamen, 361005, China
qyhong@xmu.edu.cn

Abstract. Currently, the recording playback attack has become a major security risk for speaker verification. The text-independent or text-dependent system is being troubled by it. In this paper, we propose an effective text-prompted system to overcome this problem, in which speaker verification and speech recognition are combined together. We further adopt speaker-adaptive hidden Markov model (HMM) so as to improve the verification performance. After HMM-based speaker adaptation, this system needs not to be retrained at each verification step. Experimental results demonstrated that the proposed method had quite good performance with the equal error rate (EER) lower than 2% and was also robust for different cases.

Keywords: recording playback, speaker verification.

1 Introduction

The objective of speaker recognition is to find out or verify the speaker's identity from the utterances. This technique has many real-world applications, e.g. bank security, telephone transaction, information retrieval, mobile payment and so on. Compared with traditional biometric authentication technologies, speaker recognition has the advantages of easiness and convenience. Specifically, it is the best choice of remote authentication.

Speaker recognition includes the type of text-dependent, text-independent and text-prompted. For the text-dependent system, the user should read the same content during registration and verification. The content should be short and easy to remember. For the text-independent system, the user can freely say any content. But whether it is text-dependent system or text-independent system, they both have such security risks: if someone else use high-quality recording equipment to record the target speaker's voice, and then playback it, the system might be easily attacked.

To overcome this problem, we proposed a text-prompted system based on Viterbi-GMM framework [1] in which each verification step which required a speech segmentation and re-adaptation of Gaussian mixture model (GMM) [2]. In this work, we

---

[*] Corresponding author.

Z. Sun et al. (Eds.): CCBR 2014, LNCS 8833, pp. 385–393, 2014.

adopted speaker-adaptive hidden Markov model (HMM) based on initial-final sub-word unit. This novel framework needs not re-training of HMM or GMM. Each verification step can still be conducted based on the prompted text. Our work combines the advantages of HMM and GMM, which are different from the HMM-based verbal information verification (VIV) system [3,4]. Moreover, since it requires a few accesses without speaker verification, VIV system still has the risk of impostor attack from different speaker.

This paper is organized as follows. Firstly, we describe the baseline system of speaker verification based on Gaussian mixture model. Secondly, we address the HMM-based speaker-adaptive system. Thirdly, experimental results are presented and analyzed. Finally, we give the conclusion and direction of future works.

2   Speaker Verification System

To build the baseline speaker verification system, we adopt the GMM-UBM (Universal Background Model) framework [2,5]. GMM is a probabilistic model, which is composed of the linear combination of several Gaussian probability density functions. GMM can be used to characterize the speaker's feature space. Compared with HMM, the computation of GMM is much smaller.

From our former work [2], it was found that the GMM-UBM framework, originally proposed for text-independent system, can also work well for text-dependent system. To build the GMM-based system, we first train a UBM with plenty of data, and then adapt it to the target speaker model (GMM) which is based on the algorithm of maximum a posteriori probability (MAP) [5].

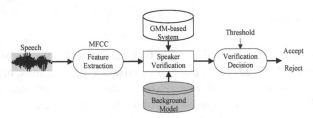

Fig. 1. GMM-based speaker verification system

In the GMM-based system, the distribution of feature vectors extracted from a speaker's utterance $X = \{x_t, 1 \leq t \leq T\}$ is modeled by a weighted sum of K mixture components, which can be defined as

$$p(x_t \mid \lambda) = \sum_{k=1}^{K} c_k N(x_t, \boldsymbol{\mu}_k, \boldsymbol{\Sigma}_k) \tag{1}$$

where λ is the brief notation of the GMM parameters $\lambda = \{c_k, \boldsymbol{\mu}_k, \boldsymbol{\Sigma}_k\}$ $1 \leq k \leq K$, and the mixture component $N(x_t, \boldsymbol{\mu}_k, \boldsymbol{\Sigma}_k)$ denotes a Gaussian density function with the mean vector $\boldsymbol{\mu}_k$ and covariance matrix $\boldsymbol{\Sigma}_k$,

Given a segment of speech X and a target-speaker GMM λ, the speaker verification task consists in determining whether X was spoken by λ or not. This task is often stated as basic hypothesis test between two hypotheses: X is from the hypothesized speaker λ (H_0), and X is not from the hypothesized speaker λ (H_1). A log-likelihood ratio (LLR) between these two hypotheses is counted and compared to a decision threshold θ. The LLR test is given by:

$$LLR = \log P(X \mid H_0) - \log P(X \mid H_1) \tag{2}$$

If LLR is not less than decision thresholdθ, H_0 is accepted, otherwise H_1 is accepted.

The GMM-based speaker verification system has relatively robust performance for short utterance, such as six-digit string. However, it can't detect the text content of speech and might be cheated by the recording playback. To avoid this risk, we adopt the HMM-based speaker-adaptive and text-prompted system in which each verification utterance has different text content.

3   Speaker-Adaptive and Text-Prompted System

HMM has been widely used for automatic speech recognition (ASR) [6]. To adopt it into text-prompted system, a straight method is to build a speaker-independent (SI) recognizer and then use it to detect the text content of utterance. If the content is correct, speaker verification will be conducted subsequently. However, the intra-speaker and inter-speaker variability between the training and testing conditions might cause the performance to degrade greatly. Therefore the challenge of this method is that the accuracy of SI recognizer should be high enough. Otherwise it might lead to a wrong judgment. Another problem is that SI recognizer can't identify the impostor speaker. Its score can't be utilized for speaker verification.

In this work, we apply an effective method which combines speech recognition and speaker recognition. As shown in Figure 2, speaker-adaptive (SA) recognizer for target speaker will be adapted from SI recognizer based on MLLR[6]. For digit-string text-prompted system, we use 19 initial-final sub-word HMM models (*sil, sp, b, a, _e, er, j, iou, l, ing, q, i, s, an, i_one, _w, u, _y, iao*) for ten Chinese digits (including 0,1,2,3,4,5,6,7,8,9). The target speaker will have his respective sub-word models after the adaptation.

Generally, getting reliable optimized sub-word models more than ten registered utterances are required as the adaptation data.

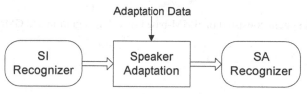

Fig. 2. The speaker adaptation process from speaker-independent (SI) recognizer to speaker-adaptive (SA) recognizer

When doing verification, the SA recognizer of target speaker will generate a corresponding grammar for each prompted text. For example, a six-digit string is randomly generated as "4-0-7-3-9-6". Then its grammar based on HTK [6] can be designed as follows.

$digit1 = si;
$digit2 = ling;
$digit3 = qi;
$digit4 = san;
$digit5 = jiu;
$digit6 = liu;

(SENT-START [$digit1] [$digit2] [$digit3] [$digit4] [$digit5] [$digit6] SENT-END)

With the above constrained grammar, the target speaker's correct utterance will have the right result and higher score. On the other hand, the impostor attack including recording playback with other digit string such as "5-3-7-2-4-8" will be recognized as a wrong result and will have lower score.

Another advantage of our proposed method is that it can fuse the average score of recognized words of HMM-based speech recognition (represented as *scoreASR*) and the score of GMM-based speaker verification (represented as *scoreVPR*). The whole fused system is illustrated in Figure 3. The final verification decision will be based on the fused score (represented as *scoreFused*), which is calculated as follows.

$$scoreFused = 1/(1 + \exp(-(scoreASR/2 + \alpha * scoreVPR)))) \tag{3}$$

where α is a weight to be adjusted so as to make a balance of two scores.

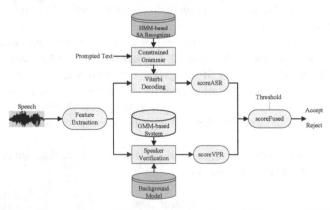

Fig. 3. The fused system consisted of HMM-based speech recognition and GMM-based speaker verification

4   Towards a Robust System

To deploy a robust system for practical applications, especially for mobile devices, we should also consider the impact of speech coder, noise and other issues. The first problem is speech coder, such as AMR, which is widely used for mobile phone and has generally encoding rate lower than 8bps. But for PCM16 WAV code, it may have the encoding rate of 128bps or 256bps. Therefore, we must transfer these different speech codec into a uniform format, and conduct necessary model adaptation for them. For example, we have trained a PC-based SI recognizer with the encoding rate of 128bps. Then we can down-sample the data of 256bps into 128bps and use some of them to adapt the SI recognizer.

The second problem is noise. Under the noisy environment, it is very possible that both SI recognizer and SA recognizer have some wrong results, which will deteriorate the fused score and thus lead to a wrong decision. To solve this problem, one solution is to build different recognizers for silent and noisy cases.

There are usually some silences in the beginning or end point of the speech signal. They should be removed to avoid affecting the subsequent verification process. End-point detection is also known as VAD (Voice Activity Detection), the purpose of which is to identify the beginning and ending points of speech utterance. In our system, silence is deleted based on the energy of window (with the time length of 2s), which has demonstrated more robust than the energy of frame (generally 0.02s).

It is also important to select the content of prompted text. For dynamic-digit string, two same connected digits are not preferred. Digit "1" should be avoided since it has two pronunciations (_y+i and _y+iao) in Chinese. Generally, six or eight random digits are suitable. For some special cases, 0~9 or telephone numbers are also good choice since they can be easily remembered by the user. To have a good user experience, it might be better to allow few errors of recognized digits.

Another challenge is model registration. Since this system requires the user to speak the prompted text one by one, there may have some non-correspondences in the training utterances, which will lead to a deviated model. If possible, the user should be required to conduct the model registration in silent environment. And the system should have necessary checking mechanism to assure the training utterances in matching the prompted text.

5   Experimental Results

5.1   Speech Database

Speech database included development data and evaluation data. The data of baseline system was sampled in 8000Hz and digitalized with 16bit. MFCC features were extracted with 32-dimension including 16-dimension static coefficients and their first-order differential coefficients. To reduce the impact of noise, cepstral mean and variance normalization were also conducted after the feature extraction.

1. We first trained a UBM with 128 mixtures based on more than 10000 speaker's speech data with the content of "0~9". This outputted a robust UBM for speaker verification.
2. Based on speech data (with the content of "0~9") of 174 speakers, we trained a HMM-based SI recognizer with 19 speaker-independent initial-final sub-word models of ten digits.
3. The first evaluation data set of text-prompted speaker verification was recorded from PC, which included 24 speakers. Each person recorded the random six-digit string of 0 to 9 ten times. All the recorded data was sampled in 8000Hz and digitalized with 16bit. The prompted six-digit digit strings were randomly generated and had the text contents such as "5-3-6-9-2-7 "," 4-2-0-5-8-3", "7-4-8-3-4-5" and others.
4. Another evaluation data set was recorded from mobile phone, which included 30 speakers. All the data were sampled in 8000Hz and digitalized with 16bit. We also used more than 16000 digit-string utterances with the same sampling rate as development data.

5.2   Experimental Results

Experiments were conducted to compare the performances of GMM/HMM-based speaker verification and our proposed fused system, SI and SA recognizer, different speech codec.

5.2.1   Impostor Attack

The text-prompted system should effectively prevent impostor speaker, even the speaker knows the password. This experiment evaluated the performance of the same digit string for different speaker. There were in total 149 true tests and 3515 impostor tests. The experimental results were plotted in DET [7] curve.

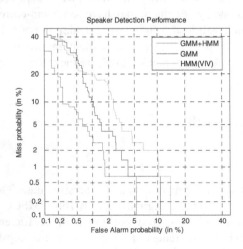

Fig. 4. Verification results of fused system (HMM+GMM) ,GMM-based and HMM-based system

It can be seen that the fused system (GMM+HMM) had better performance than GMM-based system or HMM-based system (which was proposed as VIV [3]). The equal error rate (EER) of our proposed fused system is lower than 2%.

5.2.2   SI and SA Recognizer

For HMM-based speech recognition, we also compared the performances of SI recognizer and SA recognizer. It should be mentioned that both SI and SA recognizer couldn't effectively distinguish the true and imposter speakers. So after finishing speech recognition, the score should be further fused with the score of GMM-based speaker verification.

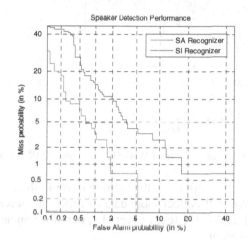

Fig. 5. Verification results of SA recognizer and SI recognizer

From Figure 5, we can see that the SA recognizer had better performance than the SI recognizer. The reason was that HMM-based SA recognizer could get higher score for target speaker and lower score for imposter speaker, which made the fused system more discriminative.

5.2.3   Different Speech Codec

We selected widely-used AMR to evaluate the impact of low encoding rate. We first transferred the PCM16 data of 128bps into AMR data of 5.15bps, and then transferred the AMR data back to PCM16 data of 128bps. The verfication results of original WAV data and resampled AMR data are as follows.

6   Conclusions

In this work, we have successfully built a speaker-adaptive and text-prompted system, in which a random digit string was prompted for verification. Only when the registered user correctly uttered the prompted digits in turn, the verification process could be successful. Since the impostor cannot predict the content in advance, there would be no way to attack the system by recording playback. Specially, our system fused the scores of HMM-based speech recognition and GMM-based speaker verification. Experimental results have demonstrated that the proposed fused system had better verification performance and its EER could reach the standard lower than 2%.

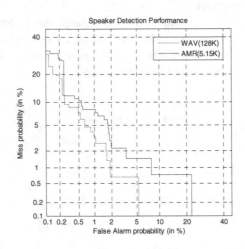

Fig. 6. Verification results of WAV(128bps) and AMR(5.15bps)

In the future, we'll further optimize the performance of whole system in order to make it more robust. We will collect more data of different speech codec and sampling rate. And we will deploy the text-prompted system for remote authentication of e-commerce and cloud security.

Acknowledgments. This work was partly supported by the National Natural Science Foundation of China (Grant No. 61105026) and Shenzhen Science and Technology Project (Grant No. JC201006030859A).

References

1. Weichen, L., Qingyang, H., Sheng, W., Dawei, L.: Text-prompted speaker recognition system based on Viterbi-GMM. In: NCMMSC 2013, Guiyang, China (August 2013)
2. Chen, W., Hong, Q., Li, X.: GMM-UBM for Text-Dependent Speaker Recognition. In: 2012 Third IEEE/IET International Conference on Audio, Language and Image Processing (ICALIP 2012), July 16-18, Shanghai, China (2012)
3. Li, Q., Juang, B.-H., Lee, C.-H.: Automatic verbal information verification for user authentication. IEEE Transactions on Speech and Audio Processing 8(5), 585–595 (2000)
4. Li, X., Chen, K.: Mandarin verbal information verification. In: ICASSP 2002, pp. I-833–I-836 (2002)
5. Reynolds, D.A., Quatieri, T.F., Dunn, R.B.: Speaker Verification Using Adapted Gaussian Mixture Models. Digital Signal Processing 10, 19–41 (2000)

6. Young, S., Evermann, G., Gales, M., Hain, T., Kershaw, D., Moore, G., Odell, J., Ollason, D., Povey, D., Valtchev, V., Woodland, P.: The HTK Book (for HTK Version 3.4), http://htk.eng.cam.ac.uk/prot-docs/HTKBook/htkbook.html
7. Doddington, G.R., Przybocki, M.A., Martin, A.F., Reynolds, D.A.: The NIST speaker recognition evaluation – overview, methodology. Systems, Results, Perspective, Speech Communication 31, 225–254 (2000)
8. Matsui, T., Furui, S.: Speaker adaptation of tied-mixture-based phoneme models for text-prompted speaker recognition. In: 1994 IEEE International Conference on Acoustics, Speech, and Signal Processing, ICASSP 1994, vol. 1. IEEE (1994)
9. Al-Hassani, M.D., Kadhim, A.A.: Design A Text-Prompt Speaker Recognition System Using LPC-Derived Features. In: The 13th International Arab Conference on Information Technology ACIT 2012, December 10-13 (2012)

Optimization of Pathological Voice Feature Based on KPCA and SVM

Houying Wang and Weiping Hu[*]

Guangxi Key Lab of Multi-source Information Mining & Security,
Electronic Engineering College, Guangxi Normal University,
Guilin, 541004, China
huwp@gxnu.edu.cn

Abstract. The correlation and redundancy of the pathological voice features, which is assorted to the feature set by the random or artificial combinations of these features, always affect the detection effect of the voice. In this paper, we present a method of optimization of pathological voice feature based on KPCA and SVM. Thus, the feature parameters are processed, the correlation and redundant information eliminated, and the representable information extracted for recognition by KPCA. Our experiments based on KPCA show that the highest recognition rate of vowel /a/ is 97.47%, the average recognition rate 91.85%, while these two rates of vowel /i/ are 91.39% and 84.15% respectively. Compared with the traditional combination method, the average recognition rate has effective improvement in our experiment based on KPCA.

Keywords: pathological voices, feature parameters, Kernel-based Principal Component Analysis(KPCA), Support Vector Machine(SVM), optimization.

1 Introduction

As we know, the health of people's voice influence their daily life. For this sake, the detection and diagnosis of pathological voice are important. In recent years, researchers working in this area have put forward some objective, noninvasive and efficient detection methods to diagnose the patients with the lesion of throat and vocal cords early [1].

The lesion of throat makes voice signal different, which can be analyzed to diagnose the lesion degree of throat and vocal cords. The voice signal has a property of short-time stability. Thus, in the detection of pathological voice, researchers would like to extract linear feature parameters of acoustics by short-time analysis technology. However, these acoustic features representing the property of voice have their limitations [2]. The recent study reveals that the voice signal, in which exists the phenomenon of eddy current [2] and occurs chaotic mechanism [2], is a complex and nonlinear process. Therefore, nonlinear time analysis is used to describe the pathology features of voice for making up for the deficiency of the traditional acoustic features.

---

[*] Corresponding author.

Z. Sun et al. (Eds.): CCBR 2014, LNCS 8833, pp. 394–403, 2014.

In study [3], it is confirmed that in the recognition of pathological voice, parameters of nonlinear feature have a better effect. In the automatic detection and evaluation of pathological voice, only when we own features with enough kind of information, can we make a better classifier. Nevertheless, a single feature parameter just contains some information which is unable to represent the features of the whole voice and satisfy the requirement of recognition. Hence, we group some single feature parameter to the detection of voice. Besides allowing for adopting the feature parameter set to describe the voice signal comprehensively, we have to avoid the redundancy and relative information between and in the features themselves. By using correlation to analyze the feature set of voice, we adopt an optimization algorithm of KPCA for feature parameters to eliminate the features containing redundance and little information and remain the most important feature parameters. Our experiments show that the method based on KPCA increases the rate of detection effectively and achieve our aim at optimizing features.

2   Database

The database of our experiments, which came from clinical cases [4], was collected in a super quiet room indoors. We got voice sampling for the people without any laryngeal disease and patients diagnosed with some laryngeal disease [4]. We classified voices of normal persons whose average age was 25 to a comparison group: vowel /a/ and /i/, voices of patients with some laryngeal disease [4] whose mean age was 27 to the other group vowel /a/. Their phonating time lasted from 3 to 4 seconds, sampled 3 times, and the sample frequency was 16kHz. 17 kinds of feature parameters representing the property of linearity and nonlinear kinetics of the voice were selected for this experiment. In this experiment, definitions and parameters of features quote documents [3],[4],[8].

3   Kernel-Based Principal Component Analysis

KPCA is based on and similar to Principal Component Analysis (PCA). PCA is a relatively good feature extraction algorithm in the linear feature space. But in the primary nonlinear feature space, it has a poor performance. Thus the primary nonlinear data should be mapped to a high-dimensional nonlinear space. KPCA meets the requirement of mapping data matrix to a new space to lower the dimension of information and we can extract the linear features at last. It has been proved by academic fields that KPCA has a better ability to deal with nonlinear data set than PCA.

The basic principle of the kernel function method is to project a nonlinear space onto a high dimensional space(feature space) and then process data with the help of a nonlinear function in the feature space. The key of the process lies in the introduction of kernel function and the calculation of kernel function of the original space, a form which the calculation of inner product of feature space is converted to. The feature space has been non-linearized before. This process greatly simplifies the amount of the calculation and enhances the ability of the nonlinear data processing at the same time.

3.1   Theory of KPCA [5,6]

Assume the training sample $x_1, x_2,..., x_M$, sample space is non-linear space, and $\{x_i\}$ denote the input space. Suppose we map the non-linear data into a feature space F , assuming map ϕ , defined by:

$$\Phi : R^d \rightarrow F$$
$$x \rightarrow \xi = \Phi(x) \tag{1}$$

With the help of Φ , the kernel function maps data ^{x} to the F by Φ, and the data of the feature space obtained by the map satisfies the condition of the center , that

$$\sum_{\mu=1}^{M} \Phi(x_\mu) = 0 \tag{2}$$

the covariance matrix of feature space can be computed by

$$C = \frac{1}{M} \sum_{\mu=1}^{M} \Phi(x_\mu)\Phi(x_\mu)^T \tag{3}$$

eigenvalues and eigenvectors of the covariance matrix

$$v \in F, \quad Cv = \lambda v, \quad \lambda \geq 0 \tag{4}$$

Then we seek eigenvalues and their nonzero eigenvectors of the following this equation:

$$(\Phi(x_v) \cdot Cv) = \lambda(\Phi(x_v) \cdot v \tag{5}$$

all feature vectors can be expressed as linear spanning $\Phi(x_1), \Phi(x_2),..., \Phi(x_M)$,and can be expressed as follows:

$$v = \sum_{i=1}^{M} \alpha_i \Phi(x_i) \tag{6}$$

Eq. (3), (4), (6)into the following equation:

$$\frac{1}{M} \sum_{\mu=1}^{M} \alpha_\mu (\sum_{w=1}^{M} (\Phi(x_v) \cdot \Phi(x_w)\Phi(x_w)\Phi(x_\mu))) = \lambda \sum_{\mu=1}^{M} (\Phi(x_v) \cdot \Phi(x_\mu)) \tag{7}$$

where $v = 1, 2,..., M$.

Define matrix $M \times M$ as kernel function K [6]:

$$K_{\mu v} := (\Phi(x_\mu) \cdot \Phi(x_v)) \tag{8}$$

Following Eq. (8) obtain:

$$M \lambda K \alpha = K^2 \alpha, \text{ simplified by: } M \lambda \alpha = K \alpha \tag{9}$$

By Eq(9)obtain eigenvalue λ and eigenvector α, compute projections of the image of a test point onto the Eigenvectors V^k in F according to :

$$(v^k \cdot \Phi(x)) = \sum_{i=1}^{M} (\alpha_i)^k (\Phi(x_i), \Phi(x)) \tag{10}$$

Next step ,Inner product of Eq.(10) is substituted for kernel function. When Eq.(2) is not established, we need to adjust this function:

$$\Phi(x_\mu) \rightarrow \Phi(x_\mu) - \frac{1}{M} \sum_{v=1}^{M} \Phi(x_v) \tag{11}$$

3.2   Kernel Function

Kernel function[6] defined by:

$$k_{ij} = k(x_i)\phi(x_j) = \phi(x_i)\phi(x_j) \tag{12}$$

where $x_i (i = 1, 2, ..., M)$, $k_{ij} \mapsto K(x_i, x_j)$ As symmetry of kernel function, i.e.

$k_{ij} = k_{ji}$,which can reduce the amount of calculation. In feature space,the center of kernel matrix k [6]is Eq(13) ,i.e.modified kernel.

$$k_{ij} = k_{ij} - \frac{1}{M} \sum_{r=1}^{M} k_{ir} - \frac{1}{M} \sum_{r=1}^{M} k_{rj} + \frac{1}{M^2} \sum_{r,s=1}^{M} k_{rs} \tag{13}$$

3.3   Implement the Following Procedure for KPCA

Step 1. n features and m samples of the information,which constitute $m \times n$ data matrix.

Step 2. Select Gaussian kernel function parameters in which σ [6]is important. Then calculate the kernel matrix according to Eq.(8).In the experiments, the algorithm employed two parameters: (1)Gaussian kernel function, (2) the size of σ [50,100] with the step 0.1.

Step 3. Gain the modified kernel matrix KL according to Eq.(8).

Step 4. Calculate eigenvalues $\lambda_1, ..., \lambda_n$ and the corresponding eigenvectors $v_1, ..., v_n$ of KL by improved Jacobi iterative method[7].

Step 5.   Obtain eigenvalues $\lambda_1^{'} > ... > \lambda_n^{'}$ and the corresponding eigenvectors $v_1^{'},...,v_n^{'}$.

Step 6. Obtain $\alpha_1,...,\alpha_n$ by uniting orthogonal eigenvectors.

Step 7. Calculate cumulative contribution rate of variance $\eta_1,...,\eta_n$ if $\eta_t \geq \eta$, where η is setted up, there are t principal components and eigenvectors $\alpha_1,...,\alpha_t$.

Step 8. Calculate $Y = KL \cdot \alpha$, a projection of the modified kernel matrix KL onto extracted feature vectors, where $\alpha = (\alpha_1,...,\alpha_t)$.

The projection Y here is the one that has been dimension reduced from the primary data by KPCA. t denotes the number of the feature vectors selected, $t < n$.

3.4   Support Vector Machine

Support vector machine (SVM) is a novel and trainable machine-learning algorithm proposed by Vapnik et al. based on statistical learning theory (SLT) [9]. SVM uses the Kernel mapping to map the sample space to a high-dimensional feature space, which transforms the nonlinear separable problem into linearly separable problem. Thus, SVM gets a wide application in solving the essentially nonlinear problem such as classification, regression, novelty detection and other issues.

SVM aims to find an optimal hyper-plane in the feature space that separates the groups and maximizes the classification margin. By employing statistical learning theory, the optimal separating hyper-plane

$$\langle w, x \rangle + b = 0 \tag{14}$$

Can be obtained by minimize $\dfrac{\|w\|^2}{2}$ or in other words optimizing the following problem.

$$\min_{w,b,\varsigma} \frac{1}{2}\|w\|^2 + C \sum_{i=1}^{n} \varsigma_i, \; subjected \; to \; y_i\left(\left\langle w_i, x_i \right\rangle + b\right) \geq 1 - \varsigma_i, \; \varsigma_i \geq 0, \; i = 1,\cdots,n \tag{15}$$

Where C is a penalty parameter to be chosen by the user and $\varsigma_i \geq 0, \; i = 1,\cdots,n$ are slack variables. A larger C corresponds to assigning a higher penalty for misclassification.

By introducing Lagrange multipliers and quadratic programming (QP) methods, the dual optimal problem is solved. The dual problem is formulated as

$$\max W(\alpha) = \sum_{i=1}^{n} \alpha_i - \frac{1}{2}\sum_{i=1}^{n}\sum_{i=1}^{n} \alpha_i y_i \alpha_j y_j \langle x_i, x_j \rangle \text{,subjected to } \sum_{i=1}^{n} \alpha_i y_i = 0 \text{ , } \alpha_i \in [0,C], i = 1,\cdots,n. \quad (16)$$

Where α_i are the support vectors. The decision function is

$$f(x) = \text{sgn}\left(\sum_{i=1}^{n} \alpha_i y_i \langle x \cdot x_i \rangle + b \right) \quad (17)$$

where $\langle x \cdot x_i \rangle$ is defined as K, the so-called kernel function.

For nonlinear transformation $\phi(x)$, the decision function for nonlinear SVM is given by

$$f(x) = \text{sgn}\left(\sum_{i=1}^{n} \alpha_i \langle \phi(x), \phi(x_i) \rangle + b \right) \quad (18)$$

May know by above, in SVM classification, the final decision function depends on the number of support vectors and their weights. Meanwhile, kernel function also plays an important part. Different kernels make different SVM algorithms. Radical Basis Function (RBF) is used in our algorithm.

4   Experiments and Results

In this paper, the experimental data contains, recordings of sustained phonation of vowel /a/, 78 healthy and 73 pathological files, vowel /i/, 78 healthy and 80 pathological files. Take 5000 sampling points for each data before feature extraction, 17 kinds of characteristic parameter sets used for pattern recognition are trained and tested by SVM. Then, we train and test set by using crossvalind in MATLAB. There are 100 randomly selections of training set and the corresponding test set, which can be obtained the maximum recognition rate and the average recognition rate of 100 times results of SVM recognition.

4.1   Recognition Results and Analysis for Parameters Set of Combination Features

Feature parameters of the experiment are as follows: Traditional acoustic features parameters: fundamental frequency, Mel frequency cepstral coefficients, linear prediction cepstrum coefficient, frequency jitter percentage, absolute frequency jitter, frequency perturbation quotient, amplitude jitter percentage, amplitude jitter, amplitude perturbation quotient. Nonlinear features parameters: approximate entropy, sample entropy, fuzzy entropy, multiscale entropy, the second-order Renyi entropy, Shannon entropy, box dimension, Hurst parameter.

4.1.1   Recognition for Combinations of Different Dimensions of Conventional Acoustic Feature Parameters in the Traditional Method

With the nine kinds of traditional acoustic feature parameters above, we train and recognize arbitrary combination sets of 2-9 dimensions. We also select the best recognition rate (in the same dimensional composition and the highest recognition rate of the combination) for each dimension in identifying.The result is as Tab 1. *feature dimension (*fd*).

In Tab 1, the results show the combination of these parameters in conventional method. That is to say, when the dimension is 2, we can get the highest rate of 92.00% and the aver rate of 80.75% for vowel /a/. Vowel /i/ can obtain the highest rate of 85.33% and the aver rate of 73.85%.

Table 1. Recognition rate for 9 kinds of traditional acoustic parameters in conventional method

fd	vowel /a/ (100%)		vowel /i/ (100%)		fd	vowel /a/ (100%)		vowel /i/ (100%)	
	max	average	max	average		max	average	max	average
2	92.00	80.75	85.33	73.85	6	89.33	78.20	82.67	70.36
3	90.67	80.79	81.33	73.86	7	88.00	77.69	81.13	69.43
4	89.33	79.28	82.67	73.85	8	86.67	78.29	81.33	68.57
5	88.00	78.43	82.67	71.48	9	89.33	78.32	80.32	63.56

4.1.2   Recognition for Combinations of Conventional Acoustic Feature Parameters in KPCA

With the above nine kinds of traditional acoustic feature parameters, we train and test arbitrary combination sets of two-nine-dimensions and get the recognition rate and the result as Tab 2. *feature dimension (*fd*).

Table 2. Recognition rate for 9 kinds of traditional acoustic parameters in KPCA method

fd	vowel /a/ (100%)		vowel /i/ (100%)		fd	vowel /a/ (100%)		vowel /i/ (100%)	
	max	average	max	average		max	average	max	average
2	91.58	83.69	82.78	75.58	6	89.41	80.58	78.86	70.03
3	89.45	82.05	84.11	75.58	7	84.67	78.88	73.56	70.00
4	85.68	79.32	81.13	73.52	8	84.77	78.33	71.86	69.12
5	88.56	79.85	82.47	74.59	9	84.11	77.91	74.51	68.11

In Tab 2,in the KPCA, the results show that combination of these parameters can get the highest rate of 91.58% and the average rate of 83.69% for vowel /a/, namely the dimension being 2. Vowel /i/ at the dimension being 3 is obtained: the highest rate of 84.11%, the aver rate of 75.58% .

Compare Tab1 with Tab2: The aver recognition rate of employing KPCA is about 2% higher than conventional method. But, the max recognition rate is a little declined.

4.1.3   Recognition for Combinations of Different Dimensions of Nonlinear Dynamic Feature Parameters in the Traditional Method

With previous kinds of nonlinear dynamic feature parameters, we train and test arbitrary combination sets of two-eight dimensions. Select the best recognition rate (ditto(1)) for each dimension in identifying. The result is as Tab 3. *feature dimension (fd).

Table 3. Recognition rate for 8 kinds of nonlinear dynamics feature parameters in conventional method

fd	vowel /a/ (100%)		vowel /i/ (100%)		fd	vowel /a/ (100%)		vowel /i/ (100%)	
	max	average	max	average		max	average	max	average
2	96.67	87.93	84.00	78.07	6	97.33	89.32	85.33	75.69
3	96.00	90.49	88.00	78.33	7	97.33	89.92	88.00	75.25
4	96.00	87.55	86.67	77.41	8	93.33	88.99	84.00	75.53
5	96.00	90.41	88.00	76.83					

In Tab 3,the results show that combination in conventional method , namely the dimension being 3, we can get the highest rate of 96.00%, the average rate of 90.49% for vowel /a/. Vowel /i/ are obtained the highest rate of 88.00%, the aver rate of 78.33%.

4.1.4   Recognition for Combinations of Nonlinear Dynamics Feature Parameters in KPCA Method

With previous kinds of nonlinear dynamics feature parameters, we train and test arbitrary combination sets of two-eight dimensions. Selecting the recognition rate, the result is as Tab 4.*feature dimension (fd).

Table 4. Recognition rate for 8 kinds of nonlinear dynamics feature parameters in KPCA

fd	vowel /a/ (100%)		vowel /i/ (100%)		fd	vowel /a/ (100%)		vowel /i/ (100%)	
	max	average	max	average		max	average	max	average
2	96.00	90.12	87.78	81.44	6	96.00	90.10	87.93	78.01
3	97.07	91.25	87.12	81.48	7	92.00	88.58	85.79	77.81
4	95.63	90.18	88.44	81.55	8	91.39	87.62	86.12	78.15
5	97.47	91.85	89.79	79.64					

In Tab 4 and the KPCA, the results show that combination of these parameters can get the highest rate of 97.47% and the aver rate of 91.85% for vowel /a/, namely, the dimension being 5. Vowel /i/ at the dimension being 4 is obtained: the highest rate of 88.44%, the aver rate of 81.55%.

Compare Tab3 with Tab4: The aver recognition rate of employing KPCA is more than 3% higher than conventional method. The max recognition rate is slightly improved.

The above analysis show that the feature set extracted from KPCA improves the recognition rate. According to the results of previous section, we select different dimension sets coming from the entire above conventional acoustic feature parameters and nonlinear dynamic feature parameters train and test in KPCA. The result is as Tab 5. *feature dimension (fd).

Table 5. Recognition rate for 17 kinds of feature parameters in KPCA

fd	vowel /a/ (100%)		vowel /i/ (100%)		fd	vowel /a/ (100%)		vowel /i/ (100%)	
	max	average	max	average		max	average	max	average
2	97.07	90.19	90.07	83.22	10	96.08	88.00	88.74	82.65
3	97.07	89.39	89.40	83.74	11	88.00	77.69	81.13	69.43
4	96.36	90.51	90.73	84.19	12	86.67	78.29	81.33	68.57
5	97.37	91.31	91.39	84.15	13	89.33	78.32	80.32	63.56
6	97.33	91.28	90.73	84.11	14	90.07	85.41	83.44	78.18
7	94.04	88.18	89.40	83.61	15	90.03	85.40	79.47	74.64
8	94.04	88.58	90.07	83.41	16	89.69	85.57	78.15	75.82
9	95.68	87.69	87.42	82.75	17	88.00	84.11	76.82	73.95

In Tab 5, the results show the point when the dimension of the feature parameters extracted from the KPCA is 5, the best recognition effect is obtained: the highest rate of 97.37% and the aver rate of 91.31% for vowel /a/,and for vowel /i/ the highest rate of 91.39%, the aver rate of 84.15%.

Results above reveal: a: The fact that the recognition rate of combination sets of nonlinear feature parameters is greatly higher than that of traditional acoustic features shows that the dynamic nonlinear features have a favorable separating capacity. b: For vowel /a/,the recognition rates of the normal one and the pathological one are both higher than for vowel /i/ respectably. Therefore, the great mass of researchers at home and abroad would like to put the vowel /a/ to use. c: The sets of feature parameters based on KPCA bringing a better average recognition rate than that of the traditional method also make clear that KPCA can produce a fine effect on features optimization.

5   Conclusions

The combination identification analysis of the feature parameters of the voice has been carried on by the experiment using traditional combination method and the experiment based on KPCA. The results make clear that the KPCA method exceeds the conventional means in the optimization of feature parameters combination. KPCA method picks over the useful components of feature parameters, which could reach a higher recognition rate than the one using the traditional combination method and the one based on the whole parameters. The fact that the identification effect of the parameter set would achieve its peak while the dimensionality ranges from 2 to 5 shows that it is effective to employ KPCA to optimize the feature parameters combination. The optimized feature parameter set lays a foundation for the improvement of the detection rate of the pathological voice.

However, the computational cost of our method is a little large, so we shall improve this point in future work.

Acknowledgements. This work supported by the National Natural Science Foundation of China (No. 61062011, No. 61362003), Guangxi Key Lab of Multi-source Information Mining & Security, Guangxi Normal University. *Corresponding author: huwp@gxnu.edu.cn.

References

1. Huami, J., Shuping, N.: Due and counter measures of teachers voice ailments.. Journal of xinghai conservatory of Music. In: No. 2: pp. 100–103(June 2006)
2. Liang, C., Xiongwei, Z.: Study the nonlinear characteristics of the speech signal. Journal of PLA Science and Technology 5(7), 11–17 (2007)
3. Junfen, G., Weiping, H.: Recognition and study of pathological voice based on nonlinear dynamics SVM. Journal of Biomedical Engineering 29(3), 5–8 (2011)
4. Yingji, G., Weiping, H.: Recognition and study of pathological voice based on HHT. Computer Engineering and Applications 43(34), 217–219 (2007)
5. Scholkopf, B., Smola, A., Muller, K.: Nonlinear Component analysis as a Kernel eigenvalue problem. Nearal Computation 70(5), 1299–1319 (1998)
6. Qi, K., Kang, W., Bingyao, H.: An Kernel optimization for KPCA based on Gaussianly estimation. International Journal of Bio-Inspired Computation 6(2), 91–107 (2014)
7. Nayu, J.: Comparative analysis Jacobi iteration method and Gauss-seidel iterative method convergence. Journal of Yuxi Normal University 25(4) (2009)
8. Bingxin, Z., Weiping, H.: Recognition entropy of pathological voice based on support vector machines. Journal of Biomedical Engineering (5), 546–552 (2013)
9. Vapnik. V. The Nature of Statis tical Learning Theory. Springer, N. Y.

Text-Independent Writer Identification Using Improved Structural Features

Youbao Tang[1], Wei Bu[2], and Xiangqian Wu[1,*]

[1] School of Computer Science and Technology,
Harbin Institute of Technology, Harbin150001, China
[2] Department of New Media Technologies and Arts,
Harbin Institute of Technology, Harbin150001, China
{tangyoubao,buwei,xqwu}@hit.edu.cn

Abstract. This paper presents a method based on two structural features for text-independent writer identification, i.e. SIFT descriptor (SD) and triangular descriptor (TD). For SD, we modify the original SIFT algorithm to make the SD possess orientation information, called modified SIFT descriptor (MSD). Acodebookis constructed by clustering the MSDs extracted from training samples. Then the bag of word technique is used to compute a MSD histogram (MSDH) as a feature vector for writer identification. For TD, it is designed to represent the unique relationship between three selected points. A TD histogram (TDH) of the TD occurrences is computed as another feature vector by tracking the contour points of a handwriting image. The distances between MSDHs and TDHs are computed and combined as the final dissimilarity measurement for the handwriting images. Experimental results on two public challenging datasets demonstrate the efficiency of the proposed method.

Keywords: text-independent writer identification, MSDH, TDH.

1 Introduction

Handwriting is a behavioral biometric which can be used for writer identification. Text-independent writer identification aims to determine the unknown writer's identify among a number of known writers by using their handwriting images. Recently, due to its importance for forensic analysis and documents authorization, text-independent writer identification has attracted an increasing interest. And a series of international writer identification contests [1-3] have been successfully organized.

A number of various approaches for text-independent writer identification have been proposed in the previous researches. Plamondon et al. [4] presented a comprehensive survey of early research literatures with respect to automatic writer identification. In general, the existing approaches can beclassified into two categories: texture-based approaches and structure-basedapproaches.The texture-based approaches [5-8]need an amount of handwriting to extract stable and powerful

---

*Corresponding author

Z. Sun et al. (Eds.): CCBR 2014, LNCS 8833, pp. 404–411, 2014.
© Springer International Publishing Switzerland 2014

features. Actually,most of time it's unrealistic to collect a large amount of handwriting data.To overcome this problem, more and more structure-based approacheshave been proposed.The structure-based features are more intuitionistic and strong than the texture-based ones and can be roughly divided into contour-based directional features[9, 10], local contour pattern based features [11, 12], connected-componentsbased features [10, 12-14], and local descriptors based features [15, 16]. This paper analyzes the shortcomings of the contour-based directional features and the local descriptors based features and presents variants of them to improve the performance of writer identification.

For the contour-based directional features, the contour-hinge feature [10]is widely used. Its main idea is to consider two contour fragments attached at a common end pixel and, subsequently, compute the joint probability distribution of the orientations of the two legs of the obtained "contour-hinge" [10].The limitation of this feature is that it cannot distinguish the situations when the orientations of the legs are same but the lengths are different. To disambiguatethese situations, this paper designs a triangular descriptor to reflect the uniqueness of the contour-hinge.Then based on the triangular descriptors, a feature vector is extracted to represent the individuality of handwriting for writer identification. The experimental results show that the proposed feature is superior to the original contour-hinge feature [10].

For the local descriptors based features, the SIFT based feature[15, 16] is widely used due to the robustness and invariance of SIFT.Since the orientation information of SIFT keypoints is discarded, the SIFT descriptors based feature cannot reflect the orientation characteristic of handwriting which has been proved as an important clue for writer identification as shown in[10].In this work, the orientation information is integrated into the SIFT descriptors by modifying the original SIFT algorithm, called the modified SIFT descriptor (MSD). And the bag of word model is used to compute a histogram of MSD (MSDH) as a feature vector.The experimental results demonstrate MSDH gets better performance than the previous SIFT descriptor based feature [16].

The rest of this paper is organized as follows: Section 2 describes the proposed method in detail. Section 3 reports our experimental results and analyses for writer identification. Finally, the conclusions are presented in Section4.

2   Methodology

2.1   Modified SIFT Descriptor Histogram (MSDH) Extraction

Modified SIFT Descriptor Extraction.Scale invariant feature transform (SIFT), presented by Lowe [17] for distinctive scale-invariant features extraction from images, has been widely and successfully applied in many fields such as computer vision and image retrieval.The SIFT algorithm can be briefly described as four steps: (1) scale-space construction, (2) key point localization, (3) orientation assignment, and (4) key point descriptor extraction. SIFT descriptor has the rotational invariance due to the third step which eliminates the orientation information of the key points by computing their dominative orientation. However, the orientation information of handwriting, which is an important part of personal writing style, should be maintained.

Hence, this workneglects the computation of dominative orientation for each keypoint in SIFT algorithm. The horizontal direction is assigned as the orientation of keypoints. Then a SIFT descriptor for each keypoint is generated. Since the third step of the original SIFT algorithm is modified, we call the final generated SIFT descriptor as modified SIFT descriptor (MSD). In this work, MSDs are used to reflect the structures of the image regions centered at the SIFT keypoints and preserve the orientation information of these structures. Therefore, MSDs provide very important information of handwriting to distinguish different writers.

Codebook Construction and MSDH Extraction.Given a handwriting document image, we use the modified SIFT algorithm to obtain a large amount of keypoints and extract their MSDs. It's easy to understand that the locations of detected keypoints are almost totally different between the query and reference handwriting images since the handwriting for writer identification is text-independent. So it is impossible to directly use the traditional local feature matching algorithm for writer identification. To deal with this problem, we use the Kohonen SOM clustering algorithm to generate a codebook with size N on the MSDs of the keypoints extracted from the training samples. In this work, the parameter N can be determined by using the training dataset.

After obtaining the codebook, we extract the MSDH feature by taking into account the frequency of MSD occurrences in a handwriting image. Given a handwriting image I, manyMSDs are extracted from I. For each MSD, the distance between it and each codeword of the codebook is computed. Then the index of the smallest distance is obtained by sorting the distancesvector and the frequency of the corresponding codeword adds one. All MSDs is processed to get a histogram of the MSD occurrences, and the histogram (MSDH) is normalized as the final feature vector for writer identification.

2.2 Triangular Descriptor Histogram (TDH) Extraction

To further improve the performance of writer identification, this paper extracts another feature from the contour of handwriting image. First of all, triangular descriptor (TD) is designed to represent the unique relationship between three points. As shown in Fig. 1, given three points (P_0, P_1, P_2), a triangle can be determined. Unlike the contour-hinge presented in [10] which only uses two angles (φ_1 and φ_2 as shown in Fig. 1), this paper employs two angles (φ_1 and φ_2) and two side lengths (the lengths of line segment P_0P_1 and P_0P_2, denoted l_1 and l_2) to represent the relationship between these three points. $\varphi_1(\varphi_2)$ measures the clockwise rotation which aligns $P_0P_1(P_0P_2)$ to right horizontal direction. So the values of the angles are between $0°$ and $360°$. If only two angles (φ_1 and φ_2) are used as done in[10], such as two similar triangles whose sides are parallel cannot be distinguished as shown in Fig. 1(a). But if two additional side lengths are used together, those kinds of triangles can be identified as different ones, as shown in Fig. 1(a). The tetrad[$\varphi_1, \varphi_2, l_1, l_2$] is defined as the triangulardescriptor (TD), which can uniquely determine a triangle.

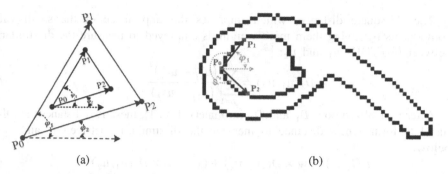

(a)   (b)

Fig. 1. (a) The definition of the triangular descriptor. It consists of two angles (φ_1 and φ_2) and two side lengths (the lengths of P_0P_1 and P_0P_2). (b) The process of the triangular descriptor histogram (TDH) extraction. Suppose p_0 is the current tracking point. p_1 and p_2 are two contour points beside p_0, and the number of contour points between p_0 and p_1, p_0 and p_2 is n, here $n=9$ is provided as an example. A triangular descriptor of these three points is computed. After tracking all contour points of a handwriting image, the TDH can be obtained as a feature for writer identification.

After defining the triangular descriptor, we binarize the handwriting image by using the threshold obtained by Otsu's algorithm, then extract the contour image by using canny operator. In order to form a feature vector for writer identification, this paper takes into account the frequency of the triangular descriptors occurrence by tracking the contour points of handwriting image, as shown in Fig. 1(b). If we directly compute the joint probabilitydistribution of these four elements in the tetrad as a feature, the dimension of the feature vector will be too large to save the memory and improve the performance. To deal with this problem, this paper separately computes the joint probabilitydistribution$P_1$of the first two elements and$P_2$of the last two elements, then concatenates them together as the final feature $P = [P_1, P_2]$, called triangular descriptor histogram (TDH). During computing P_1, the angle is quantized in m directions with interval $360°/m$, so the histogram P_1 has m^2 bins. During computing P_2, the side length is normalized with maximum $\sqrt{2}n$and minimum 0, where n is the number of contour points between current contour point and another selected contour point, then quantized into l sections with interval $1/l$, so the histogram P_2 has l^2 bins. At last, the dimension of P is $M = m^2 + l^2$.In this work, the parameters n, m, and l can be determined by using the training dataset.

2.3   Feature Matching

Let I_1 and I_2 denote two handwriting images, and let $v_1 = (v_{11}, v_{12}, ..., v_{1N})$ and $v_2 = (v_{21}, v_{22}, ..., v_{2N})$ denote their MSDHs, and $u_1 = (u_{11}, u_{12}, ..., u_{1M})$ and $u_2 = (u_{21}, u_{22}, ..., u_{2M})$ denote their TDHs.

In this work, the Mahanttan distance is adopted to measure the dissimilarity between two MSDHs v_1 and v_2:

$$D_1(v_1, v_2) = \sum_{i=1}^{N} |v_{1i} - v_{2i}| \tag{1}$$

The chi-square distance, which improves the importance of the small value components by giving them more weight, is employed to measure the dissimilarity between two TDHs u_1 and u_2:

$$D_2(u_1, u_2) = \sum_{j=1}^{M} \frac{(u_{1j} - u_{2j})^2}{(u_{1j} + u_{2j})} \tag{2}$$

After normalized both D_1 and D_2 into interval [0, 1], these two distances are then fused to form a new distance to measure the dissimilarity between I_1 and I_2 as below:

$$D(I_1, I_2) = w \times D_1(v_1, v_2) + (1 - w) \times D_2(u_1, u_2) \tag{3}$$

where w is a weight and can be determined by using the training dataset.

3   Experiments

The proposed method is evaluated on two public datasets: IAM [18] and ICDAR 2013 writer identification contest dataset (called ICDAR2013 dataset) [3].

The IAM dataset [18] contains 1539 English handwriting document images from 657 writers. There are 158 writers owning 3 or more handwriting samples. We modify the IAM dataset as described in[10] in our experiments by keeping only the first two documents for those writers who contribute more than two documents and splitting the document roughly in half for those writers with a unique page in the original set.

The ICDAR2013 dataset [3] consists of a training dataset and a test dataset, containing 100 writers and 250 writers, respectively. Each writer is asked to copy four pages of text in two languages (two in English and two in Greek). And the number of text lines that are produced by the writers ranges between two and six.

The most popular criterions including the "leave-one-out" strategy and the Top-N performance for each dataset are employed to evaluate the proposed method on the same dataset. The "leave-one-out" strategy means that for each handwriting document sample, the distances to all other samples of these datasets are computed[3, 10]. The TOP-N performance criterion is defined as that a correct hit is considered when at least one document image of the same writer is included in the N most similar document images with K-nearest-neighbors as [3, 10].

3.1   Parameters Optimization

We use the ICDAR2013 training dataset to construct the codebookand determine the parametersmentioned in the feature extraction process, i.e. the size of codebook$N$, the number of contour points between current point and another selected point n, the orientation bins m, the side length bins l, and the weight w with free searching method. This is done by sampling for the best performance of writer identification on training dataset over $100 \leq N \leq 1000$at intervals of 50, $4 \leq n \leq 24$at intervals of 2, $10 \leq m \leq 30$at intervals of 1, $5 \leq l \leq 20$at intervals of 1, $0 \leq w \leq 1$at intervals of 0.01. The parameter $N$and w are independent with others, so we train them alone. While another three parameters n, m, and l are jointly determined. The experimental results have best performance when N=550,n=16, m=24, l=10, w=0.61.This group parameters will be used in the following experiments.

3.2   Experimental Results

Table 1 lists the writer identification results and the test writer numbers of the proposed method and other approaches which use the same evaluation criterions on IAM. For fair comparison, we give the results of the approaches whose test writer numbers are about 650. From Table 1, firstly, we can see the proposed method of MSDH and TDH gets the best performance, which reflects the efficiency of the proposed method. Secondly, the performance of the proposed feature TDH is much better than the contour-hinge featurepresented in [10]. The Top-1 performance of contour-hinge feature is 81% while 90.1% for the proposed TDH with improving 9.1%.That's because the triangular descriptor can represent the unique relationship between three contour points while contour-hinge cannot. Therefore, TDH is more powerful to capture the individuality of handwriting than contour-hinge feature. Thirdly, the proposed MSDH gets better performance than the approach presented in [15], although both of them are based on SIFT descriptors.That's because MSD integrates the orientation information of the structure centered at the SIFT keypoints while the approach presented in [15] don't, and the orientation information is helpful to distinguish different handwritings.

Table 1. Top-n performance of different approaches for writer identification on the IAM dataset (%)

Approach	Writers	Top-1	Top-5	Top-10
Grapheme emission(GE) [10]	650	80	N/A	94
Contour-hinge(GH) [10]	650	81	N/A	92
GH+GE [10]	650	88	N/A	97
GMF [11]	657	90	95	96.3
Fiel et al [15]	650	90.8	96.5	97.5
Tang et al [12]	657	92.6	96.4	97.3
Ghiasi et al [13]	650	93.7	N/A	97.7
MSDH	657	95.1	97.4	98.2
TDH	657	90.1	95.7	96.7
MSDH+TDH	**657**	**97.1**	**98.8**	**99.2**

Table 2 presents the performance of the proposed method and other approaches on the entire ICDAR2013 dataset and different language sub-datasets. From this table, we can see the proposed method of MSDH and TDH gets the best results inhybrid-languages and different languages (i.e. Greek and English) tests,which demonstrate that the proposed method is language-insensitive.We has to mention that the participantapproach HIT-ICG and CVL-IPK which also extract the SIFT descriptor based features. The performance of MSDH is better than HIT-ICGand CVL-IPKas shown in Table 2, which further demonstrates that MSDH with orientation information of handwriting is more powerful than these SIFT descriptor based approaches withoutorientation informationfor writer identification.

Table 2. Top-n performance of different approaches for writer identification on the entire ICDAR2013 dataset and different language sub-datasets(%)

Approach	Entire dataset			Greek sub-dataset			English sub-dataset		
	Top-1	Top-5	Top-10	Top-1	Top-5	Top-10	Top-1	Top-5	Top-10
CS-UMD-a [14]	95.1	98.6	99.1	95.6	98.6	**99.2**	94.6	**98.4**	98.8
CS-UMD-b [14]	95.0	98.6	**99.2**	95.2	**98.8**	99.0	94.4	**98.4**	**99.0**
HIT-ICG[3]	94.8	98.0	98.3	93.8	97.2	97.8	92.2	96.4	96.8
TEBESSA-a [3]	90.3	96.7	98.3	91.0	96.8	97.8	86.0	94.4	96.0
TEBESSA-c[3]	93.4	97.8	98.5	92.6	98.0	98.4	91.2	96.2	96.6
CVL-IPK [16]	90.9	97.0	98.0	88.4	96.8	97.8	91.4	95.8	97.2
MSDH	95.4	98.0	98.6	95.0	98.2	98.8	94.6	97.4	98.4
TDH	91.6	96.2	97.5	90.0	95.8	97.0	89.2	94.2	95.6
MSDH+TDH	**96.4**	**98.7**	**99.2**	**96.0**	**98.8**	**99.2**	**95.2**	**98.4**	**99.0**

From Table 1 and Table 2, we observe that the performance of the proposed method drops little from IAM dataset to ICDAR2013 dataset, such as Top-1 performance from 97.1% to 96.4 and Top-5 performance from 98.8% to 98.7%. And we analyze the samples in these two datasets and find that the average amount of handwritings in samples of IAM dataset is much more than those in ICDAR2013 dataset. These demonstrate that the proposed method is robust to the amount of handwriting. Although both of MSDH and TDH get good performance, their fusion performance improves slightly. The possible reason is that TDH is used to capture the orientation information of handwriting and MSDH also captures some orientation information. So after weighted sum fusion, MSDH and TDH have someredundancy.

4   Conclusions

In this paper, we propose a novel method for text-independent writer identification by usingtwo improved structural features, i.e. MSDH and TDH.The experiments on two public challenging datasets demonstrate the efficiency of the proposed method. According tothe experimental results and analysis, three conclusions can be obtained: 1) the proposed triangular descriptor can uniquely define the relationship between three points; 2) the orientation information of the keypoints is integrated into SIFT descriptors, which further improves the distinguishability of writers' individuality; 3)the proposed method is robust to the amount of handwriting and can work well on different languages and hybrid languages. The proposed method has a good application prospect for text-independent writer identification.

Acknowledgments. This work was supported by the Natural Science Foundation of China (Grant No. 61073125 and 61350004) and the Fundamental Research Funds for the Central Universities (Grant No.HIT.NSRIF.2013091 and HIT.HSS.201407).

References

1. Louloudis, G., Stamatopoulos, N., Gatos, B.: ICDAR 2011 Writer Identification Contest. In: International Conference on Document Analysis and Recognition, Beijing, pp. 1475–1479 (2011)
2. Louloudis, G., Gatos, B., Stamatopoulos, N.: ICFHR 2012 Competition on Writer Identification Challenge 1: Latin/Greek Documents. In: International Conference on Frontiers in Handwriting Recognition, Bari, pp. 829–834 (2012)
3. Louloudis, G., Gatos, B., Stamatopoulos, N., Papandreou, A.: ICDAR 2013 Competition On Writer Identification. In: International Conference on Document Analysis and Recognition, Washington, pp. 1397–1401 (2013)
4. Plamondon, R., Lorette, G.: Automatic Signature Verification and Writer Identification - The State of The Art. Pattern Recognition 22, 107–131 (1989)
5. Said, H.E.S., Tan, T.N., Baker, K.D.: Personal Identification Based on Handwriting. Pattern Recognition 33, 149–160 (2000)
6. He, Z., You, X., Tang, Y.Y.: Writer Identification of Chinese Handwriting Documents Using Hidden Markov Tree Model. Pattern Recognition 41, 1295–1307 (2008)
7. He, Z., You, X., Tang, Y.Y.: Writer Identification Using Global Wavelet-Based Features. Neurocomputing 71, 1832–1841 (2008)
8. Du, L., You, X., Xu, H., Gao, Z., Tang, Y.: Wavelet Domain Local Binary Pattern Features for Writer Identification. In: International Conference on Pattern Recognition, Istanbul, pp. 3691–3694 (2010)
9. Bulacu, M., Schomaker, L., Vuurpijl, L.: Writer Identification Using Edge-Based Directional Features. In: International Conference on Document Analysis and Recognition, Edinburgh, pp. 937–941 (2003)
10. Bulacu, M., Schomaker, L.: Text-Independent Writer Identification and Verification Using Textural and Allographic Features. IEEE Transactions on Pattern Analysis and Machine Intelligence 29, 701–717 (2007)
11. Li, X., Ding, X.: Writer Identification of Chinese Handwriting Using Grid Microstructure Feature. In: International Conference on Biometrics, Alghero, pp. 1230–1239 (2009)
12. Tang, Y.B., Wu, X.Q., Bu, W.: Offline Text-Independent Writer Identification Using Stroke Fragment and Contour Based Features. In: International Conference on Biometrics, Madrid (2013)
13. Ghiasi, G., Safabakhsh, R.: Offline Text-Independent Writer Identification Using Codebook and Efficient Code Extraction Methods. Image and Vision Computing 31, 379–391 (2013)
14. Jain, R., Doermann, D.: Writer Identification Using an Alphabet of Contour Gradient Descriptors. In: International Conference onDocument Analysis and Recognition, Washington, pp. 550–554 (2013)
15. Fiel, S., Sablatnig, R.: Writer Retrieval and Writer Identification Using Local Features. In: International Workshop on Document Analysis Systems, Queensland, pp. 145–149 (2012)
16. Fiel, S., Sablatnig, R.: Writer Identification and Writer Retrieval using the Fisher Vector on Visual Vocabularies. In: International Conference onDocument Analysis and Recognition, Washington, pp. 545–549 (2013)
17. Lowe, D.: Distinctive Image Features from Scale-Invariant Keypoints. International Journal of Computer Vision 60, 91–110 (2004)
18. Marti, U.V., Bunke, H.: The IAM-Database: an English Sentence Database for Offline Handwriting Recognition. International Journal on Document Analysis and Recognition 5, 39–46 (2002)

An Effective Optical Component to Increase the Illumination Uniformity of Extended LED Light Source

Yonghua Tang and Weiqi Yuan

Shenyang University of Technology, Computer Vision Group, Shenyang, 110870, China

Abstract. The design of light source is crucial for the availability of palmprint, hand shape and high quality image of Handmetric identification. After the small (small lighting area, Gao Liangdu) LED light source is added at the front end of an appropriate optical component, it may assist to redistribute the LED flux in receiving specific distant source within a specific range. It may also favor in reducing the volume of light source. Such can be done during the improvement of the uniformity of illumination. The light's utilization of surface is also objective. This paper analyses in detail of the track's changes before and after the light through optical components by comparing the use of flux distribution and optical component. The results show that the uniformity is improved after luminous flux component's distribution.

Keywords: Highlight LED, small light source, optical components, luminous flux.

1 Introduction

The design of light source is crucial for the availability of palmprint, hand shape and the high quality image of Handmetric identification. The distribution of hand image's light has more uniformity. The higher the contrast, the identity recognition effect will be better. Therefore, a light source for the hand image's acquisition needs as much irradiation's uniform as possible for the position of hand. The light intensity should be moderate. The light's condition in target images matters in getting a satisfying image. Since the source of LED light is with low power consumption, high brightness and other characteristics are widely used in all walks of life. The acquisition if image is no exception. Hand image acquisition device generally uses LED light source a lot lower brightness which constitutes a surface light source. We increase the light guiding plate in the front when necessary. In order to follow the uniform light, we try to avoid the uneven and adverse situation in hand after intensity of light irradiation target's distribution. The hand image's capturing of the source is ideal. It can be used for hand identification. But for this kind of source of large volume, the overall power consumption brings great inconvenience.

The bright LED light source can guarantee the overall light conditions, reducing the number of luminous tube, thereby reducing the size and power source. But the biggest problem is brought about by the non-uniform distribution of the light intensity in the target region. The distribution which is directly used for hand image acquisition

Z. Sun et al. (Eds.): CCBR 2014, LNCS 8833, pp. 412–418, 2014.

proves not ideal in effect. Therefore, when we appropriate optical components in the front end of the light source, LED fluxes during the surface's redistribution. The uniform illumination effects while improving the receiving surface of light utilization.

2   Theoretical Basis

In this paper, eight 2W blue LED light-emitting tubes cover areas in the source 72mm * 72mm. The middle position of the light source is a 1/3 inch camera. As shown in figure 3, in order to keep LED luminously emitting two times until it accepts the reasonable distribution of light source, the ideal intensity distribution and higher efficiency in the palm of your hand matter a lot. A single concave lens and reflector combination mode are used as the basic model for analysis and the design of optical components of the optical guide.

According to the refraction principle, a concave lens is of divergence of light. By setting the parameters of concave lens, it can be balanced in distribution. LED fluxes during for the improving of illumination uniformity. According to the principle of reflection, specular reflection by irradiating the light may receive surface outside the collection to the receiving surface. It can improve the utilization rate. In this paper, the flat surface concave lens belongs to the radius of circular surface R. R will be called the curvature radius of lens. The undetermined parameters include the lens center thickness and the curvature radius of lens according to the obtained region's specific distance and its optical component in front of the light efficiency and uniformity.

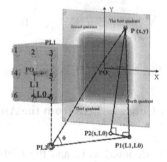

Fig. 1. Light source and optical components in the acceptance of the flux distribution

The surface center for light receiving is set to XY plane origin, being denoted as PO`. As the origin, the light receiving plane to PO` point will be paid in the plane into four quadrants, as shown in fig2.The relative position of four symmetrical quadrants and the light source are studied. The source of light rests on the intensity distribution of four quadrants. Therefore, this paper analyses the intensity distribution of the first quadrant.

3   Theoretical Analysis

3.1   Corresponding to an Arbitrary Angle Radius R 'and the Concave Lens Radius r

As shown in figure 2, ABCD are respectively for the plane concave lens. T is set as the center of a concave lens. Installing the optical component (the circular radius concave curvature radius of lens is r), the light source outside length is u, the A point as the center to rotate at any angle ξ, $\xi \in \left[0, \frac{\pi}{4}\right]$ form a new section, the radius of the new section denoted as r' . According to the Pythagorean theorem $r^2 = (r')^2 + d^2$, concave lens center section distance is $d = r \times \arcsin(\quad \frac{\pi}{4} - \xi)$,$\in [0, \frac{\sqrt{2}}{4}r]$ is the circular section radius

$r' = \sqrt{r^2 - d^2}$. Width corresponding to the optical component under section section is $a = \frac{u}{\cos \xi}$, $\xi \in \left[0, \frac{\pi}{4}\right]$.

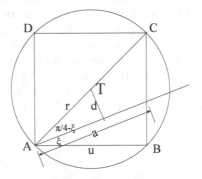

Fig. 2. Light guide assembly plan

3.2   Any light through a Concave Lens from the Angles of Incident Angle and Light Plane $\Delta \delta$

The LED's luminous point is denoted as O, and the Light plane to plane as XY. XY vertical direction is Z. The light source and the concave lens center line and XY plane angle is α, $\alpha \in \left[0, \frac{\pi}{2}\right]$. The light source and the concave lens center line and a particular light angle are γ, $\gamma \in [0, \alpha]$. The particular outgoing rays and XY plane angle is α-γ. A central concave lens is recorded as o', the intersection of specific light and concave lens is D. The fovea lens thickness is h, the o' distance optical component surface distance is $r' + h$. The angle of Oo' and $o'D$ is β, and the angle of OD与O'D is δ. Reflection of the outgoing light rays to deviate from the original direction angle is $\Delta \delta$, as shown in figure 3.

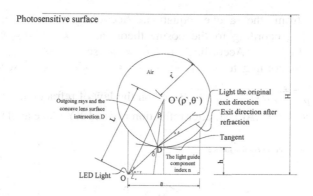

Fig. 3. Light in the exit plane refraction diagram

The polar coordinates equation of taking O as the origin, and O' as the center if $(\rho')^2 + \rho^2 - 2\rho\rho'\cos(\theta - \theta') = (r')^2$, and (ρ',θ') if the polar circle of o'. Any point coordinates of circular is (ρ,θ), radius is r'. As shown in figure 3, $\rho' = L = \sqrt{(c + h)^2 + (\frac{a}{2})^2}$, $\theta = \alpha$, so the polar coordinates can be expressed as $L^2 + \rho^2 - 2L\rho\cos(\theta - \alpha) = (r')^2$. the polar coordinates corresponding to D points is (ρ_D, θ_D), and $\theta_D = \alpha - \gamma$, so ρ_D is from $L^2 + \rho_D^2 - 2L\rho_D\cos(\theta_D - \alpha) = (r')^2$. So $\rho_D = \frac{-(2L\cos(\theta_D - \alpha)) \pm \sqrt{(2L\cos(\theta_D - \alpha))^2 - 4(L^2 - (r')^2)}}{2}$, that is $\rho_D = L\cos(\theta_D - \alpha) \pm \sqrt{(r')^2 - L^2\sin^2(\theta_D - \alpha)}$ According to $\theta_D = \alpha - \gamma$, $\rho_D = L\cos(\gamma) + \sqrt{(r')^2 - L^2\sin^2(\gamma)}$. As shown in figure 3, D should be close, that is $\rho_D = L\cos(\gamma) - \sqrt{(r')^2 - L^2\sin^2(\gamma)}$, and $(r')^2 - L^2\sin^2(\gamma) \geq 0$, $\sin(\gamma) \leq \frac{(r')}{L}$. According to the cosine theorem in $\triangle Oo'D$, $\beta = \arccos\frac{L^2 + (r')^2 - \rho L}{2L'}$. The angle between the incident ray OD and the normal $o'D$ is $\delta = \beta + \gamma$, and the angle between the plane and Z direction is $\varepsilon = \frac{\pi}{2} - (\alpha - \gamma - \Delta\delta)$, as shown in figure 4. A function of exit angle of single LED light intensity and light is $f(\delta)$, δ is the front light direction and the light source plane angle, $\delta \in [0, \frac{\pi}{2}]$. the function relation after optical components is $g(\delta)$, $g(\delta) = f(\delta - \Delta\delta)$.

3.3 Analysis of Optical Components of Reflected Light

As shown in Figure 4, with an outgoing light rays to light guide, components reflects wall Q. The reflected light reflected wall to the concave lens M, Q point normal to M to extend the line from point P, handed over to the o' vertical point N. The light and XY plane angle is ζ, light reflection in the light guide assembly angle of incidence is Ω, deviate from the original direction of light $\Delta\zeta$. The angle between $O'N$ and $O'M$ is ω. The angle between $O'N$ and $O'Q$ is ψ, angle between $O'M$ and $O'Q$ is φ, MP is m. QP is p. The distance from Q to light plane XY, Q is the origin for the polar coordinate systems center, coordinate of O' is (ρ', θ'), and $\theta' = \arctan\frac{r' + h - h'}{\frac{a}{2}}$, $h' = a \times \tan\zeta$, $\rho' = \sqrt{(c + h - h')^2 + (\frac{a}{2})^2}$, so equations in polar coordinates is $(c + h - h')^2 \cdot (\frac{a}{2})^2 + \rho'^2 - 2\rho'\sqrt{(c + h - h')^2 + (\frac{a}{2})^2}\cos\theta - \theta' = \arctan\frac{r + h - h'}{\frac{a}{2}} - (\gamma)$. Polar coordinates of M is (ρ_M, θ_M),

$\theta_M = \varsigma$, ρ_M is from the above equation. According to $\tan \psi = \dfrac{a/2}{r+h-h}$, $v = \arctan \dfrac{a/2}{r+h-h}$. According to the cosine theorem, $\cos \phi = \dfrac{(\rho)^2 + (\varsigma)^2 - \rho_i^2}{2\rho r}$, so $\phi = \arccos \dfrac{(\rho)^2 + (\varsigma)^2 - \rho_i^2}{2\rho r}$. According to $\omega = \psi - \phi$, so $\cos \omega = \dfrac{r+h-h}{r+m}$, and $m = \dfrac{r+h-h}{\cos \omega} - r$. According to $\sin \omega = \dfrac{a/2 - p}{r+m}$, $p = \dfrac{a}{2} - \sin(\omega \times (r+m))$. According to the

sine theorem, $\dfrac{\Omega}{p} = \dfrac{\varsigma}{m}$, so $\Omega = \dfrac{p}{m} \times \varsigma$. Based on the law of refraction, $n = \dfrac{\sin(\Omega + \Delta\varsigma)}{\sin \Omega}$, so

$\Delta\varsigma = \arcsin(n \times \sin \Omega) - \Omega$. At last, after refraction ray and XY plane angle is $\varsigma - \Delta\varsigma$.

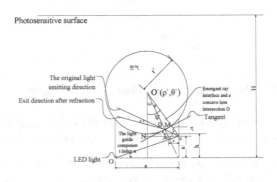

Photosensitive surface

The original light emitting direction

Exit direction after refraction

$O'(\rho',\theta')$

Emergent ray interface and a concave lens intersection D

Tangent

The light guide componen t index n

LED light   O

Fig. 4. Reflect light refraction of Plane Graphs

The emission from point O, the q-point reflection of light, and a light beam are equivalent to the existence of virtual point symmetry. Point coincides with the q-point emission, i.e. M, Q, 3.1. Similarly, the source of each point is equivalent to the existence of a mirror. The mirror point constitutes a virtual source matrix with 3U larger. Virtual light's source in the matrix virtual light comes through optical component scattering on receiving plane (photosensitive plane) to fill light. It plays at the same time the light uniformity and the dual purpose of raising the utilization rate of light. As shown in Figure 5, the A LED and AB ξ angle emission by reflected light, the equivalent of a mirror A` emitted light, virtual light matrix diagram in TA, TB, TC, TD is a rectangular area with the formation of ABCD 3U as light source of U.

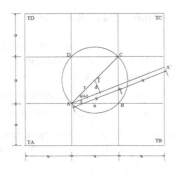

Fig. 5. Equivalent diagram of the actual light source

4   The Experiment of Flux Comparison

In this paper, 8 power is 2W with wavelength of 450nm blue light length of 75mm square LED source comparison experiment. Single LED illumination is shown in figure 6.

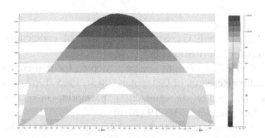

Fig. 6. Single LED illumination map

Optical component samples and main parameters include the center height with h=10mm, length u=75mm, size 75mm*75mm, curved surface radius r=10mm. The distance from source to receiver H=300mm receive on the surface and illuminant center coaxial, area 200mm*200mm. The received plane illumination is shown in figure 7. In Figure 7, the bottom coordinates for the luminous flux which received surface physical dimension coordinate. The longitudinal direction corresponds with the receiving surface of each coordinate of a point light intensity.

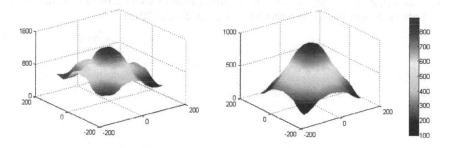

Fig. 7. Comparison of illuminance

Fig. 7 shows that, at the receiving plane, the flux variation range corresponds to each coordinate point and reduces significantly. The illumination uniformity is improved basically consistent with the previous theoretical results.

5   Conclusion

Through theoretical analysis, experiment shows that the increase in the front end of the light source of small LED. Optical components produce a more uniform light in front of the light source and specifically receive plane illumination effect. The next step will use the hand image acquisition of the optical components in the field. Further analysis using image difference before and after the optical components will influence on the subsequent processing research.

References

1. Weiqi, Y., Jun, W., Zonghui, G.: Study and design of contactless palm vein imaging system. Micro Computer Information 28(10), 46–48 (2012)
2. Weiqi, Y., Hong, S.: Design of lignt source structure for non-contract palmprint images acquisition. Application Research of Computers 28(5), 1965–1967 (2011)
3. Weiqi, Y., Kang, D.: Study on contactless palmprint images sampling equipment. Microcomputer and Application 1, 16–19 (2010)
4. Weiqi, Y., Deqi, K.: Design of palm three modal acquisition device based on multispectral. Instrument Technique and Sensor (10), 35–41 (2013)
5. Weiqi, Y., Lili, W., Ningning, Z.: Design and realization of hand three-modal image acquisition system. Transducer and Microsystem Technologies 32(5), 78–85 (2013)
6. Chenhui, W., Fengxu, G., Xinjing, S., et al.: Design of multi-modal image acquisition device of palmprint and 3D hand-shape. Techniques of Automation & Applications 30(7), 76–79 (2011)
7. Qieni, L., Chang, X., Wenhua, J.: Calculation of scattering light distribution of large bubbles by geometrical optics approximation model. Journal of Tianjin University 45(12), 1089–1095 (2012)
8. Yanyan, S., Lu, H., Xiaoyu, S., et al.: General laws of reflection and refraction for metasurface with phase discontinuity. Acta Phys. Sin. 62(10), 104–201 (2013)
9. Zhuowei, Z., Zhouping, S., Xishun, X.: Application of vector form of reflection law in LED lighting design. Physics and Engineering 12(2), 21–22 (2012)

Nuclear Norm Based Bidirectional 2DPCA

Yu Ding, Caikou Chen, Ya Gu, and Yu Wang

College of Information Engineering, Yangzhou University
yzcck@126.com

Abstract. This paper develops a new image feature extraction and recognition method coined bidirectional compressed nuclear-norm based 2DPCA (BN2DPCA). BN2DPCA presents a sequentially optimal image compression mechanism, making the information of the image compact into its up-left corner. BN2DPCA is tested using the Extended Yale B and the CMU PIE face databases. The experimental results show that BN2DPCA is more effective than N2DPCA, B2DPCA, LPP and LDA for face feature extraction and recognition.

Keywords: Nuclear norm, two dimensional principal component analysis, feature extraction, classification.

1 Introduction

Principal component analysis (PCA) is a classical dimension reduction and data representation technique, which has been successfully applied into the areas of pattern recognition and computer vision [1] Many PCA-based face representation and recognition techniques have been developed to preprocess a two-dimensional image by transforming it into a long vector. This must lead to the loss of the structural information of the image, which is very important for kinds of analysis and recognition tasks. To address this problem, many techniques which directly based on image matrix have been proposed. One of representative methods is two-dimensional principal component analysis (2DPCA), which was originally proposed by Yang et al. [2]. 2DPCA has been successfully applied in pattern recognition, computer vision and signal process community [3, 4]. However, 2DPCA just works in the row directions of images and disregards the data compression in vertical direction. So, its compression rate is far lower than that of one-dimensional PCA. Moreover, the other drawback of 2DPCA is that it needs more coefficients than the traditional PCA for the representation of images. This must lead to consuming more time to compute distance (similarity) in classification phase and larger storage for large-scaled databases. So, many bi-directional 2DPCA (B2DPCA) methods have been developed for solving these weaknesses. B2DPCA [5] aims to simultaneously eliminate the correlation in the row and column directions. Both PCA and 2DPCA are all based on L_2-norm metric which is not robust to grossly corrupted or outlying observations. Thus, their performance and applicability are limited by a lack of robustness to outliers, which are ubiquitous in many applications like face recognition and computer vision.

Some recent works on the alleviating of this problem have been explored in the literature including robust PCA [6] and low-rank matrix recovery (LR) [7, 8, 13, 14].

Z. Sun et al. (Eds.): CCBR 2014, LNCS 8833 , pp. 419–425, 2014.

They are converted into a nuclear norm-based minimization problem. Nuclear norm is essentially the convex envelope of the matrix rank [7, 8, 9]. Fornasier et al. [7] presented an efficient algorithm to solve the nuclear-norm-minimization problem by converting the nuclear norm problem into Frobenius norm problem in conjunction with the iteratively reweighted strategy. Inspired by the work of Fornasier et al., Zhang et al. [10] proposed nuclear-norm-based 2DPCA, termed as N2DPCA. N2DPCA used nuclear norm to measure the reconstruction error rather than F-norm. Nevertheless, similar to classical 2DPCA, N2DPCA also worked in the row direction and ignored the correlation in the vertical direction.

Considering the drawback of N2DPCA, we propose a modified N2DPCA method, coining bidirectional N2DPCA (BN2DPCA), to overcome the disadvantage of N2DPCA. The initial idea behind BN2DPCA is to perform N2DPCA twice: the first one is in horizontal direction and the second is in vertical direction. After the two sequential transforms with N2DPCA, the information of the image is compacted into its up-left corner. Ultimately, the effectiveness of the proposed method is verified on two well-known face databases, the Extended Yale B and the CMU PIE.

2   Related work

2.1   2DPCA

Suppose there are a set of M training-image samples. The ith training image is denoted by an $m \times n$ matrix A_i. Assume that the training images are scaled to have zero mean. Let $U \in \Re^{n \times q}$ denote a projection matrix, the idea behind 2DPCA is to project an image A, an $m \times n$ random matrix, onto U by the linear transformation $Y = AU$. Then an optimal projection matrix U^* is found through the following model which is based on the minimum reconstruction error criterion:

$$\min \quad J(U) = \sum_{i=1}^{M} \left\| A_i - A_i U U^T \right\|_F^2 \tag{1}$$

$$\text{s.t.} \quad U^T U = I$$

It is well recognized that model (1) can be equivalently expressed by maximizing the following generalized total scatter criterion [2]:

$$\max \quad J(U) = U^T G_t U$$

$$\text{s.t.} \quad U^T U = I \tag{2}$$

where $G_t = \frac{1}{M} \sum_{i=1}^{M} A_i A_i^T$ is called the image's total scatter matrix. Thus, the solution of model (1), the resulting optimal projection matrix U^* can be obtained by computing orthonormal eigenvectors of G_t corresponding to the first q largest eigenvalues.

2.2   Nuclear Norm Based 2DPCA (N2DPCA)

It is well-known that 2DPCA adopts F-norm metric for measuring the error (distance) between the original sample and the reconstructed one. Similar to 2DPCA, techniques with F-norm metric are however not very robust to outliers. It is also well recognized that nuclear norm is more robust to outliers. Therefore, N2DPCA was developed to apply the nuclear norm metric for measuring the similarity between samples.

The objective of N2DPCA is to minimize the following reconstruction error with nuclear norm:

$$\min \quad J(\mathbf{U}) = \sum_{i=1}^{M} \left\| \mathbf{A}_i - \mathbf{A}_i \mathbf{U}\mathbf{U}^\mathrm{T} \right\|_*$$

$$\text{s.t.} \quad \mathbf{U}^\mathrm{T}\mathbf{U} = \mathbf{I}_q \tag{3}$$

The solution of model (3) can be obtained by transforming the nuclear norm based optimization problem into a series of F-norm based optimization problems. Thus, the model (3) can be reformulated as

$$\min \quad J(\mathbf{U}) = \sum_{i=1}^{M} \left\| \mathbf{W}_i(\mathbf{A}_i - \mathbf{A}_i \mathbf{U}\mathbf{U}^\mathrm{T}) \right\|_\mathrm{F}^2$$

$$\text{s.t.} \quad \mathbf{U}^\mathrm{T}\mathbf{U} = \mathbf{I} \tag{4}$$

where $\mathbf{W}_i$ is defined by $\mathbf{W}_i = ((\mathbf{A}_i - \mathbf{A}_i\mathbf{U}\mathbf{U}^\mathrm{T})(\mathbf{A}_i - \mathbf{A}_i\mathbf{U}\mathbf{U}^\mathrm{T})^\mathrm{T})^{-\frac{1}{4}}$.

3   Bi-directional 2DPCA Based on Nuclear Norm (BN2DPCA)

3.1   Idea

Compared with classical F-norm-based 2DPCA, N2DPCA not only makes good use of structural information of image but is also more robust to outliers. Nevertheless, N2DPCA just works in the row directions of images and disregards the data compression in vertical direction. So, its compression rate is far lower than of one-dimensional PCA. Moreover, the other drawback of N2DPCA is that it needs more coefficients than the traditional PCA for the representation of images. This must lead to taking more time to compute distance (similarity) in classification phase. Then, it needs larger storage for large-scaled databases.

In this section, a simple but effective method will be presented to overcome the above drawbacks of N2DPCA. Our idea is just to perform N2DPCA twice in horizontal direction and vertical direction. Specifically, given an image $\mathbf{A} \in \mathfrak{R}^{m \times n}$, we obtain the first projection matrix $\mathbf{U} \in \mathfrak{R}^{n \times q}$ and its feature matrix $\mathbf{B} \in \mathfrak{R}^{m \times q}$ after performing the first N2DPCA transformation. Then, we transpose $\mathbf{B}$ and feed $\mathbf{B}^\mathrm{T}$ into N2DPCA again. We find that the transform matrix $\mathbf{V}$. Projecting $\mathbf{B}^\mathrm{T}$ onto $\mathbf{V}$ and we obtain $\mathbf{C}^\mathrm{T} = \mathbf{B}^\mathrm{T}\mathbf{V}$. The resulting feature matrix of $\mathbf{A}$ is $\mathbf{C} = \mathbf{V}^\mathrm{T}\mathbf{B}$.

In this whole procedure, the first N2DPCA transformation $\mathbf{B} = \mathbf{A}\mathbf{U}$ performs the compression of 2D-data in horizontal direction, making the information pack into a small number of columns. While the second N2DPCA transformation $\mathbf{C} = \mathbf{V}^\mathrm{T}\mathbf{B}$ performs the compression of 2D-data in vertical direction, eliminating the correlations between columns of image $\mathbf{B}$ and making its information further compact into a small number of rows. Finally, the information of the entire image is squeezed into the up-left corner of the image matrix.

3.2   Transformation

Now, let us describe the detailed implementation of BN2DPCA. After the first N2DPCA transforms in horizontal direction, we get the feature matrix **B** of the image sample **A** using the objective function (3). Constructing the objective function which is based on $\mathbf{B}^{\mathrm{T}}$, we have

$$\min \quad J(\mathbf{V}) = \sum_{i=1}^{M} \left\| \mathbf{W}_i (\mathbf{B}_i^{\mathrm{T}} - \mathbf{B}_i^{\mathrm{T}} \mathbf{V} \mathbf{V}^{\mathrm{T}}) \right\|_{\mathrm{F}}^2 \tag{5}$$

$$\text{s.t.} \quad \mathbf{V}^{\mathrm{T}} \mathbf{V} = \mathbf{I}$$

where $\mathbf{W}_i$ is defined by $\mathbf{W}_i = ((\mathbf{B}_i^{\mathrm{T}} - \mathbf{B}_i^{\mathrm{T}} \mathbf{V} \mathbf{V}^{\mathrm{T}})(\mathbf{B}_i^{\mathrm{T}} - \mathbf{B}_i^{\mathrm{T}} \mathbf{V} \mathbf{V}^{\mathrm{T}})^{\mathrm{T}})^{-\frac{1}{4}}$ and $\mathbf{B}_i = \mathbf{A}_i \mathbf{U}$.

Suppose $\mathbf{V} = \left[\mathbf{v}_1, \mathbf{v}_2, \cdots, \mathbf{v}_p \right]$ are the solution of the objective function (5). The N2DPCA feature matrix of $\mathbf{B}^{\mathrm{T}}$ can be obtained by

$$\mathbf{C}^{\mathrm{T}} = \mathbf{B}^{\mathrm{T}} \mathbf{V} \tag{6}$$

Thus,

$$\mathbf{C} = \mathbf{V}^{\mathrm{T}} \mathbf{B} = \mathbf{V}^{\mathrm{T}} \mathbf{A} \ \mathbf{U} \tag{7}$$

The resulting feature matrix **C** is a $p \times q$ matrix, which is much less than the N2DPCA feature matrix **B** and the original image **A** since p and q are always chosen much smaller than m and n.

After a transformation by BN2DPCA, a feature matrix is obtained for each image. Then, a nearest neighbor classifier with nuclear norm is used for classification. Here, the nuclear-norm distance between two arbitrary feature matrices, $\mathbf{C}_i$, $\mathbf{C}_j$, is defined by

$$d(\mathbf{C}_i, \mathbf{C}_j) = \left\| \mathbf{C}_i - \mathbf{C}_j \right\|_* \tag{8}$$

3.3   BN2DPCA Based Image Reconstruction

Given an image **A**, we get its feature matrix $\mathbf{C} = \mathbf{V}^{\mathrm{T}} \mathbf{A} \mathbf{U}$ after the BN2DPCA trans-formation. Since the two projection matrices, **V**, **U** are orthonormal, it is easy to obtain the reconstructed image of sample **A**:

$$\tilde{\mathbf{A}} = \mathbf{V} \mathbf{C} \mathbf{U}^{\mathrm{T}} \tag{9}$$

where $\mathbf{V} = [\mathbf{v}_1, \mathbf{v}_2, \ldots, \mathbf{v}_p]$ and $\mathbf{U} = [\mathbf{u}_1, \mathbf{u}_2, \ldots, \mathbf{u}_q]$.

4   Experiment

The proposed BN2DPCA method was used for face recognition and tested on two standard face image databases: the Extended Yale B [11] and the CMU PIE [12]. After performing BN2DPCA, we obtain two projection matrices $\mathbf{U}$ and $\mathbf{V}$ for each image, and then one gets the projected image feature matrix $\mathbf{C} = \mathbf{V}^{\mathrm{T}}\mathbf{A}\mathbf{U}$ for each image. Finally, the nearest neighbor classifier based on nuclear norm metric is employed for classification.

4.1   Experiments on the Extended Yale B Database

The Extended Yale B database [16] contains 38 subjects, each of which consists of 64 frontal images under different illuminations. Every image is resized to 96×84. We choose 10 images from each class, which are divided into five groups.

The experiment uses group 4 {(23, 24)} for training, and the remaining groups {1(7, 8); 2(12, 13); 3(16; 19); 5(28, 29)} for testing. Fig. 1 shows the recognition rates of each method versus the dimensions. From Fig. 1, we can see that BN2DPCA gives better results than N2DPCA, B2DPCA, LDA and LPP. Table 1 shows the average top recognition rate and the average consumption time.

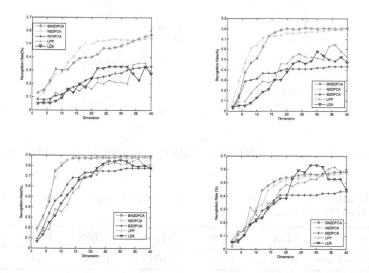

Fig. 1. The recognition rates of BN2DPCA, N2DPCA, B2DPCA, LPP and LDA versus the dimensions. The group 4 of the Extended Yale B database is used for training the projection matrix. (a) Group 1 is used for testing. (b) Group 2 is used for testing. (c) Group 3 is used for testing. (d) Group 5 is used for testing.

Table 1. The average CPU time (s) consumed for testing and the average top recognition rates of BN2DPCA, N2DPCA, B2DPCA, LPP and LDA versus the dimensions.

Method	BN2DPCA	N2DPCA	B2DPCA	LPP	LDA
Recognition rate(%)	0.745	0.734	0.525	0.657	0.662
Dimension	30×40	64×40	30×40	80×1	80×1
CPU time	107	112	1.1	1.5	1.3

4.2   Experiments on the CMU PIE Face Database

The CMU PIE face database contains 68 subjects in total. Images of each person were taken across 13 different poses, under 43 different lighting conditions, and with 4 different expressions. The subset of pose C9 is chosen for experiment. Each image is rescaled to 64×64 pixels.   Next, we select the first 6 images (2,4,6,8,10,12) per person for training, and the other 6 images (1,3,5,7,9,11) for testing.

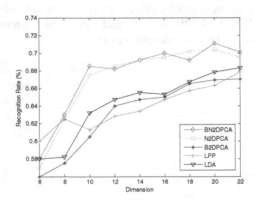

Fig. 2. Recognition rates of BN2DPCA, N2DPCA, B-2DPCA, LPP, LDA on different dimensions

Table 2. The average CPU time (s) consumed for testing, the top recognition rates (%) of the four methods on PIE database

Method	LDA	LPP	B2DPCA	N2DPCA	BN2DPCA
Recognition rate	0.682	0.669	0.671	0.704	0.711
Dimension	80×1	80×1	30×40	64×40	30×40
CPU time (s)	1.1	1.17	1.24	110.1	107

Then the average recognition rates of each method versus the dimensions are shown in Fig. 2 and the running time of each method are listed in Table 1. Fig. 2 indicates that the performance of BN2DPCA is still better than those of N2DPCA, B2DPCA, LPP and LDA.

5   Conclusion

This paper presents the bi-directionally compressed nuclear norm which is based 2DPCA model. The key idea is simple and effective by just performing N2DPCA twice: the first one is in horizontal direction and the second in vertical direction. Experimental results on face image databases demonstrate the proposed method outperforms N2DPCA.

References

1. Jolliffe, I.T.: Principal component analysis, 2nd edn. Springer, New York (2002)
2. Yang, J., Zhang, D., Frangi, A.F., Yang, J.Y., Two-dimensional, P.C.A.: a new approach to appearance-based face representation and recognition. IEEE Trans. Pattern Analysis and Machine Intelligence 26(1), 131–137 (2004)
3. Wang, D., Lu, H.: Object Tracking via 2DPCA and L1-regularization. IEEE Signal Processing Letters 19(11), 711–714 (2012)
4. Jeong, Y., Kim, H.S.: New speaker adaptation method using 2-D PCA. IEEE Signal Processing Letters 17(2), 193–196 (2010)
5. Zhang, D.Q., Zhou, Z.H. (2D)2PCA: 2-directional 2-dimensional PCA for efficient face representation and recognition. Neurocomputing 69, 224–231 (2005)
6. Candès, E., Li, X.D., Ma, Y., Wright, J.: Robust principal component analysis? Journal of the ACM 58(3) (2011)
7. Fornasier, M., Rauhut, H., Ward, R.: Low-rank matrix recovery via iteratively reweighted least squares minimization. SIAM Journal on Optimization 21(4), 1614–1640 (2011)
8. Fazel, M.: Matrix Rank Minimizati on with Applications, PhD thesis, Stanford University (2002)
9. Fazel, M., Hindi, H., Boyd, S.: A rank minimization heuristic with application to minimum order system approximation. In: Proceedings of the American Control Conference, vol. 6, pp. 4734–4739 (2001)
10. Zhang, F.L., Qian, J.J., Yang, J.: Nuclear Norm Based 2DPCA. In: Second IAPR Asian Conference on Pattern Recognition (2013)
11. Lee, K.C., Ho, J., Driegman, D.: Acquiring linear subspaces for face recognition under variable lighting. IEEE Trans. Pattern Analysis and Machine Intelligence 27(5), 684–698 (2005)
12. Sim, T., Baker, S., Bsat, M., The, C.M.U.: Pose, illumination, and expression (PIE) Database. In: the 2002 International Conference on Automatic Face and Gesture Recognition (2002)
13. He, R., Tan, T., Wang, L.: Robust Recovery of Corrupted Low-RankMatrix by Implicit Regularizers. IEEE Trans. Pattern Anal. Mach. Intell. 36(4), 770–783 (2014)
14. He, R., Sun, Z., Tan, T., Zheng, W.-S.: Recovery of corrupted low-rank matrices via half-quadratic based nonconvex minimization. In: CVPR 2011, pp. 2889–2896 (2011)

Design of an Embedded Multi-biometric Recognition Platform Based on DSP and ARM

Jiaqi Li, Yuqing He, Zhe Zou, and Kun Huang

Key Laboratory of Photoelectronic Imaging Technology and System,
Ministry of Education of China, School of Optoelectronics,
Beijing Institute of Technology, Beijing 100081, China
yuqinghe@bit.edu.cn

Abstract. Thedual-core embedded system can make the system have higher efficiency of simultaneous running in the recognition algorithm and controlling the peripheral equipments. This paper presents a study of an embedded multi-biometric recognition system based on DSP and ARM which can realize the face and iris image acquisition, recognition, datastorage and input/output control. The ARM is used as a host to communicate with peripherals. The DSP performs the multi-biometric image acquisition and recognition. The host port interface (HPI) is used to implement the communication between DSP and ARM. We design the HPI strobe signal and the hardware device driver based on the embedded Linux to realize the data exchange and communication. Experimental results show that the dual-core embedded system has greater storage capacity and higher interactive ability.

Keywords: DSP, ARM, HPI, multi-biometric recognition.

1 Introduction

There are many biometric features such as face, iris, fingerprint, palm print, handwriting, and vein pattern. Each biometric feature has its advantage and drawback. A multiple biometric system using multiple applications to capture different types of biometrics allows the integration of two or more types of biometric recognition systems in order to meet the strict performance requirements imposed by various applications[1].Among all biometric features, face recognition is widespread because it has many advantages such as being non-intrusive, user-friendly. It can be easily captured. But, it is susceptible to change as the ambient light and the position of the subject's head [2][3]. On the other side, iris recognition is the most accurate method. It has the lowest false recognition rate studied widely and it has a broad usage [4]. It is feasible to integrate the face and iris as both of them can be captured in a distant by non-contacting imaging device.

Embedded system is widely-adopted in a myriad range of systems because of the portable size and configurability [5]. Most multi-biometric recognition embedded system use the single core processor. The use of single processor like DSP or FPGA may have excellent computing speed. But it is weak to control the equipment like SD

Z. Sun et al. (Eds.): CCBR 2014, LNCS 8833 , pp. 426–433, 2014.

card, LCD and network transmission equipment. Also, the ARM is widely used for its perfect processing performance and low power consumption. But its calculation speed is limited to its system architecture. In paper [3], the core of system is Intel XScale PXA255 400Mhz processor with 64MB RAM and 32MB flash, and in paper [6], their system is designed around a Cyclone® II 2C35 FPGA manufactured by ALTERA which connected to 8-MB SDRAM, 512-KB SRAM and 4-MB Flash. Both of their systemshave limited computing speed and storage capacity. Some research use the dual-core embedded systems[4][8].But those systems are closed systems. That is to say, the data of the biometric feature cannot be stored in the systems' external storage devices or transmitted through the network for deeper research.

In our embedded system, we use the DSP combined with the ARM. In this way, the system can make full use of the two processors and make up the disadvantages of each other. The computing processer is DSP which has perfect calculation speed. The microcontroller is ARM which can achieve the functions of controlling peripheral equipment. This mode can make the DSP only achieve the biometric recognition algorithm and free from various logical control. The ARM runs the embedded Linux operating system and controls external devices. Based on the Linux kernel, the char device driver for HPI is applied to communicate between DSP and ARM. In this way, the ARM can achieve data exchanges and share resource with DSP. Through the program running in the ARM, the system can store the biometric features in the SD card automatically and control the peripheral devices. The applications of the system provide us convenience to update the system database and do the further research. In this way, the system can work as a multi-biometric acquisition and recognition system.

The paper is organized as follows. In Section 2, we outline the structure of the dual-core system and the working flow of the recognition algorithm based on the dual-core system. Section 3 analyzes the communication between the DSP and ARM. Next in Section 4, we describe the implements of the devices' drives. The experimental results are given in Section 5. Final section is the conclusions.

2   The Structure of the Dual-Core System

The biometric recognition system we design is a dual-core system which contains DSP (TI TMS320DM642) and ARM (SAMSUNG S3C6410).To maintain the consistency of system resources management, the main work of DSP is implementation and acceleration of the biometric recognition algorithm and working only with the DSP's RAM and SDRAM. The ARM controls and manages the peripherals through the device drive running on the operation system. The peripherals include display device like LCD. The network interface device is like network card, communication equipment like HPI and storage device like SD card, etc. LCD can be an interactive interface between dual-core embedded system and users. Network card can work as a network interface to transmit the biometric features and images to the terminal server through the network protocol like TCP/IP. The terminal console can control the ARM to receive the instructions of the user and achieve data transmission and the system initialization. The output control signal can send the result of recognition to specific device such as the door or others. In our dual-core system the ARM acts to be the host and the DSP is the slave. HPI is the bilateral control interface the ARM can send the control signal from the users to manage the work of DSP, also the DSP can send interrupt signal of HPI when the transmission is ready then the ARM can access DSP's memory and external storage space and store the biometric features in the SD card. Figure 1 shows the system's structure diagram.

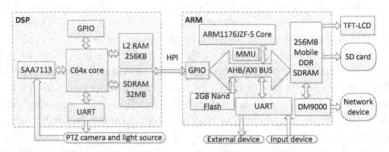

Fig. 1. The systematic diagram

We use Adaboost to do the face detection [9][10]. Based on the face position and the eye's color feature, we locate the iris position. The PTZ camera and light source is controlled by the UART to capture the iris image [7]. After performing feature extraction, the features and imagesare transmitted to the ARM through the HPI. At last, the ARM can match the features in the database or store the features and images in the SD card. The system is controlled by the external terminal console signal. The terminal console can send UART signal which can control system in registering or deleting users' biometric information to manage the database. The output control signal send the operating result to users. Figure 2 shows the working flow of the system.

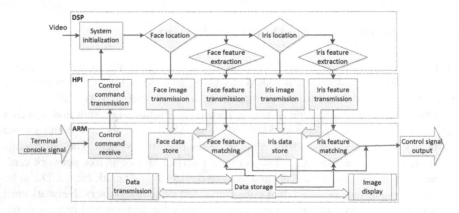

Fig. 2. The working flow of dual-core system

3   Communications between DSP and ARM

The dual-core system we designed has already been introduced in Section 2.We have already achieved the control of PTZ camera and light source in paper[7].As the communication is the most important part to dual-core embedded system, in this paper we mainly talk about the implement of HPI in data exchange and storage. The DSP is used to implement the main algorithm and we use ARM to communicate to DSP to receive the recognition results, facial features and biometric images through HPI, the DSP transmits the biometric feature and images of face and iris in the width of 32 bits. The ARM can control the DSP's work by writing the relevant registers. In this way, the HPI we design is the bidirectional data communication interface.

3.1   The Hardware Connection of HPI

HPI is a parallel port through which a host processor can directly access the CPU memory space. The host device functions as a master to the interface, which increases the ease of access [11]. The host and DSP can exchange information via internal or external memory. Through the HPI, an external host like ARM is capable of accessing the entire DSP memory map except the L2 registers, Interrupt selector registers and Emulation logic. As shown in Figure 3 the C64x has 32 external data pins HD [31–0]. As a result, the C64x HPI supports either a 16-bit or 32-bit external pin interface. We use 32-bit-wide host port (HPI32) because S3C6410 is the 32 bit RISC microprocessor.HPI have some interface control signals such as HCNTL0/1, $\overline{\text{HR}}$ / $\overline{\text{W}}$, $\overline{\text{HDS1}}$, $\overline{\text{HDS2}}$, $\overline{\text{HCS}}$, $\overline{\text{HRDY}}$ and so on. They are used for the connection with ARM.

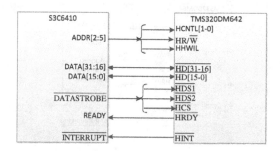

Fig. 3. The communications between DSP and ARM

3.2   The Data Strobe Signal of HPI

In order to enable the HPI, we must implement the data strobe signal. In this section, we design the time sequence of the enable signals. $\overline{\text{HCS}}$ serves as the enable input for the HPI and must be low during an access.$\overline{\text{HCS}}$, $\overline{\text{HDS1}}$ and $\overline{\text{HDS2}}$ those three signal generate internal strobe signal $\overline{\text{DATASTROBE}}$ according to the logic which require $\overline{\text{HCS}}$ low level and opposite of $\overline{\text{HDS1}}$ and $\overline{\text{HDS2}}$.$\overline{\text{DATASTROBE}}$ is low only when both $\overline{\text{HCS}}$ is low and either (but not both) $\overline{\text{HDS1}}$ or $\overline{\text{HDS2}}$ is low. The time point of the falling edge of $\overline{\text{DATASTROBE}}$ responses the last jumped signal of the three. Figure 4 shows the internal logic and the sequence chart of the signals we design. The frequency of the $\overline{\text{DATASTROBE}}$ determines the speed of HPI. We write PWM driver of the ARM based on the embedded Linux to control the frequency and ensure the stability of the transmission.

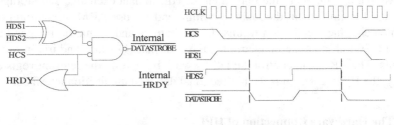

(a) The internal logic diagram   (b)The sequence chart of the signals

Fig. 4. The data strobe signal we design

3.3   Access Control Select

The HPI samples the controlling signal $\overline{\text{HR}/\text{W}}$ and HCNTL[1–0] to determine which register is to be read or written by the ARM. The states of these two pins select access to the HPI address (HPIA), HPI data (HPID), or HPI control (HPIC) registers. HPID can be accessed with an optional automatic address increment. The Internal structure of C64x HPI is shown in Figure 5.

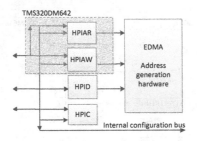

Fig. 5. HPI Internal structure diagram

The ARM begins HPI accesses by performing the following tasks in this order:

1. Initializing the HPI control register (HPIC), which is used for port setting.
2. Initializing the HPI address register (HPIA).HPIA contains two registers, one is the HPI address write register (HPIAW) and the other is HPI address read register (HPIAR).In our system, HPIAW is the writing address information of the control signal received from the ARM, and the HPIR is the reading address of data of the biometric features and images stored in the DSP's SDRAM.
3. Writing data to or reading data from the HPI data register (HPID). The EDMA carries the data stored in the HPIA through the address generation in fast speed.

4   The Device Driver of Hardware Device

As we use the embedded Linux operating system to make our system, we can have more Interaction function. We write the hardware device driver to make the Linux could control the external devices. There are three kinds of device in Linux: char device, block device and network device. We define the HPI as the char device and SD card as the block device. The main difference between the two kinds of the device is the data access interface. Consider about the multi functions of our system, we embed the Linux operating system in the S3C6410[12], and its Linux kernel version is 3.0.1.

4.1   The Char Device Driver of HPI

HPI is considered to be the peripheral of the ARM's RAM. The communication between ARM and DSP is the operations of the several registers: HPIC, HPIA and HPID. In Linux system, the operation to the char device is just like operating the common files. Structfile_operations of the Linux kernel is the operation interface to all the char devices. The internal members of the Struct are actually a series of function points. The definition of HPI driver's operation structure is in the below. The operations include open, close, read, and write and so on, the char device driver of HPI offers the access of the functions.

```
Structfile_operations HPI_FOPS={
    .owner = THIS_MODULE,
    .open = HPI_open,
    .release = HPI_release,
    .ioctl = HPI_ioctl,
    .read = HPI_read,
    .write = HPI_write,};
```

Each member's name of the Struct corresponds to a system call of Linux. When user processing use system calls to read or write the device file, the system calls will find the correspond device driver through the main equipment number (unsigned int major) and use the read or write function to control the HPI device.

4.2   The SD Card Driver

After receiving the processing results from the DSP through the HPI, the ARM will match the biometric features with the database store in the SD card, then store the facial features and the iris images in the SD card by block device driver as the SD card belongs to the block device. The SD card can make up the defect of small storage capacity of the embedded system. As the Linux kernel has supported the SD card perfectly, we just have to change some kernel configuration and add the hot plug function of the SD card. At last, we mount the SD card to the file node of the block device we create in the application program. In this way, we can read and write the SD card just like the operation of a common file.

5   Experimental Results

In view of the above design, we make the experiment by PTZ camera we already introduced in paper [7] and the dual-core system. Our DSP development board has a 32MB SDRAM and 256KB RAM, we allocate 128KB RAM as the Cache. The ARM development board we used is based on ARM1176JZF-S core, dominant frequency is 667MHz and it has 256 DDR SDRAM and 2GB NAND Flash. Figure 6 shows the picture of our dual-core embedded system.

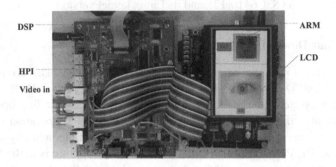

Fig. 6. The experimental platform of the dual-core embedded system

The maximum transmission rate of HPI we design can be 4MB/s through the HPI device driver. We can easily store the facial features and images of faces and iris in the SD card and automatic classification by the recognition results. We can store about 0.4 million face or iris images with resolution of 640×480 pixels. Compared to the single processor based on the DSP which has only 32MB SDRAM in our previous work[7], this system has bigger storage space which can be as big as 32GB, which means we can store a thousand times of biometric features than the single DSP.

All the program code is stored in the DSP's rest RAM and the data like the cascade classifiers and features are stored in the SDRAM. In the DSP program, all the floating variables and operations in the system are replaced with the fixed point counterpart. The time of extraction of face and iris running based on the algorithm of LBP and Gabor on the DSP core is about 160ms.The recognition performance is related to the specific biometric algorithm, and this paper focuses on the design and implementation of the hardware platform of the dual-core embedded system, so we don't evaluate the recognition rate.The results shows that the dual-core embedded system has acceptable speed and it can also store huge numbers of biometric images which can be used as the database for deep research.

6   Conclusions

This paper describes an embedded multiple biometric acquisition and identification system. The face/iris detection and recognition are implemented. The system can also store the facial features and iris images automatically in few seconds. According to the characteristics of ARM and DSP, we make full use of the advantages of ARM in system control and the DSP in image processing. By the use of HPI device driver based on embedded Linux system, reliable communication and data exchange are available between the two processers. In future study, we will focus on the cutting and integration of our experimental system. And as the Linux system has excellent network function, the encrypt transmissions of facial and iris features through Internet is also needed.

Acknowledgements. This work is supported by National Science Foundation of China (No. 60905012, 60572058) and International Fund of Beijing Institute of Technology.

References

1. Klugler, D.: Advance security mechanisms for machine readable travel documents, Technical report, Federal Office for Information Security (BSI), Germany (2005)
2. Kumar, V.K.N.: Internet Passport Authentication System Using Multiple Biometric Identification Technology. International Journal of Information Technology and Computer Science 5(3), 79–89 (2013)
3. Pun, K.H., Moon, Y.S., Tsang, C.C., Chow, C.T., Chan, S.M.: A face recognition embedded system. In: Defense and Security. International Society for Optics and Photonics (2005)
4. Yoo, J.H., Ko, J.G., Chung, Y.S., Jung, S.U., Kim, K.H., Moon, K.Y., Chung, K.: Design of Embedded Multimodal Biometric Systems. In: 3rd International IEEE Conference on Signal-Image Technologies and Internet-Based System, pp. 1058–1062 (2007)
5. Wang, Y., He, Y., Hou, Y., Liu, T.: Design Method of ARM Based Embedded Iris Recognition System. In: International Symposium on Photoeletronic Detection and Imaging: Technology and Applications, ISPDI (2007)
6. Hentati, R., Bousselmi, M., Abid, M.: An Embedded System for Iris Recognition. In: 5th International Conference on Design and Technology of Integrated Systems in Nanoscale Era, Hammamet (2010)
7. Gan, C., He, Y., Li, J., Ren, H., Wang, J.: An Embedded Self-adaptive Iris Image Acquisition System in a Large Working Volume. In: Sun, Z., Shan, S., Yang, G., Zhou, J., Wang, Y., Yin, Y. (eds.) CCBR 2013. LNCS, vol. 8232, pp. 361–369. Springer, Heidelberg (2013)
8. Zhu, X.J., Xie, M.: Multiple Biometric Recognition System with the Function of Real-time Display. In: 2007 5th International Conference on Communications, Circuits and Systems, pp. 990–994 (2007)
9. Viola, P., Jones, M.: Robust real-time face detection. International Journal of Computer Vision 57(2), 137–154 (2004)
10. Dong, W., Sun, Z., Tan, T.: A design of iris recognition system at a distance In: Proceedings of the Chinese Conference on Pattern Recognition (CCPR), pp. 553–559 (2009)
11. Texas instruments incorporated. TMS320C6000 DSP host port interface(HPI) reference guide[EB/OL], http://www.ti.com
12. Samsung electronics incorporated. S3C6410X_User's Manual_Rev1.10[EB/OL], http://www.samsungsemi.com

Standardization of Gas Sensors
in a Breath Analysis System

Yujing Ning, Guangming Lu, Ke Yan, and Xia Zhang

Shenzhen Graduate School, Harbin Institute of Technology, Shenzhen, China
luguangm@hit.edu.cn

Abstract. Breath analysis systembased on electronic nose(e-nose) uses gas sensors to detect biomarkers in breath. Then the health situation of peoplecanbe estimated by analyzing the responses of the sensors. As we know,Even for the same kind of gas sensor, the physical and chemical characteristics of each copy are not same. Therefore, theoutput results are usually not same when measuring the same sample by different breath analysis devices of the same model.This situation will greatly confine the application of the devices. In this paper, a self-designed breath analysis system isintroduced, then, a standardization method is proposed to counteraction the individual difference.The results show that our method is effective. It reduces the error caused by the device variance.

Keywords: e-nose, breath analysis, gas sensor, standardization.

1 Introduction

Breath analysis is a noninvasive approach for clinical applications. By analyzing the concentrations of the biomarkers in breath, we are able to detect disease, monitor disease progression or therapy [1].Many research results show the validity of breath biomarkers in diseases. For instance,breath concentration of volatile organic compounds (VOCs), such as cyclododecatriene, benzoic acid, and benzene, are much higher in lung cancer patients'breath than in control groups [2], acetone is more abundant in the breath of diabetics [3], andammonia is significantly elevated in patients with renal diseases[4].

Compared with other methods, such as blood test and urine test, breath analysis has many advantages. Firstly, breath analysis is a noninvasive method, and it is painless to users. Secondly, the test resultscan beobtained immediately since the breath analysis system can work in real time. Lastly, the sample collecting process is easy.The users can do it by themselves.

With the development of sensor technology, the electronic nose (e-nose) for breath analysis has drawn much attention.E-nose is an instrument that combines gas sensor array and pattern analysis techniques for the detection, identification, or quantification of volatile compounds [5]. As we know,even for the same kind of gas sensor, the outputs of different copiesare different from each other because of their physical or chemical characteristics.Furthermore, the components, such as integrated chips,

Z. Sun et al. (Eds.): CCBR 2014, LNCS 8833 , pp. 434–441, 2014.

resistors and capacitor in one e-nose, also have a certain error range. All of these influence the output results when taking the same sample by two e-noses of the same model.This kind of situation will greatly influence the application of the devices, so the e-nose standardization step is necessary before releasing.

This paper focuses on the individual differences of the designed e-noses, and proposes an e-nose standardization method to reduce the differences.At first, we use different e-noses to measure the standard gas dataset. Then, a standardization model is built so that the data collected by one e-nose can be standardized to the reference e-nose's response. The experiments show that the proposed method is effective.

2   The Self-designed e-nose

The self-designed breath analysis system includes two parts: a device to measure breath and a set of algorithms to analysis the data. Fig. 1 shows the working flow of breath analysis device.

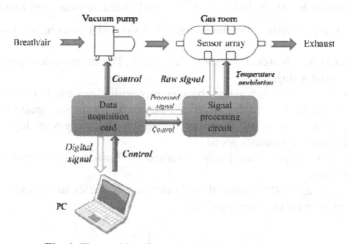

Fig. 1. The working flow of self-designed e-nose

The appearance of the breath analysis device is shown in Fig.2(a). There is one rubber tube on the top of the device, which connects to the gas chamber within the system. The gas isinjected into the gas chamber by a micro vacuum pump. The gas chamber contains a sensor array whichcan measure the gas. Then the signals of the sensorsarefiltered, amplified, digitized and sent to computer for further analysis.

The sensor array comprises 11 gas sensors (S1-S11) to measure the VOCs, carbon dioxide, humidity and temperature in breath samples, including 6 ordinary metal oxide semiconductor (MOS) sensors, 3 temperature modulated MOS sensors, one carbon dioxide sensor, and one temperature-humidity sensor.

Fig. 2(b) shows how the subject's breath is collected into a Tedlargas bag. The person is asked to take a deep breath into the gas bag through a disposable mouthpiece after 10-15 minutes calm breath. There is an airtight box between the mouthpiece and the gas bag which is filled with disposable hygroscopic material to absorb the water vapor in the breath. The hygroscopic material is silica gel which is stable and does not react with the components involved in the breath samples. Then the gasbag is plugged onto the connector of the device and the computer software will control the device to finish the measurement process automatically.

 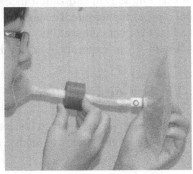

(a) breath analysis device   (b) Exhaled air is collected with a gas bag

Fig. 2. Snapshot of the breath analysis device and its working interface

Two typical breath signalsare shown in Fig. 3. The measurement processwill take 144s and consist 4 stages.

1) Baseline stage (1s): purge the chamber with clean air. Let sensors stay in a steady state. Record the values of baseline for future data analysis.

2) Injection stage (7s): Pump is turned on. Breath gas is injected into the chamber at a constant speed.

3) Reaction stage (56s): Pump is turnedoff. Sensors are reacting with the gas particles.

4) Purge stage (80s): Purge the chamber again. Fresh air is drawn into the gas room to push the breath gas out.

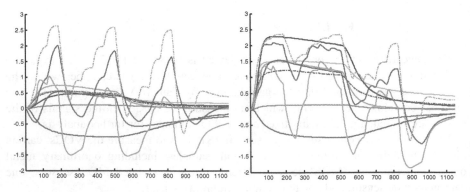

Fig. 3. Two typical breath signals: Healthy sample(left), and diabetic sample (right)

The data analysis part includes signal preprocessing, feature extraction, standardization and classification, as shown in Fig. 4.

Signal preprocessing can eliminate the irrelevant information and compensate the drift. For each gas sensor, the baseline value is estimated by its average response in the baseline stage. Then it is subtracted from the response of the corresponding sensor.

Feature extraction is to find a low-dimensional mapping $f: x \in R^N \to y \in R^M$ ($M < N$) that preserves most of information in the original feature vector x [7]. For this breath analysis system, we employed discrete wavelet transform to extract features of samples, and we find that Haar wavelet has good performance.

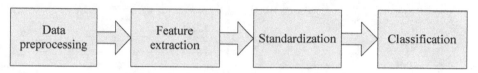

Fig. 4. The working flow of data analysis stage

As the key part of this paper, the standardization stage will be introduced in details in the next section. Finally, support vector machine (SVM) with a Gaussian kernel is used as a classifier for the features.

3   Device Standardization Method Based on Least Square Linear Fitting

From experiments, we observe that the output signals are different when we use two devices with the same type sensor array to measure the same sample, then, the purpose of standardization is to unify the data.

For standardization, some standard gas is necessary. Here, we choose acetone and hydrogen as standard gas since they are the main component in breath, especially in diabetesor dyspepsiapatients' breath. According to [3], the concentration of breath acetone in healthy subjects is ranged from 0.22 to 0.80 ppm, while that in subjects with type 2 diabetes is from 1.76 to 3.73 ppm. For subjects with type 1 diabetes, breath acetone could be as high as 21 ppm [9]. So we prepared acetone and hydrogen samples in 8 kinds of concentration (0.1, 0.2, 0.5, 1, 2, 5, 10, 20 ppm).For each device, we measure the same sample twice. Then we get 16 output data for each device.

In the sensor array, there are three sensors (S1,S2,S3)particularly sensitive to acetone gas and four sensors (S4, S5, S6, S7) sensitive to hydrogen gas. Thus, we take an observation on these sensors when we measure one standard gas sample. The differences are obvious, as shown in Fig. 5. The blue lines and red lines stand for the output of sensors in device 1 and device 2, respectively. However, the signals have the same characteristics since they go up or fall down at the same time. We can consider to standardize the output data by fitting methods.

There are many fitting algorithms, such as linear, nonlinear, univariate, and multivariate methods. For linear and univariate fitting algorithm, the models are relatively simple and the variances are small. The nonlinear and multivariate fitting algorithms can construct complex models, but they also have large variance, which may lead to overfitting.

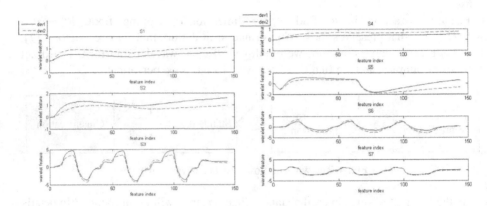

Fig. 5. The output of the same type sensor in two devices: acetone gas (left), hydrogen gas (right)

Since the maximum value can effectively reflect the changing of the sensor [10]. We extract the maximum value of the Haar wavelet feature of each sensor from the 8 kinds of concentration samples. As it shows in Fig. 6, each mark stands for a sensor. It is clear to see that these 16 points of each sensor lies in a line. So we use least square linear fitting algorithm on the features.

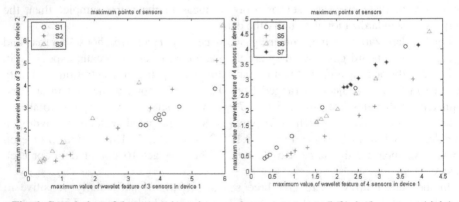

Fig. 6. Correlation of the sensors' maximum values: acetone gas (left), hydrogen gas (right)

Least square fitting minimizes the sum of the errors' squares to find a function thatfits the data best. By counting the points(x_iy_i)we get a curve $y = \varphi x$which let the partial bias to be the smallest.

$$\min \sum_{i=1}^{m} \delta_i^2 = \sum_{i=1}^{m} (\varphi(x_i) - y_i)^2 \tag{1}$$

Let the data measured on device 1 to be$x_{i,j}$i $= 1,2 \dots m$j $= 1,2 \dots$ n, and take device 1 as the slave device. Let the data measured on device 2 to be$y_{i,j}$($i = 1,2, \dots, m$) ($j = 1,2 \dots$ n), and take device 2 as the master device. Here the index j ranges from 1 to 16, andthe index i stands for the feature index that we extracted by Haarwavelet. Sothe standardization model is

$$y_{i,j} = a_i x_{i,j} + b_i \tag{2}$$

wherea_i, b_irepresent the standardization coefficients of the $i'th$ feature. The fitting results are shown in Fig. 7.

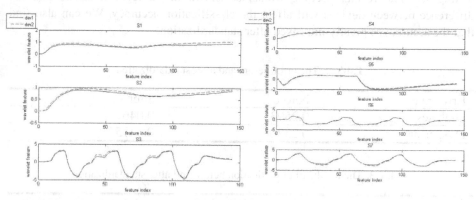

Fig. 7. The fitting results: acetone (left), hydrogen (right)

4 Experiments and Analysis

In order to evaluate the efficiency of standardization, we construct a dataset from health people, the simulated diabetes patients and dyspepsia patients. The simulated diabetes and dyspepsiasamples are gotten by mixing acetone and hydrogen into healthy people's breath, respectively, as shown in Table 1.

Table 1. The number of samples collected by two devices

Samples	Device 1	Device 2
Healthy people	48	48
Simulated Diabetes patients	40	40
Simulated Dyspepsia patients	40	40

After the least square linear fitting on device 1(slave device) and 2 (master device), we have got a set of coefficients based on the standard gas samples, then we can use the standardization coefficients to standardize the sample data output by device 1 to make it close to device 2. Here we present two ways to evaluate the effect of standardization.

First, we define the average error between two devicesas

$$Error = \frac{1}{mn} \sum_{j=1}^{n} \sum_{i=1}^{m} (x_{i,j} - y_{i,j})^2 \tag{3}$$

Where the index i stands for the feature index that we extracted by Haarwavelet, the index j stands for the sample numbers. The smaller it is, the more similar between the two devices. Table 2 shows the results.

Second, we can prove the standardization results by classifying the healthy people and simulated patients. If the training dataset and testing dataset are both from device 1, the classification accuracy rate is 93.24%. If we take the sample data collected by device 2 to be the training set, and the sample data collected by device 1 to be the testing set. The results become worse, as shown in Table 3. It shows that the difference between devices will affect the classification accuracy. We can also find that the accuracy is greatly improved after standardization.

Table 2. The error before and after standardization

Error rate	before	after
Diabetes	0.2593	0.0467
Dyspepsia	0.2520	0.0475

Table 3. The results of classification before and after standardization

Accuracy rate	Before standardization	After standardization
Diabetes	64.41%	86.62%
Dyspepsia	62.53%	87.42%

5 Conclusion

In this paper, the problem of individual difference between e-nose has been studied, device standardization is achieved by applying the least square algorithm. The experiments proved that the difference between two devices' responses have been decreased indeed after standardization.The errors between device 1 and 2 are decreased and the classification accuracy is increased.

Acknowledgments. The work is supported by the NSFC fund (61020106004, 61271344, 61332011), and Key Laboratory of Network Oriented Intelligent Computation, Shenzhen, China.

References

1. Risby, T.H., Solga, S.: Current status of clinical breath analysis. Appl. Phys. B: Lasers Opt. 85(2-3), 421–426 (2006)
2. Phillips, M., Altorki, N., Austin, J., Cameron, R., Cataneo, R., Greenberg, J., Kloss, R., Maxfield, R., Munawar, M., Pass, H., et al.: Prediction of lung cancer using volatile biomarkers in breath. Cancer Biomarkers 3(2), 95–109 (2007)
3. Deng, C., Zhang, J., Yu, X., Zhang, W., Zhang, X.: Determination of acetone in human breath by gas chromatography–mass spectrometry and solid-phase microex-traction with on-fiber derivatization. Journal of Chromatography B 810(2), 269–275 (2004)
4. Davies, S., Spanel, P., Smith, D.: Quantitative analysis of ammonia on the breath of patients in end-stage renal failure. Kidney International 52(1), 223–228 (1997)
5. Gutierrez-Osuna, R.: Pattern analysis for machine olfaction: a review. IEEE Sens. J. 2, 189–202 (2002)
6. Yan, K., Zhang, D., Wu, D., Wei, H., Lu, G.: Design of a breath analysis system for diabetes screening and blood glucose level prediction. IEEE Trans. Biomed. Eng., 1–9 (2014)
7. Balaban, M.O., Korel, A.Z., Folkes, R.G.: Transportability of data between electronic noses: mathematical methods. Sens. Actuators B: Chem. 71(3), 203–211 (2000)
8. Distante, C., Leo, M., Siciliano, P., Persaud, K.: On the study of feature extraction methods for an electronic nose. Sensors and Actuators B: Chemical 87(2), 274–288 (2007)
9. Turner, C., Walton, C., Hoashi, S., Evans, M.: Breath acetone concentration decreases with blood glucose concentration in type I diabetes mellitus patients during hypoglycaemic clamps. J. Breath Res. 3(4), 46004 (2009)
10. Guo, D., Zhang, D.: A novel breath analysis system based on electronic olfaction. IEEE Transactions on Biomedical Engineering 57(11), 2753–2763 (2010)

Discriminative Super-Resolution Method
for Low-Resolution Ear Recognition

Shuang Luo, Zhichun Mu, Baoqing Zhang

School of Automatic, University of Science and Technology Beijing
Beijing 100083, China
Mu@ies.ustb.edu.cn

Abstract. The available images of biometrics recognition system in real-world applications are often degraded and of low-resolution, making the acquired images contain less detail information. Therefore, biometrics recognition of the low-resolution image is a challenging problem. It has received increasing attention in recent years. In this paper, a two-step ear recognition scheme based on super-resolution is proposed, which will contribute to both human-based and machine-based recognition. Unlike most standard super-resolution methods which aim to improve the visual quality of ordinary images, the proposed super-resolution based method is designed to improve the recognition performance of low-resolution ear image, which uses LC-KSVD algorithm to learn much more discriminative atoms of the dictionary. When applied to low-resolution ear recognition problem, the proposed method achieves better recognition performance compared with the present super-resolution method.

Keywords: Super-resolution, Low-resolution, Ear recognition, Label constraint dictionary learning, Sparse coding.

1   Introduction

Biometrics, the technology of identifying or verifying an individual based on human physiological or behavioral characteristics, has been a hotspot of modern security technique development in the past few years [1]. Because of its special merits, the interest in ear recognition has grown significantly. Even though current ear recognition systems have reached a certain level of maturity, their success is limited to high-resolution ear images acquired in controlled conditions [2], [3]. However, under uncontrolled environment, the quality of the acquired images always varies with changes of the imaging conditions such as illumination, distance, device, etc. The resolution of image obtained from the above scenarios makes it difficult to perform perfect recognition. Low-resolution recognition describes a situation that images in probe and gallery set have different dimensions, referring to matching low-resolution images with high-resolution images. Generally speaking, there exist two kinds of methods to solve the low-resolution recognition problem. One is two-step method which focuses on reconstructing high-resolution (HR) image from one or more observed low-resolution (LR) images, and then recognizes with HR image. The other one is the direct method, such as work in [4].

Z. Sun et al. (Eds.): CCBR 2014, LNCS 8833 , pp. 442–450, 2014.

In general, the super-resolution reconstruction method is an ill-posed problem. In order to solve this problem, many approaches have been developed. Baker et al. [5] proposed a Gaussian pyramid based method and reconstructed HR images by finding the nearest gradient vector in training data according to the input LR image. Freeman et al. [6] described the LR image and the HR image as a Markov network in which LR image and HR image were divided into small patches separately. Wang et al. [7] proposed a global method that used PCA to find the observed LR face image relationship with the training LR images, and then reconstructed the HR image by using this relationship. Previous methods aimed to reconstruct better visual quality of images. With the development of signal processing technology and compressive sensing theory, sparse coding is considered as a good way for data representation. Yang et al. [8] applied sparse coding model on both HR and LR image patch space to learn dictionaries, and then obtained the HR image. This method achieved good results. Then, Zeyde et al. [9] improved Yang's method and proposed a super-resolution method using K-SVD algorithm to train dictionary, which achieved less visual artifacts and produced sharper result with the improvement of peak signal to noise ratio (PSNR). The above super-resolution approaches tended to reconstruct detail feature. But they didn't take into account the prior knowledge of special feature like structure and class information of human face or ear. These key discriminative features, in fact, may be important for face or ear recognition. In real-world ear recognition system, most of existing super-resolution-based methods can obtain a good appearance of LR ear image. But they maybe lack of discriminative information which contributes to recognition performance. Therefore, in this paper, a two-step ear recognition method based on super-resolution is proposed so as to adapt to special features and reconstruct HR ear image from LR ear image. The proposed super-resolution-based method uses learned dictionary which takes label information as discriminative constraint to reconstruct ear image.

2   Background and Related Work

The basic idea of super-resolution method based on sparse coding aims to find the sparse codes of the input LR image. Then, it assists to utilize the assumption of the same representation of LR and HR until it generates the HR image output. According to the sparse representation, a signal $y \in \Re^n$ can be represented as a sparse linear combination of elements from an over-completed dictionary $D = [d_1, d_2, \ldots, d_k], (k > n)$, which can be represented as $y = D\alpha$, in which α is the sparse codes of   signal y. For an input signal y and the known dictionary D, sparse codes α can be obtained by the following optimization problem:

$$\arg \min_{\alpha} \|y - D\alpha\|_2 + \lambda \|\alpha\|_0 \qquad (1)$$

The above formulation is a L0-norm regularized problem, which is NP-hard. There was research in which the L1 norm can approximate the sparsest solution of L0 norm [13]. Reformulate (1), the minimization of L1 norm is presented as follows:

$$\underset{\alpha}{\arg\min} \|y - D\alpha\|_2 + \lambda \|\alpha\|_1 \tag{2}$$

Yang et al. [8] proposed an approach of super-resolution based on sparse coding. LR dictionary D_l and HR dictionary D_h were obtained from training data by the following optimization:

$$\underset{D_l, D_h, \alpha}{\min} \left\| \tilde{D} \alpha - \tilde{y} \right\|_2^2 + \lambda \|\alpha\|_1 \tag{3}$$

Where $\tilde{D} = \begin{bmatrix} FD_l \\ \beta P D_h \end{bmatrix}$ and $\tilde{y} = \begin{bmatrix} Fy \\ \beta w \end{bmatrix}$, F is feature extraction operator, y is LR patch of training data, λ is weighting factor, P extracts the region of overlap patch, w contains overlap values of HR image. By optimizing (3), sparse codes α can be achieved. Thus, the HR image patch can be reconstructed as $x = D_h\alpha$, supposing that LR image and corresponding HR image have the same sparse codes.

Zeyde et al. [9] trained the LR and HR dictionaries in a different way. They firstly trained LR dictionary D_l and obtained the sparse codes α by the following optimization:

$$\underset{D_l, \alpha}{\arg\min} \|y - D_l\alpha\|_2 + \lambda \|\alpha\|_0 \tag{4}$$

y is the LR patch in training data. Efficient K-SVD dictionary learning algorithm was applied to solve (4). After that, the HR dictionary D_h was trained in order to satisfy the similarity between LR and the corresponding HR image as follows:

$$D_h = \underset{D_h}{\arg\min} \|x - D_h\alpha\|_2^2 \tag{5}$$

Where x represents the HR patch in training data. In their solution, Pseudo-Inverse method was applied to solve (5). In the reconstruction stage, the sparse codes of an input LR image were obtained by using Orthogonal Matching Pursuit (OMP) algorithm. The corresponding HR image was reconstructed using the same sparse coding of LR image.

In both [8] and [9], solving the L1-norm problem like (2) is computationally demanding, which is a limit for real-time applications. For this reason, Timofte et al. [10] proposed more efficient super-resolution methods referring to Global Regression (GR) and Anchored Neighborhood Regression (ANR), in which Global Regression was an efficient offline method and it contributed to real-time applications. They reformulated the reconstruction problem as a least square regression regularized by the L2-norm. Their method of reconstruction stage is the following optimization:

$$\min_{\beta} \| y - N_l\beta \|_2^2 + \lambda \| \beta \|_2 \tag{6}$$

In their formulation, y is the input LR feature, N_l corresponds to the neighborhood in LR space, β is the coefficient. The solution of (6) is a Ridge Regression problem which has a closed-form. This method retains the qualitative performance of state-of-art methods, and at the same time is very efficient.

3   The Proposed Method

In the two-step low-resolution ear recognition method, our goal is to reconstruct good visual quality of LR ear image and to improve the performance of recognition. Therefore prior knowledge is generally introduced. In the prior knowledge of ear image, label information might not be ignored. Jiang et al. [11] proposed a dictionary learning method incorporating both reconstruction error and classification error. It optimized it via using the K-SVD algorithm, referring to LC-KSVD algorithm. Inspired by the work of [10] and [11], we propose an efficient super-resolution approach for LR ear image in order to remain both high frequency detail and discriminative information. The proposed method includes three main steps. Step 1 is prepared for training data. Step 2 is the training dictionary stage. Step 3 is the reconstruction stage.

1)   For every original HR ear image in training data $z_i \in \Re^N$, LR training data is obtained by removing its high frequency information through two-time interpolation (first scale down and then scale up). In our notation, LR training data is represented as $z_l^i \in \Re^N = (z_i \downarrow)\uparrow$. To get HR training data, the low frequency information is removed from the original HR training image by this operation: $z_h^i = z_i - z_l^i$. LR and HR training data are image vectors which are represented as $z_l = \{z_l^1, z_l^2, \ldots, z_l^i\}$ and $z_h = \{z_h^1, z_h^2, \ldots, z_h^i\}$. The first and second gradient features in four directions based on image patch of size $\sqrt{n} \times \sqrt{n}$ are extracted for feature by operator $R_k : \Re^N \to \Re^n$, in which k means the location k of the i-th image. $p_l^k = R_k \times z_l$. $p_h^k = R_k \times z_h$ is the patch-based feature. In order to reduce the time of training dictionary, PCA method is applied on the patch feature vector for reducing dimension. The patch-based training feature vector $\{p_l^k\}$ and $\{p_h^k\}$ are finished for dictionary learning.

2)   According to the LC-KSVD algorithm, in order to train a discriminative dictionary, class label matrix $H = [h_1, h_2, \ldots, h_k] \in \Re^{M \times k}$ (M means class number of training data) is needed, in which each vector

$h_i = [0,0,\ldots1\ldots0,0]^T \in \Re^M$ is corresponding to an input patch p_l^k. In this step, sparse codes X and LR dictionary D_l are obtained by optimizing the objective function

$$< D_l, A, X >= \arg\min_{D_l, A, X} \left\| p_l^k - D_l X \right\|_2^2 + \alpha \left\| Q - AX \right\|_2^2 \quad s.t. \forall i, \left\| x_i \right\|_0 \le T.$$

A is a linear transformation matrix. $Q = [q_1, q_2, \ldots, q_N]$ is the 'discriminative' sparse codes of input $\{p_l^k\}$, computed by H showed in [11]. α balances the reconstructive and discriminative power of learned dictionary. If we assume that $\{p_l^k\}$ and the corresponding $\{p_h^k\}$ have the same discriminative sparse codes X. HR dictionary D_h can be computed by $\{p_h^k\} = D_h X$.

3) In this step, for a given LR ear image y in testing data, the same method in step 1 is applied to extract patch feature $\{y_l^k\}$. Calculate a projection matrix P through using Global Regression method in [10]. The HR patches $\{y_h^k\}$ can be directly obtained by $\{y_l^k\} * P$ using the same constraints of the formulation (6).

The algorithm of super-resolution is shown as follows:

Algorithm: Label-constraint GR super-resolution

Input: $\{p_l^k\}, \{p_h^k\}, H, \alpha, T, y_l^i$

Output: y_h^i

1. Initialize $D^{(0)}$ with H using K-SVD; Initialize Q with $D^{(0)}$ and H; Initialize $X^{(0)}$; Compute $A^{(0)}$ by $A = QX^T(XX^t + I)^{-1}$.

2. Define $y_{new} = \begin{pmatrix} \{p_l^k\} \\ \sqrt{\alpha}Q \end{pmatrix}, D_{new} = \begin{pmatrix} D^{(0)} \\ \sqrt{\alpha}A^{(0)} \end{pmatrix}$; Solve

$$< D_{new}, X >= \arg\min_{D_{new}, X} \{\left\| Y_{new} - D_{new} X \right\|_2^2\} \quad s.t. \forall i, \left\| x_i \right\|_0 \le T \text{ using K-SVD}$$

to update D_{new}; Obtain X and D_l from D_{new}.

3. Compute $D_h = (\{p_h^k\}) X^T (XX^T)^{-1}$.

4. Compute $P = D_h (D_l^T D_l + \lambda I)^{-1} D_l^T$.

5. Compute HR patch $y_h^i = P * y_l^i$.

In our notations, y_l^i is the i-th image (the LR image of testing data). y_h^i is the corresponding HR image after reconstruction. $\{p_l^k\}$ and $\{p_h^k\}$ are image patches of training data for dictionary learning.

4 Experimental Result

In this section, we carry out experiments on both subsets of UND and USTB II ear database. Firstly, we show the reconstruction result of our proposed method from 20×12 LR ear images to 60×36 HR ear images (reconstruction result is 54×30 as a result of overlap patches) when the scale factor is defined as 3. Secondly, we use PCA method as a baseline to test the recognition performance of reconstruction ear image of our method with the super-resolution method of original Global Regression.

4.1 Experiment on UND Ear Database

The ear images in UND database contain different poses and illumination of each ear. In our experiment, we choose 400 car images of 200 people (about two ear images per person) from UND database Collection J2 [12] as training set, from which we choose 61 ear images (about one ear image per person) as probe set and 264 ear images(about four ear images per person) as gallery set. In our experiment, training image patch is 3×3 with overlap of 1 pixel between adjacent patches. Fig. 1 demonstrates visual result of super-resolution methods.

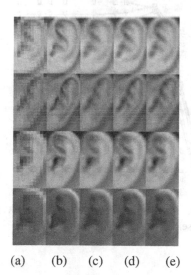

(a)   (b)   (c)   (d)   (e)

Fig. 1. Super-resolution result on the UND database (a) Input LR image (b) Original HR image (c) Bicubic interpolation (d) GR of [10] (e) Our method.

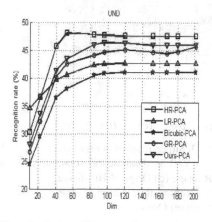

Fig. 2. Recognition result on the UND database.

Table 1 shows the average PSNR of the entire ear images in probe set when using different dictionary size. The results show that the PSNR of our method is slightly below GR method. In Fig. 2, the dictionary size of reconstruction is 200. Our method achieves a higher recognition rate than GR method. In our experiment, when the dictionary is much larger, the reconstruction result may obtain the same recognition rate of the original image. LR-PCA (HR-PCA) means matching LR (HR) ear image to LR (HR) ear image through using PCA method. Experiment on USTB II Ear Database

For experiment on USTB II database, we choose 80 ear images (four images per person) as the probe set, and the other 80 ear images as gallery set. We choose the gallery set for training data of PCA. Fig. 3 shows the reconstruction result of ear images. Table 2 shows PSNR result of USTB II database. In Fig. 4, the size of the learned dictionary is 200. The recognition rate of LR-PCA and GR-PCA are almost the same after 100-D features. Recognition rate of our method is higher than the GR method.

Experiment on both UND and USTB show that recognition rate of LR-PCA is higher than Bicubic-PCA. This result indicates that the resolution of pure ear image may not be the key factor of recognition performance. We will do more experiments on this in the future.

(a)   (b)   (c)   (d)   (e)

Fig. 3. Super-resolution result on the USTB II database (a) Input LR image (b) Original HR image (c) Bicubic interpolation (d) GR of [10] (e) Our method

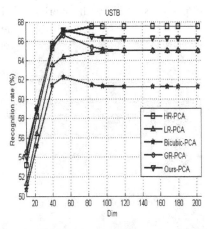

Fig. 4. Recognition result on the USTB II database.

Table 1. PSNR on UND database

Dictio nary size	PSNR		
	Bicubic	GR of [10]	ours
200	30.39	32.54	32.22
400	30.39	32.55	32.42
800	30.39	32.53	32.28
1200	30.39	32.53	32.40

Table 2. PSNR on USTB II database

Dictio nary size	PSNR		
	Bicubic	GR of [10]	ours
200	31.33	33.14	32.79
400	31.33	33.14	32.90
800	31.33	33.15	32.80
1200	31.33	33.14	32.97

5   Conclusions

In this paper, a two-step low-resolution ear recognition scheme based on super-resolution is proposed. Compared with the existing method, the proposed method in the paper utilizes more discriminative information. We therefore achieve better recognition performance with good visual quality of images.

Acknowledgments. This paper is supported by (1) National Natural Science Foundation of China under the Grant No. 61170116; (2) National Natural Science Foundation of China under the Grant No. 60973064; (3) Fundamental Research Funds for the Central Universities (FRF-SD-12017A).

References

1. Jain, A.K., Flynn, P., Ross, A.A.: Handbook of Biometrics. Springer (2007)
2. Mu, Z., Yuan, L., Xu, Z., Xi, D., Qi, S.: Shape and Structural Feature Based Ear Recognition. In: Proceedings of the 5th Chinese Conference on Biometric Recognition, Guangzhou, China, pp. 663–670 (2004)
3. Zhang, B., Mu, Z., Li, C., et al.: Robust Classification for Occluded Ear via Gabor Scale Feature-Based Non-negative Sparse Representation. Optical Engineering 53(6), 061702 (2013)
4. Li, B., Chang, H., Shan, S., et al.: Low-resolution Face Recognition via Coupled Locality Preserving Mappings [J]. IEEE Signal Processing Letters 17(1), 20–23 (2010)
5. Baker, S., Kanade, T.: Hallucinating Faces. In: Proceedings. Fourth IEEE International Conference on Automatic Face and Gesture Recognition, 2000, pp. 83–88. IEEE (2000)
6. Freeman, W.T., Pasztor, E.C., Carmichael, O.T.: Learning Low-level Vision [J]. International Journal of Computer Vision 40(1), 25–47 (2000)
7. Wang, X., Tang, X.: Hallucinating Face by Eigentransformation. IEEE Transactions on Systems, Man, and Cybernetics, Part C: Applications and Reviews 35(3), 425–434 (2005)
8. Yang, J., Wright, J., Huang, T.S., et al.: Image Super-resolution via Sparse Representation. IEEE Transactions on Image Processing 19(11), 2861–2873 (2010)
9. Zeyde, R., Elad, M., Protter, M.: On single image scale-up using sparse-representations. In: Boissonnat, J.-D., Chenin, P., Cohen, A., Gout, C., Lyche, T., Mazure, M.-L., Schumaker, L. (eds.) Curves and Surfaces 2011. LNCS, vol. 6920, pp. 711–730. Springer, Heidelberg (2012)

450   S. Luo, Z. Mu, B. Zhang

10. Timofte, R., Smet, V.D., Gool, L.V.: Anchored Neighborhood Regression for Fast Example-based Super-resolution. In: IEEE Int. Conf. Computer Vision (2013)
11. Jiang, Z., Lin, Z., Davis, L.S.: Label Consistent K-SVD: Learning A Discriminative Dictionary for Recognition. IEEE Transactions on Pattern Analysis and Machine Intelligence 35(11), 2651–2664 (2013)
12. http://www.cse.nd.edu/~cvrl/CVRL/Data_Sets.html
13. Baraniuk, R.G.: Compressive sensing. IEEE Signal Processing Magazine 24(4) (2007)

Multimodal Finger Feature Recognition
Based on Circular Granulation

Jinjin Peng, Yanan Li, Ruimei Li, Guimin Jia, and Jinfeng Yang

Tianjin Key Lab for Advanced Signal Processing,
Civil Aviation University of China, Tianjin, China
jfyang@cauc.edu.cn

Abstract. Finger has three biometric modalities, fingerprint (FP), finger-vein (FV) and finger-knuckle-print (FKP).Taking these modalities as a whole has a natural advantage in convenience and universality for personal identification. In this paper, a new finger recognition method based on granular computing is proposed. The used granular space consists of three layers and is constructed in a bottom-up manner. For the finger recognition, a coarse-to-fine granular matching scheme is proposed. Experiments are performed on a self-built image database with three modalities to validatethe reliability and performance of the proposed method.

Keywords: Finger-knuckle-print, Finger-vein, Fingerprint, Granular computing, Circularization.

1   Introduction

With the increasing demandof personal authentication accuracy, the traditional unimodal biometric recognition technique has been proved ineffectivein the real situation. Therefore, multimodal biometric techniquehas become an alternative in many applications [1].

The multimodal biometric fusion can be divided into four levels:the pixel level, the feature level, the matching score level and the decision level [2]. Among these levels, the feature level fusion is considered powerful in discrimination. Feature-level fusion is of consideration in feature compatibility and complementarity. Unfortunately, although a lot of work has been done in fusion at feature level, the fusion theory is undesirablein addressing feature fusion problem [3].

GrC is an approach that can solve problems using knowledge from multiple levels of information granularity [4]. Since Zadeh proposed this concept in 1979 [5], GrC has rapidly developed and implemented [6,7].It is also becoming an important problem-solving approach in the artificial intelligence. [8] proposed the tolerance granular computing model and applied it to image segmentation, [9] used granulation method for pedestrian detection, [10] applied granular feature to face recognition. These researches indicate that GrC can have good performance in image analysis and recognition.

Z. Sun et al. (Eds.): CCBR 2014, LNCS 8833 , pp. 451–457, 2014.

In this paper, GrC is used to solve a finger-based recognition problem. Here, a finger trait is composed of FP, FV and FKP. To address the fusion-recognition problem of FP, FV and FKP, this paper proposed a three-layer granular modal. Firstly, we enhance the consistency and compatibility of FP, FV and FKP.The three modalities are normalized to a same aspect. In a granular modal, the construction of the basic granules plays a key role.Therefore, circularization based on minutiae is used to obtain basic granules, whose intension and extension is respectively Gabor feature and circle. Then, a bottom-up multi-granularity granular model based on the basic granules is constructed [8]. The recognition approach is a top-down method. To evaluate the performance of this method, a self-built database with three modalities is used here. The experimental results validate that the method proposed performs reliable and precise in feature fusion and personal identification.

2   Circles Extraction

As minutiae-based features are very informative in FP, FV and FKP images, circularized granulation based on minutiae is introduced to construct the basic granule.

To improve the compatibility of FP, FV and FKP, the images of the three modalities have been normalized to the same size 166×166, as shown in Fig.1. (a) (Left: FP, Middle: FV, Right: FKP). Fig.1. (b) (Left: FP, Middle: FV, Right: FKP)shows the filter results of FP, FV and FKP. Since the imaging principles and texture structures of the three modalities are different, Gabor filter [11] is used to filter FV images, and Steerable filter [12] is applied for filtering FP and FKP images here.

Then, a thresholdmethod in [13] is used to acquire the binary images.The results are provided in Fig.1. (c) (Left: FP, Middle: FV, Right: FKP).In order to provideenough minutiae and ensure that the minutiae in the three modalities are the same, the binary images of the three modalities are superimposed to a fusion binary. The result is show in Fig.1. (d). Then, a thinning algorithm in [13] is used here to extract the skeleton of the fusion binary image, as provided in Fig.1. (e).

In order to extract the minutiae from skeleton image, a cross number concept for a 3×3 regionis used here [14]. After the reductionof feature dimension, the results are shown in Fig.2. (a). Based on the detected minutiae, we can obtain unique circles, as illustrated in Fig.2. (b).

3   Granular Initialization

A granule can be represented by a 2-tuple $G = (IG, EG)$. IGdenotes the intension of the granule, which describes generality characteristic of all objects in the granule. In this paper, IG is represented by $(i_1, i_2, \cdots, i_n)$. EGdenotes the extension of the granule, a set containing all the objects in the granule.

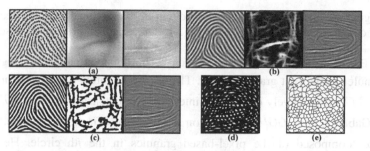

Fig. 1. The preprocessing results (a)Normalization images (b) Filtered images (c) Binary images (d) Combined binary image (e) Skeleton image of (d)

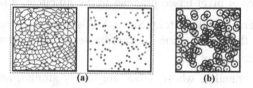

Fig. 2. Circularization (a) Minutiae extraction(b) Circle extraction

Each pixel in an image modality can be regarded as a pixel-basedgranule $G^i_{0_{\text{modal}}}$. The vector expression of $IG^i_{0_{\text{modal}}} \left(= \left(g^{0_i}_{1_{\text{modal}}}, g^{0_i}_{2_{\text{modal}}}, \cdots, g^{0_i}_{8_{\text{modal}}} \right) \right)$ consists of 8 Gabor coefficients obtained by Gabor transformation [11]. $EG^i_{0\,\text{modal}}$ is the ith pixel in an image modality. The granules with the same coordinatein FP FV and FKP images are fused to form an original granule G^i_0 ($i = 1, \cdots, n$).$n$is the number of the pixels in a finger image combined by three image modalities.Here, $IG^i_0 = \left(IG^i_{0_{FP}}, IG^i_{0_{FV}}, IG^i_{0_{FKP}} \right)$, EG^i_0 is the correspondingpixel in the finger image. The fusion process is shown in Fig.3.

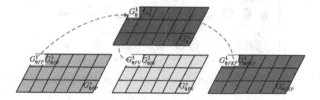

Fig. 3. Three modalities original granules fusion

4 Granulation and Recognition

4.1 Three-Layer Granulation

As mentioned above, a normalized finger image contains 27556 pixels, so GrC process is very time-consuming when using the original pixel-based granules. To improve granular matching efficiency, a bottom-up hierarchical granular recognition model is constructed, as illustrated in Fig. 4. The granular process is described as follows.

Step 1Based on circularization in Section 2.The obtained circles are regarded as basic granules in the first granular-layer. That is, the jth circle is a basic granule. G_1^j, IG_1^j and EG_1^j respectively denote the intension.The extension of G_1^j. IG_1^j consists of local Gabor feature GG_1^j and location information LG_1^j of the granule. EG_1^j is a granule-set composed of the pixel-based granules in the jth circle. Here, GG_1^j $\left(=g_{1FP}^{j1},\cdots,g_{1FP}^{j8},g_{1FV}^{j1},\cdots,g_{1FV}^{j8},g_{1FKP}^{j1},\cdots,g_{1FKP}^{j8}\right)$ is an average absolute deviation (AAD) Gabor feature of pixel-based granules in the jth circle. $LG_1^j\left(=\left(x_j,y_j\right)\right)$ is the coordinate of the center of the circle. Since AADs may be same for two circles in different locations, the introduction of coordinate of the center of the circle can increase the discrimination of IG_1^j.

Step 2The basic granules, whose GG_1s are highly similar, are clustered to form second layer granules by K-means analysis.Here,DBE algorithm is used to obtain the optimal cluster number K[15]. Each cluster is a 2-layer granule G_2^k. IG_2^k and EG_2^k respectively denote the intension and the extension of G_2^k ($k=1,\cdots,K$). GG_2^k is an AAD Gabor feature of the1-layer granules in the kth class.

Step 3 A 3-layer granuleconsists of all the 2-layer granules in a finger image, GG_3 is an AAD Gabor feature of all the2-layer granules. EG_3 contains all the 2- layer granules. Thus, each finger can be represented by a granule G_3.

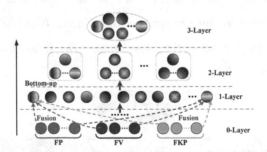

Fig. 4. Threelayer bottom-up granulation process based on fusion original granules

4.2   Recognition

GrC is a method that can solve problem from coarse granularity to fine granularity. Thus, a top-down granular recognition process is conducted here. A granular descriptor (GrD) consists ofGGand LG in the first granular layer. In the second and third granular layer, the GrDs consist of CGs solely. The recognition process is described as follows.

Step 1 The similarity between GrD_3 and GrD_3' of two finger images is measured by $Sim_3 = \cos(GrD_3, GrD_3')$. If $Sim_3 \geq T_3$ (T_3 is the decision threshold in the third granule layer), the two finger images match in the third granule layer. Since the 3-layer granules are extremely coarse, a successful matching behavior in the third granule layer cannot ensure that the two finger images are from the same individual. Then, granule matching in the second granule layer is further conducted.

Step 2 Assume there are M_2 and N_2 2-layer granules in two finger images respectively. $Sim_{2mn} = \cos(GrD_2^m, GrD_2'^n)$ ($m = 1, 2, \cdots, M_2$, $n = 1, 2, \cdots, N_2$) is the similarity between GrD_2^m and $GrD_2'^n$ .If $Sim_{2mn} \geq T_2$ (T_2 is the decision threshold in the second granule layer), the two granules are similar, then the match score of the two finger images in the second layer can be obtained using $Score_2 = 2S_2/(M_2 + N_2)$). If $Score_2 \geq Ts_2$ (Ts_2 is the matching threshold in the second granule layer), the two finger images match in the second granule layer. Since the second layer granules are still relatively coarse, granule matching in the first granule layer is needed.

Step 3 Assume there are M_1 and N_1 1-layer granules in two finger images. The similarity between GG_1^m and $GG_1'^n$ is $Sim_{1mn} = \cos(GG_1^m, GG_1'^n)$ and the distance between LG_1^m and LG_1^n ($m = 1, 2, \cdots, M_1, n = 1, 2, \cdots, N_1$) is Dis_{1mn} .If $Sim_{1mn} \geq T_1$ and $Dis_{1mn} \leq D_1$ (T_1 is the decision threshold and D_1 is the distance thresholdin the first granule layer), the two granules are similar, and the match score of the two finger images in the firstgranule layeris $Score_1 = 2S_1/(M_1 + N_1)$. If $Score_1 \geq Ts_1$ (Ts_1 is the matching threshold in the firstgranule layer), the two finger images match in the firstgranule layer. If $Sim_3 \geq T_3$, $Score_2 \geq Ts_2$, $Score_1 \geq Ts_1$ are satisfied at the same time, the two finger images are believed to be from an identical individual.

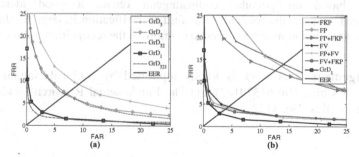

Fig. 5. ROCcurves(a) Comparison of single layer and multi-layer(b) Comparison of single modal and multimodal

5   Experiments

Here,a self-built database which contains 600 finger-vein images, 600 fingerprint images and 600 finger-knuckle-print imagesfrom 60 individuals is used.

In the experiments, circles with radius $r = 8$ is used to obtain basic granules. The thresholds Ts_1, Ts_2 and D_1 are empirical values ($Ts_1 = 0.5$, $Ts_2 = 0.5$, $D_1 = 10$ are using here). Firstly, GrD is used as feature vector for matching in each granular layer solely.Then, multilayer-granular recognition experiments are conducted. The results are shown in Fig. 5. (a). The results of uni-modal and bimodal identifications are shown in Fig. 5. (b). Table.1 illustrates the matching time of a finger image. The experiments (see Fig. 5. (a)) show that the multilayer-granular recognition performs best. The reason is that the discrimination of fine granule is better than that of coarse granule and the discrimination is enhanced using multilayer-granular information. However, Table.1 shows that multilayer-granular recognition can reduce the time cost since the non-matched granules in the high layer are neglected for granule matching in the low layer. As shown in Fig. 5. (b), the results prove that the performance of multimodal identification is better than that of single modal and bimodal.

Table 1. Recognition perfomance

Performance	3-layer	2-layer	3-2-layer	1-layer	3-2-1-layer
EER (%)	9.3	7.1	6.7	2.8	2.1
Time cost (s)	0.026	0.631	0.517	11.265	8.808

6   Conclusion and Future Work

In this paper, a new biological recognition method based on three finger traits (FP, FV and FKP) is proposed. Here,a bottom-up 3-layer granular model is conducted. Base on the same database.Some experiments are conducted. The results show that finger recognition based on granular computingcan obtain a good identification performance. However, the method needs further verification in large databaseand a more proper granulation method is needed to improve the recognition accuracy rate.

Acknowledgement. This work is jointly supported by National Natural Science Foundation of China (No.61379102) and The Fundamental Research Funds for the Central Universities (No. 3122014C003).

References

1. Jain, A.K., Ross, A., Prabhakar, S.: An Introduction to Biometric Recognition. IEEE Transactions on Circuits and Systems for Video Technology 14(1), 4–20 (2004)
2. Gudavalli, M., Babu, A.V., Raju, S.V., Kumar, D.S.: Multimodal Biometrics–sources, Architecture & Fusion Techniques: An Overview. In: International Symposium on Biometrics and Security Technologies, pp. 27–34. IEEE Press, New York (2012)

3. Yang, J., Zhang, X.: Feature-level fusion of fingerprint and finger-vein for personal identification. Pattern Recognition Letters 33(5), 623–628 (2012)
4. Yao, Y.: Interpreting Concept Learning in Cognitive Informatics and Granular Computing. IEEE Transactions on Systems, Man, and Cybernetics 39(4), 855–866 (2009)
5. Zadeh, L.A.: Fuzzy Sets and Information Granulation Advances in Fuzzy Set Theory and Application. North Holland Publishing Press, Netherlands (1979)
6. Bargiela, A., Pedrycz, W.: Toward a Theory of Granular Computing for Human-Centered Information Processing. IEEE Transactions on Fuzzy Systems 16(2), 320–330 (2008)
7. Yao, J., Vasilakos, A.V., Pedrycz, W.: Granular Computing: Perspectives and Challenges. IEEE Transactions On Cybernetics 43(6), 1977–1989 (2013)
8. Zheng, Z.: Image Texture Recognition based on Tolerance Granular Space. Journal of Chongqing University of Posts and Telecommunications 21(4), 484–489 (2009) (in Chinese)
9. Chan, Y., Fu, L., Hsiao, P., Lo, M.: Pedestrian Detection Using Histograms of Oriented Gradients of Granule Feature. In: 4th IEEE Intelligent Vehicles Symposium, pp. 1410–1415. IEEE Press (2013)
10. Bhatt, H.S., Bharadwaj, S., Singh, R., Vatsa, M.: Recognizing Surgically Altered Face Images using Multi-objective Evolutionary Algorithm. IEEE Transactions on Information Forensics and Security 8, 89–100 (2013)
11. Yang, J., Shi, Y.: Finger-Vein ROI Localization and Vein Ridge Enhancement. Pattern Recognition Letters 33(12), 1569–1579 (2012)
12. Freeman, W.T., Adelson, E.H.: The Design and Use of Steerable Filter. In: IEEE Transaction on Pattern Analysis and Machine Intelligence, pp. 891–906. IEEE Press, New York (1991)
13. Vlachos, M., Dermatas, E.: Vein segmentation in infrared images using compound enhancing and crisp clustering. In: Gasteratos, A., Vincze, M., Tsotsos, J.K. (eds.) ICVS 2008. LNCS, vol. 5008, pp. 393–402. Springer, Heidelberg (2008)
14. Yu, C., Qin, H., Zhang, L., Cui, Y.: Finger-Vein Image Recognition Combining Modified Hausdorff Distance with Minutiae Feature Matching. Journal of Biomedical Science and Engineering 1(4), 280–289 (2009)
15. Wang, L., Leckie, C., Ramamohanarao, K., et al.: Automatically Determining the Number of Clusters in Unlabeled Data Sets. IEEE Transactions on Knowledge and Data Engineering 21(3), 335–350 (2009)

A Multimodal Finger-Based Recognition Method Based on Granular Computing

Yanan Li, Jinjin Peng, Zhen Zhong, Guimin Jia, and Jinfeng Yang

Tianjin Key Lab for Advanced Signal Processing
Civil Aviation University of China, Tianjin, China
jfyang@cauc.edu.cn

Abstract. Finger-based biometrics is widely used in identity authentication. In this paper, viewing fingerprint (FP), finger-knuckle-print (FKP) and finger-vein (FV) as the constitutions of finger trait, a new multimodal finger-based recognition scheme is proposed based on granular computing (GrC). First, the ridge texture features of FP, FV and FKP are extracted using the feature extraction scheme of Orientation coding and Magnitude coding (OrientCode& MagCode) which combines orientation and magnitude information extracted by Gabor filtering. Combining the OrientCode and MagCode feature maps in a color-based manner respectively, we then constitute the original feature object set of a finger. To represent finger feature effectively, they are granulated at three levels of information granularity in a bottom-up manner based on GrC. Moreover, a top-down matching method is proposed to test the performance of the multilevel feature granules. Experimental results show that the proposed method achieves higher accuracy recognition rate in multimodal finger-based recognition.

Keywords: Multimodal Biometrics, Fingerprint, Finger-knuckle-print, Finger-vein, Granular Computing.

1 Introduction

Multimodal biometrics technology has become an attractive research direction in personal identification [1-2]. A multimodal biometric system usually contains two or more biometric modalities in a single identification system for performance improvement [3-5]. How to reliably and effectively fuse the multimodal features together, however, has still been a puzzling problem in practice.

Recently years, the research on granular computing (GrC) has attracted many researchers and practitioners. The basic idea of GrC is the using of information granules during complex problem solving [6-7]. Since Zadeh first introduced the concept of GrC in 1979 [7], many related applications have been proposed [8-10]. Firstly, Zheng proposed a tolerance granular space model (TGSM) to study some problems in pattern recognition [8]. Then, Li proposed a method for MRI and MRA image fusion based on TGSM [9]. Further, Bhatt proposed face feature granulation scheme for face recognition [10]. These works imply that GrC is a new way to deal with the complex multimodal biometrics recognition problems.

Z. Sun et al. (Eds.): CCBR 2014, LNCS 8833 , pp. 458–464, 2014.

In this paper, viewing the finger trait as the combination of a fingerprint(FP), finger-vein(FV) and finger-knuckle-print(FKP) [3][4][11], we adopt a novel method to study the problems of multimodal finger-based recognition based on GrC. As ridge texture information dominates over these three biometric characteristics with a compatible feature space. Therefore, a finger itself can be viewed as a coarse-granularity information granule with plenty of ridge texture.

In the proposed method, we adopt the combination of OrientCode [11-13] and MagCode [11] scheme for finger feature extraction. First, a bank of even-symmetric Gabor filters [14-15] with six orientations is used to exploit the orientation and magnitude features in FP, FV, FKP images. Second, the Orientation coding and Magnitude coding [11-13] are respectively conducted with the orientation and magnitude features to obtain the three-modal finger feature-maps. Third, combining the OrientCode and MagCode feature-maps into a single color-feature map respectively, we then constitute the original feature object set of a finger. Finally, each original object is granulated into non-overlapping rectangle granules [9] in a bottom-up manner to construct the multilevel feature granules (FGs). To evaluate the performance of the multilevel FGs, a top-down matching method is proposed. Experimental results show that the proposed method yields high identification accuracy in finger-based recognition.

2   The Proposed Method

2.1   Finger Image Acquisition and Feature Extraction

To obtain FP, FV and FKP images, we have designed a homemade imaging device, which can capture these three modality images automatically and simultaneously when a finger is available, as shown in Fig.1(a). In the proposed imaging system, the fingerprints and finger-knuckle-prints are imaged by reflected lights, and the finger-veins are imaged using the near infrared light in a transillumination manner.

After capturing the finger images, we first apply the methods in [3,11] to extract the ROI images of FP, FV and FKP, and all ROIs are normalized to 160*160 pixels, as shown in Fig.1(b). Feature extraction is essential for original feature object set construction and finger feature granulation. Considering specific ridge texture information dominates over these three biometric characteristics, the used feature extraction method should be powerful in image texture description.

In the spatial domain, Gabor filters have been widely used for analyzing texture information, and have been demonstrated that they are effective in finger texture information exploration [14-15]. Therefore, the feature extraction scheme of Orientation Coding and Magnitude Coding [11-13], which combines orientation and magnitude information extracted by Gabor filtering is used to extract the ridge texture information of finger images. First, a bank of even-symmetric Gabor filters [15] with 6-orientations is used here to exploit Gabor orientation and magnitude features in FP, FV, FKP images. Second, the Orientation coding [11-13] and Magnitude coding [11] methods are respectively implemented here to obtain the OrientCode and MagCode feature-maps, as shown in Fig.1(c) and Fig.1(d).

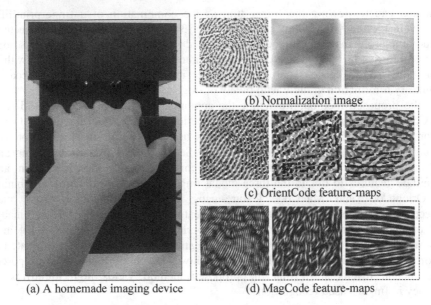

(a) A homemade imaging device

(b) Normalization image

(c) OrientCode feature-maps

(d) MagCode feature-maps

Fig. 1. A homemade imaging device and finger feature extraction results (Left: FP, Middle: FV, Right: FKP)

2.2   Feature Granulation

In order to effectively express the feature structure of the fingers, we adopt a bottom-up method to construct the multilevel feature granules (FGs). Here, FGs are generated as the following procedure.

Step 1: Select the original feature object set

Here, we combine FP, FV and FKP feature-maps in a color-based manner to form RGB-OrientCode and RGB-MagCode feature-maps. Then these two maps are used to constitute the original feature object set of a finger. Here we defined $O_0 = (x, y, R, G, B)$, where x, y is coordinate value, R, G, B denote the FP, FV, FKP feature-map respectively. O_1 represents the original feature object, which is defined as:

$$O_1 = \left\{ \bigcup_{FP} \{O_{i,j}\} \right\} \cap \left\{ \bigcup_{FV} \{O_{i,j}\} \right\} \cap \left\{ \bigcup_{FKP} \{O_{i,j}\} \right\} \tag{1}$$

Therefore, structure of the 0-layer feature granules are constructed here by a 2-tuple $G_0^1 = (IG_0^1, EG_0^1)$, and the intension and extension of 0-layer granules are respectively defined as $IG_0^1 = (x, y, mapR, mapG, mapB), EG_0^1 = \{x | x \in O_1\}$.

Step 2: Construct the 1-layer feature granules

According to the merger rules of the granularity grid [9], we can construct 1-layer FGs $G_1^1 = (IG_1^1, EG_1^1(\eta_1^1 | tr_1^1))$, the extension $EG_1^1(\eta_1^1 | tr_1^1) = \left\{ x | (x, \eta_1^1) \in tr_1^1{}_{(cp_1, w_1, DIS_1, D_1)} \right\}$. Here, we use the rectangle granule as the shape of the feature granules, where $cp(\alpha, \beta | DIS, D) = (dis_1(\alpha, \beta | \omega) \le d_1) \wedge (dis_2(\alpha, \beta | \omega) \le d_2), dis_i(\alpha, \beta | \omega) = |\alpha_i - \beta_i|, \omega = (1,1,0,0,0)$

$DIS = \{dis_1, dis_2\}, D = \{d_1, d_2\}, \eta_i^1 \in Grid_i^1, Grid_i^1 = \{(x,y) | x = 8i+1, y = 8j+1\}$, i and j are integers, η_i^1 denotes the position of the G_i^1. The histogram of the code-map as the intension of the FGs. Therefore, the original feature object is granulated as rectangle granules with the size of 8*8 pixels, which denoted as 1-layer FGs.

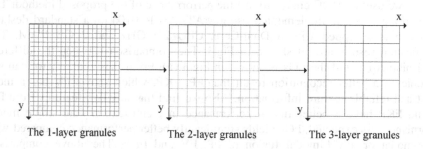

The 1-layer granules   The 2-layer granules   The 3-layer granules

Fig. 2. The 3-layer bottom-up granulation process

Step 3: Recursively, calculating the $i+1$-layer FGs $G_{i+1}^1 = (IG_{i+1}^1, EG_{i+1}^1(\eta_{i+1}^1 | tr_{i+1}^1))$, where $EG_{i+1}^1(\eta_{i+1}^1 | tr_{i+1}^1) = \{x | (x, \eta_{i+1}^1) \in tr_{i+1(cp_{i+1}, w_{i+1}, DIS_{i+1}, D_{i+1})}^1 \land x \in EG_i^1\}$. If this step continues to execute, the extension of the highest-level granules will eventually contain only one original object. In this paper, FGs are generated considering three granularity levels, and the granulation process is shown in Fig.2.

2.3   The Proposed Multimodal Finger-Based Recognition Method

Considering the multimodal finger-based recognition can be analyzed at different granularity levels, a top-down recognition method is proposed in this paper. The coarse-granularity information is an abstract description of the finger feature, instead the fine-granularity information represents a specific description of the finger feature. Therefore, we first analyze the problem at a coarse-granularity level. And for the problems cannot be solved at coarse granularity levels, we could address them at a fine-granularity level. Here, we use the histogram intersection H(FG^1,FG^2) [16] as the similarity measurement of two FGs. First, we calculate the similarity between two finger images based on orientation coding and magnitude coding which called Sim_{ori} and Sim_{mag} respectively. Then fuse these two similarity coefficients together as the final matching metrics, we define the similarity between two finger images as

$$Sim_i(F^1, F^2) = (1-\lambda) \cdot Sim_{ori}^i + \lambda \cdot Sim_{mag}^i \tag{2}$$

where $Sim_{ori}^i(F^1, F^2) = \sum_{r=0}^{N_i-1} H(FG_r^1, FG_r^2)$, i is the index number of the granular layer, N_i is the number of granules in the ith-layer, λ is used to control the distribution of Sim_{mag} to Sim and it is set to 0.25 in our experiment. If $Sim_i \geq T_i$ (T_i is the threshold of the ith-layer), then the two finger images are similar in the ith-layer. Hence, if $Sim_3 \geq T_3$, $Sim_2 \geq T_2$ and $Sim_1 \geq T_1$ are all satisfying, we believe that the two finger images are from the same individual.

3   Experimental Results

To evaluate the performance of the multimodal finger-based recognition system based on GrC, a self-constructed database which totally contain 600 sets of FP-FV-FKP images are used in this experiment.

Here, we use the ROC curves to test the performance of the proposed method. The proposed algorithm is implemented using MATLAB R2010a on a standard desktop PC which is equipped with a Dual-Core, CPU 2.7 GHz and 2 GB RAM. The identification results are all shown in Fig.3. The comparison between the different modal biometrics and the FGs is shown in Fig.3 (a). From these curves, we can see FV achieves a better recognition result than FP, FKP, which shows FV has a more robust and reliable texture information. Also we find that any two features from FP, FV and FKP have a better fusion performance in identification than single modal performance. As expected, FGs yields significantly better performance compared with single-modal or any bimodal fusion of FP, FV and FKP. The above comparison shows that the proposed method can effectively achieve information complementary between different features. It is helpful for multimodal identification performance improvement. Fig.3 (b) shows the ROC curves generated by the different granularity levels and Table.1 lists the corresponding EER and its matching time costs. From which we can clearly see that the 1-layer FGs make a lower EER compared with two other layers, indicating that the matching performance in fine-granularity space outperforms coarse-granularity space.

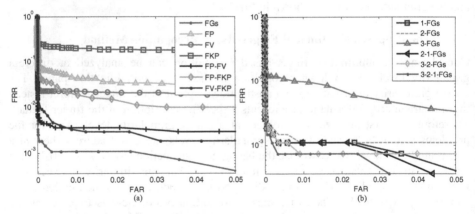

Fig. 3. ROC curves. (a) Comparisons between different modal biometrics and FGs. (b) Comparisons between different granularity levels

Table 1. Matching results from different levels FGs

Granular level	1-level	2-level	3-level	3-2-level	2-1-level	3-2-1-level
EER(%)	0.1638	0.19	0.98	0.1636	0.1635	0.135
Matching Time(s)	0.1403	0.0374	0.0184	0.0352	0.1336	0.1333

Further, from the presented results in Table.1, we can draw the conclusion that the coarse-granularity information has the higher matching efficiency, and the fine-granularity information has the higher matching accuracy. So, the combination of coarse-granularity information and fine-granularity information can keep the recognition efficiency in the premise of accuracy. Therefore, we can see that the top-down matching method of 3-2-1-FGs achieves the best accuracy recognition result and has the lowest time costs, here the threshold of 3-layer and 2-layer FGs are respectively set as $T_3=0.9089$, $T_2=0.8458$ to ensure low recognition error rate in the two high layer. Therefore, the top-down recognition method of multilayer FGs performs better in finger-based recognition both in efficiency and accuracy.

4   Conclusion

A new multimodal finger-based recognition scheme based on granular computing has been proposed in this paper. First, the ridge texture features of the FP, FV and FKP were both extracted by the OrientCode&MagCode method. Second, combining the OrientCode and MagCode feature-maps in a color-based manner respectively, we then constitute the original feature object set of a finger. Finally, three levels FGs were constructed in a bottom-up manner. Experimental results have shown that FGs are much more reliable and precise in multimodal finger-based identification. Moreover, the top-down matching method of multilevel FGs has a good performance in reducing the matching costs as well as improving the accuracy of finger-based recognition.

Acknowledgements. This work is jointly supported by National Natural Science Foundation of China (No.61379102) and the Fundamental Research Funds for the Central Universities (No. 3122014C003).

References

1. Ross, A., Jain, A.K.: Information fusion in biometrics. Pattern Recognition Letters 24(13), 2115–2125 (2003)
2. Ross, A., Jain, A.K.: Multimodal biometrics: An overview. In: 12th European Signal Processing Conference, pp. 1221–1224. IEEE Press (2004)
3. Yang, J.F., Zhang, X.: Feature-level fusion of fingerprint and finger-vein for personal identification. Pattern Recognition Letters 33(5), 623–628 (2012)
4. Yang, J.F., Hong, B.F.: Finger-vein and fingerprint recognition based on a feature-level fusion method. In: Fifth International Conference on Digital Image Processing, pp. 88782T–88782T-5. IEEE Press (2013)
5. Hong, L., Jain, A.K., Pankanti, S.: Can Multibiometrics Improve Performance? In: Proceedings of IEEE Workshop on Automatic Identification Advanced Technologies, pp. 59–64. IEEE Press, New Jersey (1999)
6. Miao, D.Q., Wang, G.Y., Liu, Q.: Granular computing: past, present and prospect. Science Publishing House, Beijing (2007) (in Chinese)

7. Yao, J.T., Vasilakos, A.V., Pedrycz, W.: Granular Computing: Perspectives and Challenges. IEEE Transactions on Cybernetics 43(6), 1977–1989 (2013)
8. Zheng, Z., Hu, H., Shi, Z.Z.: Tolerance granular space and its applications. In: IEEE International Conference on Granular Computing, pp. 367–372 (2005)
9. Li, Z.G., Meng, Z.Q.: Technique of medical image fusion based on tolerance granular space. Application Research of Computers 27(3), 1192–1194 (2010) (in Chinese)
10. Bhatt, H.S., Bharadwaj, S., Singh, R., Vatsa, M.: Recognizing Surgically Altered Face Images using Multi-objective Evolutionary Algorithm. IEEE Transactions on Information Forensics and Security 8, 89–100 (2013)
11. Zhang, L., Zhang, L.: Online finger-knuckle-print verification for personal authentication. Pattern Recognition 43(7), 2560–2571 (2010)
12. Zhang, L., Zhang, L., Zhang, D.: Ensemble of local and global information for finger-knuckle-print recognition. Pattern Recognition 44(2010), 1990–1998 (2011)
13. Kong, A.W.K., Zhang, D.: Competitive coding scheme for palmprint verification. In: 17th International Conference on Pattern Recognition, pp. 520–523. IEEE Press (2004)
14. Lee, T.S.: Image representation using 2D Gabor wavelet. IEEE Transactions on Pattern Analysis and Machine Intelligence 18(10), 957–971 (1996)
15. Yang, J.F., Shi, Y.H., Yang, J.L.: Finger-vein Recognition Based on a Bank of Gabor Filters. In: Asian Conference on Computer Visio., pp. 374–383 (2009)
16. Swain, M., Ballard, D.: Color indexing. International Journal of Computer Vision 7(1), 11–32 (1991)

An Intelligent Access Control System Based on Multi-biometrics of Finger

Shenghong Zhong, Xiaopeng Chen, Dejian Li, Wenxiong Kang[*] Feiqi Deng

School of Automation Science and Engineering, South China University of Technology,
Guangzhou, 510640, P.R. China
auwxkang@scut.edu.cn

Abstract. To address limitations of existing biometric access control systems in "smart" living environments, we introduce the design and construction of an intelligent access control system based on multi-biometrics of the finger. We formulate our system on three aspects: hardware structures, feature extraction and matching algorithm design, and software framework. By taking advantage of the high uniqueness of fingerprints and the strong anti-counterfeiting performance of finger veins, the system has considerable improvement in security and accuracy. In addition, it enables a security solution with a combination of pyro-electric sensor, voice message, video intercom, and the burglar alarm, etc. The experimental results show that the equal error rate is 0.27% and the time consumption of authentication is about one second, which demonstrates that our system meets the requirements of an access control system.

Keywords: Multi-biometrics, Access Control System, DSP, Fingerprint Recognition, Finger-Vein Recognition.

1 Introduction

Tremendous developments in science and technology are leading to the concept of "smart homes". As the key device of the security system in smart homes, an intelligent access control system is designed to allow authorized people in and prevent malicious invasion. Smart cards and passwords are easily stolen and duplicated, which leads to such systems being poor at anti-counterfeiting. However, biometric recognition[1] can overcome that. Unique human body characteristics such as irises, fingerprints, and voice patterns are difficult to steal or copy, making a biometrics-based system more secure. Despite the increasing number of biometrics-based authentication systems, the present equipment has not yet satisfied the requirements of simultaneous safety, reliability, multi-functionality, and low power consumption.

According to the analysis above, we design and implement an access control system based on fingerprint and finger-vein recognition. The system has the following characteristics: (1) For a better user experience, the system is equipped with video

---

[*] Corresponding author.

Z. Sun et al. (Eds.): CCBR 2014, LNCS 8833 , pp. 465–472, 2014.

intercom, voice message, burglar alarm, etc. (2) The system uses pyro-electric sensors to sense the body heat, so that the device can switch between standby and working mode to keep the energy consumption low. (3) To improve security, the system has the ability to detect violent and coerced unlocking. (4) The system combines two biometrics and utilizes efficient methods of feature extraction and matching to achieve high accuracy and security. This paper mainly focuses on the introduction of hardware design and optimization of image processing algorithms. But, the software framework of the system and the experimental results of authentication accuracy and time consumption are also discussed.

2   System Scheme

As shown in Fig. 1, the system has two kinds of parts: indoor components and outdoor components. The body sensor module is composed of a pyro-electric sensor that can detect whether there is a person outside. The image collection module includes a fingerprint acquisition instrument, a monochromatic camera for capturing finger-vein image, and an 850 nm near-infrared light supply. The heart of the system is a control board, which consists of a core board, an expansion board and some expansion interfaces. The human-interactive module consists of a keypad and an LCD. The video intercom module is divided into an intercom and a visualization module. The intercom includes voice ICs, two microphones, and two speakers; the visualization module includes a CMOS imaging sensor, a TFT color LCD, a FIFO IC, and an SD card.

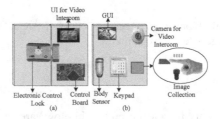

Fig. 1. Structure chart of the system: (a) Indoor components. (b) Outdoor components

When nobody is close to the door, the system remains in standby mode, in which only the pyro-electric sensor and electronic lock are active. When the pyro-electric sensor detects people nearby, it sends out a high-level signal to activate the rest of the system. That is, the core board initializes, and the visualization module starts to collect video images and display it on the TFT LCD in real time. Meanwhile, a picture is collected and stored in the database every 3 seconds. Visitors ring the doorbell; the owner can observe them through the TFT LCD or communicate with them through the intercom and decide whether to open the door. If the owner does not answer, visitors can use the video intercom to leave a message. For the owner himself, two options are provided to open the door: (1) Using finger recognition. (2) Entering the password. In the case of unlocking through violence or coercing the owner, the system will send alarm messages via the GSM module embedded in the system.

3   Hardware Design

The hardware design, which is the foundation of the whole system, must take into account factors such as size, stability, and maintenance cost. To avoid concentrating all chips on one circuit board, the hardware design of the system is divided into two parts: the core board is responsible for resource management and scheduling, while the expansion board connects the core board with other function modules. This sub-module design approach makes hardware debugging and troubleshooting easier. In addition, if there is a need to upgrade the system, we just need to modify the corresponding module.

Fig. 2 shows the structure of the core board circuit. The center of DSP is surrounded by SDRAM, flash memory, FIFO, clock circuit, power supply, reset circuit, JTAG circuit, etc. The FIFO is used as a data buffer when collecting images. We add two SDRAMs for image processing, considering the amount of image data to be processed. The FLASH chip stores codes, fonts, and the user's finger sample data. The SDRAM, FLASH data bus, and the address bus, are mounted on the DSP bus; the DSP bus also connects to the CPLD bus simultaneously through the external bus so that they can work cooperatively.

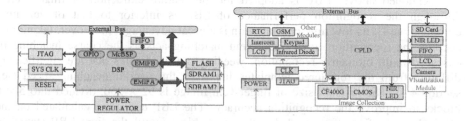

Fig. 2. Structure of core board   **Fig. 3.** Structure of expansion board

The expansion board integrates a CPLD logic controller and some functional modules. As shown in Fig. 3, RTC, fonts, keypad, and other modules are directly controlled by the DSP through the external bus. In the visualization module, except the SD card (which is controlled directly by DSP), the other devices are controlled by the CPLD. The image collection module collects fingerprint images from CF400G and finger-vein images from an infrared-sensitive CMOS-based camera and sends the image data back to DSP through the CPLD and external bus.

4   Image Processing Algorithm

In our system, fingerprints and finger veins are adopted for identity recognition with the improved image processing algorithm. Since the finger-vein images collected in our system have little rotation and a simple background, the LBP algorithm[2] is adopted for feature extraction. Fingerprint images have a complex background, yet the texture can be distinguished obviously by their difference in gray values; therefore the traditional minutiae extraction[3] is utilized for feature extraction.

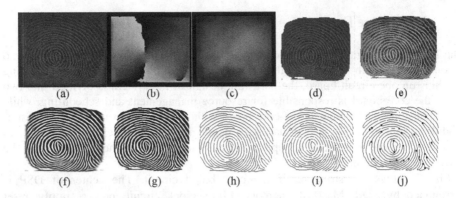

Fig. 4. Fingerprint processing steps: (a) original image, (b) orientation field, (c) gradient magnitude image, (d) background removing, (e) image enhancing, (f) texture enhancing, (g) image binarization, (h) fingerprint thinning, (i) deburring, and (j) minutiae extraction.

4.1   Feature Extraction of Finger Vein

As mentioned above, LBP is adopted for the feature extraction of finger veins. Although the recognition performance of LBP is inferior to that of curvature computation[4], its low time consumption is a great advantage. Moreover, taking into account the recognition time, finger-vein matching acts as the coarse matching of cascaded multi-biometric recognition, weeding out candidates that are significantly different from the registered templates improves the overall matching speed (see section 4.4). The original size of finger-vein image is 92×250, divided into 3×8 blocks to improve the recognition accuracy. The LBP codes are calculated on the original image first, then pooled within each block, until the final LBP statistical histograms of 3×8 blocks are spliced together to represent the finger-vein image.

4.2   Feature Extraction of Fingerprints

The feature extraction of fingerprints[5] can be divided into two sections: image preprocessing and minutiae extraction. The processing steps are showed in Fig. 4.

Preprocessing. Unlike the LBP algorithm used on finger veins, where the results of background separation appear largely unaffected by image preprocessing, the texture clarity of fingerprints has a great impact on the precision of feature extraction. Therefore, sufficient preprocessing should be conducted to obtain clearer texture, which can be summarized as follows:

1) Fingerprint ROI location: After computing the orientation field and gradient magnitude of the original fingerprint image, the background is removed by utilizing the gradient magnitude to obtain the fingerprint ROI.

2) Texture enhancement: After image enhancement by histogram equalization, the fingerprint can be further enhanced by the Gabor filter based on the orientation field.

3) Texture extraction: After the intelligent binarization is based on orientation field, fingerprint thinning, and deburring, clear fingerprint textures are obtained for the final processing.

Minutiae Extraction. To process the singular points, ending points, and bifurcation points of minutiae of fingerprint, the feature extraction process requires the orientation field. In our system, the orientation field is first computed on an image downsampled by ½ from the original one; the obtained orientation image then gets upsampled to the original size. The integral image is adopted during computation so as to reduce time consumption. During the process of code designing, each algorithm is encapsulated into an independent function with code optimized according to the specific entrance parameters, which can boost speed and enhance code portability simultaneously.

4.3   Feature Matching

Since the features of finger-vein are represented by its LBP code histogram, the matching of two finger-vein images is decided by comparing the intersectant area of their histograms with a preset threshold, which is determined through sufficient training experiments. We adopt the minutiae-matching method mentioned in Patil and Zaveri[6] for fingerprints in our system. Although our system's acquisition device constrains the location of the fingers, even a slight positional or angular offset during image acquisition affects the quality of fingerprint matching. Therefore, the fingerprint images should first be aligned[7] for better results. A fast alignment method is adopted: Suppose we have two minutia points to match; we choose one minutia from the upper area of each fingerprint ROI. Then, we calculate the coordinate and angle offset of the two ridges associated with those two referenced minutia points. Further, we transform each set of minutiae to a new coordinate system whose origin is at the referenced point. In the matching stage, the similarity of two point sets is calculated after each alignment. The the matching result is decided by comparing the similarity with a preset threshold.

4.4   Cascaded Fusion

Because the information contained in fingerprint and finger veins is complementary, the score-level fusion is conducted on them to further improve recognition precision. Considering the time consumption and security concerns of our system in practical applications, a three-step cascaded fusion strategy is adopted for identity authentication:

Step 1. Compare the candidate finger-vein image with a registered finger-vein image that is sequentially selected from the user registration database. If the matching score is bigger than the preset finger-vein threshold, jump to step 3; otherwise execute step 2.

Step 2. Judge whether the candidate image matches all the registered finger-vein images in the user registration database. If yes, the identification fails and the process ends; otherwise return to step 1 and execute again.

Step 3. Compare the two corresponding fingerprint images. Conduct a weighted SUM fusion on the fingerprint and finger-vein matching scores. If the final score is bigger than the preset threshold, the candidate is a genuine user; otherwise return to step 1.

During the training experiments, the preset threshold and the optimal fusion weights of fingerprint and finger-vein can be obtained by the ROC curve after fusion. Then the minimum value of finger-vein threshold selected as the preset finger-vein threshold in our system can be calculated based on the fusion formula while the fingerprint-matching score is set to the maximum value.

5   Software Framework

To synthesize the factors of system workflow, module driver characteristics, and development difficulty, we divide the DSP/BIOS[8] real-time kernel TI provides into three parts as: the underlying driver, the application program, and the task scheduling. The underlying driver is closely related to the hardware design; it directly controls the hardware of the system including memory reading and writing, image acquisition, GPIO and LCD operations. Application program is the main part of the software design. It is composed of different task management functions in the system. Every task management function contains an infinite loop. Semaphores and email are adopted for communication between these loops.

6   Experimental Results

6.1   Recognition Precision

To the best of our knowledge, there is no public joint database that contains fingerprint and finger-vein image collected simultaneously. Thus, to verify the performance of our system, we built a new database containing 370 fingerprint images and 370 finger-vein images (74 fingers, with five images per finger). The EER of fingerprint, finger-vein, and fusion recognition are tested in this section, with the experimental results shown in Fig. 5. Among them, the EER of minutiae-based fingerprint and LBP-based finger-vein recognition are 3.22% and 3.06%, respectively. To compare the validity, we also conducted the experiments using ORB-based fingerprint and template-based finger-vein recognition for comparison. Their EER is 5.83% and 7.04%, respectively, which demonstrates that the aforementioned methods are more suitable for our database. Finally, after fusion of minutiae-based fingerprint and LBP-based finger-vein recognition, the EER of fingerprint recognition reaches 0.27% with a weight of 0.7, which proves that the weighted SUM fusion can improve the precision of system efficiently.

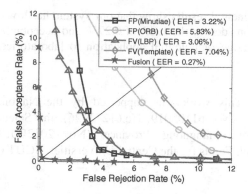

Fig. 3. The EER of our system

6.2 Time Consumption

The identification process contains four steps: feature extraction of finger-vein, feature matching of finger-vein, feature extraction of fingerprint, and feature matching of fingerprint. Experiments demonstrate that the average time consumption of the first three steps is 47 ms, 0.5 ms, and 900 ms, respectively. After adopting a fast matching method for fingerprints, the time consumption of matching intra-class and inter-class decrease to 2 ms and 12 ms, respectively. Additionally, the cascaded fusion adopted in our system can reduce the computation time. Our experiments show that about three-fourths of the user registration database is filtered by the preset finger-vein threshold during the finger-vein matching. So, fingerprint matching only needs to execute on the remaining one-fourth of the database.

To illustrate the time consumption of the whole system, we suppose that there are 50 registered finger images in the database. The total time consumption will be longest when an imposter wants to break into the system because the matching result is decided after traversing the whole database, with a value of $47 + 0.5 \times 50 + 900 + 12 \times ¼ \times 50 = 1122$ ms. That is to say, the worst-case identification procedure can complete within 1122 ms, which demonstrates that our proposed system can satisfy the requirements of practical application.

7 Conclusion

Aiming to address the limitations of existing biometric access control systems, we propose and implement an intelligent entrance guard system based on fingerprint and finger-vein recognition. The work entails hardware construction, algorithms design, and software implementation. In terms of hardware, the equipment integrates a fingerprint reader, infrared lights, and a CMOS image sensor to acquire the fingerprint and finger-vein images simultaneously. Utilizing a pyro-electric sensor reduces power consumption. In algorithms design, LBP and minutiae extraction are adopted for quick feature extraction of finger-vein and fingerprint, respectively. Then, a cascaded fusion strategy is used to improve the recognition accuracy with low time-consumption. Experimental results show that our system has low energy consumption and high security; considering the EER of 0.27% and acceptable time consumption. This offers a wide range of potential application to laboratories, offices, and other settings.

Acknowledgments. This work was supported by the National Natural Science Foundation of China (No. 61105019, No.61273126). the Science and Technology Planning Project of Guangdong Province (No. 2012B010100021) and the Fundamental Research Funds for the Central Universities, SCUT (No. 2014ZG0041)

References

1. Jain, A.K., Ross, A., Prabhakar, S.: An introduction to biometric recognition. IEEE Transactions on Circuits and Systems for Video Technology 14, 4–20 (2004)
2. Park, Y.H., Tien, D.N., Lee, E.C., Park, K.R., Kim, S.M., Kim, H.C.: A multimodal biometric recognition of touched fingerprint and finger-vein. In: 2011 International Conference on Multimedia and Signal Processing (CMSP), vol. 1, pp. 247–250. IEEE (2011)
3. Feng, J., Zhou, J.: A performance evaluation of fingerprint minutia descriptors. In: 2011 International Conference on Hand-Based Biometrics (ICHB), pp. 1–6. IEEE (2011)
4. Song, W., Kim, T., Kim, H.C., Choi, J.H., Kong, H.-J., Lee, S.-R.: A finger-vein verification system using mean curvature. Pattern Recognition Letters 32, 1541–1547 (2011)
5. Vaikole, S., Sawarkar, S., Hivrale, S., Sharma, T.: Minutiae feature extraction from fingerprint images. In: IEEE International Advance Computing Conference, IACC 2009, pp. 691–696. IEEE (2009)
6. Patil, A.R., Zaveri, M.A.: A Novel Approach for Fingerprint Matching Using Minutiae. In: 2010 Fourth Asia International Conference on Mathematical/Analytical Modelling and Computer Simulation (AMS), pp. 317–322. IEEE (2010)
7. Lee, C., Choi, J.-Y., Toh, K.-A., Lee, S.: Alignment-free cancelable fingerprint templates based on local minutiae information. IEEE Transactions on Systems, Man, and Cybernetics, Part B: Cybernetics 37, 980–992 (2007)
8. Instruments, T.: Tms320c6000 dsp/bios 5.32 application programming interface (api) reference guide. Literature number: SPRU403O (2007)

Cascaded Convolutional Neural Network
for Eye Detection Under Complex Scenarios

Lang Ye, Mingming Zhu, Siyu Xia, and Hong Pan[*]

School of Automation, Southeast University,
Nanjing, 210096, China
syelang@126.com, yaoxinreaps@163.com,
{xsy,enhpan}@seu.edu.cn

Abstract. Eye detection is a preliminary yet important step for face recognition and analysis. It is a challenging problem especially for unconstrained images. We propose a coarse-to-fine eye detection approach by using a two-level convolutional neural network which follows a biologically-inspired trainable architecture. The first level of our network roughly detects initial bounding boxes, whereas the second level judges whether the detected bounding boxes belong to eyes or not and deletes the non-eye bounding boxes. All remaining bounding boxes yielded from the two-level network are finally merged to give the accurate locations of detected eyes. Experimental results demonstrate the effectiveness of our method for eye detection under complex scenarios.

1   Introduction

Over the last twenty years, face recognition has been extensively investigated in computer vision and pattern recognition society. Since face recognition is often based on normalized face images and normalization of input face images mainly depend on eye location, thus, eye detection is a crucial step for face recognition. Besides, many other practical applications, such as security authorization systems, human robot interaction, driver drowsiness or sleep detection etc., need to solve the fundamental and important problem of eye detection.

Many approaches have been proposed for eye detection in recent years. Broadly speaking, these approaches can be classified into two categories [1]: the active infrared (IR)-based approaches and the traditional image-based passive approaches. Eye detection based on active IR illumination is a simple yet effective approach [2]. But it requires an active IR lighting and many face images in real applications are not IR illuminated, so it is not widely used.

The commonly used approaches in the image-based passive methods include template based methods, appearance based methods and feature based methods. In template methods, segments of an input face image are compared with previously stored face template images, then the similarities between the input face and face templates are evaluated using a correlation measure. The drawback of this approach is that it cannot deal with eye variations in scale, expression, rotation and illumination.

---

[*] Corresponding author.

Z. Sun et al. (Eds.): CCBR 2014, LNCS 8833 , pp. 473–480, 2014.

Yuille et al. [3] proposed a deformable template to extract face features; however, the performance of their method relies greatly on the initial position of the template. Appearance based methods detect eyes according to their photometric appearance. These methods convert the eye detection problem to a two-category (eye and non-eye) classification problem. To train an effective classifier such as support vector machine (SVM) [4], Adaboost [5] and neural network [6], it usually requires a large amount of training data. Feature based methods explore the characteristics of eyes such as shape, intensity and gradient information. Usually these methods are effective, but may result false detections (e.g. wrongly classify eyebrows into eyes [1]) in low contrast images.

Although numerous eye detection methods have been developed, many problems, such as low detection accuracy under unconstrained conditions and the detection efficiency, still exist. In this paper, we focus on improving the eye detection accuracy under unconstrained scenarios by using a cascaded convolutional neural network.

The remainder of the paper is organized as follows. In section 2, we describe the structure of our eye detector and how it works. Section 3 discusses the training details of our network and gives some detection results. Section 4 concludes our work.

2   The Proposed Method

Recently, convolutional neural network(CNN) introduced by LeCun et al.[7] has achieved great success in many vision tasks such as image classification[8], pedestrian detection[9], text recognition[10], and face parsing[11]. Convolutional neural network has a biologically inspired structure that can automatically learn a unique set of features optimized for a given task. In this paper, cascading two levels of CNN, we propose a novel CNN structure to improve the eye detection accuracy directly using the raw color values of image pixels. In particular, the first level detects the rough bounding boxes of possible eye patches. The second level judges whether the rough bounding boxes belong to eyes or not and deletes the non-eye bounding boxes. All remaining bounding boxes yielded from this two-level network are finally merged to give the accurate location of detected eyes. Next, we describe the detail of our network and how it works.

2.1   Cascaded Network Architecture

Fig.1 illustrates the framework of our eye detector. For the convenience of representation, we refer to the first level of the convolutional neural network as CNN_1 and the second level of the convolutional neural network as CNN_2. The input of CNN_1 is an image of 18x32 pixels with normalized intensity channel. It consists of two stacked feature stages, both stages containing the following four layers: a filter bank layer (convolution layer), a rectification layer, a contrast normalization layer, and an average subsampling layer, followed by a classification module. Fig.2 illustrates the deep structure of CNN_1. CNN_2 has the same structure as CNN_1. Next, we elaborate each layer involved in the CNN.

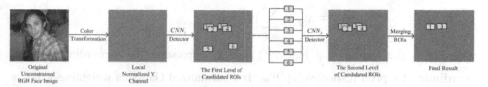

Fig. 1. The framework of our detector using a two-level cascaded convolutional neural network. The input is an unconstrained image. A transformation from RGB color space to YUV color space is applied first. The normalized intensity component Y is extracted for eye detection. The yellow rectangles label the position of candidate bounding boxes (ROIs) yielded from CNN_1. Then CNN_2 judges them respectively and deletes the non-eye bounding boxes. Finally, we merge the remaining adjacent bounding boxes to generate the final detection result.

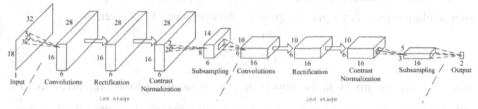

Fig. 2. The structure of convolutional neural network CNN_1. All layers are illustrated by cuboids whose length, width and height denote the number of maps, and the size of each map, respectively. The small squares represent the local receptive of neurons in different layers.

Filter Bank Layer. the input feature map x_i is convolved by a trainable filter k_{ij}, such that the output feature map y_j is expressed as

$$y_j = \sum_i k_{ij} * x_i + b_j \tag{1}$$

where $*$ is a 2D convolution operator and b_j is a trainable bias parameter. Each filter extracts a special feature from different receptive fields of input.

Rectification Layer. It is a nonlinear layer that activates useful features from filter bank layer. Given an input x, the activity function f is given in Eq.(2)

$$f(x) = | \tanh(x) | \tag{2}$$

The absolute rectified sigmoid function is proved to be useful in natural image recognition [12].

Contrast Normalization Layer. This layer is employed after rectification layer enforcing the local competition between adjacent features in a feature map, and between features at the same spatial location. The local contrast normalization is inspired by visual neuroscience models [13, 14]. It can be separated into two steps: subtractive normalization and divisive normalization. For a given pixel feature map x_{ijk}, the output of subtractive normalization is given in Eq.(3):

$$v_{ijk} = x_{ijk} - \sum_{ipq} w_{pq} \cdot x_{i,j+p,k+q} \qquad (3)$$

where i is the feature map index; j and k represents the x-coordinate and y-coordinate of a pixel respectively; w_{pq} is a normalized Gaussian weighting window with a size of $p \times q$ such that $\sum_{pq} w_{pq} = 1$. The divisive normalization is given by:

$$y_{ijk} = \frac{v_{ijk}}{\max(c, \sigma_{jk})} \qquad (4)$$

where $\sigma_{jk} = (\sum_{ipq} w_{pq} v_{i,j+p,k+q}^2)^{1/2}$ and c is set to $mean(\sigma_{jk})$.

Average Subsampling Layer: This layer computes the average values of each subsampling region. For a given region R_j, the operation s_j is given by:

$$s_j = \frac{1}{|R_j|} \sum_{i \in R_j} a_i \qquad (5)$$

where a_i are the pixels in the region R_j. A subsampling local region results in a reduced-resolution output feature map. It makes the extracted feature robust to small variations in the location of input image.

The first feature stage in CNN_1 consists of 6 filters with sizes of 3x5, which perform convolution over the input image. The convolution responses are put into the following rectified sigmoid function. The subtractive and divisive local normalization is applied after the rectified sigmoid. The last layer of the first feature stage is a subsampling operation using 2x2 kernels by 2x2 strides.

The second-stage feature extractor is fed with the output of the first feature stage. It extracts 16 output feature maps using 3x5 kernels followed by the same operations with the first feature stage. All the mapping from input features to output features are completely connected. Finally, the extracted features are fed into the classifier which has only one layer.

2.2   Detection Procedure

In this subsection, we describe how our cascaded convolutional network is used to detect eyes within the entire input image. In order to detect eyes with varying sizes, we subsample the input image by a factor of 1.2 from its original size to the network's size 18x32. Then, the first level of network CNN_1 uses an 18x32 window to scan across the multi-scale images constructed above and generates a group of regions of interest (ROIs) image patches. These ROIs represent eyes. The second level of network, CNN_2, decides whether all the ROIs yielded from CNN_1 are eyes or not and deletes the ROI that it judges as non-eye. Finally, we merge all ROI candidates in the following way. For each input image, all the ROI candidates are sorted by the correlation coefficients in a descending order. Then, the ROI candidate with the highest correlation coefficient is chosen as a positive region and all other regions near this region are deleted. We repeat this step until no region is left. The whole detection procedure is illustrated in Fig.3, where each row gives an example.

Fig. 3. Examples of detection procedure. The first column is the original image. The second column shows the ROIs yielded from the CNN_1 detector with green rectangles. The blue rectangles in the third column are the remaining ROIs yielded from the CNN_2 detector. The fourth column is the final detection result labeled by red rectangles.

From Fig.3, we can see that CNN_1 detector generates many ROIs which include eye and non-eye patches, while CNN_2 detector efficiently discards those non-eye patches and keeps the eye patches obtaining an accurate detection result.

3   Experiments

3.1   Network Training

We collected 8300 eye samples with varying illumination conditions, resolutions and gazes from the development set of Public Figures Face Database [15]. For the background samples, taking into account of the most possible environments where eyes occur, we first collected 3330 face images and changed the grayscale of eye pixels to 128. Then, we decomposed these images into multi-scale levels and chose 6 patches from each image to generate negative samples. In this way, we obtained a total of 8000 negative images. Finally, we split the whole samples into training and validation datasets with 500 samples per class in the validation set.

According to the input size of our network, we resize all the datasets to 18x32 which meet the common aspect ratio of eyes. Then, we convert images from RGB format to YUV format and pre-process them with local contrast normalization by a 7x7 kernel on the Y channel which is used to train our models. The U and V channels are discarded. And no sample distortions were employed to augment datasets for improving invariance.

We adopt standard fully supervised training using a stochastic gradient descent strategy to minimize the loss function of mean squared error. The parameters in all layers are updated simultaneously during the learning procedure. The gradients are computed using the back-propagation method. To boost our model's rejection ability, we employ the bootstrapping technique to improve the detection performance. The bootstrapping procedure is conducted as follows. Firstly, we train the network using the original datasets. Secondly, we run the network on a set of images which do not have eyes and add the extracted samples which are judged as eyes to the existing negative dataset. Thirdly, we train the network on the new dataset again until it converges. We perform one bootstrapping pass which extracts 5000 negative samples. Then, we apply the extracted samples to learn the CNN_1. Based on the trained CNN_1, we conduct the same procedure to train the CNN_2.

3.2   Detection Results

We created a dataset including 597 images with 1307 eyes from LFPW [16] which were suitable for our experiments. LFPW was a public dataset for evaluating the performance of face detection in unconstrained conditions. The containing faces showed large variations in pose, illumination and expression. Using this dataset, we conducted different experiments to evaluate the performance of our model under different configurations. Firstly, we applied the trained networks CNN_1 and CNN_2 to conduct experiments respectively. Secondly, we cascaded CNN_1 and CNN_2 to do the same experiment. Finally, to compare with the performance of convolutional neural network, we employed the cascaded Adaboost classifier with Haar-like feature provided by OpenCV to detect eyes on the same dataset. The individual CNN was implemented using the EBLearn C++ open-source package [17].

Experimental results are listed in Table 1. We report detection results in terms of precision rate and recall rate, and the third column in Table 1 gives the standard f - measure which combines precision rate and recall rate in one measurement, i.e. $f = 2 * Precision * Recall / (Precision + Recall)$. We see in Table 1 that the individual CNN_1 has a precision rate of 55% and a recall rate of 68%, while individual CNN_2 outperforms CNN_1, as it achieves a 73% precision rate and a 76% recall rate, respectively. This verifies that bootstrapping is an important step to improve the detection performance. The results of the last row in Table 1 show that cascaded CNN_1 and CNN_2 achieve the best performance which even beats the method of cascaded Adaboost classifier with Haar-like feature. The main reason why cascaded CNN_1 and CNN_2 method achieves higher performance than other methods is that CNN_2 can effectively reject the non-eye bounding boxes yielded from CNN_1, and the common effect of CNN_1 and CNN_2 remains more confident bounding boxes to merge.

Some detection examples resulted from our cascaded CNN_1 and CNN_2 approaches are shown in Fig.4. The first column images in Fig.4 (a) have dark backgrounds and the people in it have different poses. The scenarios in the second column images are complex. The third column images demonstrates that our detector is also effective for multiple persons. Fig.4(b) gives some false positive and false negative detections. The false positive detections come from mouth and figures similar to eyes. Adding the color information in the network may filter out these false positives.

Table 1. Experimental results of selected LFPW dataset with different configurations

Method	Precision	Recall	f	Detected eye patches
Haar-like+Adaboost	0.82	0.76	0.79	994
CNN_1	0.55	0.68	0.61	892
CNN_2	0.73	0.76	0.74	995
$CNN_1 + CNN_2$	**0.93**	**0.91**	**0.92**	**1187**

(a) Correct detection examples.   (b) Some false detection examples.

Fig. 4. Detecting examples resulted from our cascaded CNN_1 and CNN_2 method

4   Conclusion

We propose a cascaded two-level convolutional neural network method for eye detection. The first level of convolutional neural network CNN_1 is trained after one bootstrapping round. The second level of convolutional neural network is trained on the basis of CNN_1 and one further bootstrapping round. Experimental results demonstrate our method significantly improves the detection accuracy of human eyes under complex scenarios.

Acknowledgments. This work is supported by Jiangsu Natural Science Foundation (JSNSF) under Grant BK20131296 and BK20130639.

References

1. Khairosfaizal, W.W.M., Noráini, A.: Eyes detection in facial images using circular hough transform. In: 5th International Colloquium on Signal Processing & Its Applications, CSPA 2009, pp. 238–242. IEEE (2009)
2. Morimoto, C., Koons, D., Amir, A., Flickner, M.: Real-time detection of eyes and faces. In: Workshop on Perceptual User Interfaces, pp. 117–120 (1998)
3. Yuille, A.L., Hallinan, P.W., Cohen, D.S.: Feature extraction from faces using deformable templates. International Journal of Computer Vision 8(2), 99–111 (1992)
4. Chen, S., Liu, C.: A new efficient svm and its application to real-time accurate eye localization. In: The 2011 International Joint Conference on Neural Networks (IJCNN), pp. 2520–2527. IEEE (2011)
5. Wang, P., Ji, Q.: Multi-view face and eye detection using discriminant features. Computer Vision and Image Understanding 105(2), 99–111 (2007)
6. Rao, P.S., Sreehari, S., et al.: Neural network approach for eye detection. arXiv preprint arXiv:1205.5097 (2012)
7. LeCun, Y., Bottou, L., Bengio, Y., Haffner, P.: Gradient-based learning applied to document recognition. Proceedings of the IEEE 86(11), 2278–2324 (1998)
8. Krizhevsky, A., Sutskever, I., Hinton, G.E.: Imagenet classcation with deep convolutional neural networks. NIPS 1(2), 4 (2012)
9. Sermanet, P., Kavukcuoglu, K., Chintala, S., LeCun, Y.: Pedestrian detection with unsupervised multi-stage feature learning. In: 2013 IEEE Conference on Computer Vision and Pattern Recognition (CVPR), pp. 3626–3633. IEEE (2013)
10. Wang, T., Wu, D.J., Coates, A., Ng, A.Y.: End-to-end text recognition with convolutional neural networks. In: 2012 21st International Conference on Pattern Recognition (ICPR), pp. 3304–3308. IEEE (2012)
11. Luo, P., Wang, X., Tang, X.: Hierarchical face parsing via deep learning. In: 2012 IEEE Conference on Computer Vision and Pattern Recognition (CVPR), pp. 2480–2487. IEEE (2012)
12. LeCun, Y., Kavukcuoglu, K., Farabet, C.: Convolutional networks and applications in vision. In: Proceedings of 2010 IEEE International Symposium on Circuits and Systems (ISCAS), pp. 253–256. IEEE (2010)
13. Lyu, S., Simoncelli, E.P.: Nonlinear image representation using divisive normalization. In: IEEE Conference on Computer Vision and Pattern Recognition, CVPR 2008, pp. 1–8. IEEE (2008)
14. Pinto, N., Cox, D.D., DiCarlo, J.J.: Why is real-world visual object recognition hard? PLoS Computational Biology 4(1), e27 (2008)
15. Kumar, N., Berg, A.C., Belhumeur, P.N., Nayar, S.K.: Attribute and simile classiers for face verication. In: 2009 IEEE 12th International Conference on Computer Vision, pp. 365–372. IEEE (2009)
16. Belhumeur, P.N., Jacobs, D.W., Kriegman, D., Kumar, N.: Localizing parts of faces using a consensus of exemplars. In: 2011 IEEE Conference on Computer Vision and Pattern Recognition (CVPR), pp. 545–552. IEEE (2011)
17. Sermanet, P., Kavukcuoglu, K., LeCun, Y.: Eblearn: Open-source energy-based learning in c++. In: 21st International Conference on Tools with Articial Intelligence, ICTAI 2009, pp. 693–697. IEEE (2009)

A People Counting Method Based on Universities' Surveillance Videos and Its Application on Classroom Query

Yang Liu and Huayu Wu

School of Information Science and Engineering,
Shenyang University of Technology, Shenyang, China
{Yang Liu,liuyangxx@}sut.edu.cn

Abstract. In this paper, we present a new people counting method based on universities' surveillance videos. Firstly, we set the threshold value for the HSV space V channel pixel-based on the color of hair so as to detect the head regions. Secondly, we fit the function of the head size and space coordinate and then remove the connected regions which are too big or too small. Finally, we detect the motion using the improved frame difference method and remove the static regions. This method has solved the problems of that the feature is not obvious when students are in different positions with different sizes due to the perspective effect of cameras. There is false detection due to the interference of static entities such as bags and basketballs on tables and chairs. Experimental results show that the average correct detecting rate can reach 87.71%. By calculating, the detected classroom occupancy rate and the actual classroom occupancy rate are almost at the same.

Keywords: People counting, Frame difference method, Video analysis, Function fitting method.

1   Introduction

Currently, the university's classroom is the main place for students to study because of the shortage of studying rooms. But it is difficult to find a classroom to study in. Students often need to look for classroom for a long time because they do not know which classroom has no lesson and which classroom has fewer people. At the same time, classroom with video surveillance has become more and more prevalent. But the utilization rate of the surveillance video is not high.

Based on the above consideration, a rapid and efficient system is required to monitor and query the classroom occupancy rate. This paper proposes a method of people counting based on the surveillance video. And then people can calculate the occupancy rate of the classroom. Currently, researches on people counting are mainly divided into two categories. One is based on method of pedestrian detection[1-2], which detects pedestrians by extracting the human body or the contour, texture, color and other characteristics of the head. Then calculate the number on the basis of pedestrian detection. The other one is based on the global features[3-6]. Firstly, the feature of the

Z. Sun et al. (Eds.): CCBR 2014, LNCS 8833 , pp. 481–488, 2014.

foreground area is extracted, such as area, length of the edge and texture characteristics. Then the number of statistics is given by using regression algorithm.

The method of people counting basing on surveillance video in classroom mainly has the following problems. Firstly, the human density in classroom is so high that the detail is not obvious. Secondly, people in different positions of the picture are with different sizes due to the perspective effect of cameras. Thirdly, there is false detection due to the interference of static entities such as bags and basketballs on tables and chairs.

2   Algorithm

According to the mentioned problems, this paper presents a method of people counting on color, size, and motion detection. Then, the classroom occupancy rate is given. Disturbance factors like light, windows are found in the classroom, so we first eliminate the Influence of them and get the student candidate area. Secondly, binary image will work on this image based on the hair color and get the head candidate area. Thirdly, the article analyzes the functional relation of the head size and space coordinate. Finally, detect moving object using the improved frame difference method and remove the stillness area. The algorithm flowchart is shown in Fig. 1.

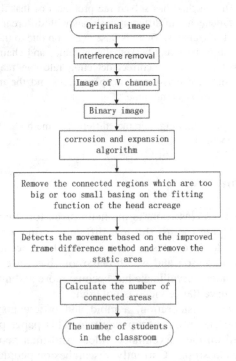

Fig. 1. The flowchart of the new people counting method

2.1   Interference Removal

Fig. 2(a) shows the image of classroom from the surveillance video. The camera is static and the students with small movements in classroom. So a binary image shown in Fig. 2(b) is created as a layer mask to distinguish between the interference area and the useful area. Fig. 2(c) shows the experimental result which shows that the interference is removed effectively by means of the "and operation".

Fig. 2. Remove the interference area from the image. (a) The original image. (b) The layer mask. (c) Interference removal image.

2.2   Hair Candidate Area

Color space is a space coordinate system describing color attribute values in nature. RGB color space is the most common color space and it is the foundation of other color spaces. H, S, V in HSV color space respectively hue, saturation and brightness and V is from 0 to 1.

It comes out that head is the easiest feature to recognize after observation of the interference removal image. The hair's color is the most obvious information on behalf of the head. A large number of experiment prove that setting the threshold value of HSV space V channel pixel can effectively detect the hair's color and can be less affected by illumination changes and shadow7. Fig. 3(a) shows the image of V channel. The experiment found that binary image by the V value is set to 0.25 which can effectively extract the head candidate area. Fig.3 (b) shows the result of binary image.

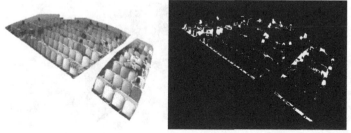

Fig. 3. Hair candidate area based on the hair's color of V. (a) The image of V channel from its HSV color space. (b) The binary image based on the hair's color.

2.3   Function Fitting

Due to the perspective effect of cameras, people in different positions of the picture have different sizes. This article collects the acreage of the head in different coordinates. The acreage of the head and its coordinate presents obvious nonlinear relationship, so we use a function as follows fitting the function.

$$S = ax^b + cy^d \tag{1}$$

S is the acreage of the head. x is abscissa and y is ordinate. a, b, c, d are coefficients of the function. The finally fitting function is below and the fitting result shows in Fig. 4.

$$S = 242.8511x^{-0.6807} + 0.0083y^{1.2408} \tag{2}$$

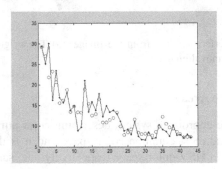

Fig. 4. The function fitting result based on the acreage of the head in different coordinates

There are many connected regions after binary image. Firstly, dealing with the image using corrosion and expansion algorithm and structural element holds a circle of 3 pixels radius. Then we remove the connected regions which are too big or too small basing on the fitting function of the head acreage. More than 4/3 and less than 1/2 of the area of predicted head are removed. Detection result shows in Fig. 5.

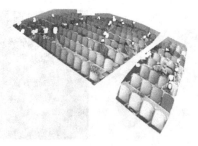

Fig. 5. The detection result which is removed the connected regions which are too big or too small

2.4   The Improved Frame Difference Method

There is false detection due to the interference of static entities such as bags and basketballs on tables and chairs. We need a method of motion detection. Since the captured video images form a fixed camera, there are important motion detection methods such as optical flow method[8], frame difference method[9] and background subtraction method[10]. The traditional frame difference method[11] is by selecting three continuous frames and doing difference and "AND" operation.

Since the movement is not obvious in the classroom, the traditional frame difference method cannot detect the movement. This article presents an improved frame difference method. It can realize a one-minute frame capturing every five seconds and perform difference of the adjacent images. Then comes the "AND" operation of all the results from difference operation. $f(x,y,t)$ is the current frame when time is t and $f(x,y,t+5)$ and $f(x,y,t+10)$ are two frames followed by 5 adjacent seconds. Frame difference operation between 5 adjacent seconds is:

$$D_{t,t+5}(x,y,t) = f(x,y,t) - f(x,y,t+5) \tag{3}$$

$$D_{t,t+10}(x,y,t) = f(x,y,t+5) - f(x,y,t+10) \tag{4}$$

$D_{t,t+5}(x,y,t)$ is the difference result between the current frame $f(x,y,t)$ and the next frame $f(x,y,t+5)$. $D_{t,t+10}(x,y,t)$ is the difference result between the next two frames $f(x,y,t+5)$ and $f(x,y,t+10)$. The "AND" operation of the difference results and the cumulative frame differential results are obtained as follows:

$$D(x,y,t) = D_{t,t+5}(x,y,t) + D_{t,t+10}(x,y,t) + ... + D_{t,t+60}(x,y,t+60) \tag{5}$$

Cumulative frame difference results shows in Fig. 6(a). It shows that this method can effectively detect the movement. We can extract the motion area by binary image and the result shows in Fig. 6(b).

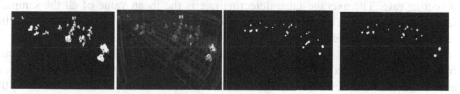

Fig. 6. Result of the method basing on the improved frame difference and the finally head area which is removed the static subject. (a) Cumulative frame differential results. (b) Binary image. (c) Original head candidate image. (d) Head area.

The original head candidate image shows in Fig. 6(c) which can remove the interference of shadow and black bag, etc. Then the head area shows in Fig. 6(d). Calculate the number of connected area as the number of students in the classroom. The classroom occupancy rate is the ratio of the number of students and the number of seats.

3   Experiment Results and Analyses

The experimental surveillance video is from the camera in classroom G104. The number of seats in the classroom is predetermined and G104 has 171 seats. In order to contrast the experiment results, we definite the evaluation indicator[12] as follows:

(1)The Correct Detecting Rate: The ratio of r_d and s_sum. r_d is the number of the head which is correctly detected and s_sum is the real number of students in classroom.

$$r\_ratio = r\_d / s\_sum \qquad (6)$$

(2)The False Detecting Rate: The ratio of w_d and s_sum. w_d is the number of the heads which is falsely detected.

$$w\_ratio = w\_d / s\_sum \qquad (7)$$

(3)The Missing Rate: The ratio of m_d and s_sum. m_d is the number of the head which is not detected.

$$m\_ratio = m\_d / s\_sum \qquad (8)$$

(4)The Actual Classroom Occupancy Rate: The ratio of s_sum and z. z is the number of the seating in classroom.

$$fz\_ratio = s\_sum / z \qquad (9)$$

(5) The Detected Classroom Occupancy Rate: The ratio of m_d and z.

$$tz\_ratio = s\_d / z \qquad (10)$$

The average correct detecting rate is the mean value of all the samples' correct detecting rate. The average false detecting rate is the mean value of all the samples' false detecting rate. The average missing detecting rate is the mean value of all the samples' missing detecting rate.

The experiment is done in the platform of MATLAB2010. The 9 images come from the same camera in G104. The number of students in the classroom is different and the time is different. The image is 1280×720. From Table 1 we can find that the mean value of right detecting rate can reach 87.71% and the average false detecting rate can reach 5.18% and the average missing detecting rate can reach 7.11%.

The method can effectively detect the number of students in the classroom. As shown in Fig. 7, the detected classroom occupancy rate and the actual classroom occupancy rate are almost the same and can be used to query the classroom occupancy rate.

Table 1. The testing results of the algorithm and its analyses

time	s_sum	s_d	r_d	w_d	m_d	r_ratio	w_ratio	m_ratio	fz_ratio	tz_ratio
10:29	16	16	16	0	0	1	0	0	0.0935	0.0935
12:19	16	15	15	0	1	0.9375	0	0.0625	0.0935	0.0877
14:32	18	17	15	1	2	0.8333	0.0555	0.1111	0.1052	0.0994
15:17	23	24	20	2	1	0.8695	0.0869	0.0434	0.1345	0.1403
16:27	23	23	19	2	2	0.826	0.0869	0.0869	0.1345	0.1345
18:22	22	21	19	1	2	0.8636	0.0454	0.0909	0.1286	0.1228
19:17	24	24	20	2	2	0.8333	0.0833	0.0833	0.1403	0.1403
20:31	31	30	26	2	3	0.8387	0.0645	0.0967	0.1812	0.1754
22:00	46	45	41	2	3	0.8913	0.0434	0.0652	0.269	0.2631

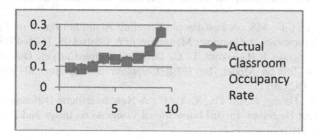

Fig. 7. Comparison between fz_ratio and tz_ratio

4   Conclusion

This paper presents a people counting method basing on head detection and motion detection for the counting of students in classrooms. The method has solved the problems of the high density of people in classrooms. The detail is not obvious since people are in different positions of the picture with different sizes. Due to the perspective effect of cameras, there is false detection. For the interference of static entities such as bags and basketballs on tables and chairs, similar problem may occur as well. Experimental results show that the average correct detecting rate can reach 87.71% and the average false detecting rate can reach 5.18%. The average missing detecting rate can reach 7.11%. Through calculating, the detected classroom occupancy rate and the actual classroom occupancy rate are almost at the same and can be used to query the classroom occupancy rate. It greatly saves the resources and provides the convenience for the students. At the same time, it provides the guarantee to the development of classroom occupancy rate query system basing on the surveillance video.

References

1. Zeng, C.-B., Ma, H.-D., C.: Robust Head-shoulder Detection by PCA-based Multilevel HOG-LBP Detector for People Counting. In: 20th International Conference on Pattern Recognition, Istanbul, pp. 2069–2072 (2010)
2. Conde, C., Moctezuma, D., Martin, D.D., MS: Gabor And HoG-based Human Detection for Surveillance in Non-controlled Environments. J. Neurocomputing 100, 19–30 (2013)
3. Gao, C.-W., Huang, K.-Q., Tan, T.-N., C.: People Counting Using Combined Feature. In: 2011 3rd Chinese Conference on Intelligent Visual Surveillance, Beijing, pp. 81–84 (2011)
4. Chan, A.B., Vasconceloos, N., MS: Counting People with Low-level Features and Bayesian Regression. J. IEEE Transactions on Image Processing. 21, 2160–2177 (2012)
5. Tan, X.-H., Wang, X.-F., Zhou, X., MS.: People Counting Based on A Variety of Population Density. J. Journal of Image and Graphics 18, 392–398 (2013)
6. Hajer, F., Jean-Luc, D., C.: People Counting System in Crowded Scenes Based on Feature Regression. In: 20th European Signal Processing Conference, Bucharest, pp. 136–140 (2012)
7. Qiang, W., Yan, F., MS.: A Fast People Counting Algorithm Based on Fusion of Color and Shape Information. J. Computer Measurement & Control 09, 1671–4598 (2010)
8. Senst, T., Evangelio, R.H., Sikora, T., C.: Detecting People Carrying Objects Based on An Optical Flow Motion Model. In: IEEE Computer Society, pp. 30–306. IEEE Press, Washington, DC (2011)
9. Weng, M.-Y., Huang, G.-C., Da, X.-Y., C.: A New Interframe Difference Algorithm for Moving Target Detection. In: 3rd International Congress on Image and Signal Processing, pp. 28–289 (2010)
10. Mohamed, S.S., Tahir, N.M., Adnan, R.: Background Modeling and Background Subtraction Performance for Object Detection. In: 6th International Colloquium on Signal Processing and Its Applications, pp. 236–241 (2010)
11. Gao, M.-F., Liu, D., M.S.: Moving Object Detection Based on Block Frame Differential and Background Subtraction. J. Computer Utility Research 01, 299–302 (2013)
12. Yuan, C.-M.: Research and Implementation of Train Traffic Detection System Based on Video Analysis. D. Southwest Jiaotong University (2013)

The Study of Feature Selection Strategy in Electrocardiogram Identification

Chen Chen, Gang Zheng, and Min Dai

School of Computer and Communication Engineering,
Tianjin University of Technology, 300384, Tianjin , China
yffschenchen@163.com, {zhenggang,daimin}@tjut.eud.cn

Abstract. Identification based on electrocardiogram (ECG) is an emerging hot spot in biometric identification. Feature selection is one of the key research points on it. In the paper, features are firstly calculated from fiducial points of ECG. Secondly, the initial feature set is composed of amplitude, interval, slope, area and some clinical indexes. Thirdly, a feature selection strategy is proposed. The strategy uses stepwise discriminant analysis to calculate the contribution (weight) of each feature for ECG identification. On the basis of contribution sorting, accumulative recognition rate is calculated. Furthermore, a key feature subset for ECG identification is acquired when accumulative recognition rate reaches a steady level. Fourthly, the identification procedure works on key feature subset. ECG data from both PTB and laboratory is used in experiments. Experimental results show that the identification accuracy of the two data sets is 99.7% and 94.8% respectively.

Keywords: ECG identification, Biometric, Feature selection, Stepwise discriminant analysis, Feature set, Feature weight.

1 Introduction

ECG identification is based on ECG signal features. Feature selection is a classic problem [1] in pattern recognition. In general, the scope of initial feature set is large when containing most feature information. This may cause dimension curse [2, 3]. Also, correlation and redundancy among features may affect accuracy and efficiency of recognition. Therefore, it is significant to sort features according to certain rules and select a feasible feature set, which is a subset of initial, named key feature subset.

This paper discusses feature selection strategy for ECG identification. ECG is biological potential waveform of human heart. It varies from person to person [4, 5]. Each living person has ECG signal. Each person's ECG is relatively stable in a certain period of time (normal decades). Under different situations (like pressure, anxiety, running, resting, etc.), ECG reflects heart condition (including geometric structure, size, location, etc.). Namely, each person's ECG is different. Namely, ECG satisfies the universality, stability, and uniqueness of biometric identification [5, 6]. To sum up, ECG is a kind of feasible biometric signal for identification [7-11].

Z. Sun et al. (Eds.): CCBR 2014, LNCS 8833, pp. 489–497, 2014.

One heartbeat interval of ECG is usually composed of P wave, QRS complex and T wave. It contains abundant identification information. Peaks and troughs (P, Q, R, S and T), onsets and offsets of waveform (P1, P2, Q', S', T1 and T2) are called fiducial points, as shown in figure 1. Features (like amplitude, interval, slope and area) are calculated from these fiducial point coordinates.

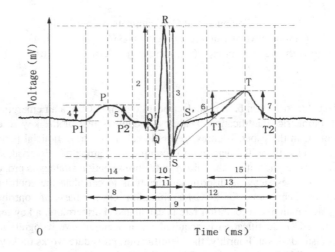

Fig. 1. Diagram of ECG waveform features (partial)

ECG biometric identification is a living identification. It has strong security to avoid the danger of imitation (like fake finger in fingerprint identification) [12]. Researchers have done much research on it and made some promising achievements. Most of the studies were based on features. This paper reviewed related works from the following aspects: experiment dataset, tester amount, identification method (PCA-Principal Component Analysis, MD- Mahalanobis Distance, LDA-Linear Discriminant Analysis, WL- Wilks' Lambda, RBF NN- RBF Neural Network, TM-Template Matching, AT- Adaptive Threshold, DTW- Dynamic Time Waveform), selected features and recognition rate. They are shown in table 1.

In the existing studies on the feature based ECG identification, the scope of feature is large and different. They have not reached a broad consensus in feature selection. They have also led to poor generality of initial feature set and the difference in recognition rate, as shown in table 1.

In the paper, we propose a strategy. Firstly, we sort all initial features according to their contribution to identification. The contribution rate is evaluated by weight. Secondly, a classifier is used for selecting feature in descending order of sorting. When the cumulated recognition rate is steady, a key feature subset is acquired. Ultimately, we use the key feature subset for identification and get better recognition accuracy.

Table 1. Previous works of feature based ECG identification

	Author	Dataset	Tester Amount	Identification Method	Selected Features	Recognition Rate (%)
1	Biel[13]	lab collect	22(healthy)	PCA	10	100
2	Kyoso[14]	lab collect	9 (healthy)	MD,LDA	3	90+
3	Israela[15]	lab collect	29 (healthy)	WL,LDA	15	100
4	Wang[16]	lab collect	10 (healthy)	RBF NN	8	100
5	Wang[17]	lab collect	13 (healthy)	LDA	15	100
6	Singh[18]	MIT-BIH	15(patients) 10 (healthy)	TM,AT	20	99
7	Shorten[19]	MIT-QT	719 beats	DTW	3	98.5

2   Selection of Initial Feature Set

Compared with features selected from previous works, both features in common sense and main parameters used for clinical heart disease diagnosis are selected as our initial feature set (including 26 features), as shown in table 2 (amp.-amplitude, int.-interval). Description of part features is shown in figure 1.

Features used for previous experiments were commonly calculated from ECG fiducial points. The accuracy of locating points by algorithm automatically has huge impact on ECG identification accuracy. The missing location of any point would enlarge the error in feature calculation and lead to low identification rate.

In order to explore the real value of features for ECG identification, we locate fiducial points and calculate features manually. This is expected to acquire the real contribution of each feature for identification. It can help us find out the key feature subset that can be applied to further ECG identification.

Table 2. The initial feature set

No.	Feature	Description	No.	Feature	Description	No.	Feature	Description
1	Heart Rate	heartbeats per minute	10	I_R	Q-S int.	19	S_{PP2}	P-P$_2$ slope
2	H_{QR}	Q-R amp.	11	I_{QRS}	Q'-S' int.	20	$S_{Q'Q}$	Q'-Q slope
3	H_{RS}	R-S amp.	12	I_{QT}	Q'-T$_2$ int.	21	S_{QR}	Q-R slope
4	H_{T1T}	T$_1$-T amp.	13	I_{ST}	S'-T$_2$ int.	22	S_{RS}	R-S slope
5	H_{TT2}	T-T$_2$ amp.	14	I_P	P$_1$-P$_2$ int.	23	$S_{SS'}$	S-S' slope
6	H_{P1P}	P$_1$-P amp.	15	I_T	T$_1$-T$_2$ int.	24	S_{T1T}	T$_1$-T slope
7	H_{PP2}	P-P$_2$ amp.	16	S_{ST}	S-T slope	25	S_{TT2}	T-T$_2$ slope
8	I_{PR}	P$_1$-Q' int.	17	$S_{S'T}$	S'-T slope	26	$A_{SS'T}$	area of S, S' and T
9	I_{PT}	P-T int.	18	S_{P1P}	P$_1$-P slope			

3   Feature Selection Strategy

This paper uses stepwise discriminant analysis in the evaluation of the identification contribution rate of each feature in the initial feature set. They are sorted by their contribution rate (namely, weight) in descending order. In training procedure, we use features in descending order and calculate the cumulative recognition accuracy. When the accuracy reaches a steady status, the key feature subset is acquired and can be used for later classification accuracy test. The specific process is shown in figure 2.

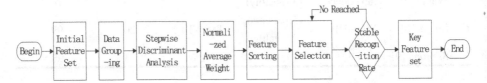

Fig. 2. The flow chart of feature selection strategy

3.1   Stepwise Discriminant Analysis

At the beginning, there is no feature in discriminant model. Features are introduced one by one through stepwise discriminant analysis. The model needs to be tested in each step. Feature outside the model with the largest contribution to discriminant ability will be joined to each step of the model. Then, features in the model which do not meet the criterion will be excluded. This is because of the fact that the new intro-duced features are likely to make the contribution of features in the model less signif-icant. This process will not stop until all features in model meet the criterion remain-ing in the model. Features outside the model do not meet the criterion.

For testers G_1, G_2, ..., G_k. Each tester has n_i groups of heartbeat interval features, m features are extracted from each interval. Each group of feature can be described as

$$X_{(j)}^{(i)} = (X_{(j1)}^{(i)}, X_{(j2)}^{(i)}, \cdots X_{(jm)}^{(i)})^T, \quad (i=1,2,\ldots,k; j=1,2,\ldots,n_i; n=n_1+n_2+\ldots+n_k, m=26) \ .$$

According to the principle of the multivariate analysis of variance, stepwise dis-criminant analysis is used to measure contribution ability of features. Wilks' lambda statistics is also in use. We define A: matrix of within group dispersion, B: matrix of between group dispersion and T: total dispersion matrix, and sample average vector

$\bar{X} = \dfrac{1}{n}\sum\limits_{i=1}^{k}\sum\limits_{j=1}^{n_i}X_{(j)}^{(i)}$, average vector of sample i $\bar{X}^{(i)} = \dfrac{1}{n_i}\sum\limits_{i=1}^{n_i}X_{(j)}^{(i)}$.

$$A = \sum_{i=1}^{k} A_i = \sum_{i=1}^{k}\sum_{j=1}^{n_i}(X_{(j)}^{(i)} - \bar{X}^{(i)})(X_{(j)}^{(i)} - \bar{X}^{(i)})^T \ . \tag{1}$$

$$B = \sum_{i=1}^{k} n_i(\bar{X}^{(i)} - \bar{X})(\bar{X}^{(i)} - \bar{X})^T \ . \tag{2}$$

$$T = \sum_{i=1}^{k}\sum_{j=1}^{n_i}(X_{(j)}^{(i)} - \bar{X})(X_{(j)}^{(i)} - \bar{X})^T = A+B \ . \tag{3}$$

The likelihood ratio statistic is derived from likelihood ratio principle

$$\Lambda = |A|/|T| \ . \tag{4}$$

The subset X^* has q features. It calculates partial Wilks' lambda statistics and the significant level of F test on outside features. We can know whether the adding feature X_t is in or not.

$$\Lambda(X_t \mid X^*) = \Lambda(X^*, X_t)/\Lambda(X^*) \ . \tag{5}$$

$$F = \frac{n-k-q}{k-1} \cdot \frac{1-\Lambda(X_t \mid X^*)}{\Lambda(X_t \mid X^*)} \sim F_\alpha(k-1, n-k-q) \ . \tag{6}$$

If $F \geq F_{in} = F_\alpha(k-1, n-k-q) = 3.84$ （F distribution, $\alpha=0.05$）, feature X_t should be added in. Similarly, we can get to the point whether to move feature X_p out from subset X^* or not.

$$F = \frac{n-k-q+1}{k-1} \cdot \frac{1-\Lambda[X_p \mid X^*(p)]}{\Lambda[X_p \mid X^*(p)]} \sim F_\alpha(k-1, n-k-q+1) \ . \tag{7}$$

If $F < F_{out} = F_\alpha(k-1, n-k-q+1) = 2.71$, feature X_p should be moved out from subset. $X^*(p)$ is the subset moving feature X_p out from X^*.

The above procedure will not stop until no new feature can be added in.

4   Experiment and Analysis

4.1   Experimental Data

Two ECG data sets used in the paper are PTB [20] and laboratory collected data set

PTB (Physikalisch-Technische Bundesanstalt) is an ECG database provided by German National Institute of Metrology for medical diagnosis. We selected 60s (about 70 heartbeat intervals) V5-lead ECG from 60 healthy testers (No. 1-60, from 17 to 85 year-old, 43 males and 17 females). Laboratory collected 90s (about 110 heartbeat intervals) V5-lead ECG from 120 healthy undergraduates (No. 61-180, from 20 to 22 year-old, 85 males and 35 females). Each tester was randomly selected. 56 and 24 complete heartbeat intervals were given to extract features for training and testing.

4.2   Experimental Procedures

4.2.1   Experimental Data Grouping

After investigating the application scale of identification (such as fingerprint attendance system, face recognition system) in daily life and previous researching literatures, our experiments take 30 testers as a unit dataset. Therefore, PTB data set can be divided into 2 groups: (1) No.1-30, (2) No.31-60; The collected data set can be divided into 4 groups: (3) A (No.61-90), (4) B (No.91-120), (5) C (No.121-150), (6) D (No.151-180); In addition, we take the growth of the amount of data into account, assembling these unit datasets separately and acquire another 12 data sets: (7) PTB No.1-60,(8) AB, (9) AC, (10) AD, (11) BC, (12) BD, (13) CD;(14) ABC; (15) ABD; (16) ACD; (17) BCD; (18) ABCD.

4.2.2   Grouping Feature Sorting

Taking No.1-30 testers from PTB for example, after using stepwise discriminant analysis, we obtained the feature sorting of this group according to their significant level of F test. The result is shown in table 3. Similar results can be acquired from other data groups.

Table 3. Result of feature sorting of No.1-30 tester in PTB

Order	Feature	F-static	No. of feature
1	H_{RS}	1349.025	3
2	S_{ST}	855.851	16
...	...	...	...
26	H_{PP2}	2.455	7

4.2.3   Calculation of Normalized Average Weight

After analyzing experimental results of the two data sets, we proposed a formula of average score w_{Xm} and normalized average weight $w_{Xm(normalized\ average)}$ of each feature (tt: test times on different data sets, slc: the number of feature selected in each experiment, $occr$: the number of occurrence of each feature in total experiments, r: the sorting of each feature in test).

$$w_{X_m} = \frac{1}{occr} \cdot \sum_{s=1}^{tt} \frac{slc\text{-}r+1}{slc}, s = 1,2,3\ldots, tt; m = 1,2,\ldots,26 \quad \cdot \tag{8}$$

$$w_{X_m(normalized\ average)} = w_{X_m} \cdot \frac{occr}{tt} = \frac{1}{tt} \cdot \sum_{s=1}^{tt} \frac{slc\text{-}r+1}{slc}, s = 1,2,\ldots, tt; m = 1,2,\ldots,26 \quad \cdot \tag{9}$$

The normalized average weight of each feature of the two data sets in descending order is shown in table 4.

Table 4. The normalized average weight of each feature in the two datasets

	PTB			Lab collect	
Order	Feature	Normalized Average weight	Order	Feature	Normalized Average weight
1	H_{RS}	0.968	1	$Area_{SST}$	0.937
2	S_{RS}	0.851	2	H_{QR}	0.933
3	I_{PT}	0.791	3	H_{TT2}	0.748
4	HR	0.780	4	I_{PT}	0.734
5	H_{T1T}	0.718	5	I_{ST}	0.656
6	$S_{S'T}$	0.663	6	I_{T1T2}	0.579
7	$Area_{SST}$	0.661	7	I_{P1P2}	0.559
8	S_{ST}	0.657	8	$S_{S'T}$	0.513
9	S_{QR}	0.633	9	I_{PR}	0.493
...	...	...	...	...	...
26	H_{PP2}	0.043	26	I_{QT}	0.000

4.2.4   Feature Selection

Features were taken as variables in stepwise discriminant analysis. They were added into feature set for training in the order of table 4. Identification rate of each experiment was obtained by cross validation. The results are shown in figure 3.

Through figure 3, we find that when the former 9 features in PTB and 17 features in collected data set are taken as key feature subset for identification, the recognition rate can reach 100% and 95.7% steadily. Therefore, to PTB and collected data set, experiments with the former 9 and 17 features can get stable identification rate.

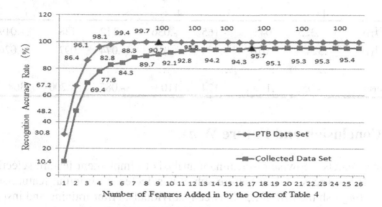

Fig. 3. The curve of identification accuracy rate

4.3   Verification and Analysis

In order to justify the performance of features selected by the proposed strategy, testers (each tester selects 24 heartbeat intervals) are selected randomly for demonstration. When choosing the selected 9 features of PTB and 17 features of collected data set as key features for identification test, the recognition rate reaches 99.7% and 94.8%.

From table 4, we get 9 key features from PTB. We can find 6 identical features and 2 similar features in the 17 key features from collected data set. To some extent, for different data sets, the selected key features are different. But features selected by stepwise discriminant analysis for identification are relatively concentrated, which means that this strategy is feasible.

4.4   Comparative Experiment

We use PCA in literature [13] to select key features. 26 eigenvalues were obtained (values greater than 1 are 7.771, 4.1731, 2.8427, 2.5282, 2.3301, 1.6728, 1.3052) in total variance explanation. According to the Kaiser rule, we acquire 7 principle components (C1{feature 4,5,25,24,3,2,17,22,21,20,16}, C2{feature 13,9,12,15,1,8}, C3{feature 7,6}, C4{feature 26,11}, C5{feature 10,23,18}, C6{feature 14}, C7{feature 19}). The coefficient of feature in components is shown in table 5. These 7 components can explain 83.8% of total variance. Then use them as new key features for identification test and get the accuracy rate of PTB and the data set collected is 99.8% and 95.6% respectively.

Compared with the method proposed by this paper, identification rate of using PCA in selection features improves slightly. While all initial features are used for identification, there is no dimension reduction actually.

Table 5. Coefficient of principle components

Feature	Component						
	1	2	3	4	5	6	7
H_{T1T}	.325	.045	-.165	-.036	-.112	.138	-.019
H_{TT2}	.324	.016	-.184	-.019	-.074	.097	-.026
...	...	...	...	...	...	...	...
S_{PP2}	-.056	.199	-.174	.110	-.087	-.200	.368

5   Conclusion and Future Work

This paper selects stepwise discriminant analysis to implement feature selection from different data sources. A key feature subset is selected from initial feature set and is used to distinguish the difference between individuals. After training and inspection, a complete strategy for feature selection and identification is obtained.

Future work will be on collecting different ECG data sources (devices) in order to finish further experiments. More works will be carried out on the feature contribution study. The target is to find universal features for ECG identification. We will focus on fiducial point's positioning algorithm. This will be the basement of ECG identification.

Acknowledgement. The paper is supported by Tianjin Key Foundation on Science Supporting Plan (10ZCKFSF00800), and Tianjin Natural Science Foundation (10JCYBJC00700) .

References

1. Harol, A., Lai, C.P., Kalska, E.: Pairwise Feature Evaluation for Constructing Reduced Representations. J. Pattern Analysis & Applications 10(1), 55–68 (2007)
2. Bishop, C.M.: Neural Networks for Pattern Recognition. Clwerendon Press, Oxford (1995)
3. Song, F.X., Gao, X.M., Liu, S.H.: Dimensionality Reduction in Statistical Pattern Recognition and Low Loss Dimensionality Reduction. J. Chinese Journal of Computers 28(11), 1915–1922 (2005)
4. Chan, A.D.C., Hamdy, M.M., Badre, A.: Person Identification Using Electrocardiograms. In: Canadian Conference on IEEE Electrical & Computer Engineering. CCECE 2006, pp. 1–4 (2006)
5. Peng, H.: A Method Based on Wavelet Transform and SVM of ECG Human Identification. J. Microelectronics & Computer 30(3), 152–155 (2013)

6. Li, J.Z., Jing, Y., Zhang, Q.L.: The Study of the Uniqueness of the ECG Waveform in Individual. J. Journal of Medical Forum 29(4), 45–46 (2008)
7. Agrafioti, F., Hatzinakos, D.: ECG Based Recognition Using Second Order Statistics. In: 6th Annual Communication Networks and Services Research Conference, CNSR 2008, pp. 82–87. IEEE (2008)
8. Odinaka, I., Lai, P.H., Kaplan, A.: ECG Biometrics: A Robust Short-Time Frequency Analysis. In: Proceedings of IEEE International Workshop on Information Forensics and Security, pp. 1–6 (2010)
9. Yang, X.L., Yan, H., Ren, Z.R.: Analytic Feature Selection of ECG Based BAB Algorithm for Human Identification. J. Chinese Journ. of Scientific Instrument 31(10), 2394–2400 (2010)
10. Chen, X.Z., Wysocki, T., Agrafioti, F.: Securing Handheld Devices and Fingerprint Readers with ECG Biometrics. In: 2012 IEEE Fifth International Conference on Digital Biometrics: Theory, Applications and Systems (BTAS), pp. 150–155 (2012)
11. Gao, Z., Wu, J., Zhou, J.: Design of ECG Signal Acquisition and Processing System. In: 2012 International Conference on Biomedical Engineering and Biotechnology (iCBEB), pp. 762–764. IEEE (2012)
12. Tian, Q.C., Zhang, R.S.: Survey on Biomitrics Technology. J. Application Research of Computer 26(12), 4401–4406 (2010)
13. Biel, L., Pettersson, O., Philipson, L.: ECG Analysis: A New Approach in Human Identification. IEEE Transactions on J. Instrumentation and Measurement 50(3), 808–812 (2001)
14. Kyoso, M., Uchiyama, A.: Development of an ECG Identification System. In: Proceedings of the 23rd Annual International Conference of the IEEE Engineering in Medicine and Biology Society, pp. 3721–3723. IEEE (2001)
15. Israel, S.A., Irvine, J.M., Cheng, A.: ECG to Identify Individuals. J. Pattern recognition 38(1), 133–142 (2005)
16. Wang, L.: Research on Identification Technology Based on ECG. D. Shandong University (2005)
17. Wang, Y., Plataniotis, K.N., Hatzinakos, D.: Integrating Analytic and Appearance Attributes for Human Identification from ECG Signals. In: 2006 Biometrics Symposium: Special Session on Research at the Biometric Consortium Conference, pp. 1–6. IEEE (2006)
18. Singh, Y.N., Gupta, P.: ECG to Individual Identification. In: 2nd IEEE International Conference on Biometrics: Theory, Applications and Systems, pp. 1–8. IEEE (2008)
19. Shorten, G.P., Burke, M.J.: A Time Domain Based Classifier for ECG Pattern Recognition. In: 2011 Annual International Conference of the IEEE Engineering in Medicine and Biology Society, EMBC, pp. 4980–4983. IEEE (2011)
20. Physiobank – Physiological Signal Archives, The ECG Signal,Archive, The MIT-BIH QT Database, http://www.physionet.org/physiobank/database

A Novel Method for Shoeprint Recognition in Crime Scenes

Xiangbin Kong, Chunyu Yang, and Fengde Zheng

Beijing Hisign Technology Co.Ltd., China
{kongxiangbin,yangchunyu,zhengfengde}@hisign.com.cn

Abstract. We present a novel method for shoeprint recognition in crime scenes. First, a preprocessing algorithm is introduced to remove the complicated background, and then Gabor features and Zernike features are extracted and fused to represent the textural and statistical features of shoeprint images. Lastly, a matching approach is also presented to solve the problem of identifying incomplete shoeprints which account for a large proportion in all the captured images. The samples in our database are directly collected from crime scenes. In the experiment, 104 probe shoeprints are tested on a gallery set containing 1,225 shoeprints. Results show that our method is practical and provides better performance in identifying crime scene shoeprint than other algorithms.

Keywords: crime scene shoeprint recognition, Gabor feature, Zernike feature, incomplete shoeprint matching.

1 Introduction

Shoeprint recognition is very important for identifying criminals and linking crime scenes but it is ignored in recent years. A study conducted by Switzerland [1] showed that about 35% of the crime scenes have usable shoeprints. Shoeprints are always used in three different tasks: (i) Compare shoeprints with all available shoes on the market to decide its brand and type. (ii)Compare shoeprints in different crime scenes (to link between crimes). (iii)Match shoeprints with the ones stored in the suspects' database. However, because of the complicated background and the incomplete marks, shoeprint recognition has been a long and challenging task. A lot of semiautomatic systems have been developed. Usually, there are 3 main steps to complete the whole process.

Image acquisition and preprocessing. A number of samples [2][3] used in recent research are generated by taking participants' shoeprints with a scanner which always have good quality. Partial images are obtained by splitting the whole image horizontally or vertically. Because the images are different in size and always have noisy parts, some image processing methods such as filtering, background removal and down sampling are applied. For bad quality images, manual work is always necessary in this step.

Feature Extraction. Different features can be chosen according to the shoeprint image quality. Philip de Chazal[2] used power spectral density(PSD) features which

Z. Sun et al. (Eds.): CCBR 2014, LNCS 8833, pp. 498–505, 2014.

calculated by squaring the absolute value of the Fourier Transform of the image. Mourad Gueham[5] also chose features in Fourier domain, but instead of magnitude, they used phase information. Maria Pavlou[3] extracted Harris-Affines(HA) and Maximally Stable Extremal Region(MSER) features to get the affine stable regions and to represent patterns and shapes. These features work well in good quality footprint images, but it fails for those images with lots of background noise because noisy area in the background will greatly affect the HA and MSER feature extraction and representation. Gharsa AlGarni[4] used Hu Moments for its invariant property under translation, rotation and scaling. However, Hu Moments method is a third order moment which limits its representation ability. It is widely used in simple shapes such as: planes, apples, trees and so on. A lot of details of the shoeprint image cannot be obtained. Other features such as SIFT, SURF are also not suitable for shoeprint feature extraction because most of the interest points will be on the noisy background, features of the prints cannot be extracted.

Matching. There is no public database for shoeprints, so all the researchers give their recognition rate based on different databases, and then make a comparison with other method on their own database. 2D correlation coefficient was considered to measure the similarity of two shoeprints in[2], and first-rank recognition rate in their database was 67%. Gaussian weighed similarity metric is also used in [3] to determine the similarity of HA and MSER features with a first-rank recognition of 87 %. Four types of similarity measures: Euclidean distance, City Block distance, Canberra distance and Correlation distance are applied in[4] with a result of 98%. All the databases used in above methods are good quality images which are not taken directly from crime scenes.

In this paper, we proposed a new shoeprint recognition method. Due to the complex background, a manual preprocessing method is introduced first. Then textural feature (Gabor features) and high order statistical feature (Zernike moments) are extracted to represent different aspects of the shoeprint image, both of the features are stable in complicated background situations. At last, we give a method to solve the matching problem of the incomplete footprints, and the matching step is accomplished by normalized coefficient measurement.

The rest of this paper is organized as follows. Section 2 describes the database and image processing algorithm. Section 3 presents our feature extraction and matching method. Section 4 shows the experimental results and comparison with other method in our database. Section 5 is devoted to discussions and conclusions.

2   Shoeprint Image Preprocessing

We captured shoeprint images from a number of crime scenes. And a total number of 1,329 shoeprints were collected. 1,121 of them are single prints that means no same pattern can be found in the database, the other 208 prints are 104 pairs, each of them has a same pattern print in the database, although some of them are incomplete. A number of the images are incomplete and have complex background. It is impossible to extract features directly from these images, so we introduce a procedure to extract the shoeprint area. There are mainly 4 steps:

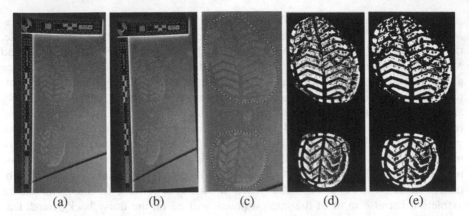

(a)   (b)   (c)   (d)   (e)

Fig. 1. Preprocessing of shoeprint images. (a)original image, (b)rotating, (c)cutting and marking, (d)thresholding, (e)noise removing.

Rotating. Most of the shoeprint images captured at the crime scene are a little bias, rotate them to the right position which shown in Fig.1. (b).

Footprint Area Cutting and Marking. Cut shoeprint image according to its bounding rectangle, then mark the contour of the shoeprints as shown in Fig.1.(c).

Thresholding. A local based thresholding method is performed. We can obtain the binary image of the shoeprint as shown in Fig.1. (d).

Noise Removing. There are always some isolated noisy areas in the binary image, so median filter and other morphology algorithms such as dilation and erosion are used to remove the noise. The result shown in Fig.1. (e) is the input image of the feature extraction step.

3   Feature Extraction and Matching

Intuitively, texture style is the most distinctive feature of the shoeprint images, so Gabor feature is an appropriate choice. And moment feature is also a useful tool to define shapes. As described before, Hu moments is incapable of representing details of the image, we choose high order Zernike moment to describe shoeprint image in another aspect. In this section, firstly, Gabor feature is introduced briefly, then we propose the Zernike moment feature. Lastly, an effective matching method is also mentioned.

3.1   Gabor Feature

Gabor filter, with its excellent ability to detect edges, is widely used in face recognition and fingerprint enhancement [6]. Here it is applied to describe shoeprint patterns.

The even-symmetric Gabor filter has the general form in equation(1):

$$h(x, y : \phi, f) = \exp\left\{-\frac{1}{2}\left[\frac{x_\phi^2}{\delta_x^2} + \frac{y_\phi^2}{\delta_y^2}\right]\right\}\cos\left(2\pi f x_\phi\right) \tag{1}$$

$$x_\phi = x\cos\phi + y\sin\phi$$
$$y_\phi = -x\sin\phi + y\sin\phi \tag{2}$$

Where ϕ is the orientation of the Gabor filter, f is the frequency of a sinusoidal wave, δ_x and δ_y are the standard deviation of the Gaussian envelope along x and y axes. In order to get all texture features in different directions and frequencies, several values of ϕ and f are applied to do the filtering. The average value and standard deviation of each filtered image are computed and then cascaded to form the Gabor features.

3.2 Zernike Moment Feature

Zernike moments are constructed using a set of complex polynomial [7] that is a complete orthogonal basis set defined on the unit circle $(x^2 + y^2) \leq 1$. It can be used to compute any order of the image, the higher the order is, more detail of the image can be represented. Besides all the advantages above, Zernike moment is rotational invariant which is a good complementary property to Gabor feature.

In this section, we will first introduce the original expression of Zernike moments [8] briefly, and then show the pseudo-Zernike expression proposed by Mukundan in [10] which is easier to realize.

Zernike polynomial expressed in polar coordinates is defined as:

$$V_{mn}(r,\theta) = R_{mn}(r)\exp(jn\theta) \tag{3}$$

where (r,θ) is the radial and angle of points on the unit circle, $j = \sqrt{-1}$, and $R_{mn}(r)$ is orthogonal radial polynomial, defined as:

$$R_{mn}(r) = \sum_{s=0}^{m-|n|} (-1)^s \frac{(m-s)!}{s!\left(\dfrac{m+|n|}{2}-s\right)!\left(\dfrac{m-|n|}{2}-s\right)!} r^{m-2s} \tag{4}$$

where $m = 0, 1, 2, \cdots$ and defines the moment's order, n depicts the angular dependence, subject to:

$$m - |n| = even\ number,\ |n| \leq m \tag{5}$$

The original Zernike moment is :

$$Z_{mn} = \frac{m+1}{\pi} \int_0^{2\pi} \int_0^1 \left[V_{mn}^*(\rho,\theta)\right] f(\rho,\theta) d\rho d\theta \tag{6}$$

From (6), we can see that compute Z_{mn} directly is very difficult and time consuming, so algorithm presented in[9][10] is applied to obtain the pseudo-Zernike moment. There are four steps in the algorithm:

1. Normalize the image to size of $N \times N$, where $-N/2 \leq x, y \leq N/2$, then transform Cartesian (x, y) to polar coordinates (ρ, θ). Two intermediate variables (r, σ) are used in the transform.

$$r = \max(|x|, |y|) \tag{7}$$

$$\sigma = \frac{2(r-x)y}{|y|} + \frac{xy}{r} \qquad if \ |x|=r$$
$$\sigma = 2y - \frac{xy}{r} \qquad if \ |y|=r \tag{8}$$

Then (ρ,θ) is defined as:

$$\rho = \frac{2r}{N}, \theta = \frac{\pi\sigma}{4r} \tag{9}$$

It can be proved that $\rho \in [1, N/2], \theta \in [1, 8r]$

2. Calculate $R_{mn}(r)$ defined in (4).

3. Get Zernike moment using formulation below:

$$C_{mn} = \frac{2n+2}{N^2} \sum_{r=1}^{N/2} R_{mn}(2r/N) \sum_{\sigma=1}^{8r} \cos\frac{\pi m\sigma}{4r} f(r,\sigma)$$
$$S_{mn} = -\frac{2n+2}{N^2} \sum_{r=1}^{N/2} R_{mn}(2r/N) \sum_{\sigma=1}^{8r} \sin\frac{\pi m\sigma}{4r} f(r,\sigma) \tag{10}$$

$$Z_{mn} = \sqrt{C_{mn}^2 + S_{mn}^2} \tag{11}$$

From (7) - (11), we can see that calculation of Z_{mn} has been greatly simplified, the algorithm is implemented to extract Zernike features of shoeprints in this paper.

3.3   Feature Matching

We use normalized correlation coefficient as similarity score:

$$score(X_1, X_2) = \frac{1}{2}\left(\frac{X_1 X_2}{\sqrt{|X_1|^2}\sqrt{|X_2|^2}} + 1 \right) \tag{12}$$

where X_1 and X_2 are feature vectors.

The whole feature extracting and matching process is: for shoeprint sample S_1 and S_2, first Gabor feature G_1, G_2 and Zernike feature Z_1, Z_2 are extracted separately, then $score_g = score(G_1, G_2)$ and $score_z = score(Z_1, Z_2)$ is calculated, the final similarity score of S_1 and S_2 is fusion of the two scores in (13).

$$score = a * score_g + (1-a) * score_z \qquad a \in [0,1] \tag{13}$$

4   Experiments

This section contains two parts. First part gives the details and parameters of our shoeprint recognition algorithm. The second part shows the result and the comparison with other methods.

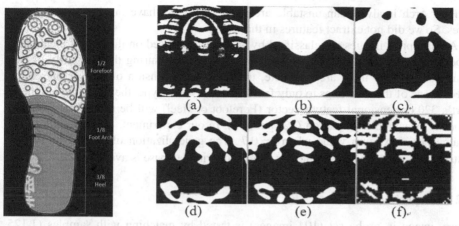

Fig. 2. Left image shows how we divide shoeprint into three parts and the corresponding ratio. Right images are shoe images reconstructed using different orders of Zernike moment. (a)original image, (b) 12 orders, (c)22 orders, (d) 32 orders, (e) 42 orders, (f)49 orders.

4.1 Implementation Details

Our shoeprint database was grouped into two sets: gallery set containing 1,225 images and probe set containing104 images. All the crime scene shoeprint images are different in size, so they are all normalized to a standard size of 256×512 pixels. Feature vector of the images is extracted as below:

Gabor Features. To obtain textures with different scales and directions, 24 filters (4 frequencies and 6 directions) are applied to extract Gabor features of the shoeprint images. Average value and standard deviation of the filtered image is calculated which makes a feature vector with $2 \times 24 = 48$ dimensions.

Zernike Features. Order of Zernike moments plays an important role in representing the shoeprint patterns. To find the right order, we reconstruct the original image by using different orders of Zernike moment. The result is shown in right part of Fig.2. Although higher order moments seem better, it will take much more time and the recognition rate was not much improved in our experiment. 32 order moments is an appropriate choice both in reconstruct ability and compute duration. 32 order moments generate a feature vector of 272 dimensions.

Shoeprint feature vector. Considering a number of shoeprint in the crime scene are incomplete in different parts, we divide shoeprint into three main parts: forefoot, foot-arch and heel, which is shown in left part of Fig. 2. Each shoeprint, in spite of its completeness, will be described by the following 960 dimensional features:

1. Gabor and Zernike feature of the original image are extracted, which make a 320 dimensional vector.

2. Forefoot of the shoeprint image which is the upper half of the image form a 320 dimensional vector.

3. Heel part of the shoeprint image which is about 3/8 of the whole image, also described by a 320 dimensional vector.

Foot Arch is always an unstable area and it does not have much distinctive features. So we did not extract features in that part.

All shoeprint images are classified by an algorithm based on their valid area into 3 types: complete, only forefoot and only heel. When measuring the similarity of two images, if both of them are complete, the first 320 dimension of the vector will be used; if one of them belongs to only forefoot or only heel type, the relatively complete part's 320 dimensional feature vector (Forefoot or Heel) will be used. The matching score is measured by equation (12) and (13). In our experiment, the recognition rate attained its maximum value when $a = 0.7$. The generalization of a will be further tested when we get more samples or other shoeprint database is available.

4.2   Experiment Results

Every image in probe set (104 images) is tested by matching with samples (1,125 images) in the gallery set. And Gabor feature score and Zernike feature score are fused using equation (13). There are not much method really based on crime scene images and it's difficult to get other databases. So we implemented the algorithm proposed in [2] and had it tested on our database. Figure (3) plots the Cumulative Match Characteristic (CMC) curve of our method and the method proposed in [2].

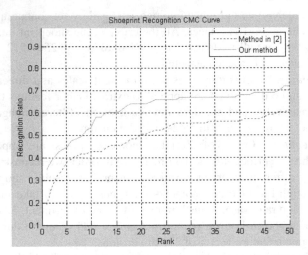

Fig. 3. CMC curve of our method (solid line) and method presented in [2] (dash line)

Table 1. 1,5,10 and 20 rank recognition rate of our method and method in [2]

Rank	1Rank	5 Rank	10 Rank	20Rank
Top Rate:		(0.4%)	(0.8%)	(1.6%)
Our Method	34.59%	44.66%	53.40%	64.08%
Method in [2]	19.42%	37.86%	42.72%	50.49%

5   Discussion and Conclusion

We have presented a novel method to identify shoeprints. There are three main key contributions. First, our whole system based on images that are taken directly from crime scene while most of other method can't do the same. Second, texture feature and moment feature are both considered in our algorithm, they define the shoeprint image in different aspects, and make good complementation. Third, our matching process solved the problem of measuring similarity between partial shoeprints. Extensive experiments showed that our approach is efficient and stable.

References

1. Girod, A.: Computer Classification of the shoeprint of Burglar Soles. J. Forensic Science 82, 59–65 (1996)
2. Philip, C., John, F., Richard, B.R.: Automated Processing of Shoeprint Images Based on the Fourier Transform for Use in Forensic Science. IEEE Transactions on Pattern Analysis and Machine Intelligence 27, 341–350 (2005)
3. Maria, P., Nigel, M.A.: Automatic Extraction and Classification of Footwear Patterns. In: 2006 Intelligent Data Engineering and Automated Learning (IDEAL), pp. 721–728 (2006)
4. AlGarni, G., Hamiane, M.: A Novel Technique for Automatic Shoeprint Image Retrieval. J. Forensic Science 181, 10–14 (2008)
5. Gueham, M., Bouridane, A., Crookes, D.: Automatic Recognition of Partial Shoeprints Based on Phase-Only Correlation. In: IEEE Conference on International Conference on Image Processing (ICIP), pp. 441–444. IEEE (2007)
6. Hong, L., Yi, F.W., Jain, A.K.: Fingerprint Image Enhancement: Algorithm and Performance Evaluation. IEEE Transactions on Pattern Analysis and Machine Intelligence 20, 777–798 (1998)
7. Zernike, F.: Diffraction Theory of the Cut Procedure and Its Improved Form, the Phase Contrast Method. Physica 1, 689–704 (1934)
8. Chin, T.: On Image Analysis By the Method of moments. IEEE Transactions on Pattern Analysis and Machine Intelligence 10, 496–513 (1988)
9. Bhatia, A.B., Wolf, E.: On the Circle Polynomials of Zernike and Related orthogonal sets. Proceedings of Cambridge Philosophical Societ 50, 40–48 (1954)
10. Mukundan, R., Ramakrisshnan, K.R.: Moment Functions in Image Analysis: Theory and applications. World Scientific (1998)
11. Rathinavel, S., Arumugam, S.: Full Shoe Print Recognition based on Pass Band DCT and Partial Shoe Print Identification using Overlapped Block Method for Degraded Images. J. International Journal of Computer Applications 26, 16–21 (2011)

Person Re-identification with Data-Driven Features

Xiang Li, Jinyu Gao, Xiaobin Chang, Yuting Mai, and Wei-Shi Zheng

School of Information Science and Technology, Sun Yat-sen University,
510006 Guangzhou, China
{lixiang651,sistjygao,littlesoliderchang,ytmai2013}@gmail.com,
wszheng@ieee.org

Abstract. Human-specified appearance features are widely used for person re-identification at present, such as color and texture histograms. Often, these features are limited by the subjective appearance of pedestrians. This paper presents a new representation to re-identification that incorporates data-driven features to improve the reliability and robustness in person matching. Firstly, we utilize a deep learning network, namely PCA Network, to learn data-driven features from person images. The features mine more discriminative cues from pedestrian data and compensate the drawback of human-specified features. Then the data-driven features and common human-specified features are combined to produce a final representation of each image. The so-obtained enriched Data-driven Representation (eDR) has been validated through experiments on two person re-identification datasets, demonstrating that the proposed representation is effective for person matching. That is, the data-driven features facilitate more accurate re-identification when they are fused together with the human-specified features.

Keywords: Person Re-identification, Data-Driven Features, PCA Network.

1 Introduction

In recent years, person re-identification in unconstrained conditions have attracted increasing research interests. The task of re-identification can be formalized as the problem of matching a given individual probe image against a gallery of candidate images. In order to tackle the problem, the human-specified appearance features are widely used for person re-identification at present, such as color and texture, which are effective to describe and distinguish an individual.

Specifically, color histograms [1,2,3], HOG like signatures [4], local binary patterns (LBP) [5], differential texture filters [6] , graph model [7], spatial co-occurrence representation model [8], and group representation [9] are current typical appearance representations. Moreover, these features can be combined as they play different roles for re-identification. For example, [10] combined 8 color features with 21 texture filters (Gabor and Schmid) and [5] employed a mixture of color histograms and LBP. However, recently works show that these human-specified features may discard some important cues which are essential for re-identification [1]. As the human-specified features are lack of a learning process, they depend too much on subjective appearance characteristics and ignore the discriminative cues. The performances of the features are not so satisfying when people's appearance undergoes large variations across disjoint

Z. Sun et al. (Eds.): CCBR 2014, LNCS 8833, pp. 506–513, 2014.

camera views. Consequently, we attempt to obtain features learned from person images, namely data-driven features, which are significantly different from existing approaches in that requiring a learning process. The data-driven features are more adaptive to the polytrope of individuals, and remedy the weakness of human-specified features. As the roles of different feature types give different appearance attributes, we further seek a distinctive and reliable representation based on the both types of features to improve person matching.

In this paper, we present a new representation to tackle the person re-identification problem that incorporate data-driven features to improve the performance of person matching. Firstly, we try to learn the data-driven features from person images. A deep learning network — PCA Network (PCANet) [11] is utilized to obtain the convolution filters (PCA filters) from pedestrian data and thereby generate the features. We choose PCANet to learn the data-driven features because it is very easy and effective to train and to adapt to different data and tasks. The features contain much effective discrimination information and provide more invariance for intra-class variability. So they compensate the drawback of human-specified features. Nevertheless, as the data-driven features describe abstract semantics of pedestrians, they could not represent basic appearance information alone very well. For this reason, we fuse the data-driven features and common human-specified features (color and texture) to produce a final appearance representation of each image. The proposed combination is refered to as eDR: the enriched Data-driven Representation.

To our best knowledge, this is the first study that the data-driven features learned by deep network are applied to person re-identification problem. Moreover, we draw insights into the symbiotic and complementary relation between the data-driven features and human-specified features. We formulate a new feature representation framework which fuses the advantages of both types of feature to work for complicated and changing pedestrians, improving the reliability and robustness in person matching. Extensive experiments conducted on two person re-identification datasets (i-LIDS [9] and ETHZ [12]) demonstrate that (i) data-driven features are significant and robust for re-identification; and (ii) proposed eDR is effective for person matching, that is, combining the data-driven features with existing human-specified features leads to more accurate person re-identification.

2   Description of the Proposed Approach

2.1   Data-Driven Features Learned by PCA Network

In this work, PCA Network (PCANet) [11] is employed to learn the data-driven features from person images. We briefly review the two-stage PCANet model below, one can build more stages if a deeper architecture is found to be beneficial for person matching.

The PCA Filters. In the PCANet, only the PCA filters need to be learned from the images. Assuming that the number of PCA filters in ℓth stage is L_ℓ and the size of all person images $\{I_i\}_{i=1}^N$ is $m \times n$.

At the first stage, for each image I_i, a $k_1 \times k_2$ patch is extracted around each pixel and all patches of the I_i are obtained: $p_{i,1}, p_{i,2}, \cdots, p_{i,mn} \in R^{k_1 k_2}$, where $x_{i,j}$ denotes the

jth vectorized patch in I_i. Then the patches are deducted patch mean and put together as $\bar{P}_i = [\bar{p}_{i,1}, \bar{p}_{i,2}, \cdots, \bar{p}_{i,mn}]$, where $\bar{p}_{i,j}$ is a mean-removed patch. The patch sets of all images are further collected, i.e., $P = [\bar{P}_1, \bar{P}_2, \cdots, \bar{P}_N] \in R^{k_1 k_2 \times Nmn}$.

In order to obtain the PCA filters, PCA is utilized to minimize the reconstruction error and the minimization problem of the first stage is formulated as

$$\hat{\Theta}^1 = \underset{\Theta^1 \in R^{k_1 k_2 \times L_1}}{\arg \min} \|P - \Theta^1 {\Theta^1}^T P\|_F^2, \quad s.t. {\Theta^1}^T \Theta^1 = I, \tag{1}$$

where I is unit matrix of size $L_1 \times L_1$. The optimal solution $\hat{\Theta}^1$ is a matrix composed of L_1 principal eigenvectors of PP^T. So the PCA filters of the first stage are built as

$$F_l^1 = f_{k_1,k_2}(\hat{\Theta}_l^1) \in R^{k_1 \times k_2}, \quad l = 1, 2, \cdots, L_1, \tag{2}$$

where $\hat{\Theta}_l^1$ denotes the lth column of $\hat{\Theta}^1$, i.e. lth principal eigenvector of PP^T, and $f_{k_1,k_2}(a)$ is a function that maps a vector $a \in R^{k_1 k_2}$ to a matrix $F \in R^{k_1 \times k_2}$. The lth filter outputs of the first stage are $I_i^l = I_i * F_l^1, i = 1, 2, \cdots N$, where $*$ denotes convolution.

At the second stage, all the patches of I_i^l are removed patch mean and formed as $\bar{Q}_i^l = [\bar{q}_{i,l,1}, \bar{q}_{i,l,2}, \cdots, \bar{q}_{i,l,mn},]$ like the first stage. Then all the patch sets of the lth filter output are assembled as $Q^l = [\bar{Q}_1^l, \bar{Q}_2^l, \cdots, \bar{Q}_N^l]$, and all Q^l are further concatenated, i.e., $Q = [Q^1, Q^2, \cdots, Q^{L_1}] \in R^{k_1 k_2 \times L_1 Nmn}$.

Repeating the same process as the first stage, the L_2 principal eigenvectors of QQ^T are formed the matrix $\hat{\Theta}^2$. The PCA filters of the second stage are then expressed as

$$F_s^2 = f_{k_1,k_2}(\hat{\Theta}_s^2) \in R^{k_1 \times k_2}, \quad s = 1, 2, \cdots, L_2. \tag{3}$$

Therefore, for each input I_i^l of the second stage, the set of L_2 outputs is

$$\partial_i^l = \{I_i^l * F_s^2\}_{s=1}^{L_2}. \tag{4}$$

Obviously, the number of ∂_i^l is L_1 for each image I_i.

Data-Driven Features. In the PCANet, hashing and histogram are used to generate the data-driven features of each image I_i after learning the PCA filters.

Specifically, for each I_i^l, the ∂_i^l are hashed as $\{H(I_i^l * F_s^2)\}_{s=1}^{L_2}$, where $H(\cdot)$ is a function whose value is one for positive entries and zero otherwise. Then ∂_i^l is transformed to a integer-valued "image":

$$\tilde{I}_i^l = \sum_{s=1}^{L_2} 2^{s-1} H(I_i^l * F_s^2), \tag{5}$$

whose every pixel is an integer in the range $[0, 2^{L_2} - 1]$. So we have L_1 images $\tilde{I}_i^l, l = 1, 2, \cdots, L_1$ for each image I_i. We partition each of them into K blocks and compute the 2^{L_2}-bins histogram of each block. Then K histograms are concatenated into one vector $h(\tilde{I}_i^l)$. Finally, L_1 vectors are further collected to form the data-driven feature vector D_i of the image I_i:

$$D_i = [h(\tilde{I}_i^1), \cdots, h(\tilde{I}_i^{L_1})]^T. \tag{6}$$

The data-driven features could contain much effective discrimination information through a learning process and are significant and robust for person re-identification.

2.2   Enriched Data-Driven Representation

As mentioned in the introduction, there is the complementary relation between data-driven features and human-specified features. Therefore, we investigate the fusion of two types of features to gain more accurate re-identification performance.

Typically, color and texture histograms are chosen as the human-specified features in this paper in that they are the mainstream features for person matching [1,5,10]. Specifically, 16-bins histogram of 8 color channels (RGB, YCbCr, HSV) and uniform LBP histograms are combined to represent people's subjective appearance, which are shown to be effective for re-identification [5]. Then the data-driven features and the human-specified features are fused to produce a global representation of each image. We denote this combination as eDR (enriched Data-driven Representation). In eDR, we suppose that D_i denotes the data-driven feature vector and H_i denotes the human-specified feature vector. For purpose of computing the similarity between two image representations $eDR_i = (D_i, H_i)$ and $eDR_j = (D_j, H_j)$, we adopt a weighted sum scheme as follows

$$dist(eDR_i, eDR_j) = \mu d(D_i, D_j) + (1 - \mu)d(H_i, H_j) \qquad (7)$$

where μ is a parameter that controls the weight between the two types of features. In order to evaluate the intrinsic properties of feature representation, $d(\cdot)$ is denoted as $\ell 1$-norm distance simply.

3   Experiments

3.1   Datasets and Evaluation

Two publically available person re-identification datasets, i-LIDS [9] and ETHZ [12], are used for evaluation. In the i-LIDS dataset, which is captured indoor at a busy airport arrival hall, there are 119 people with a total 476 person images captured by multiple non-overlapping cameras. Many of these images undergo large illumination change, considerable view angle change, and are subject to large occlusions (see Fig. 1). The ETHZ dataset contains three video sequences captured outdoor from moving cameras. It contains a large number of different people in uncontrolled conditions. The three sequences are as follows: SEQ. 1 contains 83 persons(4,857 images); SEQ. 2 contains 35 persons (1,936 images); SEQ. 3 contains 28 persons (1,762 images). The most challenging aspects of ETHZ are illumination changes and occlusions (see Fig. 1). It is noted that the two datasets have different characteristics (e.g. outdoor/indoor, large/small variations in view angle) and therefore are ideal for evaluating appearance representations.

Our motivation is to evaluate the intrinsic properties of the feature representations, so we do not use any metric learning but simply measure the similarity between two persons using the $\ell 1$-norm distance between their representations. The matching performance is measured using the averaged cumulative match characteristic (CMC) performance curves over 10 trials. The CMC curve represents the correct matching rate at

(a)   (b)

Fig. 1. (a)i-LIDS dataset. (b)ETHZ dataset

the top r ranks. For each trial, we randomly chose one image from each person to set up the gallery set and the remaining images are used as probe images.

3.2   Methods for Comparison and Implementation Details

For comparison, different components of eDR are chosen to assess the availability of the proposed representations, including the data-driven features learned by PCANet and the common human-specified features (color histograms and LBP) mentioned above. Two other human-specified representations, namely Histogram of Oriented Gradient (HOG) and strip histograms [6,10], are also used to test the performance of eDR.

In our experiments, all image samples are normalized to 128×48 pixels according to the common practice. We vary the parameter μ from 0.1 to 0.9 by a step of 0.1, and obtain the eDR by selecting optimal μ. For the PCANet, the filter size is $k_1 = k_2 = 7$, the number of filters is $L_1 = L_2 = 8$, block size is 32×32, and the overlapping region between blocks is half of the block size. For human-specified features, we extract the features from blocks of person images inspired by [13]. This method could contain more local appearance information and is popular for representing people's appearance at present. Specifically, we use 16×16 pixels overlapping blocks, and define with a 8 pixels step in both the horizontal and vertical directions, resulting in 75 blocks for each image. Then each block feature vector is made of 16-bins histogram of 8 color channels and uniform LBP histograms. Finally, all blocks are concatenated to form the features of each image. In addition, strip histograms is a combined representation which divides a person image into 6 horizontal strips and uses the color histograms and texture filters for each strip.

3.3   Performance Analysis

We first present some experiments on the i-LIDS dataset. Fig. 2 and Table. 1 give the performance of eDR as well as the performances of other different appearance repre-sentations. We report the average performances over 10 random split of 60 persons. It is evident that the data-driven features learned by PCANet perform much better than three single human-specified representations, e.g. at rank 1, PCANet achieves 6% im-provement over color histograms, 9.9% improvement over LBP, and 10.3% over HOG,

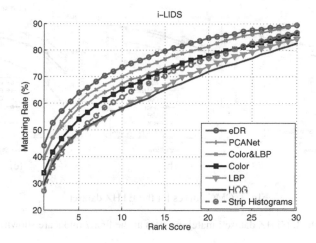

Fig. 2. CMC curves for the i-LIDS dataset

Table 1. i-LIDS dataset: top ranked matching rates

METHOD	r=1	r=5	r=10	r=20
eDR	**44.1**	**64.0**	**73.6**	**84.7**
Color&LBP	39.4	60.2	70.1	81.5
Strip Histograms	27.2	48.9	62.3	77.0
PCANet	40.0	58.1	67.5	78.0
Color	34.0	54.1	65.3	78.0
LBP	30.1	48.8	58.0	74.0
HOG	29.7	49.4	58.1	72.0

respectively. The learning features are more effective than single non-learning features because people's appearance undergoes large variations across disjoint camera views in i-LIDS dataset. This suggests that the data-driven features are more robust for person matching. It is also clear that the proposed eDR gives a significant improvement over its components and other methods. e.g. rank 1 matching rate is 44.1% for eDR, versus 39.4% for a mixture of color histograms and LBP, 40.0% for PCANet and 27.2% for strip histograms. The results show that the data-driven features further lead to more accurate re-identification when they are fused together with human-specified features.

We have also tested the proposed representation on the ETHZ dataset. Fig. 3 shows the CMC curves for the three different sequences, and the results are also summarized in Table. 2. From the figure and table, we can see that the performance of eDR is better than that of all other methods. Especially, on SEQ. 2 and 3, PCANet alone performs little bit worse than using color histograms. We think that it is because the appearance of same pedestrian show little change in ETHZ dataset and the human-specified features play a more important role. So we still consider that the data-driven features can yet be regarded as the robust appearance features for polytropic pedestrians.

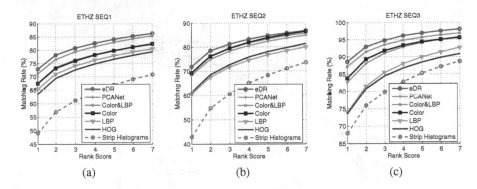

Fig. 3. CMC curves for the ETHZ dataset

Table 2. ETHZ dataset: matching rates at the first 7 ranks are shown

METHOD	SEQ.1							SEQ.2							SEQ.3						
	1	2	3	4	5	6	7	1	2	3	4	5	6	7	1	2	3	4	5	6	7
eDR	**72.9**	**78.2**	**80.8**	**82.7**	**84.1**	**85.3**	**86.3**	**71.9**	**78.5**	**81.2**	**83.2**	**84.8**	**85.8**	**86.8**	**88.6**	**92.9**	**94.8**	**96.2**	**96.9**	**97.6**	**98.0**
Color&LBP	71.2	76.5	79.4	81.4	83.0	84.3	85.5	69.5	76.3	79.4	81.8	83.3	84.7	85.8	87.2	91.5	93.5	94.8	95.7	96.4	96.9
Strip Histograms	49.0	56.9	61.2	64.4	67.0	69.1	70.9	42.9	54.8	60.7	65.1	68.3	71.1	73.6	68.0	76.0	79.9	82.8	85.3	87.2	88.7
PCANet	67.5	73.5	76.4	78.4	79.9	81.2	82.2	68.3	75.0	78.3	80.6	82.3	83.7	84.9	82.6	88.1	91.1	92.9	94.1	95.0	95.8
Color	67.5	73.2	76.0	78.2	79.9	81.2	82.4	69.3	76.2	79.5	81.9	83.9	85.3	86.6	83.8	89.3	91.8	93.4	94.4	95.1	95.6
LBP	65.4	71.0	74.1	76.3	78.0	79.3	80.5	60.6	67.6	71.7	74.5	76.8	78.5	80.0	74.0	81.5	85.5	88.0	89.9	91.4	92.7
HOG	63.5	69.4	72.6	74.9	76.6	78.1	79.4	61.3	68.6	72.7	75.8	78.1	79.7	81.4	73.7	80.8	84.5	86.7	88.4	89.8	90.9

From all the results above, we consider that the data-driven features are significant and remedy the limitation of existing human-specified features, in describing an individual. Furthermore, the relationship between two types of features is complementary. Proposed eDR indeed combines the advantages of them, improving reliability and robustness in person matching.

4 Conclusion

In this study, we have addressed the problem of person re-identification by proposing a new appearance representation. The data-driven features learned from person images by PCANet are utilized for compensating the drawback of common human-specified features, and both types of features are fused to produce a final appearance representation of each person image. We test our representation on two public datasets (i-ILDS and ETHZ), showing that person matching can benefit from proposed method.

Acknowledgment. This research was funded by Specialized Research Fund for the Doctoral Program of Higher Education No. 20110171120051.

References

1. Liu, C., Gong, S., Loy, C.C., et al.: Person Re-identification: What Features are Important? In: European Conference on Computer Vision, Workshops and Demonstrations, pp. 391–401. Springer, Heidelberg (2012)
2. Park, U., Jain, A.K., Kitahara, I., et al.: Vise: Visual Search Engine Using Multiple Networked Cameras. In: IEEE International Conference on Pattern Recognition, vol. 3, pp. 1204–1207 (2006)
3. Farenzena, M., Bazzani, L., Perina, A., et al.: Person Re-identification by Symmetry-Driven Accumulation of Local Features. In: IEEE Conference on Computer Vision and Pattern Recognition, pp. 2360–2367 (2010)
4. Schwartz, W.R., Davis, L.S.: Learning Discriminative Appearance-Based Models Using Partial Least Squares. IEEE Transactions on Computer Graphics and Image Processing, 322–329 (2009)
5. Mignon, A., Jurie, F.: PCCA: A New Approach for Distance Learning from Sparse Pairwise Constraints. In: IEEE Conference on Computer Vision and Pattern Recognition, pp. 2666–2672 (2012)
6. Gray, D., Tao, H.: Viewpoint Invariant Pedestrian Recognition with an Ensemble of Localized Features. In: Forsyth, D., Torr, P., Zisserman, A. (eds.) ECCV 2008, Part I. LNCS, vol. 5302, pp. 262–275. Springer, Heidelberg (2008)
7. Gheissari, N., Sebastian, T.B., Hartley, R.: Person Reidentification Using Spatiotemporal Appearance. In: IEEE Conference on Computer Vision and Pattern Recognition, vol. 2, pp. 1528–1535 (2006)
8. Wang, X., Doretto, G., Sebastian, T., et al.: Shape and Appearance Context Modeling. In: IEEE International Conference on Computer Vision, pp. 1–8 (2007)
9. Zheng, W.S., Gong, S., Xiang, T.: Associating Groups of People. In: British Machine Vision Conference, London (2009)
10. Zheng, W.S., Gong, S., Xiang, T.: Re-identification by Relative Distance Comparison. IEEE Transactions on Pattern Analysis and Machine Intelligence 35(3), 653–668 (2013)
11. Chan, T.H., Jia, K., Gao, S., et al.: PCANet: A Simple Deep Learning Baseline for Image Classification? arXiv preprint arXiv:1404.3606 (2014)
12. Ess, A., Leibe, B., Van Gool, L.: Depth and Appearance for Mobile Scene Analysis. In: IEEE International Conference on Computer Vision, pp. 1–8 (2007)
13. Pedagadi, S., Orwell, J., Velastin, S., Boghossian, B.: Local Fisher Discriminant Analysis for Pedestrian Re-identification. In: IEEE Conference on Computer Vision and Pattern Recognition, pp. 3318–3325 (2013)

A Similar Interaction Model for Group Activity Recognition in Still Images

Xiaobin Chang, Xiang Li, Yuting Mai, and Wei-Shi Zheng

School of information science and technology, Sun-Yet Sen University
510006 Guangzhou, China
{littlesoliderchang,lixiang651,ytmai2013}@gmail.com,
wszheng@ieee.org

Abstract. This paper addresses the group activity recognition in the still image. We formulate an alternative discriminant contextual model on feature level. On the one hand, it mines the person-joint-context feature model, which describes the interaction of a focal person and its surrounding context. In the meanwhile, the surrounding context is featured with the relative pose, relative location and the scene background. On the other hand, a similar interaction model is formed to learn the interactive correlation between a focal person and its surrounding context. An optimization criterion is proposed to learn the similar interaction model. We show that the optimization problem can be optimized efficiently. Our experimental results show that the proposed model outperforms related works, even though temporal information is not available.

Keywords: Group Activity Recognition, Discriminative Model, Large Margin Learning.

1 Introduction

Group activity recognition is recently gaining increasing attentions and it has a wide range of applications, such as surveillance, entertainment and human computer interaction. So far, existing work understands group activity recognition from video sequences, such as a flow processing model over frames [1] and a tracking based collective activity modeling [2].

In this work, we propose to classify a group activity from a still image rather than relying on temporal information. As shown in Fig. 1, human can still recognize the group activity in the still images. The main challenge of recognizing group activity in still images lies in the ambiguity of single person's group activity. As illustrated in the Fig. 2, relying only on the appearances of these two single people without using any other cues is hard to distinguish those two guys, although their group activities are different. This suggests other visual cues have to be explored from the image in order to help inference. A person's activity in the group is also highly affected by other people in the group and the way how they interact . In this work, we formulate this by proposing an interaction modelling to combine those visual cues for the recognition task. What's more, the

Z. Sun et al. (Eds.): CCBR 2014, LNCS 8833, pp. 514–521, 2014.
© Springer International Publishing Switzerland 2014

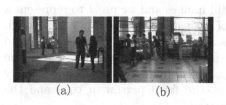
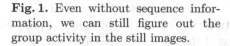

Fig. 1. Even without sequence information, we can still figure out the group activity in the still images.

Fig. 2. In the above two images, the interactive action between people are similar. However, the scene context helps distinguish walking from queuing.

scene context has not been considered before, but we think it is useful for distinguishing some activities. As illustrated in Fig. 2, the crossing and the queuing can be more easily separated under different scene backgrounds.

We believe how a person is acting in the group is highly related to the other people and the environment around him. To this end, we propose a similarity function based learning procedure to model the interactions between a person and its surroundings. An optimization model is proposed in order to find out the most likely group activity that the people involve.

Related Work. Contextual information is also developed in [3], [4]. However, there are substantial differences. First, the context modeling are different. Lan el al [3]. infers the relation action labels between individual people and thus actions have to infer during the learning. However, our model mines relation between people at the feature level without estimating the action of each person. Second, the learning strategy is completely different. Due to estimation of the human action and group activity together, Lan el al [3] formulates a latent model and perform iterative learning, and this may lead to high computational complexity. In comparison, we develop a similar interaction model that forms the interactive correlation between a focal person's activity feature and its surrounding joint context, which can be efficiently solved. [4] focuses on collective activity localization rather than recognition by making use of the contextual information. What's more, [5,6,7] do not capture interactive correlation between a focal person and its surroundingand the visual cues have not been jointly used.

In summary, the contributions of this work include: 1) formulating a person-joint-context feature modeling that describes interaction between focal person and its surrounding at feature level; 2) proposing an efficient similarity interaction model to form and learn the interactive correlation based on the person-joint-context feature in an image. Our experimental results show that our model by using the proposed model, recognizing group activity from still image is plausible and can get better results than or perform comparably to related work without using video information.

2   Approach

Suppose that all the people are found in still images and we use I to represent a person. What's more, the pose feature P of each single person is also generated. First, we choose one person I_m as the focal person. The other people around I_m including the scene can be seen as the context of I_m. Therefore, we call the context feature L_m of the focal person I_m as the joint context feature. Every person in a still image will be selected as the focal person in turn and the corresponding joint context feature is extracted.

Our interaction model formulates the connection between the focal people and its joint context based on the assumption that the action of the focal people would be highly related to the joint context if the focal people is affected by the group of people in the image. For modeling the interaction, we form the following interaction response R_c^m:

$$R_c^m = P_m^{'} * \omega_c * L_m. \tag{1}$$

R_c^m can be viewed as a similar function between P_m and L_m, where the matrix ω_c plays as a weight matrix that relates the focal person and the joint context. If R_c^m is large, it means there is a high response between them given the cth group activity; otherwise, it is not. By assembling all M individual persons' interaction responses in an image, we predict the dominating group activity of the image by

$$k = \arg \max_{c \in 1, \ldots S} R_c, \quad R_c = \sum_{m=1}^{M} R_c^m \tag{2}$$

In the following, we form a similar interaction model that learns an optimal ω_c in Sec. 2.2. After building the model, we detail the inference of activity in Sec. 2.3. Before that, we first detail the pose feature P_m and the joint context L_m in Sec. 2.1.

2.1   Feature Details

Pose of Each Focal People. The people in the pictures can be found by the person detector such as [8]. For extracting the pose feature P of each person, We will adopt the procedure in [3]. We divide the directions into 8 bins and the pose feature consists of the SVM scores on these 8 direction bins.

Interactive Action Context. The interactive action context describes the relative interaction between people. For this purpose, we use the relative pose feature to explore spatial information around a person and then we assemble them together to form the context. For extracting *relative pose feature* that reflects the interaction between the focal person I_m and the others $I_i, i \neq m$ around I_m, we first find out the max entry of the focal person's pose feature P_m, and then a cyclic shifting the others' pose feature P_i is performed to make the corresponding maximum entry of P_m be the first entry. Let RP_{mi} denote the relative pose feature of a surrounding person I_i with respect to the focal person

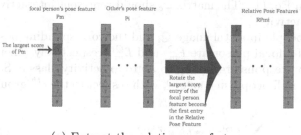

(a) Extract the relative pose feature

(b) Illustration of how to divide the space

Fig. 3. (a)Extract the relative pose; (b) The focal person is in the pink area and his direction is given by the blue arrow. The space is divided into 4 subregions and the first bin is decided by the direction of the focal person.

I_m, where $i \neq m$. We use F_{mi} to represent the composite pose feature of the person I_i with respect to the focal person I_m, and $F_{mi} = [RP_{mi}; P_i]$.

We also consider how person I_i locates around the focal person I_m. we divide the region around the focal person I_m into B subregions($B = 4$ in our model). An example is illustrated in Fig. 3(b). The bth subregion is represented by a feature vector F_m^b. F_m^b represents the dominant interactive pose information of all people located in the bth bin with respect to focal person I_m. Therefore, F_m^b is a weighted F_{mi}^b as follows $F_m^b = \sum_{i=1}^{N_b} W_{mi} * F_{mi}^b$, $W_{mi} = \exp^{-\frac{D_{mi}}{\alpha}}$, where N_b means the number of people in the bth subregion and D_{mi} is the spatial distance between I_m and I_i and α is a parameter. The farther the two people is, the smaller the distance weight is. Finally, we get *interactive action context feature* K_m of the focal person I_m: $K_m = [F_m^1; F_m^2; ...; F_m^B]$.

Scene Context. Some special group activities are more likely to take place in some kinds of scenes. For example, protests will usually take place in urban area while football usually plays in an open area. We can use the scene feature, such as [9], [10], to capture the scene context, and we employ the scene context [11] is denoted by G.

Joint Context. The joint context feature L_m of the focal person I_m then consists of interactive action context and scene context, denoted by $L_m = [G; K_m]$.

2.2 Learning

Suppose there are S group activities we concern and there are N training images $\{Q_i, s_i\}$, $i \in 1, ..., N$ where $s_i \in \{1, \cdots, S\}$ is the label of group activity that image Q_i belongs to. We form the connection between a focal person's activity feature P_m and its surrounding context L_m by the group activity weight matrix

ω_c in the similarity function Eq. (1). The matrix ω_c should represent interactive structure of the cth group activity.

Suppose there are M_{Q_i} people in a still image Q_i and the corresponding pose and join context features of a focal person are $P_m^{Q_i}$ and $L_m^{Q_i}$, respectively. Then, Eq. (1) gives the interaction response regarding to a group activity class c. So, the interaction response over all people in image Q_i with respect to the cth group activity is

$$R_c^{Q_i} = \sum_{m=1}^{M_{Q_i}} (P_m^{Q_i})' * \omega_c * L_m^{Q_i} \tag{3}$$

We wish the match interaction response is larger than non-match interaction response in order to distinguish group activities. That is

$$R_{s_i}^{Q_i} > R_t^{Q_i}, t \neq s_i \tag{4}$$

More generally, we define a margin δ between the responses of ground truth group activity and the other group activites.

$$\sum_{m=1}^{M_{Q_t}} (P_m^{Q_t})' * \Delta_{kl} * L_m^{Q_t} > \delta. \tag{5}$$

The final formulation becomes:

$$\min_{\Delta_{kl}, \xi^{Q_t}} \frac{1}{2}||\Delta_{kl}||_F^2 + \sum_{\forall t, s_t = k \text{ or } l} \xi^{Q_t}, \quad s.t. \sum_{m=1}^{M_{Q_t}} (P_m^{Q_t})' * \Delta_{kl} * L_m^{Q_t} > 1 - \xi^{Q_t}, \ \xi^{Q_t} \geqslant 0$$

Based on the above model, we learn all the Δ_{kl}, where $k, l \in 1, 2, ..., S$, $k \neq l$.

2.3   Inference

There are two methods to figure out the group activity of a still image.

Least Square. We learn Δ_{kl} in the last section, where $k, l \in 1, 2, ..., S$, $k \neq l$. Note that we compute the interaction response of an image based on weight matrix ω_c for each group activity in Eq. (3). Since $\Delta_{kl} = \omega_k - \omega_l = -\Delta_{lk}$, we can figure out all the weight matrices ω_c, $c \in \{1, 2, ..., S\}$ from the Δ_{kl}, $k, l \in \{1, 2, ..., S\}$, $k \neq l$ using least squares minimization technique. After that, we can make a prediction on the group activity of an image by using Eq. (2)

Voting Scheme. Rather than computing weight matrix ω_c explicitly, we develop a voting scheme based on Δ_{kl}, $k, l \in \{1, 2, ..., S\}$, $k \neq l$ directly. First, for a probe image Q, we first compute pose feature P_m of each person and compute the corresponding joint interaction context for each focal person L_m. Then we compute the value

$$\sum_{m=1}^{M} P_m' * \Delta_{kl} * L_m. \tag{6}$$

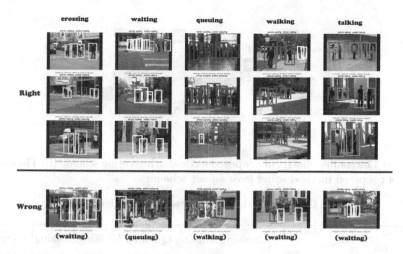

Fig. 4. Demonstration of match and non-match group activity. Different color boxes indicate the activity of a person. Collective activities: crossing, waiting, queuing, walking, talking, correspond to colors: yellow, white, blue, red, green.

If Eq. 6 is larger than 0, that means Q is more likely from k^{th} group activity rather than from l^{th} one. Hence, we vote k^{th}th group activity class once; otherwise, we vote l^{th} group activity class. We compute Eq. 6 on every Δ_{kl} $k, l \in \{1, 2, ..., S\}$, $k \neq l$ and take the group activity class that gets the maximum votes as our prediction for the probe image Q.

3 Experiments

3.1 Dataset

We select the Collective Activity Dataset that is proposed in [12] for evaulation. This dataset contains images of 5 group activity classes, including crossing, waiting, queuing, walking and talking. In each image, there is a dominating group activity class we need to recognize. The challenge of this dataset can be illustrated by Fig. 4. We follow the same setting as in [3]: randomly choosing one fourth of the video clips from each activity category to form the test set and the rest of the video clips are used for training.

3.2 Results and Analysis

Comparison with Existing Works. Our still image based model can achieve better performance than the video based ones. We compare the results of existing methods in Table 1 and show some confuse matrices of them. As shown in the Table1 and the confuse matrices in Fig. 5 , we find that our model achieve better average performance than [3], [7] and [1]. These results verify that even without the sequence information, group activity can also be recognized based on the

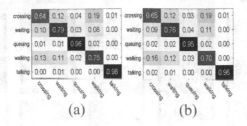

(a)   (b)

Fig. 5. (a) The confuse matrix of proposed method using voting scheme (b) The confuse matrix of proposed method using least square scheme

Table 1. Comparing the result between the different models

Method / Activities	Crossing	Waiting	Queuing	Walking	Talking	Accuracy
Our Model (Voting Scheme)	64%	79%	96%	75%	98%	82.4%
Our Model (Least Square)	65%	76%	95%	70%	96%	80.4%
Gist + SVM	40%	53%	88%	54%	97%	66.5%
Dense SIFT + SVM	53%	71%	100%	64%	100%	77.6%
Joint Context Feature + SVM	58%	34%	17%	53%	31%	38.7%
Lan's [3]	68%	69%	76%	80%	99%	78.4%
Kaneko's [7]	67%	84%	86%	49%	75%	72.2%
Khamis's [1]	68%	58%	79%	62%	88%	71%

context information. What's more, our similarity function learning scheme can capture the different structures of interactions in different group activities.

Importance of Learning Interaction in Image. We show that without learning the interaction would make the prediction unsatisfactory. In Table 1, we conduct a typical image categorization methods Dense SIFT+SVM and Gist+SVM for comparison. The results show these two models failed to recognize the images of walking, waiting and the crossing, because the scene backgrounds of these 3 group activity are very similar. In contrast, our model explores the interactive action context, so we can distinguish these activities better.

Least Square Scheme vs. Voting Scheme. We develop two inference methods, namely the least square scheme and the voting scheme. As shown in Table1, we find that the voting scheme outperforms the least squares scheme on almost all group activities. Because the voting scheme directly use $\Delta_{kl}, k \neq l, k, l \in 1, 2, 3..., S$ for prediction, and Δ_{kl} is the global solution of the optimization problem. The least square scheme uses $\omega_c, c \in 1, 2, 3, ..., S$, which is computed from Δ_{kl}, and thus the estimation of ω_c may not be optimal.

4   Conclusion

A new model has been proposed for predicting a group activity in a still image. The model extracts the person-joint-context that describes how context are acting around a focal person. Based on that, a similar interaction model is formed to model the interactive correlation between a focal person and its surrounding context. By introducing an efficient optimization criterion which can be reduced to a quadratic programming problem, we learn the parameters of the similar interaction model and are able to infer different group activities efficiently. Our model outperforms the related works that based on videos.

Acknowledgment. This research was funded by Specialized Research Fund for the Doctoral Program of Higher Education No. 20110171120051.

References

1. Khamis, S., Morariu, V.I., Davis, L.S.: A flow model for joint action recognition and identity maintenance. In: CVPR (2012)
2. Choi, W., Savarese, S.: A unified framework for multi-target tracking and collective activity recognition. In: Fitzgibbon, A., Lazebnik, S., Perona, P., Sato, Y., Schmid, C. (eds.) ECCV 2012, Part IV. LNCS, vol. 7575, pp. 215–230. Springer, Heidelberg (2012)
3. Lan, T., Wang, Y., Yang, W., Robinovitch, S.N., Mori, G.: Discriminative latent models for recognizing contextual group activities. PAMI 34(8), 1549–1562 (2012)
4. Odashima, S., Shimosaka, M., Kaneko, T., Fukui, R., Sato, T.: Collective activity localization with contextual spatial pyramid. In: ECCV Workshop (2012)
5. Kaneko, T., Shimosaka, M., Odashima, S.: Viewpoint invariant collective activity recognition with relative action context. In: ECCV Workshop (2012)
6. Khuram, W.C., Savarese, S.S.: Learning context for collective activity recognition. In: CVPR (2011)
7. Kaneko, T., Shimosaka, M., Odashima, S., Fukui, R., Sato, T.: Consistent collective activity recognition with fully connected crfs. In: ICPR (2012)
8. Felzenszwalb, P., McAllester, D., Ramanan, D.: A discriminatively trained, multi-scale, deformable part model. In: CVPR (2008)
9. Heitz, G., Koller, D.: Learning spatial context: Using stuff to find things. In: Forsyth, D., Torr, P., Zisserman, A. (eds.) ECCV 2008, Part I. LNCS, vol. 5302, pp. 30–43. Springer, Heidelberg (2008)
10. van Gemert, J., Geusebroek, J.M., Veenman, C., Snoek, C., Smeulders, A.: Robust scene categorization by learning image statistics in context. In: CVPR Workshop (2006)
11. Oliva, A., Torralba, A.: Modeling the shape of the scene: a holistic representation of the spatial envelope. IJCV, 145–175 (2001)
12. Choi, W., Shahid, K., Savaese, S.: What are they doing?; collective activity classification using spatio-temporal relationship among people. In: ICCV workshop (2009)

A New Hand Shape Recognition Algorithm Unrelated to the Finger Root Contour

Fu Liu[1], Lei Gao[1], Wenwen LI[1, 2], and Huiying Liu[1]

[1] College of communication Engineering, Jilin University, Changchun 130022,China
[2] College of Mechanical Engineering, Baicheng Normal University, Baicheng 137000, China
liufu@jlu.edu.cn

Abstract. For the problems of the finger root deformation caused by hands' locations' inaccurate and a big error of hand shape feature's extraction. Taking advantage of its role as Finger contour high stability, a present algorithm of hand location is improved. An algorithm is presented for Hand shape recognition which is without the connection with the finger root contour. This method first locates the finger's central axis, and then extracts finger geometric features that are none of the finger root's contour. The final statistical characteristic difference between different fingers is adopted to recognize the shape of hands. The method in this paper is good to solve the problem of large deformation at the finger root contour and the big error of the finger root's location. We can extract the hand's shape's features with high stability. The recognition rate can reach to 99.51%.

Keywords: Hand shape recognition, Curve fitting, Finger geometric features, Finger central axis.

1   Introduction

Recently, biometric technology is widely used in the field of identity authentication. Due to the advantages, such as the acquisition convenience and high stability, hand shape recognition plays an important role in the field of biometric [1].

Hand's shape is mainly composed of two parts: palm shape and finger shape. The palm shape of the same individual will show great difference due to the degree of the open palm. However, fingers will not. Therefore, in the hand shape recognition, the finger's features are mainly used due to its stability. The existing hand shape recognition algorithms mainly includes two categories: one is selecting the geometry of the fingers[1-6],the other is using finger contour as the features, which is an algorithm of contour matching in the spatial domain or polar domain[7-10].

After analyzing the existing hand shape recognition algorithms, it shows that difficulty of hands' shape recognition algorithm was due to the different open extent of the palm, which brought about a big difference on the root contour. It also led to problems about hand shape positioning inaccuracies and the error in the extraction of hand shape features. To this issue, this paper presents a hand shape's recognition algorithm which was irrelevant with finger root contour. The contour deformation of finger root has little effect on hand location. The hand shape feature extraction. The recognition rate is high.

Z. Sun et al. (Eds.): CCBR 2014, LNCS 8833, pp. 522–529, 2014.

2   Hand Shape Location

Traditional hand shape location is by locating fingertip and finger root point. The algorithm of hand shape location in this paper is locating the axis of the finger. First, we get the axis slope of the finger, and then we locate the fingertips.

The algorithm of axis slope of the finger is mainly based on the idea of finger contour's fitting with the point proposed in paper [10]. However, there is not too much explanation in it. Leqing Zhu followed the idea and elaborated concrete steps of finger outline binomial which fit in paper [11]. However, he used the finger outline to fitting. The fitted straight line is still affected by the finger root points. The influences of finger root location's inaccuracies on fitted line slope were not considered. This paper still follows the method of finger outline binomial fitting. We re-select the length and position of the finger contour which is needed in fitting and discussions. Experimental results show that the proposed and improved algorithm in this paper could solve the finger axis slope. It was basically irrelevant with finger root point location.

Steps in this article to solve fingers axis slope were: firstly, the hand shape location's algorithm in paper [1] was used to separate each finger outline from the whole hand shape contour; then curvature method was used to locate fingertips, as the curvature method applied finger contour feature to locate fingertips with high accuracy. According to fingertips, the curvature method delimited left and right finger's contours. Finally, binomial curve's fitting algorithm was used to fit for the left and right finger contour respectively.

We use the least square method to fit the finger edges with straight line. Assuming the lines expressed as:

$$y = k_d x + b_d \tag{1}$$

Then

$$k_d = \frac{\sum\limits_{c=g_d}^{m_d} x_c^d * \sum\limits_{c=g_d}^{m_d} y_c^d - (m_d - g_d + 1) * \sum\limits_{c=g_d}^{m_d} \left(x_c^d * y_c^d\right)}{(\sum\limits_{c=g_d}^{m_d} x_c^d)^2 - (m_d - g_d + 1) * \sum\limits_{c=g_d}^{m_d} (x_c^d)^2} \tag{2}$$

$$b_d = \frac{\sum\limits_{c=g_d}^{m_d} y_c^d - k_d * (\sum\limits_{c=g_d}^{m_d} x_c^d)}{(m_d - g_d + 1)} \tag{3}$$

Where $\{(x_c^d, y_c^d) \mid c = 1, ..., t_d\}, d(d = 1, 2, ..., 8)$, is finger unilateral contour labels, t_d is finger's unilateral contour length, $g_d, m_d (1 \le g_d < m_d \le t_d)$ is the start and the end points on contour segment which are needed in fitting respectively, (x_1^d, y_1^d) is the fingertips, $(x_{t_d}^d, y_{t_d}^d)$ is the finger root points.

The fitted straight line of both sides of the finger contour could be obtained by fitting finger's left and right outline. The fingers axis slope k' could be calculated according to the two fitted straight lines.

$$k' = \tan((\arctan k_1 + \arctan k_2)/2) \tag{4}$$

k_1 and k_2 were straight line slopes of the left and right finger contours respectively.

Assuming the line ab shown in Fig. 1 is the side contour of the finger, a is fingertip point, b is the finger root point, the red line is the contour segment selected in fitting. a_1 and b_1 are the endpoints of red segment. The length of line ab is P and the length of line a_1b_1 is L.

$$x = L/P \tag{5}$$

The x directly determines the contour length of the line used in fitting. Or rather, x determines g_d, m_d in formula (2).

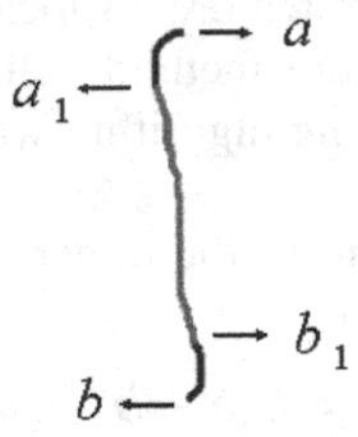

$$a_1 - \left\{ \begin{array}{l} \rightarrow a \\ \\ \\ \\ \end{array} \right.$$

$$b - \left. \begin{array}{l} \\ \end{array} \right\} \rightarrow b_1$$

Fig. 1. Shows variation of x

Fig. 2 is a contour fitting diagram of different x, the red line is the fitted straight line of the left side contour. The blue line is the fitted straight line of the right side contour. The green line is the axis of the finger.

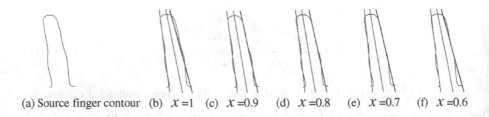

(a) Source finger contour   (b) $x = 1$ (c) $x = 0.9$ (d) $x = 0.8$ (e) $x = 0.7$ (f) $x = 0.6$

Fig. 2. Picture of finger contour fitting

3   Hand Shape Recognition

3.1   Hand Shape Features Extraction

In traditional hand shape recognition, finger root contour deformation has great influences on the accuracy of hand shape recognition. A group of hand shape features unrelated to finger root contour was extracted in this paper, which could improve hand shape recognition's accuracy. Experimental results show that it was difficult to obtain stable hand shape features due to the relatively large degree of freedom of thumb when extracting hand shape feature. So it only needed to extract hand shape features of the other four fingers except thumb.

Starting from the top of the finger axis, then along a central axis, a vertical straight line is drawn for every 10 pixels. Until the number of the intersections of finger contour and the vertical line is less than 2, the distance between the two intersections of the finger contour and the vertical line is the hand feature. $V_i = [Q_i, W_i^1, W_i^2, ..., W_i^n]$ represents the feature vectors, where i is the number of fingers, ($i = 1,2,3,4$), Q_i is the number of the features and $W_i^1, W_i^2, ..., W_i^n$ is the hand shape features. As shown in Fig. 3.

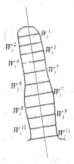

Fig. 3. Picture of Feature selection signal

3.2   Hand Shape Recognition

Features of hand shape recognition are the difference between the standard hand shape and the tested hand shape. In order to improve the recognition speed without reducing recognition rates, hand recognition process is divided into two steps, initial recognition and precise recognition.

3.2.1   Initial Recognition

Assuming $M_i(i = 1,2,3,4)$ are the eigenvectors of standard hand shape, $N_i(i = 1,2,3,4)$ are the eigenvectors of test hand shape, the approach of extracting M_i and N_i is same as V_i.

$$C_i = |M_i(1) - N_i(1)| \ , i = 1,2,3,4 \tag{6}$$

Experiments show that all of C_1, C_2, C_3, C_4 of the same person are 0 or 1, so if any one of C_1, C_2, C_3, C_4 is greater than 1, the two hand shapes are considered not the same person's hands. Instead, if all of C_1, C_2, C_3, C_4 are 0 or 1, the two hand shapes need be precise recognized.

3.2.2   Precise Recognition

$$D_i(j) = |(M_i(j+1) - N_i(j+1)) / \max(M_i(j+1), N_i(j+1))| \tag{7}$$

Where $i = 1,2,3,4$, $j = 1,2,..., \min(M_i(1), N_i(1)) - 1$, to avoid error of hand features vector caused by fingers root contour deformation, j is not equal to $\min(M_i(1), N_i(1))$.

$S_i^{\geq n}$ is equal to the number of $D_i(j)$ greater than n, where n is a threshold.

$$G^{\geq n} = \sum_{i=1}^{4} \left(S_i^{\geq n} \right) \tag{8}$$

The smaller value of $G^{\geq n}$, the greater the degree of similarity between two hands. In the experiments of hand shape recognition, if $G^{\geq n}$ is smaller than the threshold T, then we can consider that the two hand shapes belong to the same person, if $G^{\geq n}$ is greater than the threshold T, we can consider that the two hand shapes belong to the different persons.

4   Experimental Results and Analysis

In this paper, a hand-shaped collection instrument is designed, as shown in Figure 4. The features of the instrument are that the plane of the hand parallel to the plane of the camera. The distance of them is fixed. So when collecting the hand images, we can avoid the angle's fluctuations between the plane of the hand and the plane of the camera. For the two-dimensional image of the hand, some hand location algorithms can solve the rotation, translation and scaling problems. But, it is incompetent to the distortion of hand characteristics caused by angle fluctuations.

Fig. 4. Image acquisition device

In order to verify the superiority of algorithm of hand shape location in this paper, x takes 0.6, 0.7, 0.8, 0.9 and 1, n takes 0.02, 0.03, 0.04, 0.05, 0.06 and 0.07, T takes 8,9,10,11,12,13 and 14 in the experiment, a total of 210 groups experiments. The matching experiments used the database from the above equipment. The images from the first 50 persons and the images of 10 right hands each person belongs to the 500 images in all. The experiments consisted of 124 750 matching times, including 2 250 times Intra-class matching, and 122 500 times Inter-class matching. The change relations among n, x, T and the recognition rate were showed in Fig.5. The points represent the highest recognition rate with a fixed value of n, a fixed value of x and a optimal value of T. The highest recognition rate reached 99.51%. Fig.6 (a) and (b) are experiment results, when n is 0.04 and x is 0.8. Fig.6 (a), the Intra-class matching refers to the matching with different images from the same person. The Inter-class matching refers to the matching with images from different persons. In Fig.6 (b), the FRR is the false rejecting rate. The FAR is the false accepting rate. When characteristic difference is equal to 12, the FRR is 0.83%, the FAR is 0.49%.

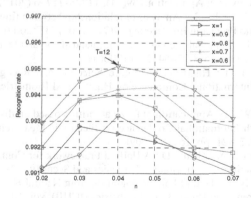

Fig. 5. Accuracy curve of hand shape recognition

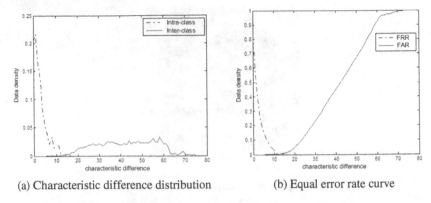

(a) Characteristic difference distribution   (b) Equal error rate curve

Fig. 6. Results of n equaling 0.04 and x equaling 0.8

5   Conclusion

This paper analyzes the present algorithms of hand shape recognition. The degree of palm open makes bigger difference and ultimately result in inaccuracy of finger root contour. The present hand shape location and the great error of hand shape features extraction come about the low rate of hand shape recognition. In order to solve this problem, this paper improves the algorithm of hand shape location and extracts the finger geometric features which are none of the finger root contour. Experiments show that the algorithm has a higher recognition rate, which can reach 99.51%.

References

1. Guo, J.-M., Hsia, C.-H., Liu, Y.-F., et al.: Contact-free hand geometry-based identification system. Expert Systems with Applications 39(14), 11728–11736 (2012)
2. Yuan, W.-Q., Zhu, C.-Y., Ke, L.: Analysis of relationship between finger width and recognition rate. Optics and Precision Engineering 17(7), 1730–1736 (2009)
3. Kumar, A., Zhang, D.: Personal recognition using hand shape and texture. IEEE Transactions on Image Processing 15(8), 2454–2461 (2006)
4. Yuan, W.-Q., Jing, L.-T.: Hand-Shape Feature Selection and Recognition Performance Analysis. In: 2011 International Conference on Hand-Based Biometrics (ICHB), vol. 1(6), pp. 17–18 (2011)
5. Zhang, J.-M., Gao, W.-X.: Application of fuzzy algorithm based on distance in hand-shape identification. In: 9th International Conference on Electronic Measurement & Instruments, ICEMI 2009, 2-818, 2-821, pp. 16–19 (2009)
6. Kanhangad, V., Kumar, A., Zhang, D.: A Unified Framework for Contactless Hand Verification. IEEE Transactions on Information Forensics and Security 6(3), 1014–1027 (2011)
7. Bakina, I., Mestetskiy, L.: Hand Shape Recognition from Natural Hand Position. In: 2011 International Conference on Hand-Based Biometrics (ICHB), vol. 1(6), pp. 17–18 (2011)
8. Yoruk, E., Konukoglu, E., Sankur, B., et al.: Shape-based hand recognition. IEEE Transactions on Image Processing 15(7), 1803–1815 (2006)

9. Duta, N.: A survey of biometric technology based on hand shape. Pattern Recognition 43(11), 2797–2806 (2009)
10. Ma, Y.L., Pollick, F., Hewitt, W.T.: Using B-spline curves for hand recognition, Pattern Recognition. In: Proceedings of the 17th International Conference on ICPR 2004, vol. 3, pp. 274–277, 23–26 (2004)
11. Zhu, L.-Q.: 2D Finger Shape Recognition Based on Local Zero-Order Moment Features. In: 2nd International Congress on Image and Signal Processing, CISP 2009, vol. 1(4), pp. 17–19 (2009)

An Image Thinning Processing Algorithm for Hand Vein Recognition*

Qi Li[1,2], Jianjiang Cui[2], Hongxing Sun[1], and Zhendong Wang[1]

[1] School of Electronic and Information Engineering, University of Science and Technology Liaoning, 114051 Anshan, Liaoning, China
[2] College of Information Science and Engineering,
Northeastern University, 110819 Shenyang, China
Liqi_as@163.com

Abstract. In this paper, an improved algorithm of thinning hand vein's image is proposed in order to meet the requirements of post feature extraction and the recognition for hand vein recognition system. First, the image is enhanced and smoothed. Then, the image is segmented by using dynamic threshold segment algorithm. Finally, the segmented image are smoothed, thinned and deburred. The simulative experiments show that the proposed algorithm is effective and is able to obtain a vein skeleton with less distortion.

Keywords: image processing, hand vein, thinning, deburring.

1 Introduction

As an emerging biometric recognition technology, the recognition of human hand vein has the unique advantage of non-contact, internal characteristics and living recognition. Hence, it has a great potential and a strong practical significance both as the primary method of identity recognition and auxiliary methods of combination with other recognition methods [1-4].

Hand vein image is captured by an infrared camera. Many factors have impact on the quality of the acquired image, such as time, place, light intensity; hand back's size, thickness and the capturing angle. Different quality of images will make the subsequent image feature extraction and feature matching more difficult, which affects the recognition results. Therefore, image processing is the focus of hand vein recognition system. In this paper, what the hand vein image acquired originally is the input of image acquisition system. In order to satisfy the requirement of post feature extraction and the recognition for the hand back vein's recognition system, the output of image processing should contain valid information of hand back vein skeleton.

* This work is supported by the National Natural Science Foundation of China Grant NO.61273003; the General Research Project for the Education Department of Liaoning province under Grant No. L2013120; the National Science Foundation for Young Scholars of China under Grant No. 71301066.

Z. Sun et al. (Eds.): CCBR 2014, LNCS 8833, pp. 530–534, 2014.
© Springer International Publishing Switzerland 2014

2 Smoothing and Segmenting Vein Image

The collected vein image in Fig.1 is processed by background removal, extracting effective area and normalization, respectively. Then vein image obtained by histogram equalization is medium filtered by using 5 × 5 windows templates [5]. Smoothed image is shown in Fig.2. Image is segmented by NIBlack segmentation method [6] and the image segmentation vein is shown in Fig. 3.

 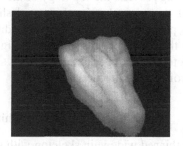

(a) Original image   (b) The image with background removed

Fig. 1. original image and the image with background removed

Fig. 2. Vein image after smoothing   **Fig. 3.** Vein image segmented by NIBlack

In this paper, the method of area elimination and median filtering method are used to denoise image. Fig. 4 shows the result of a denoised image.

Fig. 4. Denoised vein image   **Fig. 5** Segmented vein image

3   Thinning and Recovering Vein Image

3.1   Thinning Vein Image

Hand vein's skeleton can be obtained by thinning algorithm as the basis of feature extraction and feature recognition. Hence, the thinning results directly affect the efficiency and accuracy of recognition. To maintain the original features of the image, in thinning process, the topology of the original image should be preserved, the continuity of the original vein-of-choroid should be kept and breakage should be reduced. This paper adopts an improved condition thinning algorithm by Kejun Wang, etc [2]. The thinning effect is shown in Fig.5. From the experimental results, a wide vein skeleton with single pixel and with smaller distortion is obtained. However, vein-of-choroid is still attached to glitches.

3.2   Removing Glitches from Thinned Vein Image

The thinned wide vein skeleton with single pixel has been obtained through a series of processing. But some tiny glitches are produced in this process. In order to effectively extract and recognize vein feature, they need to be removed [7].

Common method for the removing of glitches is as follows: locate a point in the vein image and in its eight neighborhood areas we find a point whose pixel value is 1 while vein foreground is white. In order to determine the direction of this point with pixel value of 1, we track down it and set the counter as *lineL* to calculate the number of tracking points until reach the crossing point. Set the value of threshold as *th*. If *lineL* <*th*, these tracking points are treated as glitches and set their pixel values to 0. However, this method is defective in tracking. For the non-endpoints, if there are two points whose values are 1 in the eight neighborhood areas, it is hard to implement for the algorithm to tell the right tracking direction. In this paper, this method has been improved as follows: when tracking, the current point is set to 0, and then we judge the direction of the point with the value of 1 in eight neighborhood areas and track down until the crossover point is reached. If *lineL*> *th*, then these tracked points are set to 1.

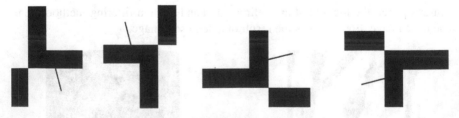

Fig. 6. A special kind of glitches' tail ends

When tracking a glitch from head to end, the test reaches the crossing point and stops tracking by judging the number of the points with the value of 1 in eight adjacent areas. But there is a special kind of glitch tail end. These points are marked by black line shown in Fig. 6 in which the number of points with the value of 1. In eight neighborhood areas, it is equal to the number of crossing points. So in tracking, such special glitch tail end will be mistaken for a crossing point, which makes the tracking stop in advance so that the glitch cannot be removed completely as shown in Fig.7.

The image in the yellow box area of Fig.5 is enlarged shown in Fig. 7 (a), where the green rectangle in upper area marks this special kind of glitch tail end and below is the usual glitches. From Fig. 7 (b), it can be seen that the glitch are mistaken for the crossing point because glitches are not removed completely. Fig.7 (c) shows that these special glitch tail ends are removed effectively by the proposed algorithm.

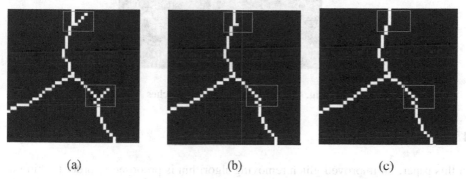

(a)   (b)   (c)

(a) Glitches in the yellow box of Fig.4 (b) Glitch tail ends removed not completely (c) Glitch tail ends removed by the proposed algorithm

Fig. 3. Results of removing the glitches

The improved removing glitches algorithm includes the following steps:

Step1 First, we scan the image point by point from left to right and from top to bottom. We then judge whether the current point's pixel value is 1. If it is 1, go to **Step2**; or else continue **Step1**.

Step2 Judge if the number of the point's pixel value of 1 in eight neighborhood areas is greater than 1. If it is greater than 1, go to **Step1**. If it is equal to 1, go to **Step3**.

Step3 Add 1 to the line length variable $lineL$ and judge the direction of the next point with pixel value of 1 in the neighborhood. Move the current point to the next point and put the former point's coordinates into the vector array, setting its pixel value to 0.

Step4 Calculate the number of the point's pixel value of 1 in eight neighborhood areas. If it is equal to 1, then repeat **Step3**, or else go to **Step5**.

Step5 Determine whether it is a special glitch tail endpoint. If it is a special glitch endpoint, set the pixel value to 0 and go to **Step6**, or else directly go to **Step6**. If the length variable $lineL$ is smaller than th, repeat **Step1**, or else set the point's pixel value in coordinates to 0.

Step6 If $lineL$ is less than th, repeat **Step1**, or else set the point in coordinates to 0.

In this paper, the threshold is set to 10. The line whose length is less than 10 is identified as glitches to be needed to be removed. Experiments show that glitches can be effectively removed after the above thinning recovery and the results are shown in Fig.8.

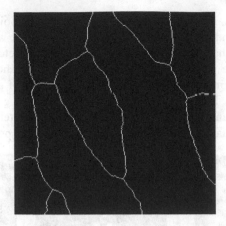

Fig. 4. Image after removing glitches

4   Conclusion

In this paper, an improved glitch removing algorithm is proposed in order to thin image and repair glitches. The proposed algorithm can effectively remove glitches and a special kind of glitch tail end. Experiments show that single pixel-wide vein skeleton with less distortion can be obtained and proved that the proposed algorithm is effective for hand vein pretreatment and provides good preparation for subsequent feature extraction and vein recognition.

References

1. Hashimoto, J.: Finger vein authentication technology and its future. In: 2006 Symposium on VLSI Circuits, Kawasaki, pp. 5–8 (2006)
2. Wang, J.G., Yau, W.Y., Suwandy, A., et al.: Person recognition by fusing palm print and palm vein images based on "Laplacian palm". Representation Pattern Recognition 41(5), 1514–1527 (2008)
3. Crisan, S., Tarnovan, I.G., Crisan, T.E.: A low cost vein detection system using near infrared radiation. In: IEEE Sensors Applications Symposium, pp. 51–56. IEEE, San Diego (2007)
4. Wang, L., Leedham, G.: A Thermal Hand Vein Pattern Verification System. In: Singh, S., Singh, M., Apte, C., Perner, P. (eds.) ICAPR 2005. LNCS, vol. 3687, pp. 58–65. Springer, Heidelberg (2005)
5. Han, X.: Research on Algorithm for Human Dorsal Hand Vein Recognition. Jilin University (2007)
6. Wang, K., Guo, Q., Zhuang, D., et al.: The Study of Hand Vein Image Processing Method. In: Proceedings of the 6th World Congress on Intelligent Control, Dalian, China, pp. 10197–10201 (2006)
7. Zhang, L.: Research and Achievement on Algorithm for Human Palm-Dorsa Recognition, Changchun University of Science and Technology (2008)

Classification of Patients with Alzheimer's Disease Based on Structural MRI Using Locally Linear Embedding (LLE)

Zhiguo Luo, Ling-Li Zeng, and Fanglin Chen[*]

College of Mechatronics and Automation, National University of Defense Technology,
Changsha, Hunan 410073, P.R. China
fanglincheng@nudt.edu.cn

Abstract. Several methods have been used to classify patients with Alzheimer's disease (AD) or its prodromal stage, mild cognitive impairment (MCI) from cognitive normal (CN) based on T1-weighted MRI. In this study, we used LLE to discriminate 453 subjects form the ADNI database. We conducted six pair wise classification experiments: CN (cognitive normal) vs. sMCI (MCI who kept stability and had not converted to AD within 18 months, stable MCI — sMCI), CN vs. cMCI (MCI who had converted to AD within 18 months, converters MCI — cMCI), CN vs. AD, sMCI vs. cMCI, sMCI vs. AD, and cMCI vs. AD. Each of them was repeated for 10 times. The proposed method got the average accuracy of 0.67, 0.79, 0.85, 0.72, 0.75 and 0.65, respectively. The outcomes suggested that the LLE method is useful in the clinical diagnosis and the prediction of AD.

Keywords: Alzheimer's disease, mild cognitive impairment, locally linear embedding.

1 Introduction

Alzheimer's disease (AD) is one of the major dementia that affects the elders' life quality. It has a trend of growing worse [1], since AD is a chronic and nonreversible disease. It is hard but important to diagnose it in its early stage. Doctors' diagnosis may not be the same for their different subjective factors. Machine learning methods may be helpful due to its objectivity. For such advantages, machine learning methods have attracted researchers' considerable interest in the area of neuroimaging.

Voxel-based morphometry (VBM) have been widely used in the analysis of neuroimaging data, such as the early diagnosis and prediction of AD. Since it is hard to take full use of the features of the MRI image because of the obstruction of noise, taking all the voxels as features directly may not get good performance and high accuracy. Dimension reduction is designed to solve this problem, and LLE may show its advantage.

---

[*] Corresponding author.

Z. Sun et al. (Eds.): CCBR 2014, LNCS 8833, pp. 535–540, 2014.

In this research, we tried to explore whether LLE benefits the classification of individuals with various levels of cognitive deficits. We designed six pairwise experiments via using LLE. LLE was first introduced in the year 2000 and widely used in face recognition [2], image classification [3], remote sensing [4] and feature fusion [5]. More recently, LLE has also been used in MRI, such as hippocampus' shape analysis in AD [6] and functional MRI [7]. The overall goal of our study was to see if LLE can improve the classification performance of individuals with AD through basing on brain MRI data from multisite. Specifically, we tried to see if the method of using LLE can get better classification performance than the tradition methods that do not use LLE in the classification experiment of sMCI and cMCI. If so, the new method may assist doctors to make more accurate prediction on the development trend of MCI, which can be meaningful for both prevention and later treatment.

The rest of this paper is organized as follows. In section 2, we depict the experimental data and give a further explanation of the LLE method. In section 3, we compute the classification performances of the VBM method using LLE in some aspect including accuracy, sensitivity, specificity and ROC curve. In section 4, we make a conclusion and discuss the limitations of this study.

2   Materials and Methods

2.1   Subjects

Data used in this study were obtained from the Neuroimaging Initiative (ADNI) database for Alzheimer's Disease.

The ADNI was initiated in 2003, and it was the result of many co-investigators' endeavor including the Food and Drug Administration, National Institute on Aging, the National Institute of Biomedical Imaging, Bioengineering of America, non-profit organizations and also some private medicine corporations. The Chief Investigator of ADNI is Michael W. Weiner, MD in University of California San Francisco. The ADNI planned to spend 60 million US dollars and five years recruiting 800 adults from over 50 sites in America and Canada aging from 55 to 90. They consisted of about 200 people with early AD, 200 cognitive normal older individuals and 400 people with MCI. The purpose of the ADNI was to help researchers and clinicians detect AD in its early time and develop new treatments to monitor their efficacy, to reduce the time and cost of clinical experimentations, and to improve the quality of lives of AD patients. For up-to-date information, please consult: http://www.adni-info.org.

In this study, we downloaded 453 subjects of whom 122 were with AD, 101 with cMCI, 110 with sMCI and 120 CN. All of the subjects had serious clinical and cognitive assessments when they had their MRI scans. Those assessments include: (MMSE) (CDR-SOB) 1) MMSE (The minimental state examination) afford a all-around assess of psychosis and 2) CDR-SOB (the clinical dementia rating sum of boxes) assess the functional and cognitive impairment. If you want to find more details about the tests, please consult the ADNI website www.loni.ucla.edu/ADNI

A resume of the data of each group is provided in Table 1.

Table 1. Group demographics and clinical summary

	CN	sMCI	cMCI	AD
No. of subjects	120	110	101	122
Male (%)	45.8	64.6	58.4	50.0
Age (years)	75 ± 15	72 ± 16	72 ± 17	73 ± 18
MMSE	27.5 ± 2.5	27 ± 3	26.5 ± 3.5	22.5 ± 4.5
CDR-SOB	0 ± 0	0.5 ± 0	0.5 ± 0	0.75 ± 0.25

All of the subjects underwent the standardized 1.5 T MRI protocol of ADNI at each site, respectively. Details about the standardized 1.5 T MRI protocol, you can consult http://www.loni.ucla.edu/ADNI/Research/Cores/index.shtml.

2.2   LLE

LLE algorithm is a new recently-proposed dimension reduction method for nonlinear data. The low dimensional data can keep the topological relation of the original data after being treated. It has been widely used in image data classification and clustering, multidimensional data visualization, character recognition, and bioinformatics fields.

The LLE algorithm can be divided into three steps: (1) finding K nearest neighbors of each sample point; (2) calculating local reconstruction weight matrix of each sample point using the sample point's neighbor points; (3) calculating the output of the sample point via its local reconstruction weight matrix and nearest neighbors.

The first step of the algorithm is to calculate K nearest neighbors of each sample point. K is a preestablished value. Euclidean distance is used.

The second step of the LLE algorithm is to calculate the local reconstruction weight matrix of the sample point. Here we defined an error function as shown below:

$$\min \varepsilon(W) = \sum_{i=1}^{N} \left| x_i - \sum_{j=1}^{k} w^i_j x_{ij} \right|^2 \tag{1}$$

Where x_{ij} ($j=1,2...k$) are the K neighbor points of x_i, and w^i_j are the weights between x_i and x_{ij}, and it must meet the conditions:

$$\sum_{j=1}^{k} w^i_j = 1 \tag{2}$$

To get the W matrix, we need to construct a local covariance matrix Q^i.

$$Q^i_{jm} = \left(x_i - x_{ij} \right)^T \left(x_i - x_{im} \right) \tag{3}$$

By combining (2) with (3) and adopting the Lagrange multiplier method, we can obtain the local optimization reconstruction weight matrix:

$$w_j^i = \frac{\sum\limits_{m=1}^{k} \left(Q^i\right)^{-1}_{jm}}{\sum\limits_{p=1}^{k}\sum\limits_{q=1}^{k} \left(Q^i\right)^{-1}_{pq}} \tag{4}$$

In the actual operation, Q^i may be a singular matrix and thus it must be regularized, as shown below:

$$Q^i = Q^i + rI \tag{5}$$

Where r is the regularization parameter, and I is a unit matrix of $K \times K$.

The last step of the LLE algorithm is mapping all the sample points into a low dimensional space. The mapping condition is as follows:

$$\min \varepsilon(Y) = \sum_{i=1}^{N} \left| y_i - \sum_{j=1}^{k} w_j^i y_{ij} \right|^2 \tag{6}$$

Among them, (Y) is the loss function value, y_i is the output vector of x_i, and y_{ij} $(j=1,2...k)$ are the K neighbor points of y_i, and it must satisfy two conditions, i.e.:

$$\sum_{i=1}^{N} y_i = 0 \tag{7}$$

$$\frac{1}{N} \sum_{i=1}^{N} y_i y_i^T = I \tag{8}$$

Where I is a unit matrix of $m \times m$.

3   Results

We designed six pairwise of experiments. In each of those experiments, we first pretreated every MRI data into a vector, and then we randomly chose half of each class as training set and the rest as testing set. And then, we used LLE to reduce dimension. Finally we used linear SVM to do the classification. All the experiments were repeated for 10 times. Thus, we had the average accuracy, sensitivity and specificity described as [1]. Then, we had the ROC curves of those experiments.

The outcomes of those experiments are provided in Table 2.

Table 2. Outcomes of classifications using LLE. ACR: accuracy; SEN: sensitivity; SPE: specificity

	ACR	SEN	SPE
CN vs. sMCI	0.67	0.66	0.70
CN vs. cMCI	0.79	0.78	0.80
CN vs. AD	0.85	0.84	0.86
sMCI vs.cMCI	0.72	0.71	0.72
sMCI vs. AD	0.75	0.76	0.75
cMCI vs. AD	0.65	0.66	0.68

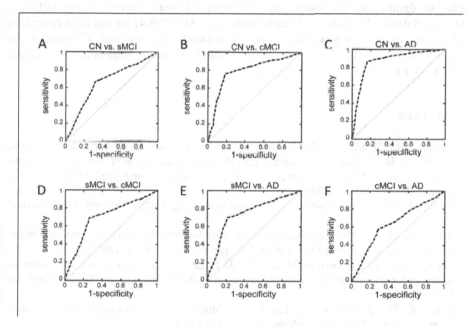

Fig. 1. ROC curves of pairwise classifications using LLE

As what we mentioned above, the severities of the four stages of AD should be CN< sMCI<cMCI<AD, so the classification performance should increase from CN vs. sMCI to CN vs. cMCI, and then CN vs. AD. In Table 2 and Fig. 1, we can see that the outcomes of the experiment obey this phenomenon, typically ACR(CN vs. sMCI)< ACR(CN vs. cMCI)< ACR(CN vs. AD) and the area under the ROC curve area(CN vs. sMCI)< area(CN vs. cMCI)< area(CN vs. AD). We can also see that ACR(cMCI vs. AD)< ACR(sMCI vs. AD)< ACR(CN vs. AD), and area(cMCI vs. AD)< area(sMCI vs. AD)< area(CN vs. AD).

4   Discussion

In this study, we computed the performance of LLE if this method is suitable for the classification of AD. The outcome showed that LLE did have good classification performances, suggesting that the LLE method may be choice. It should be noted that, although [8] have described a method of choosing the optimal parameters K and D, and we used cross-validations of the parameters to get the higher accuracy, in order to save time, we limited K in 5-30 and D in 5-15 so the outcomes we got in LLE were not the best in all probability. The performance of LLE was satisfying.

In conclusion, in this paper we used LLE in the classification of AD in MRI data. It shows that LLE have good performance in the experiments. In the future, we will try to use the method introduced by [8] to improve the calculate efficiency together with the performance of LLE.

Acknowledgements. We thank the Alzheimer's Disease Neuroimaging Initiative (ADNI) (National Institutes of Health Grant U01 AG024904) for the Data collection and sharing for this project. This work was supported by National 973 program of China (2013CB329401) and National Natural Science Foundation of China (61203263, 61375034).

References

1. Cuingnet, R., Gerardin, E., Tessieras, J., Auzias, G., Lehericy, S., Habert, M.-O., Chupin, M., Benali, H., Colliot, O.: Automatic classification of patients with Alzheimer's disease from structural MRI: A comparison of ten methods using the ADNI database. NeuroImage 56, 766–781 (2010)
2. Chang, H., Yeung, D.Y.: Robust locally linear embedding. Pattern Recognit. 39, 1053–1065 (2006)
3. Zheng, Z., Jie, Y.: Non-negative matrix factorization with log gabor wavelets for image representation and classification. J. Syst. Eng. Electron. 16, 738–745 (2005)
4. Ma, L., Member, S., Crawford, M.M., Tian, J.: Local manifold learning-based k —nearest-neighbor for hyperspectral image classification. IEEE Trans. Geosci. Remote Sens. 48, 4099–4109 (2010)
5. Sun, B.Y., Zhang, X.M., Li, J., Mao, X.M.: Feature fusion using locally linear embedding for classification. Trans. Neural Netw. 21, 163–168 (2010)
6. Yang, W., Lui, R., Gao, J.H., et al.: Independent componenet analysis-based classification of Alzheimer's disease MRI data. J. Alzheimers Dis. 24, 775–783 (2011)
7. Mannfolk, P., Wirestam, R., Nilsson, M., Sthlberg, F., Olsrud, J.: Dimensionality reduction of FMRI time series data using locally linear embedding. MAGMA 23, 327–338 (2010)
8. Shen, H., Wang, L.B., Liu, Y.D., Hu, D.W.: Discriminative analysis of resting-state functional connectivity patterns of schizophrenia using low dimensional embedding of fMRI. NeuroImage 49, 3110–3121 (2010)

Author Index